New Media Applications in Digital Education

Wan Nor Ashiqin Wan Ali
https://orcid.org/0000-0003-2489-2843
Universiti Malaysia Perlis, Malaysia

Syed Zulkarnain Syed Idrus
Universiti Malaysia Perlis, Malaysia

Mohd Noorulfakhri bin Yaacob
https://orcid.org/0000-0002-0938-7833
Universiti Malaysia Perlis, Malaysia

Izati Nabila Marzuki
https://orcid.org/0000-0001-6740-7655
Universiti Malaysia Perlis, Malaysia

IGI Global
Scientific Publishing
Publishing Tomorrow's Research Today

Vice President of Editorial	Melissa Wagner
Director of Acquisitions	Mikaela Felty
Director of Book Development	Jocelynn Hessler
Production Manager	Mike Brehm
Cover Design	Jose Rosado

Published in the United States of America by
IGI Global Scientific Publishing
701 East Chocolate Avenue
Hershey, PA, 17033, USA
Tel: 717-533-8845 | Fax: 717-533-7115
Website: https://www.igi-global.com E-mail: cust@igi-global.com

Library of Congress Cataloging-in-Publication Data

LCCN: 2025035307 (CIP Data Pending)
ISBN13: 9798337351575
Isbn13Softcover: 9798337351582
EISBN13: 9798337351599
British Cataloguing in Publication Data
A Cataloguing in Publication record for this book is available from the British Library.

Table of Contents

Detailed Table of Contents

Educational gamification promises increased student engagement, but applications remain superficial, using points, badges, leaderboards without pedagogical foundation, risking motivation loss. This chapter bridges theory and practice via motivational psychology, especially Self-Determination and Flow Theory. Using the MDA framework (dynamics, mechanics, components), showing how elements serve pedagogical purposes via classroom scenarios. The approach transforms gamification into learning structures supporting autonomy, competence, relatedness. Emphasizing equity and inclusivity, addressing how competitive systems favor certain profiles, presenting strategies for diverse learners. Five stages are detailed: goal setting, student analysis, narrative development, task design, feedback systems. Examining risks like technology addiction, attention distraction, excessive competition offers prevention strategies. Effective educational gamification must be guided by pedagogical philosophy and ethical values over technical decisions.

This chapter explores the integration of Artificial Intelligence (AI) with Extended Reality (XR) technologies (encompassing virtual, augmented, and mixed reality) in university/college-level computer science (CS) education. The chapter examines how AI and XR-based CS teaching make learning experiences more personalized, immersive, adaptive, and interactive. AI in CS education supports functions such as data analysis, content development automation, and learner engagement, complementing rather than replacing human instructors. The chapter highlights how AI+XR technologies can aid in teaching and learning complex CS courses and topics. It covers theoretical foundations and a literature review, emphasizing XR innovations. Additionally, the chapter addresses ethical and equity concerns to promote inclusive implementation. Aimed at educators, researchers, and developers, the chapter offers a framework and actionable strategies to leverage AI and XR for more effective, immersive, and intelligent CS education in higher education settings

Finding effective pedagogical techniques and tools to improve teaching methods is essential for educational growth. An alternative approach suggested is using comics, which are popular and inexpensive to produce. Comics are a popular, accessible entertainment enjoyed by many and easily shared on social media for quick, widespread information. This paper explores how comics enhance understanding, drawing on Eisner and McCloud's theories about storytelling through texts and images. Their views show how combining pictures and text can improve comprehension and memory. This paper also offers a new perspective on using comics as a learning tool, illustrated with a case study of a comic featuring classical mythology stories to clarify its explanation. The selected comics, based on stories from classical Wayang mythology—socialized through traditional performances in Indonesia, especially Java and Bali for centuries—serve as a case study, as they have traditionally conveyed guidelines for human behavior.

This study explores the use of social media for educational purposes among 100 pre-service teachers from various programs and year levels in a state university in the

student reactions. Drawing on experimental evidence, the study compared two groups of MBA students; one exposed to continuous instrumental background music and another taught without it. Findings revealed a significant positive difference in both engagement (reaction) and knowledge acquisition (learning), though the effect on learning was smaller in magnitude. By situating these results within established frameworks such as the Kirkpatrick Model and theories like the Arousal-Mood Hypothesis and Self-Determination Theory, this chapter highlights the nuanced relationship between music, cognition, and emotion. It makes the case for strategically integrating music into educational and corporate learning settings as a tool to foster attention, motivation, and engagement, while also acknowledging limitations and contextual considerations.

P. Karthik, St. Francis Evening College, Bengaluru, India
Velaga SriSai, School of Business and Management, Christ University, Bengaluru, India
Dhara Vinod Parmar, Design and Merchandising, Parul Institute of Design, Parul University, Waghodia, India
Nishant Bhuvanesh Trivedi, Animation and Design, Parul Institute of Design, Parul University, Waghodia, India
Vandana Aggarwal, University Institute of Teachers Training and Research, Chandigarh University, Mohali, India
D. Ramya, Department of English, Kongu Engineering College, Erode, India
M. Suresh, KPR Institute of Technology, Kovai, India

This chapter explores how digital tools can improve Social and Emotional Learning (SEL) and help develop students holistically. It looks at how educational technology can fall within three distinct categories of SEL: technology-enhanced gamified learning, online collaboration spaces, and classroom-based Artificial Intelligence (AI)-driven feedback and evaluation. This chapter emphasizes using interactive approaches that foster self-awareness, empathy, responsible decision-making, and interpersonal skills—using data-driven approaches in order to make the student more aware of their own learning. This chapter discusses the benefits and challenges; the equity issues; and provides tangible ideas and strategies for educators and policy-makers. By connecting the principles of SEL with digital innovations, the chapter demonstrates ways that we can create meaningful, richer, inclusive, and emotionally safe learning conditions for students in both formal, and informal settings.

Micro and nano learning are changing education today, bringing bite-sized and focused learning short units that are made with today's digital learner in mind. With multimedia, they can use mobile, and interactive content, ensuring flexibility and engagement and allowing just-in-time knowledge acquisition. Micro and nano learning leverage principles of cognitive science and are proven to lead to better retention of learning when implemented using spaced repetition principles and contextually relevant learning. In the digital education era, the micro-formats support personalized learning pathways, skill-based training, and opportunities for rapid upskilling. This chapter will focus on theoretical foundations, technological enablers, and practical possibilities for microlearning and nanolearning, and discuss their impact on lifelong learning, corporate learning, and formal education context while acknowledging the challenges of design, assessment opportunities, and opportunities for integration into larger educational ecosystems.

In an era of rapid technological change and learner-centered pedagogy, integrating new media into education has become imperative. This chapter examines the shift from capacity building to competence enhancement in teacher professional development (TPD) for digital pedagogy. It moves beyond basic digital literacy to focus on adaptive expertise, pedagogical innovation, and critical digital citizenship. Drawing on global frameworks, national policies, and case studies, it calls for inclusive,

personalized, effective learning experiences and inspire sustained interest in creative digital tasks.

Preface

The rapid evolution of technology in the 21st century has transformed how knowledge is created, disseminated, and consumed. The convergence of artificial intelligence (AI), immersive media, gamification, and digital pedagogy has profoundly redefined the landscape of teaching and learning. As the global education system continues to embrace digital transformation, educators face the dual challenge of integrating innovative tools while maintaining humanistic values at the core of learning. *New Media Applications in Digital Education* responds to this challenge by presenting a comprehensive exploration of how new media technologies can be harnessed to enhance learning outcomes, teaching practices, and institutional strategies. The book gathers interdisciplinary research and pedagogical innovations from scholars and practitioners committed to shaping the next generation of education.

This volume investigates the intersection of technology, pedagogy, and human learning, focusing on how new media tools, ranging from AI to extended reality (XR), contribute to effective teaching and meaningful learning experiences. The chapters examine practical applications and theoretical insights across diverse educational settings, revealing how educators can employ new media to foster engagement, inclusivity, and lifelong learning. By bridging traditional educational paradigms with digital innovations, this book offers an evidence-based perspective on rethinking learning in a world increasingly mediated by technology.

The subject matter aligns with global trends in digital transformation in education, which emphasize learner-centered pedagogies, data-driven assessment, and competency-based learning frameworks. It also reflects Malaysia's national education agenda and the broader Southeast Asian aspiration to prepare digitally literate, critical, and creative citizens. In doing so, the book situates new media not as a peripheral aid but as an integral component of modern education policy, curriculum design, and teacher professional development.

In the current educational landscape, technology is both an enabler and a disruptor. Artificial intelligence, virtual reality, and social media ecosystems are redefining not only how students learn but also how teachers teach, and institutions assess performance. The post-pandemic era has intensified the urgency for digital fluency, with educators expected to adapt rapidly to hybrid and remote learning models. Within this context, *New Media Applications in Digital Education* offers a timely and scholarly response to these global shifts. It highlights how AI-driven personalization, gamified learning environments, and interactive media can create more adaptive, immersive, and equitable educational ecosystems.

Globally, there is a movement toward Education 4.0, a framework aligning education with the Fourth Industrial Revolution. This book positions itself within that movement, demonstrating how technology can foster critical thinking, collaboration, creativity, and communication—the essential 21st-century skills. By examining both opportunities and ethical implications, it encourages readers to engage critically with the transformative potential of digital media while remaining mindful of the social and pedagogical responsibilities it entails.

The book is designed for a diverse readership that includes academics, educators, teacher trainers, policy makers, students, and industry practitioners. For scholars and researchers, it provides empirical studies and conceptual frameworks that advance the discourse on digital pedagogy and technology-enhanced learning. For educators, it offers concrete classroom strategies and tools to integrate new media effectively. Policy makers will find valuable insights into how digital education aligns with national and institutional development goals, while students and practitioners can use the discussions to deepen their understanding of emerging educational technologies.

CHAPTER OVERVIEW

Chapter 1: Rethinking Gamification: From Surface-Level Mechanics to Pedagogical Design

Moving beyond reward-based learning, this chapter redefines gamification as a deep pedagogical approach rooted in motivation, engagement, and cognitive development. It presents a framework for designing meaningful gamified experiences aligned with learning outcomes rather than superficial competition.

Chapter 2: Integrating AI and XR for Smarter Learning in Computer Science Education: Teaching in the Age of Intelligence and Immersion

Here, the authors combine artificial intelligence with extended reality to create immersive and adaptive learning experiences in computer science education. The chapter demonstrates how these technologies enable personalized instruction and experiential learning through simulation and intelligent feedback.

Chapter 3: Comics as a Practical Learning Tool to Improve Comprehension: A Case Study of Wayang Comic in Delivering Character Education Content

This study illustrates how culturally inspired comics can serve as a pedagogical tool for moral and character education. Through visual storytelling, students engage with complex ethical concepts, enhancing comprehension and cultural identity formation.

Chapter 4: Integration of Social Media in Education: Opportunities, Challenges, and Pedagogical Implications

Social media has become an indispensable educational tool, yet it presents challenges in ethics, attention, and authenticity. This chapter evaluates its role in collaborative learning, digital citizenship, and knowledge co-creation, offering guidelines for safe and productive use in classrooms.

Chapter 5: Assessing the Future: Tools and Trends in Media-Rich Learning Environments

Assessment in the digital era requires innovative tools that go beyond traditional testing. This chapter explores the integration of multimedia, analytics, and formative assessment methods to measure complex learning outcomes effectively.

Chapter 6: Harnessing the Power of Background Music: Enhancing Learning and Student Engagement

This unique contribution examines how background music can influence cognitive performance, concentration, and emotional regulation in educational settings. The findings reveal the potential of auditory media to enhance engagement and retention.

Chapter 7: Digital Pathways to Social and Emotional Learning: Leveraging Technology for Holistic Student Development

Here, the authors bridge emotional intelligence and technology, showing how digital platforms can foster empathy, collaboration, and self-awareness. It positions social-emotional learning (SEL) as essential to digital citizenship and lifelong learning.

Chapter 8: Microlearning and Nano-Learning in Transforming Pedagogy in the Digital Education Era

The chapter discusses bite-sized learning strategies that cater to modern learners' short attention spans. It explores how microlearning and nano-learning enhance flexibility, retention, and accessibility in both formal and informal education contexts.

Chapter 9: Professional Development of Teachers for New Media Integration in Teaching and Learning: From Capacity to Competence

Teacher professional development remains a cornerstone of educational transformation. This chapter outlines strategies for equipping educators with digital competencies, emphasizing reflective practice, collaboration, and ongoing learning.

Chapter 10: Empowering Educators for the Digital Age: A Faculty Development Framework for New Media Integration

Complementing the previous chapter, this work presents a structured framework for faculty development focused on new media. It emphasizes institutional support, leadership, and innovation in embedding digital pedagogy into higher education.

Chapter 11: Artificial Intelligence and Adaptive Learning Technologies

A complementary exploration of AI, this chapter provides a comparative analysis of adaptive systems in various disciplines. It discusses ethical implications, data privacy, and the pedagogical shift toward learner autonomy and continuous improvement.

Chapter 12: GenAI – Opportunities, Disruptions, and the New Learning Paradigm

Generative AI represents both promise and disruption in education. This chapter critically examines its implications for creativity, authorship, and assessment, urging institutions to balance innovation with academic integrity.

Chapter 13: Exploring User Experience in Virtual and Desktop Animation Interfaces from a Usability Perspective

This chapter presents usability research on virtual and desktop animation interfaces, revealing how interface design influences learner engagement, motivation, and comprehension in creative disciplines.

Chapter 14: VR to Stimulate: Extending the Expertise of Psychology Lecturers to Use VR in Teaching Modules

Focusing on psychology education, this chapter showcases a case study on how virtual reality enhances experiential learning, empathy development, and lecturer confidence in integrating immersive tools.

Chapter 15: Digital Creativity: The Influence of Thinking Styles on Motivation in Video Production Education

Concluding the collection, this chapter explores how individual thinking styles shape motivation and creativity in video-based learning. It reinforces the idea that digital creativity is not merely technical but deeply cognitive and effective.

New Media Applications in Digital Education contributes to the global dialogue on how education can evolve in the face of technological disruption. The book underscores that innovation in education must remain grounded in pedagogy, ethics, and equity. By combining empirical research, conceptual reflection, and practical guidance, it bridges the gap between theory and classroom implementation. Its emphasis on AI, digital pedagogy, media integration, and 21st-century skills aligns with international education standards and supports Malaysia's commitment to digital transformation and lifelong learning.

Ultimately, this volume serves as a comprehensive reference for understanding, designing, and implementing new media in education. It invites educators, researchers, and policy makers to rethink traditional paradigms, embrace interdisciplinary collaboration, and harness technology to cultivate adaptive, creative, and socially responsible learners. Through its multifaceted perspectives, the book positions itself as a critical resource for those seeking to navigate, and shape, the dynamic future of digital education.

Chapter 1
Rethinking Gamification: From Surface-Level Mechanics to Pedagogical Design

Abdullah Yasin Gunduz
https://orcid.org/0000-0003-2370-6199
Usak University, Turkey

ABSTRACT

Educational gamification promises increased student engagement, but applications remain superficial, using points, badges, leaderboards without pedagogical foundation, risking motivation loss. This chapter bridges theory and practice via motivational psychology, especially Self-Determination and Flow Theory. Using the MDA framework (dynamics, mechanics, components), showing how elements serve pedagogical purposes via classroom scenarios. The approach transforms gamification into learning structures supporting autonomy, competence, relatedness. Emphasizing equity and inclusivity, addressing how competitive systems favor certain profiles, presenting strategies for diverse learners. Five stages are detailed: goal setting, student analysis, narrative development, task design, feedback systems. Examining risks like technology addiction, attention distraction, excessive competition offers prevention strategies. Effective educational gamification must be guided by pedagogical philosophy and ethical values over technical decisions.

INTRODUCTION

With the technological transformation in the field of education over the last decade, the concept of gamification has received great interest from educators seeking alternatives to traditional teaching methods. Gamification is defined as the use of game design elements and game thinking in non-game contexts (Deterding, Dixon,

DOI: 10.4018/979-8-3373-5157-5.ch001

Khaled & Nacke, 2011) and promises to increase student motivation and strengthen class participation. However, a significant portion of the applications observed in educational institutions remain far from the true potential of gamification and occur in the form of integrating superficial mechanical elements into classrooms without being based on a pedagogical foundation.

The main problem this situation creates is the conceptual confusion between gamification as entertaining activities and learning. As emphasized by Kapp (2012), effective gamification is not just adding game elements, but an experience design process aligned with learning objectives. Applications encountered in many educational institutions occur in the form of adding game-like elements to existing curricula without analyzing students' real learning needs. This approach leads to superficial applications criticized by Dicheva, Dichev, Agre, and Angelova (2015).

Longitudinal research in undergraduate courses provides concrete examples of this superficiality. When gamification elements such as badges and leaderboards were implemented without connection to learning objectives, students initially showed increased engagement but demonstrated declining intrinsic motivation over the semester, with some developing negative attitudes toward the course material itself (Hanus & Fox, 2015). The study revealed that students in the gamified condition spent more time on tasks but showed lower final exam performance compared to control groups, suggesting that attention focused on earning rewards rather than understanding content. Similarly, empirical testing of leaderboard effects demonstrated that while some students increased time-on-task, the competitive ranking system created anxiety and reduced academic performance particularly among students who scored lower (Landers & Landers, 2014). These cases illustrate how game elements, when applied without pedagogical grounding, can inadvertently undermine the learning outcomes they aim to enhance.

From a critical perspective, gamification has potential risks including technology addiction, reduced attention spans, and excessive competitive environments requiring careful consideration (Twenge & Campbell, 2018). Merve, an eighth-grade science teacher, plans to use gamification to make the topic of cell division more engaging for her students. However, the challenges she faces reflect the general problems most educators experience. She needs guidance on how to integrate game elements with pedagogical goals, how to include students with different learning styles, and how to prevent the negative side effects of the process. Understanding the potential of gamification in educational contexts requires establishing a solid theoretical foundation based on the fundamental theories of motivational psychology. Self-Determination Theory, developed by Deci and Ryan (2000), reveals that human motivation is shaped around three basic psychological needs. Autonomy refers to the individual's feeling of directing their behaviors with their own will; competence refers to the feeling of being able to cope with challenges; and relatedness refers to the feeling of connecting with others.

Meeting these three needs is critically important in the context of educational gamification. As emphasized by Ryan and Deci (2017), autonomy-supportive learning environments strengthen students' intrinsic motivation. Meeting the need for competence constitutes one of the strongest aspects of gamification. Flow Theory, developed by Csikszentmihalyi (1990), explains the psychological foundations of this situation. Flow state is the optimal experience state where a person focuses on an activity with complete concentration.

Supporting the need for relatedness requires the integration of social learning theories into educational gamification. The social constructivist approach put forward by Vygotsky (1978) emphasizes that learning occurs within social interaction processes. A meta-analysis study conducted by Hamari, Koivisto, and Sarsa (2014) reveals that gamification applications containing social elements show longer-term motivational effects compared to individually focused systems.

Recent meta-analytic evidence provides additional support for the critical role of implementation quality. A comprehensive analysis of gamification studies found that while gamification generally produces positive effects on motivation and engagement, the magnitude and sustainability of these effects depend on theoretical grounding and design quality (Sailer & Homner, 2020). Systems incorporating collaborative learning structures showed more consistent positive outcomes compared to those emphasizing individual competition. Furthermore, systematic reviews reveal that many applications fail due to insufficient attention to motivational theory, with successful implementations consistently demonstrating clear connections between game mechanics and psychological need satisfaction (Koivisto & Hamari, 2019). These findings emphasize that effective gamification design requires careful attention to how social interaction is structured around learning goals, not merely whether social elements are present.

However, serious difficulties are experienced in the process of transforming this theoretical potential into practice. As pointed out by McGonigal (2011), games have powerful mechanisms that create motivation, but effective use of these mechanisms in educational contexts requires a careful design process. The commonly encountered mistake is adding game elements independently of learning objectives, thus causing students to focus only on reward mechanisms.

The affective filter hypothesis put forward by Krashen (1982) explains why this situation is problematic. When students make efforts only for external rewards, they may develop negative attitudes toward the learning process. A comprehensive meta-analysis conducted by Deci, Koestner, and Ryan (1999) empirically demonstrated that unexpected and controlling external rewards reduce intrinsic motivation.

An important dimension of effective gamification design is the issue of inclusivity and equity. Traditional competition-focused gamification approaches can only support certain student profiles and exclude students with other learning styles. The player types taxonomy developed by Bartle (1996) shows the existence of individuals with different motivation sources. This approach, expanded by Yee (2006), reveals that player motivations are shaped in dimensions of achievement, social interaction, and immersion.

In light of this theoretical framework, the main purpose of this chapter is to systematically present the design principles, application strategies, and evaluation methods necessary to realize the educational potential of gamification. The chapter seeks answers to four basic research questions. First, how educational gamification should be designed to support students' intrinsic motivation and not create external reward dependency is examined. Second, how gamification systems that will include students with different learning styles and motivation profiles should be developed is addressed. Third, how a balance should be established between pedagogical goals and game mechanics in gamified learning environments is analyzed. Finally, which measurement and analysis methods should be used to evaluate the long-term educational effects of gamification is investigated.

In the process of seeking answers to these questions, strategies that combine theoretical foundations with practical applications and can be used directly by educators in classroom environments are presented. The aim is for gamification to cease being an entertainment additive and become a systematic pedagogical approach that improves the quality of learning processes.

FUNDAMENTAL BUILDING BLOCKS

To ground theoretical foundations in a practical framework, the hierarchy of dynamics, mechanics, and components of gamification systems is examined. Understanding this triple structure in the context of educational gamification is critically important because designing each layer in alignment with pedagogical goals determines the overall effectiveness of the system (Hunicke, LeBlanc & Zubek, 2004; Werbach & Hunter, 2012).

For systematic understanding of this framework, Table 1 presents the relationship between dynamics, mechanics, and components along with pedagogical examples.

Table 1. MDA Framework of Gamification System and Pedagogical Applications

Layer	Definition	Educational Function	Example from Merve's Class
Dynamics	Conceptual frameworks and long-term experience character	Adding meaning to the learning journey	"Cell Detectives" narrative, researcher identity
Mechanics	Operational rules and interaction processes	Structuring learning activities	Task completion rules, collaboration protocols
Components	Concrete, observable interface elements	Providing motivation and progress tracking	Points, "Mitosis Master" badge, team rankings

As seen in Table 1, each layer should be designed to support the layer above it. In Merve's example, the cell detective narrative (dynamic) feeds the task-based research process (mechanics), while this process is experienced by students through points and badges (components).

In Merve's process of gamifying the cell division topic, how these three layers interact can be concretely observed. The system she will design to help her students learn mitosis and meiosis processes requires an integrated structure extending from the conceptual framework of dynamics to the operational rules of mechanics and finally to the concrete elements of components. This systematic approach shows that gamification is not just adding superficial elements, but a holistic design process serving pedagogical purposes.

Dynamics

Dynamics represent the conceptual frameworks that constitute the highest level of the gamified learning system. To understand how this theoretical framework is applied in practice, it would be appropriate to focus on the experience in Merve's classroom. These elements determine the general character of students' experiences within the system and create long-term motivational effects. In educational contexts, dynamics are metaphorical structures that draw the big picture of the learning process and give meaning to students' educational journeys.

Progress Dynamic

Progress dynamic constitutes one of the most fundamental elements of educational gamification. This dynamic provides students with the opportunity to track their own learning processes and concretely observe their development. The powerful effect of clear and measurable goals on motivation plays a critical role in increasing academic success. Within the cognitive taxonomy framework, effective design of progress dynamics requires hierarchical structuring of learning objectives. In Merve's cell division lesson, students can experience gradual progress starting from remembering basic concepts, moving to understanding processes, applying them in different situations, and finally analyzing complex scenarios. This approach allows each student to progress at their own pace while maintaining academic standards.

Growth mindset research shows that students make more effort when they believe their intelligence and abilities can be developed (Dweck, 2006). Therefore, balancing process-focused evaluation criteria with outcome-focused criteria is important in progress dynamic design. Students should be recognized not only for giving correct answers but also for developing problem-solving strategies, conducting error analysis, and trying creative approaches.

However, potential risks of progress dynamics should also be considered. Overly focused progress tracking can create performance anxiety in students and reduce risk-taking behaviors. Students who are constantly evaluated may focus only on appearing successful rather than learning new things. Therefore, progress dynamics should be designed to support students' ownership of their own development processes.

A seventh-grade history classroom illustrates this principle in practice. The teacher designed a progress tracking system where students advanced through levels representing increasing historical thinking complexity: from identifying basic facts in primary sources, to analyzing author perspective and bias, to evaluating multiple conflicting accounts, and finally to constructing evidence-based historical arguments. Crucially, students could revisit earlier levels to strengthen foundational skills without penalty, and progress visualization emphasized individual growth trajectories rather than fixed class positions. One student who initially struggled with source analysis spent additional time at that level, received targeted feedback on identifying author purpose, and eventually demonstrated mastery before advancing to comparative analysis. This approach reduced anxiety about falling behind peers while maintaining clear expectations for historical thinking development aligned with disciplinary standards.

Narrative Dynamic

Narrative dynamic is a powerful tool that adds contextual meaning to gamified learning experiences. The critical role of story structures in humans' processes of organizing and remembering complex information has special importance in educational contexts. Narrative dynamic transforms abstract concepts into concrete experiences, enabling students to form emotional connections with the subject.

The hero's journey archetype offers a powerful template in effective narrative dynamic design (Campbell, 1949). This structure positions students as heroes of their own learning processes and frames academic challenges as obstacles to overcome. In Merve's lesson, students can take on the role of researchers solving mitosis and meiosis mysteries as "Cell Detectives."

Given that learning is a process that occurs within social and cultural contexts, narrative structures provide students with frameworks to understand these contexts. When complex scientific processes are presented within narrative dynamics, students can form deeper connections with the subject. This approach yields effective results especially in teaching abstract concepts.

However, excessive use of narrative dynamics carries some risks. If story elements overshadow academic content, students may focus on the entertaining narrative and miss the actual learning objectives. Therefore, narrative dynamics should be used in careful balance to support pedagogical goals.

Relatedness Dynamic

Relatedness dynamic represents the practical application of social learning theories in gamified environments. The fact that individuals learn by observing others, imitating, and establishing social interaction emphasizes the importance of social elements in educational gamification design. Comprehensive research shows that collaborative learning methods yield superior results compared to competitive and individual learning approaches in terms of academic achievement, social skills, and self-esteem.

In Merve's classroom, students can form collaborative teams to understand cell division processes. Each team can research different stages of mitosis and meiosis processes and teach each other. This approach both supports academic learning and develops social skills. The positive interactions established among students increase learning motivation while also improving the classroom climate.

However, relatedness dynamics also have potential problems. Unstructured group work can lead to some students remaining passive and others taking excessive load. Therefore, relatedness dynamics should be supported with mechanisms that ensure active participation of every student. Clear role distributions, individual accountability systems, and regular group evaluations can minimize these problems.

While these listed dynamics constitute the abstract conceptual framework, mechanics make this framework operational with concrete rules and processes.

Mechanics

Mechanics refer to the operational rules and processes of the system that enable dynamics to be put into practice. These elements determine how students will act within the system, what actions they can perform, and what the consequences of these actions will be. Mechanics serve as a critical bridge that transforms abstract dynamics into concrete experiences.

Task Mechanics

Task mechanics is the fundamental mechanism where learning objectives are transformed into concrete action plans. It is known that the clarity and structural level of learning tasks have a powerful effect on academic success. Therefore, systematic design of tasks is critically important for the effectiveness of gamified learning environments. Effective task mechanics should systematically include nine fundamental stages of the learning process. These stages include gaining attention, informing learning objectives, recalling prerequisite knowledge, presenting new material, providing learning guidance, eliciting performance, providing feedback, assessing performance, and enhancing retention and transfer (Gagné, 1985).

In Merve's cell division lesson, task mechanics can be applied as follows. First, examples of cell division in daily life can be presented to attract students' attention. Then, the goal of comparing mitosis and meiosis processes can be explained. After students' prior knowledge is recalled, new processes can be presented with interactive simulations. Guidance can be provided at each stage and students' performances can be evaluated.

Within the framework of multiple intelligence theory, task diversity enables students with different learning preferences to experience success (Gardner, 1983). Students with strengths in different intelligence areas can learn through linguistic tasks, logical-mathematical tasks, spatial tasks, and kinesthetic tasks. This diversity allows all students in the classroom to reveal their potential.

Feedback Mechanics

Feedback mechanics constitutes one of the most critical components of the learning process. Research has proven that the effect of effective feedback on student success is stronger than many educational interventions (Hattie & Timperley, 2007). Therefore, careful design of feedback mechanisms in gamified learning systems is necessary.

Formative feedback principles emphasize that feedback should be timely, specific, understandable, and actionable. In Merve's gamified system, students can receive immediate feedback when they simulate cell division processes. When wrong steps are taken, the system can not only say "wrong" but also explain at which stage the error was made and how it can be corrected.

It is observed that formative assessment processes create particularly strong positive effects for low-achieving students. This finding emphasizes the strategic importance of feedback mechanisms in gamified learning environments in terms of equity and inclusivity. Feedback systems designed to support all students' development can reduce differences in academic achievement.

Collaboration Mechanics

Collaboration mechanics represents the operational application of social learning theories. Systematic design of collaborative learning processes encourages both cooperation and personal responsibility through balancing individual accountability and group rewards. This balance is necessary for students to value both individual development and group success.

Given the effect of goal structure on group dynamics and student motivation, careful design of collaboration mechanisms is critically important. In Merve's classroom, student teams can work on different projects about cell division, targeting both individual learning and group success. This approach minimizes the negative effects that competitive environments would create while increasing learning motivation. However, collaboration mechanics also have potential problems. Unstructured group work can create negative effects such as social loafing and groupthink. Therefore, collaboration mechanics should be supported with clear roles, individual accountability, and effective group dynamics management. Regular group evaluations and role rotations can minimize these problems.

Components

Components refer to the concrete elements of the gamified learning system that can be directly observed and interacted with by students. These elements constitute the user interface of the system and play a critical role in shaping students' motivational experiences. The design of components should ensure effective communication of underlying dynamics and mechanics.

Point System

The point system constitutes one of the most common components of gamified learning environments. However, the educational value of points is closely related to design philosophy and implementation method. While controlling external rewards can weaken intrinsic motivation, informational rewards can strengthen intrinsic motivation by supporting feelings of competence (Deci & Ryan, 1985).

In effective point system design, points should be connected not only to achievement outcomes but also to effort, development, and innovative thinking in the learning process. In Merve's system, students can earn points for correctly completing the mitosis process, as well as for making creative explanations, helping peers, or conducting error analysis. This approach encourages students to make process-focused rather than just outcome-focused efforts.

Authentic assessment principles can be used to increase the pedagogical value of the point system. These principles emphasize that assessment processes should be designed to be connected to real-life problems, require complex thinking skills, and enable students to monitor their own learning. In this way, points become not just performance indicators but learning tools.

Badge System

The badge system functions as a mechanism for recognizing and rewarding students' various achievements. Motivational climate research reveals that task-oriented climate creates more sustainable learning motivation compared to ego-oriented climate. Therefore, the diversity principle is critically important in badge system design.

Multi-dimensional criteria such as creativity, cooperation, leadership, perseverance, and social responsibility should be integrated into the badge system alongside academic success. In Merve's classroom, process-focused badges such as "Team Player," "Creative Thinker," and "Question Asker" can be used alongside academic badges like "Mitosis Master" and "Meiosis Expert." This diversity ensures recognition of students with different strengths.

It is observed that the effect of badge systems on student motivation is directly related to design quality. Badges given only for rare achievements carry prestige value, while badges that can be obtained too easily lose their motivational value. Therefore, a careful balance of difficulty gradation and meaningfulness should be established in badge system design.

Leaderboard

The leaderboard constitutes one of the most controversial components of gamified learning environments. When analyzed within the framework of social comparison theory, it is seen that traditional ranking approaches carry potential benefits and risks. Upward social comparison can be a source of motivation for some students, while it can create a motivation-reducing effect for others.

Alternative leaderboard designs have been developed to solve this problem. The multiple category approach ranks students in different dimensions and thus creates a more inclusive recognition system (Christy & Fox, 2014). In Merve's classroom, leaderboards can be created in different categories such as academic success, development speed, cooperation, and creativity. This approach ensures that each student has the opportunity to stand out in their own strengths.

Alternatively, personal development-focused leaderboards compare students with their own past performances. This approach supports the development of self-efficacy perception and enables students to focus on their own development processes. Given that accessible role models have a positive effect on motivation, this approach can produce more inclusive results. In terms of general design principles of components, user experience theories provide important guidance. Design principles include visibility, feedback, constraints, mapping, consistency, and affordances. Systematic application of these principles enables students to use the gamified system effectively.

Finally, evaluating components in terms of cultural sensitivity is critically important. It should be considered that students from different cultural backgrounds may have different approaches to competition, cooperation, and authority relationships. Therefore, considering cultural diversity and providing flexible options in the design of gamification components is important.

CULTURAL CONTEXT AND ADAPTATION CHALLENGES

The effectiveness of gamification strategies varies significantly across cultural contexts, requiring educators to adapt design principles to local values and learning traditions. Cultural dimensions such as individualism versus collectivism, power distance, and uncertainty avoidance fundamentally shape how students respond to competitive and collaborative game elements (Hofstede, 1980). In cultures emphasizing collective harmony over individual distinction, leaderboard systems ranking students publicly may create discomfort and reduced engagement, as visible performance comparison conflicts with cultural values prioritizing group cohesion.

Language considerations represent practical challenges in multicultural classrooms. Systems relying heavily on text may disadvantage students with limited language proficiency, requiring visual symbols, audio support, and simplified interfaces to ensure equitable access (Vygotsky, 1978).

STEP-BY-STEP CLASSROOM IMPLEMENTATION

Transforming the theoretical potential of educational gamification into practice requires following a systematic design process. This process follows a logic that progresses from learning objectives to evaluation strategies and finally to instructional activities. For developing user-centered solutions, systematic application of empathy building, problem identification, idea generation, prototype development, and testing phases is necessary.

Merve's experience as an eighth-grade science teacher gamifying the cell division topic provides an opportunity to observe the practical application of this five-stage design process. The integration of systematic instructional design principles with game design principles enables the creation of systems that are effective both educationally and motivationally.

This integration process is carried out within the framework of the five-stage systematic approach shown in Figure 1.

Figure 1. Educational Gamification Design Process

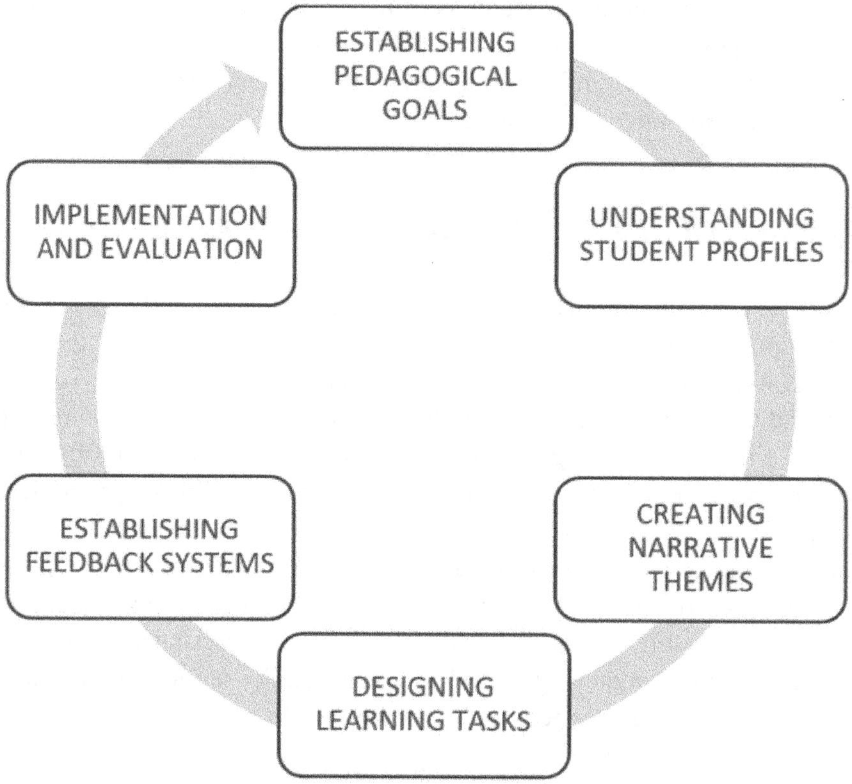

The process shown in Figure 1 adopts an iterative rather than linear approach. Feedback obtained at each stage enables re-evaluation of previous stages, offering continuous improvement opportunities. Merve's cell division project was developed by systematically following these five stages.

Step 1: Pedagogical Goal Setting Process

The first and most critical stage of educational gamification design is establishing clear and measurable pedagogical goals. Effective learning objectives should clearly define what students will be able to do, under what conditions they can do it, and what the acceptable performance level is. These goals should be expanded to include 21st-century skills alongside academic achievements.

In the process of determining learning outcomes for the cell division topic, students are targeted to be able to recall mitosis and meiosis processes, understand differences between these processes, apply appropriate division types in different situations, and analyze the importance of processes in living organisms. Within the cognitive taxonomy framework, learning objectives are structured hierarchically from the recall level to the evaluation level.

Alongside academic achievements, critical thinking, creativity, collaboration, and communication skills are also included among the goals. Students are expected to question scientific processes, form hypotheses, and share their findings with peers. Learning cell division terms as verbal information, analyzing processes as mental skills, and developing problem-solving approaches as cognitive strategies are targeted. Among the goals established in this example are students being able to explain the four stages of the mitosis process in correct order, analyze the contribution of meiosis process to genetic diversity, and select appropriate division types for different organisms. These goals are designed in connection with real-life problems to create authentic learning experiences.

A four-level approach is adopted in evaluating goals in terms of measurability. Specific measurement criteria are developed for student satisfaction, knowledge and skill acquisition, application of what is learned, and long-term effects.

Step 2: Analysis of Student Characteristics

The second critical stage of effective gamification design is in-depth analysis of the characteristics of the target student population. Determining the gap between students' current ability levels and potential development areas is critically important for practical application of the zone of proximal development.

Systematic analysis of the profiles of a thirty-student classroom requires identifying strengths in different intelligence areas based on multiple intelligence theory. In a typical classroom, it can be observed that approximately one-third are strong in linguistic intelligence, one-fourth excel in spatial intelligence, and one-fifth prefer kinesthetic learning.

Learning style analysis reveals student preferences in terms of environmental, emotional, sociological, and physical factors. In terms of environmental factors, it is determined that most students learn better in medium-level light and quiet environments, and motivation levels vary in terms of emotional factors. In terms of sociological factors, it is observed that group work is preferred over individual work. Educational adaptation of player typology typically reveals four basic profiles in classrooms. Achievement-oriented students prefer clear goals and reward systems, while explorer-profile students enjoy discovering new information. Socializing students are active in group activities, while competition-oriented students are motivated by ranking and comparison systems.

Motivation analysis shows that students exhibit different preferences in achievement, social interaction, and immersion dimensions (Yee, 2006). This analysis provides critical guidance in designing elements that appeal to different motivation profiles in the gamified system.

Within the framework of the digital native concept, students' technology usage habits are examined. It is observed that most of today's students actively use mobile devices, have short attention spans, and prefer visual-interactive content. Cultural diversity analysis reveals that students from different socioeconomic backgrounds show variation in their approaches to competition and cooperation. Surveys, individual interviews, and classroom observations are used for systematic conduct of student needs analysis. The multi-source data collection approach ensures more comprehensive and reliable formation of student profiles.

Step 3: Narrative Framework Development

The third design stage of the gamified learning experience is creating a consistent and motivational narrative framework based on pedagogical goals and student profiles. Systematic application of narrative thinking mode in educational contexts transforms abstract concepts into concrete experiences, enabling students to form emotional and cognitive connections with the subject.

Utilizing narrative-based learning approaches, developing the “Cell Detectives Academy” theme for the cell division topic enables positioning students as researchers solving mysteries of the cell world in the role of young scientists. Utilizing the hero's journey archetype, students experience academic challenges as obstacles to overcome as heroes of their own learning processes. Within this narrative framework, students are welcomed as trainee researchers accepted into the “Cell Detectives Academy.” The academy director assigns them the task of clarifying mysterious events occurring in cell division processes. Within the framework of narrative transportation theory, the effect of how much students immerse themselves in the narrative world on learning is considered.

Story form theory provides important guidance in narrative design. The conflict element as the laboratory accident where mitosis and meiosis processes are confused, the tension element as the necessity to distinguish correct processes, and the solution element as successful detective work form the basic structure of the narrative.

Given that adolescent students are in the process of identity search, enabling students to choose their own areas of expertise in the narrative has special importance.

By assuming roles such as “Mitosis Expert,” “Meiosis Researcher,” or “Genetic Analyst,” personal development needs are met.

In accordance with multicultural education approach, narrative contents are designed to represent students from different cultural backgrounds. This academy includes researchers from different countries and characters representing various scientific traditions. Story structure principles are used to ensure narrative consistency. The opening hook as the laboratory accident, character development as students' increasing scientific competence, climax as solving the most complex case, and resolution as the graduation process from the academy form the main outline of the narrative.

Step 4: Structuring Learning Activities

The fourth design stage of the gamified learning system includes detailed design of learning tasks and interaction cycles based on pedagogical goals and narrative framework. By utilizing learning principles from good games, organic integration of educational content with game mechanics is achieved.

Designing various tasks within the “Cell Detectives Academy” theme requires establishing balance between task difficulty and students' ability levels. While initial tasks require recall of basic concepts, progressive tasks target complex analysis and synthesis skills. Optimal experience conditions of flow theory are considered in each task design.

In designing task progression, the area between what students can do independently and what they can do under guidance is targeted. Using dynamic difficulty adjustment mechanisms ensures each student encounters appropriate challenges at their own level. Task diversity is provided within the cognitive taxonomy framework. Tasks are designed including “Mitosis Memory Game” at the recall level, “Process Explanation Task” at the understanding level, “Cell Simulation” at the application level, “Comparative Case Analysis” at the analysis level, “New Organism Design” at the synthesis level, and “Scientific Article Review” at the evaluation level.

The four components of the motivation model are used as the basic framework in designing task cycles. Each task cycle is designed to systematically include attention-getting, interest-creating, confidence-building, and satisfaction-providing dimensions. In the “Laboratory Accident Solving” task example, the process beginning with an interesting problem enables students to use their existing knowledge, provides guidance for successful solution, and makes it possible for them to reach a satisfying solution at the end.

The experiential learning cycle is used in the temporal organization of learning cycles. Concrete experience as cell division simulations, reflective observation as process analysis, abstract conceptualization as forming theoretical frameworks, and active experimentation as application in new situations are systematically integrated. Collaborative learning principles provide a guiding framework in integrating social interaction elements. In the "Research Teams" task, the principles of positive interdependence, individual accountability, face-to-face promotive interaction, social skills, and group processing are applied (Johnson & Johnson, 1989).

Authentic instruction standards are used in evaluating the real-life connection of tasks. Designed tasks reflect real-life problems such as cancer research, reproductive technologies, and aging processes, require higher-order thinking skills, and include interdisciplinary approaches. The feedback model is used in designing task feedback systems. Feedback is balanced in four categories: task level, process level, self-regulation level, and person level. In this system, students receive detailed feedback not only about correct/incorrect information but also about the strategies they use and their learning processes.

Step 5: Creating Evaluation and Monitoring Systems

The fifth and final design stage of the gamified learning system is developing comprehensive feedback and progress tracking mechanisms that monitor, evaluate, and guide student performance. Systematic presentation of information aimed at closing the gap between current performance and targeted performance is intended. Creating a multi-layered feedback structure in the "Cell Detectives Academy" system requires clarifying success criteria before each task to ensure goals are clear. The quality of current performance is determined with detailed rubrics and actions to close the gap are defined with specific recommendations (Sadler, 1989).

Considering the strong positive effect of formative assessment processes, the system ensures students receive immediate and constructive responses to every action. When a wrong step is taken in cell division simulation, the system not only indicates the error but also explains at which stage the problem occurred and how it can be corrected.

The principles of mastery learning model are used in designing the progress monitoring system. The principle that all students can reach learning objectives when sufficient time and appropriate instructional conditions are provided is applied through individualized progress tracking and flexible time management. A systematic approach is adopted in diversifying feedback types. A wide range is offered from simple confirmation to detailed explanation in the complexity dimension, from immediate feedback to delayed analysis in the timing dimension, from fixed messages to personalized recommendations in the adaptability dimension.

Information design principles are considered in designing progress visualization systems. Indicators are designed that enable students to understand their performance quickly and accurately in accordance with criteria of maximizing data-ink ratio, maintaining graphical integrity, and preventing data distortion.

Within the framework of self-regulated learning theory, integration of self-assessment mechanisms is necessary. Developing students' skills in planning, monitoring, and evaluating their own learning is targeted. In this system, students regularly evaluate their own performance and determine future goals. Considering that peer assessment processes provide learning gains for both evaluating and evaluated students, inclusion of social feedback mechanisms is important. Peer feedback is systematized through structured rubrics and evaluation forms.

By utilizing learning analytics technologies, it is possible to develop the analytical dimension of the progress tracking system. Analysis of data collected from student behaviors can enable optimization of learning processes. This approach is critically important for early detection of which subjects students struggle with and development of appropriate intervention strategies.

The five-stage systematic design process detailed above plays a critical role in transforming the theoretical foundations of educational gamification into practical applications. To summarize this process and provide readers with a quick reference, Table 2 below presents the description of each stage, its theoretical basis, practical application example (cell division scenario), and potential risks with solutions. This table provides a holistic view of the design process, facilitating educators' adaptation in their own classrooms.

Table 2. Five-Stage Systematic Design Process Summary

Stage	Description	Theoretical Basis	Practical Application Example	Potential Risk and Solution
1. Pedagogical Goal Setting	Clarifying learning outcomes and objectives	Bloom's taxonomy, Gagné's conditions of learning	Understanding and applying mitosis/meiosis processes	Risk: Goals inconsistent with game elements. Solution: Use SMART criteria
2. Student Profile Analysis	Evaluating different learning styles and motivation types (Bartle/Yee)	Multiple intelligence theory (Gardner), growth mindset (Dweck)	Grouping according to explorer/social/competitive profiles	Risk: Lack of inclusivity. Solution: Apply surveys and pre-tests
3. Narrative Theme Development	Creating story-based context (hero's journey)	Flow theory (Csikszentmihalyi), social constructivism (Vygotsky)	Cell "adventure": Students as "cell heroes" conduct division simulation	Risk: Cultural incompatibility. Solution: Integrate local elements

continued on following page

Table 2. Continued

Stage	Description	Theoretical Basis	Practical Application Example	Potential Risk and Solution
4. Learning Task Design	Creating progressive tasks and cycles	Self-determination theory (Deci & Ryan), MDA framework	Simulation tasks, collaborative challenges	Risk: Excessive competition. Solution: Establish individual and group progress balance
5. Feedback System Setup	Immediate, constructive feedback mechanisms	Formative assessment (Sadler), feedback power (Hattie & Timperley)	Badges, progress bars, and peer assessment	Risk: External motivation trap. Solution: Design focused on intrinsic achievement

As summarized in Table 2, this five-stage process transforms gamification from a superficial tool into a pedagogical design philosophy. While this summary helps educators adapt the process to their own contexts, the following section addresses the potential risks and ethical dimensions of gamification.

IMPORTANT CONSIDERATIONS

Realizing the theoretical potential of educational gamification in practice requires recognizing the traps frequently encountered in the design process and systematically evaluating ethical dimensions. Current literature observes that a significant portion of educational gamification applications fail to achieve expected learning outcomes and in some cases create negative side effects. The fundamental cause of these problems is focusing on superficial elements of gamification and ignoring basic principles of motivational psychology.

When systematic analysis of problems encountered in gamification applications is conducted, it is seen that most errors stem from failure to support basic psychological needs. Particularly, controlling use of external reward systems damages students' sense of autonomy, while overly competitive environments fail to meet relatedness needs. In terms of ethical evaluations, gamification applications require fundamental principles including non-maleficence, beneficence, respect for autonomy, and justice.

A particularly important ethical dimension is considering the long-term effects of gamification systems on students. Responsible use of games' powerful motivational effects requires designers to prioritize student welfare. This responsibility includes a holistic approach encompassing not only academic success but also students' psychological health, social development, and ethical values.

BALANCING INTRINSIC AND EXTRINSIC MOTIVATION

One of the most critical traps of educational gamification relates to the overjustification effect. This phenomenon refers to the decline of interest in an activity below initial levels when external rewards are removed after being added to intrinsically motivated activities (Deci, 1971). In the gamification context, this effect can manifest as natural satisfaction students derive from the learning process being damaged by external reward systems.

Comprehensive meta-analysis studies show that unexpected and controlling rewards reduce intrinsic motivation, but informational rewards based on student choice can support intrinsic motivation. This finding provides critical guidance on how reward systems should be structured in gamification design. The risk of technology addiction constitutes one of the most serious side effects of modern gamification applications. There are growing concerns that excessive use of digital tools can negatively affect students' social skills and deep thinking capacities. Particularly, game designs based on instant gratification mechanisms can create impatience and constant stimulation-seeking in students.

Attention distraction problems are frequently overlooked risks in gamified learning environments. Visual effects, audio alerts, and continuous feedback mechanisms can distract students from main learning content. This situation can lead students toward superficial learning strategies, hindering deep analytical thinking.

In gamification design that protects intrinsic motivation, autonomy-supportive instructional strategies should be used as the basic framework. These strategies include taking student perspective, acknowledging student initiations, providing options, avoiding controlling language, and being patient. Systematic application of these strategies in gamified learning environments can minimize potential negative effects of external rewards.

Performance-contingent reward strategies hold special importance in reward design. This approach connects rewards not only to task completion but also to process-focused criteria such as creativity, effort, development, and learning strategies. Thus, students are recognized and rewarded not only for results but also for the learning process itself.

Flow theory principles provide critical guidance in gamification design that supports intrinsic motivation. Creating flow state requires tasks to be appropriately challenging for student ability levels, contain clear goals, and provide immediate feedback. When these conditions are met, students can focus on activities with full concentration without needing external rewards.

Sustaining motivation beyond initial novelty requires deliberate strategies. Longitudinal research reveals a common pattern: initial enthusiasm in weeks 1 to 4, declining engagement as novelty diminishes, and stabilization at moderate levels after 8 to 10 weeks (Hanus & Fox, 2015). Meta-analysis confirms stronger effects in short-term studies compared to longer interventions (Sailer & Homner, 2020). Successful implementations integrate progressive complexity preventing stagnation, meaningful choice supporting autonomy, and explicit connections between activities and real-world competencies to maintain engagement beyond superficial point accumulation.

The five fundamental problems of rewards defined as not working, damaging relationships, hindering creativity, killing intrinsic motivation, and creating addiction contain critical warnings that gamification designers should consider. To prevent these problems, reward systems should be designed to support student autonomy and be informational and choice-based. The triad of autonomy, mastery, and purpose offers valuable guidance as alternative motivation strategies. This approach focuses on strengthening students' intrinsic motivation sources by reducing dependence on external rewards. Systematic support of these three elements in gamified learning environments can create sustainable motivation.

TECHNOLOGY ADDICTION AND ATTENTION DISTRACTION RISKS

One of the most serious side effects of modern gamification applications is the risk of technology addiction. Continuous reward systems, instant gratification mechanisms, and designs based on social approval-seeking can develop excessive dependence on technological tools in students. This situation can lead students to lose learning motivation outside gamified environments.

Dopamine-based reward cycles are critically important for understanding the neurological effects of gamification systems. Activities supported by continuous small rewards can create habits in the brain's reward centers and dull students' natural curiosity. This process can cause students to participate only in activities that promise rewards and lose their intrinsic motivation.

Increased screen time is an inevitable consequence of gamified educational applications. There is growing scientific evidence about the negative effects of prolonged screen exposure on students' physical health, sleep quality, and social skills. Particularly in adolescent students, excessive screen use has been shown to increase depression and anxiety risk. Shortened attention span constitutes one of the most problematic effects of digital gamification tools. Continuous stimulation and rapid feedback cycles can cause students to struggle with academic tasks requiring long-term concentration. This situation can negatively affect the development of higher-order cognitive skills such as deep reading, complex problem-solving, and creative thinking.

The multitasking fallacy is a frequently observed problem in gamified learning environments. Visual effects, audio alerts, and simultaneous feedback mechanisms cause students to try to cope with multiple stimuli simultaneously. However, scientific research shows that the human brain cannot truly multitask and this situation reduces learning quality.

Instant gratification addiction is a side effect of gamification systems that conflicts with long-term learning objectives. Students accustomed to continuous small successes and rapid rewards may struggle to make efforts for long-term goals. This situation can hinder the development of values such as patience, perseverance, and continuous effort required for academic success.

Social isolation risk is a potential consequence of individual gamification experiences. Increased interaction with digital tools can lead to decreased face-to-face social interactions. This situation can negatively affect the development of students' empathy, social problem-solving, and communication skills. Various preventive strategies must be developed to minimize these risks. Balanced technology use, regular digital detox periods, physical activity integration, and inclusion of face-to-face social interaction opportunities in gamification design are critically important.

SOCIAL AND PSYCHOLOGICAL RISKS OF COMPETITION

While the use of competitive elements in gamified learning environments has motivation-enhancing potential, it carries significant social and psychological risks. Within the achievement goal theory framework, it is seen that competitive environments direct students toward performance goals and this overshadows learning goals. This situation can lead to negative consequences such as students avoiding risk-taking, decreased help-seeking behaviors, and preference for superficial learning strategies.

Social interdependence theory analyzes the effects of competitive goal structures on group dynamics. Since one person's success requires another's failure in competitive environments, negative interactions and hostility can develop among group members. In educational contexts, this means deterioration of classroom climate and reduction of social learning opportunities.

Research shows that collaborative learning structures are superior to competitive structures in terms of academic achievement and social skills. These findings support prioritizing collaborative elements in gamification design.

Self-esteem and confidence problems constitute one of the most serious side effects of competition-focused gamification. Continuous comparison and ranking systems can create feelings of inadequacy in low-performing students. This situation can negatively affect students' academic self-perceptions and develop resistant attitudes toward learning.

Social exclusion risk is an inevitable consequence of competitive gamification systems. In systems where academically strong students are continuously highlighted, struggling students can become increasingly marginalized. This situation leads to hardening of classroom social hierarchies and reduction of equal learning opportunities.

Increased anxiety and stress are natural consequences of intensely competitive environments. Students under continuous evaluation, ranking, and comparison pressure can develop performance anxiety. This situation can negatively affect creativity and risk-taking behaviors in the learning process.

Cheating and ethical violations constitute one of the unexpected side effects of competitive systems. Students under winning pressure may tend to violate academic honesty principles. This situation can negatively affect students' moral development, leading to long-term character problems.

From justice and equity perspectives, competition-focused gamification systems contain serious ethical problems. The principle that social arrangements are unacceptable when they do not improve the situation of the least advantaged individuals requires questioning competitive gamification systems.

Alternative approaches must be developed to solve these problems. Collaborative learning models can provide both personal accountability and positive interdependence by linking individual development with group success. These models enable each student to contribute to group success starting from their own development level.

Structural approaches can support academic learning while developing students' social skills by providing specific interaction structures. Integration of these structures into gamified activities can create strong alternatives to competition-focused systems.

Individual progress competition offers an alternative to traditional competition models. This approach encourages development-focused competition by comparing students with their own past performances rather than others. Thus, motivational benefits of competition are preserved while negative effects of social comparison are minimized.

FAIR ASSESSMENT AND INCLUSIVITY CHALLENGES

Designing evaluation and grading processes fairly and inclusively in gamified learning systems is critically important for ensuring educational equity. When evaluation systems are biased, certain student groups can be systematically disadvantaged, preventing equal access to educational opportunities.

A frequently encountered problem in traditional gamification applications is that evaluation criteria are one-dimensional and recognize only certain types of achievements. Within the multiple intelligence theory framework, multi-dimensional evaluation approaches must be developed against this problem. Recognition of various competencies such as creativity, collaboration, leadership, perseverance, and social responsibility alongside academic success in gamified systems enables students with different strengths to experience success.

Cultural bias risk is an important factor to consider in gamification system design. Students from different cultural backgrounds may show variation in game experiences, competition perceptions, and social interaction preferences. Systems that do not consider these differences can systematically disadvantage certain cultural groups.

Language and communication barriers constitute one of the important challenges of gamification applications in multilingual classrooms. Students whose native language is different may struggle to understand game instructions, and this situation can negatively affect their academic performance. Against this problem, multilingual support mechanisms must be integrated into gamification systems.

Socioeconomic factors are important variables that can create injustice in gamified learning environments. Access to technological resources, home environment support, and cultural capital differences can cause students to show different success levels in gamified systems. To prevent this situation, equal access opportunities must be provided and alternative participation paths must be developed.

Protecting the fair evaluation rights of students with special educational needs is a topic requiring special attention in gamification system design. Within the framework of legal regulations, flexible evaluation options, time extension opportunities, and alternative presentation modalities must be provided for these students.

Gender bias is an important source of injustice overlooked in gamification systems. Traditional game types and competition formats can favor certain genders. To prevent this situation, gender-neutral design principles must be adopted and various game types must be integrated.

Algorithmic bias risk constitutes a serious problem in technology-supported evaluation systems. A concrete example of algorithmic bias is seen in artificial intelligence-supported gamification systems. For example, when algorithms evaluating student performance perpetuate gender bias in historical data, male students may systematically receive higher scores in gamified activities in STEM fields (Barocas & Selbst, 2016). This situation can lead to decreased motivation of female students toward STEM fields and negative effects on their academic self-efficacy perceptions. Therefore, automatic evaluation algorithms used in gamification systems must be regularly audited for fairness and bias detection techniques must be used.

Data privacy and security issues are critically important for protecting student data collected in gamified systems. There is a risk of misuse of detailed data collected about student performance, behavior patterns, and personal preferences. To minimize this risk, strict data protection protocols must be implemented.

Inclusive design principles provide fundamental guidance for ensuring gamification systems are accessible to all students. Implementation of design recommendations that enable students with visual, auditory, motor, and cognitive difficulties to use the system effectively is critically important.

Fairness of peer evaluation processes requires that social dynamics do not negatively affect evaluation results. It should be considered that unstructured peer evaluation processes can turn into popularity contests and prevent objective learning evaluation. To prevent this problem, anonymous evaluation systems and structured feedback forms should be used.

Transparent sharing of evaluation results and protection of students' appeal rights are indispensable components of fair systems. Securing students' rights to appeal evaluation results, request explanations, and seek re-evaluation supports the legitimacy of the system and student trust.

The various risks addressed in this section and the preventive strategies developed against them are summarized in Table 3.

Table 3. Gamification Risks and Preventive Strategies

Risk Category	Specific Risks	Preventive Strategies	Merve's Teacher Application
Motivational	External reward dependency, intrinsic motivation loss	Informational rewards, process-focused evaluation	Creative explanation points, development-focused badges
Technological	Screen addiction, attention distraction	Balanced use, regular breaks	Weekly digital detox, physical activity integration
Social	Excessive competition, social exclusion	Collaboration-focused design, multiple evaluation	Team projects, recognition in different ability areas
Pedagogical	Narrative overshadowing content, superficial learning	Clear learning objectives, deep analysis tasks	Scientific method emphasis in detective process

The strategies summarized in Table 3 aim to minimize potential risks of gamification while maximizing educational benefits. These strategies, which each educator can adapt to their own context, provide fundamental guidance for responsible gamification practice. In light of this systematic analysis of potential risks, an evaluation of the chapter's general findings can be made.

DISCUSSION

The systematic design framework presented addresses the gap between current implementation quality and theoretical potential in educational gamification. This gap can be significantly reduced through structured approaches grounded in motivational psychology and learning theory (Dicheva, Dichev, Agre & Angelova, 2015). The framework depends not only on technical design processes but also on managing complex dynamics requiring pedagogical understanding and ethical sensitivity.

This framework's application is demonstrated through the cell division case study presented throughout the chapter. Merve's implementation of the five-stage design process within the "Cell Detectives Academy" theme illustrates how theoretical principles can be operationalized in classroom environments. The case reveals that effective gamification requires holistic integration with pedagogical goals rather than technological supplementation, with each design decision reflecting the interplay between motivational theory, learning objectives, and student characteristics.

KEY CONTRIBUTIONS

Integration of Self-Determination Theory with the MDA framework provides theoretically grounded design guidance addressing motivational superficiality in current implementations. By linking game dynamics, mechanics, and components to psychological needs for autonomy, competence, and relatedness, the framework offers clear direction for avoiding external motivation dependency that undermines sustained engagement (Ryan & Deci, 2017). This integration represents advancement beyond purely mechanical approaches to gamification design.

The five-stage design process operationalizes abstract theoretical principles into actionable steps applicable across educational contexts. Anchoring each stage in established learning theory (Bloom's taxonomy in goal setting, Kolb's experiential learning cycle in activity design, formative assessment principles in feedback systems) ensures pedagogical rigor while maintaining practical feasibility (Gagné, 1985; Sadler, 1989). The case study demonstrates translation from theory to specific classroom decisions about narrative development, task design, and feedback mechanisms. Extended treatment of potential harms and ethical considerations provides necessary counterbalance to promotional gamification discourse, enabling informed decisions rather than uncritical adoption.

ADDRESSING THE RESEARCH QUESTIONS

The four research questions posed at the beginning require holistic perspectives focused on educational philosophy and student welfare. First, supporting intrinsic motivation while preventing external reward dependency requires systematic application of Self-Determination Theory principles. Design should prioritize mechanisms meeting autonomy needs through choice in learning paths and progress control, competence needs through dynamic difficulty adjustment and constructive feedback, and relatedness needs through collaborative tasks and social interaction (Ryan & Deci, 2017). Informational reward strategies prove essential, with rewards providing performance information rather than exerting control (Deci, Koestner, & Ryan, 1999).

Second, including students with different learning styles and motivation profiles requires integrating Multiple Intelligence Theory with player typology (Gardner, 1983; Yee, 2006). Effective design offers varied activity types and progress paths for achievement-oriented, social interaction-oriented, exploration-oriented, and mastery-oriented students. Universal Design for Learning principles enable this diversity through multiple representation, action and expression, and engagement strategies implemented via flexible task options and personalized feedback systems.

Third, balancing pedagogical goals with game mechanics requires learning objectives to guide element selection, with each mechanic grounded in clear pedagogical justifications (Kiili, 2005). Game elements function as organic learning process components rather than decorative additions. Fourth, evaluating long-term effects requires comprehensive assessment across multiple levels including satisfaction, knowledge acquisition, behavioral transfer, and sustained impact, with transfer and long-term levels demanding more complex methodologies than traditional short-term measurements.

PRACTICAL IMPLICATIONS

For practitioners, design should begin with pedagogical goals rather than game mechanics, ensuring each element serves specific learning objectives aligned with curriculum standards. Preliminary assessment of student characteristics (learning styles, motivation profiles, cultural backgrounds, technology access) enables customization preventing one-size-fits-all approaches that systematically exclude diverse learners. Pilot testing before full implementation allows refinement based on actual responses rather than designer assumptions.

School administrators support effective implementation through professional development focused on motivational psychology and game design principles, dedicated planning time for collaborative design reducing individual burden while enabling knowledge sharing, shared resource repositories preventing duplication, and technical infrastructure with reliable support. Without institutional support structures, well-designed initiatives may fail due to unsustainable workload or inadequate resources (Dichev & Dicheva, 2017).

LIMITATIONS

The framework contains certain limitations. First, development through a single lesson example (cell division) means applicability across disciplines has not been empirically tested. Second, cultural context factors were addressed from one educational system perspective, limiting validity in different cultural structures. Third, technological infrastructure analysis remained general without detailed technical requirements. Finally, long-term impact assessment was presented theoretically without longitudinal data support.

FUTURE RESEARCH DIRECTIONS

Future research should prioritize longitudinal studies examining sustained effects on academic achievement and intrinsic motivation beyond initial engagement periods. Research tracking students across multiple semesters can reveal whether motivational benefits persist or diminish over time (Hanus & Fox, 2015). Cross-cultural comparative research remains essential for understanding how cultural dimensions influence effectiveness (Hofstede, 1980). Investigation of adaptive technologies integrating artificial intelligence with gamification offers promising directions for personalized learning experiences, with machine learning algorithms enabling dynamic adjustment to individual needs (Koivisto & Hamari, 2019). Additionally, neuroscientific approaches examining how gamified environments affect cognitive processing through neuroimaging technologies could inform more effective design strategies (Palaus, Marron, Viejo-Sobera, & Redolar-Ripoll, 2024). Research addressing special needs populations and examining effectiveness for students with autism spectrum disorder, learning difficulties, and physical disabilities would advance inclusive education objectives.

CONCLUSION

Educational gamification stands at a critical juncture between transformative potential and superficial application. Current practice too often involves adding game elements to existing curricula without pedagogical foundation, producing short-term engagement increases without sustained learning benefits or meaningful skill development. The framework presented offers an alternative path: theoretically grounded design balancing motivational enhancement with deep learning, intentionally including diverse learners, and acknowledging potential harms requiring active mitigation.

Realizing educational potential requires moving beyond technological determinism. The assumption that game mechanics automatically improve learning must give way to pedagogy-centered design where understanding of motivational theory, learning processes, and student diversity guides technical decisions. This shift positions gamification not as a tool to motivate resistant students through entertaining tricks, but as a carefully designed learning environment supporting psychological needs for autonomy, competence, and relatedness while developing critical thinking, collaboration, and lifelong learning dispositions valued in contemporary society.

Responsibility for quality implementation extends beyond individual teachers to include institutional support, comprehensive professional development, and policy frameworks ensuring equitable access and ethical practice. When implemented with pedagogical rigor grounded in established theory, cultural responsiveness honoring diverse learning traditions, and ethical sensitivity prioritizing student welfare, gamification can create transformative learning experiences supporting both engagement and achievement. When implemented superficially without theoretical foundation or careful attention to unintended consequences, gamification risks perpetuating educational inequities, damaging intrinsic motivation, and providing only fleeting engagement divorced from meaningful learning. The choice between these outcomes depends on willingness to ground practice in rigorous theory, critically examine implementation assumptions, and prioritize long-term student welfare over short-term engagement metrics or technological novelty. The principles, strategies, evidence-based warnings, and systematic design process presented throughout this chapter aim to guide this essential work toward outcomes genuinely serving student learning and development.

REFERENCES

Barocas, S., & Selbst, A. D. (2016). Big data's disparate impact. *California Law Review, 104*, 671.

Bartle, R. (1996). Hearts, clubs, diamonds, spades: Players who suit MUDs. *Journal of MUD Research, 1*(1), 19–34.

Campbell, J. (1949). *The hero with a thousand faces*. Pantheon Books.

Christy, K. R., & Fox, J. (2014). Leaderboards in a virtual classroom: A test of stereotype threat and social comparison explanations for women's math performance. *Computers & Education, 78*, 66–77. DOI: 10.1016/j.compedu.2014.05.005

Csikszentmihalyi, M. (1990). *Flow: The psychology of optimal experience*. Harper & Row.

Deci, E. L. (1971). Effects of externally mediated rewards on intrinsic motivation. *Journal of Personality and Social Psychology, 18*(1), 105–115. DOI: 10.1037/h0030644

Deci, E. L., Koestner, R., & Ryan, R. M. (1999). A meta-analytic review of experiments examining the effects of extrinsic rewards on intrinsic motivation. *Psychological Bulletin, 125*(6), 627–668. DOI: 10.1037/0033-2909.125.6.627 PMID: 10589297

Deci, E. L., & Ryan, R. M. (1985). *Intrinsic motivation and self-determination in human behavior*. Plenum Press. DOI: 10.1007/978-1-4899-2271-7

Deci, E. L., & Ryan, R. M. (2000). The "what" and "why" of goal pursuits: Human needs and the self-determination of behavior. *Psychological Inquiry, 11*(4), 227–268. DOI: 10.1207/S15327965PLI1104_01

Deterding, S., Dixon, D., Khaled, R., & Nacke, L. (2011). From game design elements to gamefulness: Defining gamification. *Proceedings of the 15th International Academic MindTrek Conference*, 9-15. DOI: 10.1145/2181037.2181040

Dicheva, D., Dichev, C., Agre, G., & Angelova, G. (2015). Gamification in education: A systematic mapping study. *Journal of Educational Technology & Society, 18*(3), 75–88.

Dweck, C. S. (2006). *Mindset: The new psychology of success*. Random House.

Gagné, R. M. (1985). *The conditions of learning and theory of instruction* (4th ed.). Holt, Rinehart & Winston.

Gardner, H. (1983). *Frames of mind: The theory of multiple intelligences*. Basic Books.

Hamari, J., Koivisto, J., & Sarsa, H. (2014). Does gamification work? A literature review of empirical studies on gamification. *Proceedings of the 47th Hawaii International Conference on System Sciences*, 3025-3034. DOI: 10.1109/HICSS.2014.377

Hanus, M. D., & Fox, J. (2015). Assessing the effects of gamification in the classroom: A longitudinal study on intrinsic motivation, social comparison, satisfaction, effort, and academic performance. *Computers & Education, 80*, 152–161. DOI: 10.1016/j.compedu.2014.08.019

Hattie, J., & Timperley, H. (2007). The power of feedback. *Review of Educational Research, 77*(1), 81–112. DOI: 10.3102/003465430298487

Hofstede, G. (1980). *Culture's consequences: International differences in work-related values.* Sage Publications.

Hunicke, R., LeBlanc, M., & Zubek, R. (2004). MDA: A formal approach to game design and game research. *Proceedings of the AAAI Workshop on Challenges in Game AI*, 1-5.

Johnson, D. W., & Johnson, R. T. (1989). *Cooperation and competition: Theory and research.* Interaction Book Company.

Kapp, K. M. (2012). *The gamification of learning and instruction: Game-based methods and strategies for training and education.* Pfeiffer.

Kiili, K. (2005). Digital game-based learning: Towards an experiential gaming model. *The Internet and Higher Education, 8*(1), 13–24. DOI: 10.1016/j.iheduc.2004.12.001

Koivisto, J., & Hamari, J. (2019). The rise of motivational information systems: A review of gamification research. *International Journal of Information Management, 45*, 191–210. DOI: 10.1016/j.ijinfomgt.2018.10.013

Krashen, S. D. (1982). *Principles and practice in second language acquisition.* Pergamon Press.

Landers, R. N., & Landers, A. K. (2014). An empirical test of the theory of gamified learning: The effect of leaderboards on time-on-task and academic performance. *Simulation & Gaming, 45*(6), 769–785. DOI: 10.1177/1046878114563662

McGonigal, J. (2011). *Reality is broken: Why games make us better and how they can change the world.* Penguin Press.

Palaus, M., Marron, E. M., Viejo-Sobera, R., & Redolar-Ripoll, D. (2024). Neural basis of video gaming: A systematic review of neuroimaging studies. *Frontiers in Human Neuroscience, 18*, 123–145.

Ryan, R. M., & Deci, E. L. (2017). *Self-determination theory: Basic psychological needs in motivation, development, and wellness*. Guilford Publications. DOI: 10.1521/978.14625/28806

Sadler, D. R. (1989). Formative assessment and the design of instructional systems. *Instructional Science*, *18*(2), 119–144. DOI: 10.1007/BF00117714

Sailer, M., & Homner, L. (2020). The gamification of learning: A meta-analysis. *Educational Psychology Review*, *32*(1), 77–112. DOI: 10.1007/s10648-019-09498-w

Twenge, J. M., & Campbell, W. K. (2018). Associations between screen time and lower psychological well-being among children and adolescents. *Psychological Science*, *29*(12), 1947–1954. PMID: 30406005

Vygotsky, L. S. (1978). *Mind in society: The development of higher psychological processes*. Harvard University Press.

Werbach, K., & Hunter, D. (2012). *For the win: How game thinking can revolutionize your business*. Wharton Digital Press.

Yee, N. (2006). Motivations for play in online games. *Cyberpsychology & Behavior*, *9*(6), 772–775. DOI: 10.1089/cpb.2006.9.772 PMID: 17201605

Chapter 2
Integrating AI and XR for Smarter Learning in Computer Science Education:
Teaching in the Age of Intelligence and Immersion

Miguel A. Garcia-Ruiz
https://orcid.org/0000-0002-7048-7286
Algoma University, Canada

Randy Lin
https://orcid.org/0000-0002-3907-1995
Algoma University, Canada

Somang Nam
https://orcid.org/0000-0002-7785-9003
Algoma University, Canada

Sathaporn Hu
https://orcid.org/0009-0000-8249-9586
Algoma University, Canada

Mahreen Nasir
Algoma University, Canada

Pedro C. Santana-Mancilla
https://orcid.org/0000-0002-4184-0116
Universidad de Colima, Mexico

ABSTRACT

This chapter explores the integration of Artificial Intelligence (AI) with Extended Reality (XR) technologies (encompassing virtual, augmented, and mixed reality) in university/college-level computer science (CS) education. The chapter examines how AI and XR-based CS teaching make learning experiences more personalized, immersive, adaptive, and interactive. AI in CS education supports functions such as data analysis, content development automation, and learner engagement, complementing rather than replacing human instructors. The chapter highlights how

DOI: 10.4018/979-8-3373-5157-5.ch002

AI+XR technologies can aid in teaching and learning complex CS courses and topics. It covers theoretical foundations and a literature review, emphasizing XR innovations. Additionally, the chapter addresses ethical and equity concerns to promote inclusive implementation. Aimed at educators, researchers, and developers, the chapter offers a framework and actionable strategies to leverage AI and XR for more effective, immersive, and intelligent CS education in higher education settings

INTRODUCTION

Immersive computer technologies such as virtual reality (VR) and augmented reality (AR) have been used in higher education since the 1990s, supporting a number of knowledge areas, including computer science, where students have used 3D simulations of real-life scientific and technical information (Burke et al., 2025). Systematic reviews about VR and AR found that the applications of these technologies in university/college courses have yielded persistent learning and better spatial representations of technical computing information, offering a more hands-on learning experience (Hajirasouli & Banihashemi, 2022; Pirker et al., 2020). As Rauschnabel et al. (2022) point out, extended reality (XR) is an umbrella term where "X" serves as a variable encompassing immersive technologies such as VR, AR, and mixed reality (MR). XR has been highly useful to support learning of complex structural information, such as in molecular biology taught at the university level (Garcia-Bonete et al., 2019), making abstract information more salient. Multisensory information in XR can be used to support understanding of complex structures (Garcia-Ruiz et al., 2019, 2022). Garcia-Bonete et al. (2019) also demonstrated that XR educational materials can be developed in a short time, using freely available, open-source software tools. In addition, there is a growing convergence between research in immersive technologies and artificial intelligence (AI), which have traditionally been separate fields. There is a need for the integration of AI and XR as applications increasingly involve cutting-edge areas such as machine learning and large-language models (LLM), for example, for developing educational content and conversational agents in a VR environment (Moore et al., 2022). However, there are challenges and opportunities in creating intelligent virtual environments by combining techniques from both fields. Examples include systems that guide users with built-in knowledge, immersive environments with semi-autonomous user avatars, and those featuring independent intelligent agents (Luck & Aylett, 2000). The integration of AI and XR in computer science education creates immersive, interactive learning environments where abstract computer science concepts can be visualized in 3D space, for example, making complex algorithms and data structures more tangible and easier to understand. AI-powered adaptive systems can provide personalized feedback and guidance within these virtual environments, adjusting the learning experience to each student's pace and learning style. This combination enables hands-on experimentation with code in risk-free virtual spaces while offering intelligent tutoring that helps students debug, optimize, and understand their programs more effectively (Manfredi et al., 2023).

The mission of this chapter is to explore and critically examine the integration of AI into teaching and learning with XR technologies in computer science (CS) education, creating smarter, more adaptive, and engaging educational experiences. XR is an umbrella term encompassing VR, AR, and MR. VR is a computer-generated 3D environment that is interactive and immersive. AR technology allows overlaying digital content onto the physical environment to enhance the user's real-world experience. XR also includes mixed reality (MR), a technology that blends the real world with digital elements, allowing interaction between the two (Rauschnabel et al., 2022). AI in education refers to the use of intelligent computer systems that can simulate human thinking and behavior to support teaching, learning, and educational management (Holmes & Tuomi, 2022). These intelligent systems can analyze data, adapt to learners' needs, automate processes, and even interact with students in natural ways. AI in education can transform how education is delivered and experienced, in a way to augment teacher-to-student instruction, making learning more personalized, efficient, and data-informed.

As the educational landscape increasingly embraces immersive technologies (Tene et al., 2024), the convergence of AI and XR presents unprecedented opportunities to personalize learning, enhance interactivity, and automate educational support systems in computer science education. This chapter aims to provide a comprehensive overview of how AI can enhance the pedagogical potential of XR across CS education in higher education. For example, AI+XR can support teaching and learning of computer science courses that require spatial reasoning and the analysis of complex systems, such as computer graphics, human-computer interaction, computer networks, data visualization, and mathematics for CS, among other computing areas.

This chapter describes theoretical foundations, practical applications, emerging tools, and real-world case studies. It illustrates how AI-enhanced XR can support teaching and learning of CS courses in higher education. In addition, the chapter also addresses the ethical, equity, and implementation challenges that must be navigated to ensure responsible and inclusive adoption of AI+XR in CS education.

AI and XR have specific roles in the support of CS education, based on their own technological characteristics:

AI's Role (Holmes & Tuomi, 2022):

- Personalized Learning: AI can create adaptive learning environments, provide individual tutoring, and track personalized learning patterns to tailor education to each student.
- Enhanced Engagement: AI can generate content and interact with students in personalized ways, such as with AI tutors that guide learning rather than providing direct answers.
- Teacher Support: AI can assist teachers with lesson planning, rubric creation, and provide data-driven insights into student performance.
- Evaluation: AI can assist teachers with the evaluation of student performance and analyze data to help with decision-making within a class.

XR's Role (Burke et al., 2025):

- Immersive Experiences: XR technologies create immersive and interactive environments that can bring CS lessons to life.
- Exploration and Curiosity: XR allows for hands-on, exploratory learning, making complex subjects more engaging and easier to understand.
- Real-World Application: XR can provide realistic simulations and scenarios that improve skills-based learning and assessment in CS education.
- Learning Abstraction by Visualization: AI techniques, such as deep learning, require students to be able to abstract various programming concepts. For instance, an algorithm like gradient descent is like a "ball rolling down into the valley." However, the valley is not a 3D valley like a real-world valley. Rather, it is a high-dimensional valley, something that a normal human being cannot imagine. The best a student can do is to develop skills to create analogies and to abstract a myriad of concepts.

The Fusion of AI and XR (Grassini, 2025):

- Dynamic and Adaptive Environments: AI can power dynamic XR environments that respond to individual learner needs, making learning more effective.
- Scalable Personalization: The combination allows for personalized learning experiences to be delivered at scale.
- Increased Access: By creating accessible and adaptable learning, the AI-XR fusion can help bridge educational gaps and increase access to quality education.

- New Type of Evaluation: XR affords the instructors a new method of evaluation, e.g., immersive oral examinations, remote and immersive student presentations.

The objective of this chapter is to show educators, instructional designers, researchers, and edtech developers actionable insights and forward-looking strategies to harness the use of AI and XR for transformative learning experiences in computer science education. In addition, the chapter will serve as a practical guide for shaping the future of intelligent, immersive CS education.

BACKGROUND

Extended Reality, or XR, is an overarching term for technologies that merge the digital and physical reality realms, where users employ interactive multisensory information (Khlaif et al., 2024; Rauschnabel et al., 2022). XR is a rapidly evolving set of technologies reshaping various fields with education being a prime example. XR provides highly immersive learning experiences that blend physical classrooms with dynamic, virtual elements. For example, students could interact with an interactive 3D model of a quantum computer right in a classroom. XR technologies include:

- **Virtual Reality (VR):** This technology immerses a user in a computer-generated 3D digital environment, also called virtual world or virtual environment (Burdea & Coiffet, 2024; LaValle, S.M., 2023), ideally surrounding the user's field of view. The 3D virtual environment generated in VR is generally graphic, but it can also be auditory, where users rely on 3D sounds. In VR, users interact with the virtual environment using special haptic devices, but this is not always the case. Users can also interact with a regular mouse or keyboard and visualize a 3D virtual environment on a computer screen.
- **Augmented Reality (AR):** Unlike VR, AR overlays digital information and content onto a user's view of the real world (Craig, 2013; Kamińska et al., 2023). This is often accessed through a mobile device, like a phone or tablet, or specialized glasses or an XR headset. This technology enhances the user's real-world experience by overlaying digital content onto the physical environment.
- **Mixed Reality (MR):** MR blends the real world with digital elements, allowing interaction between the two (Kent et al., 2021; Speicher et al., 2019).

XR technologies provide various degrees of immersion and presence, depending on the type of technology used. VR is generally more immersive than AR and MR, since in VR ideally, a virtual environment will surround a user by wearing a VR headset. Although many researchers use the terms presence and immersion indistinctively, presence is a subjective experience where the user feels the illusion of "being there", inside a virtual environment (Slater, 2018). This feeling is supported by user immersion, achieved by stimulating the human senses through multisensory information played in the virtual environment, and interacting with it using special devices such as haptic devices, a 3D display, etc. Immersion (and hence presence) is very useful in learning complex scientific and technological information (Dede et al., 1999). The immersive quality of XR experiences helps bridge the gap between abstract concepts and their practical applications, making learning more concrete and experiential. Immersion helps learners tackle increasingly complex tasks by engaging and motivating them. For example, Larson & Chambers (2020a) show empirical evidence that AR motivates students to learn computer programming. Their literature review synthesizes research on AR-based methods in programming classrooms, discussing how AR's visual and spatial feedback can enhance motivation, engagement, and academic performance, which are related to immersion.

Extended reality can be used in combination with AI to support computer science education. AI in education refers to the use of intelligent computer systems that simulate human behavior and thinking to support teaching, learning, and educational management (Wang et al., 2024). The combination of XR + AI can enhance CS education in a number of ways (Allison et al., 2025; Gu et al., 2024; Horvath & Goldschmid, 2025), including:

- Visualizing abstract concepts: XR environments, especially VR, can transform abstract ideas like data structures and algorithms into interactive 3D objects, making them easier to grasp.
- Computer architecture: AR can overlay information onto physical hardware. Students can point a device at a computer and see digital labels explaining each component and its function, or visualize data flowing through the different parts.
- Immersive and personalized practice: AI enables XR systems to adapt to individual student needs, providing customized feedback and challenges in a safe, immersive space.
- AI-powered coding assistants: AI tools can act as "pair programmers," providing code suggestions, explaining bugs, and offering corrections in real time. This gives students instant feedback and exposes them to modern software development practices (Garcia-Ruiz et al., 2023).
- Virtual labs: In a VR environment, students can practice cybersecurity scenarios, troubleshoot networks, or manage data centers without real-world

risk. The AI behind the simulation can adjust the difficulty and introduce new challenges based on the student's performance.

- Real-time skill assessment: By tracking student interactions within an XR environment, AI can objectively assess skill and performance. In this case, AI identifies patterns in students' actions and provides insights that an instructor might certainly miss.
- Dynamic learning support: AI complements XR by providing contextual and adaptive support, e.g. using a chatbot to support student learning, making learning more efficient and accessible.
- Intelligent tutoring systems: AI tutors can provide personalized instruction, adaptive feedback, and helpful hints based on a student's individual learning progress. They can assess student performance and offer tailored reading materials and exercises.
- On-demand debugging: When a student encounters a code bug, an AI agent can help pinpoint the cause and suggest corrections. This is particularly valuable for beginners learning the critical skill of debugging.
- Contextual information: In an AR scenario, AI can deliver information about a physical or virtual object exactly when and where it is relevant. This reduces cognitive load by providing information in the context of the task, rather than requiring students to seek it out separately.
- Develop XR content and assets using generative AI: AI can be useful to develop compelling textures, 3D objects, sound effects, and even XR coding automatically.

LITERATURE REVIEW

Integrating AI with XR in STEM education is most impactful when grounded in established learning theories (Tenney et al., 2023). Rather than treating AI+XR merely as novel technologies, their pedagogical affordances can be aligned with constructivist, experiential, immersive, and social learning frameworks. This theoretical alignment ensures that AI+XR applications are based on sound pedagogy, providing both educators and learners with robust foundations for effective teaching and learning. CS educators should know the supporting learning theories in order to adjust and adapt their AI+XR applications more effectively. The following shows a non-exhaustive list of learning theories that support XR and AI in education.

THEORETICAL GROUNDING

Constructivist Learning

Constructivism is a learning theory stating that learners derive meaning by actively constructing their own knowledge through interaction and personal experiences with their environment (Tenney et al., 2023). XR environments embody this principle by allowing students to manipulate, explore, and test hypotheses in immersive contexts (Okorie et al., 2024). For example, Mukasheva et al. (2023) developed a VR application to visualize bubble and selection sorting methods, aiming to improve students' comprehension of programming concepts. Results showed that 76.9% of students using the VR tool achieved higher performance in implementing sorting tasks. The findings suggest that VR-based constructive visualization enhances understanding and offers promising directions for future research in CS education. AI can augment constructivism by offering adaptive scaffolding. Intelligent agents can monitor learners' interactions, detect misconceptions, and provide timely feedback aligned with the learner's zone of proximal development (ZPD). The ZPD is the gap between what a learner can do on their own and what they can achieve with guidance from a more knowledgeable person, such as a teacher or peer, or in this case, an AI agent acting like a tutor or learning companion (Haw & Muthu, 2023). A recent review highlights that constructivist principles are central to VR and XR learning, particularly in STEM domains (Marougkas et al., 2023).

Experiential and Immersive Learning

Experiential learning theory (Kolb et al., 2001; MCLeod, 2025) posits that students' knowledge develops through cycles of concrete experience, reflection, abstraction, and experimentation. XR technologies are uniquely suited to delivering the "concrete experience" phase, providing students with safe and interactive simulations of complex systems (Crogman et al., 2025), for example, distributed networks, robotics, or cybersecurity scenarios. AI can extend this cycle by facilitating reflection and abstraction. For instance, AI systems can generate summaries of a student's interactions, highlight decision points, and pose reflective prompts. Adaptive sequencing further allows experiences to progress in difficulty, ensuring that learners encounter challenges calibrated to their skill level. (Lin et al., 2025). Obourdin et al. (2024) propose the FAIRI framework (Fair, Adaptive, Immersive, Responsive, Interactive) for immersive learning, underscoring how adaptive AI features reinforce XR's experiential value.

Situated and Authentic Learning

Situated learning theory asserts that knowledge is best acquired within authentic contexts (Brown et al., 1989). XR environments can replicate real-world tasks, such as learning a second language in a real and authentic context (Yan et al., 2024). Situated learning can be applied to learning complex CS based on a real-world situation, such as tailoring cybersecurity training to teach real attacks (Noble et al., 2025). By situating abstract CS concepts in realistic, embodied activities, XR enhances transferability of learning to professional contexts. AI contributes by dynamically adjusting scenarios and embedding intelligent agents that act as collaborators, adversaries, or mentors. For example, an AI-driven "cyber adversary" in a VR cybersecurity module can alter its tactics in real time, forcing learners to apply adaptive problem-solving strategies. Such branching and adaptive scenarios reflect authentic complexity without overwhelming the learner. Studies demonstrate that XR's authenticity supports skill development and learner engagement, particularly when coupled with adaptive AI components (Rana & Chicone, 2025a)

Social Constructivism and Collaborative Learning

Vygotskian perspectives emphasize that knowledge is socially co-constructed. Multi-user XR platforms enable collaborative learning (Zhou et al., 2024), allowing students to learn together computer science topics and co-create XR contents that will allow students to learn CS topics such as human-computer interaction within shared immersive environments (Vasilchenko et al., 2020). Students can visualize each other's contributions in real time, promoting co-construction of knowledge in a shared virtual environment. AI strengthens collaboration by acting as a coach or mediator. Intelligent agents can monitor group dynamics, encourage quieter students to participate, and provide context-sensitive hints to keep groups aligned. This aligns with the principles of cognitive apprenticeship, where experts (human or AI) model processes and gradually fade support (Ramadhani Fajri et al., 2025).

Connectivism and Networked Learning

Finally, connectivism learning theory underscores that knowledge exists across distributed networks of people, multiple information sources, and technologies supporting them (Alam, 2023; Siemens, 2005). In this sense, XR allows students to socially construct new knowledge and discuss information in collaborative virtual environments (Myara, 2024).

AI enhances this by recommending pathways, highlighting critical nodes, and linking learners to relevant external resources. For example, in a VR environment visualizing a software dependency graph, AI might highlight modules for deeper inspection or suggest related documentation. This creates a dynamic and adaptive knowledge ecosystem aligned with connectivist ideals (Mallek et al., 2024).

Together, these theories illustrate a layered pedagogical rationale for AI+XR in CS education:

- Constructivism: provides active exploration based on previous knowledge.
- Experiential learning: ensures reflection and iterative growth with active learning.
- Situated learning: grounds activities in authentic contexts.
- Social constructivism: fosters collaboration.
- Connectivism: situates learning within broader knowledge networks.

Taking into account the learning theories summarized above, AI acts as the adaptive, intelligent layer that personalizes, scaffolds, and orchestrates XR experiences. This alignment offers a theoretical roadmap for designing effective AI+XR interventions that are not only engaging but also pedagogically rigorous.

Worldwide Adoption of XR and AI in Higher Education

Educational institutions around the world are constantly researching and applying AI and XR. A 2020–2024 PRISMA-guided review of 295 studies shows XR (VR/AR/MR) is rapidly expanding in higher education across six continents and 48 countries, with the U.S. leading publications. VR dominates usage (58%), most work occurs in undergraduate settings (81%), and science is the most studied area (21%). The study identified three main domains regarding XR usage: knowledge acquisition (51%), psychomotor learning (35%), and affective learning (14%), with XR commonly used for simulation, visualization, problem-solving, and gaming. Key challenges include student impact concerns, inauthentic environments represented with XR, costs/time, and usability/technical issues, highlighting clear gaps and priorities for future research.

A study conducted by Zhuang et al. (2024) examines China's large-scale use of VR simulations to counter declining mastery of theoretical knowledge in math and the sciences. Through cases in telecommunications, civil, and chemical engineering, it shows how VR builds realistic physical/social settings, visualizes abstract concepts, and lets students adjust parameters and environments, strengthening hands-on, "learning-by-doing" interaction with ideas. Framed by situated learning, the study helps contextualize theory, deepen engagement, and reduce "abstraction shock," offering practical guidance for universities seeking to improve students' grasp of foundational theory. In addition, China's higher education sector is rapidly mainstreaming AI across teaching, student support, and operations, backed by national policy guidance and university-level initiatives. Recent empirical studies show active classroom adoption (e.g., AI chatbots for tutoring and feedback) and generally positive student intentions to use such tools, while also surfacing concerns around pedagogy and ethics that institutions must address. At the leadership level, Chinese universities report strong strategic interest on AI, tempered by challenges in data governance, staff capacity, and integration with existing systems (Packer & Huang, 2025).

A bibliometric review of 126 Scopus/WoS papers maps how VR is being studied in Latin American higher education, an area where research remains limited and unsystematized. Most work comes from social sciences, engineering, business, and medicine, clustered into five themes: functional aspects of VR as a tool, VR-based teaching strategies, behavioral factors, educational outcomes, and user competencies/readiness. Notably, 74.6% of publications emphasize functional issues, such as access, feasibility, usefulness, virtual environments, and links to AI, highlighting a practical, infrastructure-focused research agenda and clear opportunities to deepen pedagogy- and outcome-driven studies (Pozzo et al., 2024). Similarly, AI is reshaping higher education across Latin America and the Caribbean by personalizing learning, streamlining research and administration, and expanding access and efficiency. Yet AI adoption is uneven across Latin America: infrastructure gaps, scarce homegrown AI innovation, and limited faculty upskilling/retention and AI knowledge slow progress. The result is a region poised for impact but needing coordinated investment, capacity building, and policy to scale AI's benefits (Molina & Medina, 2025).

Advances in XR have pushed immersive tech into everyday work and learning, offering vast creative potential for pedagogy. To understand both the opportunities and constraints and to gauge Europe's current position, Schwaiger (2021) analyzed 25 EU-funded projects focused on XR-based learning. The evaluation maps indicate XR is most promising in education, where its limits currently lie, and what gaps remain for future European initiatives. The study shows that there is a high percentage of young learners who are already familiar with virtual worlds and immersive simulations, which may facilitate the use of XR in education. However, the author found that Europe has few teachers, trainers, and educators who are knowledgeable of XR technologies, and people who know how to correctly apply XR in educational settings. Across Europe, the state of the art in AI for higher education is marked by student support, paired with an emphasis on governance, transparency, and human-rights–aligned use. Universities are piloting generative AI for feedback and tutoring, analytics for early-warning and personalization, and policy bodies are framing adoption under EU values (e.g., requirements for explainability, privacy, and accountability). Still, implementations remain uneven across systems, highlighting needs in institutional policy, staff development, and quality assurance.

A recent Council of Europe survey synthesizes national strategies and practices, underscoring both the momentum and the gaps that must be closed for trustworthy and scalable AI in European higher education (Chounta, 2024)

AI and XR for CS Education Research

The following examines relevant research on the use of AI and XR to support higher education, particularly in teaching CS topics. We believe that the application of AI+XR technologies in CS education has recently increased, mainly due to technological advances in XR hardware such as enhanced displays, audio systems, and faster microprocessors. In addition, the emergence of more accessible consumer-grade XR devices, such as the Meta Quest XR headset series (Romoser et al., 2024) and inexpensive Google Cardboard-like VR headsets (Cherner & Fegely, 2023), where learners can use their own cellphones to run VR applications, has reduced the cost barrier for educational institutions. Despite this, some educational institutions from developing countries may not afford to acquire those types of XR technologies yet. We also believe that improved usability of XR and AI software development tools, and more XR development tools based on open standards (Abeywardena, 2023; Pomerantz & Rode, 2020), have increased the use of XR and AI in education.

Garg et al. (2025) and Cinar et al. (2024) described a VR application developed and assessed for its effectiveness in teaching Python programming language, including a collection of data types and structures, to electrical and electronic engineering students. This application utilizes gamification and personalization features, alongside a virtual assistant and example generator powered by wit.ai (a text-to-speech tool) and Meta Voice SDK (a tool to develop voice interaction experiences), to provide an immersive and interactive learning experience. A study with 48 participants compared the VR application to a traditional booklet. Users from the two groups wore EEG headsets to measure engagement and attention. Results from this study indicated a statistically significant improvement in Python comprehension from VR users. In addition, the EEG analysis showed higher levels of engagement and attention in the VR group, compared to the booklet group. These findings strongly suggest that VR technology can enhance focus and improve learning outcomes in software development education.

Pirker et al. (2020) carried out a systematic review of papers regarding how VR is used in CS education, highlighting both its potential and the challenges faced. While studies dating back years ago reported on the promise of VR in this field, the recent availability of affordable, high-quality head-mounted displays (HMDs) has opened up new possibilities for innovative teaching approaches in classrooms and for self-regulated learning. The review emphasizes that professionally-designed VR environments for teaching and learning computer science can cover a wide range of topics, such as coding, and should leverage interaction, immersion, visualization, playful design, metaphors, and social experiences to enhance learning, and are most effective with VR headsets while considering school equipment limitations. It also recommends using teleportation for locomotion to prevent cybersickness, minimizing environmental risks, simplifying controls, and incorporating age-appropriate stories to boost student motivation. When VR was used in the classroom, careful embedding within the overall teaching sequence was crucial, prioritizing higher levels of technological immersion, thus enhancing engagement and motivation. The study recommends that instructors include an introductory phase and provide support for students to navigate the experience and manage cybersickness.

A systematic review written by Agbo et al. (2021) examined the use of VR in CS education over the past decade through bibliometric and content analysis. Researchers analyzed 971 articles from Web of Science and Scopus, with a more detailed review of 39 selected studies. The findings show that while VR research in CS education declined between 2013 and 2016, interest has grown again since 2017. The study identified leading scholars and emerging research hotspots in the field. CS topics taught with the help of VR include human-computer interaction, serious games (video games that support learning and entertainment), and video game development. The study concludes that while VR is increasingly used in CS education, more cross-institutional collaboration and rigorous application methodologies are needed. The paper's future research indicates that authors will explore the pedagogical aspects of VR in CS education.

Larson & Chambers (2020b) conducted a systematic review of existing literature on using AR modalities to teach computer programming (including algorithmic structures and computational thinking) in higher education using AR-based marker-based systems. The review acknowledges the limited research explicitly focused on the higher education computer programming environment, but it also considers generalizable methodologies. While the current empirical evidence suggests that AR-based learning can enhance student motivation and performance, the literature shows significant opportunities for future research in AR for supporting CS education. This includes studies validating AR models and applications, developing frameworks and protocols, and examining the long-term impact of the novelty effect to gather measurable academic achievement data.

A study conducted by Lampropoulos, Keramopoulos, Diamantaras & Evangelidis (2023) evaluated the effects of combining AR, gamification (the use of gaming elements to make learning more engaging and fun), and serious games in CS education through a mobile application. Based on an experiment with 117 students and applying a 49-item questionnaire, the research found that integrating these technologies yielded significant educational benefits. The mobile application was found to be an effective tool that enriches the educational experience and fosters interactive, inclusive, and student-centered learning environments. Its use led to increased student motivation, engagement, self-efficacy, and immersion. Students from the study reported a more enjoyable learning experience, cultivated social skills, and experienced a heightened sense of belonging. The AR application also improved students' cognitive skills, including computational and critical thinking. The study concluded that the combination of AR, gamification, and serious games holds potential for fostering both students' cognitive and social-emotional development. The active involvement of students in the software design and development process was also highlighted as a key factor in achieving these positive outcomes.

Horvath & Goldschmid (2025) explored the integration of AR and VR into computer science curricula in higher education, showing how these technologies can enhance learning by bridging the gap between theory and practice. This exploratory study found student engagement, motivation, and comprehension through interactive, hands-on experiences. Case studies from a computer science bachelor's program show that VR and AR applications support the development of critical skills, such as spatial reasoning, problem-solving, and practical application in areas such as AI, cybersecurity, and software development. Despite the benefits found in the study, challenges such as high implementation costs, technical demands, and faculty training remained significant barriers. Future research indicated in this paper that the authors will create reusable and cost-effective immersive applications. An ongoing project involving a VR-based lab for digital communications is cited as a promising example. In addition, the paper highlights a broader adoption of AR and VR to enhance technical learning, skill development, and job readiness in computer science education.

Grassini (2025) explored emerging XR and AI technological trends in education. The paper focused on how AI and XR can make learning more personalized and engaging. Grassini found that AI enables customization by adapting content to individual learning patterns, where XR offers immersive 3D environments. This, in turn, will enhance interaction and simulate real-world experiences of technical information, such as that learned in CS courses. The chapter shows evidence-based reviews and case studies based on AI-powered virtual tutors and XR-based labs. The case studies showed how AI and XR improve accessibility and skill development. In addition, the paper discusses key challenges, which include data privacy, equity, and ethical issues. The chapter concludes with pedagogical strategies for responsibly integrating AI and XR, emphasizing their potential to transform the education system.

AI and XR have been explored to support cybersecurity education, a critical CS area that requires learning abstract concepts, complex structured information, and safe technical practice environments. Rana & Chicone (2025b) examined in a book chapter how AI, VR, and AR can improve cybersecurity training. The chapter highlights key cybersecurity applications, such as network threat simulations, by using immersive learning environments and AI-driven personalization to enhance engagement and learning effectiveness. Rana & Chicone also discuss the development of intelligent interaction tools and automated assessments to support adaptive learning. Security concerns unique to VR/AR systems are addressed in the chapter, such as hardware vulnerabilities and data privacy, showcasing real-world examples, such as the Meta Quest headset exploit, used to illustrate potential cybersecurity risks. The chapter concludes by exploring future directions, learning security threats of IoT and 5G using XR. The chapter noted current limitations in hardware, haptic feedback, and the lack of VR standards. Overall, the chapter presents AI-enhanced VR/AR as a promising yet evolving approach to advancing cybersecurity education and training. Similarly, Spencer (2025) investigated the gap between current cybersecurity education and the advancement of technologies such as immersive environments, decentralized web platforms, and AI. The author argues that current educational programs are not sufficiently equipping students to address emerging cyber threats, despite the increasing influence of technologies such as VR, AR, and AI on digital interactions. By using a mixed-methods approach, the study analyzed top cybersecurity curricula. It reviewed 137 academic publications on cyber-safe learning, consulted 18 industry professionals, and developed 10 pedagogical use cases involving immersive technology. In addition, the author conducted a case study on an AI tutoring system, which shows benefits such as improved engagement and personalized learning. Key threats identified include deepfake avatars and biometric spoofing. The paper proposes a framework for integrating these innovations into cybersecurity education, including immersive simulations, interdisciplinary modules on AI ethics, and blockchain security. The paper points out the need to ensure equitable access and address ethical concerns. The study concludes by recommending future research on cross-cultural adoption and the long-term impact of AI-powered tutoring on cybersecurity.

AI+XR have been used and researched for supporting teaching and learning of computer programming in CS education. A study conducted by Manfredi et al. (2023) addresses challenges in Pair Programming (PP), an Agile software development methodology where two software developers work together on one computer, by focusing on its remote alternative, also called Distributed Pair Programming (DPP). While DPP offers similar benefits, team compatibility issues remain, especially in educational contexts. To tackle this, the researchers developed a Mixed Reality (MR) application using HoloLens (a mixed-reality headset) and a conversational virtual avatar integrated with Visual Studio Code (an integrated software development environment). This system simulates a PP experience by providing real-time coding suggestions through an animated, interactive avatar. It enables solo developers to learn and practice PP even without a human partner, offering a novel solution to the limitations of traditional DPP methods. In addition, Dyulicheva & Glazieva (2021) explore the use of serious games enhanced by AI and immersive technologies in education. The paper discusses how these technologies enable adaptability and personalization through image recognition, emotion detection, speech analysis, and intelligent agents to simulate realistic interactions to develop game complexity. The study also reviews user-friendly tools—such as Aurora Neverwinter Nights, Scratch with AI, Metaverse Studio, and CoSpaces Edu, allowing teachers and students to create educational games with little or no programming skills. The authors highlight the potential of these technologies to support game-based and project-based learning and suggest that future research should focus on developing educational games that integrate immersive technologies with machine learning.

Konecki et al. (2023) highlight the growing importance of programming applications in today's world, especially with the rise of AI, where even small coding errors can have serious consequences. Despite the demand for skilled programmers, programming remains difficult to learn, with high failure rates in courses. Traditional methods have had limited success, prompting the need for new solutions. The paper explores VR as a potential tool to make programming concepts more engaging and easier to understand, aiming to boost student motivation and learning outcomes. It presents research on the use and acceptance of VR in programming education and discusses new approaches for improving student success. Tsai & Lai (2022) developed an AR logic programming teaching system designed for elementary students, based on seventh-grade structured programming concepts. The system uses AR and game-based materials to help students build foundational programming logic through simple command tasks. A quasi-experimental study with 42 fifth and sixth-graders compared the AR-based system with traditional teaching. Results showed that both groups improved, but the AR group performed significantly better on post-tests. Additionally, using the ARCS motivation model, the AR group demonstrated notably higher learning motivation, especially in the "Attention" category. Overall, the study confirms that AR-based programming instruction can effectively boost both learning outcomes and student motivation. Although this study was applied to middle-school students, this could be replicated for higher education learners.

According to the literature review analyzed in this section, the use of AI and XR in education, particularly for teaching and learning computer science topics, is increasing due to these benefits: enhanced engagement and motivation, improved learning outcomes, immersive real-world simulations, personalized learning and AI-driven adaptive learning, accessibility and inclusivity with more affordable consumer-grade XR devices, and skill development beyond technical knowledge. However, the literature reported challenges, such as complexities in setting up XR infrastructure, security, ethical considerations, and the need for rigorous research and pedagogy.

Our Experience Developing XR Contents with Generative AI in a CS Course

The first author developed and taught a senior undergraduate course focused on an introduction to XR, in which computer science students explored how generative AI can support the development of medium and high-fidelity prototypes in VR and AR. The course had 18 students, taught during one regular semester (3 class-hours per week) in the Fall of 2024. In the course, student teams were tasked to develop virtual simulations of industrial machines and industrial processes. Students used generative AI tools throughout the course to assist with ideation, 3D asset creation, coding, and development of voice features. These tools enabled quicker prototyping and encouraged greater creative exploration, particularly benefiting students with limited technical skills.

Despite the advantages regarding rapid prototyping using AI tools, the integration of generative AI also revealed a number of challenges. For example, students encountered issues related to inconsistent content quality (some AI-generated 3D models had low quality and wrong components), complex or confusing AI tool interfaces, and a growing dependency on automated assistance. Students also identified some authorship issues, such as originality (for example, students asked questions about who is the author of the AI-generated 3D models, the AI tool or the student writing the instructions?) and potential biases in AI-generated content. These discussions emphasized the need for critical engagement with AI, not just its immediate technical usage.

It is important to note that the course highlighted the importance of embedding AI tools, ethical awareness, and intentional design practices into XR education. As generative AI becomes more integrated into CS courses, they should provide a meaningful space to examine both the AI potential and its limitations, including authorship and intellectual property issues using AI, preparing students to collaborate thoughtfully and responsibly with AI technologies. Figure 1 shows a student testing an XR application in the course. The student is wearing a Meta Quest 3, a popular XR headset. Both controls are used to select and manipulate 3D objects in the 3D virtual world that he is viewing on the XR headset.

Figure 1. A student playing an XR prototype in the classroom.

As Figure 1 shows, the students in the computer lab are using high-end gaming computers used to develop and test 3D objects and virtual worlds. It was also possible to run the 3D worlds on the XR headset running as stand-alone applications.

Figure 2 shows an example of a virtual prototype made by one of the student teams. The team dedicated quite an amount of time to improve the realism of the environment, such as the floor quality and the accuracy of movements, since they watched videos of real conveyors as an example. The conveyor simulator loaded crates on the cargo ship. Students from the team were able to control the load speed using the XR headset controls and change environmental variables such as fog, to increase its realism.

Figure 2. A screenshot of a virtual world showing a cargo ship loader simulation.

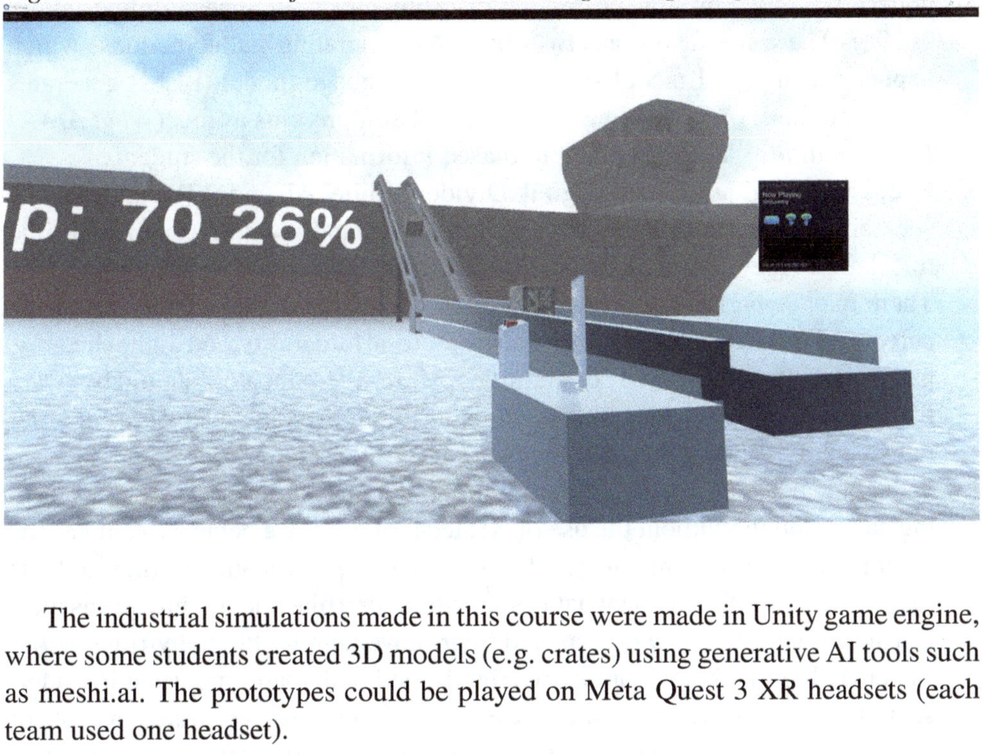

The industrial simulations made in this course were made in Unity game engine, where some students created 3D models (e.g. crates) using generative AI tools such as meshi.ai. The prototypes could be played on Meta Quest 3 XR headsets (each team used one headset).

MAIN FOCUS OF THE CHAPTER

Issues, Controversies, Problems

While the integration of AI and XR holds great promise for enhancing CS education, it also introduces a set of critical concerns that must be addressed to ensure effective, efficient, ethical, and inclusive implementation. Additionally, the AI+XR technologies should effectively and securely support CS courses' learning objectives. This chapter explores the following key concerns:

1. Ethical and Privacy Implications: The use of AI in XR environments may involve the collection of vast amounts of user data, including behavioral patterns, emotional responses, and sometimes biometric feedback. Concerns include data ownership, informed consent, surveillance risks, and the potential misuse of personal and sensitive information in educational contexts (Hu et al., 2024; Kourtesis, 2024).
2. Bias and Fairness in AI Algorithms: AI applications in XR can be used to personalize learning or assess performance, which may amplify biases present in their training data. Also, biases can affect learners from marginalized or underrepresented groups, prompting discriminatory outcomes (Holmes et al., 2019a). There are also concerns about AI generating hallucinations, which happen when an AI model such as a large language model (LLM) generates incorrect, false, or misleading information that it presents as fact (*What Are AI Hallucinations?*, 2023), leading to biased information for the students.
3. Accessibility, Equity, and Digital Divide: While AI and XR can enhance accessibility for some students (e.g., through adaptive interfaces or real-time translation), they can also exacerbate existing inequities in access to technology. There may be barriers related to the existing challenges and limitations of the current AI and XR technologies, infrastructure, affordability, and digital literacy, particularly in underserved communities. Moreover, educators should be aware that some XR devices may require students to remove their eyeglasses in order to use them in educational XR applications (Abdelsalam & Mostafa, 2025).
4. Pedagogical Effectiveness: Although some CS concepts such as machine learning can be taught without the use of XR technologies, we believe that it has the potential to unlock more effective teaching methods. Instead of asking students to imagine multidimensional data using white- or a blackboard drawing as aids, instructors can show 3D objects and their movement within the virtual world. This may help with developing imaginative skills that are important to understand models. Furthermore, the instructors can better demonstrate concepts of immersive analytics, which require XR. There is a need to critically assess how and to what extent AI-enhanced XR supports learning outcomes, or if it risks prioritizing technological novelty over pedagogical value (Dede, 2009).
5. Teacher Roles and Training: As AI takes on roles traditionally held by educators, for example, tutoring and assessment, concerns arise about the evolving role of the teacher/instructor. It is necessary to discuss the need for professional development, teacher/instructor agency, and pedagogical strategies for integrating AI/XR tools in a way that supports and amplifies rather than replaces human instruction (Holmes et al., 2019b). Unless the teachers rely on pre-designed XR materials, they should at least know how to code in a low-code XR development environment

6. System Integration and Scalability: Integrating AI and XR into existing educational systems poses logistical and technical challenges, from platform compatibility to content standardization, technology and software setup, etc. Issues related to scalability, interoperability, and sustainable implementation models need to be addressed (Rana & Chicone, 2025b). Technicians and educational technologists must work together with instructors/teachers to make system integration more effective.
7. Psychological and Cognitive Risks: Extended use of immersive XR environments, especially when combined with AI-driven interactions, may raise concerns about learner fatigue, distraction, cybersickness, and physiological or cognitive overload. Research on user experience and well-being to propose balanced and safe learning designs is needed (Rana & Chicone, 2025c).

These concerns are addressed further in the chapter to provide a balanced and critical perspective, ensuring that the exploration of AI-enhanced XR in CS education is grounded in both innovation and responsibility.

SOLUTIONS AND RECOMMENDATIONS

This section discusses and points out solutions and recommendations regarding ethical concerns, bias and fairness in XR data, technology accessibility, pedagogical effectiveness, system integration, and psychological and cognitive risks in X/AI educational applications. These solutions and recommendations are student-centered, and are intended to provide a safe, efficient, and effective CS learning environment with XR and AI.

1. Ethical and privacy implications

The vast amounts of student data that can be collected in AI/XR environments raise serious privacy and ethical concerns. The following are some recommendations:

- Obtaining approval from a research ethics board: Prior to collecting and analyzing student data, the instructor must first submit the study design to their institutional research ethics board (REB).
- Establish clear, transparent policies: Educational institutions should develop and communicate clear data privacy policies, detailing what data is collected, how it will be used, and for how long it will be stored. These policies should be easy for both students and educators to understand. To ensure that data are used properly, educators are encouraged to outline how the data will be

collected at the beginning of the semester. They must let students know about this. If the educators are also running scientific evaluations of the study using their students as a sample, they must, in the clearest possible manner, let the students know. If the students choose to opt out of the study, they cannot be barred from attending classes.

- Collect only what is necessary: Collect only the data that is necessary for educational and evaluation purposes. Use data anonymization and robust encryption techniques to protect sensitive information. It is important to note that at small institutions, it may be easy for someone to identify individual students based on their quasi-identifiers. A quasi-identifier is a small piece of identity information. On its own, it cannot be used to identify the originator. However, when combined, they can be used to identify individuals.
- Empower user control: Provide students with control over their data, including clear consent mechanisms and options to review or delete their information.
- Long-term data storage: Today, researchers are encouraged to adopt the open science framework which involves long-term storage of data and making them available for public dissemination. If the open science framework is adopted, extreme care must be taken to ensure confidentiality. If anonymity is not possible, it may be necessary to abandon the framework.

2. Bias and fairness in AI algorithms

The use of AI in XR can create or amplify biases found in the AI training data (for example, when training machine learning systems). This potentially leads to discriminatory outcomes for marginalized students. We recommend the following solutions and recommendations:

- Diversify datasets: Researchers must ensure that training data for AI models is diverse and representative of all student populations. Seek out and include data from underrepresented groups to mitigate inherent biases in the AI algorithm.
- Implement fairness by design: Integrate fairness considerations into the AI development process from the beginning, rather than attempting to fix biases after the fact, including building bias detection and mitigation techniques into the AI algorithms.
- Establish human oversight: Educators must provide oversight to AI systems, bringing nuance and context that AI algorithms lack. This ensures accountability and helps catch biases that the AI might miss.

- Develop AI literacy: Educate students and teachers on how to identify and critically evaluate potential biases and hallucinations in AI-generated content. This should be done since the first time the AI is used in XR applications.

3. Accessibility and digital divide

While AI and XR technologies offer potential learning benefits in CS education, they can also widen the digital divide for students with disabilities and students in underserved communities who lack access to necessary technology. We recommend these solutions:

- Affordability: Focus on inclusive technologies that can afford accessibility, not just the latest gadgets. Not all AI and XR tools require expensive hardware to be effective and useful. Many can be accessed through devices that are already common, such as smartphones, tablets, or desktop computers. There are XR applications that work on simple, low-cost equipment, such as Google Cardboard (or similar) VR headsets, which can still provide a valuable immersive experience without a huge financial investment. By prioritizing and opting for such cross-platform tools that work across different operating systems and devices, schools can ensure more students have a way to participate and use XR+AI applications. Adopt devices with accessibility in mind.
- Partnership: Seek funding and partnerships to close the gap. School districts, governments, and private companies can work together through public-private partnerships to secure grants and funding for technology. Some XR technology companies could offer discounted educational tools and content, which can help schools with limited budgets.
- Infrastructure: Develop and support shared infrastructure. Create community-based digital access points, such as kiosks or dedicated spaces in libraries, where students can use AI and XR equipment. This would provide high-speed internet and tech access to anyone who needs it. In addition, Invest in robust school network upgrades to handle the demands of these technologies. Some schools may lack the necessary internet speeds, especially in rural areas.
- Accommodate different types of visions: When purchasing XR hardware, schools should prioritize devices that are adjustable for different pupil distances and eye widths. Many newer devices include this functionality. Seek out devices that come with spacer inserts, which create space for students to wear their glasses comfortably while using the headset. For students who

wear reading or prescription glasses, provide prescription lens inserts for the devices if possible, or work with tech vendors who offer this option.

- Encourage critical thinking: Instead of letting AI and XR lead the learning, educators should design activities that encourage critical thinking, creativity, and collaboration. The XR technologies should be a way to enhance these skills, not a replacement for them. In addition, those technologies should be considered as tools only, and not base the whole curriculum exclusively on XR applications.
- Provide alternative course delivery methods: Offer alternative or non-XR learning modalities. Recognize that for some students, even with accommodations, XR+AI might not be suitable. It is crucial to provide alternative learning options to include everyone in an equitable experiential learning process.
- Inform the students of the accessibility settings: Some XR technologies include accessibility features in their settings, for example, displaying colors that support colorblind users. Make sure to know those features and use them if necessary.

4. Pedagogical effectiveness

The adoption of AI/XR in CS education should prioritize genuine learning benefits over technological novelty. The following are some proposed solutions and recommendations:

- Focus on evidence-based design: Rigorously assess and evaluate how AI-enhanced XR supports specific learning outcomes. Research is needed to move beyond anecdotal evidence and toward measurable academic achievement data. In addition, use standard questionnaires to evaluate the ease of use (usability) of technology, for example, use the SUS or UEQ questionnaires to evaluate whether students feel comfortable using AI+XR technologies, whether they are used efficiently and effectively, and if those are satisfactory to use (Brooke, 1996; Dafiotis et al., 2025).
- Enhance abstract, intangible concepts: Utilize XR to visualize complex, multi-dimensional data in computer science, which is a major pedagogical benefit. Instructors can use 3D objects and virtual environments to demonstrate concepts that are difficult to explain with traditional methods.
- Facilitate higher-order thinking: Integrate AI and XR to facilitate critical thinking, problem-solving, and creative exploration. For instance, AI-driven simulations can be used to model complex cybersecurity scenarios.

- Design for meaningful experiences: Educators should design meaningful learning experiences that leverage AI/XR tools to support and amplify human instruction, not replace it. Use blended learning with XR/AI technologies. Blended learning is an educational approach that combines traditional, in-person instruction with digital, online components to create a more comprehensive and flexible learning experience (Bernard et al., 2014; Osborn-King, 2005).

5. Teacher Roles and Training

Educators should be involved in the pedagogical design of the XR/AI technology applications, working along with technicians and educational technologists. The following are some suggestions and recommendations:

- Provide comprehensive training: Educational institutions must invest in professional development programs that equip teachers with skills in AI/XR tool integration, data analysis, and content development.
- Foster a learning community: Encourage collaboration among educators to share best practices and collectively refine approaches to AI/XR integration.
- Create an online knowledge base where educators, technicians, and educational technologists can share information and instructions about how to set up XR+AI applications, etc. This can be very useful, especially when new XR gadgets need to be installed and for new educators who are starting to use XR and AI. Useful tools for creating knowledge bases include MediaWiki (Barrett, 2008). Even a Google Drive folder with shared documents can be used for that purpose.
- Involve teachers in development: Actively involve educators in the design and deployment of AI/XR tools. Their input is crucial for ensuring the technology is relevant, effective, and adopted successfully.

6. System integration and scalability

Integrating AI/XR into existing CS educational curricula can be complex, posing logistical and technical challenges. Our solutions and recommendations are the following:

- Adopt standardized platforms: Prioritize platforms and tools that are interoperable and adhere to open standards (e.g. OpenXR) to reduce compatibility issues. For example, some game engines, such as Godot, allow for multiplatform XR development and AI development (Ranaweera & Mahmoud, 2024).

This open source game engine contains standard techniques, and options for creating stunning visual effects, such as particle systems that may enhance immersion.

- Leverage cloud-based solutions: Utilize cloud-based XR and AI platforms to simplify deployment, reduce infrastructure costs, and enhance scalability across multiple locations. Some game engines, like Unity, allow for cloud-based XR project management. Online tools such as GitHub can also help to conduct XR software version control.
- Use robust APIs and libraries: Ensure that AI/XR solutions can seamlessly integrate with existing well-documented APIs and libraries for XR and AI development.
- Implement sustainable models: Develop sustainable implementation models that consider long-term content standardization, technology setup, and ongoing maintenance.

7. Psychological and cognitive risks

The extended use of immersive AI/XR environments can introduce psychological and cognitive risks in students, such as fatigue, distraction, and cybersickness. We have these solutions and recommendations:

- Design with limits and wellbeing in mind: Developers should build multisensory experiences that take into account cognitive load management, balance engagement with potential overload, and propose shorter, focused, and clear XR sessions. Short XR usage sessions, about 15 minutes or less, should be enough.
- Educate on healthy usage habits: Teach students about responsible XR habits, for example, limiting session duration and taking breaks.
- Mitigate cybersickness: In XR design, utilize locomotion techniques like teleportation to prevent cybersickness, which is a common issue in immersive environments. Cybersickness is one of the main issues that will hinder learning with XR.
- Prioritize ethical design: Ensure that AI-driven interactions do not become manipulative or compromise student autonomy. AI applications should be designed to support independent thought, not replace it.
- Promote balanced learning: Encourage a balance between AI/XR-enhanced learning and human-only interactions. Create collaborative, human-centric spaces for discussion and creative activities.

FUTURE RESEARCH DIRECTIONS

The convergence of XR and AI technologies is reshaping computer science education through emerging transformative trends, which imply future research opportunities:

- Future CS learners will need to use AI-driven personalized virtual environments where students can manipulate code in 3D space, with intelligent tutors providing real-time guidance. These systems will adapt to individual learning styles, automatically adjusting complexity and presentation methods based on student performance patterns.
- More research is needed on human-centered AI (HCAI) to improve the design and application of AI in XR for CS education. HCAI studies and designs AI systems to amplify human abilities, enhance user experience, and prioritize human needs, values, and ethical considerations over simply replacing human roles. This approach ensures AI technologies are inclusive, transparent, accountable, and beneficial to people by embedding human-centered design principles and ethical safeguards into the learning system development process (*What Is Human-Centered AI?*, 2021). As AI becomes more prevalent, computer science curricula should integrate ethics training within immersive scenarios where students can explore the consequences of algorithmic decisions in realistic virtual environments, fostering responsible development practices.
- More research on intelligent virtual assistants and agents in XR is needed. These conversational tutors act in real-time to answer questions, guide learners, or simulate peers/teachers in virtual labs, which can enhance autonomy and presence within XR learning.
- We project that the XR job market will significantly increase, with the introduction of new job roles, such as VR or AR Support Technician, XR Gameplay Engineer, and XR/AI educational technologist. Educational programs will need to be adapted to prepare students for emerging job roles in the XR/AI intersection.
- Research will be needed regarding using XR+AI to support the teaching of emerging CS areas such as quantum computing. XR+AI can make abstract quantum computing concepts tangible, with AI assistants helping students understand quantum algorithms through interactive 3D visualizations and simulations.
- Recent studies show that combining AI-driven personalization with immersive XR environments delivers the highest levels of cognitive, emotional, and social engagement, compared to AI-only or traditional instruction (Hmoud

et al., 2025). Research could be aimed at how XR's immersive power boosts emotional connection and motivation, and how AI can add adaptive pathways and feedback, creating an enriched, learner-centered experience in CS courses.

- A potential research regards students' level of interaction with the Generative AI tools used for developing XR prototype contents. Possible research questions include: what are the most effective prompts that students need to write in the generative AI tools? How does the 3D model generation vary across different AI tools? Incorporating these and other related questions can assist in evaluating further the effectiveness of the generative AI tools.
- Ultimately, longitudinal research is needed regarding the use of XR+AI in CS learning and teaching, conducting studies that span more than one year, to identify learning gains and technical issues over a long period of time. In addition, mixed-methods research (including quantitative and qualitative studies) should be conducted to support the findings.

Having analyzed the literature review and our own experiences using XR and AI in the classroom, we consider that future research in AI+XR in computer science education should focus on developing adaptive, human-centered learning systems that personalize instruction based on real-time data. Student performance, behavior, and engagement should be studied. More research is needed about how AI can effectively take into account learner interactions in immersive 3D environments to dynamically adjust content difficulty, provide context-aware feedback, and support diverse learning styles. In addition, research is needed to assess the role of intelligent virtual agents and conversational tutors in enhancing student autonomy, collaboration, and presence in XR learning spaces. Investigating ethical considerations—such as data privacy, algorithmic bias, and emotional well-being—will also be essential in guiding responsible integration. Furthermore, interdisciplinary research should examine how XR+AI can make abstract or emerging CS topics (like quantum computing or cybersecurity) more accessible through interactive visualizations and simulations. Longitudinal and mixed-methods studies will be vital to measure the sustained educational impact, technical challenges, and pedagogical effectiveness of these technologies over time.

CONCLUSION

This chapter demonstrates that the integration of AI and XR in computer science education holds transformative potential when aligned with established learning theories such as constructivism, experiential learning, situated cognition, social constructivism, and connectivism. Together, these theories provide a solid pedagogical foundation for designing immersive, adaptive, and personalized learning experiences. AI enhances XR by providing intelligent scaffolding, adaptive feedback, and real-time personalization, while XR contributes immersive environments that make abstract computer science concepts tangible and engaging.

Practical implications emerge across multiple stakeholder groups. For CS educators, AI+XR offers powerful tools to support comprehension, engagement, and authentic skill development, but effective implementation requires training, evidence-based instructional design, and careful consideration of inclusivity. For policymakers, the findings underscore the need for investment in infrastructure and maintenance of XR equipment and software, equitable access, ethical guidelines, and frameworks to ensure responsible adoption of these emerging technologies. For researchers, this chapter points to key areas requiring further investigation, including longitudinal studies, usability and engagement analyses, the role of intelligent agents in XR environments, and ethical issues surrounding data privacy and algorithmic bias. Ultimately, while AI and XR technologies cannot replace the critical role of human instructors, they can significantly augment teaching and learning in higher education. Their responsible integration can help shape more personalized, interactive, and equitable pathways for the future of computer science education.

Having reviewed dozens of studies about positive applications of XR and AI in higher education, why is AI+XR not widely used in teaching/learning computer science courses? One reason is that there are few available XR examples and applications for CS education yet. Another reason is a lack of solid guidelines and frameworks for developing compelling and pedagogically sound instructional design regarding AI+XR in CS education. In addition, not all the CS courses are suitable for teaching with XR and AI. There are cases where CS concepts and topics are better explained using 2D educational materials, such as 2D lists in data structures.

Despite the powerful capabilities of XR and AI, instructors remain a critical human factor in the learning and teaching process, especially in CS education. These technologies can personalize content, simulate complex environments, and provide adaptive feedback, but they cannot fully replace the pedagogical insight, emotional intelligence, and contextual judgment of a human educator. Instructors play a key role in curating and interpreting XR+AI experiences, guiding students through abstract or ethically sensitive topics, and adapting instruction based on nuanced, real-world classroom dynamics that automated systems may overlook. Instructors must ensure that technology is used responsibly and inclusively, bridging gaps in digital literacy, supporting diverse learner needs, and fostering meaningful human interaction, which is crucial for developing communication and teamwork skills. In addition, instructors should serve as ethical role models, helping students reflect on the broader implications of AI and XR. Their presence brings empathy, mentorship, and critical thinking into the learning process, elements that no algorithm or avatar can fully replicate. Ultimately, XR+AI should augment, not replace, the instructor's role, empowering them to create deeper, more engaging, and more personalized learning environments.

Future work should explore how AI and XR can be systematically integrated into diverse areas of computer science education, with an emphasis on evidence-based design and evaluation. Studies could investigate long-term impacts on student learning, equity, and accessibility, as well as compare AI+XR against traditional instructional methods. This should include student-centered design studies, including usability and learning engagement analyses. Further work is also needed to develop scalable frameworks, test adaptive AI agents in authentic CS tasks, and assess collaborative XR environments. Finally, researchers should examine ethical considerations, including transparency of AI scaffolding and inclusivity of XR access, to ensure responsible and equitable adoption.

The key takeaways of this chapter are the following:

- AI+XR integration works best when grounded in pedagogy, aligning with constructivism, experiential, situated, social, and connectivist learning theories ensures meaningful impact.
- Educators can use AI+XR to make abstract CS concepts tangible, provide adaptive feedback, and enhance collaboration, but they must be trained to design and guide these experiences effectively.
- Policymakers should prioritize equitable access, infrastructure support, and ethical frameworks to ensure responsible adoption of AI+XR in education.
- Researchers should focus on longitudinal studies, usability and engagement analyses, and ethical issues such as bias, privacy, and inclusivity in AI-driven XR learning.
- Human instructors remain essential. XR and AI technologies should augment, not replace, the empathy, guidance, and ethical oversight that teachers bring to CS education

ACKNOWLEDGMENT

This research was supported by Algoma University's 2024-2026 Teaching Innovation Fellowship.

The authors used large language models (LLMs) and AI editing tools to support writing and editing. Responsibility for the final content remains entirely with the authors

REFERENCES

Abdelsalam, M., & Mostafa, M. (2025). *Bridging the Digital Divide: AI, VR, and AR for Equitable K-12 Education*. https://papers.ssrn.com/sol3/papers.cfm?abstract_id=5124551

Abeywardena, I. S. (2023). OXREF: Open XR for Education Framework. *International Review of Research in Open and Distance Learning, 24*(3), 185–206. DOI: 10.19173/irrodl.v24i3.7109

Agbo, F. J., Sanusi, I. T., Oyelere, S. S., & Suhonen, J. (2021). Application of Virtual Reality in Computer Science Education: A Systemic Review Based on Bibliometric and Content Analysis Methods. *Education Sciences, 11*(3), 142. DOI: 10.3390/educsci11030142

Alam, D. A. (2023). *Connectivism Learning Theory and Connectivist Approach in Teaching and Learning: A Review of Literature, 12*(2).

Allison, J., Hwang, G.-J., Mayer, R. E., Pellas, N., Karnalim, O., de Freitas, S., Ng, O.-L., Huang, Y.-M., Hooshyar, D., Seidman, R. H., Al-Emran, M., Mikropoulos, T. A., Schroeder, N. L., Roscoe, R. D., & Sanusi, I. (2025). From Generative AI to Extended Reality: Multidisciplinary Perspectives on the Challenges, Opportunities, and Future of Educational Computing. *Journal of Educational Computing Research, 63*(6), 1327–1363. DOI: 10.1177/07356331251359964

Barrett, D. J. (2008). *MediaWiki*. O'Reilly Media, Inc.

Bernard, R. M., Borokhovski, E., Schmid, R. F., Tamim, R. M., & Abrami, P. C. (2014). A meta-analysis of blended learning and technology use in higher education: From the general to the applied. *Journal of Computing in Higher Education, 26*(1), 87–122. DOI: 10.1007/s12528-013-9077-3

Brooke, J. (1996). SUS: A "Quick and Dirty" Usability Scale. In *Usability Evaluation In Industry*. CRC Press.

Brown, J. S., Collins, A., & Duguid, P. (1989). Situated Cognition and the Culture of Learning. *Educational Researcher, 18*(1), 32–42. DOI: 10.3102/0013189X018001032

Burdea, G. C., & Coiffet, P. (2024). *Virtual Reality Technology* (Third). John Wiley & Sons.

Burke, D., Crompton, H., & Nickel, C. (2025). The Use of Extended Reality (XR) in Higher Education: A Systematic Review. *TechTrends, 69*(5), 998–1011. Advance online publication. DOI: 10.1007/s11528-025-01092-y

Cherner, T., & Fegely, A. (Eds.). (2023). *Bridging the XR technology-to-practice gap: Methods and strategies for blending extended realities into classroom instruction.* AACE, Association for the Advancement of Computing in Education.

Chounta, I.-A. (2024). *The State of Artificial Intelligence and Education Across Europe—Education—Www.coe.int*. Education. https://www.coe.int/en/web/education/-/the-state-of-artificial-intelligence-and-education-across-europe-2

Cinar, O., Rafferty, K., Cutting, D., & Wang, H. (2024). AI-Powered VR for Enhanced Learning Compared to Traditional Methods. *Electronics (Basel), 13*(23), 4787. DOI: 10.3390/electronics13234787

Craig, A. B. (2013). *Understanding Augmented Reality: Concepts and Applications* (1st ed.). Morgan-Kaufmann.

Crogman, H. T., Cano, V. D., Pacheco, E., Sonawane, R. B., & Boroon, R. (2025). Virtual Reality, Augmented Reality, and Mixed Reality in Experiential Learning: Transforming Educational Paradigms. *Education Sciences, 15*(3), 303. DOI: 10.3390/educsci15030303

Dafiotis, P., Sylaiou, S., Stylianidis, E., Koukopoulos, D., & Fidas, C. (2025). Evaluating Uses of XR in Fostering Art Students' Learning. *Multimodal Technologies and Interaction, 9*(4), 36. DOI: 10.3390/mti9040036

Dede, C. (2009). Immersive Interfaces for Engagement and Learning. *Science, 323*(5910), 66–69. DOI: 10.1126/science.1167311 PMID: 19119219

Dede, C., Salzman, M. C., Loftin, R. B., & Sprague, D. (1999). Multisensory Immersion as a Modeling Environment for Learning Complex Scientific Concepts. In Feurzeig, W., & Roberts, N. (Eds.), *Modeling and Simulation in Science and Mathematics Education* (pp. 282–319). Springer New York., DOI: 10.1007/978-1-4612-1414-4_12

Dyulicheva, Y. Y., & Glazieva, A. O. (2021, December 18). *Game based learning with artificial intelligence and immersive technologies: An overview*. S&SE@*SW 2021: 4th Workshop for Young Scientists in Computer Science & Software Engineering*, Kryvyi Rih, Ukraine.

Garcia-Bonete, M.-J., Jensen, M., & Katona, G. (2019). A practical guide to developing virtual and augmented reality exercises for teaching structural biology. *Biochemistry and Molecular Biology Education, 47*(1), 16–24. DOI: 10.1002/bmb.21188 PMID: 30475432

Garcia-Ruiz, M., Nasir, M., & Rahman, Z. (2023, May 15). *Using AI Software Tools to Support Teaching Coding: A Double-edged Sword. Upper Peninsula Teaching and Learning Conference (UPTLC)*, Lake Superior State University, Sault Ste. Marie, Michigan, USA.

Garcia-Ruiz, M., Santana-Mancilla, P., Gaytán-Lugo, L., & Iñiguez Carrillo, A. (2022). Participatory Design of Sonification Development for Learning about Molecular Structures in Virtual Reality. *Multimodal Technologies and Interaction, 6*(10), 1–20. DOI: 10.3390/mti6100089

Garcia-Ruiz, M. A., Santana-Mancilla, P. C., & Gaytan-Lugo, L. S. (2019). A usability study of an interactive auditory display for supporting learning of molecular structure. *Proceedings of EdMedia '19,* The Association for the Advancement of Computing in Education.

Garg, A., Sharma, R. B., Tripathi, S., Kumar, K. S., Varshney, A. K., & Sharma, A. (2025). AI-Powered Virtual Reality: Transforming Education Beyond Conventional Approaches. *2025 International Conference on Intelligent Control, Computing and Communications (IC3)*, 398–403. DOI: 10.1109/IC363308.2025.10956771

Grassini, S. (2025). Beyond Textbooks: AI, XR, and the New Era of Learning. In *Futuristic Insights on Education Components—How education can meet the demands of an ever-changing world*. UNESCO Regional Center for Educational Planning.

Gu, Y., Feijoo-Garcia, M. A., Zhang, Y., Magana, A. J., Benes, B., & Popescu, V. (2024). An XR Environment for AI Education: Design and First Implementation. *2024 IEEE Conference on Virtual Reality and 3D User Interfaces Abstracts and Workshops (VRW)*, 157–162. DOI: 10.1109/VRW62533.2024.00032

Hajirasouli, A., & Banihashemi, S. (2022). Augmented reality in architecture and construction education: State of the field and opportunities. *International Journal of Educational Technology in Higher Education, 19*(1), 39. DOI: 10.1186/s41239-022-00343-9

Haw, S.-C., & Muthu, K. S. (2023). *Proceedings of the International Conference on Computer, Information Technology and Intelligent Computing (CITIC 2022)*. Springer Nature.

Hmoud, M., Daher, W., & Ayyoub, A. (2025). From experience to engagement: A mixed methods exploration of learning environments using artificial intelligence and extended reality. *Frontiers in Education*, *10*, 1617132. Advance online publication. DOI: 10.3389/feduc.2025.1617132

Holmes, W., Bialik, M., & Fadel, C. (2019a). Artificial Intelligence in Education Promises and Implications for Teaching and Learning. In *(1st ed.). Center for Curriculum Redesign: Boston, MA, USA. (2019)*. Center for Curriculum Redesign. https://circls.org/primers/artificial-intelligence-in-education-promises-and-implications-for-teaching-and-learning

Holmes, W., Bialik, M., & Fadel, C. (2019b). Artificial Intelligence in Education Promises and Implications for Teaching and Learning. In *(1st ed.). Center for Curriculum Redesign: Boston, MA, USA. (2019)*. Center for Curriculum Redesign. https://circls.org/primers/artificial-intelligence-in-education-promises-and-implications-for-teaching-and-learning

Holmes, W., & Tuomi, I. (2022). State of the art and practice in AI in education. *European Journal of Education*, *57*(4), 542–570. DOI: 10.1111/ejed.12533

Horvath, A., & Goldschmid, R. (2025). Extended Abstract—Immersive Education: Utilizing the Potential of Immersive Technologies in Computer Science Higher Education. *Immersive Learning Research - Academic*, 162–167. DOI: 10.56198/508qgt70

Hu, Y., Tutschku, K., Boeva, V., Goswami, P., Abghari, S., & Sundstedt, V. (2024). Towards an Ethical and Data Privacy Metrology for AI-Enriched Human-Centered XR Systems. *2024 IEEE International Conference on Metrology for eXtended Reality, Artificial Intelligence and Neural Engineering (MetroXRAINE)*, 119–124. DOI: 10.1109/MetroXRAINE62247.2024.10796457

Kamińska, D., Zwoliński, G., Laska-Leśniewicz, A., Raposo, R., Vairinhos, M., Pereira, E., Urem, F., Ljubić Hinić, M., Haamer, R. E., & Anbarjafari, G. (2023). Augmented Reality: Current and New Trends in Education. *Electronics (Basel)*, *12*(16), 3531. DOI: 10.3390/electronics12163531

Kent, L., Snider, C., Gopsill, J., & Hicks, B. (2021). Mixed reality in design prototyping: A systematic review. *Design Studies*, *77*, 101046. DOI: 10.1016/j.destud.2021.101046

Khlaif, Z. N., Mousa, A., & Sanmugam, M. (2024). Immersive Extended Reality (XR) Technology in Engineering Education: Opportunities and Challenges. *Technology. Knowledge and Learning*, *29*(2), 803–826. DOI: 10.1007/s10758-023-09719-w

Kolb, D. A., Boyatzis, R. E., & Mainemelis, C. (2001). Experiential Learning Theory: Previous Research and New Directions. In *Perspectives on Thinking, Learning, and Cognitive Styles*. Routledge.

Konecki, M., Konecki, M., & Vlahov, D. (2023). Using Virtual Reality in Education of Programming. *2023 11th International Conference on Information and Education Technology (ICIET)*, 39–43. DOI: 10.1109/ICIET56899.2023.10111156

Kourtesis, P. (2024). A Comprehensive Review of Multimodal XR Applications, Risks, and Ethical Challenges in the Metaverse. *Multimodal Technologies and Interaction*, *8*(11), 98. DOI: 10.3390/mti8110098

Lampropoulos, G., Keramopoulos, E., Diamantaras, K., & Evangelidis, G. (2023). Integrating Augmented Reality, Gamification, and Serious Games in Computer Science Education. *Education Sciences*, *13*(6), 618. DOI: 10.3390/educsci13060618

Larson, K., & Chambers, R. (2020a). AR in the Computer Programming Classroom: A Review of the Literature. *2020 IEEE International Conference on Teaching, Assessment, and Learning for Engineering (TALE)*, 436–443. DOI: 10.1109/TALE48869.2020.9368329

Larson, K., & Chambers, R. (2020b). AR in the Computer Programming Classroom: A Review of the Literature. *2020 IEEE International Conference on Teaching, Assessment, and Learning for Engineering (TALE)*, 436–443. DOI: 10.1109/TALE48869.2020.9368329

LaValle, S. M. (2023). *Virtual Reality*. Cambridge University Press., https://lavalle.pl/vr/ DOI: 10.1017/9781108182874

Lin, C.-J., Lee, H.-Y., Wang, W.-S., Huang, Y.-M., & Wu, T.-T. (2025). Enhancing reflective thinking in STEM education through experiential learning: The role of generative AI as a learning aid. *Education and Information Technologies*, *30*(5), 6315–6337. DOI: 10.1007/s10639-024-13072-5

Luck, M., & Aylett, R. (2000). Applying artificial intelligence to virtual reality: Intelligent virtual environments. *Applied Artificial Intelligence*, *14*(1), 3–32. DOI: 10.1080/088395100117142

Mallek, F., Mazhar, T., Shah, S. F. A., Ghadi, Y. Y., & Hamam, H. (2024). A review on cultivating effective learning: Synthesizing educational theories and virtual reality for enhanced educational experiences. *PeerJ. Computer Science, 10*, e2000. DOI: 10.7717/peerj-cs.2000 PMID: 38855256

Manfredi, G., Erra, U., & Gilio, G. (2023). A Mixed Reality Approach for Innovative Pair Programming Education with a Conversational AI Virtual Avatar. *Proceedings of the 27th International Conference on Evaluation and Assessment in Software Engineering*, 450–454. DOI: 10.1145/3593434.3593952

Marougkas, A., Troussas, C., Krouska, A., & Sgouropoulou, C. (2023). Virtual Reality in Education: A Review of Learning Theories, Approaches and Methodologies for the Last Decade. *Electronics (Basel), 12*(13), 2832. DOI: 10.3390/electronics12132832

MCLeod. S. (2025, March 19). *Kolb's Learning Styles & Experiential Learning Cycle*. https://www.simplypsychology.org/learning-kolb.html

Molina, E., & Medina, E. (2025). *AI Revolution in Higher Education*. The World Bank.

Moore, N., Ahmadpour, N., Brown, M., Poronnik, P., & Davids, J. (2022). Designing Virtual Reality–Based Conversational Agents to Train Clinicians in Verbal De-escalation Skills: Exploratory Usability Study. *JMIR Serious Games, 10*(3), e38669. DOI: 10.2196/38669 PMID: 35793129

Mukasheva, M., Kalkabayeva, Z., & Pussyrmanov, N. (2023). Visualization of sorting algorithms in the virtual reality environment. *Frontiers in Education, 8*, 1195200. Advance online publication. DOI: 10.3389/feduc.2023.1195200

Myara, J. (2024). The Applications and Uses of Immersive Virtual Reality: A Multisensory Approach to Effective and Efficient Academic Pedagogy. *PCOM Capstone Projects*. https://digitalcommons.pcom.edu/capstone_projects/52

Noble, E. R., Ask, T. F., & Knox, B. J. (2025). Tailored Extended Reality Environments for Education and Training in Cybersecurity: Engagement Beyond Awareness. *2025 IEEE Global Engineering Education Conference (EDUCON)*, 1–9. DOI: 10.1109/EDUCON62633.2025.11016494

Obourdin, G., de Maeyer, S., & Van den Bossche, P. (2024). Unlocking the power of immersive learning: The FAIRI instructional design proposition for adaptive immersive virtual reality. *Computers & Education: X Reality, 5*, 100084. DOI: 10.1016/j.cexr.2024.100084

Okorie, P. N., MacDowell, P., & Olson, B. (2024). Applying a Constructivist Approach to Designing Virtual Reality Experiences that Facilitate Authentic Learning for Adolescents. *The Journal of Applied Instructional Design, 13*(4). Advance online publication. DOI: 10.59668/2033.18640

Osborn-King, R. (2005). Can 'Blended Learning' Be Redeemed? *E-learning, 2*(1).

Packer, H., & Huang, F. (2025). Can China's universities power it to victory in the global AI race? *Times Higher Education (THE)*. https://www.timeshighereducation.com/depth/can-chinas-universities-power-it-victory-global-ai-race

Pirker, J., Dengel, A., Holly, M., & Safikhani, S. (2020). Virtual Reality in Computer Science Education: A Systematic Review. *26th ACM Symposium on Virtual Reality Software and Technology*, 1–8. DOI: 10.1145/3385956.3418947

Pomerantz, J., & Rode, R. (2020). Exploring the Future of Extended Reality in Higher Education. *EDUCAUSE Review*. https://er.educause.edu/articles/2020/6/exploring-the-future-of-extended-reality-in-higher-education

Pozzo, D. N., Roa, I. G., Gonzalez Beleño, C. A., Arévalo Fajardo, B. Y., Herrera Cantillo, C. P., & Guerrero, V. C. (2024). Perspectives and applications of virtual reality in higher education: An analysis of Latin America's publications. *Procedia Computer Science, 238*, 962–967. DOI: 10.1016/j.procs.2024.06.120

Ramadhani Fajri, B., Mohd Kamaruzaman, F., Omar, M., Lofandri, W., & Samala, A. D. (2025). Smart Teaching Factory: Integrating Extended Reality, Artificial Intelligence, and Animated Simulations for Transformative Vocational Education. *Salud, Ciencia y Tecnología, 5*, 1769. DOI: 10.56294/saludcyt20251769

Rana, S., & Chicone, R. (2025a). AI-Enhanced Virtual and Augmented Reality for Cybersecurity Training. In *Fortifying the Future* (pp. 101–131). Springer., https://ouci.dntb.gov.ua/en/works/7A561EB2/ DOI: 10.1007/978-3-031-81780-9_5

Rana, S., & Chicone, R. (2025b). AI-Enhanced Virtual and Augmented Reality for Cybersecurity Training. In Rana, S., & Chicone, R. (Eds.), *Fortifying the Future: Harnessing AI for Transformative Cybersecurity Training* (pp. 101–131). Springer Nature Switzerland., DOI: 10.1007/978-3-031-81780-9_5

Rana, S., & Chicone, R. (2025c). AI-Enhanced Virtual and Augmented Reality for Cybersecurity Training. In Rana, S., & Chicone, R. (Eds.), *Fortifying the Future: Harnessing AI for Transformative Cybersecurity Training* (pp. 101–131). Springer Nature Switzerland., DOI: 10.1007/978-3-031-81780-9_5

Ranaweera, M., & Mahmoud, Q. H. (2024). Deep Reinforcement Learning with Godot Game Engine. *Electronics (Basel), 13*(5), 985. DOI: 10.3390/electronics13050985

Rauschnabel, P. A., Felix, R., Hinsch, C., Shahab, H., & Alt, F. (2022). What is XR? Towards a Framework for Augmented and Virtual Reality. *Computers in Human Behavior, 133*, 107289. DOI: 10.1016/j.chb.2022.107289

Romoser, C., Nelson, R., & Ferrill, T. (2024, April 1). *Recreational Therapists' Usability Perceptions of the Meta Quest 2 VR System. | EBSCOhost.* DOI: 10.18666/TRJ-2024-V58-I2-12077

Schwaiger, M. (2021). Europe Needs to Integrate Immersive Learning Quickly at All Education Levels – But How? What to Learn From 25 EU Projects in This Field. *Journal of Elementary Education, 14*(Spec.Iss), 63–85. DOI: 10.18690/rei.14.Spec.Iss.63-85.2021

Siemens, G. (2005). Connectivism: A Learning Theory for the Digital Age. *International Journal of Instructional Technology & Distance Learning, 2*(1). http://www.itdl.org/Journal/Jan_05/article01.htm

Slater, M. (2018). Immersion and the illusion of presence in virtual reality. *British Journal of Psychology, 109*(3), 431–433. DOI: 10.1111/bjop.12305 PMID: 29781508

Speicher, M., Hall, B. D., & Nebeling, M. (2019). What is Mixed Reality? *Proceedings of the 2019 CHI Conference on Human Factors in Computing Systems*, 1–15. DOI: 10.1145/3290605.3300767

Spencer, A. D. (2025). *The Future of Immersive, AI-Driven, and Decentralized Technologies in Cybersecurity Education and Cyber Science.* RAIS Conference proceedings, Princeton, NJ.

Tene, T., Marcatoma Tixi, J. A., Palacios Robalino, M., Mendoza Salazar, M. J., Vacacela Gomez, C., & Bellucci, S. (2024). Integrating immersive technologies with STEM education: A systematic review. *Frontiers in Education, 9*, 1410163. Advance online publication. DOI: 10.3389/feduc.2024.1410163

Tenney, K., Stringer, B. P., LaTona-Tequida, T., & White, I. (2023). Conceptualizations and Limitations of STEM Literacy across Learning Theories. *Journal of Microbiology & Biology Education, 24*(1), e00168–e22. DOI: 10.1128/jmbe.00168-22 PMID: 37089236

Tsai, C.-Y., & Lai, Y.-C. (2022). Design and Validation of an Augmented Reality Teaching System for Primary Logic Programming Education. *Sensors (Basel), 22*(1), 389. DOI: 10.3390/s22010389 PMID: 35009929

Vasilchenko, A., Li, J., Ryskeldiev, B., Sarcar, S., Ochiai, Y., Kunze, K., & Radu, I. (2020). Collaborative Learning & Co-Creation in XR. *Extended Abstracts of the 2020 CHI Conference on Human Factors in Computing Systems*, 1–4. DOI: 10.1145/3334480.3381056

Wang, S., Wang, F., Zhu, Z., Wang, J., Tran, T., & Du, Z. (2024). Artificial intelligence in education: A systematic literature review. *Expert Systems with Applications, 252*, 124167. DOI: 10.1016/j.eswa.2024.124167

What is human-centered AI? (2021, February 9). IBM Research. https://research.ibm.com/blog/what-is-human-centered-ai

Yan, W., Lowell, V. L., & Yang, L. (2024). Developing English language learners' speaking skills through applying a situated learning approach in VR-enhanced learning experiences. *Virtual Reality (Waltham Cross), 28*(4), 167. DOI: 10.1007/s10055-024-01061-5

Zhou, Q., Wang, B., & Mayer, I. (2024). Understanding the social construction of the metaverse with Q methodology. *Technological Forecasting and Social Change, 208*, 123716. DOI: 10.1016/j.techfore.2024.123716

Zhuang, T., Xu, X., & Zhang, Y. (2024). Contextualizing and visualizing abstract theoretical knowledge for situated learning: Large-scale VR-supported higher education in China. *Virtual Reality (Waltham Cross), 29*(1), 4. DOI: 10.1007/s10055-024-01075-z

ADDITIONAL READING

Asra, S. A., & Wickramarathne, J. (2024, December). Artificial Intelligence (AI) in Augmented Reality (AR), Virtual Reality (VR) and Mixed Reality (MR) Experiences: Enhancing Immersion and Interaction for User Experiences. In TENCON 2024-2024 IEEE Region 10 Conference (TENCON) (pp. 1700-1705). IEEE.

Li, Y., Wang, X., Chen, Z., & Zhang, H. (2024). Recent advances and future directions in extended reality (XR): Exploring AI-powered spatial intelligence. arXiv preprint arXiv:2504.15970. https://arxiv.org/abs/2504.15970

Maathuis, C., Cidota, M. A., Datcu, D., & Marin, L. (2025). Integrating Explainable Artificial Intelligence in Extended Reality Environments: A Systematic Survey. *Mathematics, 13*(2), 290. DOI: 10.3390/math13020290

KEY TERMS AND DEFINITIONS

Artificial Intelligence (AI): AI is the simulation of human cognitive functions, such as learning, reasoning, problem-solving, and perception, in computers. AI computing systems can process vast amounts of data to recognize patterns, make decisions, and perform tasks that typically require human intelligence.

AI in education: the development and application of intelligent computer systems that can simulate human thinking and behavior to support teaching, learning, and educational management.

Augmented Reality (AR): A technology that overlays digital information, such as images, text, and sounds, onto the real world (generally a real-time video feed), enhancing a user's perception and experience of the real world without replacing it.

Extended Reality (XR): An umbrella term for all immersive technologies, including virtual reality (VR), augmented reality (AR), and mixed reality (MR). It creates interactive and immersive experiences by blending or extending digital content with the physical world, offering a spectrum of realities that range from digital overlays to fully simulated environments.

Generative AI: Generative AI is a type of AI that creates new, original content—such as text, images, music, video, and code—by learning from and mimicking patterns in large datasets. Powered by complex models, it takes user inputs, called prompts, to generate novel responses that are based on its training data, enabling applications from chatbots to media creation for supporting XR experiences.

Mixed Reality (MR): a technology that blends the physical and digital worlds, allowing virtual objects and information to interact with and be integrated into the real-world environment. MR enables both digital and real-world elements to interact with each other.

Presence: A psychophysiological effect that makes the user feel as if they are physically inside the virtual world. This is generally achieved using immersive XR technologies, although this can be achieved (at a lesser level) in other media such as movies and books.

Virtual Reality (VR): A multisensorial and computer-generated three-dimensional (3D) environment that a user can explore and interact with. User interactions typically include visual, auditory, and sometimes tactile feedback. The goal is to create a strong sense of presence.

Chapter 3
Comics as a Practical Learning Tool to Improve Comprehension:
A Case Study of Wayang Comic in Delivering Character Education Content

Danendro Adi
https://orcid.org/0009-0001-0311-3313
Bina Nusantara University, Indonesia

Muhizam Mustafa
University Sains Malaysia, Malaysia

ABSTRACT

Finding effective pedagogical techniques and tools to improve teaching methods is essential for educational growth. An alternative approach suggested is using comics, which are popular and inexpensive to produce. Comics are a popular, accessible entertainment enjoyed by many and easily shared on social media for quick, widespread information. This paper explores how comics enhance understanding, drawing on Eisner and McCloud's theories about storytelling through texts and images. Their views show how combining pictures and text can improve comprehension and memory. This paper also offers a new perspective on using comics as a learning tool, illustrated with a case study of a comic featuring classical mythology stories to clarify its explanation. The selected comics, based on stories

DOI: 10.4018/979-8-3373-5157-5.ch003

from classical Wayang mythology—socialized through traditional performances in Indonesia, especially Java and Bali for centuries—serve as a case study, as they have traditionally conveyed guidelines for human behavior.

1. INTRODUCTION

Enhancing teaching methods requires effective, accessible tools. While multimedia and IT-based solutions are popular, they can be costly and quickly outdated. Comics offer a low-cost (Aleixo & Sumner, 2017), widely enjoyed alternative that supports mass information sharing via social media (Kearns & Kearns, 2020). Though the term "comic" originally referred to humor, especially in English-language media since the 1880s, commonly called *the funnies,* which humor to mock the policies of public figures, comic books evolved from newspaper strips and were first published in the U.S. in 1934 (Ajidarma, 2011). Similarly, early Indonesian comics began as strip collections, the intention of being funny.

Since comics contain a clear narrative and visual storytelling, they have been recognised as an attractive and successful educational tool. (Akcanca 2020; Das and Singh 2022). The concept of using graphic narrative in education dates back to the late 1940s in the USA when Hutchinson (1949) reported a study on the use of comics, mainly newspaper strips, in schools (Kearns & Kearns, 2020). Although there was a negative public image of comic books in the 1950s, several studies in the USA have been published suggesting the possibilities of using comics in educational settings in the following decades.

In 1950s Indonesia, comics were often considered as uneducational children's reading and blamed for promoting laziness (Bonneff, 2008). However, the combination of text and images provided a useful tool to address learning and literacy issues. A notable genre, *Wayang* Comics, adapted traditional puppet theatre stories and served as an alternative educational medium—especially for aspiring puppeteers—at a time when access to formal *Wayang* literature and resources was limited.

After decades of research, comics in the U.S. are now widely used in education and have gained academic recognition across subjects like geography, linguistics, and medical humanities. Studies also highlight their benefits for children with learning difficulties (Aleixo & Sumner, 2017). Comics blend words and images, which makes them distinctive, approachable, and emotionally compelling. Although the Dual Coding Theory, developed by Allan Paivio, is not unique to comics, it supports comics as powerful instructional tools by explaining how the brain receives information through both visual and verbal channels.

1.1. Introduction to the Problem

Character education and cultural preservation are two important aspects in the formation of a young generation with integrity and national identity. Oral tradition and storytelling that are passed down from one generation to the next have historically been used in Indonesia to teach character education. These traditions impart moral, religious, and educational values (Rosa, 2019). Wayang has long been a vehicle for advancing these ideals because it is a beloved traditional puppet show among Indonesians, particularly on the islands of Java and Bali. But as digital media like social media, streaming services, and online games have grown in popularity, young people's focus has turned away from the traditional performances. As a result, *Wayang* is no longer a primary source of character education, raising concerns about the erosion of cultural identity and the increasing influence of external values that may not align with national character. However, today's young generation considers traditional *Wayang* performance economically inefficient; the long 7-9 hours duration of the performance does not align with the dynamics of modern society that require consuming time effectively and efficiently.

The declining frequency of *Wayang* being performed in cities and urban area, coupled with the waning interest of the younger generation in traditional *Wayang* performances, poses a significant threat to the sustainability of Indonesia's cultural heritage. In addition to this cultural concern, the educational values embedded within *Wayang* performances—values that are well-suited for character development—are increasingly overlooked by the younger audience. As access to global information becomes more seamless, there is rising concern that the younger generation will be exposed to influences that do not reflect the nation's cultural and moral identities. To close this gap, a new method that is tailored to today's learning styles and media choices is required. Wayang comics arose as an alternative for packaging cultural material in easily accessible media, both in print and digital formats.

The foundational principles of *Wayang* that embrace innovation, integrating popular media like comics can help revitalize interest in *Wayang* mythology among younger audiences while promoting its educational values. Using *Wayang* stories in modern formats not only preserves cultural heritage but also leverages local wisdom to shape character and personality—values that remain relevant today. Comics, as a widely favored and adaptable medium, offer a practical way to deliver such content. Given the digital fluency of today's youth, other media like animation, digital games, and interactive audiovisual tools can also be effective. However, unlike comics, animations are passive and limit user control over information flow, which may reduce their educational effectiveness (Tversky, Morrison & Betrancourt, 2002; Yang, 2008).

Comics are inexpensive, simple to create, making them easily accessible and circulated. Producing instructive movies or animations, on the other hand, necessitates specialised technology, trained workers, and high-end gadgets for pleasant watching. Comic books, on the other hand, can be delivered in print or downloaded through common mobile phones, making them more accessible to people of all socioeconomic backgrounds.

Wayang comics, in particular, are an effective medium for teaching virtues such as honesty, courage, and responsibility while strengthening cultural identity. They have strong instructional potential, as supported by cognitive and comedic theory, but organised application is required to prevent pupils from focusing primarily on visuals at the expense of learning outcomes.

In terms of research in the field of comics, previous research has often emphasized stereotypical views of comics as merely humorous and child-oriented, overlooking the medium's evolution over the past three decades into a diverse and stylistically rich form that resonates with audiences across age groups (Farinella, 2018). In this chapter, it not only discusses how comics can be used for academic purposes but also discusses the results of an examination of existing *Wayang* comics as a practical medium that brings the exoticism of unique traditional performances both visually and in the delivery of messages, to produce novelty in terms of research in the field of comic. Through this study, the objectives of the research can be achieved, which are firstly, to identify what educational value is contained in existing *Wayang* comics that are relevant to the younger generation, and secondly, to find a way to convey the message so that what is conveyed becomes more understood and remembered.

2. RESEARCH PROCEDURES AND METHODS

This study used a qualitative research approach to investigate the presence and role of Wayang comics in delivering educational information. The analysis focused on both textual and visual elements as the data, in line with the inherent characteristics of comics as a medium that integrates narrative and imagery to communicate. The data collected from this examination from the existing *Wayang* comic, then be analyzed using content analysis (Krippendorff, 1999) to identify the educational messages within the mythology. As for the process carried out in more detail, first, the data derived from the dialogue sentences and visualization extracted from several scenes which contain messages. Then, the words, sentences, and expressions in the dialogue of a specific scene will be identified and labeled or "coded' as keywords or short phrases that include verbs to indicate actions or adjectives to describe behavior. Finally, the codes will be grouped into categories aligned with exemplary character traits such as good behavior, honesty, responsibility, and respect for others, along with other noble characters (Lickona, 1992).

Furthermore, this chapter explains how comics are used to deliver messages in a unique way, using features found only in comics. Drawing on comic theory and cognitive theory, the research offers recommendations for enhancing message delivery to improve comprehension and retention, particularly in relation to everyday contexts.

3. THEORIES

To clarify how comics can effectively convey educational content, this chapter explores two key theoretical frameworks: cognition theory—specifically Allan Paivio's "Dual Coding" theory—and comic theory, as developed by Will Eisner and Scott McCloud. While Paivio's theory describes how verbal and visual stimuli improve memory and comprehension, Eisner and McCloud offer fundamental insights into the composition and purpose of comics.

3.1. Theory of Cognition

The brain processes written information by identifying each letter and symbol (picture with a specific meaning) to produce a word. To read a series of words, the brain firstly needs to match the shape of the letter with the symbol that has been stored as memories obtained from the previous process, possibly when the brain is introduced to the symbol when learning to recognize letters in order to learn to read. The brain then combines a series of letters to form words, words into sentences, sentences into paragraphs, and so on. Although this happens rapidly, it still takes more time than interpreting visual information. Images are processed more quickly because they bypass the complex decoding steps required for reading (Malamed, 2009). The ability to translate an image into a certain meaning is related to the human ability to process information. In the human information-processing system that consists of three main structures: sensory memory, working memory, and long-term memory, the data obtained through the senses is transformed into meaningful information. All data received through the eyes as external stimuli, such as color and shape in an image, register in sensory memory. The information is then sent to working memory, where it is paired with existing knowledge in order to be interpreted and understood. At this stage, the brain will process each written text or image with a certain meaning that has been stored as memories, as previously explained.

However, working memory has a limited capacity that affects to the person's cognitive abilities. The new information can be quickly fade away unless the information is manipulated (Malamed, 2009). For example, the information can deliberately memorized or repeated until it stored in long-term memory and can be retrieved by working memory so can be used as a prior knowledge to complement the next new sensory information.

The *human information-processing system* scientifically explains how information is processed, stored, and retrieved when needed, while *The "Dual coding" theory* provides a clearer picture of how messages in visual and verbal form are received by the human brain through two channels. The theory was first explained in 1971 by Allan Paivio, who proposes that both a visual and a verbal code contribute to cognitive processing and overall comprehension and memorability. The theory explains that material in both a verbal and visual manner would improve both the comprehension and retention of information (Kearns & Kearns, 2020). This theory underpins the study's choice to use comics, as they combine verbal and visual stimuli to support message retention.

Paivio stated that the human brain has two basic processing systems: verbal and nonverbal. Information is processed through both verbal channels (word and voice) and visual channels (pictures and non-textual visuals). These channels can operate independently, in parallel, or in an integrated fashion simultaneously (Sadoski et al, 1991). In relation The Dual Coding theory to *human information-processing system*, verbal information, such as text, is processed through the verbal channel as identified by Paivio. In this *system,* textual information must be aligned with symbols stored as memories derived from prior knowledge for proper interpretation. Conversely, nonverbal information, received through the eyes as external stimuli, registers in sensory memory before moving to working memory. Here, sensory data is combined with prior knowledge, enabling quicker interpretation of nonverbal information.

According to the Dual Coding theory, neither channel of information processing is more prominent than the other; both are necessary for communicating information and improving comprehension. A study by Carlson, Chandler, and Sweller (2003) found a significant difference in learning outcomes between groups who used text-based teaching materials and those that used a combination of text and visuals. The study's findings revealed that the group learning with diagrams and a combination of text and graphics outperformed the group that relied just on text. When both groups used text-based learning tools, their results were similar. This conclusion is consistent with the Dual Coding Theory, which proposes that mixing words and visuals improves comprehension. Thus, combining pictures with written informatio increases deeper learning, surpassing the effectiveness of employing either alone. (Hayikaleng, 2019).

In terms of conveying information, visual and textual each offer unique strengths in conveying information. Visuals communicate quickly, transcend age and location, and evoke emotions and memories, while words communicate accuracy and entertainment through language and sentences (Hall, 2011). When visual and textual are combined, they enhance comprehension and retention more effectively. Images have long served as powerful tools for communication, not just aesthetically but also functionally—contributing to a shared visual "language." Tailoring visual styles to audience preferences can further improve memorability and support long-term learning.

3.2. Comic theory: Images, time, and space

Comic readers are not just reading a series of words; in fact, the images in comics are also "read" as a part that is integrated with the words. The images mentioned by McCloud refer to all the visual elements that are arranged to narrate the story, including characters, settings, or other objects in the form of images. Other visual elements exclusively only contained in comics can be other symbols, such as dialog balloon, thought balloons, or areas to place words representing sounds or dialog. Because of the need to accommodate the text and convey speech, the balloon is given a "hook" to show the direction of origin of the dialog or thought. In addition to the "balloon" that is often visualized as not resembling a round balloon because it wants to be adjusted to the words contained in it, the space for words can also be in the form of a box called caption. The words in the caption are presented as narrative text, conveying information about events, descriptions of thoughts, or explanations beyond what is expressed through speech balloons.

The space for words in a *balloon* is the same as a panel as a space for images that are usually given a borderline (in the form of a box or also in other forms) where the panels are placed next to each other to form a sequence, although there are also sequences consisting of several images placed in a space without a real boundary line. McCloud's definition and description is a development of Will Eisner's opinion on comic art in the book *Comics and Sequential Art.* One of the important definitions of comics from Eisner is that comics are "framing time". To make it easier to understand this meaning, Eisner explained that the panel in the comics, which is generally in the form of a square, is actually like "boxing the action", where certain actions have been captured and placed inside the box which is then arranged together with other boxes containing moments from other actions. As a result of the "framing time" described by Eisner, it forms a still image as if time stops in a scene, a certain delivery technique is needed to produce the impression of movement. The presence of certain symbols such as the arrangement of lines as an additional element, makes the still image give the illusion that it can be "read" as a motion. In addition to the existence of certain forms to bring still images to life in the panel, through visual techniques such as depictions of facial expressions and body postures, captured action can also build the reader's emotions.

As explained above, in general, images are contained within a space, a panel. The arrangement of panels in sequence can also visually depict the change of moment in a certain time, in addition to illustrating the different times between one panel and another. Based on this, it can be said that the panel also plays a role in bringing readers through a specific time span according to the scene being narrated. This occurs because the action in a certain panel leads to the next action in the following panel, separated by the space between the panels (gutters), which serves as a space for the reader to imagine the moments not shown visually, allowing the "framing time" of one panel to connect with the next.

In addition to certain scenes placed in the panel, other images, as described by McCloud, are presented to express sounds or dialogue. The sound visualization is built through shapes that explain certain conditions, such as dialogue balloons, thought balloons, and balloons to explain other sound sources that each have a different shape, as a symbol of certain meaning according to its function. Another way to visualize sounds or sound effects can also be created without balloons but through the shapes and arrangements of letters that represent the character of the sound. The placement of dialogue in the frame is also related to "boxing the action" which is explained by Eisner that there is a certain action that has been captured and placed inside the box where the action in question includes a visualization of dialogue and sound effects so that "Framing time" explained by Eisner does not only refer to presenting a moment visually at a certain time but also sound that is visualized through certain techniques that presented at the same time.

3.3. Synthesis from the Theories

Based on the theoretical explanation above, in the interest of education, visual and textual merging can help in improving the understanding of the information conveyed. However, in conveying messages through text and visuals, it is also necessary to pay attention to the target reader, in the sense that it is necessary to adjust the visual form and delivery style to match the reader's preference. This is not conveyed in the dual coding theory, which theoretically does not discuss visual or language style. It is not impossible that the information conveyed cannot be accepted by the reader because it ignores one of the two elements. For example, conveying information to children in a language or visual style that is more suitable for teenagers or adults will result in the information conveyed being ineffective and potentially result in confusion for those who receive it. This is directly related to comic theory where the arrangement of scenes on the panel which is as a space to convey messages at a certain time has an important role in the success of conveying information which has an impact on increasing understanding of the message conveyed. The theory of "framing time" is uniquely implemented in comics, which allows the same message to be conveyed in the visualization of different scenes and dialogues in different time frames in a comic so that in addition to producing variations in visual narratives, it also makes the reader remember a message that is deliberately conveyed repeatedly in different frames.

By looking at the characteristics of comics and comic theories that can be associated with cognition theory, the use of comics can be an alternative medium to support learning. Although based on the Dual Coding Theory, the combination of verbal code and visual code does not have to refer to comics, it can be in the implementation of infographics or diagram, but the combination of these two elements implemented in media that apply comic theory produces new strengths in terms of conveying information through forms that are proven to be acceptable across generations and technological changes. The arrangement of frames in comics also adapts to digital media, does not have to be placed juxtaposed as mentioned by McCloud, and can be arranged vertically to accommodate the needs of digital media, such as in web comics, where the way to view the panel by scrolling the interface vertically is different from print comics. Thus, it also proves that the comic theory initiated by Eisner and McCloud is able to adapt to changes in media and technology.

4. CASE STUDY OF *WAYANG* COMIC IN DELIVERING CHARACTER EDUCATION CONTENT

Wayang is one of Indonesia's oldest traditional art forms, and it plays an important role in cultural preservation. UNESCO designated it a World Masterpiece of Humanity's Oral and Intangible Heritage (Purwanto, 2018). Wayang was used as a storytelling medium to teach younger generations about ethics, knowledge, culture, and religion. Elders would use drawings on cloth or ancient paper stretched between two wooden poles to narrate stories that contained meaningful messages by pointing at the drawings with sticks. This practice is the origin of *Wayang Beber,* the oldest form of puppet theater in Indonesia (Lysloff et al., 1992), in which the *Dhalang,* a puppeteer, narrates a story while presenting the traditional painting that illustrates the story (Lombard, 1996).

The stories of *Wayang* are considered Javanese mythology that reflects real life. Each of the figures on the mythology represents various human characters (Wijayanti, 2023), and their noble values become role models in behavior (Anderson, 2016). However, the world of *Wayang* gives the viewer the freedom to extract their own values, leading to varied interpretations of the conveyed messages (Santosa, 2023). With these facts that have lasted for hundreds of years, it can be said that *Wayang* is not only a performance but also a guide for behavior (Setiawan, 2017).

There have been several arguments about the origin of the word "*Wayang*". Some suggest it comes from *"Ma Hyang"*, which means towards the Deity or God Almighty (Febriyanti & Santoso, 2023).

For the Javanese, *Wayang* holds three interconnected meanings. First, it refers to the story—most commonly drawn from the *Mahabharata* and *Ramayana*, though other tales like *Panji* also exist. Second, *Wayang* as puppets used to narrate the story, such as Wayang kulit (leather puppets) and Wayang golek (wooden puppets), handled by a *Dhalang* (puppeteer). Third, it signifies the performance itself, including *Wayang Orang* (man/woman) ballet which does not required puppets or puppeteer. The puppet forms are believed to be inspired by ancient Javanese temple reliefs, such as those at Penataran Temple (14th century), and were later stylized to align with Islamic teachings that discouraged figural representation (Sumarsam, 2018). Despite these varied interpretations, all three meanings are seen as part of a unified cultural universe—what Wahyudi (2012) calls the Javanese *Mahabharata* or *Ramayana*, enriched with local elements distinct from their Indian origins.

Traditional Wayang performances contain a variety of artistic expressions, including fine art in the embodiment of the puppet itself, theatrical art in the Wayang performances, musical art in the *Gamelan* orchestra, and *Sinden* singing performances that accompany the puppeteer in animating the puppets. Language and dialogues telling stories performed by puppeteers are other examples of literary arts. All of these arts can be enjoyed as a complete performance that creates a sacred atmosphere.

4.1. *Wayang* as Traditional Educational Media

The Javanese have used pictorial media for a long time to narrate a story or message. In addition, it can also be known that the values contained in *Wayang* have long been popularised through traditional performances and become part of the life of the Javanese, usually performed as part of rituals to mark an event or celebration such as *Ruwatan*, village cleaning ritual, which is believed to give safety and avoid calamity, and also gets abundant blessings (Mulyono, 1983). During the Religious Propagation of Islam in the Island of Java, *Wayang* became a medium for *da'wah,* conveying Islamic teaching. As a historical fact, Sunan Kalijaga, one of the Nine Islamic Scholars (*Walisongo*) during the era of Islam's dissemination on the island of Java, acculturated the *Wayang* culture by incorporating elements of Islamic values into the *Wayang* stories, which reflect the social values of society. (Setiawan, 2017). Given the facts that have persisted for hundreds of years, it can be said that *Wayang* performances for the Javanese serve not only as *Tontonan* or performance but also as *Tuntunan* or guidance. (Setiawan, 2017). Moreover, several studies indicate that *Wayang* performances positively influence younger generations.

For instance, Wayang has enhanced students' critical thinking skills and fostered children's storytelling abilities (Nugraheni et al, 2022).

Based on these facts, *Wayang* has been proven to be involved in education such as the use of wayang as a learning tool to improve cognitive abilities and *Wayang* as a media to conveying educational messages or *da'wah*.

4.2. *Wayang* and Comic Adaptation

The main foundation of *Wayang* which are *Hamot,* openness to receive external influences; *hamong*, the ability to filter new elements; and *Hamemangkat,* to become something new (Harsrinuksmo, 1999) that has become the basic for its durability and development throughout the ages and allows the creation of new forms in storytelling and visual exploration, Including conveying the *Wayang* classical mythology through comics, so that it can be said that *Wayang* comics are a good medium to introduce the Wayang universe (Bonneff, 2008).

The birth of the *Wayang* comic actually resulted from social issues caused by the comic itself. In the 1950s, Indonesian comics emerged in various genres, including superhero stories. Ideas inspired by Western popular culture were seen as a threat to the sustainability of national cultural values and accused as the cause of laziness. To address this, some publishers gave a new orientation that comics should reflect national culture and contribute to shaping the nation's identity. Eventually, in 1954, a new type of comic appeared, commonly called the *Wayang* comic—an expression that describes comics inspired by the classical *Wayang* repertoire, *Mahabharata* and *Ramayana,* which has been part of Indonesia for hundreds of years and is considered a reflection of national values that able to respond the concern (Bonneff, 2008). This evolution was part of a broader movement affecting all areas of art creation (Bonneff, 2008). Driven by ideological ideas under Sukarno (1945–1965), which aimed to reduce Western influence and strengthen "National Identity" (Lombard, 1996), this genre became uniquely Indonesian and was well received by audiences because it was seen as more educational and aligned with the nation's culture (Bonneff, 2008). Since its debut in the early sixties, *Wayang* comics maintained popularity into the 1970s. However, unlike in the traditional *Wayang* performance that complete theatrical art displayed, *Wayang* comics as popular art displaying sequential images that illustrate a scene combined with written literature so that the skill of the comic artist is needed in visualizing scenes that are arranged in panels, especially in displaying scenes that are not present in traditional performances, such as presenting action scenes to be more dynamic. In addition, in terms of art in comics, the comic artist has freedom in terms of determining visual styles and character visualizations. Although it refers to the traditional performance, there is no standard reference for the visualization. This is actually a characteristic of every *Wayang* comic; even though it narrates the same play, the comic artists are allowed to express their own visual preference, which is part of the *Wayang* comics uniqueness, in contrast to *Wayang* performance which have a similarity on each character and the way of performing it also tends to be similar between one *Wayang* character to another.

Wayang Comics succeeded in merging two opposite things: comic as a commercial and mass popular art, and *Wayang* as a noble art that originally appeared in literature, interpreted as fine art and theater, popularized through traditional performances (Ajidarma, 2021). With the characteristics of comic, which communicates through text and images, it has advantages compared to other popular media, which is enjoyed by a wide range of audience demographics. The Long sacred rituals of the traditional *Wayang* performance are transformed into a more practical medium that makes *Wayang* comics contribute to creating the generation who appreciate the traditional art that threatened to be forgotten (Bonneff, 2008). Although *Wayang* comics refer to the traditional *Wayang* performances that are delivered in local languages, especially Javanese, Sundanese, and Balinese, *Wayang* comics successfully strengthen their national identity by using Bahasa Indonesia.

Visualization in *Wayang* comics, especially in the characters, generally refers to *Wayang Orang*, visualized in the Western version of three-dimensional realism makes it more likely to be explored and dramatise the sequences, such as fighting or war, which in the traditional *Wayang* performance are displayed symbolically (Bonneff, 2008). Even though the visual element in most *Wayang* comics is inspired by Wayang *Orang*, the comic artists have modified the visualisation according to their interpretation, not exactly the same as on the traditional performance, this actually makes it more appealing to readers who are not familiar with traditional performances. In this case, *Wayang* comics are a medium that can adapt to the visual tastes of its readers, making it possible to attract the interest of a wider audience. For readers who are familiar with the traditional *Wayang* performance, they can still easily recognize the represented characters; it could be deliberately done so that the reader's mind is connected to the traditional art.

4.3. Dewa Ruci: The Behavioral Guidance

The *Dewa Ruci* mythology, written by Raden Ngabehi Yasadipura I in 1796 and first published in print in 1870, was well received by the Javanese and often performed as a standalone episode in traditional *Wayang*. Due to its sacred and spiritually profound nature, not all puppeteers choose to perform it. Rich in moral teachings, *Dewa Ruci* has also been adapted in Javanese ethical literature. Its educational values are conveyed both implicitly and explicitly, particularly in the final segment, where a dialogue delivers core guidance on ethical behavior—considered the heart of the story (Wahyudi, 2012).

Among the messages contained in Dewa Ruci, one of the important messages that suitable for the younger generation is about the tenacity of a student to acquire knowledge that emphasizes, firstly, the importance of perseverance, persistence, and belief—while educational institutions and teachers are merely facilitators in achieving goals. Secondly, it highlights working earnestly and seriously, daring to face all risks at every step, and continuously learning until success is achieved (Supanggah, 2002). Supanggah's opinion, as explained above, is supported by Musbikin (2010), who hopes that the story of Dewa Ruci can be part of Character Education. Musbikin emphasizes that the story teaches many valuable life lessons, with the most important being the persistence of a student in pursuing knowledge until he succeeds (Musbikin, 2010).

The following is a summary of the episode: Bima, the second older brother of the Pandawa brothers, was ordered by his teacher, Durna, to look for the water of life (Tirta Perwitasari). Initially, he was directed to look for it on Mount Candradimuka where there were two giants incarnate of gods who would test his resolve. After meeting and fighting, Bima managed to kill them, and the two giants returned to their actual being. They told Bima that there was no living water in that place. As Bima goes back to his teacher and explains his experience, Durna expresses his joy because Bima passed the initial test of his determination and loyalty to his teacher. Then Bima was asked to look for the water in its actual location, at the bottom of the sea. Before leaving, Bima asked permission from his siblings and family, who were worried about his decision. When diving to the bottom of the sea, Bima was attacked by a giant dragon and managed to kill the dragon with his thumbnail. Then, he met a figure who resembled Bima, only smaller, named Dewa Ruci. During this meeting, Dewa Ruci shared teachings that primarily guide Bima on how to act kindly toward others and to keep God in mind to prevent misfortune. After listening to Dewa Ruci's "admonition", Bima left Dewa Ruci's body and returned to meet his teacher Durna. Bima considers Durna to be a true teacher, which led him to success, and never has any prejudice against him even though Durna is also the teacher of his enemy, the Kurawas, who could deliberately put him in danger.

The story above, told through the traditional *Wayang* performance, also conveys implicit philosophical lessons. However, these lessons are often weakened or lost in their comic adaptations because of format limitations. The delivery style in comics prioritizes story clarity, although it also implicitly conveys educational messages, guiding the reader through panels filled with writing and images that narrate the story from beginning to end. The ability to follow the narrative in the comic also depends on the reader, making it possible for them to only grasp what they see and read. This contrasts with the traditional lengthy performances in a sacred atmosphere during the night, which give the audience a chance for contemplation and deep reflection, enabling them to interpret the implied meanings conveyed. The characteristics of storytelling through visual imagery and written language may cause readers of Dewa Ruci comics to be more captivated by the aesthetic presentation than by the educational message it conveys. Furthermore, many action sequences capture attention, such as the iconic confrontation between Bima, the protagonist, and a formidable giant serpent, which causes the underlying message articulated by Supanggah, emphasizing "the tenacity of a student to acquire knowledge," to become increasingly overshadowed.

4.4. Implicit and Explicit Educational Content on the Comics

To preserve classical mythology and traditional arts, the story of *Dewa Ruci* is shared not only through *Wayang* performances but also via accessible media like novels and comics. As part of the *Mahabharata* epic, *Dewa Ruci* has been a recurring theme in Indonesian comics. R. A. Kosasih's 1955 version marked a milestone in the golden age of Indonesian comics. Teguh Santosa followed with a serialized version in 1983, later reissued in 2017 and again in 2024 as a collectible limited edition item. The only digital adaptation is Akhmad Fadly's *Dewa Ruci*, published on Webtoon Indonesia in 2016 and still accessible to this day. This study uses these three versions as case studies to explore how educational content is conveyed through comics.

The educational content in the *Dewa Ruci* story can be divided into two parts: implicit messages during Bima's quest for Tirta Perwita, and explicit teachings during his encounter with Dewa Ruci. In the first part, Bima's actions and dialogue subtly convey values, while the second part delivers direct moral and philosophical lessons—considered the core of the *Dewa Ruci* narrative. Although the explicit content varies across the three comics studied, they share common themes that will be discussed further. To begin, this study will first examine the explicit educational content in the scene where Bima meets Dewa Ruci.

A clear example of explicit message delivery is found in the 1955 Dewa Ruci comic, on the eleven (11) panels contains dialogue between Bhima and Dewa Ruci. For explanation purposes in this study, the dialogue originally presented in Indonesian is translated into English as shown in the Table 1 bellow

Table 1. Explicit educational message on Dewa Ruci Comic 1955 version

Panel	Dialog
1	Dewa Ruci: "It is not the teacher who teaches the virtuosity that must be worshipped, but the teacher who is in each of us".
2	Dewa Ruci: "It is not the king who sits on the throne that is worshipped, but the true king, the One Almighty".
3	Dewa Ruci: "It is not the parents who give birth to us that must be worshipped, but the true parents, who are the One who created this universe".
4	Teachers, Kings, and Parents are enough for us to be respected, not to be worshipped. Worship means obeying all the command
5	Dewa Ruci: "Teacher is not necessarily right in his orders as you are experiencing now".
6	Dewa Ruci: "Many kings forget themselves in their rule, do as what he pleases for the people".
7	Dewa Ruci: "Many parents are messed up their own family".
8	Bhima: "How to warship to the non-existent?"
9	Dewa Ruci: "There is an existence or not is the same for those who have come to know the true life"
10	Dewa Ruci: "Doing good to other people, not envying other people's property, it also has a kind of worship."
11	Dewa Ruci: "Able to control lust, calm and unfaltering by all temptations, it becomes a kind of worship".

Based on the sentence collected in the comic, several topics related to the value of education were obtained. The topic of educational content embedded in the dialogue, as in panels one to nine (1-9), is about the belief that only God is the one to be worshiped. Then panel ten (10) suggests us to do good to others, and panel eleven (11) reminds us to control ourselves from lusts and temptations.

Among the three *Dewa Ruci* comics, only the 2016 version omits the full storyline. The pivotal dialogue between Bima and Dewa Ruci appears briefly at the end as a concluding statement. Unlike the 1955 and 1983 versions, which offer more detailed narratives, the 2016 comic presents the educational message in a single panel with a clear, literal meaning during Bima's encounter with Dewa Ruci: "Follow His commands and avoid His prohibitions; those who do good will receive goodness. Keep the Creator in your thoughts, and you will certainly steer clear of disaster."

According to the creator of the comic, this was done deliberately so that readers could enjoy this comic until the end without having to read the long dialogues as in the original story. Although the message of Dewa Ruci conveyed to Bima in the three comics of Dewa Ruci is different, in terms of sentences and portions shown by the number of panels used to convey these teachings, in essence, it is about the spiritual relationship between humans and God, the message to always remember God, do good and control the desires to get the goodness and avoid disaster.

In addition to the explicit teachings conveyed in the three comics in the scene of Bima's meeting with Dewa Ruci, based on the examination of the three Dewa Ruci comics, it was also found that there were messages conveyed in other parts of the storyline. The implicit educational content in this section is no less important than that contained in the scene that narrates Bima's meeting with Dewa Ruci.

The data collected from this examination will then be analyzed using content analysis (Krippendorff, 1999) to identify the implicit educational messages within the mythology. This section will begin by presenting dialogue sentences extracted from several scenes where Bima follows his teacher's orders to seek the water of life, which contain implicit messages. Then, the words, sentences, and expressions in the dialogue of a specific scene will be identified and labeled or "coded' as keywords or short phrases that include verbs to indicate actions or adjectives to describe behavior. Finally, the codes will be grouped into categories aligned with exemplary character traits (Lickona, 1992) such as Integrity, Respect, and Perseverance, enabling the identification of themes within the messages.

The evidence of an implicit message on the three Dewa Ruci comics as shown in Table 2, which contain other educational messages obtained through coding and categorisation to identify themes of the educational message.

Table 2. Implicit Educational Message on the Three Dewa Ruci Comics

Comic	Bima Searchig for the Water of Life			
	Scene Dialogues	**Code**	**Category**	**Theme**
Dewa Ruci 1955	Bima: "I don't care about the trick. What's important is that I have to follow the teacher's orders."	I don't care about the trick follow the teacher's orders	Integrity	Never doubt and suspicious to his teacher The steadfastness of a student in carrying out his teacher's orders
Dewa Ruci 1983	Bima: "But this is a master's order to his disciple! We met face to face and none of the Kurawas was present in Sokalima" Bima: "When it comes to Tirta Perwita Sari, I cannot let anything stop me!" Caption: "Bima remained unhinged. His Four brother couldn't stop him, so they let Bima go on his journey to Mount Candradimuka".	this is a master's order to his disciple I cannot let anything stop me! Bima remained unhinged	Integrity	Never doubt and suspicious to his teacher The steadfastness of a student in carrying out his teacher's orders
Dewa Ruci 2016	"To attain significant objectives or aspirations, it requires steadfast, determination, and a commitment to perseverance".	Steadfast, determination, and a commitment	Perseverance	A relentless attitude and dedication to achieving goals.

Another implicit message that is only found in Dewa Ruci 1983 are written on the caption to describing of a student's respect for his teacher, as follows

"Bima stepped in boldly. In his own peculiar way, he paid his sembah *to Resi Durna, the teacher of Pandawa and Kurawa".*

"And After sembah *saying his bidding farewell, Bima left Sokalima"*

While in the Dewa Ruci 2016 visualising Bratasena doing *sembah* to Durna, the movement of raising both hands in front of the chest with the palms facing each other and the fingers tightly pointing upwards and the elbows slightly bent, the head slightly lowered with the gaze of the eyes downwards with a calm and respectful facial expression. This attitude is commonly found in Javanese society as a gesture of respect for elders, teachers, and those who are considered to have a higher position. Thus, the 2016 Dewa Ruci Comic contains educational content conveyed through words and the readers are also introduced through visualization in the scenes.

The message contained in this comic is not only in textual form but also visual. As explained in the previous section about comic theory, comics have a unique way of communicating, namely combining images with writings where each has its strengths and when combined will support each other and make the information conveyed easier to understand. This is in line with the theory of cognition, The Dual Coding theory, which was conveyed by Paivio so that in this part he applies a content analysis method where the provision of "code" in the form of symbols, which includes image

5. VISUAL-NARRATIVE TECHNIQUES AND THE EFFECTIVENESS OF EDUCATIONAL CONTENT DELIVERY

In comics, educational messages are conveyed not only through images but also through written text placed in speech balloons or captions—each functioning as a narrative space, much like panels do for visuals. Balloons, often shaped to fit the dialogue, represent spoken or internal thoughts, while captions provide narrative context, background information, or character insights. These elements form a unique storytelling structure exclusive to comics. According to cognitive theory, combining text and visuals enhances comprehension. Analysis of the three *Dewa Ruci* comics reveals that this structure—through both explicit and implicit messaging—helps readers better understand and retain the story's educational content. Moreover, specific technical delivery methods support message clarity. These techniques will be discussed in detail in the following section

Part of the structure of the comics is a unique characteristic that only exists in comics, which is the space for images, including panels and its transitions, and space for words or dialogue in balloons and captions to place textual narration that are not conveyed in balloons. The existence of space for words is inseparable from the presence of the panel as a space for images that complements each other according to the needs of the storytelling. Referring to the important of comic definition from Eisner as "framing time" which explains that the panel in comics is actually "boxing the action" where certain actions have been captured and placed inside the box which is then arranged together with other boxes containing moments from other actions, thus, the framed textual narratives is part of the storytelling structure in comics.

Back to the results of the examination of the three Dewa Ruci comics, the space for words and the space for images in these comics to convey educational content to the readers, even though the comic creator was not aware of it. From the examination of the three Dewa Ruci comics, it was found that there are delivery techniques as part of the comic structure that can provide a reading experience that impacts the level of understanding of the message conveyed. As for the structure of the three comics, there are messages that contain educational content in written text and visuals that are delivered repeatedly, not only in the same comic part of the whole storyline but also possibly conveyed repeatedly in the same scene. In addition, there is also a technique for simultaneously conveying two events in different settings. The delivery technique invites the reader to quickly move from one scene setting to another to make the reader see other events simultaneously. The use of these two techniques to deliver educational content is explained in more detail in this section.

5.1. Repetitive Message.

An examination of the three Dewa Ruci comics reveals repetition in the messages related to education. This repetition appears not only in the dialogue balloons but also in the captions of all three comics studied. In the storyline of the 1983 Dewa Ruci comic, where Bima is directed by Durna to find the holy water, there is a dialogue between Bima and his Pandawa brother Arjuna: "But this is a teacher's order to a student!" and Arjuna responds, "I appreciate Bima's attitude of obeying the teacher's orders!" These two lines, in effect, convey the same message about obeying the teacher's orders. The repeated message delivery is also seen in the 2016 Dewa Ruci comic about Bima's perseverance, which is shown differently from that in his predecessor comic, where it appears in dialogue. In Dewa Ruci 2016, the message is repeated twice in different scenes: first when Batara Bayu gives Bratasena the nickname, "A Knight Who Has High Aspirations and Never Gives Up," and again when Durna releases Bima to carry out his orders, with the sentence, "To achieve great goals or desires, it takes strong determination and never giving up." In line with the characteristics of comics that communicate both verbally and visually, the repeated delivery of messages is not only through writing as described above but also through visualizing scenes of sembah, an attitude commonly shown in Javanese society as a gesture to show respect to elders, teachers, and those deemed to hold a higher status. Contained in the 2016 Dewa Ruci Comics, different from the one in the predecessor Dewa Ruci comic, which contains the word *sembah* repeatedly in the caption; in the 2016 Dewa Ruci Comic, it is conveyed repeatedly visually. In this comic, Bratasena is visualized doing *sembah* when meeting with his teacher, also shown when he meets with Batara Indra and Batara Bayu, in the comic showing the gesture of raising both hands in front of the chest with the palms facing each other and the fingers tightly pointing upwards, and the elbows are slightly bent, the head slightly lowered with eyes looking down with a calm and respectful expression.

The repetition in delivering educational content may not be intentional by the comic creator to make the reader remember the message conveyed. However, referring to the *human information-processing system* described in detail in the previous section, the repetitive delivery of information can affect the brain's ability to store what is conveyed. New information received as a stimulus can quickly fade unless it is deliberately memorized, which often requires receiving it repeatedly so that it is also necessary to convey the information repeatedly until it is stored in long-term memory. This is supported by the results of the questionnaire, fully explained in the previous section, showing that most respondents who read the 2016 Dewa Ruci comic argued that the educational content from the story of Dewa comic emphasizes persistence in seeking knowledge and steadfastness in carrying out orders.

5.2. Adjusting Time and Space to Enhance Understanding.

As in movies and other textual narrative products, by certain delivery techniques, comics can also convey two events at once. This delivery technique is actually commonly applied by comic creators, not something unique only found in comics, but to apply it requires the involvement of other visual elements that are uniquely only found in the comic structure. The change of setting and time of the story in the comic usually uses captions to explain the reader textually that there has been a change of place and time different from that contained in the previous panel. However, there is also a transition between panels and changes in the panel's shape that takes readers to a different storytelling setting. As explained in the previous section, captions have the function to textually narrating something that accompanies a scene in a panel, can be as the character introduction, story background explanations, the location of a scene, and others, as well as inviting the reader to move to other scenes that occur in the same or in different timespan. The use of captions to provide explanations that takes the reader quickly navigating through spaces and times as in the story contained in the panel sequent. As an example of its application, the information in the caption begins with a change in the setting of the story in a sentence with a description of the place as in the 1955 comic Dewa Ruci: “Let’s leave Bhima's journey. Now back to Hanoman who is heading home to his hermitage." Through this sentence, the readers are invited to move to another location as well as indicate that at that point the reader is already in a different story setting. To take the reader back to the previous location, as it is indicated with a sentence in the caption on the scene panel as follow "Let's leave the Pandawa family negotiations. Now we are following Bhima's journey again". The placement of the caption is accompanied by the panel that visualising Bhima's journey, so at that point, the reader has returned to the main storyline.

The findings serve as evidence that certain methods can be applied to instantly shift the story setting to another, either simultaneously or at a different time. As mentioned above, the structure of the comic can be used to show other events in different places and times. This technique can help clarify the message in the story of Dewa Ruci. Moving time and space within the story can lead the reader to a setting that is more relevant to the current context, such as highlighting the implicit message conveyed in the story.

This storytelling technique can transport the reader to another setting that is more relevant to the current context, serving as a translation of the implicit message within the story. Its goal is to clarify the conveyed message, making the educational content easier for the reader to understand and apply in daily life. The technique ensures that the information becomes clearer in its practical use.

An example of a variation in the storyline of Dewa Ruci, which is also related to the current context, is using a storytelling technique that takes the reader to different settings within the overall story. This includes different dimensions of time and place, creating more varied versions of the story. It is exemplified by various events with contexts relevant to the younger generation, such as comic readers. For example, the variation of the Dewa Ruci story with the application of the storytelling techniques above is intended to help readers better understand the message conveyed within the context of everyday life, as follows:

Bima was ordered by his teacher, Durna, to find the water of life (Tirta Perwitasari) on Mount Candradimuka. Meanwhile, in a different place and time, a teenager named Bima, who loves to play soccer and aspires to be a famous player, was asked by his coach to go somewhere to improve his skills. Always ready to follow instructions, Bima immediately went to the location his coach mentioned. In his story, he was told to search for the water of life on Mount Candradimuka, where two giants, gods' incarnations, would test him. After fighting and defeating them, the giants revealed their true forms as *Batara* (God) Indra and *Batara* Bayu. They told Bima there was no living water there. Meanwhile, the teenage soccer enthusiast reached the place specified by his coach. Facing a tough opponent, he demonstrated determination, impressed the opponent, who then advised him to practice endurance and skills and to meet his coach. Bima returned and shared his experiences; his teacher, Durna, was pleased, recognizing Bima's determination and loyalty. Bima was then sent to find water at the bottom of the sea. He dived and fought a giant snake, killing it with his thumbnail. He later encountered Dewa Ruci, who told Bima to enter his body through his ear. Inside, Bima saw a peaceful space but was urged by Dewa Ruci to return with wisdom on living rightly and doing good. Following this guidance was akin to finding the water of life. Bima left his body, returned to the world, and expressed gratitude to Durna, whom he regarded as a true teacher despite being the teacher of his enemy. Later, as a dedicated soccer player, Bima trained diligently, following advice from opponents and his coach. He was amazed by his fitness improvements and believed that his disciplined training would lead to success if approached sincerely.

6. CONCLUSION

Based on *Wayang*'s foundation that offers openness to innovation, integrating popular media like comics offers a strategic way to engage younger audiences while preserving cultural heritage and promoting timeless moral values. Comics are effective because they are accessible, affordable, and adaptable to numerous technological advances as well as reader characteristics throughout generations. Unlike audio-video production, which includes animation and digital games, comics demand few resources and are easily accessible via mobile devices. This study looks at the Dewa Ruci mythology as a case study to see how comics may communicate character education. Comics can improve message clarity and memorability by combining certain visual and narrative techniques.

6.1. Application for Character and Cultural Education

Wayang comics are utilised in education not only as a learning tool, but also to teach character traits such as integrity and perseverance, as well as to enhance awareness of the country's cultural identity. Through the application of the visual-narrative techniques to improve the effectiveness of Educational Content Delivery, as explained in the previous section, this medium has the potential to be a great instructional tool for conveying educational messages contextually and practically. Thus, *Wayang* comics can be implemented for character and cultural education, which can be embedded in character education subjects or Language Lessons with the topic of discussion about the value of educational in Wayang stories in an integrative thematic learning model.

The learning objective is that students are able to identify the character of the *Wayang* characters and the moral message of certain *Wayang* stories and understand their relevance in daily life. So that in learning activities with this method, students in addition to reading comics to understand the message conveyed through the analysis of the story, it is also necessary to reflect to understand its relevance to the lives of each student.

The proposed stages of learning activities begin with an introduction where the teacher or facilitator opens by explaining the learning objectives and the relevance of *Wayang* culture. Furthermore, students were asked to read the comic to the end, followed by a group discussion discussing the characters of the characters in the story and the moral message contained in it. The learning session was closed with a joint reflection discussing its relevance to today's context.

6.2. Recommendation for Further Research

This scientific writing can be used to develop a new type of *Wayang* comic, namely an educational *Wayang* comic in that implements visual-narrative techniques as mentioned above, not only for educational purposes but also commercially. This chapter also provides new opportunities for further research in terms of measuring the effectiveness of comics in increasing the understanding of the message conveyed, further measuring the level of awareness of traditional culture that has an impact on changing the behavior of the students involved.

REFERENCES

Ajidarma, S. G. (2011). *Panji Tengkorak: Kebudayaan dalam Perbincangan*, KPG (Kepustakaan Populer Gramedia)

Ajidarma, S. G. (2021). *Ngobrolin Komik*. Pabrik Tulisan.

Akcanca, N. (2020). An alternative teaching tool in science education: Educational comics. *International Online Journal of Education & Teaching*, *7*, 1550–1570.

Aleixo, P. A., & Sumner, K. (2017). Memory for biopsychology material presented in comic book format. *Journal of Graphic Novels & Comics*, *8*(1), 79–80. DOI: 10.1080/21504857.2016.1219957

Anderson, B., R O'G. (2016). *Mitologi dan Toleransi Orang Jawa*, MataBangsa, Yogyakarta, 4th print, Translated from *Mythology and the tolerance of the Javanese*, 1965

Bonneff, M. (2008). *Komik Indonesia*. Kepustakaan Populer Gramedia.

Das, A. K., & Singh, A. K. (2022). Comics: An Alternative Medium for Education and Social Progress. *ECS Transactions*, *107*(1), 8847–8854. DOI: 10.1149/10701.8847ecst

Farinella, M. (2018). The potential of comics in science communication. *JCOM, Journal of Science Communication*, *17*(01), Y01. DOI: 10.22323/2.17010401

Febriyanti, P., Santoso, R. B. (2023). *Nilai Keislaman dalam Cerita Wayang Kulit dengan Lakon Babad Alas Wanamarta di Kabupaten Karanganyar*, Jurnal Keislaman, Volume 06, Nomor 01, Maret 2023

Hall, A. (2011). *Illustration*. Laurence King Publishing.

Hayikaleng, N. (2019) *The Effects of Using Dual-Coding Theory in Teaching English Reading Comprehension among Vocational Students at Narathiwat Technical College*, International Journal of Arts Humanities and Social Sciences Studies Volume 4 Issue 6 July 2019.

Kearns, C., & Kearns, N. (2020). The role of comics in public health communication during the COVID-19 pandemic. *Journal of Visual Communication in Medicine*, *43*(3), 139–140. DOI: 10.1080/17453054.2020.1761248 PMID: 32643470

Krippendorff, K. (1999). *Content Analysis: An Introduction of its Methodology*. SAGE Publications.

Lickona, T. (1992). *Educating for Character; how Our School Can Teach Respect and Responsibility*. Bantam Books.

Lombard, D. (1996). *Nusa Jawa Silang Budaya 1: Batas Batas Pembaratan*. Gramedia Pustaka Utama.

Lysloff, R., Kant-Achilles, M., Seltmann, F., & Schumacher, R. (1992). *Review of Wayang Beber*, by M. Kant-Achilles, F. Seltmann, & R. *Asian Music*, *24*(1), 146–151. DOI: 10.2307/834457

Malamed, C. (2009) Visual Language for Designer: Principles for Creating Graphics that People Understand. Rockport.

McCloud, S. (1993). *Understanding Comic: The Invisible Art*. Kitchen Sink Press.

Mulyono, S. (1983). *Simbolisme and Mistisisme dalam Wayang*. CV Haji Masagung.

Musbikin, I. (2010). *Serat Dewa Ruci: The Mystery of the Water of Life*. Diva Press.

Purwanto, S. (2018). Pendidikan Nilai Dalam Pagelaran Wayang. *Jurnal Pendidikan Islam*, *06*(01), 1–30.

Rosa, S. (2019) *Teaching Character Through Oral Stories in Indonesia And Malaysia*, Journal of Southeast Asian Studies, Volume 24(2), December 2019, 176-190, ISSN 1823-4127/e-ISSN 2600-8653

Sadoski, M., Paivio, A., & Goetz, E. T. (1991). Commentary: A Critique of Schema Theory in Reading and a Dual Coding Alternative [Published By: International Literacy Association]. *Reading Research Quarterly*, *26*(4), 463–484. DOI: 10.2307/747898

Santosa, I. B. (2023). *Alam Batin Jagat Wayang*. DIVA Press.

Setiawan, E. (2017) *Makna Filisofi Wayang Purwa dalam Lakon Dewa Ruci*, Kontemplasi.

Tversky, B., Morrison, J. B., & Betrancourt, M. (2002). Animation: Can it facilitate? *International Journal of Human-Computer Studies*, *57*(4), 247–262. DOI: 10.1006/ijhc.2002.1017

Wahyudi, A. (2012) Lakon Dewa Ruci: Cara Menjadi Jawa. Yogyakarta

Wijayanti, F. (2023) *Analysis of Character Values in the History of Wayang Beber Wonosari, Gunung Kidul Regency, Special Region Province of Yogyakarta.* Nagri Pustaka: Journal of Education, Historical Studies, and Culture.

Yang, G. (2008). Graphic Novels in the Classroom. *Language Arts*, *85*(3), 185–192. DOI: 10.58680/la20086181

Chapter 4
Integration of Social Media in Education:
Opportunities, Challenges, and Pedagogical Implications

Hana An L. Alvarado
https://orcid.org/0009-0006-6550-616X
Mindanao State University - Tawi-Tawi College of Technology and Oceanography, Philippines

Lydia A. Omar
https://orcid.org/0009-0000-5259-2739
Mindanao State University - Tawi-Tawi College of Technology and Oceanography, Philippines

Meekyla Anne A. Aripin
https://orcid.org/0009-0008-5515-2841
Mindanao State University - Tawi-Tawi College of Technology and Oceanography, Philippines

Sarah-Shane L. Jamma
https://orcid.org/0009-0000-2699-6967
Mindanao State University - Tawi-Tawi College of Technology and Oceanography, Philippines

Potchong M. Jackaria
https://orcid.org/0009-0006-1678-4841
Mindanao State University - Tawi-Tawi College of Technology and Oceanography, Philippines

DOI: 10.4018/979-8-3373-5157-5.ch004

ABSTRACT

This study explores the use of social media for educational purposes among 100 pre-service teachers from various programs and year levels in a state university in the Philippines. Using a mixed-methods design, data were gathered through a structured questionnaire with both Likert scale items and essay-type questions. Quantitative results revealed that social media is widely used for announcements, sharing materials, and coordinating task, while activities such as discussions, feedback, and assessment remain underutilized. Alongside its benefits, challenges were identified, including distraction from academic work, exposure to misinformation, poor time management, and reduced face-to-face interaction. Qualitative responses further illustrated how students negotiate its dual role as both efficient academic tool and a source of disruption. Triangulation underscored tensions between accessibility, focus and information access and credibility. The study recommends promoting digital literacy, mindful use, and structured pedagogical integration of social media in teacher education programs.

INTRODUCTION

In today's digital age, education is much influenced by digital technologies, particularly by social media. Social media serves as one of the powerful tools shaping students' academic and personal lives. The different social media platforms are no longer just entertainment spaces (Astleitner & Schlick, 2025). Rather, it has become an important means of communication, self-expression, information sharing, and most importantly, teaching and learning (Chen et al., 2011). It is already part of the students' daily routines from waking up every day, checking updates or announcements, watching short videos, joining online discussions, to collaborating on projects with classmates (Galindo-Dominguez et al., 2025).

Social media is so salient that it seems impossible to imagine our lifestyle, including education, without its presence. It plays a salient role in the students' interaction with their peers or teachers and in accessing information (Lahiry et al., 2019). There are instances where students utilized Facebook Messenger to form a group chat, YouTube to watch tutorials, and TikTok for short clips to find further information. On the teachers' part, they adopt these tools to engage their learners more, provide them with reminders, communicate with their students, and even make announcements (Arco, 2023; Merelo et al., 2023).

In the Philippines, access to the formal digital learning platforms is limited, even though social media offers a more accessible and cost-effective alternative for advancing educational experiences (Manca & Renieri, 2016). However, despite its growing influence, its integration in the educational context remains contested. There are several concerns about its utilization in the classroom. Some of the concerns raised include distractions, procrastination, addiction, and misinformation (Ma et al., 2025). Social media may also hinder students' attention, focus, engagement, or worst, their overall well-being (Brailovskaia et al., 2018; Wang et al., 2025).

Although it offers opportunities, it also comes with disadvantages and risks. While some scholars have investigated the potential of digital tools in learning, there's still a need for research that addresses this in a specific educational context. In regions such as Southern Philippines, it is salient to understand how educators and students utilize the social its benefits and pitfalls. Hence, this chapter hopes to address this need by providing an in-depth investigation of social media utilization in education, its pros and cons, drawing from the pre-service teachers' experiences. The pre-service teachers' perspectives provide a valuable contribution to how these platforms can be utilized and maximized for academic purposes. Particularly, this chapter seeks to answer the questions below:

1. What are the social media platforms most commonly used by the pre-service teachers for academic purposes?
2. What is the overall popularity of various social media platforms among pre-service teachers?
3. For what purposes do the pre-service teachers primarily utilize social media in relation to their education?
4. How do pre-service teachers perceive the ways their instructors utilize social media in teaching-related activities?
5. What negative effects do pre-service teachers experience when using social media for academic purposes?

By answering this question, the chapter intends to contribute to the understanding of contextualized utilization of social media in education. Specifically, the chapter provides practical information and insights for educators, students, and policymakers on social media utilization.

LITERATURE REVIEW

This section reviewed recent studies on the utilization of social media platforms in the educational context. It is organized thematically. Drawing first from the general popularity of social media, usage, and its negative effects.

Popularity of Social Media

Recently, social media has become one of the most dominant forces shaping global communication, culture, and education. Recent data shows that social media access has reached remarkable levels, with over 5.41 billion user identities worldwide as of 2025, equivalent to 65.7 percent of the global population. On average, users spend about 19 hours weekly across multiple platforms, including Facebook, TikTok, YouTube, and Instagram, emphasizing its relevance in everyday life (DataReport, 2025). This event is not limited to entertainment but extends into how individuals interact with one another, access knowledge, and engage with learning opportunities (Gottfried, 2024).

The utilization of these platforms among young people, especially students, is very important nowadays. Studies highlight that platforms or applications such as TikTok, Instagram, and YouTube, and many other social media platforms, control the online activities of adolescents and young adults, who engage with these platforms not only for pastime or for their leisure time but also for accessing and gathering information and educational content (Purnama & Asdlori, 2023). Similarly, in Bangladeshi universities, it has also become an important part of students' routines. Applications like Facebook, WhatsApp, YouTube, and Instagram are commonly used, and their widespread adoption is largely due to cheap internet access and the availability of smartphones. As a result, students remain active on these platforms multiple times a day, relying on them for entertainment, social interaction, and academic purposes, which makes social media a main aspect of student life (Chowdhury, 2024).

From a global perspective, social media has also redefined what it means to learn and collaborate. Students in Africa, Asia, and the Middle East used social media platforms to exchange notes, join academic forums, and participate in knowledge-sharing communities (Shater et al., 2024). In South Africa, found that more than 80 percent, specifically 84.5 percent of surveyed students use social media for at least four hours daily, with many acknowledging its dual role as both a tool for academic support and a source of distraction (Lukose & Agbeyangi, 2025). Similarly, at the University of the UAE, it was reported that students are dependent on these platforms for accessing resources and also peer interaction (Shater et al., 2024).

However, the popularity of these platforms differs from different country. In Ghana, learners were found to use these platforms most intensively for information sharing, education, entertainment, and social bonding, which is Facebook, Instagram, and WhatsApp being the most popular platforms, while lesser-known platforms such as Flickr, SoundCloud, and MySpace saw very limited use (Odoom et al., 2025). In the United States, platforms such as TikTok, YouTube, and Instagram emerged as the most popular platforms among early adolescents, with usage rates above 64% while WhatsApp is barely used (Nagata et al., 2025). In addition, 16 countries in Asia, including Bangladesh, China, India, Indonesia, the Philippines, Singapore, and South Korea, social media platforms Facebook and Instagram remain the most popular across Asia, followed by LinkedIn, TikTok, and WhatsApp, with usage patterns varying by age and gender (AlAfnan, 2024). While the United States barely used the WhatsApp platform, in contrast, in Mexico, WhatsApp is the most popular social media platform, followed by Facebook and Instagram, that widely utilized by students for communication, entertainment, and social interaction (Maciel-Saldierna et al., 2024).

Furthermore, from the local perspective, in the Philippines, the popularity of social media is equally visible. The Philippines often ranks among the highest in global social media usage. Filipino students are exposed to platforms such as Facebook Messenger for group chats, YouTube for tutorials, and TikTok for short-form learning content in their daily study routines (Salisi et al., 2019). Additionally, Filipino pre-service teachers of Baguio Central University, regarding the usage of these platforms in the education context, like Facebook, Messenger, and YouTube, are usually used for academic purposes, with participants spending 3 to 4 hours daily on social media. It is reported that Filipino pre-service teachers consider social media as moderately useful for entertainment, academic purposes, socializing with other people, and accessing information means the social media is important during their training (Sebullen, 2023).

The Use of Social Media for Teaching and Learning

The utilization of social media in schools has changed the teaching and learning methods of teachers and learners. Platforms like Facebook, WhatsApp, and Twitter, that made for communicating and socializing, have now become useful tools in education that help with learning. A study shows that social media not only helps students and teachers talk with each other but also supports group learning, encourages active participation, and gives access to many learning materials (Sahoo & Pradhan, 2025).

According to Güney (2023), using social media platforms such as Facebook, YouTube, and Twitter gives good chances in K–12 education by allowing personalized learning, building teamwork and communication, giving access to a wide range of learning materials, and connecting learners to a worldwide group of classmates and experts. Additionally, Manca and Renieri (2016) said that platforms such as Facebook and YouTube have a strong ability to improve interaction, teamwork, and creativity in higher education. Similarly, in Malaysian colleges and universities found that using it supports teamwork among students and researchers, improves communication and sharing of knowledge, and has a good effect on school performance. Social media has a good effect when students use it carefully and responsibly in schools, which can change learning spaces by allowing interactive, group-based, and resource-filled experiences that go beyond regular classrooms (Al-Rahmi et al., 2015). In addition, according to the study of Astleitner and Schlick (2025), college students looked at their role in building identity, supporting learning, and being used alongside other activities. Their study showed that social media has many uses in education since it allows students to manage their online identity, take part in group learning, improve inner motivation, and build self-confidence. The study also found that students utilize it not just for educational purposes, but also as entertainment, rest, and escape from reality. There are many effects of these platforms on both the social and school life of students, suggesting that their careful use in classrooms can help learning while also meeting students' social and emotional needs.

Ningtyas et al. (2024) explored the utilization of it in learning, specifically for science education. Their research highlights that when platforms are effectively integrated in education, they can enhance and support the learning of the students through visualization, collaboration, gaining more knowledge, and student-centered learning. However, authors emphasized that there are some possible risks and problems in integrating it. This includes the privacy issues as well as the need for proper training or utilization of these platforms in schools. Ningtyas et al. (2024) also highlighted that Facebook is a valuable tool that can be used in higher education. It offers many benefits, including improving interaction between the instructors and their students, and even among students. This can also help boost the students' performance in school, access easier learning materials, and encourage higher participation in class. However, Chugh and Ruhi (2018) noted that while there are some risks and challenges, such as privacy issues, teachers can make rules, and good practices can help maximize the pros of using these platforms.

At Ghana University, students have found that social media has many important benefits for learning. It has been found that Social media improves communication skills by allowing students to connect more easily with classmates and teachers, and also helps students academically. Social media is used to easily access information for learning, such as articles, videos, tutorials, and discussion forums, helping students add to what they learn in class with easily available information. Furthermore, these social media platforms support group learning by giving chances where students can share ideas and work on projects together with their peers, and also join academic talks beyond the limits of classrooms. The interactive nature of social media strengthens collaboration with their classmates and helps build critical thinking and problem-solving skills. These benefits show that when social media is used well in schools, it can improve the overall learning experience of college students (Demuyakor, 2020).

Negative Effects of Social Media Use

Given the many benefits of social media, there are also cons or disadvantages of using it. Its excessive use has been widely associated with negative mental health outcomes, particularly among adolescents and young adults. Nagata et al. (2025) found that higher social media usage during early adolescence contributed to increased depressive symptoms over time. Furthermore, restricting social media use led to measurable improvements in well-being, emphasizing the detrimental impact of prolonged exposure. Platforms such as Instagram and TikTok often present idealized and curated images, which can lead users to engage in frequent social comparison, resulting in body dissatisfaction, lowered self-esteem, and heightened anxiety (Burnell et al., 2025). Einstein et al. (2023), it creates pressures to conform to unrealistic beauty standards, particularly among female adolescents. In addition, a "Fear of Missing Out" (FoMO) has become one of the factors in causing mental stress to the users of social media. Young users often feel FoMO when they think their friends are doing fun activities without them. Another, Azhari et al. (2022) and Yao et al. (2025) found that this kind of feeling has been linked to loneliness, mood swings, poor sleep, and overall mental strain. Moreover, these mental health problems are made worse because of the easy access to social media, which pushes users to stay online all the time and strengthens negative emotions.

Moreover, its utilization also harms academic performance and the students' thinking ability (Cao et al., 2018). The study of Yan et al. (2017) noted that students who spend too much time on these platforms often show lower grades and less focus in class. Aligning with the research of Ma et al. (2025) that using social media too much in different ways can lead to burnout in learning and lower academic results among college students. Overuse of social media can also cause information overload, where the brain is flooded with too much content, making it harder to focus on difficult tasks. Also, Wang et al. (2025) add that this mental tiredness, often called "media fatigue," affects not only school performance but also decision-making, problem-solving, and critical thinking skills.

While the utilization of social media has improved K-12 education. However, its usage also has negative effects or challenges. The challenges of using social it can cause distraction to the students from their academics, also to the students' privacy and safety concerns, the possibility of misuse of these platforms, such as cyberbullying or plagiarism, and the lack of sufficient teacher preparedness to integrate these tools effectively in K-12 education. Moreover, the study on social media in K–12 contexts remains limited. It is said that it needs more empirical studies before large-scale implementation of this in education (Güney, 2023). In addition, it revealed significant limitations such as access obstacles, some of which could be addressed through adaptation and training, while others remained too difficult to handle within

K–12 educational contexts or settings (Arco, 2023). Social media's actual integration into teaching remains limited due to cultural resistance, pedagogical concerns, and institutional barriers (Manca & Renieri, 2016).

Social media puts users at risk, especially of online bullying and harassment. Because people can hide their identity online, they are more likely to show harmful behavior that they might not display in person (Chatzakou et al., 2019). Studies show that teenagers who are victims of cyberbullying often struggle with low self-esteem, depression, and even suicidal thoughts, with female students being more affected (Extremera et al., 2018; Albikawi, 2023). Reviews of many studies also confirm that those who face online harassment are two to three times more likely to harm themselves or think about suicide compared to those who are not bullied (Mahzunah et al., 2024). Research in countries like Vietnam and China also shows a strong link between cyberbullying, depression, and suicidal behavior, where self-image and emotional stress play an important role (Nguyen et al., 2020; Chu et al., 2022). Overall, these studies show that constant exposure to online harassment damages emotional health, reduces well-being, and increases the risk of long-term psychological problems such as hopelessness and suicidal thoughts (Brailovskaia et al., 2018).

In summary, the related review literature shows that social media has become an important part of students' daily lives across the world, including in the Philippines, UAE, South Africa, and other countries, where platforms like Facebook, YouTube, Instagram, and TikTok are commonly utilized not just for fun or entertainment but also for communication and academic purposes. Studies agree that these platforms can be a useful tool in education because they allow students to share ideas, work with their classmates, and easily access learning materials and tutorials. Social media also encourages motivation, creativity, and participation, making learning more interactive and engaging both inside and outside of the classroom. Also, teachers and students benefit from the ability of social media to connect people and provide resources that may not be available in traditional learning settings. However, given the many benefits of it, the research underscores the perceived negative impacts of it, especially when it is used too much. Overuse of social media often leads to distraction from academic activities, lower school performance, information overload, and reduced focus on studies. Furthermore, another serious issue regarding its utilization of it are the mental health problems such as stress, anxiety, depression, and cyberbullying, which can really affect students' well-being. Overall, the literature shows that social media has both pros and cons, which means using social media should be balanced to support learning as well as avoid the negative impacts on the person.

METHODOLOGY

This section explains the research design, research participants, research instruments, data collection, and statistical data analysis of this study.

Research Design. This study employed a mixed-method design that combines both the quantitative and qualitative approaches. This explored the utilization of the pre-service teachers among the different programs and year levels of social media. The quantitative data focuses on pre-service teachers' levels of agreement, frequency of the specific behaviour, and their perceptions on the usage of the different social media platforms. The qualitative data elicits in-depth narratives, experiences, and reflections.

Research Participants. The respondents of this study were 100 pre-service teachers from a state university in the southernmost part of the Philippines, Tawi-Tawi. Participants were drawn from various academic programs and year levels. The diversity provided a more holistic picture of how social media is integrated at different stages of teacher preparation. The selection of respondents was chosen using the purposive sampling technique. This is appropriate because the study required participants with direct and meaningful experiences of utilizing social media for academic purposes. Through deliberately targeting pre-service teachers with varying levels of exposure and engagement, this study ensured the richness and relevance of the data, as well as capturing the heterogeneity of experiences across programs and year levels.

Research Instrument. The instruments used in this study were divided into two sections, designed to collect both quantitative and qualitative data. The first section of the questionnaire consisted of Likert scale items that measured the commonly used social media platforms, the purpose of their utilization, teachers' utilization for teaching-related activities, and perceived negative effects of using them. The second section was essay-type questions. It encourages the participants to articulate their experiences, reflections, and provide concrete examples of how they used it for academic purposes.

Data Collection. The data of this study were collected through face-to-face sessions in the 1st semester of the school year 2025-2026. Through the face-to-face sessions, it ensures that the participants fully understand the questions, as well as being able to seek more clarification if needed. Before the data collection, the participants were briefed on the aim and purpose of this study. And to maintain the ethical standards, the participants' anonymity and confidentiality were assured.

Statistical Data Analysis. This study involved both quantitative and qualitative data. For the quantitative data, the numerical responses were tallied and analysed. The frequencies as well as the percentages were computed to present the results on the social media usage, purpose of the utilization, teachers' utilization for teaching-related activities, and its perceived negative effects. The qualitative data from the essay responses were subjected to thematic analysis. This qualitative data was used to triangulate the quantitative findings, providing in-depth insights into the motivations and lived experiences of the pre-service teachers' use of it in education. Hence, the combination of quantitative and qualitative data ensures that the study captured both measurable trends and rich narratives from the participants, presenting the utilization of social media, the benefits it offers, and the risks it poses in the educational contexts.

RESULTS AND DISCUSSION

The result and discussion sections are structured based on the statement of the problem, critically reflecting the perspectives and experiences of participants regarding the use of social media in education. This section is divided into four parts, beginning with the most commonly used platforms, and the overall popularity of different platforms used, the purpose of their utilization, teachers' utilization for teaching-related activities, and the perceived negative effects.

Commonly Used Social Media Platforms by Pre-Service Teachers

The survey results show the distinct patterns in the distribution of social media use among the 100 pre-service teachers. It highlights which social media platforms are most utilized in their academic routines.

Figure 1. Commonly Used Social Media Platforms

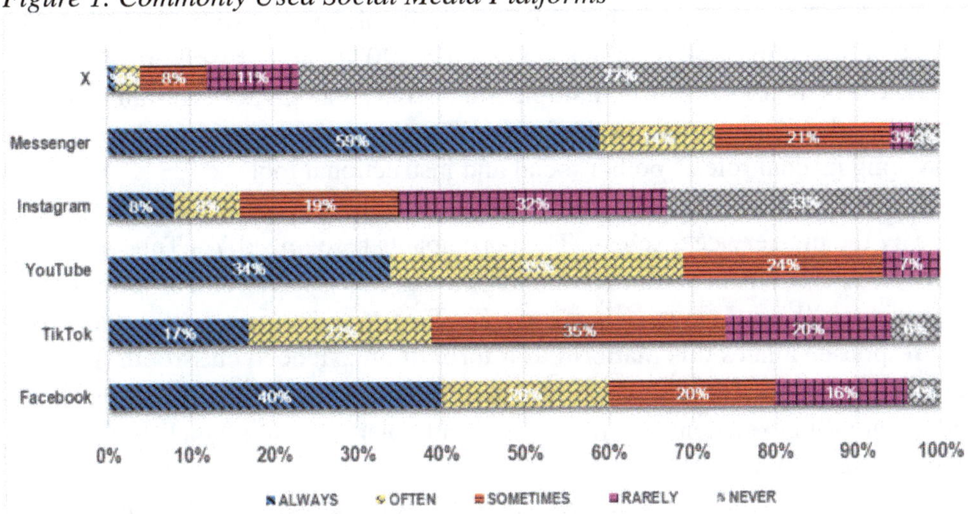

Note. This figure shows the frequency of social media usage among the pre-service teachers across the six prominent platforms (X (formerly Twitter), Messenger, Instagram, YouTube, TikTok, and Facebook). The responses are categorized into five levels: ***Always, Often, Sometimes, Rarely,*** *and* ***Never.***

The Messenger emerged as the most frequently utilized social media platform, reporting 59% of the participants answering "Always." Only 3% of the participants selected "Rarely" and "Never" categories. One pre-service teacher explained, "*I used the messenger app and it has been very effective both for me and my teacher in communicating and sharing info about educational-related tasks...*" This demonstrates that Messenger served as a communication channel among students as well as to their instructors. Relating to this response, Pedroso et al. (2023) had noted that Messenger is an essential platform that is utilized for enhancing academic skills, facilitating communication of academic inquiries, as well as for disseminating tasks that need to be accomplished. Another participant supported this by noting that, "*The most effective approaches teachers use are the utilization of applications like Messenger, which is known for sharing and disseminating information...*" These responses underscore that Messenger evolves from a casual messaging tool into an indispensable platform for communication, resource sharing, and group collaboration in academic settings.

Similarly, Facebook followed closely with 40% of the respondents selecting "Always" and 20% "Often." The students frequently highlighted its central role for announcements, reminders, and access to supplementary resources. One pre-service teacher remarked, "*I used Facebook or a FB group page to know if there are announcements. I also used it to find some learning resources.*" Another student shared, "*I used Facebook when my teachers created pages where they post announcements and reminders."* These responses confirm that Facebook continues to function not only as a social networking site but also as an academic support space through group pages that disseminate information. Chowdhury (2024) similarly reported that students actively use this platform multiple times a day, not only for entertainment but also for academic purposes, particularly in disseminating information or updates, reinforcing its dual role as both a social and instructional tool.

Moreover, YouTube also rated prominently, with 34% "Always" and 35% "Often" usage by the pre-service teachers. The participants recognized YouTube as both a source of entertainment and an accessible place of educational content. One student emphasized, *"When I am studying, I use YouTube to watch some video tutorials."* This response situates this platform as a form of an extended classroom. It offers free and on-demand tutorials that support self-paced learning. Earlier studies have found that Filipino students are more exposed to platforms like YouTube for video tutorials (Salisi et al., 2019).

Furthermore, most of the students reported a moderate pattern of use of TikTok. TikTok revealed that 35% of the participants reported "Sometimes" and 22% "Often." This indicates that even though TikTok is increasingly popular, several students acknowledged its potential for short-form educational content, particularly for quick tips for exam preparation. Its uneven adoption for academic purposes reflects its dual nature as both a leisure activity and an emerging micro-learning space. Similarly, Adnan et al. (2021) and Purnama and Asdlori (2023) noted that TikTok's short learning content is highly effective for keeping students' attention, especially for complex topics. These studies suggest that though TikTok is widely associated with entertainment, it possesses potential as a supplementary educational tool if properly used in a learning context.

In contrast, Instagram and X (formerly Twitter) were the least utilized social media platforms and hold limited relevance in the pre-service teachers' academic routines. Instagram recorded high percentages in the lower usage categories, reporting "Rarely" (32%) and "Never" (32%). While X showed overwhelming disuse, with 77% selecting "Never." As one student reported, *"I used Twitter or X for my personal and entertainment, but not really for school or classes at all."* This response suggests that while students may engage with these two platforms socially, they do not perceive them as useful in supporting academic tasks. In the same manner, Nagata et al. (2025) revealed that both Instagram and X (formerly Twitter) continue to have less usage for educational purposes, strengthening their limited value in the academic context. Aside from these reasons, the result may also relate to the fact that social media popularity differs by region. In the context of this study, Facebook is the most popular platform in the Philippines.

Overall, these findings reveal a clear stratification of social media use among the pre-service teachers. Messenger, Facebook, and YouTube dominate and are consistently embedded in the daily lives of the participants as practical tools for communication and learning. TikTok is an emerging supplementary tool for educational resources and short video tutorials. On the other hand, Instagram and X remain marginal or less utilized, indicating that it was utilized for entertainment rather than as serious academic tools. For educators, this stratification implies that integrating widely adopted platforms into teaching practices, particularly Messenger for communication, Facebook for coordination, and YouTube for instructional content, can enhance accessibility and engagement.

Overall Popularity of Social Media Used by the Pre-Service Teachers

Beyond the simple frequency counts, the overall popularity of social media platforms provides macro-level perspectives on which digital spaces pre-service teachers find most essential to their academic lives.

Figure 2. Overall Popularity of Social Media Platforms

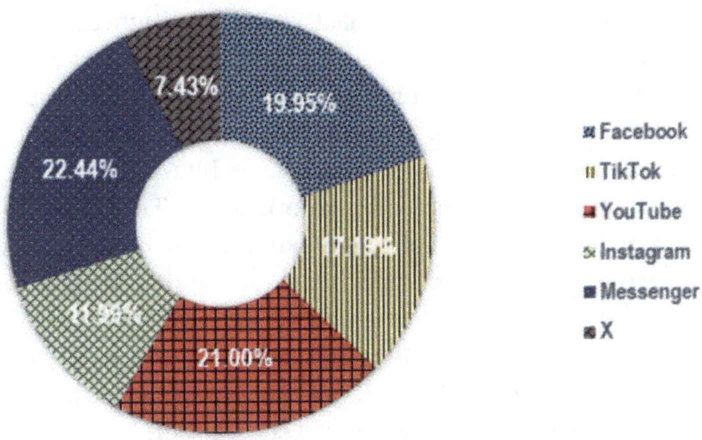

Note. This figure presents the distribution of pre-service teachers' preferred social media platforms. Percentages reflect the proportion of participants who identified each platform as their most commonly used. **Messenger (22.44%), YouTube (21%), Facebook (19.95%), TikTok (17.19%), Instagram (11.99%),** *and* **X (7.43%).**

The results revealed that Messenger ranked as the most prominent platform (22.44%), a finding that resonates with studies highlighting the centrality of instant messaging tools in fostering collaborative learning and peer support. Its dominance can be attributed to its synchronous and asynchronous affordance to the users. It allows pre-service teachers to engage in real-time consultations, coordinate with group mates, and maintain peer-to-peer academic support. This reflects how Messenger has evolved into an indispensable tool for academic collaboration, reflecting how students adapt technology to fit pedagogical and social demands. Sahoo and Pradhan (2025) also reported that what makes Messenger a preferable platform for working collaboratively with others is the ease of its use and flexibility.

Following closely is YouTube (21%), underscoring the growing reliance on video-based learning. YouTube's widespread use highlights the strong reliance of pre-service teachers on video-based learning for both independent study and reinforcement of classroom lessons. This aligns with Nacak et al. (2020), noting that YouTube functions as an informal yet powerful educational platform, providing learners to revisit lectures, access tutorials, and explore explanations that complement classroom instruction.

While Facebook ranked third (19.95%), it revealed that participants blend their academic and non-academic engagement. Students pointed out that they used it because most of their professors utilized it for posting announcements and uploading learning materials. This finding supports prior studies that show how Facebook bridges formal and informal learning environments (Manca & Ranieri, 2016). More importantly, Facebook continues to function as an environment for not just announcements and knowledge-sharing, it also serves as a community-building.

Meanwhile, TikTok (17.19%), predominantly associated with entertainment, has now begun serving as a site for micro-learning. Several students acknowledged that TikTok can provide quick tips or short lessons for specific subjects or even government exams. This aligns with recent research that the TikTok short video content allows students to engage with academic resources in bite-sized form, letting it be used as a micro-learning tool (Purnama & Asdlori, 2023). The growing popularity of TikTok among pre-service teachers suggests that educators must acknowledge unconventional learning spaces where digital natives already spend much of their time.

Furthermore, Instagram (11.99%) and X (7.43%) ranked the lowest among the social media platforms. Participants described Instagram as visually oriented and less suited for academic content. While X was perceived as fragmented and less efficient for learning. These results indicate that students are not prevalent in using these two social media platforms in their academic practices. As one participant emphasized, *"Instagram is not used for educational purposes, it's not that connected or beneficial in gathering information /knowledge."* These findings reaffirm that not all widely available and recognized platforms can serve as effective and efficient academic tools (Manca & Renieri, 2016).

Overall, these findings reveal that pre-service teachers utilized social media platforms that offer accessibility, immediacy, multi-functionality, and access to academic resources. Messenger and YouTube were frequently used because they directly address the needs of communication, as well as for supplementary learning. While Facebook provides a space for academic coordination and community engagement. However, Instagram and X remain underexplored and underutilized for academic purposes. This distribution highlights the importance of aligning the teaching strategies with the platforms that students are already utilizing. Also, critically engaging with the limitations and risks of these spaces. In doing so, educators can harness the transformative potential of these platform media to support collaboration and engagement, while also remaining attentive to the challenges of distraction, credibility, and uneven accessibility. Educators must ensure that the social media integration enhances their academic engagement rather than disrupts or hinders meaningful learning.

Purpose of Social Media Utilization

The results show the primary academic-related purposes for which pre-service teachers utilized various social media platforms.

Figure 3. Purpose of Social Media Utilization

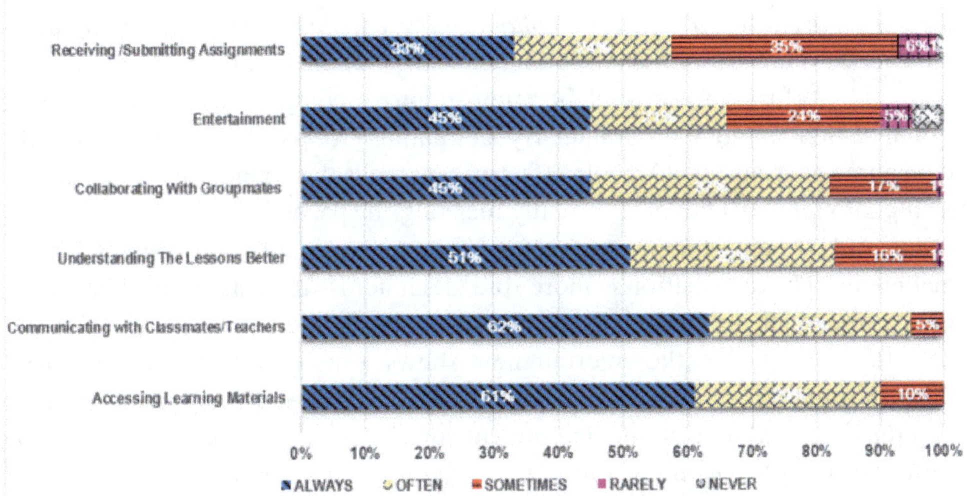

Note. This figure displays the frequency with which pre-service teachers utilize social media for different purposes. Reported uses of it include receiving/submitting assignments, entertainment, collaborating with group mates, understanding the lessons better, communicating with classmates/teachers, and accessing learning materials. The responses are categorized into five levels: ***Always, Often, Sometimes, Rarely,*** *and* ***Never****.*

The findings highlight that pre-service teachers primarily turn to these platforms for academic-related purposes. This underscores its functions as an essential education enabler of learning. A huge majority of the respondents reported always or often using social media to access learning materials (90%) and communicate with classmates and teachers (93%). These patterns illustrate how social media has evolved into a parallel academic environment. It has become a space for sustaining academic connectivity, enabling students to remain updated, share files, and even clarify lessons/discussions beyond the four corners of the classroom. As one student corroborated, *"It helps me as a student to access learning materials and information faster and easily."* One student even highlighted, *"Using these platforms increased access to information, faster communication, collaboration among students, and increased engagement through interactive content."* This is consistent with Sebullen (2023), who noted that students utilize it for academic purposes, increase engagement with other people, and facilitate immediate access to information.

Another major reason cited was understanding lessons better (83%), followed closely by collaborating with groupmates (82%). One participant explained, *"It can give me some knowledge and information that helps me to solve the problem that I've encountered in the classroom."* Another participant highlighted, *"The benefits of using it for learning make it easier for the given topic to be understood by the learners. It is easily accessible to all, where we can enhance our prior knowledge or ideas."* While one student remarked, *"The benefits I see using it for teaching and learning are that it increases engagement and interaction through discussions, comments, and shares. It facilitates collaborative learning and enables group work and projects."* These responses were aligned with Al-Rahmi et al. (2015), who found that digital platforms foster collaboration, improve comprehension, and deepen communication among the students. By facilitating group projects, peer feedback, and resource-sharing, social media effectively extends the boundaries of classroom learning into informal but academically meaningful spaces.

Moreover, the entertainment aspect (66%) remains a major purpose of utilizing social media. The distribution is more spread out across the categories. Unlike academic uses, which are strongly concentrated in higher frequencies in the "Always" and "Often" categories, the entertainment shows a more balanced pattern. This reflects the dual role of social media platforms in the students' lives. It can be used for productivity and relaxation. One student corroborated, *"I used social media for entertainment and sometimes, I used it for getting new information."* Demuyakor (2020) similarly noted that the balance between leisure and learning is a central dynamic in students' digital lives. This duality emphasizes the challenge of ensuring that the educational potential of social media is harnessed without being undermined by its capacity to distract.

Lastly, the lowest frequency was viewed in receiving or submitting assignments (57%), reported "Always" or "Often." There are also responses that fell under "Sometimes" (35%). While some students noted that they occasionally used social media to submit work and requirements, formal submissions still largely occurred through more structured Learning Management Systems (LMS). As one student noted, *"Sometimes, I used to send my reports and submit assignments..."* This indicates that although it is embedded in learners' academic routines, its role in official assessment practices remains supplementary rather than central.

Overall, the findings affirm that it has become an integral component of the academic routines and daily lives of the pre-service teachers, serving as a space for communication, collaboration, and ultimately, access to resources, while also serving as a space for relaxation or entertainment. However, the same platforms also raise challenges in balancing their benefits with their risks. Students themselves acknowledged that constant connectivity could lead to distraction or a tendency to prioritize leisure over learning. These findings emphasize that the utilization of it in higher education can be a transformative tool, but its risks must also be recognized.

Teachers' Utilization of Social Media for Teaching-Related Activities

The results below show how university instructors utilized social media for academic purposes. Drawn from the pre-service teachers' experiences, the data will provide invaluable insights into the current instructors' strategies. This will provide insights into the utilization of these platforms for teaching.

Figure 4. Teachers' Utilization of Social Media Platforms

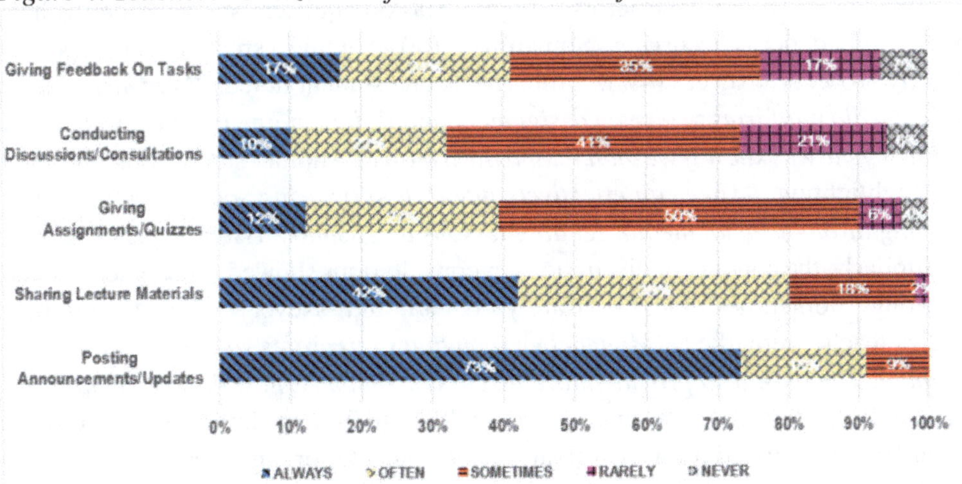

Note. This figure shows the frequency with which the instructors of the pre-service teachers utilize social media. Reported uses of it include giving feedback on tasks, conducting discussions/consultations, giving assignments/ quizzes, sharing lecture materials, and posting announcements/updates. The responses are categorized into five levels: ***Always, Often, Sometimes, Rarely,*** *and* ***Never.***

The most consistent practice reported by the pre-service teachers was posting announcements and updates, where 73% percent of the respondents selected "Always" or "Often."

One participant explained, *"They use group chats to post announcements, share videos related to the topic, and give announcements."* This suggests that social media functions as an essential channel for logistical coordination that ensures immediacy and accessibility.

Next, sharing lecture materials ranked as the second most frequent practice (80%), indicating "Always" or "Often." Students expressed that instructors distributed PDFs, slides, and supplementary resources through these platforms. As one student noted, *"They used it by giving and sending PDFs regarding the lesson, submitting requirements, giving feedback, etc."* Another respondent emphasized, "*As of today's generation, we are living in an area of modernization; it is very effective for teachers to use social media as an efficient and convenient way to communicate with their learners and disseminate educational materials."* These practices position social media as informal repositories of academic resources. Merelo et al. (2023) similarly found that messaging apps and social platforms are increasingly used by instructors to communicate with their students and share learning materials, sometimes augmented with chatbots to enhance their teaching.

In contrast, more interactive and demanding practices were less common in the teaching practices of the instructors. Assigning tasks or quizzes was described by half of the respondents as occurring "Sometimes" (50%), while a smaller share reported "Rarely" (6%) or "Never" (4%). Similarly, as one student noted, "*My teacher uses social media platforms to give an assignment or quiz by sending it in the group chats so that he/she will know if we understand the lecture."* Another student corroborated this, highlighting, *"They can effectively integrate it by using social media in their learning through social media, sending lessons and usually assignments or tasks."*

Similarly, the conduct of discussions or consultations showed a dispersed pattern reporting "Sometimes" (41%), "Rarely" (21%), and "Never" (6%). As one pre-service teacher remarked, "*My teacher sometimes integrates social media into the teaching. They use it to provide more discussions. Sometimes, they also entertain some consultations, and it's very convenient.*" These findings indicate that although the instructors utilized it for coordination and consultation, they remain hesitant to use it for assessment-related activities. Providing feedback through social media presented a more uneven pattern. The participants reported varied experiences with "Always" (17%), "Often" (24%), and "Sometimes" (35%). While a few teachers used these platforms to give feedback through chats, others still relied more on traditional channels. As one participant reflected, *"Some of my teachers use it to provide some feedback on our assignments, tasks, or performances."* This finding underscores that the feedback function of social media is still underutilized compared to its communication and resource-sharing roles.

Overall, the findings highlight that teachers utilize it primarily for communication and resource sharing. While the platforms' accessibility and immediacy make them effective tools for coordination, their potential for fostering engagement, collaboration, and ultimately, formative assessment remains largely untapped. This reflects broader patterns in higher education, where it serves as a logistical aid rather than a fully integrated pedagogical tool. Thus, intentional strategies are needed to reposition social media not only as a tool for announcements but also as a meaningful extension of the learning environment.

Perceived Negative Effects of Social Media for Academic Purposes

The result below shows the extent of the negative effects of the social media platforms as perceived by pre-service teachers.

Figure 5. Perceived Negative Effects of Social Media Utilization

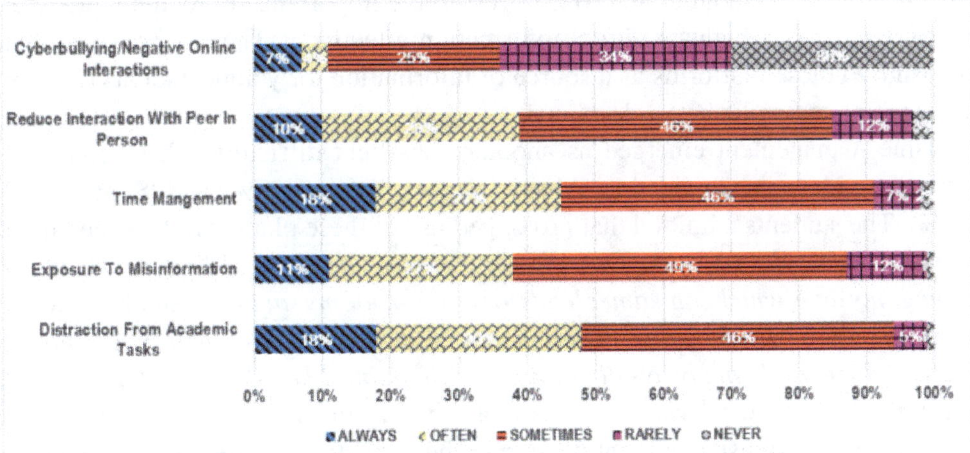

Note. This figure displays the frequency of the perceived negative effects of social media among the pre-service teachers. Reported uses of it include cyberbullying/negative online interactions, reducing interaction with peers in person, time management, exposure to misinformation, and distraction from academic tasks. The responses are categorized into five levels: ***Always, Often, Sometimes, Rarely,*** *and* ***Never.***

The most prominent perceived negative effects of social media for academic purposes when integrating it into their academic routines were distraction from academic tasks, reporting "Always" (18%), "Often" (30%), and "Sometimes" (46%). Nearly all respondents acknowledge distraction from schoolwork as a negative effect of social media. One student admitted, *"The negative experiences or challenges that I have encountered in social media are a distraction."* Another participant corroborated this, *"Negative experiences I encountered while using social media are like distractions, being left behind because I focus more on online and not on academics, can't manage my time well because I was too hooked by the technology."* These findings reinforce Lukose and Agbeyangi's (2025) observation that social media tools can be both academic support at the same time can be a source of distraction, particularly for those who are using longer hours every day. This distraction can undermine not only individual productivity but also the cultivation of self-regulated learning skills that pre-service teachers are expected to model for their future students.

Exposure to misinformation was another prominent issue, reported as "Sometime" (49%) and "Often" or "Always" (38%). While it offers quick and easy access to resources, students still raised concerns and doubts about the credibility of sources. One student corroborated, *"Many the information is not reliable."* Another participant said, *"There are a lot of experiences or so-called challenges encountered while using social media, such as false information, unreliable sources used for any educational purposes."* These responses reflect the ongoing tension between the democratization of knowledge online and the persistence of unreliable or misleading content. Jabbour et al. (2023) stressed the importance of media literacy to enable students to evaluate digital information effectively. They emphasized that exposure to these platforms as a source of information for young students to them more aware and make better decisions.

Time management emerged as another consistent difficulty. These concerns were also widespread, indicating "Always" (18%), "Often" (27%), and "Sometimes" (46%). The students admitted that prolonged use of these platforms displaced time intended for academic work. One pre-service teacher noted, *"I find it difficult to manage my time, which sometimes leads to setting aside my studies."* Another student supported this, *"The negative experience was the time management. Every time I use social media, I am always distracted by other apps like TikTok, Instagram, and other platforms to watch videos."* This supports Katsitadze et al. (2025), who found that due to the extensive amount of time in the use it fosters procrastination and it becomes an interference in accomplishing their academic tasks.

On the other hand, in terms of social dimension, it was reported that pre-service teachers perceived that it reduced interaction with their peers in person, indicating "Sometimes" (46%), "Often" (29%), and "Always" (10%). While not as pronounced as distraction or misinformation, this theme still points to a subtle but meaningful shift in how students relate to one another. One student explained, *"Some common experiences or challenges that I encountered while using social media include less interaction with my friends or classmates, and also cyberbullying."* This response indicates a perception that online connectivity may come at the expense of in-person engagement. Güney (2023) similarly noted that social media can be misused in ways such as cyberbullying or plagiarism. There is also an insufficient teacher preparedness to integrate these social media tools effectively in K-12 education.

Cyberbullying or negative online interactions were reported as less prevalent in the survey with 30% of the students indicating "Never," and 34% indicating "Rarely." At first glance, these figures might suggest that cyberbullying is not a widespread concern in the context of social media for learning. However, the qualitative responses point to its significance. As one student reflected, *"There are several negative experiences I've encountered while using social media for educational purposes. It includes mental health concerns, privacy concerns, and cyberbullying."* While reported by a few participants, this response indicates the profound consequences of cyberbullying. It has been shown to have long-term effects, such as increased depressive symptoms over time (Nagata et al., 2025). Thus, these findings suggest that the lower prevalence of cyberbullying in our data should not be equated with lower importance or disregarded. Instead, it underscores the need for educators, together with the institutions, to take preventive measures against it.

Taken together, these findings underscore that although social media is widely utilized in education, its integration also brings risks. The findings further suggest that the teacher education programs must go beyond encouraging the use of these digital platforms, highlighting the necessity of integrating digital literacy and the mindful utilization of social media among the future educators. Thus, ensuring that the future educators are equipped enough to maximize the educational potential of these platforms while mitigating their risks.

CONCLUSION

The findings of this study highlight the role of the different social media platforms in the academic lives of the pre-service teachers. It shows how these platforms, such as Messenger, YouTube, Facebook, and X (formerly Twitter), serve as spaces for communication, immediacy, and flexible modes of learning. Yet, these benefits are inseparable from their wider cultural and geographic contexts. Sometimes, what is widely adopted in one country may be peripheral in another. For instance, WhatsApp is negligible in North America but functions as a primary academic channel in many Asian countries. This distinction highlights the importance of interpreting the utilization and integration of it in higher education as culturally and contextually situated rather than assuming its universal applicability.

The results of this study reveal that social media is a double-edged tool. The pre-service teachers expressed that these platforms became an extended classroom. It is a space where students and teachers exchange resources. These platforms can sustain academic engagement in ways that conventional ways often fail to support. However, there are some persistent challenges in integrating it. Challenges include distraction, fragmented attention, and exposure to misleading content or misinformation. Interestingly, the cyberbullying appeared less prevalent in the survey responses. However, these results do not mean cyberbullying should be dismissed. Several studies have shown that even limited instances of cyberbullying can lead to serious consequences. It includes heightened stress and, worst, depressive symptoms. It seems here that pre-service teachers perceive everyday challenges, the distraction and misinformation as more frequent and immediate, underlying risks of cyberbullying must not be overlooked. Furthermore, data privacy is an equally significant concern that needs to be recognized. As students submit their assignments, participate in discussions, and share their personal information, their digital footprints are exposed, and they may be misused and accessed by others. This highlights a point of a core tension. These platforms enable immediacy and connection; they also heighten the risks that demand a stronger pedagogical approach and institutional protections.

Moreover, the study also opens avenues for future inquiry. Comparative investigations between social media platforms and the learning management systems (LMS) are needed to clarify the differences in usability, accessibility, and pedagogical functions. Similarly, cross-national and longitudinal research could further reveal a deeper understanding of how digital spaces develop across contexts. It could also explore how institutional regulations mediate the balance between opportunities and risks in online learning environments. These insights, however, must be considered in light of the study's limitations. Since this research was conducted within a single institution, its generalizability is constrained. Social media preferences differ widely across countries, but still, the large sample of this study offers meaningful evidence of how pre-service teachers navigate both the advantages and challenges of these platforms in their academic routines.

In conclusion, social media can serve as a powerful and destructive tool for students. Its potential to foster collaboration and engagement is undeniable, but it also has risks. For educators and institutions, the question is no longer whether to integrate social media in education or not, but how to integrate it responsibly while mitigating its risks. And its integration into education is an unavoidable reality in the digital age. Educators should realize that its advantages extend beyond just accessing information and providing immediacy in terms of communication. This can be a space where learning and growth can happen, offering opportunities to encourage engagement with others. Thus, this study hopes to maximize and leverage the benefits of using it for education as well as mitigate the risks it holds. By fostering not only digital literacy but also digital mindfulness, ensuring that the teachers of the future generation are equipped with the competencies and skills needed to guide their students in the digital era.

Recommendations on Responsible Utilization of Social Media Platforms in Teacher Education

Based on the findings of this research, there are several recommendations to maximize the utilization of it in the academic context:

Reinforcing digital literacy and media literacy skills. One of the perceived major challenges of future teachers in utilizing it was their exposure to unreliable and misleading content. Teachers can include tasks that enhance and equip pre-service teachers on how to evaluate and critique online source content through verification or fact-checking content activities. Future teachers must strengthen their digital and media literacy skills to be able to distinguish unreliable information and sites.

Maximize platforms already embedded in pre-service teachers' lives. The teacher educators can leverage these social media platforms for posting announcements, sharing materials, consultations, and even video-based learning. However, their use should remain intentional and linked to clear learning objectives rather than being used as a default communication channel. Given their prevalent usage, these platforms can be used as a supplement to the existing learning management system of the universities if available.

Foster digital mindfulness in teacher preparation. As the pre-service transition into professional practice, their current digital habit will shape and may reflect in their pedagogical approaches. Institutions should therefore instill principles of digital mindfulness in the future generation of teachers, as they will be the role models of the young ones. Digital mindfulness is not viewed as beneficial or harmful, but as a powerful tool whose effectiveness depends on how the teachers utilize and manage it inside and outside the classroom. By equipping future educators on how to critically, effectively, and creatively harness social media platforms, it can ensure that future classrooms can leverage its strengths while mitigating its potential risks.

Develop institutional policies on responsible academic use of social media. Institutions must craft policies and guidelines that address data privacy, ethical communication, and appropriate conduct in online academic spaces. Such frameworks ensure that while social media remains accessible for the students, its use aligns with broader educational goals and safeguards the well-being of all learners.

Future Works. Lastly, future research should explore comparative investigation between social media platforms and comprehensive Learning Management Systems (LMS). These studies can deeply examine the variation in usability, accessibility, and the pedagogical affordances of these two platforms in facilitating teaching and learning, and assessment.

Finally, these recommendations emphasize the need for a balanced and critical approach to the integration of these platforms in education. Rather than viewing social media as a threat, this study advocates for their thoughtful and effective integration in the classroom. By equipping the pre-service with the vital skills, strategies, and awareness on how to thoughtfully integrate and navigate social media platforms, the institutions cultivate educators who are prepared to engage and delve into the digital technologies in ways that can enhance student learning while still preserving academic integrity and well-being.

REFERENCES

Adnan, N. I., Ramli, S., & Ismail, I. N. (2021). Investigating the usefulness of TikTok as an educational tool. [IJPTL]. *International Journal of Practices in Teaching and Learning, 1*(2), 1–5. https://ir.uitm.edu.my/id/eprint/52140/

Al-Rahmi, W., Othman, M. S., & Yusuf, L. M. (2015). The role of social media for collaborative learning to improve the academic performance of students and researchers in Malaysian higher education. *International Review of Research in Open and Distance Learning, 16*(4). Advance online publication. DOI: 10.19173/irrodl.v16i4.2326

AlAfnan, M. A. (2024). Social media personalities in Asia: Demographics, platform preferences, and behavior based analysis. *Studies in Media and Communication, 12*(3), 349–363. DOI: 10.11114/smc.v12i3.6925

Albikawi, Z. F. (2023). Anxiety, depression, self-esteem, internet addiction, and predictors of cyberbullying and cybervictimization among female nursing university students: A cross-sectional study. *International Journal of Environmental Research and Public Health, 20*(5), 4293. DOI: 10.3390/ijerph20054293 PMID: 36901301

Arco, L. J. P. (2023, March). Possibilities and limitations of social media in education processes during the pandemic: The teachers perspective. In *CTE Workshop Proceedings* (Vol. 10, pp. 315-325). https://doi.org/DOI: 10.55056/cte.552

Astleitner, H., & Schlick, S. (2025). The social media use of college students: Exploring identity development, learning support, and parallel use. *Active Learning in Higher Education, 26*(1), 231–254. DOI: 10.1177/14697874241233605

Azhari, A., Toms, Z., Pavlopoulou, G., Esposito, G., & Dimitriou, D. (2022). Social media use in female adolescents: Associations with anxiety, loneliness, and sleep disturbances. *Acta Psychologica, 229*, 103706. DOI: 10.1016/j.actpsy.2022.103706 PMID: 35973307

Brailovskaia, J., Teismann, T., & Margraf, J. (2018). Cyberbullying, positive mental health and suicide ideation/behavior. *Psychiatry Research, 267*, 240–242. DOI: 10.1016/j.psychres.2018.05.074 PMID: 29940454

Burnell, K., Meter, D. J., Andrade, F. C., Slocum, A. N., & George, M. J. (2025). The effects of social media restriction: Meta-analytic evidence from randomized controlled trials. *SSM. Mental Health, 7*, 100459. DOI: 10.1016/j.ssmmh.2025.100459

Cao, X., Masood, A., Luqman, A., & Ali, A. (2018). Excessive use of mobile social networking sites and poor academic performance: Antecedents and consequences from stressor-strain-outcome perspective. *Computers in Human Behavior, 85*, 163–174. DOI: 10.1016/j.chb.2018.03.023

Chatzakou, D., Leontiadis, I., Blackburn, J., Cristofaro, E. D., Stringhini, G., Vakali, A., & Kourtellis, N. (2019). Detecting cyberbullying and cyberaggression in social media. [TWEB]. *ACM Transactions on the Web, 13*(3), 1–51. DOI: 10.1145/3343484

Chen, S., Diao, Y., & Zhang, J. (2011, September). Social media: Communication characteristics and application value in distance education. In *2011 International Conference on Electrical and Control Engineering* (pp. 6774-6777). IEEE. https://doi.org/DOI: 10.1109/ICECENG.2011.6056919

Chowdhury, E. K. (2024). Examining the benefits and drawbacks of social media usage on academic performance: a study among university students in Bangladesh. *Journal of Research in Innovative Teaching & Learning*. https://doi.org/DOI: 10.1108/JRIT-07-2023-0097

Chu, X., Yang, S., Sun, Z., Jiang, M., & Xie, R. (2022). The association between cyberbullying victimization and suicidal ideation among Chinese college students: The parallel mediating roles of core self-evaluation and depression. *Frontiers in Psychiatry, 13*, 929679. DOI: 10.3389/fpsyt.2022.929679 PMID: 35845449

Chugh, R., & Ruhi, U. (2018). Social media in higher education: A literature review of Facebook. *Education and Information Technologies, 23*(2), 605–616. DOI: 10.1007/s10639-017-9621-2

DataReport. (2025, January). Digital 2025: Global overview report. https://datareportal.com/reports/digital-2025-global-overview-report

Demuyakor, J. (2020). Analysis of social media utilization by students in higher education: A critical literature review of Ghana. *Journal of New Media and Mass Communication, 6*(1), 1–7. DOI: 10.18488/journal.91.2020.61.1.7

Einstein, D. A., Dabb, C., & Fraser, M. (2023). FoMO, but not self-compassion, moderates the link between social media use and anxiety in adolescence. *Australian Journal of Psychology, 75*(1), 2217961. DOI: 10.1080/00049530.2023.2217961 PMID: 40666004

Extremera, N., Quintana-Orts, C., Mérida-López, S., & Rey, L. (2018). Cyberbullying victimization, self-esteem and suicidal ideation in adolescence: Does emotional intelligence play a buffering role? *Frontiers in Psychology, 9*, 367. DOI: 10.3389/fpsyg.2018.00367 PMID: 29623058

Galindo-Domínguez, H., Bezanilla, M. J., & Campo, L. (2025). Relationship between social media use and critical thinking in university students. *Education and Information Technologies, 30*(5), 6641–6665. DOI: 10.1007/s10639-024-12953-z

Gottfried, J. (2024). Americans' social media use. *Pew Research Center, 31*. https://janeaddams-il.aauw.net/files/2025/04/Soc-media-use-Americans.pdf

Güney, K. (2023). Considering the Advantages and Disadvantages of Utilizing Social Media to Enhance Learning and Engagement in K-12 Education. *Research in Social Sciences and Technology, 8*(2), 83–100. DOI: 10.46303/ressat.2023.13

Jabbour, D., Masri, J. E., Nawfal, R., Malaeb, D., & Salameh, P. (2023). Social media medical misinformation: impact on mental health and vaccination decision among university students. *Irish Journal of Medical Science (1971-), 192*(1), 291-301. https://doi.org/DOI: 10.1007/s11185-022-02936-9

Katsitadze, N., Kharadze, N., & Pirtskhalaishvili, D. (2025). The impact of social media on students' effective time management. *Baltic Journal of Economic Studies, 11*(1), 200–210. DOI: 10.30525/2256-0742/2025-11-1-200-210

Lahiry, S., Choudhury, S., Chatterjee, S., & Hazra, A. (2019). Impact of social media on academic performance and interpersonal relation: A cross-sectional study among students at a tertiary medical center in East India. *Journal of Education and Health Promotion, 8*(1), 73. DOI: 10.4103/jehp.jehp_365_18 PMID: 31143790

Lukose, J. M., & Agbeyangi, A. O. (2025). Is social media hindering or helping Academic Performance? A case study of Walter Sisulu University Buffalo City Campus. *arXiv preprint arXiv:2501.03611*. https://doi.org//arXiv.2501.03611DOI: 10.48550

Ma, X., Liu, Q., & Zhang, W. (2025). The impact of multidimensional excessive social media use on academic performance: The moderating role of mindfulness. *Frontiers in Psychology, 16*, 1579509. DOI: 10.3389/fpsyg.2025.1579509 PMID: 40625430

Maciel-Saldierna, M., Méndez-Garavito, I. R., Elizondo-Hernandez, E., Fuentes-Orozco, C., González-Ojeda, A., Ramírez-Ochoa, S., Cervantes-Pérez, E., Vicente-Hernández, B., Vázquez-Sánchez, S. J., Chejfec-Ciociano, J. M., & Cervantes-Guevara, G. (2024). Social Media Use and Fear of Missing out: An Exploratory Cross-Sectional Study in Junior High Students from Western Mexico. *Pediatric Reports, 16*(4), 1022–1033. DOI: 10.3390/pediatric16040087 PMID: 39585041

Mahzunah, A. K., Sari, I. Y., Paradela, B. V., Murti, B., & Tursina, E. (2024). The Impact of Cyberbullying on Self-Harming Behavior and Suicidal Thoughts among Adolescents: A Meta-Analysis. *Journal of Health Promotion and Behavior, 9*(4), 357–369. DOI: 10.26911/thejhpb.2024.09.04.07

Manca, S., & Ranieri, M. (2016). Facebook and the others. Potentials and obstacles of social media for teaching in higher education. *Computers & Education, 95*, 216–230. DOI: 10.1016/j.compedu.2016.01.012

Merelo, J. J., Castillo, P. A., Mora, A. M., Barranco, F., Abbas, N., Guillén, A., & Tsivitanidou, O. (2023). Chatbots and messaging platforms in the classroom: An analysis from the teacher's perspective. *Education and Information Technologies, 29*(2), 1903–1938. DOI: 10.1007/s10639-023-11703-x PMID: 37361787

Nacak, A., Bağlama, B., & Demir, B. (2020). Teacher candidate views on the use of YouTube for educational purposes. *Online Journal of Communication and Media Technologies, 10*(2), e202003. DOI: 10.29333/ojcmt/7827

Nagata, J. M., Memon, Z., Talebloo, J., Li, K., Low, P., Shao, I. Y., Ganson, K. T., Testa, A., He, J., Brindis, C. D., & Baker, F. C. (2025). Prevalence and patterns of social media use in early adolescents. *Academic Pediatrics, 25*(4), 102784. DOI: 10.1016/j.acap.2025.102784 PMID: 39800219

Nguyen, H. T. L., Nakamura, K., Seino, K., & Vo, V. T. (2020). Relationships among cyberbullying, parental attitudes, self-harm and suicidal behavior among adolescents: Results from a school-based survey in Vietnam. *BMC Public Health, 20*(1), 476. DOI: 10.1186/s12889-020-08500-3 PMID: 32276608

Ningtyas, P. K., Widarti, H. R., & Parlan, P. (2024). Exploring the Use of Social Media in Science Learning Environments: A Systematic Literature Review. *Journal of Science Learning, 7*(2), 178–186. https://eric.ed.gov/?id=EJ1440831. DOI: 10.17509/jsl.v7i2.67071

Odoom, D., Agyepong, L., Dick-Sagoe, C., & Mensah, E. O. (2025). Unveiling the social media landscape: Exploring factors influencing usage patterns among tertiary education students in Ghana. *Education and Information Technologies, 30*(3), 3861–3883. DOI: 10.1007/s10639-024-12944-0

Pedroso, J. E., Tubola, L. F. A., & Aquidado, E. J. (2023). Facebook Messenger: As Means of Communication for Academic Inquiries. *Journal of Digital Learning and Distance Education, 2*(2), 491–505. DOI: 10.56778/jdlde.v2i2.116

Purnama, Y., & Asdlori, A. (2023). The role of social media in students' social perception and interaction: Implications for learning and education. [TACIT]. *Technology and Society Perspectives, 1*(2), 45–55. DOI: 10.61100/tacit.v1i2.50

Sahoo, P., & Pradhan, J. S. (2025). Exploring the Role of Social Media in Promoting Collaborative Learning: A Systematic Review. *JOURNAL OF DIGITAL LEARNING AND DISTANCE EDUCATION, 3*(12), 1423–1435. DOI: 10.56778/jdlde.v3i12.502

Salisi, J. C. V., Aravejo, M. C. V., Eguia, G. C., Maranan, R. S. B., & Du, M. R. (2019). Social media use, perceived depression and academic performance of college students in a Philippine Higher Education Institution. *Cabrini Journal of Allied Medicine, 3*(2), 0. https://www.academia.edu/download/75923790/10.-Social-Media-Use-Perceived-Depression-and-Academic-Performance-among-College-Students.pdf

Sebullen, M. T. (2023). Assessing Pre-Service Teachers' Perceptions of the Practicality of Social Media in the Educational Arena. *Cognizance journal, 3*(7), 58-70. https://www.researchgate.net/publication/372216086

Shater, A., & Abualrish, M. A., & Al_manei, M. M. A. (. (2024). The Impact of Social Media Usage on Academic Performance: A Study of the Professional Educational Diploma Program in UAE. *American Journal of Education and Technology, 3*(3), 71–79. DOI: 10.54536/ajet.v3i3.2996

Wang, X., Zhao, X., & Yu, C. (2025). The influence of information and social overload on academic performance: the role of social media fatigue, cognitive depletion, and self-control. *Revista de Psicodidáctica (English ed.)*, 500164. https://doi.org/ DOI: 10.1016/j.psicoe.2025.500164

Yan, H., Zhang, R., Oniffrey, T. M., Chen, G., Wang, Y., Wu, Y., Zhang, X., Wang, Q., Ma, L., Li, R., & Moore, J. B. (2017). Associations among screen time and unhealthy behaviors, academic performance, and well-being in Chinese adolescents. *International Journal of Environmental Research and Public Health, 14*(6), 596. DOI: 10.3390/ijerph14060596 PMID: 28587225

Yao, X., Zhao, J., Chao, W., Gao, D., Wang, M., & Zhao, G. (2025). Relationship Between Fear of Missing Out and Social Media Fatigue: Cross-Lagged Panel Design. *Journal of Medical Internet Research, 27*, e75701. DOI: 10.2196/75701 PMID: 40680183

Chapter 5
Assessing the Future: Tools and Trends in Media-Rich Learning Environments

Gurashish Kour
https://orcid.org/0009-0002-2831-2754
Central University of Jammu, India

Raj Madhu
https://orcid.org/0009-0001-0516-3365
Central University of Jammu, India

Biswabhusan Pradhan
https://orcid.org/0000-0001-6011-0605
Central University of Jammu, India

Asit K. Mantry
Central University of Jammu, India

ABSTRACT

This chapter examines the transformation of assessment practices in media-rich learning environments, highlighting the shift from traditional summative evaluations to dynamic, learner-centred approaches. It explores how emerging technologies including Artificial Intelligence (AI), Virtual and Augmented Reality (VR/AR), gamification, data analytics, and digital storytelling enable more authentic, interactive, and formative assessments that capture not only knowledge but also creativity, collaboration, and critical thinking. By embedding assessment within immersive and technology-mediated contexts, educators can promote learner autonomy, resilience, and lifelong learning.. The chapter advocates for human-centric, equitable, and

DOI: 10.4018/979-8-3373-5157-5.ch005

sustainable assessment designs that balance innovation with inclusivity, ultimately empowering learners with the competencies required to thrive in the 21st century digital ecosystem.

INTRODUCTION

Education today moves from traditional environment to media-rich environment assessments, It is going deeper and deeper into digitally immersive media-rich environments, and now-a-days, assessment must evolve to capture not just students' knowledge, but also creativity, engagement and critical thinking by using multimedia tools, simulations, gamification and Artificial Intelligence (AI) that focus on shaping students learning, and traditional pen and paper assessments are increasingly out of synchronous with educational realities. This chapter explores how media-rich environment is helpful in transforming assessment practices, not just in functionality but in actual learning also. The main question comes to mind is how can we assess what matters in the digital age, and in what ways that is human-centric, equitable and reflective in real world skills also? Measuring outcome is one thing; assessment must now support lifelong learning, learner autonomy and inclusivity. Through this paper, the researcher explores the shift from static, summative evaluations to dynamic and comprehensive evaluations, formative feedback systems empowered by technology that are rooted in pedagogy. This chapter aims to guide educators and researchers in designing assessment approaches that embrace complexity, creativity and cognitive-emotional development in the technology-mediated classrooms.

SIGNIFICANCE OF THE CHAPTER

The chapter explores how digital tools, when used thoughtfully, digital tools ranging from multimedia portfolios to AI-based analytics can promote deeper engagement, self-awareness, and resilience in learners. These tools allow for more dynamic, interactive, and student-centred forms of assessment that go beyond traditional tests to capture how learners think, collaborate, create, and respond to real-world challenges. Crucially, the emphasis is not just on what students know, but on how they come to know how they process information, adapt to new contexts, and communicate their understanding through diverse media. This approach encourages a more holistic view of learning that values process as much as product. Educators, instructional designers, and policy-makers are offered here a research-informed and inclusive framework for creating assessment practices that are equitable, psychologically safe, and aligned with the complex competencies needed in the 21st century such as critical thinking, empathy, adaptability, and digital fluency. By adopting such a framework, stakeholders can design assessments that not only evaluate but also empower learners.

LITERATURE REVIEW

Media-rich learning environments are evolving due to the increasing availability of digital technologies and the internet (Caladine, 2008) (Dos Santos et al., 2025). These environments aim to enhance learning through interactive and immersive experiences (Vashisht, 2024). Current trends involve the integration of artificial intelligence (AI), augmented reality (AR), and virtual reality (VR) to create personalized and engaging educational settings (Asmae, 2025) (Anute & Geetali Tilak, 2024).

Evolution of Media-Rich Learning Environments

Media-rich learning environments have evolved from traditional, text-based, teacher-directed models to more interactive, multisensory, and student-centred approaches due to the rise of digital technologies. These environments now incorporate multimedia content, interactive simulations, digital storytelling, and virtual spaces (Han, 2022; McLoughlin, 2011). The integration of multimedia technology into education allows traditional educational materials to be translated into interactive electronic forms through multimedia authoring tools (Han, 2022). Teachers can design and incorporate multimedia elements into content to convey messages in a multi-sensory learning environment. The focus in education is shifting towards using multimedia as the instructional media and a platform in teaching and teaches (Han, 2022). Digital technologies can positively affect student learning in higher education, especially when teachers use them to encourage student engagement in constructive and interactive learning activities (Niemi et al., 2014). Interactive multimedia integrates text, audio, video, animations, and interactive elements to create dynamic, engaging, and effective learning experiences (Kalogeras, 2019).

Rise of Emerging Technologies in Assessment

Numerous technologies are being used for assessment methods in education. These technologies are much more efficient, individualized, and focus on comprehensive evaluation procedures for student knowledge (Ghanbaripour et al., 2024; Van Mechelen et al., 2022). Unlike traditional assessments, emerging tools such as Artificial Intelligence (AI), Learning Analytics, Virtual and Augmented Reality (VR/AR), and adaptive testing platforms allow for real-time feedback, continuous monitoring, and a deeper understanding of student learning patterns. These innovations not only measure what students know but also assess how they apply their knowledge in problem-solving and creative contexts. Furthermore, digital technologies support personalized learning by adapting assessment tasks to individual learner profiles, thereby accommodating diverse learning needs and styles. The integration of gamification elements, simulations, and interactive digital platforms has also transformed assessments into engaging experiences, reducing test anxiety while enhancing motivation. In this way, technology-driven assessment goes beyond rote memorization to evaluate critical thinking, collaboration, creativity, and other higher-order skills essential in the 21st-century knowledge economy.

Several Emerging Technologies Transforming Educational Assessment

Artificial Intelligence (AI)

AI-powered tools can help automate grading, give personalized feedback, and adjust the difficulty of assessments based on how students are doing (Rojas & Chiappe, 2024). They can analyze large volumes of student responses to spot patterns and identify where students are having trouble, making it easier for teachers to customize their teaching to better meet student needs (Rojas & Chiappe, 2024). Beyond reducing the workload for educators, AI-based assessment systems also enhance fairness and consistency by minimizing human bias in grading. Intelligent tutoring systems, for example, not only assess students but also provide step-by-step guidance, hints, or alternative explanations in areas where learners struggle, thereby creating a more supportive learning environment. Advanced natural language processing (NLP) algorithms are increasingly being used to evaluate essays, presentations, and open-ended answers, providing detailed feedback on grammar, coherence, critical thinking, and argumentation quality. Similarly, predictive analytics within AI platforms can forecast student performance trends and detect at-risk learner's early, enabling timely interventions. By integrating these capabilities into assessment practices, AI empowers both teachers and students—teachers gain actionable insights into learning progress, while students receive individualized learning pathways that foster continuous improvement and mastery of skills.

Virtual Reality (VR) and Augmented Reality (AR)

Using VR and AR can really make assessment situations feel more real, like you're actually in the scenario (Ghanbaripour et al., 2024; Van Mechelen et al., 2022). Students can show what they know and can do in a hands-on way, making tests feel more genuine and engaging for them (Ghanbaripour et al., 2024; Paananen et al., 2023). These immersive environments also allow learners to practice skills in safe, simulated settings—such as conducting scientific experiments, performing medical procedures, or handling complex machinery—before applying them in real life, thereby bridging the gap between theory and practice.

Gamification

Adding game elements to assessments can really boost how motivated and engaged students feel. Gamified tests give instant feedback and let students see how they're doing in a fun, interactive way (Ghanbaripour et al., 2024). By including features such as points, badges, leaderboards, and challenges, these assessments turn learning into an enjoyable experience while still measuring knowledge and skills effectively.

Data Analytics

Data analytics tools can carefully examine student performance data to spot trends and patterns, helping educators understand where students excel or struggle (Mhlongo et al., 2023; Rojas & Chiappe, 2024). This insight can be really useful for shaping better assessments and pinpointing students who might need a bit more support (Mhlongo et al., 2023; Rojas & Chiappe, 2024). These tech tools are also pushing us towards more ongoing, formative assessments (Sadallah, 2024). Instead of just giving a final grade, continuous assessments give students and teachers quick feedback throughout the learning process, so everyone can make timely tweaks to their strategies The goal with formative assessment is to help students grow and learn better, not just to mark their work with a grade. However, adding these new technologies into assessment practices also bring some important things to think about.

The integration of emerging technologies in assessment also raises important considerations. Looking ahead, the rise of emerging technologies in assessment is likely to continue, with increasing integration of AI, VR/AR, and data analytics. These technologies have the potential to transform assessment practices and improve student learning (Van Mechelen et al., 2022; Mhlongo et al., 2023; Adil et al., 2024). Future assessments are expected to become more adaptive, immersive, and learner-centered, providing deeper insights into skills such as problem-solving, creativity, and collaboration while supporting more personalized and equitable education. At the same time, institutions will need to address challenges such as data privacy, ethical use of AI, and the risk of over-reliance on technology that may widen existing inequalities if access is uneven. Ensuring inclusivity, transparency, and validity in technology-driven assessments will therefore be as crucial as harnessing their potential. When thoughtfully designed and responsibly implemented, however, these tools can not only complement but also enhance traditional forms of evaluation, creating a more holistic, future-ready assessment ecosystem.

GAMIFICATION AND SIMULATION-BASED ASSESSMENT

More and more, educators and trainers are turning to gamification and simulation-based assessments to boost engagement and effectiveness (Brackenbury & kopf, 2022; Brigham, 2015; Gallego-Duran et al., 2019). Gamification is all about applying game-like elements in non-game settings to make learning more motivating and fun (Lee & Lee, 2022; Gallego-Duran et al., 2019; Ha, 2025). Meanwhile, simulations create realistic scenarios that allow learners to practice skills and make decisions in a safe, controlled environment. Both methods use interactive and immersive features that help reinforce learning and improve outcomes (Brigham, 2015; Nukarinen et al., 2022; Zainuddin et al., 2024).

Gamification in Assessment

Gamification means adding game-like features—think points, badges, leader-boards, and fun challenges—to learning activities (Lee & Lee, 2022; Ha, 2025; Ghahari et al., 2023). The idea is to make studying more exciting and motivating by tapping into what drives us both internally and externally (Brigham, 2015; Gallego-Duran et al., 2019; Caballero-Hernandez et al., 2017). You can use gamification in many areas of education, from learning a new language to corporate training programs (Kessing et al., 2024; Patel et al., 2021). In assessments, it helps reduce stress, keeps students engaged, and encourages persistence, turning the evaluation process into a more enjoyable and rewarding learning experience.

Benefits of Gamification

Gamification can really help solve problems, boost engagement, and motivate people to reach their goals. It makes users feel more in control, confident, and connected, creating a fun and interactive experience (Gallego-Duran et al., 2019). By incorporating game design elements, students become more motivated to participate in learning activities (Karagiorgas & Niemann, 2017). It also encourages collaboration and healthy competition, provides instant feedback, and helps learners track their progress, which in turn supports deeper learning and skill development in both academic and professional settings.

Gamification Design

Designing engaging games isn't just about adding fun elements. It really depends on key parts like game dynamics, mechanics, and components. Game dynamics are the overall, big-picture effects that emerge from playing, while game mechanics are the specific rules and systems that shape how the game runs. Then there are the game components the individual pieces like characters and levels that make up the game world. Plus, thinking about what motivates players and keeps them interested is super important. This includes making sure the game grabs their attention, feels relevant to their goals, builds their confidence, and leaves them satisfied (Hofmann et al., 2021).

Gamification in Various Contexts

Gamification is applied in a variety of fields like education, marketing, and public health (Hjellvik et al., 2024). It helps create a lively environment for improving software processes and makes user experiences more engaging (Hjellvik et al., 2024; Song et al., 2019). By turning tasks into games, this approach encourages a more interactive experience, boosting users' sense of control, skill, and connection with others (Gallego-Duran et al., 2019).

SIMULATION-BASED ASSESSMENT

Simulation-based assessment uses computer-driven scenarios across different educational fields to help learners grasp practical skills more effectively. These simulations create situations that closely resemble real-world tasks, allowing instructors to train and evaluate a student's understanding more naturally (Jayalath & Esichaikul, 2020). It's a learner-focused approach that supports ongoing development of knowledge, skills, and competencies (Oestreich & Guy, 2022). One of the key advantages of simulation-based assessment is that it provides a safe and controlled environment where learners can experiment, make mistakes, and learn without facing real-world risks. For example, in medical education, simulations allow students to practice surgical techniques or emergency care procedures, while in aviation training, flight simulators help pilots build confidence and decision-making skills under various conditions. Similarly, in business and management studies, simulations can replicate market scenarios and organizational challenges, enabling learners to apply theoretical knowledge to practical problem-solving. These assessments also generate rich performance data, giving educators insights into not only what learners know but also how they apply their knowledge in dynamic situations. As such, simulation-based assessment bridges the gap between classroom learning and workplace application, preparing learners more effectively for real-life challenges.

Advantages of Simulation: Simulation-based education lets healthcare professionals train and be evaluated without putting patients at any risk (Bijl et al., 2024). These simulated learning environments are becoming more popular as an effective way to teach future educators (Brackenbury & Kopf, 2022). One of the key advantages is that simulations provide a safe and controlled setting where learners can practice repeatedly, make mistakes, and refine their skills without real-world consequences. This reduces anxiety and increases confidence, especially in high-stakes fields such as medicine, aviation, and engineering. Simulations also allow for standardized experiences, ensuring that every learner faces comparable scenarios and is assessed on consistent criteria. Moreover, the immediate feedback and data generated during simulations help both learners and instructors identify strengths, weaknesses, and areas requiring improvement. By bridging the gap between theory and practice, simulation-based education enhances not only technical competencies but also decision-making, teamwork, and communication skills—capabilities that are essential for professional success.

Implementation of Simulation: Simulations used for final assessments need to be carefully developed based on solid evidence. To be most effective, they should closely mimic real clinical situations, helping to select the right learners and prepare them well (Oranje et al., 2019). Effective implementation requires a structured design process that aligns learning objectives with realistic scenarios, ensuring both authenticity and reliability in evaluation. This involves incorporating elements such as standardized patients, high-fidelity mannequins, or immersive digital environments that reflect the complexity and unpredictability of real-world practice. Additionally, simulation assessments should be supported by validated rubrics and clear performance criteria so that results are consistent, objective, and defensible. Faculty training is equally important, as instructors must be skilled in facilitating simulations, providing debriefings, and interpreting performance outcomes. When carefully integrated into curricula, simulation-based assessments not only evaluate technical competence but also measure critical skills such as communication, teamwork, and ethical decision-making, offering a more holistic view of learner readiness for professional practice.

Application in Healthcare: In healthcare education, adding game elements can really boost how people learn (Brigham, 2015). Using simulation also helps make patient care safer, more effective, and more efficient (Bijl et al., 2024). Serious games and gamified simulations allow learners to practice clinical decision-making, diagnostic reasoning, and emergency responses in interactive ways that enhance motivation and retention. These methods not only make training more engaging but also create opportunities for repeated practice without risk to patients. Simulation-based training further supports interprofessional education, where medical, nursing, and allied health students can work together in realistic scenarios to strengthen teamwork and communication. By combining gamification with high-fidelity simulations, healthcare programs can improve technical skills, reduce medical errors, and foster greater confidence among trainees, ultimately contributing to higher standards of patient safety and care quality.

SHIFT FROM SUMMATIVE TO FORMATIVE AND PERFORMANCE-BASED ASSESSMENT

Unlike traditional final exams, formative and performance-based assessments like digital portfolios, student-led reflections, and peer feedback offer a more engaging, learner-centred way to evaluate understanding. These approaches encourage on-going involvement, help deepen learning, and build skills for self-regulation. Digital portfolios and student reflections are great tools for this. With digital portfolios, learners collect their work over time and reflect on their progress. This on-going process helps students grasp their learning goals, see their strengths, identify areas to improve, and become more intentional about their learning (Barrett, 2023; Lorenzo & Ittelson, 2022). Combining portfolio creation with thoughtful reflection boosts metacognitive skills, allowing learners to better understand and explain how their thinking develops (McCulloch & Sinha, 2024).

Peer Feedback

Getting students involved in peer feedback really helps them engage more actively with assessment. When students review each other's work, they not only get a clearer sense of what the assessment criteria are but also develop better judgment about quality. Over time, they become more aware of standards, learn to evaluate their own work, and improve their self-monitoring and self-assessment skills (Winstone et al., 2023; Yang & Carless, 2022). Peer feedback also fosters a sense of collaboration and shared responsibility for learning, as students learn to give constructive comments, justify their evaluations, and reflect on alternative approaches. This process not only strengthens critical thinking and communication skills but also helps reduce the traditional one-directional dependence on teacher feedback. In digital environments, peer review platforms and collaborative tools make the process more structured and transparent, allowing for anonymity, guided rubrics, and iterative revisions. As a result, peer feedback becomes a powerful mechanism for enhancing learner autonomy, building confidence, and cultivating a community of practice where students actively support one another's academic growth.

Building Metacognition and Learner Autonomy

When students actively reflect on their learning, they build important skills like taking more control of their progress and understanding how they learn best. Using different kinds of check-ins, such as self-assessments, keeping journals, and giving peer feedback, helps students become more aware of their thinking processes. It also encourages them to manage their effort and really own their learning journey (Nicol & Macfarlane-Dick, 2018; Panadero & Alonso-Tapia, 2023). As a result, they often feel more motivated, confident, and able to bounce back from challenges. Beyond improving resilience, metacognitive practices cultivate higher-order thinking skills, such as evaluating strategies, setting realistic goals, and adapting approaches when initial methods do not work. This strengthens not only academic performance but also lifelong learning habits. Moreover, digital tools—such as e-portfolios, reflective learning apps, and AI-supported feedback systems—can further scaffold metacognitive growth by offering prompts, progress tracking, and personalized insights. In this way, fostering metacognition and learner autonomy supports the development of independent, self-regulated learners who are better equipped to thrive in dynamic and uncertain learning environments.

Global Frameworks Guiding Technology Integration

There are several well-known frameworks that guide how we can bring technology into education effectively. One popular model, SAMR, helps teachers see how tech can either support or totally change their teaching. It breaks this down into four levels Substitution, Augmentation, Modification, and Redefinition with the last two encouraging truly innovative learning experiences (Puentedura, 2013). Alongside this, the TPACK framework emphasizes the importance of combining tech skills, teaching strategies, and subject knowledge to create better lessons. Recent updates have made it even clearer how teachers can customize their approaches depending on their specific context (Mishra & Koehler, 2006; Aqib et al., 2024). On a higher level, UNESCO's ICT-CFT (Version 3) sets out a broad set of skills educators need covering curriculum design, assessment, and professional growth. It offers flexible resources like Open Educational Resources (OER), and countries like Nigeria and Egypt have been successfully adopting these guidelines (UNESCO, 2018; UNESCO, 2023).

CHALLENGES HIGHLIGHTED IN THE LITERATURE

Digital Divide

The digital divide remains a tough obstacle in technology-driven education, especially in rural and low-income areas. It's all about the gaps in access to devices, internet, and the skills needed to use digital tools effectively (Mubarak et al., 2020). Poor broadband options, high costs, and limited ICT facilities hit students from disadvantaged backgrounds hardest, making it harder for them to participate in online learning (Andrey et al., 2021; Forman et al., 2020). Recent research shows these issues aren't just happening across countries but within them, too. Take India, for example: in Madhya Pradesh, only about 1% of government schools have digital libraries far below the national average of 6.1%. Smart classrooms and projectors are also scarce (Unified District Information System for Education, 2025). This means students have less access to digital resources, fewer chances to take online tests, and fewer opportunities to build digital skills. But the digital divide isn't just about infrastructure. It also involves how well students can actually use technology. Those in rural areas or underserved communities often don't have access to content in their local languages, deal with unreliable power, and struggle with inconsistent internet connections (Roberts & Townsend, 2016). Without targeted efforts that address both the physical barriers and the skills gap, using digital assessment tools fairly and broadly will remain a challenge.

Teacher Readiness

Teacher readiness is all about how confident and skilled educators feel when it comes to using technology in their teaching and assessments. Studies consistently show there's still a lot of room for improvement in digital skills, especially when it comes to using tech effectively for on-going assessments and performance feedback (Basilotta-Gomez-Pablos et al., 2022). In higher education, many instructors mention they're only moderately comfortable with digital tools used to monitor student progress or give useful feedback. When it comes to professional development, trainings are often too broad or generic, missing the mark on subject-specific strategies (Nunez-Canal et al., 2022). In K-12 settings, teachers face challenges like a lack of personalized training programs, limited access to digital resources that match their curriculum, and struggles with user-friendly tools (Kundu, 2024). There are also clear differences between rural and urban teachers. Research in China shows that rural teachers tend to have lower level of Technological Pedagogical Content Knowledge (TPACK), mainly because they have fewer training chances and less institutional backing (Li & Yang, 2024). Attitude of teachers also matter a lot. Even the resources are there, if teachers lack confidence or resist trying new tech approaches, it can hold back effective integration (Ertmer & Ottenbreit-Leftwich, 2019). To really get results, on-going, personalized professional development, collaborative learning communities, and strong support from school leaders are important for encouraging teachers to experiment and welcome new technology.

Tools Overload

While technology offers many tools for teaching, relying too much on multiple platforms without a clear pedagogical purpose can do more harm than good. This situation, often called tool overload, happens when educators add digital apps mainly for fun or to tick a box, rather than to support learning goals (Petko et al., 2016). It can cause disjointed learning, overwhelm students' brains, and make engagement drop. Research shows that technology works best when it's used intentionally to serve teaching goals, not just because tools are available (Eickelmann et al., 2017). Using lots of showy but shallow tools can distract students from true learning, encourage surface-level participation, and cause frustration for both teachers and students with multiple logins, interfaces, and expectations (Howard et al., 2021). Another challenge is when valuable tools go underused because teachers aren't trained or don't plan properly. For example, a learning management system (LMS) that can analyse student work might only be used for sharing files, missing chances for helpful feedback and progress tracking (Bond et al., 2021). To keep from overloading on tech, experts recommend sticking with fewer, versatile platforms and making sure the tools fit your learning goals.

CREATIVE DIGITAL MEDIA IN HYBRID LEARNING ASSESSMENT

Assessment through Hybrid Learning Models

Hybrid or blended learning models such as flipped classrooms, MOOCs (Massive Open Online Courses), and other blended learning approaches offer a fertile ground for integrating more authentic, embedded assessment. A systematic review of blended learning in Chinese higher education highlights how LMS-based hybrids foster stronger academic performance, cognitive engagement, and adaptability to changing educational contexts (Ashraf et al., 2022). Empirical data from a hybrid course conversion study supports that such models can equal or outperform traditional delivery, particularly in retaining students and enhancing learning outcomes (Hamza-Lup & White, 2018). Educators report that hybrid designs allow for flexibility in attendance modes, promote learner autonomy, and support authentic assessments across delivery formats. Moreover, blended environments especially those combining synchronous and asynchronous activities are seen as powerful tools for boosting engagement. Blended courses merge in-person and online components to "extend thinking and discourse over time and space," while providing differentiated, learner-centred experiences (Manwaring et al., 2017; Boelens et al., 2017). These features are particularly conducive to embedded assessments like iterative quizzes, project checkpoints, and peer review mechanisms that unfold over time.

Digital Storytelling, Blogging, and Video Essays

Digital storytelling including blogging and video essays provides dynamic avenues for assessing communication, creativity, and synthesis. A comprehensive study of digital storytelling in Australian P-12 classrooms revealed strong benefits for student engagement and educational outcomes, especially when supported by mixed-method rubrics and reflective observation tools (Smeda et al., 2014). Specifically, digital storytelling personalizes learning experiences, enhances motivation, and helps students become active learners rather than passive recipients (Smeda et al., 2014).Furthermore, student-generated video assignments in university-level science courses have been shown to serve as effective replacements for traditional assessments, combining peer review, self-evaluation, and experiential learning while creating a shared video repository for long-term academic use (Graul et al., 2020).

Global Benchmarking and Cross-Border Sharing of Assessment Practices

Digital platforms have made it increasingly practical to benchmark and share assessment practices internationally. While global benchmarking has long been researched within political and institutional governance, the same mechanisms support educational contexts, enabling comparative evaluation and shared learning. Digital platforms reduce the cost and complexity of disseminating benchmarks across borders, enabling educational institutions and organizations to compare practices, adopt innovations, and foster credibility within global networks (World Benchmarking Alliance, 2021). Through initiatives such as international assessment frameworks (e.g., PISA, TIMSS, and UNESCO-driven evaluations), institutions are able to identify best practices, highlight areas for improvement, and align their approaches with global standards. This not only enhances the quality and transparency of educational systems but also promotes equity by ensuring that learners in different regions are assessed on comparable criteria. Moreover, cross-border sharing encourages collaboration between policymakers, educators, and researchers, facilitating the exchange of digital tools, pedagogical innovations, and culturally sensitive assessment models. In a world where education is increasingly interconnected, global benchmarking serves as both a quality assurance mechanism and a driver of continuous improvement, positioning assessment as a key lever for advancing international competitiveness and cooperation in education.

CONTEMPORARY RESEARCH CONTRIBUTIONS

From Blackboard to Cloud: Digital Transformation in Education

Dos Santos et al. (2025) explore a fundamental shift in education from traditional, chalkboard-based methods to fully digital learning environments hosted in the cloud. Their study, "From Blackboard to the Cloud," examines how institutions are transitioning toward virtual learning environments, leveraging online platforms, mobile technology, and AI-driven personalization. This transformation is framed through case studies and trends highlighting changes in pedagogy, assessment strategies, teacher training, and the growing emphasis on student-centred learning. The authors also analyse persistent challenges, such as digital exclusion in underserved areas, infrastructure limitations, and resistance to technological adoption ultimately advocating for inclusive, equitable, and cloud-enabled educational ecosystems.

This research underscores the expanding role of cloud technologies in education enabling scalable digital delivery, multi-modal assessment approaches, and responsive, data-informed teaching strategies.

Immersive AR/VR and Learner Agency

A study by Vashisht (2024) closely aligns with the demonstration of how immersive technologies like AR and VR enhance conceptual understanding and learner agency. A systematic review by Wei et al. (2025) highlights the importance of different dimensions of presence—including spatial, social, and cognitive presence—in VR learning environments. The authors show how these facets of immersion significantly improve engagement, motivation, and mastery across disciplines and tasks. Battipede et al. (2024) conducted a mixed-method study ("Physics Playground") comparing immersive VR to traditional slideshow-based instruction in physics learning. While both groups exhibited knowledge gains, VR notably enhanced user satisfaction and learner confidence, suggesting immersive environments contribute positively to affective dimensions and learner self-efficacy. Beyond cognitive and affective benefits, immersive AR/VR also allows learners to take greater control over their learning pathways by enabling exploration, experimentation, and decision-making within simulated contexts. Such agency empowers learners not only to acquire knowledge but also to practice applying it in authentic, real-world scenarios—ranging from virtual science labs and engineering prototypes to cultural heritage experiences. This reinforces the idea that AR/VR can shift assessments from passive recall toward performance-based demonstrations of skills, thereby deepening both learner autonomy and long-term retention.

CONCLUSION

The transformation of assessment in media-rich learning environments highlights a decisive shift from static, summative evaluations to dynamic, formative, and learner-cantered practices. Emerging technologies such as Artificial Intelligence, Virtual and Augmented Reality, gamification, and data analytics are not merely tools but enablers of deeper engagement, creativity, and authentic skill demonstration. By embedding assessment within interactive and immersive experiences, education can better reflect the competencies needed in the 21st century critical thinking, adaptability, collaboration, and digital fluency. However, the integration of these innovations is not without challenges. Issues of digital divide, teacher readiness, and tool overload underscore the necessity of equitable access, professional development, and pedagogically sound implementation. Without careful consideration, these barriers risk reinforcing existing inequities rather than dismantling them. At the same time, opportunities such as hybrid learning models, digital storytelling, global benchmarking, and embedded performance-based assessments provide a powerful foundation for rethinking how we evaluate learning. These approaches emphasize process as much as product, valuing reflection, autonomy, and resilience alongside measurable outcomes. Ultimately, the future of assessment in media-rich environments lies in balancing innovation with inclusivity. Educators, policymakers, and researchers must work collaboratively to design frameworks that are not only technologically advanced but also human-centric, ethical, and sustainable. In doing so, assessment can move beyond measuring knowledge to empowering learners equipping them with the agency, creativity, and lifelong learning skills essential for thriving in an increasingly complex digital world.

REFERENCES

Adil, M., Song, H., Khan, M. K., Farouk, A., & Jin, Z. (2024). 5G/6G-enabled metaverse technologies: Taxonomy, applications, and open security challenges with future research directions. *Journal of Network and Computer Applications, 223*, 103828. DOI: 10.1016/j.jnca.2024.103828

Andrey, J., Evans, B., & Rathi, A. (2021). Digital inequities in education: Infrastructure, access, and opportunity. *Journal of Digital Equity*, *3*(2), 45–62.

Anute, N., & Geetali Tilak, . (2024). Revolutionizing e-Learning with AR, VR, and AI. *The Scientific Temper*, *15*(04), 3122–3126. DOI: 10.58414/SCIENTIFICTEMPER.2024.15.4.20

Aqib, M. A., Ekawati, R., & Khabibah, S. (2024). A modified Technological Pedagogical and Content Knowledge (TPACK) framework: A systematic literature review. Multidisciplinary Reviews, 8(6), Article 2025167.

Ashraf, M. A., Mollah, S., Perveen, S., Shabnam, N., & Nahar, L. (2022). Pedagogical Applications, Prospects, and Challenges of Blended learning in Chinese higher Education: A Systematic review. *Frontiers in Psychology*, *12*, 772322. Advance online publication. DOI: 10.3389/fpsyg.2021.772322

Asmae, M. (2025). Artificial Intelligence and Augmented Reality: Revolutionizing E-Learning for the Education of Tomorrow. International Journal of Innovative Science and Research Technology, 2053–2059. DOI: 10.38124/ijisrt/25feb1307

Barrett, H. (2023). Rethinking digital portfolios: Fostering reflection and engagement. *Educational Technology Journal*, *12*(1), 45–60.

Basilotta-Gomez-Pablos, V., Matarranz, M., & Casado, R. (2022). Teacher digital competence and its impact on assessment practices. *Education and Information Technologies*, *27*(1), 975–993.

Battipede, E., Giangualano, A., Boffi, P., Clerici, M., Calvi, A., Cassenti, L., Cialini, R., Weghe, T. L., Addimando, L., Lanzi, P. L., & Gallace, A. (2024). *Physics Playground: Insights from a Qualitative-Quantitative Study about VR-Based Learning*. ArXiv., DOI: 10.1007/978-3-031-88881-6_8

Bijl, A., Veldkamp, B. P., Wools, S., & de Klerk, S. (2024). Serious games in high-stakes assessment contexts: A systematic literature review into the game design principles for valid game-based performance assessment. *Educational Technology Research and Development*, *72*(4), 2041–2064. DOI: 10.1007/s11423-024-10362-0

Boelens, R., De Wever, B., & Voet, M. (2017). Four key challenges to the design of blended learning : A systematic literature review. *Educational Research Review*, *22*, 1–18. DOI: 10.1016/j.edurev.2017.06.001

Bond, M., Marin, V. I., Dolch, C., Bedenlier, S., & Zawacki-Richter, O. (2021). Digital transformation in higher education: Tools, practices, and pedagogies. *Australasian Journal of Educational Technology*, *37*(4), 1–15.

Brackenbury, T., & Kopf, L. (2022). Serious Games and Gamification: Game-Based Learning in Communication Sciences and Disorders. *Perspectives of the ASHA Special Interest Groups*, *7*(2), 482–498. DOI: 10.1044/2021_PERSP-21-00284

Brigham, T. J. (2015). An Introduction to Gamification: Adding Game Elements for Engagement. *Medical Reference Services Quarterly*, *34*(4), 471–480. DOI: 10.1080/02763869.2015.1082385

Caballero-Hernandez, J. A., Palomo-Duarte, M., & Dodero, J. M. (2017). Skill assessment in learning experiences based on serious games: A Systematic Mapping Study. *Computers & Education*, *113*, 42–60. DOI: 10.1016/j.compedu.2017.05.008

Caladine, R. (2008). *The future of rich media, learning management systems, and content management systems.*, DOI: 10.4018/978-1-59904-732-4.ch016

Dos Santos, V. de F., Balbino, J., Bueno, A. J. A., Ghisi, K. M., Bessa, W. A., Souza, O. G., & Austríaco-Teixeira, P. (2025). FROM BLACKBOARD TO CLOUD. *HOW EDUCATION IS MOVING TO ALL-DIGITAL ENVIRONMENTS*, *7*(6), 32475–32487. DOI: 10.56238/arev7n6-193

Eickelmann, B., Gerick, J., & Koop, C. (2017). ICT use in teaching and learning: A cross-national analysis. *Computers & Education*, *104*, 1–14.

Ertmer, P. A., & Ottenbreit-Leftwich, A. T. (2019). Teacher beliefs and technology integration practices. *Journal of Research on Technology in Education*, *51*(1), 1–15.

Forman, T., Kenney, B., & Wheeler, D. (2020). Barriers to digital participation: Socioeconomic and geographic perspectives. *International Journal of Digital Literacy*, *12*(3), 89–105.

Gallego-Duran, F. J., Villagra-Arnedo, C. J., Satorre-Cuerda, R., Compan-Rosique, P., Molina-Carmona, R., & Llorens-Largo, F. (2019). A guide for Game-Design-Based Gamification. *Informatics (MDPI)*, *6*(4), 49. DOI: 10.3390/informatics6040049

Ghahari, D., Chaharlangi, D., Bonato, S., Sliekers, S., Sockalingam, S., Ali, A., & Benassi, P. (2023). Educational Approaches Using Simulation for Psychiatric Risk Assessment: A Scoping Review. *Academic Psychiatry*, *48*(1), 61–70. DOI: 10.1007/s40596-023-01836-z

Ghanbaripour, A. N., Talebian, N., Miller, D., Tumpa, R. J., Zhang, W., Golmoradi, M., & Skitmore, M. (2024). A Systematic Review of the Impact of Emerging Technologies on Student Learning, Engagement, and Employability in Built Environment Education. *Buildings (Basel, Switzerland)*, *14*(9), 2769. DOI: 10.3390/buildings14092769

Graul, B., Rollins, M. L., Powers, N., & Della Corte, D. (2020). *Student created video content for assessment, experiential learning, and service*. ArXiv., DOI: 10.1119/5.0029343

Ha, Y. K. (2025). Assessing Learning Outcomes in Simulation-based Education to Recognize and Respond to Deteriorating Patients in Nursing Education: A Scoping Review. *Journal of Korean Critical Care Nursing*, *18*(1), 39–54. DOI: 10.34250/jkccn.2025.18.1.39

Hamza-Lup, F. G., & White, S. (2018). Design and assessment for hybrid courses: Insights and overviews. arXiv. https://arxiv.org/abs/1811.07273

Han, S. (2022). Flipped classroom: Challenges and benefits of using social media in English language teaching and learning. *Frontiers in Psychology*, *13*, 996294. DOI: 10.3389/fpsyg.2022.996294

Hjellvik, S., Mallam, S., Giskeodegard, M. F., & Nazir, S. (2024). Review on competency Assessment instrumentation in computer-based simulation. Technology Knowledge and Learning, 2994), 2171-2200. https://doi.org/.DOI: 10.007/s10758-024-09735-4

Hofmann, R., Curran, S., & Dickens, S. (2021). Models and measures of learning outcomes for non-technical skills in simulation-based medical education: Findings from an integrated scoping review of research and content analysis of curricular learning objectives. *Studies in Educational Evaluation*, *71*, 101093. DOI: 10.1016/j.stueduc.2021.101093

Howard, S. K., Tondeur, J., Ma, J., & Yang, J. (2021). Teacher technology integration and overload: Understanding the balance. *Technology, Pedagogy and Education*, *30*(4), 469–484.

Jayalath, J., & Esichaikul, V. (2020). Gamification to enhance motivation and engagement in blended eLearning for technical and vocational education and training. *Technology Knowledge and Learning*, *27*(1), 91–118. DOI: 10.1007/s10758-020-09466-2

Kalogeras, S. (2019). The Practice of Transmedia Storytelling Edutainment in Media-Rich Learning Environments. In Advances in Educational Technologies and Instructional Design (pp. 149–164). DOI: 10.4018/978-1-5225-5915-3.ch008

Karagiorgas, D. N., & Niemann, S. (2017). Gamification and Game-Based Learning. *Journal of Educational Technology Systems*, *45*(4), 499–519. DOI: 10.1177/0047239516665105

Kessing, D., Katzwinkel, T., & Löwer, M. (2024). Gamification as an innovative method in user experience design. *Proceedings of the Design Society*, *4*, 285–294. DOI: 10.1017/pds.2024.31

Kundu, A. (2024). Teachers' readiness for integrating digital assessment in K–12 education. *Education and Information Technologies*, *29*(2), 1457–1478.

Lee, J., & Lee, J. H. (2022). Effects of simulation-based education for neonatal resuscitation on medical students' technical and non-technical skills. *PLoS One*, *17*(12), e0278575. DOI: 10.1371/journal.pone.0278575

Li, X., & Yang, Z. (2024). Rural-urban disparities in teachers' technological pedagogical content knowledge: Evidence from China. *Education and Information Technologies*, *29*(3), 2101–2120.

Lorenzo, G., & Ittelson, J. (2022). Building reflective learners with e-portfolios. *Journal of Learning Technologies*, *8*(2), 112–128.

Manwaring, K. C., Larsen, R., Graham, C. R., Henrie, C. R., & Halverson, L. R. (2017). Investigating student engagement in blended learning settings using experience sampling and structural equation modeling. *The Internet and Higher Education*, *35*, 21–33. DOI: 10.1016/j.iheduc.2017.06.002

McCulloch, A., & Sinha, S. (2024). Portfolio practices for metacognitive skill development. *Reflective Education Quarterly*, *5*(1), 1–18.

McLoughlin, C. (2011). Leading pedagogical change with innovative web tools and social media. In Encyclopedia of E-Leadership, Counseling and Training (pp. 1-11). IGI Global. DOI: 10.4018/javet.2011010102

Mhlongo, S., Mbatha, K., Ramatsetse, B., & Dlamini, R. (2023). Challenges, opportunities, and prospects of adopting and using smart digital technologies in learning environments: An iterative review. *Heliyon, 9*(6), e16348. DOI: 10.1016/j.heliyon.2023.e16348

Mishra, P., & Koehler, M. J. (2006). Technological Pedagogical Content Knowledge: A framework for teacher knowledge. *Teachers College Record, 108*(6), 1017–1054. DOI: 10.1111/j.1467-9620.2006.00684.x

Mubarak, A., Cao, H., & Zhang, Y. (2020). Digital divide and social inclusion: A review. *Sustainability, 12*(20), 8588.

Nicol, D. J., & Macfarlane-Dick, D. (2018). Formative assessment and self-regulated learning: A model and seven principles of good feedback practice. *Studies in Higher Education, 43*(5), 798–814.

Niemi, H., Harju, V., Vivitsou, M., Viitanen, K., Multisilta, J., & Kuokkanen, A. (2014). Digital Storytelling for 21 Century Skills in Virtual Learning Environments. *Creative Education, 05*(09), 657–671. DOI: 10.4236/ce.2014.59078

Nukarinen, T., Rantala, J., Korpela, K., Browning, M. H., Istance, H. O., Surakka, V., & Raisamo, R. (2022). Measures and modalities in restorative virtual natural environments: An integrative narrative review. *Computers in Human Behavior, 126*, 107008. DOI: 10.1016/j.chb.2021.107008

Nukarinen, T., Rantala, J., Korpela, K., Browning, M. H. E. M., Istance, H. O., Surakka, V., & Raisamo, R. (2022). Measures and modalities in restorative virtual natural environments: An integrative narrative review. *Computers in Human Behavior, 126*, 107008. DOI: 10.1016/j.chb.2021.107008

Nunez-Canal, M., de Obesso, M., & Perez-Sanchez, A. (2022). Assessing digital competence: Review of tools and methods. *Education Sciences, 12*(6), 402.

Oestreich, J. H., & Guy, J. W. (2022). Game-Based Learning in Pharmacy Education. *Pharmacy (Basel, Switzerland), 10*(1), 11. DOI: 10.3390/pharmacy10010011

Oranje, A., Mislevy, B., Bauer, M. I., & Jackson, G. T. (2019). Summative Game-Based Assessment. In Advances in game-based learning (pp. 37-65). DOI: 10.1007/978-3-030-15569-8_3

Paananen, V., Kiarostami, M. S., Lik-Hang, L., Braud, T., & Hosio, S. (2023). From Digital Media to Empathic Spaces: A Systematic Review of empathy Research in Extended reality Environments. *ACM Computing Surveys, 56*(5), 1–40. DOI: 10.1145/3626518

Panadero, E., & Alonso-Tapia, J. (2023). The role of peer assessment and self-assessment in promoting metacognitive skills. *Educational Psychology Review, 35*(1), 299–315.

Patel, P., Torppa, M., Aro, M., Richardson, U., & Lyytinen, H. (2021). Assessing the effectiveness of a game-based phonics intervention for first and second grade English language learners in India: A randomized controlled trial. *Journal of Computer Assisted Learning, 38*(1), 76–89. DOI: 10.1111/jcal.12592

Petko, D., Prasse, D., & Cantieni, A. (2016). Perceived quality of educational technology use: Scale development and validation. *Computers & Education, 92-93*, 27–36.

Puentedura, R. (2013). SAMR model: A model for integrating technology into teaching. [Original framework description].

Roberts, E., & Townsend, L. (2016). The contribution of the digital economy to rural development. *Local Economy, 31*(1-2), 129–147.

Rojas, M. P., & Chiappe, A. (2024). Artificial Intelligence and Digital Ecosystems in Education: A review.Technology Knowledge and learning, 29(4), 2153-2170. DOI: 10.1007/s10758-024-09732-7

Sadallah, M. (2024). User-Centered Course Reengineering: An Analytical Approach to Enhancing Reading Comprehension in Educational Content. ArXiv. https://arxiv .org/abs/2412.11944

Smeda, N., Dakich, E., & Sharda, N. (2014). The effectiveness of digital storytelling in the classrooms: A comprehensive study. *Smart Learn. Environ., 1*(1), 6. DOI: 10.1186/s40561-014-0006-3

Song, Y., Chen, X., Hao, T., Liu, Z., & Lan, Z. (2019). Exploring two decades of research on classroom dialogue by using bibliometric analysis. *Computers & Education, 137*, 12–31. DOI: 10.1016/j.compedu.2019.04.002

UDISE. (2025). School education statistics in India. Ministry of Education, Government of India.

UNESCO. (2018). ICT competency framework for teachers (Version 3).

UNESCO. (2023, June 9). ICT Competency Framework for Teachers as a game changer for digital capacity building for teachers.

Van Mechelen, M., Smith, R. C., Schaper, M., Tamashiro, M., Bilstrup, K., Lunding, M., Petersen, M. G., & Iversen, O. S. (2022). Emerging Technologies in K-12 Education: A future HCI research agenda. *ACM Transactions on Computer-Human Interaction, 30*(3), 1–40. DOI: 10.1145/3569897

Vashisht, S. (2024). Enhancing Learning Experiences through Augmented Reality and Virtual Reality in Classrooms. 2024 2nd International Conference on Recent Advances in Information Technology for Sustainable Development (ICRAIS), 12–17. DOI: 10.1109/ICRAIS62903.2024.10811732

Wei, Z., Liao, J., Lee, L., Qu, H., & Xu, X. (2025). Towards Enhanced Learning through Presence: A Systematic Review of Presence in Virtual Reality Across Tasks and Disciplines. ArXiv. https://arxiv.org/abs/2504.13845

Winstone, N. E., Nash, R. A., Parker, M., & Rowntree, J. (2023). Engaging through feedback: Exploring student metacognition and the peer review process. *Assessment & Learning in Higher Education*, *48*(2), 234–249.

World Benchmarking Alliance. (2021). Digital companies share experiences and best practices.

Yang, M., & Carless, D. (2022). Peer feedback as a tool for enhancing evaluative judgement in higher education. *Teaching in Higher Education*, *27*(3), 343–360.

Yaseen, H., Mohammad, A. S., Ashal, N., Abusaimeh, H., Ali, A., & Sharabati, A. (2025). The Impact of Adaptive Learning Technologies, Personalized Feedback, and Interactive AI Tools on Student Engagement: The Moderating Role of Digital Literacy. *Sustainability (Basel)*, *17*(3), 1133. DOI: 10.3390/su17031133

Zainuddin, Z., Chu, S. K. W., & Othman, J. (2024). The evaluation of gamification implementation for adult learners: A scale development study based on andragogical principles. *Education and Information Technologies*, *29*(14), 18591–18620. DOI: 10.1007/s10639-024-12561-x

Chapter 6
Harnessing the Power of Background Music:
Enhancing Learning and Student Engagement

Sridevi Nair
https://orcid.org/0000-0002-1529-4297
Christ University, India

Akshita Patil
Christ University, India

ABSTRACT

Music has long been considered a universal language, but its potential in enhancing learning is still emerging as a serious academic inquiry. This chapter explores the cognitive and emotional effects of background music on learning outcomes and student reactions. Drawing on experimental evidence, the study compared two groups of MBA students; one exposed to continuous instrumental background music and another taught without it. Findings revealed a significant positive difference in both engagement (reaction) and knowledge acquisition (learning), though the effect on learning was smaller in magnitude. By situating these results within established frameworks such as the Kirkpatrick Model and theories like the Arousal-Mood Hypothesis and Self-Determination Theory, this chapter highlights the nuanced relationship between music, cognition, and emotion. It makes the case for strategically integrating music into educational and corporate learning settings as a tool to foster attention, motivation, and engagement, while also acknowledging limitations and contextual considerations.

DOI: 10.4018/979-8-3373-5157-5.ch006

INTRODUCTION

Music has often been described as the universal language of humankind, a medium that transcends barriers of culture, geography, and age (Southgate & Roscigno, 2009). Beyond its artistic and aesthetic value, researchers across disciplines have long been fascinated by its influence on the human mind. The rhythm of a melody can soothe stress, an upbeat tempo can energize, and a soft instrumental piece can create the perfect backdrop for reflection or study. In recent years, this fascination has sharpened into a practical question: can music be intentionally used to enhance learning?

This inquiry is not a modern curiosity. The educational role of music was already a subject of philosophical debate in ancient Greece. Plato, in The Republic, argued that music shaped both intellect and character, while Aristotle highlighted its role in moral and emotional education. Centuries later, cognitive psychologists and neuroscientists continue this exploration, now supported by empirical studies and experimental methods. The accumulated evidence paints an intriguing but sometimes contradictory picture. On one hand, music has been shown to improve memory, sustain attention, and elevate mood; factors that are conducive to learning (Schellenberg, 2011). On the other hand, certain studies suggest that music may distract, interfere with concentration, or overload the learner's cognitive system, particularly if the tempo, volume, or complexity are not matched to the task (Thompson et al., 2011).

This book chapter enters this debate by focusing on a practical dimension. The study explores the impact of background music on learning outcomes and learner reactions in educational settings. It draws upon an experimental study conducted among postgraduate students at a business school, where one group attended a lecture with continuous instrumental background music and another attended in silence. Findings revealed that music significantly improved learner engagement and reaction; and produced a smaller but positive effect on knowledge acquisition. These results suggest that music may not merely be an aesthetic backdrop but a potential pedagogical tool.

The relevance of this discussion extends well beyond classrooms. Today's learners; whether university students, young professionals, or employees engaged in upskilling, operate in environments characterized by information overload and continuous distraction. Learning and development (L&D) professionals face the dual challenge of delivering content that is effective while also engaging. Traditional lectures and static e-learning often fail to sustain attention in such contexts. Here, the integration of music offers an intriguing possibility. Could background music act as a low-cost, scalable intervention to sustain focus, reduce anxiety, and heighten learner receptivity?

The timing of this inquiry is particularly significant. Organizations worldwide are increasing their investment in employee learning and development, recognizing its role in retention, productivity, and innovation. Reports show that companies prioritizing continuous learning see tangible gains in profitability and employee satisfaction. But beyond these metrics, learners themselves, especially millennials and Gen Z, demand learning environments that are not only intellectually stimulating but emotionally engaging. They want learning experiences that feel meaningful, immersive, and even enjoyable. In this context, background music is not just simply an embellishment but a potential tool to create emotionally intelligent and human-centred learning environments.

At the same time, the complexity of the subject must be acknowledged. Music is not a universal enhancer. Its effects depend on genre, tempo, cultural associations, and learner preferences. What helps one learner focus may distract another. A slow instrumental track might facilitate reflection during reading but impede performance during analytical problem-solving. Thus, the central question is not whether music "works" in a general sense, but when, how, and for whom it works best (Husain et al., 2002).

This chapter, therefore, adopts a layered approach. It begins by reviewing the conceptual foundations that explain how music interacts with cognition and emotion. The study draws on theories such as Self-Determination Theory (Ryan & Deci, 2000), the Arousal-Mood Hypothesis (Husain et al., 2002), and the Kirkpatrick Model of training evaluation (Kirkpatrick & Kirkpatrick, 2006). These frameworks help to understand why music influences both affective (reaction, mood, motivation) and cognitive (knowledge acquisition, retention, performance) dimensions of learning.

The chapter then turns to the literature on background music in educational contexts, highlighting both supporting and contradictory findings. While some research confirms music's benefits for attention and memory (Schwartz et al., 2017), others caution that poorly chosen music may distract or overload learners (Moreno & Mayer, 2000). Against this backdrop, the experimental study conducted at a b-school is presented. The design was a post-test, control and experimental group design where one group of MBA students experienced a lecture accompanied by continuous background instrumental music at 60 bpm, while the other attended in silence. Their engagement was measured through a standardized reaction survey, and their learning through a multiple-choice assessment.

The results indicated that students exposed to background music reported higher engagement and scored somewhat better on the learning test. The stronger impact on reactions, compared to learning scores, suggests that music may first and foremost influence the affective domain, creating an environment of attentiveness and positivity that indirectly supports learning. This finding highlights the importance of considering learner emotions, not just cognitive outcomes, in educational design.

The remainder of the chapter situates these findings in a broader context. It discusses implications for higher education and corporate training, acknowledging the limitations of current research and proposing directions for future studies. Ultimately, it argues that music should be viewed as part of a human-centred approach to learning design, reminding us that effective education must engage both the mind and the emotions. In an age where AI platforms, digital simulations, and algorithm-driven platforms dominate conversations about the future of learning, music offers a reminder of the human, sensory, and emotional dimensions of education. By weaving melody into pedagogy, we may not only enhance focus and performance but also reimagine learning as an experience that is as engaging and memorable as it is effective.

CONCEPTUAL FOUNDATIONS: THEORIES AND THE PSYCHOLOGY OF MUSIC IN LEARNING

Understanding the impact of background music on learning requires us to go beyond anecdotal experiences and delve into the theoretical frameworks that explain how music interacts with the human mind. While the surface experience of listening to music may feel intuitive, calming, energizing, or distracting; the psychological and cognitive mechanisms underlying these effects are complex. This section explores three major theoretical perspectives relevant to music and learning: Self-Determination Theory (SDT), the Arousal-Mood Hypothesis, and the Kirkpatrick Model of learning evaluation. Together, they offer a lens through which we can interpret not only the findings of experimental studies but also the broader implications of integrating music into educational and organizational contexts.

Self-Determination Theory and Motivation in Learning

Self-Determination Theory (SDT), introduced by Deci and Ryan (1980), is one of the most influential frameworks in understanding human motivation, especially in educational psychology. Unlike behaviourist perspectives that emphasize external reinforcements such as rewards and punishments, SDT emphasizes the innate psychological needs that drive individuals to learn, grow, and flourish. According to this theory, human beings are not passive recipients of external stimuli but active agents who seek environments that support their basic needs and allow them to thrive.

At the heart of SDT lie three basic psychological needs: autonomy, competence, and relatedness. When these needs are satisfied, learners are more likely to experience intrinsic motivation or the kind of motivation that emerges from genuine interest, curiosity, and enjoyment. Conversely, when these needs are frustrated or neglected, learners may rely on extrinsic motivation, or worse, experience amotivation, a state of disengagement and lack of purpose (Ryan & Deci, 2000).

The theory is particularly useful for examining the role of **background music in learning**, because music is not only a cognitive stimulus but also a deeply emotional and personal experience. Depending on how it is introduced into a learning environment, music can either support or undermine the three needs described by SDT. The first dimension of SDT is autonomy. Autonomy refers to the sense of volition and self-direction in one's actions. Learners are more motivated when they feel that they have meaningful choices and that their preferences are respected. Autonomy does not mean complete independence, but rather the perception that one's actions are self-endorsed.

In the context of background music, autonomy comes into play in multiple ways. For instance, when learners are allowed to choose whether or not to study with music or to select the type of music they prefer, they experience a greater sense of ownership over the learning environment. A student who enjoys soft instrumental music while studying complex theories in finance or law may feel more immersed and motivated simply because the environment reflects their individual preference. This personalization reinforces the idea that the learning experience is not imposed but tailored, thereby supporting autonomy. In contrast, if music is imposed without choice, it may have the opposite effect. A learner who finds the chosen music distracting or culturally alien may feel that their autonomy has been undermined. This can lead to resistance, disengagement, or frustration. For educators and trainers, this highlights a practical insight: autonomy-supportive learning design should include options, such as toggling music on or off, or offering a range of background tracks to suit different learners. The relationship between autonomy and music also extends to tempo and rhythm. Learners often know what kind of pace helps them concentrate.

The second dimension is Competence. Competence is the need to feel effective, capable, and successful in one's activities. In learning, this translates into feeling able to master new knowledge and skills. Anxiety, distraction, or cognitive overload can undermine competence, making learners feel ineffective. Background music, when carefully chosen, can act as a facilitator of competence. Research suggests that music with specific characteristics, such as soft, instrumental tracks at moderate tempo can reduce stress and support concentration (Husain et al., 2002). By creating a calming learning environment, music may help learners focus on the material rather than on internal distractions such as nervousness or negative self-talk. When learners feel more focused and less anxious, they are more likely to succeed in mastering the material, reinforcing their sense of competence. Moreover, music can function as a mnemonic aid, reinforcing competence by strengthening memory recall. Just as many people can effortlessly remember song lyrics from their childhood, pairing information with rhythm or melody creates additional retrieval cues. In learning contexts, this can make students feel more capable of recalling facts or applying concepts, further enhancing competence. However, competence is fragile. If the music is mismatched, it can overload working memory and reduce learners' sense of effectiveness (Moreno & Mayer, 2000). Thus, supporting competence through music requires careful alignment with the type of task and the cognitive load involved.

The third psychological need, relatedness, emphasizes the human desire to feel connected, valued, and part of a larger community. Learning is not only a cognitive act but also a social one. Students learn better when they feel a sense of belonging with peers and support from instructors. Music has a unique capacity to cultivate relatedness. It is a profoundly social phenomenon, often associated with shared cultural rituals, celebrations, and emotional experiences. When used in classrooms or group training sessions, music can create a shared emotional atmosphere. For example, playing gentle instrumental music during group discussions may ease tension and encourage participation, helping students feel more connected to one another.

In organizational training, background music can create a sense of welcome and inclusivity, particularly in diverse cohorts. Participants entering a training room where music is playing may feel an immediate sense of warmth and connection, reducing the initial anxiety of group interactions. In this way, music contributes to the social fabric of learning, aligning with SDT's emphasis on relatedness. However, relatedness is culturally sensitive. Music that resonates deeply with one group may alienate another if it carries unfamiliar or negative associations.

By viewing background music through the lens of SDT, we gain a richer understanding of why learners respond differently to musical interventions. For some, music enhances autonomy, competence, and relatedness, leading to higher intrinsic motivation and engagement. For others, poorly chosen or imposed music undermines these needs, resulting in frustration or disengagement.

The Arousal-Mood Hypothesis and Its Relevance to Learning

While Self-Determination Theory helps explain how background music supports motivational needs, the Arousal-Mood Hypothesis provides a complementary lens, focusing on how music influences learners' psychological and physiological states, which in turn affect cognitive performance. Originally developed in the early 2000s through the work of Husain et al., (2002), this hypothesis argues that music does not directly alter cognitive processes such as memory or comprehension. Instead, it shapes arousal or the level of physiological activation or alertness; and mood or the affective state of the learner. These two mediators of arousal and mood, then influence how effectively learners can engage with, process, and retain information. This framework helps us understand why the same piece of music may benefit one learner but distract another, or why certain types of music improve performance in one task but hinder it in another.

Arousal refers to the physiological state of alertness or activation, often linked to the autonomic nervous system. It can range from deep relaxation to high stimulation. In learning contexts, arousal plays a critical role in determining attention and concentration. Music is a powerful arousal regulator. Fast-tempo, upbeat music often raises physiological arousal by increasing heart rate and stimulating alertness. Conversely, slow, calming music can lower arousal by reducing stress hormones and heart rate. The relationship between arousal and learning is captured in the Yerkes-Dodson Law (1908), which suggests that performance improves with arousal up to an optimal point, after which further increases in arousal lead to decline. This inverted-U relationship implies that both under-arousal (e.g., boredom, lethargy) and over-arousal (e.g., stress, overstimulation) can impair learning.

Music, then, can serve as a tool for moving learners closer to the optimal arousal level. For example, during early-morning classes, when students may feel sluggish, moderately upbeat background music can energize them and bring arousal to a productive level. In contrast, during high-stakes test preparation, when anxiety runs high, calming instrumental music can reduce arousal, helping learners concentrate without being overwhelmed. However, arousal regulation through music is not one-size-fits-all. Personality traits, prior mood, and even cultural background influence how individuals respond. An extroverted learner may thrive with upbeat tracks that boost energy, while an introverted learner may find the same tracks overstimulating and disruptive.

The other dimension is that of mood. Mood, distinct from arousal, refers to the affective state. Whether one feels happy, calm, anxious, or irritable. Positive moods are linked to greater creativity, flexibility, and openness to learning, while negative moods can hinder memory and problem-solving. Music has long been recognized as one of the most reliable ways to shift mood. Research demonstrates that listening to music can elevate positive affect, reduce negative affect, and even act as a form of emotion regulation (Isen, 2000; Thoma et al., 2013). For learners, a positive mood creates a psychological climate conducive to engagement and persistence.

Thus, the implications for learning are appear to be pleasant, calming music can reduce test anxiety and create an encouraging atmosphere for studying. Uplifting, joyful music can stimulate curiosity and creativity, particularly in brainstorming or problem-solving tasks. Conversely, mismatched music (e.g., overly dramatic or melancholic tones) may induce negative moods that interfere with motivation and focus.

A key contribution of the Arousal-Mood Hypothesis is its emphasis on the interaction between arousal and mood. Arousal provides the physiological readiness to engage, while mood provides the emotional tone. Together, they create a state that either enhances or detracts from learning.

For example:

- High arousal + positive mood: A lively, energetic state that may boost performance in active, creative, or social learning tasks.
- Moderate arousal + positive mood: A balanced state ideal for sustained attention, comprehension, and problem-solving.
- Low arousal + negative mood: A disengaged state that leads to lethargy and disinterest in learning.
- High arousal + negative mood: A stressed, anxious state that impairs concentration and recall.

Empirical studies provide compelling evidence for the Arousal-Mood Hypothesis. Husain et al., (2002) found that music in a major key with a fast tempo enhanced spatial task performance, primarily by elevating arousal and mood compared to music in a minor key or with a slower tempo. Isen (2000) further demonstrated that pleasant music can induce positive moods, which in turn increase creativity and problem-solving flexibility. Similarly, Thompson et al., (2011) showed that while moderate and pleasant background music can aid concentration, fast and loud music often disrupts reading comprehension, likely due to overstimulation and excessive arousal. Adding to this evidence, Thoma et al., (2013) highlighted that music not only enhances mood but also reduces cortisol levels, offering both psychological and physiological benefits. Together, these findings propose the central premise of the hypothesis that music affects learning indirectly, by shaping internal states of arousal and mood that then influence attention, memory, and creativity. However, some critics argue that the hypothesis oversimplifies the complexity of musical experience. Music is not merely a stimulus for arousal and mood; it carries cultural, personal, and symbolic meanings that may profoundly influence its effects on learners.

Despite these limitations, the Arousal-Mood Hypothesis provides a valuable framework for understanding how music shapes the learning process. By influencing learners' physiological readiness and emotional tone, music can create states of mind that either enhance or hinder performance. The hypothesis bridges the gap between cognitive psychology and educational practice, reminding us that learning is not a purely rational endeavour but it is also deeply shaped by how we feel in the moment. For educators and trainers, the lesson is clear: music is not a universal enhancer, but a contextual tool. When carefully matched to task demands and learner needs, it can regulate arousal, elevate mood, and create optimal conditions for learning.

LITERATURE REVIEW

The relationship between music and learning has long been a subject of interdisciplinary investigation, bringing together insights from psychology, neuroscience, education, and even organizational studies. Researchers have been intrigued by the ways auditory stimuli can alter attention, memory, emotional states, and ultimately, learning outcomes. The accumulated body of evidence paints a picture that is both promising and complex: while some findings suggest music enhances learning by creating optimal psychological conditions, others highlight its potential to distract, interfere, or overwhelm. This duality makes music a particularly rich topic for examining the interplay between cognition, emotion, and motivation in educational contexts.

One of the earliest and most publicized contributions to this field was the so-called Mozart Effect. Rauscher et al., (1993) reported that listening to Mozart's compositions could temporarily enhance spatial reasoning. Though subsequent meta-analyses questioned the robustness of this claim (Chabris, 1999), the phenomenon captured public imagination and ignited a wave of studies on how music affects cognition. Beyond Mozart, research has explored whether music influences domains such as working memory, attentional control, and comprehension. Evidence suggests that music can enhance working memory by providing additional cues that support recall. Wallace (1994), for example, showed that pairing information with melodies improved memory retention, indicating that music offers structural scaffolds for encoding and retrieval. Jäncke and Sandmann (2010) also suggested that background music may help reduce mind-wandering, thereby sustaining attentional focus. This potential to stabilize attention is especially relevant in learning environments where distractions are plentiful. At the same time, findings have highlighted limitations. Moreno and Mayer (2000) found that music with lyrics often interferes with reading comprehension, a result explained through Cognitive Load Theory. According to this framework, learners possess limited working memory resources. When verbal tasks and lyrical music compete for the same cognitive channel, overload occurs, impairing comprehension. Thus, music can enhance or impair cognition depending on how it interacts with task demands and information-processing systems.

Parallel to cognitive studies, a large body of research emphasizes music's role in shaping emotions and motivation. Music is a potent regulator of mood and has been used by learners to reduce stress, maintain motivation, and build persistence in the face of difficult tasks. This aligns with the Arousal-Mood Hypothesis (Husain et al., 2002), which proposes that music indirectly influences learning by altering physiological arousal and emotional tone. Positive moods induced by pleasant music have been consistently linked with greater creativity and flexibility. Isen (2000) demonstrated that positive affect leads to improved problem-solving and decision-making, findings echoed in educational contexts where learners exposed to background music report higher enjoyment and willingness to persist. Moreover, studies show that calming instrumental music can lower cortisol levels and alleviate test anxiety (Thoma et al., 2013). These physiological effects complement psychological ones, illustrating how music's benefits extend beyond the purely cognitive domain.

However, Thompson et al., (2011) found that while moderate, pleasant music supports concentration, excessively loud or fast-paced music disrupts reading comprehension. Thus, mood effects are not unidirectional but context-dependent. Music that elevates arousal and mood in one setting may overstimulate in another, underscoring the need for careful alignment between music, learner, and task.

Flow and Engagement in Learning

Another relevant perspective is Flow Theory, developed by Csikszentmihalyi (1990), which describes the state of complete immersion in an activity where challenges and skills are in balance. Music has been shown to facilitate flow by creating conditions of focused attention, enjoyment, and temporal distortion. Learners who experience flow are more likely to report deeper engagement and intrinsic motivation, both of which are associated with improved learning outcomes. In educational contexts, music can help trigger flow states by reducing anxiety, regulating arousal, and providing a rhythmic structure that supports task engagement. For example, students working on repetitive problem-solving tasks often find that steady, instrumental background music helps sustain focus and momentum. Flow-inducing conditions are particularly valuable in higher education and professional training, where learners face complex challenges requiring sustained concentration. However, as with mood regulation, not all music is equally effective: overly complex or distracting music can pull learners out of flow rather than supporting it.

One of the most striking features of the literature is its contradictory findings, which can be understood by examining moderating factors. The type of task is perhaps the most significant determinant. Research suggests that music aids performance more reliably in spatial and creative tasks than in verbal or text-based tasks (Hallam et al., 2002). Music characteristics also matter. For example, instrumental music tends to be less disruptive than lyrical music, while tempo and volume significantly influence outcomes.

Individual differences further complicate the picture. Personality traits, particularly introversion and extraversion, moderate responses to music. Extroverts, who often thrive in stimulating environments, are more likely to benefit from background music, while introverts may find it distracting (Furnham & Bradley, 1997). Learner preferences and cultural contexts are equally important: music that feels familiar and enjoyable to one learner may be unsettling or irrelevant to another. Such differences highlight the importance of autonomy in music selection, as emphasized in Self-Determination Theory.

Educational Practice and Applications

Despite inconsistencies in findings, educators have long experimented with music in classrooms. Hallam et al. (2002) found that background music improved arithmetic performance in primary school children, while Schellenberg (2004) reported associations between musical training and higher IQ and academic achievement. These studies suggest that music can play both a direct role by influencing cognition; and an indirect role by fostering general intellectual development.

At the higher education level, research is more limited but no less intriguing. Studies with university students show mixed results, often depending on task type and music characteristics. Yet many students self-report that music is an integral part of their study routines, especially in managing stress and sustaining motivation. In professional and workplace training, music is frequently used informally during icebreakers, group exercises, or reflective sessions; though rarely as a systematic pedagogical strategy. This indicates untapped potential for integrating music more thoughtfully into adult learning contexts.

However, some researchers highlight the impact of the use of music on the cognitive load. Cognitive Load Theory (Sweller, 1994) distinguishes between intrinsic load based on the inherent task difficulty, extraneous load due to unnecessary distractions, and germane load or resources devoted to learning. Music can either reduce extraneous load by lowering stress and creating focus, or add to it by introducing competing auditory information. For example, while instrumental music may reduce anxiety and thereby free up cognitive resources, lyrical music can act as extraneous load, interfering with verbal tasks. This perspective helps reconcile conflicting findings in the literature and offers practical guidance for educators: music should be matched to task demands to ensure it reduces rather than increases cognitive load.

Despite decades of inquiry, several gaps remain. Much of the existing evidence comes from studies on children or adolescents, with relatively few investigations focusing on adult learners in higher education. This leaves an important gap, given that university students face distinct challenges, such as managing high academic workloads, balancing professional commitments, and navigating stress in competitive environments. By focusing specifically on postgraduate learners, this study contributes to an underexplored demographic in music-and-learning research.

Another gap lies in the scope of outcomes measured. Many prior studies focus on either test performance (cognitive outcomes) or emotional responses (mood, motivation), but seldom integrate the two systematically. This study bridges that divide by examining both learning outcomes and learner reactions, drawing inspiration from frameworks like the Arousal-Mood Hypothesis and Self-Determination Theory. In doing so, it recognizes that effective learning is not only about improved test scores but also about learners' subjective experiences, which influence persistence, engagement, and long-term outcomes.

Finally, this study advances the conversation by situating the investigation within the framework of higher education pedagogy. While music has occasionally been used informally in classrooms and training contexts, it has rarely been examined as a deliberate pedagogical tool for adult learners. By providing empirical evidence of its impact on postgraduate students, the study not only addresses a scholarly gap but also offers practical implications for educators seeking innovative ways to enhance engagement and reduce stress in higher education settings.

In sum, this study fills critical gaps in the literature by focusing on adult learners, integrating both cognitive and affective measures, and highlighting the pedagogical applications of background music in higher education. It moves the discourse beyond the polarized "music helps" versus "music distracts" debate toward a more nuanced understanding of how music can be strategically used to foster motivation, well-being, and learning. The conceptual model of the study has been presented in Figure 1.

Figure 1. Conceptual Model

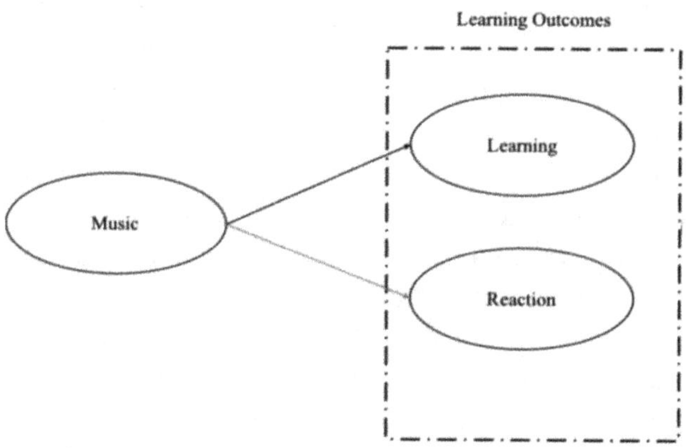

Source: Author created

METHODOLOGY

This study adopted a quasi-experimental design to investigate the impact of background music on both learning outcomes and learner reactions among postgraduate students. The design was chosen because it allows for comparison between groups exposed to different learning environments. In this case, one group worked with continuous background music and another without music, while maintaining validity by situating the experiment within a real classroom context. Unlike laboratory experiments that isolate variables under highly controlled conditions, this approach reflects the actual dynamics of higher education settings, thereby enhancing the study's relevance for educators and practitioners

Participants

The participants consisted of postgraduate management students enrolled at a leading business school in India. A total of 50 students were recruited for the study, representing a typical cross-section of young adult learners in higher education. The sample included 26 males and 24 females, with an average age of 23.6 years. All participants had prior exposure to classroom-based instruction and were familiar with conventional lecture delivery formats. None reported hearing impairments, ensuring greater uniformity in the experimental conditions. The choice of postgraduate students was deliberate, as this demographic faces distinct challenges: heavy academic workloads, high performance expectations, and stress associated with competitive career trajectories. These conditions make them a particularly relevant group for testing interventions such as background music, which has been shown to influence both stress regulation and motivation.

The sample was divided into two groups:

- Experimental Group (n = 25): Students exposed to continuous background instrumental music during the learning session.
- Control Group (n = 25): Students who completed the same learning session in silence.

Random allocation was used to reduce bias, ensuring that both groups were comparable in terms of academic background and prior exposure to the subject matter.

Materials and Learning Content

The instructional content was drawn from the management curriculum, focusing on a topic that was familiar enough for students to engage with meaningfully but not so well known as to make performance differences negligible. The material was delivered through a 30-minute lecture, identical across both conditions.

For the experimental group, instrumental background music was selected. The music was intentionally chosen to be non-lyrical, soft, and moderately paced in order to minimize verbal interference and avoid excessive arousal, aligning with evidence from prior research (Moreno & Mayer, 2000; Thompson et al., 2011). This choice was guided by findings that instrumental music is less distracting in verbal learning tasks while still capable of influencing mood and focus.

Procedure

The study followed a structured three-phase process:

1. Pre-session briefing: Students were informed that they would be participating in a study on learning experiences. However, they were not told about the specific variable of background music to minimize expectancy effects.
2. Learning session: Both groups attended the same lecture delivered by the same instructor under identical classroom conditions. For the experimental group, background music played continuously throughout the session using standard audio equipment at a comfortable volume.
3. Assessment phase: At the end of the lecture, students completed two measures:
    - A multiple-choice quiz designed to test comprehension and recall of the material, providing an indicator of learning outcomes.
    - A reaction survey consisting of Likert-scale items that measured engagement, enjoyment, and perceived effectiveness of the learning experience. This survey was adapted from established learner-reaction instruments used in training evaluation (Kirkpatrick & Kirkpatrick, 2006).

Data Analysis

Data were analysed using both descriptive and inferential statistics. Mean scores and standard deviations were computed for both learning outcomes and reaction measures. Independent samples t-tests were conducted to examine whether differences between the experimental and control groups were statistically significant. Effect sizes were also calculated to determine the magnitude of differences observed. This dual approach of measuring both cognitive (quiz performance) and affective (learner reactions) outcomes, enabled the study to move beyond narrow measures of academic achievement and explore the holistic impact of music on learning.

Ethical Considerations

Ethical approval was obtained from the institution's academic review committee prior to data collection. Participation was voluntary, and students provided informed consent before the study began. Confidentiality was assured, and no identifying information was collected in assessments. The intervention of playing instrumental background music was non-invasive and low risk, ensuring minimal ethical concerns.

ANALYSIS

This section presents the analysis of the data. Table 1 provide the descriptive statistics for the data.

Table 1. Descriptive Statistics for Reaction and Learning Scores

Variable	Group	N	Mean	Std. Deviation	Std. Error Mean
Reaction Scores	Control	25	4.11	0.53	0.11
Experimental		25	4.82	0.41	0.08
Learning Scores	Control	25	5.16	1.02	0.20
Experimental		25	6.20	0.95	0.19

Source: Author data

The descriptive statistics indicate that both reaction and learning scores were higher in the experimental group (with background music) compared to the control group (without music). To test whether the difference in reaction scores was statistically significant, an independent samples t-test was conducted. The results are presented in Table 2.

Table 2. Independent Samples t-test for Reaction Scores

Group	N	Mean	Std. Deviation	Std. Error Mean
Control	25	4.11	0.53	0.11
Experimental	25	4.82	0.41	0.08

Source: Author data

Results showed a significant difference between the control group (M = 4.11, SD = 0.53) and the experimental group (M = 4.82, SD = 0.41), $t(48) = -4.68$, $p < .001$. The effect size was medium-to-large (Cohen's $d = 0.89$), indicating that background music had a meaningful impact on learners' affective responses. This finding suggests that background music enhanced participants' engagement, attentiveness, and overall perception of the learning experience. The results align with the Arousal–Mood Hypothesis (Husain et al., 2002), which suggests that music improves learning indirectly by influencing arousal and mood. A similar analysis was conducted for learning outcomes. Results have been presented in Table 3.

Table 3. Independent Samples t-test for Learning Scores

Group	N	Mean	Std. Deviation	Std. Error Mean
Control	25	5.16	1.02	0.20
Experimental	25	6.20	0.95	0.19

Source: Author data

The experimental group (M = 6.20, SD = 0.95) outperformed the control group (M = 5.16, SD = 1.02). The difference was statistically significant, $t(48) = -2.53$, $p = .015$, with a moderate effect size (Cohen's $d = 0.72$).

These results indicate that background music not only enhanced learners' affective responses but also translated into modest cognitive benefits, as reflected in higher test scores. However, the smaller effect size compared to reaction scores suggests that music's primary impact may lie in shaping the emotional climate of learning, with cognitive improvements emerging indirectly.

DISCUSSION

The three theoretical lenses used in this study; Self-Determination Theory (SDT), the Arousal-Mood Hypothesis, and Kirkpatrick's evaluation model, are complementary and together provide a parsimonious explanation of the observed pattern of results. Instrumental background music functions first as an affective regulator, modifying arousal and mood (Arousal-Mood Hypothesis) to create an emotional climate that supports attention and positive affect. This enriched affective state satisfies basic psychological needs identified in SDT, particularly relatedness (shared atmosphere) and competence (reduced anxiety), thereby enhancing intrinsic motivation and engagement. These enhanced affective and motivational conditions manifest at Kirkpatrick Level 1 (reaction) as higher learner satisfaction and perceived engagement, and spill over into Level 2 (learning) producing modest but measurable gains in knowledge acquisition. In short: music operates primarily by shaping internal affective states and motivational conditions (Arousal-Mood + SDT), which then translate into improved learner reactions and, secondarily, to better cognitive outcomes as captured by Kirkpatrick's framework.

The results of this study highlight the layered ways in which background music interacts with human learning processes. While both reaction and learning outcomes improved in the music condition, the difference in effect sizes points to deeper psychological mechanisms at work. The much stronger effect on reaction scores highlights music's role as an affective regulator. Learning is not a purely cognitive process; it is deeply linked with emotion (Pekrun, 2014). By influencing mood states, background music helps set the emotional tone of the classroom. In this case, instrumental tracks may have acted as an emotional primer, lowering stress and creating a sense of calm that made the environment feel more welcoming. When learners perceive the learning space as positive and supportive, they tend to report higher levels of satisfaction and engagement, which was reflected in the elevated reaction scores observed.

Another explanation for these results lies in theories of attention. Music, especially instrumental pieces with a steady tempo, can serve as an attentional anchor that helps sustain focus and reduce mind-wandering. In this study, the presence of background music may have guided learners into a more attentive state, enabling them to concentrate better on the material at hand. However, this effect is more readily captured in subjective evaluations, such as reactions, than in measurable test performance, which depends on a broader range of cognitive processes. This may explain why the uplift in reactions was more pronounced than the gains in learning scores.

At the same time, music's influence extended beyond mood and engagement to learning outcomes, although to a lesser degree. The modest but significant improvement in test scores suggests that music did more than simply create a pleasant environment. Research on state-dependent learning points out that mood congruence facilitates both memory encoding and retrieval. By creating a positive emotional state, music may have primed learners to encode information more effectively, thus improving recall during assessment. Nevertheless, because this mechanism operates indirectly, its effect on learning outcomes is not as strong as its influence on affective reactions.

The Yerkes–Dodson law (1908) also provides insight into these findings. This principle suggests that performance improves with physiological arousal up to a certain point, beyond which additional stimulation becomes counterproductive. The instrumental music used here likely provided mild arousal that helped learners remain alert without overwhelming them. This balanced stimulation may account for why learning outcomes improved moderately without evidence of distraction. At the same time, the smaller effect on test performance compared to reactions indicates that even optimal arousal has limits when it comes to enhancing cognitive processes.

From the perspective of working memory, the results can also be explained through Baddeley's model (2000). Because the music was instrumental, it avoided heavy demands on the phonological loop, which would otherwise compete with verbal processing of the lecture. This reduced the likelihood of interference and allowed learners to process content without significant disruption. However, even instrumental music requires some allocation of attentional resources, which may have slightly constrained the extent to which information could be encoded. This helps explain why learning outcomes improved, but not to the same degree as self-reported engagement.

It is also important to recognize the social context of learning. Beyond shaping individual experience, music created a shared sensory atmosphere in the classroom. This collective environment may have enhanced what Goffman (1967) calls "interactional order," fostering a sense of cohesion and positive group energy. Learners were not only responding individually but were also attuned to the collective effect of their peers. Such emotional contagion may help explain why reaction scores showed a strong improvement: participants not only felt better themselves but also perceived the group as more engaged. However, this kind of collective mood does not automatically translate into better individual test scores, which remain shaped by personal factors such as prior knowledge, study habits, and cognitive ability.

Perhaps the most significant interpretive insight from this study is the gap between reactions and learning outcomes. The stronger effect on affective measures suggests that music's primary domain of influence lies in shaping perceptions, emotions, and motivation rather than directly boosting cognitive performance. This has practical implications: educators and trainers should view music as an environmental enhancer or facilitator of engagement rather than a tool that guarantees higher test scores. Put differently, music seems to prepare the soil in which learning can flourish, but it is not a substitute for high-quality teaching, curriculum design, or active learning strategies.

Finally, these findings help reconcile some of the contradictory results in the literature. Studies that reported distraction effects often used lyrical or fast-tempo music, which is more likely to interfere with verbal processing and increase arousal beyond optimal levels (Moreno & Mayer, 2000; Thompson et al., 2011). In contrast, this study employed carefully selected instrumental tracks at a moderate tempo, which struck a balance between stimulation and subtlety. This design choice highlights the importance of contextual sensitivity and that not all music will benefit learning, and the effects are highly dependent on how music is curated and applied.

The findings of this study fit within, but also extend, a long-standing debate on the role of music in learning. On one side of the debate, research has consistently demonstrated the benefits of background music for cognitive and emotional outcomes. For example, Schellenberg (2011) found that music exposure was associated with improvements in IQ, memory, and verbal ability in children. Hallam et al., (2002) similarly reported that carefully selected music enhanced motivation and concentration in classroom contexts. More recently, Schwartz et al., (2017) demonstrated that instrumental music could increase task persistence and improve the emotional experience of learning. The present study supports this body of work by showing that music can positively affect both learner reactions and immediate knowledge acquisition among postgraduate learners, a group less frequently studied in this area.

On the other side of the debate, however, there is strong evidence that music may interfere with cognitive processing under certain conditions. Moreno and

Mayer (2000), drawing from the cognitive theory of multimedia learning, argued that music can overload working memory and distract from essential processing. Thompson et al., (2011) similarly cautioned that music with lyrics or high tempo may impair reading comprehension and text-based learning tasks. These findings highlight that the benefits of music are not universal but contingent on the type of music, the nature of the task, and the learner's individual characteristics.

The present study's results contribute to reconciling these contradictory strands of research. By demonstrating significant improvements in reactions and moderate gains in learning when instrumental, moderate-tempo music was used, the study illustrates that the effects of music are highly sensitive to context and design. Unlike studies that used lyrical or fast-tempo tracks, which are more likely to interfere with verbal processing, the music chosen in this intervention minimized competition for phonological processing resources while still shaping mood and attention. This helps explain why the experimental group showed both affective and cognitive improvements.

Another contribution of this study is its focus on adult postgraduate learners. Much of the prior work in this field has concentrated on children (Schellenberg, 2004), adolescents (Southgate & Roscigno, 2009), or school settings (Hallam et al., 2002). The context of adult learners in higher education is comparatively underexplored, despite the fact that university students often operate in high-stakes, cognitively demanding environments. The present findings suggest that even in populations where learners are expected to self-regulate and manage complex information loads, music can act as a supportive environmental cue that enhances engagement and learning.

These results also align with affective neuroscience perspectives on learning, which highlight that emotional and cognitive processes are not separate but deeply integrated (Immordino-Yang & Damasio, 2007). By showing that music primarily influenced affective outcomes while also generating spillover effects on cognition, this study contributes to a growing body of evidence that learning environments cannot be fully understood without accounting for the emotional dimensions of human experience.

An important distinction to note is the short-term nature of the outcomes measured. The improvements observed in learner reactions and immediate test performance reflect effects that are likely strongest in-the-moment, aligning with the Arousal–Mood Hypothesis (Husain et al., 2002), which posits that music influences arousal levels and emotional states that subsequently impact cognitive functioning. However, the study did not assess long-term retention or motivation. Thus, while music may enhance initial attentiveness and short-term recall, whether these effects persist over days or weeks remains uncertain. This distinction is crucial for both theory and practice, as the sustainability of music's impact determines its value as a consistent pedagogical tool.

In summary, the present study confirms prior findings that music can be beneficial to learning, while also qualifying those conclusions by demonstrating that the type of music and the context of learning are crucial determinants of its impact. By situating its results within adult higher education, the study extends the literature and underscores the importance of contextualized, carefully designed applications of background music in pedagogy and training.

IMPLICATIONS

The findings of this study carry meaningful implications for educators, trainers, and learning designers seeking to optimize the emotional and cognitive climate of their classrooms and training environments. The results confirm that music has the capacity to influence learning outcomes, but they also highlight that its most reliable effect lies in shaping learners' affective engagement. This distinction is important because it suggests that music should be strategically deployed not primarily as a direct tool for boosting test performance, but rather as an environmental enhancer that improves motivation, attentiveness, and satisfaction with the learning experience.

For educators in higher education, the results suggest that carefully chosen background music can play a subtle but effective role in creating a more engaging classroom environment. Particularly in contexts where learners are exposed to long lectures, dense content, or stressful academic demands, music may function as an emotional buffer that reduces anxiety and sustains concentration. For example, instrumental music could be used at the beginning of a session to set a calm tone, or during individual reflection exercises to provide a sense of focus and containment. Importantly, the study suggests that even small interventions, such as playing low-volume, non-lyrical tracks during specific phases of a class, can make learners perceive the experience more positively.

For corporate trainers and learning and development (L&D) professionals, the findings are equally relevant. Organizations increasingly recognize that training effectiveness depends not only on content delivery but also on learner engagement and emotional connection. Music, as this study demonstrates, can act as a low-cost, scalable tool for enhancing these dimensions. It can be incorporated into training sessions to energize participants during workshops, to manage transitions between modules, or to create a reflective mood in leadership or mindfulness programs. Unlike more resource-intensive interventions such as immersive technologies, music requires minimal investment yet can produce significant improvements in learner reactions, which are closely linked to training satisfaction and motivation.

The implications extend further into the domain of digital learning environments. As learners increasingly engage with self-paced e-learning platforms and virtual classrooms, the absence of physical presence often results in disengagement and fatigue. Integrating background music into digital platforms — for example, ambient instrumental tracks in microlearning modules or adaptive music in gamified environments — could enhance emotional engagement and sustain attention. This is particularly relevant in an era where remote and hybrid learning models are becoming dominant. However, digital contexts also magnify the need for personalization: while in a physical classroom learners experience the same soundscape, in digital environments music could be made optional or adaptable to learner preference.

At the same time, the findings remind practitioners that music is not universally beneficial and must be applied thoughtfully. Learners differ in their cultural associations, personal preferences, and tolerance for background sound. What feels relaxing to one learner may feel distracting or irritating to another. Trainers and educators should therefore avoid blanket assumptions about music's benefits and instead consider offering learners some degree of choice or control over the auditory environment. This could take the form of allowing students to opt out, to select from a curated playlist, or to adjust volume according to their comfort. Such autonomy-supportive practices not only mitigate potential downsides but may also strengthen music's motivational benefits, as suggested by self-determination theory.

Another practical implication relates to the type of task and phase of learning. The present findings suggest that music is particularly effective in influencing affective engagement, which may be most useful in phases that require openness, reflection, or sustained attention. For tasks demanding heavy verbal processing, such as reading complex texts, music may offer fewer advantages and could even interfere if it is poorly chosen. Trainers and instructors should therefore align music use with task demands: employ it to energize or calm learners before a cognitively demanding activity, but avoid using it in ways that compete with the same cognitive resources required by the task.

Finally, this study underscores music's role as a symbolic signal of care. By incorporating music, educators and trainers signal that the learning environment has been intentionally designed with the learner's experience in mind. This aligns with contemporary shifts in pedagogy and L&D that emphasize human-centred design and holistic learner well-being.

LIMITATIONS

Although this study provides valuable insights into the role of background music in shaping learner reactions and knowledge acquisition, certain limitations should be acknowledged. First, the study was conducted with a relatively small and homogenous sample of 64 MBA students from a single institution, which may limit the generalizability of the findings. Future studies should test larger and more diverse samples, including learners from different educational levels, professional contexts, and cultural backgrounds.

Second, the study employed a one-shot, immediate post-test design, which captured short-term effects of music on engagement and learning. While results showed a positive impact, it remains unclear whether these effects persist over time. Music may boost immediate attentiveness and mood, but its long-term influence on retention, motivation, and transfer of learning requires further investigation.

Third, the role of individual differences in response to background music was not examined. Learners may vary in their tolerance, preferences, and sensitivity to music. For some, music may enhance focus, while for others it could act as a distraction. Factors such as personality traits (e.g., introversion–extraversion), prior exposure to music during study, or cultural associations with particular genres could moderate the outcomes.

Fourth, the study used a single type of instrumental music (non-lyrical, 60–80 bpm). While this choice was deliberate to minimize distraction, it restricts the conclusions that can be drawn about other forms of music. Different tempos, genres, or lyrical content may produce stronger, weaker, or even opposite effects on learning and engagement.

Finally, contextual factors such as delivery environment and instructional style may also influence how music interacts with learning. Since the same instructor delivered both experimental and control sessions, consistency was ensured, but it is possible that instructor characteristics or teaching style interacted with the presence of music in ways that were not measured.

Taken together, these limitations do not diminish the significance of the findings but rather point to the need for more nuanced and longitudinal research. Future investigations should account for individual learner preferences, include diverse types of music, and extend beyond immediate learning outcomes to explore long-term retention and transfer.

FUTURE RESEARCH DIRECTIONS

While this study provides evidence of the immediate benefits of background music on learner reactions and short-term knowledge acquisition, several promising avenues for future research remain.

First, longitudinal research is needed to evaluate whether the benefits of background music extend beyond the immediate classroom setting. The current design measured only short-term effects; future studies should track whether music contributes to improved retention of knowledge, sustained motivation, and transfer of learning over days, weeks, or even across semesters.

Second, the rise of digital and online learning environments presents an important context for exploration. With the growth of virtual classrooms, e-learning platforms, and corporate digital training, background music could play a role in maintaining learner focus in settings often characterized by high distraction and reduced social presence. Investigating how music interacts with features such as multimedia presentations, gamified content, or virtual breakout rooms could expand its practical relevance.

Third, cultural considerations warrant greater attention. Music is deeply tied to cultural identity, and what enhances engagement in one context may not translate effectively in another. Comparative studies across diverse cultural groups could provide insights into how music selection should be tailored to global classrooms and multinational corporations. Such cross-cultural research could also clarify whether universal patterns exist in music's impact on learning or if its effects are largely culturally contingent.

Fourth, genre-based differences represent another rich area for inquiry. This study employed non-lyrical instrumental tracks at a moderate tempo, chosen to minimize distraction. However, other forms of music—such as classical, jazz, ambient, or culturally relevant folk music—may produce different outcomes. Research comparing multiple genres, tempos, and even lyrical versus non-lyrical tracks could uncover nuanced patterns of effectiveness for different learner populations and instructional tasks.

Finally, individual differences should be systematically examined in future studies. Factors such as personality traits (e.g., introversion–extraversion), prior habits of studying with music, or musical training may moderate learners' responses. Incorporating these variables into study designs would yield more fine-grained insights and allow for more personalized recommendations regarding when and for whom background music is beneficial.

CONCLUSION

This study set out to investigate the role of background music in shaping both the affective and cognitive dimensions of learning. The findings demonstrate that music exerts a particularly strong influence on learners' reactions, significantly enhancing engagement, attentiveness, and overall satisfaction with the learning experience. Its effect on knowledge acquisition, while more modest, was still meaningful, suggesting that music not only shapes how learners feel about a session but also indirectly supports the processing and recall of information. Together, these results affirm that background music functions less as a direct cognitive enhancer and more as an environmental facilitator that creates conditions conducive to deeper learning.

In doing so, the study contributes to ongoing debates within the literature by clarifying that the effects of music are not uniform but context-dependent. The use of carefully selected, non-lyrical instrumental tracks at moderate tempo appears to strike a balance between stimulating engagement and minimizing distraction, reconciling prior contradictory findings. Importantly, the study also extends this body of work into the underexplored context of adult higher education, demonstrating that even highly self-directed learners benefit from subtle affective interventions.

For practitioners, the results point to music as a simple, low-cost, and scalable tool for enhancing the learner experience in both educational and organizational training contexts. When thoughtfully applied, music can create more welcoming and focused environments, improve learner satisfaction, and indirectly support better cognitive outcomes. However, the findings also highlight the need for sensitivity to learner preferences and task demands, reinforcing that music is most effective when tailored rather than universally applied.

Looking ahead, future research should continue to explore the conditions under which music most effectively enhances learning, examining variations in genre, tempo, cultural context, and learner characteristics. Longitudinal designs and digital learning settings also represent fertile avenues for further inquiry. Ultimately, this line of research underscores the growing recognition that learning is not simply about the transmission of knowledge but about creating emotionally engaging environments in which learners are motivated to invest their attention and effort. Background music, as this study shows, has the potential to be a valuable part of that design.

REFERENCES

Baddeley, A. D. (2000). The episodic buffer: A new component of working memory? *Trends in Cognitive Sciences*, *4*(11), 417–423. DOI: 10.1016/S1364-6613(00)01538-2

Chabris, C. F. (1999). Brief exposure to Mozart music does not enhance spatial ability: A meta-analysis. *Current Directions in Psychological Science*, *8*(4), 131–134.

Furnham, A., & Bradley, A. (1997). Music while you work: The differential distraction of background music on the cognitive test performance of introverts and extraverts. *Applied Cognitive Psychology*, *11*(5), 445–455. DOI: 10.1002/(SICI)1099-0720(199710)11:5<445::AID-ACP472>3.0.CO;2-R

Goffman, E. (1967). *Interaction ritual: Essays on face-to-face behavior*. Pantheon Books.

Hallam, S., Price, J., & Katsarou, G. (2002). The effects of background music on primary school pupils' task performance. *Educational Studies*, *28*(2), 111–122. DOI: 10.1080/03055690220124551

Husain, G., Thompson, W. F., & Schellenberg, E. G. (2002). Effects of musical tempo and mode on arousal, mood, and spatial abilities. *Music Perception*, *20*(2), 151–171. DOI: 10.1525/mp.2002.20.2.151

Immordino-Yang, M. H., & Damasio, A. (2007). We feel, therefore we learn: The relevance of affective and social neuroscience to education. *Mind, Brain and Education : the Official Journal of the International Mind, Brain, and Education Society*, *1*(1), 3–10. DOI: 10.1111/j.1751-228X.2007.00004.x

Isen, A. M. (2000). Positive affect and decision making. In M. Lewis & J. M. Haviland-Jones (Eds.), *Handbook of emotions* (2nd ed., pp. 417–435). Guilford Press.

Jäncke, L., & Sandmann, P. (2010). Music listening while you learn: No influence of background music on verbal learning. *Behavioral and Brain Functions : BBF*, *6*(1), 3. DOI: 10.1186/1744-9081-6-3

Kirkpatrick, D. L., & Kirkpatrick, J. D. (2006). *Evaluating training programs: The four levels* (3rd ed.). Berrett-Koehler Publishers.

Moreno, R., & Mayer, R. E. (2000). A coherence effect in multimedia learning: The case for minimizing irrelevant sounds in the design of multimedia instructional messages. *Journal of Educational Psychology*, *92*(1), 117–125. DOI: 10.1037/0022-0663.92.1.117

Moreno, R., & Mayer, R. E. (2000). A coherence effect in multimedia learning: The case for minimizing irrelevant sounds in the design of multimedia instructional messages. *Journal of Educational Psychology, 92*(1), 117–125. DOI: 10.1037/0022-0663.92.1.117

Pekrun, R. (2014). Emotions and learning. [UNESCO International Bureau of Education.]. *Educational Practices Series, 24*, 1–31.

Rauscher, F. H., Shaw, G. L., & Ky, K. N. (1993). Music and spatial task performance. *Nature, 365*(6447), 611. DOI: 10.1038/365611a0

Ryan, R. M., & Deci, E. L. (2000). Self-determination theory and the facilitation of intrinsic motivation, social development, and well-being. *The American Psychologist, 55*(1), 68–78. DOI: 10.1037/0003-066X.55.1.68

Schellenberg, E. G. (2004). Music lessons enhance IQ. *Psychological Science, 15*(8), 511–514. DOI: 10.1111/j.0956-7976.2004.00711.x

Schellenberg, E. G. (2011). Examining the association between music lessons and intelligence. *British Journal of Psychology, 102*(3), 283–302. DOI: 10.1111/j.2044-8295.2010.02000.x

Schwartz, R. W., Ayres, K. M., & Douglas, K. H. (2017). Effects of music on task performance, engagement, and behavior: A literature review. *Psychology of Music, 45*(5), 611–627. DOI: 10.1177/0305735617691118

Southgate, D. E., & Roscigno, V. J. (2009). The impact of music on childhood and adolescent achievement. *Social Science Quarterly, 90*(1), 4–21. DOI: 10.1111/j.1540-6237.2009.00598.x

Sweller, J. (1994). Cognitive load theory, learning difficulty, and instructional design. *Learning and Instruction, 4*(4), 295–312. DOI: 10.1016/0959-4752(94)90003-5

Thompson, W. F., Schellenberg, E. G., & Letnic, A. K. (2011). Fast and loud background music disrupts reading comprehension. *Psychology of Music, 40*(6), 700–708. DOI: 10.1177/0305735611400173

Wallace, W. T. (1994). Memory for music: Effect of melody on recall of text. *Journal of Experimental Psychology. Learning, Memory, and Cognition, 20*(6), 1471–1485. DOI: 10.1037/0278-7393.20.6.1471

Yerkes, R. M., & Dodson, J. D. (1908). The relation of strength of stimulus to rapidity of habit-formation. *The Journal of Comparative Neurology and Psychology, 18*(5), 459–482. DOI: 10.1002/cne.920180503

Chapter 7
Digital Pathways to Social and Emotional Learning:
Leveraging Technology for Holistic Student Development

P. Karthik
https://orcid.org/0000-0001-8647-1927
St. Francis Evening College, Bengaluru, India

Velaga SriSai
https://orcid.org/0000-0002-5138-6236
School of Business and Management, Christ University, Bengaluru, India

Dhara Vinod Parmar
Design and Merchandising, Parul Institute of Design, Parul University, Waghodia, India

Nishant Bhuvanesh Trivedi
Animation and Design, Parul Institute of Design, Parul University, Waghodia, India

Vandana Aggarwal
https://orcid.org/0000-0002-3006-0624
University Institute of Teachers Training and Research, Chandigarh University, Mohali, India

D. Ramya
https://orcid.org/0000-0002-7970-3483
Department of English, Kongu Engineering College, Erode, India

M. Suresh
https://orcid.org/0009-0006-5764-1660
KPR Institute of Technology, Kovai, India

ABSTRACT

This chapter explores how digital tools can improve Social and Emotional Learning (SEL) and help develop students holistically. It looks at how educational technology can fall within three distinct categories of SEL: technology-enhanced gamified learning, online collaboration spaces, and classroom-based Artificial Intelligence

DOI: 10.4018/979-8-3373-5157-5.ch007

(AI)-driven feedback and evaluation. This chapter emphasizes using interactive approaches that foster self-awareness, empathy, responsible decision-making, and interpersonal skills—using data-driven approaches in order to make the student more aware of their own learning. This chapter discusses the benefits and challenges; the equity issues; and provides tangible ideas and strategies for educators and policy-makers. By connecting the principles of SEL with digital innovations, the chapter demonstrates ways that we can create meaningful, richer, inclusive, and emotionally safe learning conditions for students in both formal, and informal settings.

INTRODUCTION

In our ever-connected, technologically advanced world, there is a collective emphasis from educators, policy-makers, and, most importantly, learners, to bolster the development of social and emotional competencies. Social and Emotional Learning (SEL) is the process in which individuals develop and enact the attitude, knowledge, and skills necessary to understand and manage emotions, set and achieve positive goals, show empathy for others, establish and maintain supportive, purposeful relationships, and make responsible decisions. SEL has generally been promoted through live interactions and experiential learning. However, with the fast-paced development of digital technologies and a global shift towards online and hybrid schooling, there are now unprecedented opportunities to incorporate SEL into digital contexts that potentially complement, enhance and, in some instances, displace traditional practices(Chouhan et al., 2021).

The rise of a variety of educational programs, including educational apps, VR (virtual reality) simulation, AI (artificial intelligence)-based feedback systems, gamified learning environments, and digital collaborative environments, has helped advance SEL beyond the four walls of the physical classroom, creating learning opportunities that are accessible, scalable, and highly personalized. Such transformation is important and timely given the global challenges that learners are facing today; thus, to explore connections to the psychological residue of the COVID-19 pandemic, heightened social isolation, a competitive labor market, and innovation through cross-cultural communication in a globalized economy. Digital avenues for SEL have enabled educators to go beyond geographic and socio-economic boundaries and afford students in diverse situations equitable access to emotionally compelling tools for growth in resilience, empathy, adaptability, and crucial people skills(Tapalova & Zhiyenbayeva, 2022).

Integrating SEL into digital tools relates closely to the demands of 21st century education that call for not only cognitive development but also emotional intelligence and collaboration as well as ethical citizenship. Research continues to provide support regarding the benefits of SEL competencies and capacity of success in academic achievement, emotional health, and mental well-being, living full lives; therefore, we encourage deliberate investments in technology that build capacity for future-ready learners (Lipschitz et al., 2023). Lastly, many digital tools include unique affordances for SEL including: virtual role-play scenarios that allow learners to practice empathy through cultural simulated representation; AI chatbots that can provide individualized emotional support that is immediate; gamified systems that reward persistence and collaborative problem solving; or allow data analysis on social or economic factors or dilemmas that educators can observe and take action in a responsive, supportive way, receive timely benefits from the social aspects of students' engagement, and determining who needs intervention and when. However, using technology intentionally for SEL purposes has challenges as well(Triyono et al., 2023).

Questions of digital equity, privacy, data ethics, and screen fatigue raise considerable challenges for educators and policy-makers, while we need to guard against turning SEL into a checklist that is algorithmically safe, thereby rendering it overly technical and deceptively devoid of the relational, precious and fundamentally human values with which SEL is concerned. Embracing and successfully operationalizing the integration of SEL into digital learning requires substantial thoughtfulness regarding pedagogical design, attention to cultural responsiveness, application of student voice and perspectives, and appropriate levels of technology to enable connections between students and their peers, educators and mentors. Ultimately, these connections, and the relationship between technology and SEL, need to be ongoing; we need to view the connections as live collaboration - one that is dynamic and leverages the potential of digital innovation, while making sure we remain firmly grounded in evidence-informed principles of SEL(John & Bates, 2024).

This chapter evaluates how digital tools can facilitate SEL within the urgency of educational change and the need for a more expansive notion of student development. It opens with an overview of the conceptual principles underpinning SEL, proffering several current conceptual models and international policy perspectives to illustrate the growing relevance of SEL in contemporary learning contexts. Next, it explores the key technological affordances and utility to illustrate how digital platforms are enabling SEL with educational examples across multiple contexts and organizations and across disciplines. Lastly, challenges, potentials for risk, and a critical consideration of ethical, cultural, and access perspectives are offered(Rout & Bhoi, 2024a).

Finally, it presents strategic options for educators, school leaders, and policy makers to prepare, implement, and evaluate technology-enabled SEL programs that are effective, inclusive, and sustainable. By taking into account both the opportunities and challenges of implementing SEL in digital learning contexts, this chapter highlights the importance of intentional balance - which recognizes technology not as the answer but as an important partner in developing emotional intelligence and social responsibility and resilience in learners(Meng et al., 2025). As education systems and educators around the world grapple with unprecedented change, the intentional integration of SEL with digital tools as part of the digital learning experience represents a compelling pathway to support human-centered learning in education systems responding to a digital world, that prepares students to not only advance their learning but to thrive in diverse, interconnected, and evolving societies.

CONCEPTUAL FOUNDATIONS OF SOCIAL AND EMOTIONAL LEARNING (SEL)

Social and Emotional Learning (SEL) is establishing itself as a guiding force in education for a whole person. SEL allows learners to develop the emotional skills, interpersonal competencies, and ethical dispositions that give them agency in a complex and interdependent world as shown in Figure 1. Academic success is critical, and it remains a powerful measure of measure student performance and success, and research shows that social and emotional competencies are equally important considerations for student personal wellness, workforce readiness, and active citizenship. SEL allows educators to go beyond awareness and understanding of emotional and social intelligence and compassion, to development of the agency to understand, express, regulate, and manage emotions, cultivate positive relationships, resolve conflicts, and make responsible value-based decisions. This section discusses the foundational competencies within SEL, the role of SEL in 21st century educational context, and the global frameworks that exist for the implementation of SEL(Meng et al., 2025; Setia et al., 2024).

Figure 1. Conceptual foundations of social and emotional learning (SEL)

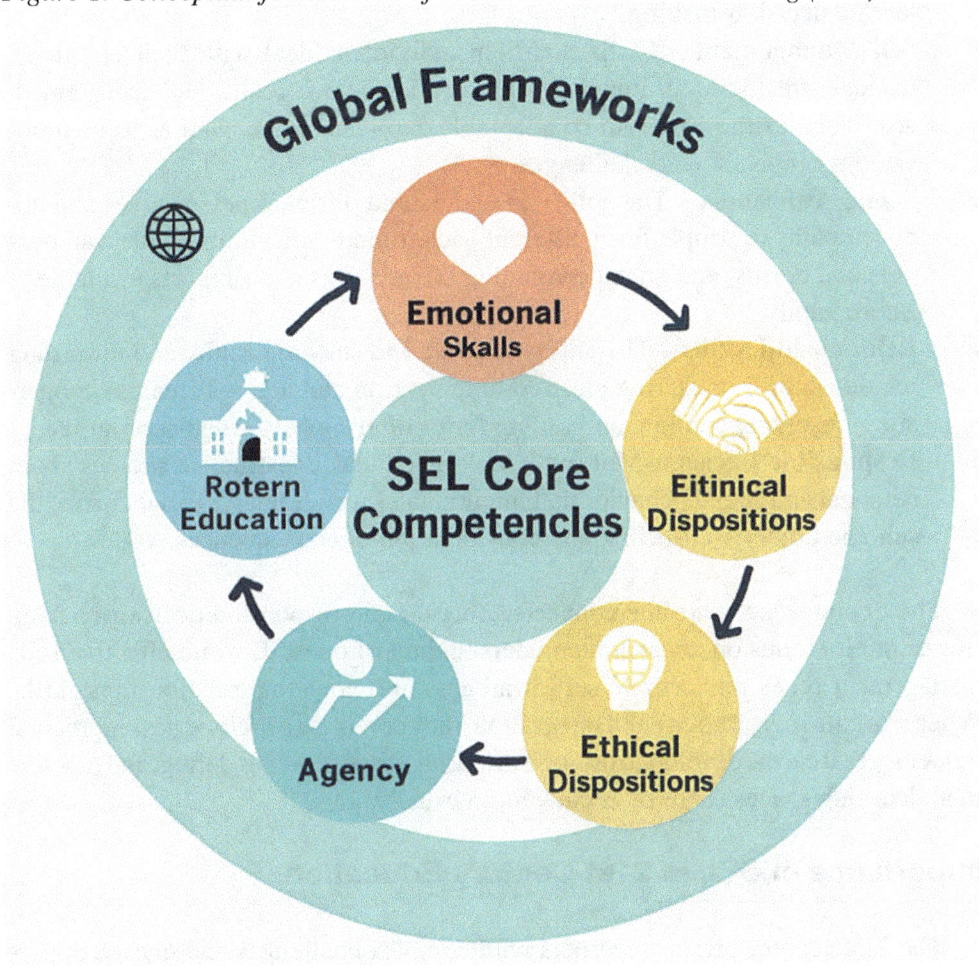

Core Competencies of SEL

The Collaborative for Academic, Social, and Emotional Learning (CASEL), is one of the most important organizations influencing the discourse on SEL, identifies five interrelated core competencies which define the foundation of SEL programing, for all ages, in any culture(Erstad et al., 2024; Rout & Bhoi, 2024a):

- **Self-Awareness** – The ability to accurately identify one's emotions, values, strengths, and limitations. This includes developing a well-grounded sense of confidence and optimism, and understanding how emotions influence behavior and decision-making.

- **Self-Management** – Skills that help individuals deal with their emotions, manage stress, control impulses, and set and achieve goals. Self-management also includes the ability to be adaptable and resilient, as well as to be motivated when faced with challenges.
- **Social Awareness** – The ability to understand different perspectives and apply empathy to people from different backgrounds and cultures; an awareness of social norms; and an understanding of resources and supports available in a community.
- **Relationship Skills** – The ability to forge and sustain healthy and rewarding relationships by fostering clear communication and active listening, cooperating, resolving conflict, and asking for or offering help when appropriate.
- **Responsible Decision-Making** – Making ethical, constructive choices about personal and social behavior that intentionally weigh safety, social norms, the self and others' well-being, and consideration of consequences.

These competencies are interconnected: for example, responsible decision-making (for example) relies on an accurate understanding of oneself, while effective self-management relies on accurate self-awareness and empathic relationships skills. When working in reciprocity and integration, they comprise a lifelong developmental trajectory that can be developed through in tentful instruction, modeling, and practice in all learning spaces (both physically and virtually).

Importance of SEL in 21st-Century Education

The 21st century presents learners with complex challenges and myriad opportunities shaped by globalization, accelerating technological change, environmental unpredictability and shifting labor market dynamics. In this context, education systems are now being asked not just to prepare learners for academic success at school and in higher education, but also to prepare them for future adaptability, resilience and cross-cultural teamwork. SEL is particularly well-aligned to recognizing the ability to adapt through fostering emotional intelligence, as it has been associated with academic success, productivity and well-being (Erstad et al., 2024; Triyono et al., 2023).

The analysis is extended to illustrate the similarities and differences in the onboarding of Social and Emotional Learning (SEL) between high- and low-income environments, including the relative capacity, resources, and cultural appropriateness of the interventions initiated. In general, high-income environments tend to be better funded, integrated within broader systems, and supported by trained educators, while low-income environments often have infrastructure, teacher capacity, and competing mandates that are less supportive of SEL. The analysis includes comparative equity and accessibility as a framing, highlighting context-based adaptations to improve equity, access, and success in SEL. Rather than export generic SEL programs that are inconsistent with local need, an equity-focused approach to SEL initiatives must carefully consider the support of community, context, and sustainability to effect equitable outcomes for SEL development globally.

Employers frequently emphasize the value of soft skills (like teamwork, problem-solving, communication, and adaptability) to them, equally or more important than technical skills from an economic perspective. SEL competencies are very closely tied to these soft skills set of competencies, and can be seen as a requisite set of skills for entering the workforce and advancing in a career. From a societal perspective, SEL equips people to participate fruitfully in different and diverse communities, navigate differences between and among people, and contribute in some way to social cohesion, especially in increasingly pluralistic societies which require negotiated social agreements to manage the rules of social interactions.

The nature of the relevance of SEL shifted when responding to the needs caused by the learning disruption from the COVID-19 pandemic. Traditional schooling disappeared and students experienced increased social isolation, and mental health needs. When learning moved online, integrating SEL and SEL into online learning spaces while teaching were not only pedagogical innovations, but also critically urgent as part of the action needed to maintain student well-being, engagement, and motivation. In this sense, SEL can be understood as the protective sphere reducing the risk of disengagement, anxiety, and conflicts and the growth sphere that takes students from surviving uncertainty to possible thriving in uncertainty.

Global Frameworks and Policy Perspectives

Across the world application of SEL is evolving in educational policy and practice through various frameworks relating to unique cultural, developmental and socio-political priorities. The CASEL framework continues to be one of the most prominent examples that inform curriculum development and teacher education or professional development across North America, Europe and Asia. The CASEL framework promotes systemic approaches to SEL that embed within classroom practices, school climate, family engagement and partnerships with community organizations(Chouhan et al., 2021; Tapalova & Zhiyenbayeva, 2022).

Universally, the United Nations Educational, Scientific and Cultural Organization (UNESCO) includes SEL within global citizenship education (GCED) and education for sustainable development as a key policy initiative. UNESCO's policy guidance indicates that socio-emotional competencies can help people develop empathy, respect for diversity and commitment to human rights; these attributes help us become the kind of person that we need to be to address critical issues of the global agenda like climate change, inequality, and conflict. UNESCO's most general position on SEL also emphasizes culturally responsive programs which recognize local communities, as long as the program demonstrates higher common human values.

Similarly, The Organization for Economic Co-operation and Development (OECD) has identified SEL-related competencies as part of the new Learning Compass 2030 framework seeing learners as "co-creators" of their future. It identifies the importance of agency, adaptability, and well-being with SEL at the forefront as it relates to these competencies. In the Asia-Pacific Region nations such as Singapore, Australia, and Japan have placed SEL as a core principle and in other circumstances articulated within "values education" or "character and citizenship education". In Africa and Latin America there is also a connection, especially around peace education, youth empowerment, and community sustainability, whereby the concepts, frameworks and practices have been adapted to the local situations. While there are a variety of cross regional perspectives, the idea of SEL as an "add-on" does not appear to be foundational anywhere. Countries are moving towards policy approaches that increasingly require it to be integrated into curriculum, pedagogy, assessment and professional development. In terms of educational technology, these frameworks also have a focus on how educational technology can support SEL through personalized learning, cross-cultural exchanges, and providing immediate feedback on emotional and social growth.

In sum, the conceptual foundations of SEL-its well-defined competencies, its focus on the skills needed for education in the 21st century, and its integration in worldwide education policy-make it a powerful and universally important element of contemporary learning. The challenge and opportunity going forward is to use technology not as a substitute for human connection, rather to add value and scale SEL so that every learner, regardless of geographical location or socioeconomic status, may have the social and emotional capacities to thrive in an increasingly unpredictable world.

DIGITAL TRANSFORMATION IN EDUCATION AND ITS RELEVANCE TO SEL

Over the past 20 years, the realization of digital transformation in higher education has quantitatively changed the way all learners have had access to education; the way they access knowledge; how they engage with other learners; and the way they learn skills. While early iterations of educational technology (EdTech) were focused on enhancing the ability to share content and extending access, EdTech has progressed significantly enough to explore some of these other facets of learning, and to increasingly advance the idea that we can actively engage a learner's social and emotional learning (SEL) as shown in Figure 2. After all, digital transformation brings this capacity to learners to develop their self-awareness, empathy, resilience, collaboration competence - all essential competencies in the quest for 21st century education(Oliveira & De Souza, 2022). Hence, mapping the relationship between digital transformation of higher education and SEL requires us to consider the development of EdTech, the impact of COVID-19 on the delivery of SEL, and the streamed pathways toward hybrid and blended models that have begun to change the boundaries of educational practice.

Figure 2. Digital transformation in education and its relevance to SEL

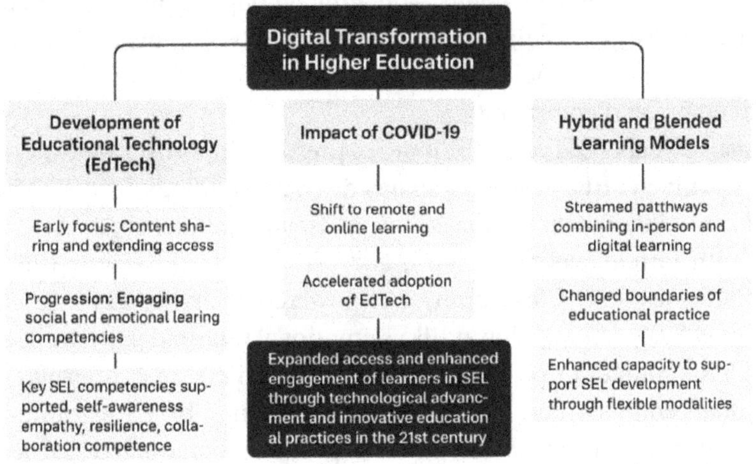

Evolution of Educational Technology (EdTech)

The field of educational technology has taken different pathways, each expanding the definition of teaching and learning(Rout & Bhoi, 2024b; Veckalne & Tambovceva, 2022).

The earliest pathway, emerging at the end of the 20th century, was primarily based on the early computer-assisted instruction, videos, and other very rudimentary multimedia-based tools, designed to replace some of the elements of the typical classroom learning environment with exercises and pictures of educational activities while supplements were offered. These early iterations of educational technology were more focused on the content than any social interactions or emotional development of the process of learning.

In the 2000s, there was a development of web-based teaching and learning platforms, and learning management systems (LMS), such as Moodle, Blackboard, and Google Classroom, that allowed for asynchronous learning and communication between the instructor and student in addition to the primary formalized learning environment. Even while focused on content delivery through media platforms, an increase in interactivity through discussion forums was available, although these platforms provided no intentional social-emotional learning (SEL) opportunities, peer interaction was encouraged, to a certain extent, and student directed engagement, self-directed learning was an option.

The arrival of Web 2.0 technologies marked a transition to participatory, user-generated content and experience. Social media, wikis, blogs, and video-sharing sites enabled learners to creatively express themselves, work together on projects, and interact with various viewpoints—creating an opportunity for utilizing digital SEL practices. These tools helped produce opportunities for developing empathetic practices, cultural understanding, and digital citizenship through the development of online dialogue and community.

In the last 10 years, EdTech's ability to expressly support state-of-the-art social-emotional-learning (SEL) is being enhanced with technology by connecting: individualized, constant, instant feedback (via artificial intelligence, or AI), immersive role-play (with virtual reality, or VR), and affinity-based rewards (via gamified learning platforms, like Class craft). AI-powered analytics provide immediate feedback on such communication skills as emotional tone and patterns in collaboration, while VR simulations provide students with immersion in role-play scenarios that teach them empathy and taking perspective. Game-based learning platforms incorporate cooperation, perseverance, and positive social behaviour as rewards, resulting in an experience that components of state-of-the-art SEL are embedded in the mechanics of learning.

In short, we have observed the continued evolution of EdTech not only as a delivery platform for knowledge, but as a facilitator of human development, so that educators can infuse SEL into both formal and informal learning experiences.

Impact of the COVID-19 Pandemic on SEL Delivery

The COVID-19 pandemic represented a landmark moment in the evolution of technology's relationship with SEL. Nearly overnight, schools of all shapes and sizes were suddenly thrust into remote learning environments, massively accelerating the trajectory of adopting digital tools and fundamentally shifting education's relationship with technology. While remote learning enabled a continuity of academic instruction, it exposed some very real challenges connected to social and emotional learning and students' overall well-being(Goulart et al., 2022).

In traditional classroom spaces, students engage with SEL practices, its objective and purpose, organically on the 'daily' - in group work, activities on the playground, informal conversations and non-verbal cues exchanged between teachers and students. The transition to online instruction disrupted and removed many of those critical student-interaction opportunities and created a feeling of isolation for many learners. Students reported feelings of loneliness, anxiety, and distancing; all of which demonstrated how quickly we need to incorporate SEL into remote and digital learning environments.

Educators reactively trialed proacting virtual SEL: integrating mindfulness practices, committee peer support discussions in shared "virtual" breakout rooms, and using digital journaling tools to invite emotional reflection. Video conferencing platforms (e.g., Zoom, Microsoft Teams) began providing space for educators not only to lecture but to create social spaces, where teachers could inquire about their student's well-being before engaging with academic content.

The COVID-19 pandemic opened up new paths for SEL delivery in multiple ways around the world. For example, there are now AI chatbots that could provide students with real-time, confidential emotional support. There are gamified applications (wellness apps) that encouraged healthy coping strategies. There are online collaborative tools (Padlet and Miro) that provided a virtual creative outlet for group work, which helped develop community and creativity. COVID-19 pointed out that the field has the potential to develop SEL in digital delivery. As long as educators are designing activities that take into account emotional engagement and social connection.

At the same time, the realities of digital equity were put on full display. Students lacking reliable and/or equitable access to a digital education (related primarily to internet access, and access to appropriate devices, while also involved in supportive home environments) were dramatically disadvantaged and typically warned about missing academic content (which was bad enough), let alone all the unfortunate SEL experiences. This also clearly showed a need for policy and infrastructure to assure equitable access to digital SEL.

Shifts Towards Hybrid and Blended Learning Models

As education systems are emerging from pandemic times, many systems are moving toward hybrid and/or blended learning that combines in-person and digital experiences. In doing so, there is much potential to enhance school-based SEL while benefiting from the flexibility, choice, personalization, and other varied modes that can be used to leverage different learning preferences(Akour & Alenezi, 2022; Goulart et al., 2022).

In hybrid learning, SEL is imbedded even across the physical and virtual environments at the same time. For instance, in-person time can explicitly foster and generate safety, trust, rapport, and group collaborative problem-solving and members can use digital platforms such as Seesaw, and Google Classroom. to allow for ongoing implementation of reflection, goal setting, and further communication with colleagues asynchronously allowing for blended opportunities and ways of working collaboratively. Likewise, blended models can create learning communities that extend beyond the actual learning times where students can keep relationships, collaborative projects, and see one another outside of the hours of school.

Hybrid methods of social and emotional learning (SEL) in social work have the benefits of being data-informed personalized, culturally collaborative, and global. For example, digital platforms could monitor learners' engagement, the frequency of collaboration, and the sentiment of communication, which means educators could check in on students demonstrating a need for support. When this is done ethically and without compromising privacy, the data could promote more effective SEL interventions. These models are constructed with care to mitigate the risk of fragmenting experiences. An effective blended SEL model would create a continuum, expanding upon the same emotional and social skills across all learning contexts. Designing an effective blended SEL model requires clearly communicating the purpose of each educator's role, systematically implementing an SEL framework, and coordinating the purpose of the digital activity with the in-class intentions of building relationships that directly impact learning.

Hence, the digital transformation of education has progressed from tools that are limited to content consumption to complex, interactive systems that can directly support SEL. In the context of education, the onset of COVID-19 accelerated this change by demonstrating both the potential, and the pitfalls, of providing SEL digitally. As hybrid and blended learning becomes more common, we have the opportunity to create inclusive and integrated experiences utilizing technology, but still human connection should be a priority, and SEL should be integrated.

TECHNOLOGY-ENABLED PATHWAYS FOR SEL

The role of technology in Social and Emotional Learning (SEL) has changed from a secondary option to a primary teaching strategy that allows educators to design flexible, individualized, and scalable learning opportunities as shown in Figure 3. Today, a depth of digital tools offers new affordances that can help design SEL competencies - whether that is through immersive simulations, online shared spaces, or by means of personalized feedback. This section explores five technology-enhanced pathways: gamification and game-based learning; virtual and augmented reality to building empathy; AI tools to support and provide emotional feedback; social media and online communities to engage in collaborative learning; and the mobile apps with microlearning to support ongoing practice of SEL(Goulart et al., 2022).

Figure 3. Roles of technology in Social and Emotional Learning (SEL)

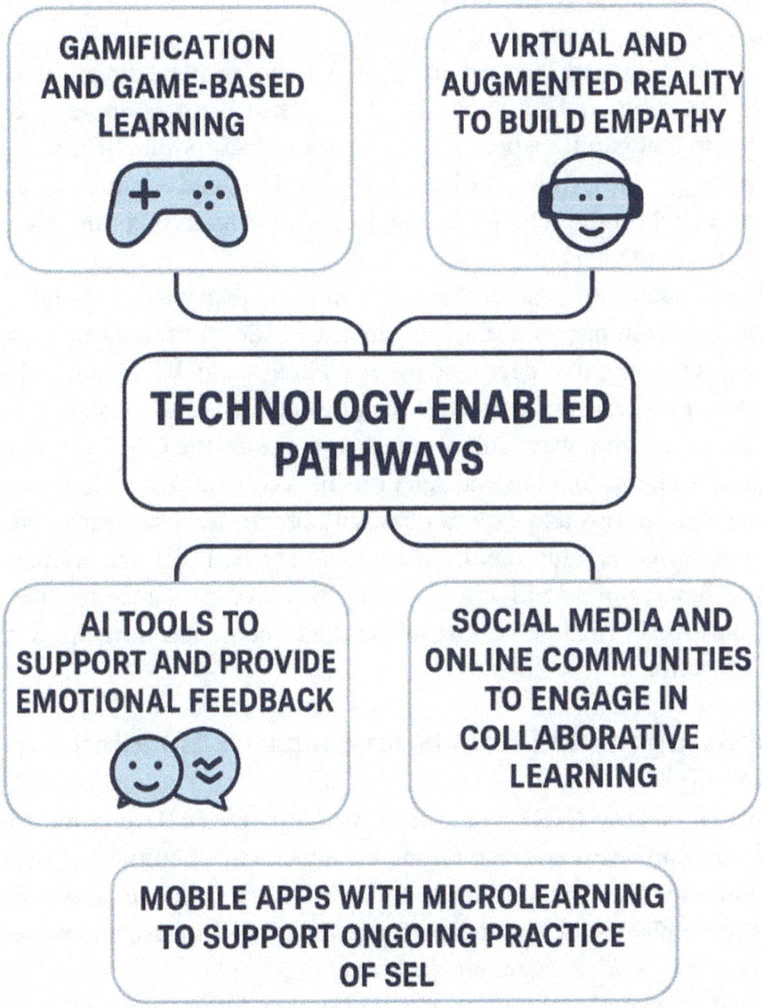

Gamification and Game-Based Learning for SEL

Gamification is the use of game elements (points, leaderboards, badges, quests, etc.) in non-game contexts, while game-based learning involves the use of entire games as the primary mode of instruction. Both gamification and game-based learning can effectively foster SEL by embedding the opportunities for students to develop social and emotional skills while participating in engaging challenges (Akour & Alenezi, 2022; Goulart et al., 2022).

In a gamified SEL setting, students might receive points for not only getting the right answers but also working cooperatively with peers, persisting with tasks, and successfully resolving conflict situations. Class craft is an example of a teacher-created platform that gamifies prosocial behavior to incorporate SEL concepts into classroom management. Minecraft Education Edition is an example of a platform that contains collaborative challenges that require effective communication and empathic attention to peers.

Game-based scenarios also make it possible to experiment socially without repercussion. For example, role-playing games can address situations from the real world—like intervening in a peer dispute or making ethical decisions while under pressure—that allow learners to practice making decisions and managing their emotions in a non-threatening way. This similarly touches on the CASEL competencies of responsible decision-making and relationship skills, making it a powerful way to link artificial scenarios and experiences with practical, behavior-based context.

The turn of phrase is intentional: Successful gamified SEL experiences require intentional design: gamified SEL learning activities should relate to specific learning objectives, not overly focus on competition, and encourage intrinsic, rather than extrinsic, motivation.

Virtual and Augmented Reality for Empathy-Building

Both Virtual Reality (VR) and Augmented Reality (AR) provide immersive experiences that can be exceptional for increasing empathy, cultural sensitivity, and perspective-taking, the foundational skills of SEL. VR contexts allow learners to "walk in someone else's shoes" and experience situations from a person's perspective (Akour & Alenezi, 2022; Mohamed Hashim et al., 2022).

One particular example is Stanford's Virtual Human Interaction Lab which created VR modules for students to live life as a person experiencing homelessness, or a person living with disabilities which can give the learners a level of awareness about social issues. Much similarly to VR, AR applications can layer information about other cultures or historical events onto a physical space and encourage students to think about other perspectives in relation to their current interactions in the world they experience.

One of the most helpful things about VR and AR as tools for empathy-building is how immersive they are, as they take engaging multiple senses to create an emotional connection that reading or discussion may not tap into, especially with not-yet-experienced situations. VR and AR can create environments that would otherwise be impossible or problematic to experience in real life (for example, navigating a refugee camp or witnessing climate change impacts on an at-risk community). Yet, the effectiveness of the approach relies upon placing VR or AR experience in context and that requires some sort of structured debriefing session afterward to help learners to process their experience, connect it to social emotional learning frameworks, and convert any realizations into behaviours.

AI-Powered Tools for Emotional Feedback and Support

AI is changing personalized social emotional learning by giving teachers insight into how students interact, changing dispositions of an emotional nature, and providing feedback. AI can be used to evaluate students' competencies with communication, collaboration, and empathy which allow educators to effectively respond to students' wellbeing. Nevertheless, ethical considerations such as data privacy, transparency and a resistance to trusting algorithmic judgement, must remain prominent in AI-based planning(Goulart et al., 2022).

Social Media and Online Communities for Collaborative Learning

When moderated and organized to encourage positive interactions, social media applications and online communities can support Self-Study (SEL) when students are able to share reflections, respond to their peers, and collaborate on projects. Educational tools such as Edmodo, Flipgrid, and Padlet support students by enabling them to engage as a social community, which allows students the opportunity to develop the social competencies of digital citizenship such as respect, tolerance, and empathy. Initiatives such as PenPal Schools promote global empathy, intercultural empathy and the building of intercultural communication skills. That said, using social media in the classroom must account for the possibility of issues such as cyberbullying, misinformation, and overexposure. Educators should create and explain guidelines about acceptable use, create opportunities for critical digital literacy and practice positive engagement.

Mobile Apps and Microlearning for Continuous SEL Practice

The role of mobile technologies is an important means of supporting the practice of SEL as it has begun to transgress the boundaries of formal learning and into the routines of daily life. Microlearning strategies, which are employed to break larger content into smaller segments, also facilitate the concept of SEL, as continuous practice allows for ongoing reflection as well as skill reinforcement and modification. Apps, such as Mood Meter from Yale Center for Emotional Intelligence, and Smiling Mind, help students track and label the emotions they are experiencing as part of their self-reflection which builds self-awareness skills and fosters emotional vocabulary that SEL does espouse. This enables students to utilize just-in-time SEL, through these mobile apps that cater to students' emotional capacities, as needs arise. The variety of tools, formats and accessibility of mobile tools can support diverse ages and contexts, as well as aid in all aspects of hybrid and blended learning model. For these tools to maximize their impact in mobile learning, SEL tools should be integrated into learning purposefully to ensure fruitful areas of consideration(Rout & Bhoi, 2024b; Soykan et al., 2023; Veckalne & Tambovceva, 2022).

Technology-enabled pathways for social and emotional learning (SEL) offer a range of scalable and varied approaches to build on emotional intelligence empathy, and collaboration. Gamification and game-based learning offer ways to translate abstract skills into dynamic challenges; VR and AR allow us to create experiences that are immersive in building empathy; AI-based tools can generate immediate and personalized emotional feedback; social media can facilitate communities of collaborators; and mobile apps can help to saturate the practice of SEL into daily life. However, enhancing feasibility does not necessarily hinge on the technology alone, rather it requires pedagogical development to incorporate ethically sound practices, including fidelity in decision-making and adhering to existing SEL Frameworks to make sure SEL tools created through technology are used for enhancement and not as a substitute for equitable and deeply human processes that are vital in the development and growth of children's' Social and Emotional Well-Being.

BEST PRACTICES

SEL in Virtual Classrooms: Lessons from Global Initiatives

International programs have shown that Social and Emotional Learning can be achieved in virtual classrooms, if it is purposeful and thoughtfully designed, and facilitated well. As part of its Future of Education and Skills Project, the OECD explored programs such as the program, which connects classrooms across the globe through collaborative projects, with a focus on empathy and cultural awareness through intentionally designed, structured exchange experiences. The Learning Passport, developed by UNICEF, has also integrated SEL into the digital learning platform, and provided displaced and distance learners an opportunity to pause and reflect emotionally before continuing in their studies. Some insight from these examples, and other experiences learning online, include, the following: structured blocks of SEL time must be delivered in online classes, students should have intentional opportunities to interact with their peers in the virtual space that are carefully designed to the needs of students, and teachers need to be trained in virtual facilitation skills that connect students emotionally with what they are learning(Greenberg, 2023)

Technology-Supported Peer Mentoring and Emotional Support Systems

Technology-enhanced peer mentoring programs can help strengthen relationship skills, resilience, and belonging. Chronus, MentorCity, and other similar platforms have built marketplaces for peer-to-peer support, creating structured and monitored peer-to-peer mentoring programs where older students mentor younger students in both academic and emotional learning. Asynchronous ways to connect, like instant messaging, using video to connect face to face, and real-time applications to work together digitally can help educate mentors and offer on-going encouragement, model positive coping strategies, and share experiences(Jones et al., 2025). The most effective systems nurture successful relationship-building through regular check-ins, guided conversation prompts, and group, individual, and peer success goals aligned with emotional and academic learning, ensuring emotional learning is considered equally to academic learning. Technology and Peer mentoring programs can also support these systems with AI-based tools to flag early signs of emotional distress and prompt relevant interventions, as long as privacy processes are in place for users in this space.

Inclusive Digital SEL Programs for Marginalized Learners

Inclusive social-emotional learning (SEL) initiatives acknowledge that marginalized learners—including those from low-income or rural backgrounds and those in conflict-affected areas—often do not have the opportunity to participate in traditional SEL practices or programming. Digital platforms Education provide offline-capable SEL content, allowing learners to engage with SEL in low-connectivity locations. Content is locally sourced and adapted, and delivered in multiple languages, increasing relevance and access. Programs that address the principles of Universal Design for Learning (UDL)—including provision for multiple means of engagement, representation, and expression—can better accommodate diverse learners' needs, including learners with disabilities. In partnership with community organizations, inclusive programming blends digital and in-person SEL offerings with local support networks(Cipriano et al., 2023).

STRATEGIC FRAMEWORK FOR IMPLEMENTING DIGITAL SEL

A successful merger of social and emotional learning (SEL) into digital education contexts requires the intentional and holistic combination of pedagogy, technology and relationships with people as shown in Figure 4. Digital tools have great potential to facilitate SEL, but their potential depends on intentional design, use of existing SEL frameworks, readiness among educators, and continual monitoring and evaluation. This section presents a strategic framework across four important dimensions: pedagogical design principles, integration of curriculum and assessment, teacher professional development, and systems for monitoring and evaluating(Karthikeyan et al., 2024).

Figure 4. Strategic framework for implementing digital SEL

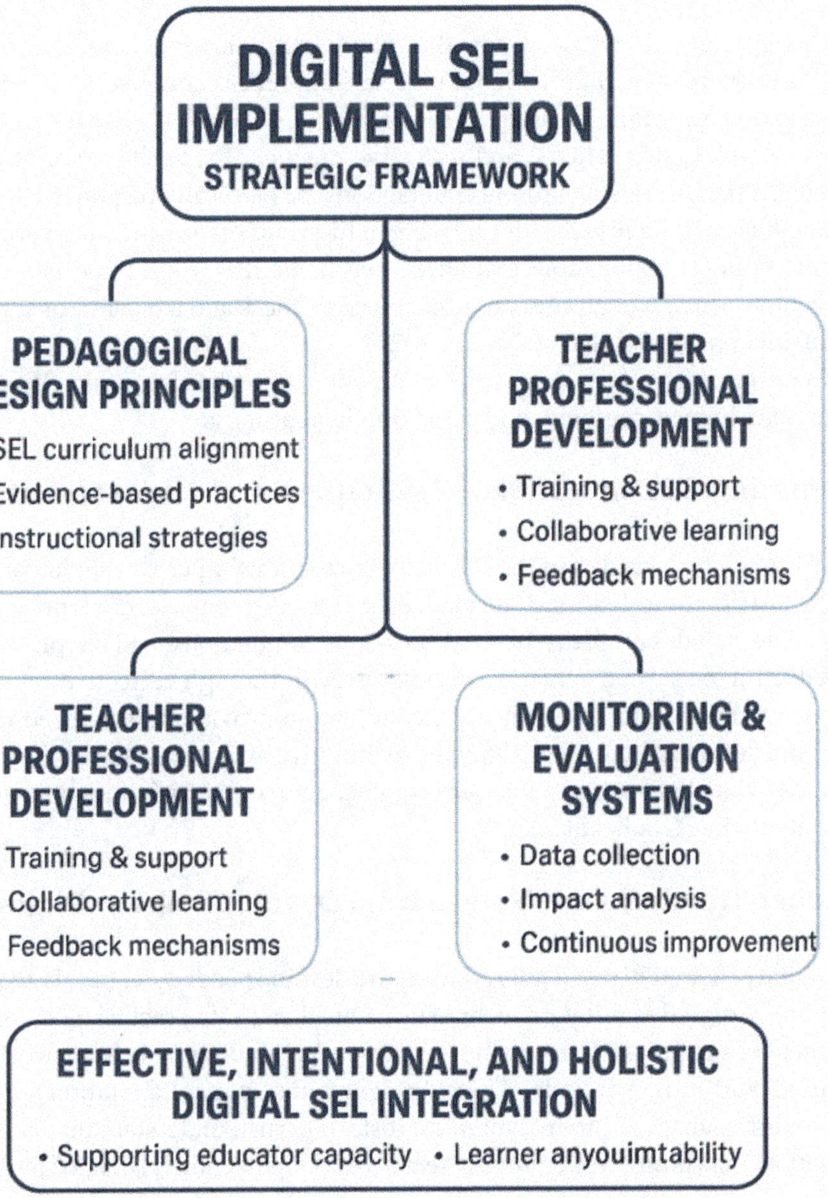

Pedagogical Design Principles for Tech-Enabled SEL

This highlights the advocacy for taking digital activities, practices, and knowledge to a place where they align with our core self-awareness competencies, experience active and experiential learning of the creativity of the digital space through the use of role-play, simulations, and reflective practices, experience social presence and connection using synchronous interactions, be culturally responsive by leading with no bias, and be mindful of both screen time and offline practice with the idea being to promote applications and reflections in the real world of online situations. The content also advocates for cultural responsiveness and a balance of screen time and offline practice(Kalaiselvi et al., 2024).

These principles ensure that the integration of technology into SEL remains intentional, human-centered, and contextually appropriate.

Integrating SEL into Digital Curriculum and Assessment

SEL must be included in the digital curriculum using cross-curricular integration, scenario-based learning, formative SEL assessments, and adaptive learning tools. This includes empathy-based discussions, simulations, and interactive stories embedded in academic subjects, tracking growth through reflective journals and peer assessments, and AI-enhanced technology to provide personalized feedback. Assessment should include qualitative/ quantitative assessment to provide feedback about emotional growth and measures of engagement, participation and quality of peer interaction(Gopi et al., 2024).

Teacher Training and Professional Development in Digital SEL

Digital SEL initiatives require educators to develop pedagogical skills, technology integration, digital facilitation techniques, ethical and safe practice, and continuous learning communities. These skills include understanding SEL frameworks, using gamified platforms, VR tools, AI feedback systems, and collaboration apps, building rapport, managing group dynamics, fostering trust, understanding data privacy regulations, and promoting culturally sensitive communication. Blended professional development models, including live workshops, online modules, and peer mentoring, can help teachers effectively integrate digital SEL into their practice(Rajkumar et al., 2024; Sarkar, Shandilya, et al., 2025).

Monitoring, Evaluation, and Impact Measurement

Continuous monitoring and evaluation are essential for successful digital SEL initiatives. Ongoing evaluation allows for responses that are relevant and timely in relation to meet the learners' needs and meet the initiative's desired outcomes. Relevant evaluation frameworks can include baseline and follow-up assessments, stakeholder evaluation feedback, learning analytics, well-being indicators, and quality improvement cycles. There are ethical ways to collect and safeguard data collection, especially where students' emotional data is concerned. Evaluation frameworks provide clarity about rates of access, frequencies of collaboration, and trends in participants' communication and sentiment (e.g. google Meets Chat).

To conclude, scaling digital SEL means you are developing a framework that incorporates pedagogically appropriate examples of digital engagement as part of the curriculum, supports development of educator capacity to develop their practice around effective how of engaging with their students, and include an effective monitoring framework to provide feedback. When the digital engagement framework is informed by these guidelines, the potential for technology to amplify SEL scale and reach is possible, creating a 'learning' environment that has mental health benefits to utilities in an academically enriched, emotively relevant way to prepare students to thrive in an interconnected world that is rapidly changing.

CHALLENGES AND ETHICAL CONSIDERATIONS

The involvement of Social and Emotional Learning (SEL) in digital spaces offers incredible possibilities but also allows very complex challenges to be considered in a way that leverages the components of digital to create equitable, safe, and culturally responsive forms of SEL(Gopi et al., 2024; Kalaiselvi et al., 2024).

Digital Divide and Access Inequality

Access is perhaps the most prominent barrier to digital SEL: The digital divide results from social, economic, and political barriers to things like devices, internet access, and digital literacies. Students from low-income, remote, or marginalized communities may face challenges that prevent them from having the infrastructure to fully participate in online SEL. This will contribute to the already existing inequities of the education system and diminish the possibilities for developing skills, especially skills such as collaboration and empathy, that are learnt through active inference at every level of learning. To continue expanding access to SEL for all learners requires a real investment in connectivity, low-bandwidth solutions, and platforms that allow offline access(Krishnamoorthy et al., 2025; Sarkar, Mahamuni, et al., 2025; Venkatasubramanian et al., 2024).

Data Privacy, Security, and Emotional Data Ethics

Digital SEL often includes the collection of sensitive emotional and behavioral data through various means, such as AI-enabled sentiment analysis, reflective logs, or monitoring peers. These insights can provide Personalized Learning with emotional data; however, emotional data raises several implications regarding privacy, consent, liability, and misuse of sensitive data. Emotional data related to students is personal information. Any breach may have lasting, life-altering reputational or psychological ramifications for students. Ethical frameworks need to guide the storage, transfer, and sharing of information related to emotional data and regulations need to be followed (GDPR, COPPA, etc). Schools and EdTech need to engage and use appropriate consent practices, anonymization, and set limitations on the use of emotional insights.

Risk of Over-Reliance on Technology for Human-Centered Learning

Technology can play a role in enhancing SEL, but excessive dependence on digital SEL risks weakening the art of SEL that is human-centered. Human-centered empathy, subtle emotional attunement and relational trust can be very difficult to achieve in fully digital environments. Without paired offline SEL activity and human interaction, digital SEL may devolve into a transactional experience that relies on algorithmic prompts instead of richer emotional frameworks. In the best case, we merge technology with teacher-facilitated inquiry and community action where teacher-learners can have tangible experiences, islanded to contextualize their digital SEL learning relationally.

Cultural Sensitivity in Digital SEL Content

SEL competencies and expressions of emotion are influenced by cultural norms and a standardized digital curriculum poses potential misalignment or alienation. Different communities are likely to demonstrate stark differences in communication styles, conflict resolution, and emotional expression. For this reason, these global SEL platforms must provide bilingual and culturally contextualized content, involving local educators in co-creating resources to make culturally relevant. By taking a culturally responsive approach, SEL platforms will not only improve student engagement by taking into account their lifestyle and beliefs, but they can also avoid reinforcing cultural bias or potentially promoting beliefs that may be misaligned to students' current context.

Figure 5. Future directions and emerging trends in Social and Emotional Learning (SEL)

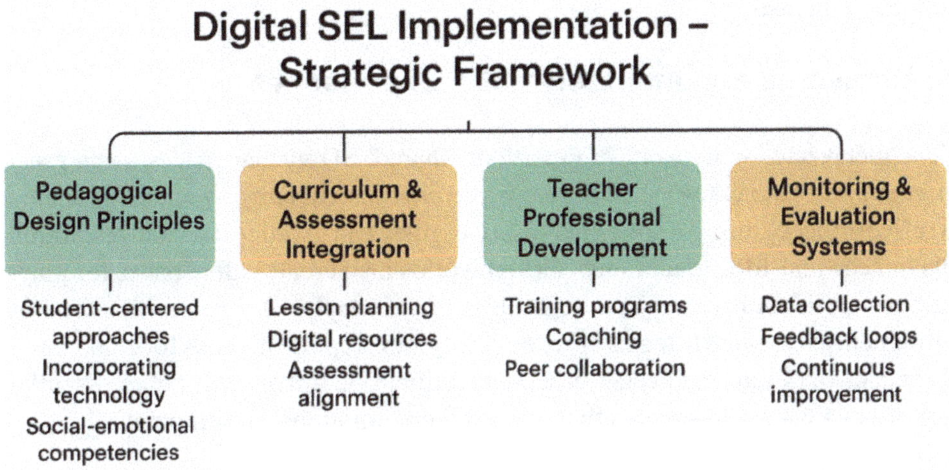

FUTURE DIRECTIONS AND EMERGING TRENDS

The field of Social and Emotional Learning (SEL) is poised to transform as technology continues to develop as a modality that can yield deep personalization, broad developer reach, and high user engagement as illustrated in Figure 5. The future of digital SEL will most likely include new innovation and development that balances human empathy with artificial intelligence capabilities to shape environments where social and emotional growth is cultivated as an inherent part of everyday learning(Sarkar, Shandilya, et al., 2025; Vaithianathan et al., 2025; Yadav et al., 2025).

AI and Emotional Intelligence in Learning Analytics

The ability of artificial intelligence (AI) to detect emotional intelligence, including voice tone, facial expressions, and diction, is extremely sophisticated. In the context of SEL, AI can provide educators with real-time learning analytics to detect students' emotional status. This can help identify disengagement, distress, loneliness, social isolation, or similar signals. The technology could prompt recommendations for activities that are most aligned with individuals' needs (e.g., "mindful breathing" as opposed to "joining a peer support task group"). Nevertheless, this development requires robust ethical standards to accompany learning analytics systems for emotional data collection, reporting, and ultimately using professionalism and ethical constructs needed to interpret what emotional data AI will suggest to teachers—AI should never fully replace human judgment in the process of making sense of emotional data analysis.

The Metaverse and Immersive SEL Experiences

The metaverse—a network of persistent, shared, 3D virtual spaces—is a great opportunity for immersive SEL. Students can practice empathy by entering avatars that reflect other cultural or social perspectives; they can practice conflict-resolution skills in near-real-life simulations. Virtual worlds also create safer spaces for play-acting and collaborative projects regardless of geography. As we see this type of environment get applied in terms of accessibility, developing methods for embedding SEL frameworks into metaverse-based educational platforms will be an essential safeguard against environments that distract from emotional development.

Cross-Sector Collaborations for Scalable SEL Solutions

No one entity can achieve sustainable scalable and effective digital SEL alone, including school systems. The only way to achieve scalable and effective digital social-emotional learning is through collaboration outside of the education system, with companies, governments, non-government organizations, mental health organizations, and community organizations coming together to co-create culturally relevant and inclusive SEL solutions. Together, we can bridge access gaps, collaborate on research, establish best practices around the world. Open source/digital SEL, co-designed training programs with mutual metrics around emotional wellbeing are ways to give flexibility, equity, and sustainability to digital SEL in different contexts.

CONCLUSION

The combination of social and emotional learning (SEL) with digital technologies presents a real transformation in how learning recognizes and meets the whole needs of learners. By utilizing technologies and tools like, AI-enhanced tracking and analytics, immersive virtual environments, gamification, and inclusive apps, educators are empowered to design lively, tailored, culturally relevant pathways for emotional and social development.

However, as we have explored in this chapter, the potential of digital SEL comes along with the tensions we need to consider. If we are going to build trust, foster long-term effectiveness, and encourage social and emotional growth with technology, we need to be aware of the realities of the digital divide, emotional data privacy, not replacing human connection with reliance on technology, and cultural responsiveness. These tensions remind us that technology is not a substitute for human connection, but it can be a purposeful tool when used thoughtfully and appropriately. The future will unfold through the use of AI-enhanced emotional intelligence tools, metaverse-based immersive environment experiences, and intersectoral partnerships that scale SLE solutions but maintain human-centered values. Success in this space requires attention to pedagogical design, ready teacher preparedness, ongoing action research, and sincere partnerships between educators, tech leaders, and communities.

When all is said and done, our aim isn't to digitize social and emotional learning; rather our aim is to humanize digital learning spaces, so that empathy, resilience, collaboration, and self-awareness are modelled and imbued in every learner's educational experience. By doing this, we can strive to prepare learners not only for academic success but more importantly the emotional complexities of the interconnected world.

REFERENCES

Akour, M., & Alenezi, M. (2022). Higher education future in the era of digital transformation. *Education Sciences, 12*(11), 784. DOI: 10.3390/educsci12110784

Chouhan, N., Khan, A., Shah, J. Z., Hussnain, M., & Khan, M. W. (2021). Deep convolutional neural network and emotional learning based breast cancer detection using digital mammography. *Computers in Biology and Medicine, 132*, 104318. DOI: 10.1016/j.compbiomed.2021.104318 PMID: 33744608

Cipriano, C., Strambler, M. J., Naples, L. H., Ha, C., Kirk, M., Wood, M., Sehgal, K., Zieher, A. K., Eveleigh, A., McCarthy, M., Funaro, M., Ponnock, A., Chow, J. C., & Durlak, J. (2023). The state of evidence for social and emotional learning: A contemporary meta-analysis of universal school-based SEL interventions. *Child Development, 94*(5), 1181–1204. DOI: 10.1111/cdev.13968 PMID: 37448158

Erstad, O., Černochová, M., Knezek, G., Furuta, T., Takami, K., & Liang, C. (2024). Social and Emotional Modes of Learning Within Digital Ecosystems: Emerging Research Agendas. *Technology. Knowledge and Learning, 29*(4), 1751–1766. DOI: 10.1007/s10758-024-09775-w

Gopi, B., Kokila, M. S., Bibin, C. V., Sasikala, D., Howard, E., & Boopathi, S. (2024). Distributed technologies using AI/ML techniques for healthcare applications. In *Social Innovations in Education, Environment, and Healthcare* (pp. 375–396). IGI Global.

Goulart, V. G., Liboni, L. B., & Cezarino, L. O. (2022). Balancing skills in the digital transformation era: The future of jobs and the role of higher education. *Industry and Higher Education, 36*(2), 118–127. DOI: 10.1177/09504222211029796

Greenberg, M. T. (2023). *Evidence for social and emotional learning in schools.* Learning Policy Institute. DOI: 10.54300/928.269

John, A., & Bates, S. (2024). Barriers and facilitators: The contrasting roles of media and technology in social–emotional learning. *Social and Emotional Learning: Research, Practice, and Policy, 3*, 100022. DOI: 10.1016/j.sel.2023.100022

Jones, S. M., McGarrah, M. W., & Kahn, J. (2025). Social and emotional learning: A principled science of human development in context. In *Social and Emotional Learning* (pp. 4–19). Routledge. DOI: 10.4324/9781003054573-2

Kalaiselvi, D., Ramaratnam, M., Kokila, S., Sarkar, R., Anandakumar, S., & Boopathi, S. (2024). Future developments of higher education on social psychology: Innovation and changes. In *Social Innovations in Education, Environment, and Healthcare* (pp. 146–169). IGI Global.

Karthikeyan, M., Vigilia, J. N., Sequeira, S. L., Priya, P. V., Ghamande, M. V., & Boopathi, S. (2024). NBA Implementation Across Engineering Disciplines for Driving Social Changes in India. In *Social Innovations in Education, Environment, and Healthcare* (pp. 240–265). IGI Global. DOI: 10.4018/979-8-3693-2569-8.ch012

Krishnamoorthy, N., Chandrasekar, J., Saqib, M., Therasa, P., Ganesh, C. S., & Boopathi, S. (2025). The Role of CO-PO Mapping in NBA Accreditation Assessments: Enhancing Educational Quality and Outcomes. In *Hispanic Leadership in Higher Education* (pp. 89–118). IGI Global.

Lipschitz, J. M., Pike, C. K., Hogan, T. P., Murphy, S. A., & Burdick, K. E. (2023). The engagement problem: A review of engagement with digital mental health interventions and recommendations for a path forward. *Current Treatment Options in Psychiatry*, *10*(3), 119–135. DOI: 10.1007/s40501-023-00297-3 PMID: 38390026

Meng, Q., Yan, Z., Abbas, J., Shankar, A., & Subramanian, M. (2025). Human–computer interaction and digital literacy promote educational learning in pre-school children: Mediating role of psychological resilience for kids' mental well-being and school readiness. *International Journal of Human-Computer Interaction*, *41*(1), 16–30. DOI: 10.1080/10447318.2023.2248432

Mohamed Hashim, M. A., Tlemsani, I., & Matthews, R. (2022). Higher education strategy in digital transformation. *Education and Information Technologies*, *27*(3), 3171–3195. DOI: 10.1007/s10639-021-10739-1 PMID: 34539217

Oliveira, K. K. de S., & De Souza, R. A. (2022). Digital transformation towards education 4.0. *Informatics in Education*, *21*(2), 283–309.

Rajkumar, V., Boopathi, S., & Jatav, S. S. (2024). Empowerment of Fisherwomen through Self-Help Groups: A Multidimensional Impact Assessment in Thoothukudi, Tamil Nadu, India. *Indian Journal of Extension Education*, *60*(4), 47–52. DOI: 10.48165/IJEE.2024.60409

Rout, B., & Bhoi, M. T. (2024a). SEL and Technology: The Role of Digital Tools in Promoting Emotional and Social Skills. *International Journal for Research in Applied Science and Engineering Technology*, *12*(12), 1584–1512. DOI: 10.22214/ijraset.2024.66086

Rout, B., & Bhoi, M. T. (2024b). SEL and Technology: The Role of Digital Tools in Promoting Emotional and Social Skills. *International Journal for Research in Applied Science and Engineering Technology*, *12*(12), 1584–1512. DOI: 10.22214/ijraset.2024.66086

Sarkar, R., Mahamuni, V. S., Chitra, M., Vijayakumar, M., Jefferson, K., & Boopathi, S. (2025). Integrating Innovation Tools and Technology in Educational Management. In *Planning Tools for Policy, Leadership, and Management of Education Systems* (pp. 121–154). IGI Global.

Sarkar, R., Shandilya, S., Anand, T., Sri, R. R., Dhanaraj, K., & Boopathi, S. (2025). Best Practices and Frameworks for Higher Education: Optimizing Learning Progressions Using Recent Tools. In *Driving Quality Education Through AI and Data Science* (pp. 51–72). IGI Global Scientific Publishing.

Setia, S., Tichy, M., Gilbert, F., & Tichy, M. L. (2024). Innovating social-emotional learning to enhance positive engagement of youth with social media: A comprehensive review of why and how. *Cureus*, *16*(9). Advance online publication. DOI: 10.7759/cureus.70130 PMID: 39463555

Soykan, E., Bastas, M., & Çakici, A. (2023). Digital transformation of education in the COVID-19 process and its psychological effects on children. *Frontiers in Education*, *8*, 1117458. DOI: 10.3389/feduc.2023.1117458

Tapalova, O., & Zhiyenbayeva, N. (2022). Artificial intelligence in education: AIEd for personalised learning pathways. *Electronic Journal of e-Learning*, *20*(5), 639–653. DOI: 10.34190/ejel.20.5.2597

Triyono, M. B., Mutohhar, F., Kholifah, N., Nurtanto, M., Subakti, H., & Prasetya, K. H. (2023). Examining the mediating-moderating role of entrepreneurial orientation and digital competence on entrepreneurial intention In vocational education. *Journal of Technical Education and Training*, *15*(1), 116–127. DOI: 10.30880/jtet.2023.15.01.011

Vaithianathan, V., Shastri, D. S., Nandakumar, V., Misba, M., Kumar, P. S., & Boopathi, S. (2025). NEP Policy Implementation Strategies in Education in India. In *Educational Philosophy and Sociological Foundation of Education* (pp. 325–356). IGI Global.

Veckalne, R., & Tambovceva, T. (2022). The role of digital transformation in education in promoting sustainable development. *Virtual Economics*, *5*(4), 65–86. DOI: 10.34021/ve.2022.05.04(4)

Venkatasubramanian, V., Chitra, M., Sudha, R., Singh, V. P., Jefferson, K., & Boopathi, S. (2024). Examining the Impacts of Course Outcome Analysis in Indian Higher Education: Enhancing Educational Quality. In *Challenges of Globalization and Inclusivity in Academic Research* (pp. 124–145). IGI Global Scientific Publishing.

Yadav, U., Pitchai, R., Gopal, V., Kumar, K. S., Talukdar, M., & Boopathi, S. (2025). Powers of Higher Education Leadership: Navigating Policy and Management in Academic Institutions. In *Navigating Leadership and Policy Management in Education* (pp. 103–136). IGI Global.

APPENDIX

SEL – Social and Emotional Learning
AI – Artificial Intelligence
VR – Virtual Reality
COVID – Coronavirus Disease
OECD – Organization for Economic Co-operation and Development
CASEL – Collaborative for Academic, Social, and Emotional Learning
UNESCO – United Nations Educational, Scientific and Cultural Organization
GCED – Global Citizenship Education
LMS – Learning Management System
AR – Augmented Reality
UNICEF – United Nations International Children's Emergency Fund
UDL – Universal Design for Learning
GDPR – General Data Protection Regulation
COPPA – Children's Online Privacy Protection Act
SLE – Social Learning Environment

Chapter 8

Microlearning and Nano-Learning in Transforming Pedagogy in the Digital Education Era

Dolly Misra

Department of Management, Aarupadai Veedu Institute of Technology, Vinayaka Mission's Research Foundation, Chennai, India

Rohini Ramesh Chandge

School of Business Management, JSPM university, Pune, India

T. P. Saravanan

https://orcid.org/0000-0002-6881-0929

Department of Management Studies, Nandha Engineering College, Erode, India

J. Rajini

https://orcid.org/0000-0002-5080-7545

Department of English, Kongu Engineering College, Erode, India

A. Arulmozhi

Department of Physics, St. Joseph's College of Engineering, Chennai, India

Pooja Rani

https://orcid.org/0000-0002-6563-4704

University Institute of Teachers Training and Research, Chandigarh University, Mohali, India

M. Kumari

https://orcid.org/0009-0006-2989-9883

SRM University, India

ABSTRACT

Micro and nano learning are changing education today, bringing bite-sized and focused learning short units that are made with today's digital learner in mind. With multimedia, they can use mobile, and interactive content, ensuring flexibility and engagement and allowing just-in-time knowledge acquisition. Micro and nano

DOI: 10.4018/979-8-3373-5157-5.ch008

learning leverage principles of cognitive science and are proven to lead to better retention of learning when implemented using spaced repetition principles and contextually relevant learning. In the digital education era, the micro-formats support personalized learning pathways, skill-based training, and opportunities for rapid upskilling. This chapter will focus on theoretical foundations, technological enablers, and practical possibilities for microlearning and nanolearning, and discuss their impact on lifelong learning, corporate learning, and formal education context while acknowledging the challenges of design, assessment opportunities, and opportunities for integration into larger educational ecosystems.

INTRODUCTION

The rapid pace of change in information technologies has transformed education, creating a shift in how information is created, delivered, and consumed. In a hyperconnected world with information overload, shorter attention spans, and increasingly personalized learner needs, the overall model for instruction is under review. Microlearning and nano-learning are the two leading innovations changing education today. Both of which reduce curriculum into bite-sized learning content. Both approaches cater to the new learning patterns of students emerging today, while also taking full advantage of the affordances of digital technologies and learning platforms, making learning flexible, fun, and on-demand. Microlearning is typically referring to small chunks of learning content designed for a precision or about a specific skills, concept, or dissertation of knowledge(Bhowmick & Sarma, 2021).

Nano-learning takes this compact learning a step further, delivering ultra-short learning events - often in less than two minutes - meant to be easily consumed and immediately applied. The transition from longer, more traditional forms of direct instruction, to smaller and more modular forms of instructional resources, reflects the advancement of technology as well as a shift in learner behavior. The acceptance of rapid approaches to learning as a valid process reflects contemporary notions of why learning is important in a sustainable, globalized economy, proving further that quickly and adaptively acquiring new skills is no longer a competitive advantage in a knowledge economy but essential for performance. Educators, trainers in the performance development context, as well as instructional designers for example, are increasingly adopting micro- and nano-learning approaches to respond to these higher expectations in our rapidly changing world and society. They are relevant for digital learners who consume and process learning from social platforms, video streams, and mobile applications in small media-intensive pieces of information. From a pedagogical perspective, micro- and nano-learning is aligned with many principles of effective learning, including the principles of cognitive load theory and chunking, as well as the tendency of spaced repetition, which makes them an effective approach to retention and transfer of knowledge(Khlaif & Salha, 2021).

There is less cognitive load in large topics when broken into smaller chunks that are small enough to encourage deep learning by small wins towards mastery. Further, these formats can be personalized and provide adaptive learning journeys for each learner to receive content according to social, experiential, and performance preferences, plus learning goals. In other words, we access small learning at the point of need which takes advantage of just-in-time training, in the corporate environment while combining the resources to create maximum productivity with minimal down-time. In formal education, micro- and nano-learning can add value as supplementary materials, reinforce knowledge and instructions from the classroom, or provide remedial learning when the prescribed curriculum cannot be completed(KAYALAR, 2022).

The emergence of mobile learning channels, cloud-based learning management systems (LMS), and artificial intelligence-assisted content distribution has increased the availability and scalability of these approaches, increasing the possibility of applying them across a wide range of educational situations and learner populations. They are not without obstacles, however- shaping content to be both short and pedagogically sound requires thoughtful instructional design, possible innovative use of multimedia, and alignment with identifiable learning objectives. In addition, when assessing in short formats, one must consider a diverse array of assessment types, and abandon the mindset of testing (e.g., traditional exams and quizzes) to consider micro-assessment opportunities, simulations, or interactive exercises. While being brief is certainly an advantage, it can also be a weakness if the micro-units are not connected together to form a coherent learning pathway that will actually build towards higher order thinking and result in skill synthesis(Dwinggo Samala et al., 2023).

While educational institutions and organizations are adopting these approaches, there is increasing demand for frameworks that ensure that the use of micro-and nano-learning is effective, scalable, and aligned to other educational frameworks. The COVID-19 pandemic has also accelerated the growth of micro-and nano-learning, as remote and hybrid approaches to learning demonstrated the need for less rigid and more accessible and flexible styles of learning. The shift to global remote and hybrid learning emphasized the need to be resilient and adaptable as educational systems, and the opportunity for formats that can be quickly created and modified. Additionally, the growth of artificial intelligence and data analytics, and the availability of new immersive technologies such as augmented and virtual reality, will help create new learning opportunities in micro-and nano-learning, especially with the interactive, context-aware, and experiential opportunities available. For example, AI-based media recommendation engines can read and respond to learner performance and change or adjust assets or sequences "on-the-fly", and AR and VR immersive experiences can deliver micro-experiences or opportunities to replicate real situations in small and engaging ways(Pham et al., 2023).

Micro- and nano-learning are developing into key elements (not merely adjuncts) of a learner-centered, technology-enabled pedagogic approach which has now grown exponentially in strength, sophistication and interest. They combine theory, digital possibilities and practical need to provide scalable and responsive learning options to a range of users. This chapter examines the origins, theory and practical details of microlearning and nano-learning to illustrate their potential for changing our educational practices and processes in the digital age. The important presumptions, design principles and digital developments which allow for pragmatically meaningful use of micro- and nano-learning are discussed, as are the constraints and challenges that will be involved in addressing their full potential(Desiderio et al., 2024).

By investigating real-world case studies, emerging trends, and future pathways, this work will encumber applicable understanding as to how educators, instructional designers, and policy makers may engage micro- and nano-learning to create learning environments that are more efficient, engaging, and inclusive. Micro- and nano-learning is indicative of a broader transition in education which de-emphasizes one-size-fits-all and allows for the flexibility, personalization, and learner agency to advance their education: it's plausible that this trend will capture the next chapter in teaching and learning in the digital age(Silva et al., 2025).

BACKGROUND: THEORETICAL FOUNDATIONS

The rise of microlearning and nano-learning to become the predominant forms of pedagogy in the digital educational period is founded in general educational theories and basic principles of neuroscience and cognitive science as shown in Figure 1. The theories will not only explain the basis for the effectiveness of these short-form learning formats, but they will also guide the design and development of the micro-learning and nano-learning interventions to optimize learner engagement, retention and application of the material. There are 4 theoretical perspectives: Cognitive Load Theory and Chunking, the Principles of Spaced Repetition, Adult Learning Theory (Andragogy), and Constructivist and Connectivism Perspectives which provide the theoretical basis for microlearning and nano-learning(Denojean-Mairet et al., 2024).

Figure 1. Background for microlearning and nano-learning

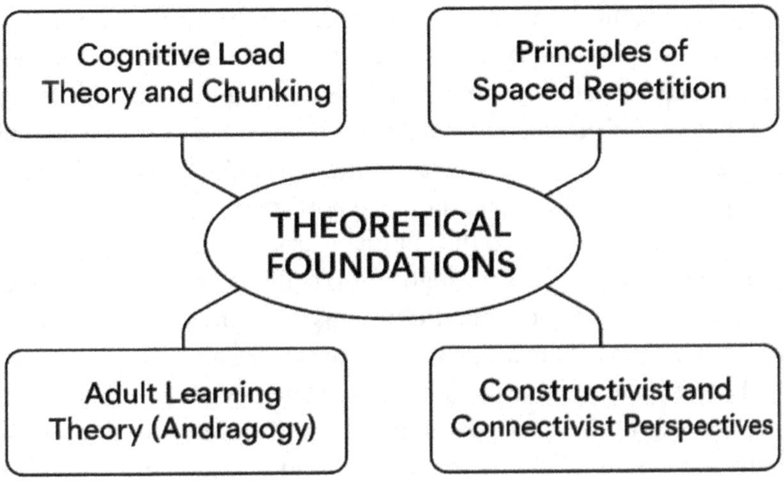

Cognitive Load Theory and Chunking

Cognitive Load Theory (CLT) developed by John Sweller and colleagues in the 1980s, posits that the human brain has a limited amount of capacity to process information in working memory. When cognitive capacity is exceeded, learning occurs, but comprehension is reduced. Microlearning and nano-learning directly address this limitation by compartmentalizing complex subject matters into smaller, manageable segments, known as "chunking." Chunking may allow information to be processed and encoded into long-term memory by limiting the extraneous cognitive load and allowing the learner to concentrate on intrinsic and germane cognitive load. In practice, chunking may facilitate the organization of learning material into independent, identifiable units of material that can be consumed individually, yet all contribute to a larger learning objective(Sarkar, Shandilya, et al., 2025). For example, an instructor may decide to create four 10-minute microlearning modules to supplement a 60-minute lecture on data analysis, with each module representing its own skill. This form of learning is more in line with the learner's cognitive capacity, which is likely to increase understanding and retention(Denojean-Mairet et al., 2024; Desiderio et al., 2024).

Principles of Spaced Repetition

Another strong cognitive science principle that supports micro- and nano-learning is spaced repetition. Spaced repetition based on the research of Hermann Ebbinghaus on the forgetting curve states that information is better remembered when reviewed over spaced intervals of time than when it is reviewed all at once in a high intensity. Microlearning modules lend themselves well to spaced repetition in that the time it takes to approve or revisit the learning is short, making it easy to consume the concept more often. In addition to this, online learning platforms can automate the schedules of spaced repetition, using algorithms to decide review intervals based on the learner's performance. Spaced repetition helps counteract the natural forgetting of memory and strengthens pathways, which decreases the amount of work that has to be done by the learner to retrieve the information later. For example, many language learning applications utilize nano-learning flashcards that pop up at spaced intervals that gradually increase to allow for the practice and retention of vocabulary. When spaced repetition is used with chunking, taking advantage of short-form learning becomes more than just a “one-off” learning experience; it becomes a process of learning that helps individuals to achieve long-term mastery(Denojean-Mairet et al., 2024).

Adult Learning Theory (Andragogy)

Adult learning theory, or andagogy, developed by Malcolm Knowles provides an important perspective on the significance of micro- and nano-learning in professional and lifelong education. In proposing his principles of adult learning, Knowles identified things like self-directed learning, drawing from prior experience, readiness to learn, and favoring problem-centered learning. Adults usually want to learn when the content is immediately useful to their work or personal objectives, and they want to be autonomous and self-regulate their learning versus following more traditional instructional learning events. Microlearning allows consumers to have short instructional events as part of the seriously shortened module, and they can do this at any time, which allows adult learners to self-regulated their learning via pacing, sequence, and extent in other learning contexts. In a corporate learning situation, an employee can stable a 5-min training video, just in time for them to perform the work they want to learn: this is probably the most autonomous and self-directing form of learning— 5 mins prior. Respecting the principles of Andragogy from Knows, micro- and nano-learning forms allow access to high-value resources for adult learners without excessive cognitive or trauma load.

Constructivist and Connectivism Perspectives

Constructivism understands learning as active knowledge construction by the learner as they have experiences, reflect, and build on knowledge, not by receiving it. Microlearning and nano-learning could be designed to align with a constructivist model using interactive scenarios, simulations, and problem-solving learning activities to encourage active learning. For example, a Learning Module on project management may present a real-world problem for learners to use a tool(s) and concepts, in a simulated learning environment. Connectivism, a more recent theory put forward by George Siemens and Stephen Downes, focuses on learning as acquiring knowledge from a distributed network of information, in which technology and social connection support newly acquired knowledge in a digital age. Micro-learning and nano-learning are fundamentally aligned with connectivism models, since learners begin to embed microlearning experience in online learning communities, share from their own social platforms, and integrate their learning into personal learning networks (PLNs). Learners do not just consume hugely miniaturized content, they curate, remix, and distribute it to allow for an ever-evolving knowledge exchange cycle. Continuous and socially connected learning experiences support the modular, shareable nature of microlearning, or even further, nano-learning facilitated learning opportunities. In networked, collegial environments, micro- and nano-learning experiences are especially relevant(Chamorro-Atalaya et al., 2024).

In summary, Exploring the theoretical basis of microlearning and nano-learning has demonstrated that these are intentional pedagogies, based on decades of research about how humans learn best, not simply a result of digital convenience. Utilizing cognitive load management, spaced repetition, adult learning principles, and the active, networked nature of knowledge construction, micro- and nano-learning provide a powerful framework for designing and implementing education that is effective and flexible.

MICROLEARNING AND NANO-LEARNING

Fast growth in digital learning ecosystems is introducing different instructional formats to meet learning needs. Among these instructional forms, microlearning and nano-learning are demonstrating great potential as flexible and effective instructional formats. Microlearning and nano-learning are similar approaches, and often used interchangeably in common vernacular, but they have important distinctions—scope, structure, and use of selected content. It is important for educators, instructional designers, and trainers within organizations to know those distinctions to utilize effectively. I highlight three areas—conceptual distinctions, duration and content coverage, and alignment to learning objectives—as a clear and differentiating framework for microlearning and nano-learning; and to effectively apply these concepts within learning and meaningful activities(Corbeil et al., 2021; Ferrera, 2023).

Conceptual Distinctions

Microlearning is the delivery of instructional content in small, self-contained amounts that are focused on a single, clearly defined concept, skill or knowledge area. Microlearning is built for fast consumption, flexibility, and accessibility, typically as part of a greater learning pathway. The key concept is "Teach less at a time, but teach it better," which allows learners to focus entirely on a specific target without cognitive overload. Microlearning can take many forms: short, sharable videos, interactive modules, infographics, quizzes, or podcasts. Microlearning can occur in a stand-alone format or sequentially, in larger units or whole "pathways" to provide comprehensive mastery over time(Kamariddinovna, 2025).

Nano-learning is even more condensed instructional content—also referred to as ultra-short learning bursts—often under two minutes, created for immediate instructional use or to reinforce an immediacy of very specific point. For example, microlearning may want to teach a small skill such as how to create a pivot table in Excel (several broader concepts), while nano-learning may want to teach that small skill's element (a single task) such as how to use the "VLOOKUP" formula. Nano-learning is particularly effective in environments where speed, accuracy, and immediacy are paramount. This includes small, just-in-time training, quick compliance reminders, or micro-assessments that a learner can integrate into their workflow.

Duration and Content Scope

Time is the paramount distinction between microlearning and nano-learning. Microlearning is typically anywhere from three to fifteen minutes, with some definitions proposing it goes up to twenty minutes depending on content complexity and learner context. Because of this duration, microlearning is spacious enough to explain a concept, model a skill and do limited practice or reflection on the same element. For instance, a 10-minute microlearning experience on "Effective Email Communication" would cover writing effective subject lines, tone, and formatting tips, alongside examples and short interactive elements(Yousef et al., 2023).

Nano-learning is very short, ranging from thirty seconds to two minutes. The scope is much smaller—it is tightly bound to a single atomic piece of knowledge or micro-skill that can be acted on immediately. A 90-second nano-learning clip might show the steps to take to hyper-link a document. The content is reduced to its essence—there is little context, and no tangential topics—so learners experience it, engage with it and act on it in the moment. The difference in scope has implications for content design. Microlearning can provide some context and background information synthesizing with other learning, and, potentially provide brief opportunities for practice, feedback, or assessment. In contrast, nano-learning usually cannot accommodate practice. Nano-learning's key intent is to facilitate retention, or reinforcement, or provide knowledge fast. Therefore, microlearning could provide and support context around content and reinforce, while nano-learning can potentially reinforce or provide performance support.

The briefness of both formats aligns well with mobile learning situations and the multitasking nature of learners today. However, the scope of both must be clearly defined in order to prevent "fragmentation" - a situation where a learner receives isolated pieces of information with no way to connect it to a larger schema for knowledge. This can complicate effective use - especially if micro- and nano-learning components are used independently of a larger curriculum or performance support system.

Learning Objectives Alignment

The effectiveness of microlearning and nano-learning depends on having clear learning objectives. In microlearning, objectives are often aimed at lower- to mid-order thinking skills - remembering, understanding, applying, and analyzing. But, because microlearning allows enough time to present a concept, place it into context, and allow for applying it, it can take on more ambitious objectives. For example, a microlearning module with the scope of "Apply simple and brief time management techniques to daily planning" could identify two techniques (e.g., Pomodoro technique, Eisenhower matrix), provide a short activity, and finish with a brief self-assessment of their planning approach(Hilsmann & Dodson, 2025; Yousef et al., 2023).

In contrast, nano-learning learning objectives should be limited to the lower order of Blooms Taxonomy - mainly remember and understand, and occasionally apply for procedural skills. The extreme shortness of nano-learning limits the ability to use higher order cognitive processes, such as evaluate or create, although nano-learning can contribute to these by at least providing a quick reference to help in a more complex process. For example, a nano-learning unit may be in the form of objectives, "Recall how to calculate gross margin (the formula)," or "Identify the keyboard shortcut for copying formatting in a spreadsheet."

Proper objective alignment will also ensure that the format is correctly utilized to support the intended depth of learning. A nano learning module occupied with complicated analysis would be detrimental, just as microlearning modules would likely not provide leveraged higher-level learning if using rote memorization. In the field, a blend will likely provide the best outcome. Use micro-learning modules to provide preliminary instruction and then follow this up with nano learning modules to reinforce key points, memory joggers and quick performance support space.

Furthermore, these two formats will also be effective when incorporated into a larger instructional strategy where they act in concert as building blocks in a performance learning continuum to accomplish a larger learning objective. For example, a corporate onboarding program strategy might consider microlearning modules to define core company values as an introduction, followed by nano learning reminders, pertaining to the employee's specific expected behaviors. In formal education, microlearning content may introduce the key principles informing a scientific methodology but use a nano learning prompt before each lab to refresh lab safety principles(Nanjappa et al., 2023).

Microlearning and nano-learning remain centered around a common pedagogical DNA: brevity, relevancy and learner-centered. The main difference is scope, as microlearning uses short and targeted lessons (that are long enough to provide some depth into conceptual understanding and limited practice), whereas nano-learning uses up ultra-focused knowledge bites that can be easily recalled or acted upon. Both contribute their value to the learning experience only when thoughtfully matched to learning outcomes, and both micro-and nano-learning are best used as a part of a larger learning ecosystem that connects and links each small 'piece' of learning to future educational or performance goals. Knowing the conceptual boundaries, length specifications and alignment requirements of these two formats will allow educators and organizations to apply them when creatively engaging learners and designing for retention and knowledge transfer in the digital era of education.

Figure 2. Evolution of learning formats in the digital era

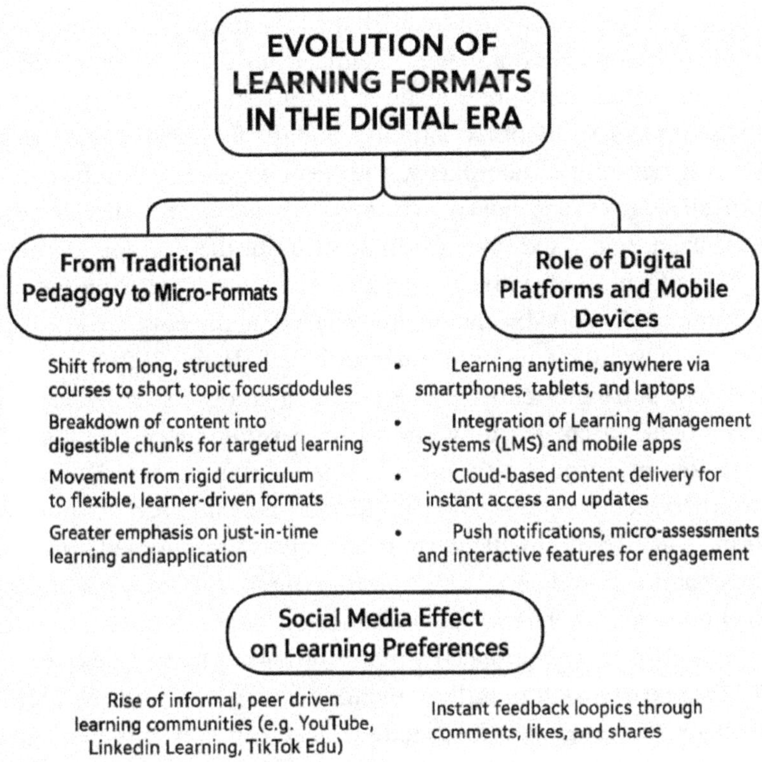

EVOLUTION OF LEARNING FORMATS IN THE DIGITAL ERA

In the last couple of decades, the transformation of ways of learning shows significant societal, technological, and cultural shifts. The shift away from standard learning, such as a pedagogy, to microlearning, and then further down to nano-learning moves beyond just a different style of delivery and uses, but is indicative of a greater, wider, systemic reconfiguration of the way knowledge is produced, accessed, and consumed in the digital era as shown in Figure 2. This transformation can be identified by the following three transformations: (1) dismantling of traditional pedagogy into micro-format (topics), (2) the role of platforms and mobile devices as fundamentally transformative technology for learning, and (3) the influence of social media on learning people and their preferences for more informal learning(-Sousa et al., 2022).

From Traditional Pedagogy to Micro-Formats

Traditional pedagogy has long been shaped by formal, structured, instructor-led, classroom or lecture sessions (with the materials typically organized into long 'blocks' of time, such as hour-long lectures or semester-long courses). Traditional pedagogy has emphasized depth, continuity, and the face-to-face experience, but it has also limited flexibility, modularity, and responsiveness to individual learning needs. In typical lectures (or other fixed format delivery) time path followed a slower, more standardized, and fixed pace for instruction in the average learner in group community; this fashion of delivery caused some learners to drag behind, and on the other end some learners disengaged from learning the content as it did not push or challenge them in any meaningful fashion(Zhu & Jiang, 2025).

Microlearning and nano-learning have emerged in contrast to the one-size-fits-all pedagogical model. Micro-learning and nano-learning adopt brevity, modularity, and learner autonomy, providing content in smaller, more focused, digestible forms that can be experienced at the learners preferred time and pace. Arguably, the shift to microformats are driven by the awareness that traditional methods of exploring or engaging content, would cease to be appropriate for the evolving skills demands of modern economies where the half-life of knowledge is continually decreasing. Learners are more broadly equipped by microformats or learning experiences to respond in the context of evolving skills demands over the long term. Microformats are also generally more aligned with knowledge transfer, attention span, cognitive load, and retention in consideration of cognitive science research evidence. Microformats have the potential to provide a more adaptive and personalized learning experience than traditional approaches considering the increasing pace of change(Vaithianathan et al., 2024).

The Role of Digital Platforms and Mobile Devices

The availability of digital platforms (especially mobile) has opened doors for all types of micro- and nano-learning- such as Learning Management Systems (LMS), Massive Open Online Courses (MOOCs), and microlearning platforms like Duolingo- to share or push specialized content to millions of learners globally. These platforms allow for any type of content, including but not limited to video, interactive quizzes, infographics, and podcasts; instructional designers can create custom content delivery in every format to meet the needs of various learner preferences(Dumitru et al., 2023; Kem, 2022).

Mobile devices, especially have proved to be helpful in capitalizing on microformats. Smartphones and Tablets are a learning platform that is in reach and accessible at any time; or preferably as an always-on, portable form of learning where it becomes part of daily practice. This commonality allows a designer or educator to have a learner engage in "just-in-time" learning in any number of moments during the day- while commuting, waiting in a line or external transition between meetings, between classes, and breaks. The learner is gaining value in a little conscious development activity. And with more designs being downloaded into the mobile app, offline access and content info is also becoming common, led by gamifying progress tracking (and potentially digital badges) the opportunities to engage and develop a behaviour becomes habitual.

A mobile-first model has also changed how the content is designed with, for example brevity, visual impact and interactive fun in thinking about content for small mobile screens. However, as the access to bandwidth progresses and the storage in the cloud (or affordable), we now can provide resources that are rich in multimedia learning wherever it may be displayed. Distance and developed regions with limited back-setting may still have immediate access to the same rich resources.

The Social Media Effect on Learning Preferences

The cultural implications of social media have dramatically influenced how individuals consume and interact with information. Social media platforms like YouTube, Instagram, TikTok, and LinkedIn have normalized bite-sized and visually stimulating content needing to "grab" our attention in seconds. The typical social media experience has become an information "stream," one that commonly blends learning, entertainment, and socialization. This shift has disrupted learner perceptions, so that students now expect concise, visually stimulating, and on demand theory-in-practice information(Dumitru et al., 2023; Marpelina & others, 2024).

Microlearning and nano-learning have obvious synergies with these consumption styles, as social media users are conditioned to scroll through short, self-contained posts or videos in a similar rhythm to micro-learning or nano-learning in short "lessons." Additionally, the interactive and shareable properties of social media may have created a level of collaboration and networking possibilities per the tenets of connectivism learning theory--which maintain that learners could share micro-learning or nano-learning modules, discuss them in online communities, and co-create user-generated content to an ecosystem of learning."

The "social proof" mechanism inherent in social media — where likes, shares, and endorsements establish credibility — also applies to educational contexts. Things such as popular microlearning videos or nano-learning tips can be disseminated quickly, reaching audiences with greater scope than the primary audience. However, this is a double-edged sword with quality concerns at times since engagement can trump educational rigor on occasion. Therefore, being engaged versus being educative is a design challenge in using micro-format for traction and reach in social media-dependent learning(Agrawal et al., 2023).

The changing learning formats of the current digital environment symbolize a fluidity of pedagogy, technology, and culture. What was once a structured time period in a classroom has been supplanted by flexible and modular formats that allow empowered learners to be in charge of their pace of learning and pathways of learning. Digital platforms make microlearning and nano-learning available in any location, while social media shapes the way we consume, distribute, and value content. All of these forces enable short-form learning to thrive, not as a substitute for education, but as a more dynamic part of a fast-paced and connected world.

Figure 3. Microlearning and nano-learning are dependent on the digital technologies

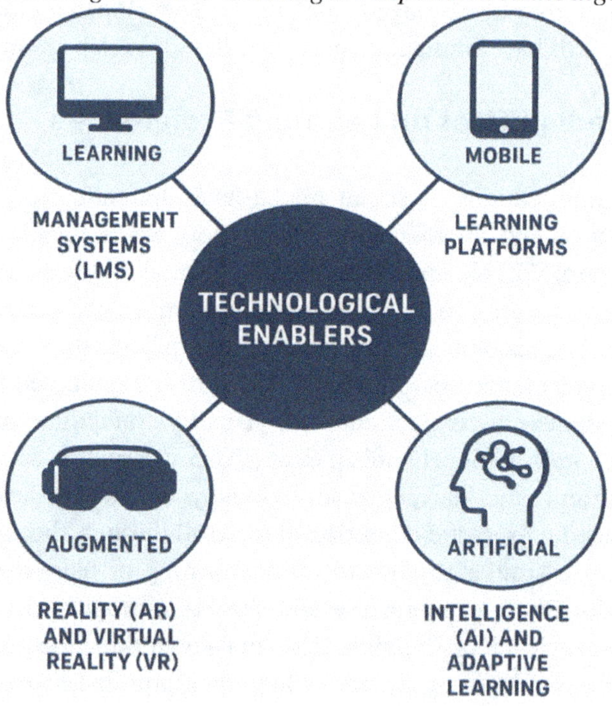

TECHNOLOGICAL ENABLERS

The expansion and efficiency of microlearning and nano-learning are dependent on the digital technologies that allow for content to be created, delivered, and personalized—while also being manageable at scale as shown in Figure 3. Without strong technology infrastructures, these immersive learning experiences would have limited reach and effectiveness. Four significant enablers—Learning Management Systems (LMS), Mobile Learning Platforms, Artificial Intelligence (AI) and Adaptive Learning, and Augmented Reality (AR) and Virtual Reality (VR)—underpin today's new learning ecosystem in microlearning and nano-learning(Astaño, 2025).

Learning Management Systems (LMS)

Learning Management Systems serve as centralized platforms for creating, delivering, managing, and tracking learning content. In the context of microlearning and nano-learning, LMS platforms have evolved to support modular, bite-sized learning units rather than exclusively long-form courses. Modern LMS tools such as Moodle, Blackboard, and Canvas offer features that allow educators and trainers to organize content into discrete lessons, each mapped to specific learning objectives(Laskar, 2024).

LMS platforms are essential for micro- and nano-learning. LMS platforms include essential time-saving features for managing micro- and nano-learning: content modularization, tracking progress, units of assessment, and reporting analytics. LMS platforms often integrate with video hosting services, gamification plugins, and social tools, all of which foster active participation and collaboration among peer learners. The scalability of LMS platforms allows organizations to provide thousands of learners with standardized microlearning programs in disparate locations while enabling centralized quality assurance.

Mobile Learning Platforms

The spread of smartphones and tablets means that short-form learning is easier to access and more flexible than ever. Mobile learning platforms are made for small screens and touch interfaces, and are built or adapted for learning on the go. And there are lots of examples of good mobile learning, such as Duolingo for languages, EdApp for workplace training, and Khan Academy's mobile app for schooling. Mobile learning platforms tackle a lot of benefits for microlearning/nano-learning, including always-available access, timely reminders, offline access, and micro-interaction. Learners can re-engage with the learning moment, support spaced repetition, keep continuity with low connectivity, and cue into mobile sessions(Marr, 2021).

Mobile learning, when looked at through mobile-first design principles considers short text, visual clarity, and responsive multisensory media, and can make sure the content is engaging, without overloading the learner; mobile learning platforms are also usually gamified with leaderboards, badges, and streaks, which are obvious motivators, generally speaking, but are especially well-suited to short-form learning engagement. In some sectors, such as healthcare, retail, and field services, mobile-based nano-learning modules are very highly regarded as just-in-time performance support, especially within the context of executing tasks that require speed in recall-time, which can directly impact accuracy or efficiency.

Artificial Intelligence and Adaptive Learning

Artificial Intelligence is now causing disruptions in learning by helping us design and best deliver micros and nanos learning experiences. AI-based adaptive learning systems examine student data such as performance history and engagement data to generate combinations of pedagogical factors for the benefit of auto adjusting the content delivered (i.e. module). As a result, each learner receives the content at the 'right' moment, maximizing relevance and efficiency. Within micro learning, AI can recommend modules of microlearning, adjust challenge/difficulty, identify weak areas, and automate repetition periods to catalyze retention and learning experience(Laskar et al., 2023).

AI's driving force can make distinctions about how the micro-units attenuate learning while also helping the learning design process to shape potential instruction by revealing who the micro-units work and not work. Learning analytics will play a key role across future education because of how close it facilitates to pedagogical strategies for learning in multiple ways. AI and Natural Language Processing are advancing chatbots as active learning companions that can assist in providing fast explanations, answering learners' questions, and guiding users through a micro-assessment in a conversational manner.

Augmented Reality (AR) and Virtual Reality (VR)

Even though microlearning and nano-learning are basically synonymous with brief, mobile-friendly content, the use of AR and VR technologies will allow us to integrate immersive learning into our microlearning and nano-learning content. Most importantly, immersive technologies offer highly engaging microlearning content in a contextual way that emulates real-world environments in shorter formats (ManiMekalai et al., 2024; Sekhar et al., 2024).

For instance, augmented reality (AR) technology allows for the overlay of digital information onto the real-life environment. For individuals engaging with learning, this means digital prompts can be used to deliver contextual, nano-learning supports while they are doing the work. Think about AR-enabled mobile apps that are now embedded in manufacturing systems, where step-by-step assembly instructions can be displayed on top of the machinery for workers. Each nano-learning prompt may only take few seconds, but it will support just-in-time, video-based learning without interrupting someone's workflow.

Using virtual reality (VR) we can develop learning scenarios that are fully immersive simulated environments, allowing people to practice skills in short durations in fully structured situations. For instance, VR microlearning modules could be developed to simulate a 5-minute sales pitch, what a safety drill may look like, or how a customer service interaction should go. The VR scenarios would have the capacity to be repeatable, and with variations, to support learning objectives without the complexity of capacity that exists with real-world training environments.

The use of AR and VR, which will likely change the way micro- and nano-learning are integrated, has the potential to create experience-based learning, increase engagement, and provide real-time feedback. Nevertheless, where these technologies can diverge from the top of mind learning objectives to learning distractions requires deliberate instructional design even if they are cost-effective to produce. The impetus for microlearning and nano-learning cannot be separated from explaining or describing the technological ecosystems that provide and/or enable them. LMS platforms structure the organizational and administrative support; mobility and mobile learning platforms provide ease of access and engagement features; artificial intelligence enables personalization and continuous improvement; and AR and VR add an in the moment learning experience within contextualized learning. These enablers provide not only a short-form learning method for delivery, they also increase effectiveness, scalability, and adaptability to different learning environments. As technology continues to evolve it will further widen the boundaries of microlearning and nano-learning to allow for a hyper-personalized, data-driven, and immersive experiences in education at any time 24/7 in a digital age.

DESIGN PRINCIPLES FOR EFFECTIVE MICRO/NANO-LEARNING

Microlearning and nano-learning are effective learning strategies, not just based on their short length and spontaneous accessibility, but on the quality of their design. Short-form content can be shallow, disconnected, or boring; ultimately becoming ineffective if does not lead to your intended learning outcome. Designing content and other learning experiences with impact in mind requires attention to instructional design principles, creative integration of multimedia, personalizing learning experiences, and integrating effective micro- and nano-learning experiences into learning programmes. In the Figure 4, Four pillars of effective micro- and nano-learning design must include (1) Instructional considerations, (2) Multimedia and interactivity, (3) Personalized and learner pathways, and (4) Curriculum or training considerations (Sarkar, Shandilya, et al., 2025; Vaithianathan et al., 2025; Yadav et al., 2025).

Figure 4. Design principles for effective micro/nano-learning

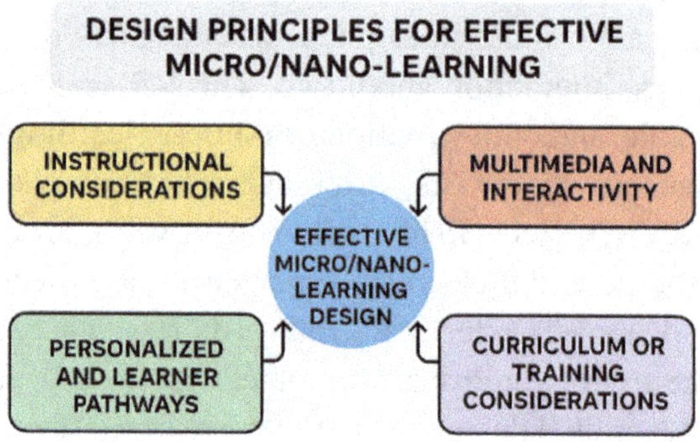

Instructional Design Considerations

The starting point for effective micro/nano-learning is clearly defined, measurable learning objectives. The first step is to have clear, measurable learning objectives. Learning objectives must be defined as simply as possible and reflect the learning or the acquisition of a skill, piece of knowledge, or competency that can be completed within the time constraints of the format. In microlearning, the objective may begin with an introduction to a concept and then include some practice but quite limited as it is microlearning. For nano-learning the emphasis can typically be on recall, demonstration, or brief method.

The principles for instructional design will pay heed to intended content, acknowledge a single primary learning objective, and be action-orientated as well as provide learners with immediate feedback that will reflect their understandings. Instructional designers must avoid overloading which would affect each learner's memory, must avoid amount and detail of unnecessary background, and engage learners in taking ownership of their learning in opportunities for practice exercises, decision making, and tasks from experience. Micro/nano-learning is brief and because of this, being precise with the use of language, intended instruction, and sequencing is important. There will be no space for information that is only peripheral to the learning goal. Each aspect must contribute to, or compliment the learning goal.

Multimedia and Interactivity

Multimedia is ideal for micro- and nano-learning since it includes visual and auditory stimulation for diverse students and will increase learning retention. Learners can learn content through video clips, animations, infographics, podcasts, and interactive infographics or diagrams quickly and most importantly, memorably. However, multimedia must be implemented in a careful way so not to produce cognitive overload or distraction (Gopi et al., 2024; Kalaiselvi et al., 2024; Vaithianathan et al., 2024).

Interactive features like clickable hotspots, in addition to many types of scenarios (i.e., branching scenarios), drag and drop activities and quizzing, promote active engagement because social presence and active learning are linked with knowledge retention of learning. If a microlearning unit was designed for workplace safety, it could use a brief (3- to 5-minute interactive video) with hazards in a workplace setting where the learner determines the hazards to avoid and receives instant feedback with knowledge checks.

Micro/nano-learning multimedia needs to be related, equitable, available, and leveraged. It should deepen understanding, reduce cognitive dissonance, employ captions, transcripts, and alternative text. The multimedia must conform to the time frame allowed by the format to ensure that the key points can be communicated. It is critical to balance aesthetics and instructional clarity, ensuring learners are engaged by the presentation of graphics and retained in learning through the value in content.

Personalization and Learner Pathways

Personalization takes micro/nano-learning beyond generic content to an individualized experience that fits personal learner needs. Adaptive learning technologies using AI, for example, allow the delivery of content sequences based on a learner's past knowledge, performance data, and preferences. If a learner shows mastery in an assessment, the system can skip microlearning units covering basic knowledge and deliver advanced modules or related nano-learning refreshers, for example (Padmavathi et al., 2025; Padmavathy et al., 2025; Priya & Boopathi, 2025).

The personalization strategies we can implement include adaptive sequencing, choice of learning, tracking and recommending progress, and contextualization. These strategies adjust content order and difficulty automatically, let learners select content topics, formats, or scenarios on which to focus, and can provide insight into learners' progress.

Learner pathways may be linear where microlearning modules must be completed in a specific order or non-linear where learners have the freedom to choose their pathway. In corporate learning environments learner pathways may relate to some form of competencies framework and in academic environments they may be related to course intended learning outcomes. Regardless, personalization provides motivation, autonomy, and relevance, which are essential components in sustaining engagement with short-form learning (Ravichandra et al., 2025; Sarkar, Parmar, et al., 2025).

Integration into Curriculum or Training Programs

Micro- and nano-learning are at their best embedded in a larger educational or training ecosystem instead of being individual resources. Embedding micro- and nano-learning ensures that, ideally, they are reinforcing, expanding or preparing the learner for deeper instruction, and encompassing the overall learning pathway. In higher education, microlearning can either be the pre-class preparation activity, a post-lecture learning activity, or supplementary support for students who struggled in class. For example, a micro-module on the Pythagorean theorem could act as a precursor to problem-solving in the classroom, providing assurance that all the students have the same foundational knowledge base (Gopi et al., 2024; Kalaiselvi et al., 2024; Saravanan et al., 2024).

In corporate training, nano-learning can serve as just-in-time learning moments within workflows, with reminders or tips delivered by mobile notifications to enhance a critical skill just-in-time to use that skill. Microlearning can supplement onboarding for organizations; it allows the unpacking and organization of complex organizational knowledge into smaller pieces of knowledge, with nano-learning to supplement the identified "knowledge" over the initial months of employment experience.

Micro/nano-learning can be effectively structured and integrated in a learning plan by mapping modules to specific competencies (or outcomes for the course), blending short-form digital content with instructor-led learning events, mentoring or group projects, incorporating nano-learning to reinforce learning over time with a structure that feeds into a larger evaluation framework. This approach will build a sustained skill building practice rather than a series of short learning interventions.

Creating impactful micro- and nano-learning does not require "just" shortening to content, but effective instructional design, thoughtfully deployed multimedia, personalization to individual learner preferences and needs, and alignment to broader learning. Instructional design provides focus and intention; multimedia and interactivity create engagement and retention; personalization creates alignment to individual life and learning goals; and alignment ensures that each of the formats contribute to a larger set of learning objectives. When these principles of design are simultaneously considered in micro- and nano-learning, the result can be more than quick information bursts, it can provide meaningful, and lasting learning experiences that meet many of the factors expected of today's digital education world.

APPLICATIONS AND USE CASES

Microlearning and nano-learning have shown flexibility in many domains, providing learners with scalable, convenient, and focused learning content (Das et al., 2024; Sharma et al., 2024).

Corporate Training and Just-in-Time Learning

Micro and nano-learning provide effective support for employees seeking new skills through rapid instructional design or on-demand performance support. For instance, an employee wanting to troubleshoot software can access a nano-learning experience mere moments before they begin the task, likely reducing downtime and error rates. Organizations use microlearning to onboard employees, conduct compliance training, and support leadership development, allowing employees to learn without displacing their work schedules.

Higher Education and E-Learning Environments

Universities, colleges, and online education providers utilize micro and nano-learning to supplement follow-up discussion of lectures, create pre-class pre-lecture primer modules, or provide brief refreshers for concepts and ideas discussed in class. Modular platforms allow students to engage with small chunks of material at flexible times, which has resulted in an effective transition to blended learning, and a degree of progress to the flipped classroom.

Professional Certifications and Continuous Learning

In industries that require regular management of credentials — like healthcare, finance, or IT — short, focused micro-learning modules prepare workers to adapt to ever-changing laws, standards, or technologies. Micro-learning modules can also be integrated into a certification application to be tracked as completing parts of professional development toward continuing education units (CEU's) .

Informal and Self-Directed Learning

Outside the formal realm of education, learners are also integrating micro and nano-learning into their own lives for personal development. Apps, podcasts and 5 to 15-min segments of video or audio allow learners to explore an entirely new skill such as learning a language, dabbling in some art form and other skills without committing to a long-time perspective. This allows learners to create their own individual micro-and-nano learning sequences promoting autonomy, self-direction, and intrinsic motivation. In all the instances cited, micro/nano is providing learners with flexibility, relevance, and immediacy to complement or supplement traditional instructional formats.

BENEFITS AND IMPACT ON PEDAGOGY

Microlearning and nano-learning have both become revolutionary pedagogical practices because they change the way knowledge is to be distributed, consumed and retained. They can clearly be beneficial for the learning experience in both the education and corporate sectors as shown in Figure 5, learner-centered learning experiences (Sarkar, Parmar, et al., 2025; Sarkar, Shandilya, et al., 2025; Yadav et al., 2025).

Figure 5. Benefits and impact on pedagogy

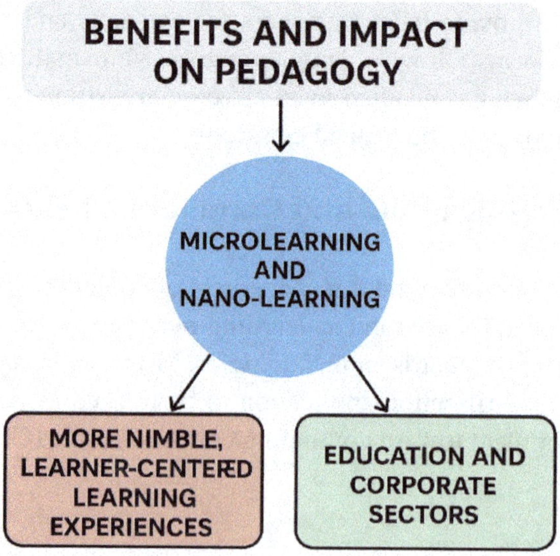

Flexibility and Accessibility

The development of short, modular content, provide opportunities for learners to interact and engage with the material at any time and from any location, thus making education a reality for anyone who has to juggle work, study and family commitments. Being able to consume and engage with the material in a mobile-friendly format and sometimes offline has eliminated previous barriers of time and place to engage with content, and in many cases has democratized the accessibility of learning.

Increased Engagement and Motivation

The concise nature of micro/nano-learning reduces cognitive fatigue and sustains attention. By integrating multimedia elements, gamification, and interactive scenarios, these methods foster active participation and higher motivation. Learners perceive immediate relevance, which strengthens commitment to the learning process (Ravichandra et al., 2025; Sarkar, Parmar, et al., 2025; Sharma et al., 2024).

Enhanced Knowledge Retention

The ability to interact with smaller components of information within micro/nano-learning can help learners reduce the experience of cognitive overload lessens and allows them to maintain their focus. Learning often uses multimedia, gamification, or interactive scenarios that promote active participation that motivates learners more effectively, making the learning experience directly relevant to them, resulting in increased commitment to the learning process.

Scalability Across Contexts

Micro/nano-learning can be quickly implemented and context-augmented in many ways across industry, higher education, and informal self-directed learning. Content can be repurposed and transformed into bite-sized modules, and AI-driven platforms can personalize a pathway for each learner at scale without sacrificing time and resources. It is these benefits that can be embedded into the pedagogy of micro/nano-learning, in which educators and organizations alike can design more responsive, learner-led systems of education—a model that focuses on the engagement of knowledge to meet need, instead of adherence to a curriculum, in the rapidly evolving digital world.

CHALLENGES AND LIMITATIONS

Microlearning and nano-learning are beneficial forms of learning but like all forms of learning there are many hurdles for educators and organizations to overcome (Vaithianathan et al., 2024).

Content Fragmentation and Lack of Depth

By breaking topics into smaller units it can become fractured if relationships are not pointed out or clearly established. In complex topics where deep analysis is required, the subject matter is easily oversimplified.

Assessment in Short-Form Learning

Assessment of learning outcomes can be more difficult in micro- and nano-learning formats. In traditional assessments assessment of learning could be missed when looking at incremental learning. Frequent assessments in micro formats could disrupt flow of learning and discourage learners.

Technological and Infrastructure Barriers

The success of microlearning relies on digital infrastructure that supports good practice, this includes ensuring mobile compatibility, strong reliable internet service, and user-friendly platform(s). In low-resource settings, at least one of these preconditions may limit the adoption of microlearning and nano-learning.

Over-Reliance on Micro-Formats

Over reliance on micro/nano-learning may dismiss the advantages of long, immersive learning experiences. It is also important to note that some skills, like critical thinking or collaborative problem-solving build on some level of sustained engagement that micro/nano learning cannot provide.

How we will address this is the purposeful alignment of micro/nano-learning with traditional learning as a complement to, not a replacement of and through intentional design focused on coherence, context, and authentic assessment strategies.

Figure 6. Future trends in micro- and nano-learning

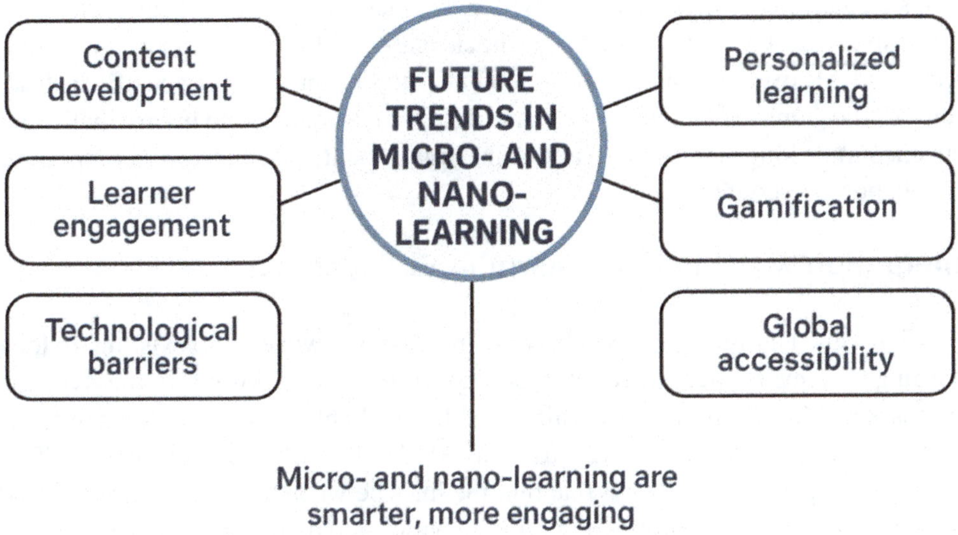

FUTURE TRENDS IN MICRO- AND NANO-LEARNING

Micro- and nano-learning will become even more impactful as education and training evolve in response to technological advancement and the changing expectations of learners as shown in Figure 6. New trends suggest a future of micro/nano-learning that is smarter, more engaging, and adapted globally (Agrawal et al., 2023; Sarkar, Shandilya, et al., 2025; Vaithianathan et al., 2024).

AI-Powered Personalization

Artificial intelligence (AI) will be made use of to increasingly drive micro- and nano-learning experiences that are personalized. AI will gather information from understanding how individual learners behave along with performance and data to provide a set of individually curated learning paths, and adjust the difficulty of content in real time, and recommend short modules to close specific knowledge gaps. Predictive analytics will allow for personalized interventions so that learning will happen in a proactive way to make sure learners have the content they need at the right time (Sarkar, Parmar, et al., 2025; Vaithianathan et al., 2025; Yadav et al., 2025).

Gamification and Immersive Technologies

Using gamification, AR, and VR will make micro/nano-learning interactive and immersive. Short VR simulations can track real-world tasks allowing practice of skills, and AR overlays can augment content with instant, context-specific instruction. All the gamified elements such as badges, leaderboards, and micro-challenges can encourage longer-term motivation and engagement, especially in a competitive or collaborative context.

Integration with Lifelong Learning Ecosystems

Micro- and nano-learning will become increasingly woven into existing lifelong learning systems to facilitate continuous upskilling and reskilling in the dynamic job market. Micro- and nano-learning will be stackable modules in competency-based frameworks, and contribute to many kinds of certification or degrees. This will create experience pathways that blur the lines between formal, non-formal, and informal learning opportunities and offer transitions no matter the stage of learning.

Global Adoption and Cross-Cultural Adaptation

As digital infrastructure and mobile networks spread across the globe, we will see micro/nano-learning deployed and adopted in a wider range of countries and regions. However, before successful global deployment occurs, content will need to be culturally adapted, language localized, as well as accounted for based on different educational values and norms. Thankfully, AI-powered language translation and localization tools will allow us to offer relevant learning experiences in context while retaining our cultural authenticity. By the end of this decade, micro- and nano-learning will be contextually adaptive, interconnected systems that complement traditional learning models and provide flexible, on-demand, and globally inclusive learning opportunities. The use of AI, immersive media, and lifelong learning strategies will solidify the role of micro/learning and nano-learning in the future of education and workplace development.

CONCLUSION

In the digital age, microlearning and nano-learning signify a shift in how we think about and develop education and training. By providing micro-sized, focused, and easily accessible experiences, micro- and nano-learning meet the demands of our changing learners who have greater expectations for usefulness, flexibility, and immediacy.

Their advantages - including increased engagement, better retention, and scalability - make them viable learning activities in a range of educational and work contexts. When intentionally woven into curriculum, training, and lifelong learning environments, micro- and nano-learning can support- not replace- more traditional pedagogical approaches, resulting in a hybrid approach to learning that optimizes efficiency and depth. However, building in limitations to micro- and nano-learning cannot be ignored. Risks surrounding content fragmentation, inadequate assessment, and over-emphasizing brevity, suggest the need for intentional build, design and integration. They should be leveraged as learning shortcuts rather than comprehensive, sustainable experiences.

Going forward, the developments in technology - especially of importance, AI, gamification, immersive media, and global adaptation - will continue to increase the potential of micro- and nano-learning. While micro and nano learning may become derivative to overarching lifelong learning strategies, these learning formats also have the potential to be key components of continuous skill formation, upskilling, reskilling, professional movement, and equitable access to quality education on a global level.

In summary, micro- and nano-learning are more than fads for the future educational landscape, which will support learning that will be always adaptive, learner- centered and truly embedded in daily life. Any future evolution of micro- and nano-learning will be based on a balance between innovation and pedagogical well-being; while supporting succinctness we need to also support suitable depth (with the appropriate prior knowledge), and while moving toward technology enhancements, we need to be true to the purpose of worthwhile learning for meaningful learning that lasts for years.

REFERENCES

Agrawal, A. V., Pitchai, R., Senthamaraikannan, C., Balaji, N. A., Sajithra, S., & Boopathi, S. (2023). Digital Education System During the COVID-19 Pandemic. In *Using Assistive Technology for Inclusive Learning in K-12 Classrooms* (pp. 104–126). IGI Global. DOI: 10.4018/978-1-6684-6424-3.ch005

Astaño, J. L. (2025). Bibliometric analysis of studies on nanolearning and microlearning. *International Journal of Studies in Education and Science*, *6*(2), 240–256. DOI: 10.46328/ijses.144

Bhowmick, D., & Sarma, I. B. D. (2021). Micro-learning: An Effective E-learning Resource with Poor Net Connectivity. In *Virtual and Classroom Learning in Higher Education: A Guide to Effective Online Teaching* (pp. 76–96). Bentham Science Publishers.

Chamorro-Atalaya, O., Flores-Velásquez, C. H., Olivares-Zegarra, S., Dávila-Ignacio, C., Flores-Cáceres, R., Arévalo-Tuesta, J. A., Cruz-Telada, Y., & Suarez-Bazalar, R. (2024). Microlearning and nanolearning in higher education: A bibliometric review to identify thematic prevalence in the COVID-19 pandemic and post-pandemic context. *International Journal of Learning. Teaching and Educational Research*, *23*(4), 279–297. DOI: 10.26803/ijlter.23.4.15

Corbeil, J. R., Khan, B. H., & Corbeil, M. E. (2021). Microlearning in the digital age. *Taylor and Francis. Doi*, *10*, 9780367821623.

Das, S., Lekhya, G., Shreya, K., Shekinah, K. L., Babu, K. K., & Boopathi, S. (2024). Fostering Sustainability Education Through Cross-Disciplinary Collaborations and Research Partnerships: Interdisciplinary Synergy. In *Facilitating global collaboration and knowledge sharing in higher education with generative AI* (pp. 60–88). IGI Global Scientific Publishing.

Denojean-Mairet, M., López-Pernas, S., Agbo, F. J., & Tedre, M. (2024). A literature review on the integration of microlearning and social media. *Smart Learning Environments*, *11*(1), 46. DOI: 10.1186/s40561-024-00334-5

Desiderio, L., Poutrain, S., Karda, M., & Kazantzidou, D. (2024). Using Artificial Intelligence And Leveraging Nano And Microlearning For Enhanced Language Acquisition: A Comprehensive Approach. *EdMedia+ Innovate Learning*, 175–185.

Dumitru, C., Radovici, M. C. M., Rasiti, G., & Veselinović, L. (2023). Science and learning in the digital era. *Der Donauraum*, *63*(1–2), 83–98. DOI: 10.7767/dedo.2023.63.1-2.83

Dwinggo Samala, A., Bojić, L., Bekiroğlu, D., Watrianthos, R., & Hendriyani, Y. (2023). Microlearning: Transforming education with bite-sized learning on the go—Insights and applications. [iJIM]. *International Journal of Interactive Mobile Technologies, 17*(21).

Ferrera, R. (2023). Nano Learning: An Analysis of The Bite-Sized Discussions on Tiktok. *Available at SSRN* 4524968. DOI: 10.2139/ssrn.4524968

Gopi, B., Kokila, M. S., Bibin, C. V., Sasikala, D., Howard, E., & Boopathi, S. (2024). Distributed technologies using AI/ML techniques for healthcare applications. In *Social Innovations in Education, Environment, and Healthcare* (pp. 375–396). IGI Global.

Hilsmann, N., & Dodson, C. (2025). Mobile Microlearning in Continuing Professional Development for Nursing: A Scoping Review. *Journal of Continuing Education in Nursing, 56*(2), 53–62. DOI: 10.3928/00220124-20250121-05 PMID: 39880017

Kalaiselvi, D., Ramaratnam, M., Kokila, S., Sarkar, R., Anandakumar, S., & Boopathi, S. (2024). Future developments of higher education on social psychology: Innovation and changes. In *Social Innovations in Education, Environment, and Healthcare* (pp. 146–169). IGI Global.

Kamariddinovna, M. E. (2025). THE ROLE OF NANO-LEARNING IN DEVELOPING DIGITAL COMPETENCE AMONG FUTURE ENGLISH LANGUAGE TEACHERS. *AMERICAN JOURNAL OF EDUCATION AND LEARNING, 3*(5), 335–341.

KAYALAR., F. (2022). Efficiency and Application of Nano-learning in Adult Education. *Proceedings of VIAC 2022 in Budapest*, 71.

Kem, D. (2022). Personalised and adaptive learning: Emerging learning platforms in the era of digital and smart learning. *International Journal of Social Science and Human Research, 5*(2), 385–391. DOI: 10.47191/ijsshr/v5-i2-02

Khlaif, Z. N., & Salha, S. (2021). Using TikTok in education: A form of micro-learning or nano-learning? *Interdisciplinary Journal of Virtual Learning in Medical Sciences, 12*(3), 213–218.

Laskar, J. H. (2024). Content-based learning to competency-based education: A paradigm shift. *Educational Reforms Journal, 18*(1), 99–110.

Laskar, J. H., Khatun, R., & Sarkar, M. C. (2023). Education. In *Resurgent India*. Ashok Yakkaldevi.

ManiMekalai. M., Veni, C., Agarwal, A., Joshi, A. A., Gururaja, H., & Boopathi, S. (2024). Harnessing VR and AR for sustainable smart manufacturing: Eco-friendly innovations. In *Reshaping environmental science through machine learning and IoT* (pp. 355–380). IGI Global Scientific Publishing.

Marpelina, L. & others. (2024). Revolutionizing history learning in the digital era: Transforming the way we learn. *KnE Social Sciences*, 912–927.

Marr, B. (2021). *Business trends in practice: The 25+ trends that are redefining organizations.*

Nanjappa, S., Ghosh, V., Acharya, S., Mukerjee, H. S., & Stl, V. (2023). Microlearning in corporate settings: Practitioner perspectives. *Human Resource Development International, 26*(5), 655–662. DOI: 10.1080/13678868.2022.2160688

Padmavathi, P., Thrimurthulu, V., Bharani, J., Sailaja, V., Kumar, N. M., & Boopathi, S. (2025). A Study on Integration of Deep Learning With IoT for Smart Engineering Solutions. In *Navigating Challenges of Object Detection Through Cognitive Computing* (pp. 125–158). IGI Global Scientific Publishing. DOI: 10.4018/979-8-3693-9057-3.ch005

Padmavathy, S., Gudipudi, N. R., & Boopathi, S. (2025). *Em povvering Small and Medium Enterprises Through Smart Technology and Talent Management.*

Pham, X. L., Nguyen, P. N., & Nguyen, T. H. (2023). Innovative approaches to learning: An examination of nano-learning research. *2023 14th IIAI International Congress on Advanced Applied Informatics (IIAI-AAI)*, 212–217.

Priya, P. K., & Boopathi, S. (2025). *Agile Approaches to Commercializing Agricultural Business: Strategies for.*

Ravichandra, T., Mariappan, M., Padmaja, C., Barnikana, N. R., Saravanan, T., & Boopathi, S. (2025). Mapping the Growth of Pedagogical Content Knowledge Across Teaching Careers. In *Current Trends and Best Practices of Pedagogical Content Knowledge (PCK)* (pp. 151–182). IGI Global Scientific Publishing. DOI: 10.4018/979-8-3693-0655-0.ch006

Saravanan, S., Chandrasekar, J., Kumar, S. S., Patel, P., Shanthi, J. M., & Boopathi, S. (2024). The Impact of NBA Implementation Across Engineering Disciplines: Innovative Approaches. In *Enhancing Higher Education and Research With OpenAI Models* (pp. 229–252). IGI Global Scientific Publishing. DOI: 10.4018/979-8-3693-1666-5.ch010

Sarkar, R., Parmar, D. V., Trivedi, N. B., Prabakaran, S., Chandra, S., & Boopathi, S. (2025). Pedagogical Contents Developments and Specialized Training for Teaching Careers. In *Global Practices in Inclusive Education Curriculum and Policy* (pp. 187–216). IGI Global.

Sarkar, R., Shandilya, S., Anand, T., Sri, R. R., Dhanaraj, K., & Boopathi, S. (2025). Best Practices and Frameworks for Higher Education: Optimizing Learning Progressions Using Recent Tools. In *Driving Quality Education Through AI and Data Science* (pp. 51–72). IGI Global Scientific Publishing.

Sekhar, K. C., Ingle, R. B., Banu, E. A., Rinawa, M. L., Prasad, M. M., & Boopathi, S. (2024). Integrating VR and AR for Enhanced Production Systems: Immersive Technologies in Smart Manufacturing. In *Human-Machine Collaboration and Emotional Intelligence in Industry 5.0* (pp. 90–112). IGI Global.

Sharma, D. M., Ramana, K. V., Jothilakshmi, R., Verma, R., Maheswari, B. U., & Boopathi, S. (2024). Integrating Generative AI Into K-12 Curriculums and Pedagogies in India: Opportunities and Challenges. *Facilitating Global Collaboration and Knowledge Sharing in Higher Education With Generative AI*, 133–161.

Silva, E. S., da Costa, W. P., de Lima, J. C., & Ferreira, J. C. (2025). Contribution of microlearning in basic education: A systematic review. *Education Sciences*, *15*(3), 302. DOI: 10.3390/educsci15030302

Sousa, M. J., Marôco, A. L., Gonçalves, S. P., & Machado, A. de B. (2022). Digital learning is an educational format towards sustainable education. *Sustainability (Basel)*, *14*(3), 1140. DOI: 10.3390/su14031140

Vaithianathan, V., Shastri, D. S., Nandakumar, V., Misba, M., Kumar, P. S., & Boopathi, S. (2025). NEP Policy Implementation Strategies in Education in India. In *Educational Philosophy and Sociological Foundation of Education* (pp. 325–356). IGI Global.

Vaithianathan, V., Subbulakshmi, N., Boopathi, S., & Mohanraj, M. (2024). Integrating Project-Based and Skills-Based Learning for Enhanced Student Engagement and Success: Transforming Higher Education. In *Adaptive Learning Technologies for Higher Education* (pp. 345–372). IGI Global.

Yadav, U., Pitchai, R., Gopal, V., Kumar, K. S., Talukdar, M., & Boopathi, S. (2025). Powers of Higher Education Leadership: Navigating Policy and Management in Academic Institutions. In *Navigating Leadership and Policy Management in Education* (pp. 103–136). IGI Global.

Yousef, A. M. F., Huang, R., Tlili, A., Garcia, M. B., Mahmoud, A. G., & Metwally, A. H. S. (2023). Small bites, big impact: The power of nanolearning. *International Conference on Smart Learning Environments*, 108–116. DOI: 10.1007/978-981-99-5961-7_12

Zhu, Y., & Jiang, H. (2025). Revolutionising education: The evolution, current landscape and future of digital learning. *International Journal of Smart Technology and Learning*, *4*(3), 278–295. DOI: 10.1504/IJSMARTTL.2025.146291

Chapter 9
Professional Development of Teachers for New Media Integration in Teaching and Learning:
From Capacity to Competence

Ratan Sarkar
https://orcid.org/0009-0008-5480-0165
Tezpur University (A Central University), India

ABSTRACT

In an era of rapid technological change and learner-centered pedagogy, integrating new media into education has become imperative. This chapter examines the shift from capacity building to competence enhancement in teacher professional development (TPD) for digital pedagogy. It moves beyond basic digital literacy to focus on adaptive expertise, pedagogical innovation, and critical digital citizenship. Drawing on global frameworks, national policies, and case studies, it calls for inclusive, context-sensitive, and sustainable TPD ecosystems. Innovative models—blended learning, micro-credentialing, communities of practice, and experiential labs—are explored for their potential to strengthen teacher agency. Persistent challenges such as infrastructure gaps, technophobia, and superficial training are addressed through actionable strategies. Ultimately, the chapter envisions teachers as transformative agents, co-creating digitally enriched, socially just, and future-ready classrooms that bridge vision with practice.

DOI: 10.4018/979-8-3373-5157-5.ch009

1. INTRODUCTION

Technological change has increasingly linked education in recent times. The worldwide digital revolution driven by the quick diffusion of the internet, mobile devices, and also artificial intelligence altered the ways of knowledge distribution and learning. Trilling and Fadel (2009) argue that this transition marks a more general social move towards a knowledge-based society in which lifelong learning, digital fluency, and adaptive thinking are essential skills. Therefore, pedagogical frameworks that were once considered stable are today under constant evolution. The traditional teacher-centered model of one-way knowledge transmission has moved towards more dynamic learner-centered paradigms for active, collaborative, and multimodal engagement. These pedagogical shifts are further sustained by the growing supply of novel media technologies, including learning management systems (LMS), open educational resources (OER), interactive simulations, and gamified platforms, as well as AI-powered tools, which makes learning personalized, situated, and available independent of place and time. The COVID-19 pandemic advanced this transition even more, indicating that in education digital tools are now a necessity. It revealed inequities in digital access, though, and demonstrated many educators were unprepared for remote and hybrid modalities (Trust & Whalen, 2020). These systemic disruptions led education systems worldwide to reconsider teacher preparation structures and models and to make a radical break with superficial digital training in favor of more profound, competence-based professional development.

1.1 Redefining the Teacher's Role in the Digital Age

Nowadays, teachers are expected to be more than transmitters of knowledge or classroom managers. But their roles have changed: they are content curators, digital designers, facilitators of inquiry, guides to online safety, and mentors of socio-emotional growth in blended environments. This new definition of teacher identity aligns with the notion of a learning architect, someone who designs educational experiences by combining digital tools with pedagogical intent (Mishra, 2019). However, the complexities of digital-age classroom demands and outdated teacher preparation systems trap many educators. Pretending that having basic ICT skills equals digital competence has led to training programs that are too focused on tools and not on pedagogical coherence, ethical implications, or contextual appropriateness (Redecker, 2017). Though ICT training teaches a teacher how to use a learning app, digital pedagogy teaches a teacher when and how that app helps learning, if at all. This is where the transition from capacity to competence is critical. Capacity-building is necessary but often involves decontextualized skill acquisition that is linear. Competence development is instead recursive, reflective, and embedded in real classroom practice. And it goes beyond "what teachers can do with digital media" to "how they adapt and modify educational experiences based on learners' needs, technological affordances, and sociocultural considerations."

1.2 New Media in Education: Scope, Tools, Challenges, and Potential

So, the landscape of educational technology is always changing, as is new media. No longer restricted to digitized texts and slide presentations, new media in education include interactive simulations, podcasts, infographics, digital storytelling, mobile apps, virtual labs, AI chatbots, and immersive learning environments in AR and VR. Such tools afford unparalleled opportunities to design multisensory, personalized, and inclusive learning experiences (Beetham and Sharpe, 2013). Further, new media platforms permitted collaborative learning worldwide. Students can interact with peers across borders through blogs, wikis, and video conferencing tools, construct knowledge mutually, and take part in authentic problem-solving tasks. These kinds of practices are based on constructivism and connectivism, the latter conceiving learning as socially constructed and distributed across networks (Siemens, 2005). These range from infrastructure gaps (particularly in rural and disadvantaged contexts), via questions relating to culturally appropriate content, to worries about data security, surveillance, and the very real algorithmic bias that's embedded in educational platforms (Selwyn 2021). In addition to this, information and media literacy expect teachers and students to develop critical media literacy: to assess the trustworthiness, pertinence, and ethical issues raised by digital content. Education professionals also face screen-time concerns, particularly in early childhood and primary education, where prolonged exposure to digital devices may impair attention spans and social development (Livingstone et al. Therefore, professional development should prepare teachers to balance innovation with caution and to make pedagogically sound decisions in a complex digital ecosystem.

1.3 From Digital Literacy to Digital Pedagogy

Among these transformations lies the need to distinguish digital literacy from digital pedagogy. Digital literacy is the functional operation of digital tools and platforms. This is a necessary first step but not sufficient. Digital pedagogy demands that educators use technology critically and reflectively in service of learning. It involves questions like, "Does this tool help understanding?" Do they support diverse learners? Does it respect equity & accessibility? In doing so, Koehler and Mishra's (2009) Technological Pedagogical Content Knowledge (TPACK) framework articulate this well: technology, pedagogy, and content knowledge need to be integrated rather than coexisting. In a similar vein, the SAMR model (Puentedura, 2013) shows how technology can go from simple substitution to task redefinition in ways that were previously unimaginable. But the development of digital pedagogy also requires capacities for openness to experimentation, resilience to failure, ethical sensitivity, and orientation towards inclusion and learner empowerment. This whole-system view of professional development is reflected in the 2017 DigCompEdu framework (Redecker, 2017), which defines six areas of educator competence, digital resources, assessment, personalization, and empowerment of learners. Development of such competencies is not linear. That requires iterative scaffolded learning in real contexts. Teachers need opportunities to reflect on practice, learn from peers, research, and co-create resources. Sadly, many professional development models are workshop-based, technocratic, and compliance-oriented and thus fail to sustain the transformative pedagogical impact required (Darling-Hammond et al., 2017).

1.4 Overview of the Chapter Structure

The chapter argues that teacher professional development (TPD) should be reframed as competence development rather than capacity building, drawing on TPACK, SAMR, DigCompEdu, and UDL to model digital pedagogy as multidimensional. The chapter reviews international and national policy contexts offering promise and risk, particularly for equity-advancing contexts. Barriers such as the digital divide, technophobia, and teacher voices are critically examined. The chapter then describes inclusive models such as blended learning, micro-credentials, virtual communities, and experiential labs based on case studies in low-resource settings. It ends with strategies and policy recommendations for reimagining TPD as systemic, participatory, and equity-driven, placing teachers as active co-creators of knowledge and technology, and competence as a pedagogical and ethical imperative for resilient and future-ready education systems.

2. THEORETICAL FOUNDATIONS AND CONCEPTUAL CLARIFICATIONS

The integration of new media in education depends not on equipment access but on teachers' competence in developing and delivering, along with reflecting on, electronic pedagogy. This particular section clarifies the difference between capacity and competence and outlines their relevance in teacher training, along with reviews of primary frameworks guiding professional development for alternative digital competence, laying the groundwork for proposing innovative, context-sensitive PD models.

2.1 Capacity vs. Competence

2.1.1 Definitional Distinctions

Capability in the context of teacher professional development typically describes the possibility of an educator to acquire and use new knowledge and skills, procedural or technical, especially in nature (OECD, 2009). It's often known as a foundational point, in which coaches are exposed to the purposeful use of tools or platforms through contact with content, models, or perhaps guided practice. Capacity-building programs usually wish to provide teachers with baseline proficiency in operating instructional technologies, including presentation software programs, LMS platforms, or maybe electronic assessment tools.

In comparison, competence represents a higher-order, multidimensional construct encompassing technical, ethical, and pedagogical, along with reflective, dimensions. It provides not just the capability to utilize technology but additionally the judgment to determine when and exactly why, and also how you can put it to use equitably and effectively in a certain teaching-learning context (Redecker, 2017). Competence comes with an understanding of socio-cultural dynamics, accessibility concerns, curriculum goals, and learner diversity (UNESCO, 2022).

The European Commission's DigCompEdu framework (Redecker, 2017) comes with a nuanced knowledge of competence by determining it as a "dynamic mixture of metacognitive and cognitive abilities, knowledge, attitudes, and values." Thus, competence is tool-dependent or static, not critically conscious, but adaptive, along with contextually grounded. It transcends a skill set and turns into a kind of commercial identity, a better way of getting in the electronic pedagogical space.

2.1.2 Historical Evolution of Capacity-Building in Teacher Education

The reputation of electronic teacher development continues to be shaped considerably by a capacity-oriented paradigm, especially in the Global South. During the early 2000s, global development agencies and tech companies, along with national governments, emphasized basic ICT education for teachers in their academic modernization agendas. Initiatives like Intel Teach, Microsoft's Partners in Learning, or maybe India's ICTSchools program centered on teacher familiarity with hardware, email, and word processing, along with essential presentation tools.

Nevertheless, these initiatives basically implemented a technocentric approach, the place that the device was prioritized over the pedagogy (Cuban, 2001). As Selwyn (2021) critically observes, such models risked turning teachers into passive recipients of technology rather than reflective agents of pedagogical transformation. Furthermore, the usefulness of these designs was usually measured quantitatively, number of teachers taught, quantity of sessions completed, instead of by any qualitative change in classroom practice or maybe learner results (Trucano, 2015).

This particular emphasis on "technical efficiency" instead of "pedagogical efficacy" rendered several capacity-building programs insufficient for supporting significant teaching change, particularly in complex or under-resourced classroom environments (Voogt et al., 2015). The gap between instruction and also transformation has since resulted in a rethinking of electronic TPD, shifting the discourse toward competence.

2.1.3 Why Competence Matters in New Media Integration

The incorporation of new media into instructional practice demands not only understanding how you can utilize something but also understanding the reason, when, and also for whom it ought to be worn (Koehler & Mishra, 2009). This calls for educators to consider pedagogically and ethically, along with contextually. For instance, utilizing AI-based writing equipment might help foster creativity in one context but reinforce dependency or bias for someone else. Furthermore, the integration of electronic media is profoundly embedded in complicated ethical terrains, digital exclusion, algorithmic bias, surveillance capitalism, misinformation, and data privacy, every one of which needs critical electronic literacy (Livingstone & Helsper, 2007; Selwyn, 2021). Competent teachers have to be equipped not simply to navigate these problems but additionally to empower their students to do exactly the same. Competence, consequently, represents a shift from conformity to company, from equipment adoption to pedagogical innovation, and from uniformity to inclusivity. It allows for teachers to become co-creators of electronic pedagogies, rather than passive users of platforms or content. As Giroux (2011) argues in the context of vital pedagogy, education should cultivate those who could interrogate predominant narratives and solutions and also utilize them in service of imagination, equity, and justice. Competence development in electronic teaching aligns directly with this ethos.

2.2 Theoretical Frameworks for Digital Pedagogical Competence

To move from aspirational rhetoric to actionable design, several theoretical frameworks have emerged to guide the development of digital competence among educators. These models offer both conceptual clarity and implementation strategies for shaping PD initiatives across varied contexts.

2.2.1 Technological Pedagogical Content Knowledge (TPACK)

Koehler and Mishra's (2009) TPACK framework extends Shulman's (1986) *Pedagogical Content Knowledge* model by introducing technology as an integral third domain. It (figure-1) posits that effective teaching with technology requires a thoughtful convergence of:

- Content Knowledge (CK) – Subject-matter expertise
- Pedagogical Knowledge (PK) – Understanding of how students learn
- Technological Knowledge (TK) – Knowledge of digital tools and platforms

Figure 1. Technological Pedagogical Content Knowledge (TPACK)

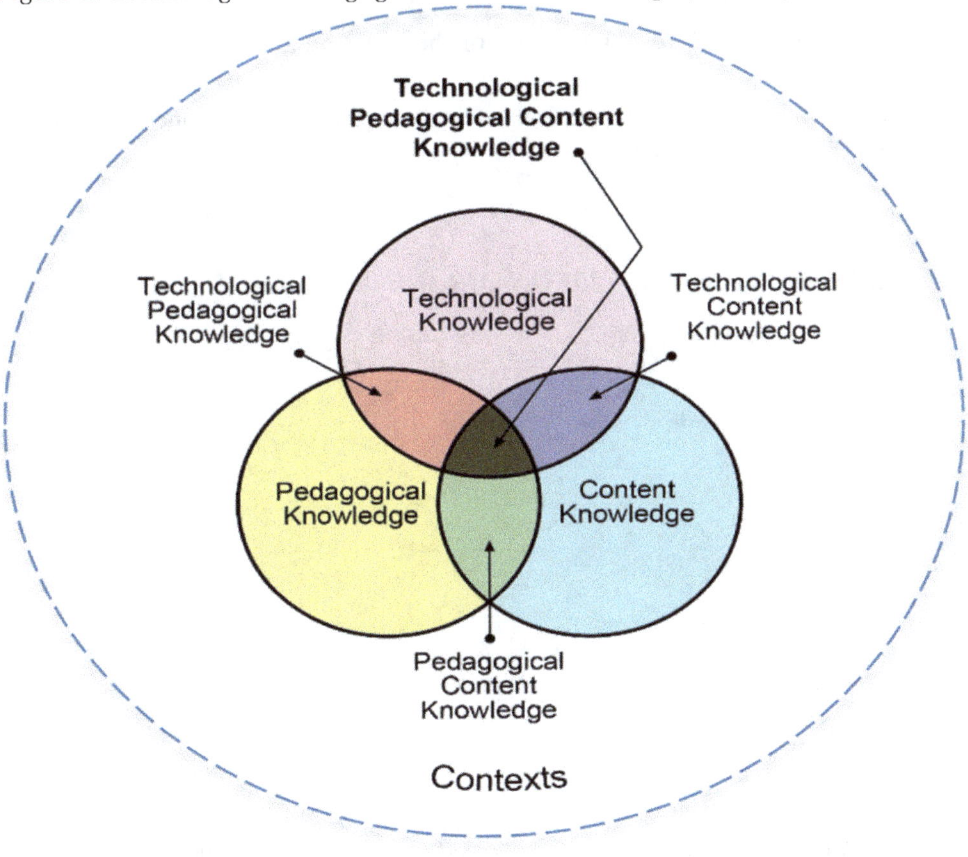

At the heart of TPACK lies the understanding that no single domain operates in isolation (see figure – 1). For instance, knowledge of technology is insufficient unless it is pedagogically sound and content-relevant. This triangulation offers a situated, integrative view of teacher competence. In PD programs, TPACK provides a flexible blueprint to help educators design lessons where media tools are not add-ons but integral to learning objectives. It fosters *design thinking*, reflection, and contextual adaptation—qualities crucial to developing real competence.

2.2.2 SAMR Model: Depth of Technology Use

Ruben Puentedura's (2013) SAMR model complements TPACK by evaluating the *depth* of *technology integration* in learning tasks (see figure -2):

1. Substitution – Tech acts as a direct substitute (e.g., digital textbook)
2. Augmentation – Tech adds some functional improvements (e.g., embedded videos)
3. Modification – Tech redesigns parts of the task (e.g., collaborative writing in Google Docs)
4. Redefinition – Tech creates entirely new tasks previously inconceivable (e.g., virtual reality field trips)

Figure 2. Ruben Puentedura's (2013) SAMR Model

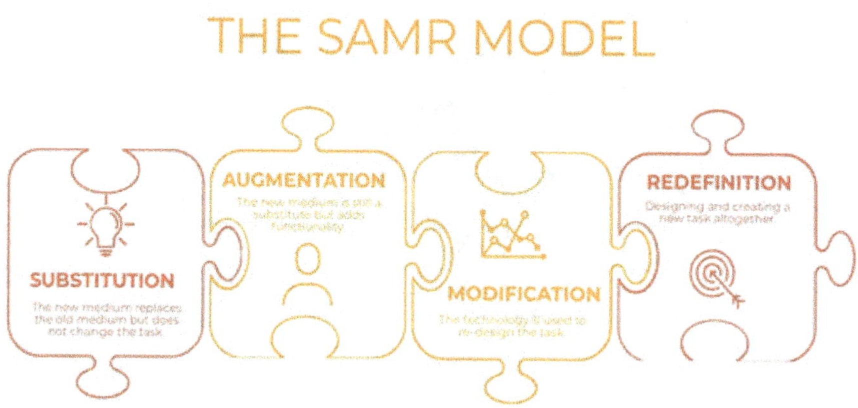

The SAMR model (as shown in figure-2) urges educators to move beyond low-level substitutions toward transformative technology use. PD programs that structure their objectives using SAMR can help teachers reflect on *impact* rather than just *usage*, thereby fostering pedagogical competence.

2.2.3 DigCompEdu Framework

Developed by the European Commission, the Digital Competence of Educators (DigCompEdu) framework (Redecker, 2017) is among the most comprehensive models for mapping teacher digital competence. It identifies six key areas (shown in figure -3):

1. Professional Engagement – Using digital tech for collaboration, professional development
2. Digital Resources – Creating, evaluating, and sharing digital content
3. Teaching and Learning – Orchestrating digital pedagogies effectively
4. Assessment – Employing tech-based formative/summative assessment
5. Empowering Learners – Personalization, accessibility, and inclusive practices
6. Facilitating Learner Digital Competence – Helping students become digitally literate

Figure 3. DigCompEdu Framework (Redecker, 2017)

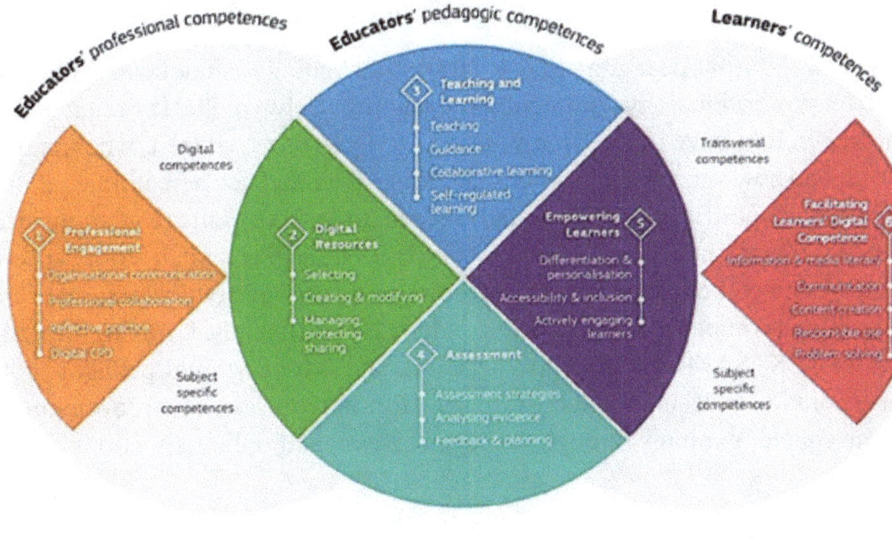

This framework places equal emphasis on professional ethics, inclusivity, and learner agency, aligning closely with UNESCO's vision for digital education (UNESCO, 2021). It has been used widely across Europe and is increasingly adopted in the Global South to develop modular, self-paced, and micro-credentialed PD programs.

2.2.4 Universal Design for Learning (UDL)

The UDL framework, developed by CAST (2018), offers a powerful lens for creating inclusive digital learning environments. It is grounded in neuroscience and advocates for multiple means of engagement, representation, and action,expression, thus addressing learner variability. In the context of digital pedagogy, UDL encourages teachers to:

- Offer varied formats (e.g., text, video, audio) to support comprehension
- Use assistive technologies (e.g., screen readers, captions) to enhance accessibility
- Allow students to demonstrate understanding in different ways (e.g., video, poster, essay)

For professional development, UDL serves a dual purpose: training teachers *about* inclusive design, and delivering PD *through* inclusive practices. It aligns particularly well with the goal of equity-oriented competence development.

2.2.5Critical Digital Pedagogy and Teacher Agency

It is critical digital pedagogy that points out technology is not neutral but constructed by power, ideology, and political economy (Selwyn, 2021; Freire, 1970). Teachers therefore have to question whose knowledge is privileged, who controls platforms, and how surveillance affects autonomy. Competence here implies ethical reflexivity, sociopolitical awareness, and resistance to technocratic reductionism, as teachers are transformative intellectuals (Giroux 1988). The switch from capacity building to competence development is an epistemological and ethical turn: capacity gives tools, and competence gives vision, judgment, and agency. Using frameworks such as TPACK, SAMR, DigCompEdu, UDL, and critical digital pedagogy, this section theoretically designs inclusive and transformative professional development, which the chapter explores through models, barriers, and policy directions.

3. GLOBAL AND NATIONAL POLICY CONTEXTS

The integration of new media and teacher competence is emphasized in global and national education policies, yet implementation often remains fragmented and tool-focused. This section reviews UNESCO frameworks and India's NEP 2020 with related digital initiatives, highlighting alignments, divergences, and the gap between policy discourse and classroom practice.

3.1 International Guidelines

3.1.1 UNESCO ICT Competency Framework for Teachers (ICT-CFT)

First released in 2008 and revised in 2011 and 2018, the ICT Competency Framework for Teachers (ICT-CFT) is a global benchmark for developing teacher capacities in digital pedagogy (UNESCO, 2022). The framework has six components: ICT in education, curriculum and assessment, pedagogy, and ICT tools and applications. - organization and administration; - teacher professional learning, at three developmental stages: technology literacy, knowledge deepening, and knowledge creation.

The framework argues that teachers need to move beyond functional digital proficiency to creative users and critically thinkers who can use technology to redesign curricula as well as learning environments (Kozma, 2008). However, implementation in low-and middle-income countries has frequently lacked contextual adaptation, so that technocentric and top-down teacher training disregarded teachers' different realities (Trucano, 2015).

3.1.2 Sustainable Development Goal 4: Quality and Inclusive Education

As part of the 2030 Agenda for Sustainable Development, SDG four refers to "ensuring access to quality education for everyone and lifelong learning opportunities" (UNESCO, 2015). Target 4.c identifies adequately trained teachers as one foundation for equitable educational outcomes. This connection was reinforced by the COVID-19 pandemonium, which highlighted digital inequity as well as the need to build teacher competence to support remote and blended learning (UNESCO, 2021). A report for 2021 by UNESCO, Reimagining Our Futures Together, envisages collaborative, inclusive, and future-focused education systems in which teacher empowerment and critical digital literacy are key reform components (UNESCO, 2021).

3.2 Indian Policy Landscape

3.2.1 National Education Policy (NEP) 2020

India's National Education Policy (NEP) 2020 recognizes the transformative power of technology in teacher education. It recommends establishing NETF as a National Educational Technology Forum for innovation and knowledge sharing, recommends blended modes of instruction, and mandates professional development (Ministry of Education, 2020).

The NEP 2020 sees teachers as agents of a reimagined learning environment and supports DIKSHA as a platform for scalable training. But scholars contend that the policy does not yet specify how such reforms will be framed for marginalized schools, tailored to special educators, or assessed for pedagogical depth. Despite introducing the language of competence, capacity-building models based on surface ICT usage often entangle implementation.

3.2.2 Digital India Initiatives: SWAYAM, DIKSHA, and NISHTHA

India's Digital India initiative includes multiple platforms supporting teacher development:

- SWAYAM, a national MOOC platform, provides free courses for students and educators with credit transfer capabilities (MoE, 2020).
- DIKSHA, launched in 2017, hosts curriculum-aligned e-content and professional development modules in multiple Indian languages (Ministry of Education, 2022).
- NISHTHA is a nationwide teacher training program delivered through blended learning to build foundational, pedagogical, and inclusive capacities among educators.

Although such platforms attempt to democratize PD access, studies indicate their contents are usually standard and of little use in multilingual, rural, or inclusive classrooms (Sandu & Taylor, 2025; Sing Yun, 2023). Assessing teachers usually involves multiple-choice questions or completion badges but not measuring changes in teacher beliefs, practices, or classroom outcomes.

And most platforms make teachers recipients rather than creators of professional knowledge, thereby undermining agency for reflective and adaptive pedagogical decision-making (Lieberman & Miller, 2014).

3.2.3 Limitations of Current Policy Implementation

In spite of progressive visions and investments, teacher professional development (PD) in India remains challenged by rural internet access (only 24% of households online, NFHS-5; IIPS and ICF, 2021), cultural marginalization of tribal and minority languages, standardized programs that do not take into account diverse classroom realities, and a lack of reflective practice that neglects inquiry and teacher-led innovation (Sharma, Mittal, & Zayan, 2023). Global frameworks such as UNESCO

ICT-CFT & SDG 4 and national policies like NEP 2020 & Digital India place digital competence at the heart of 21st-century education; however, there is still a gap between policy rhetoric and practice. Most initiatives continue to prioritize access and basic ICT training over deeper, context-responsive competence. There is a need to move towards reflective, collaborative, and transformative PD models that respect teachers' lived experiences, promote critical and ethical digital pedagogy, and allow educators to reimagine learning through technology.

4. CHALLENGES IN TEACHER PROFESSIONAL DEVELOPMENT

Teacher professional development for digital pedagogy is vital to 21st-century reform, yet its implementation faces structural, pedagogical, and ethical-cultural challenges that intersect and reinforce inequities. This section examines these barriers and stresses the need to move from fragmented capacity-building to holistic, context-responsive competence development.

4.1 Structural Barriers

4.1.1 Infrastructure Gaps and the Digital Divide

Despite significant ICT investments, the digital divide continues to hinder teacher professional development (TPD) in low- and middle-income countries like India. The *National Family Health Survey (NFHS-5)* reported that only 24% of rural households had internet access in 2021 (IIPS & ICF, 2021). Even where connectivity exists, it is often unreliable, low-bandwidth, or unaffordable, limiting both professional learning and classroom application. Teachers struggle with lack of devices, frequent power outages, insufficient technical support, and the absence of ICT policies or maintenance budgets. Such barriers reduce access to symbolic participation rather than meaningful engagement. Many teachers are registered on platforms such as DIKSHA or SWAYAM but lack resources, time, or institutional support to benefit from them (Jayalakshmi & Uma Rani, 2024). Moreover, hardware provision alone does not ensure use; as Warschauer (2003) argues, digital access is embedded in social, cultural, and institutional contexts, requiring mentorship, scaffolding, and systemic support to be effective.

4.1.2 Urban-Rural and Socio-Economic Disparities

Geographic and socioeconomic contexts significantly shape teachers' participation in professional development. Urban teachers, especially in private institutions, often benefit from better infrastructure, faster internet, peer networks, and greater familiarity with innovative practices. By contrast, rural and government school teachers face persistent disadvantages, including limited institutional support, high student–teacher ratios, poor working conditions, and gaps in both language and digital literacy. These inequities intersect with gender, as rural female teachers encounter additional obstacles such as household responsibilities, safety concerns while travelling to training sites, and social restrictions on women's internet use. A uniform digital TPD model fails to address these layered disparities and inadvertently reinforces privilege hierarchies. As Sharma, Mittal, and Zayan (2023) emphasize, such one-size-fits-all approaches hinder the development of localized, culturally grounded, and sustainable pedagogical competence.

4.2 Pedagogical Challenges

4.2.1 Technophobia and Resistance to Change

Integration of technology changes teacher identity and classroom dynamics, but many educators, especially traditional models, exhibit technophobia. That is because of limited exposure, automation fears, technology perceived as dehumanizing, and heavy workloads. Mandatory logins and dashboards push teachers into superficial compliance and turn TPD into a ritual instead of growth (Selwyn, 2021). Overcoming resistance involves mentoring, co-learning, and respecting teachers' professional judgment.

4.2.2 Overreliance on Standardized ICT Training

Current TPD tends to place tool operation above pedagogy in a technocratic logic in which technology is the end in itself (Trucano, 2015). Teachers learn apps or smartboards without design principles, creativity, or adaptability, limiting transferability, especially in low-resource classrooms. Competence requires integration rather than instruction guided by frameworks like TPACK (Koehler and Mishra, 2009).

4.2.3 Lack of Contextual Relevance

Linguistic, cultural, and regional differences; inclusion; and multigrade classroom challenges are often not taken into account in centralized TPD. Such homogenization kills motivation and applicability and disempowers teachers as passive consumers. Effective PD must emerge from teachers' lived realities through participatory, action research models that connect local knowledge, teacher experience, and community needs (Avalos, 2011).

4.3 Ethical and Cultural Issues

4.3.1 Screen Time and Mental Health

Rising digitization raised questions about teacher and student well-being. Frequent screen use leads to fatigue, sleep loss, less activity & a blurred work-life balance. Unrealistic online teaching demands created stress, anxiety, and burnout during the pandemic (Trust and Whalen 2020). Pushing efficiency in disregard of human limits risks de-professionalizing teachers. Competent pedagogy has to be humane, valuing rest, reflection, and mental health as prerequisites for innovation.

4.3.2 Data Privacy and Algorithmic Bias

Digital platforms Personal & performance data, often without transparency & consent in TPD & assessment. Risks include surveillance and punitive monitoring, biased algorithms and weak safeguards (Selwyn, 2021). Ethical pedagogy requires data literacy and critical engagement with platforms & PD modules on digital rights, ethics & data protection.

4.3.3 Linguistic and Cultural Marginalization

Digital PD platforms like DIKSHA & SWAYAM in India operate largely in Hindi and English and embed urban, middle-class, and dominant-caste perspectives. For teachers of tribal, Dalit, or minority-language communities, this leads to alienation and what Alim (2016) calls epistemic injustice—where some knowledge systems are favored and others are erased. In multilingual classrooms effective teaching demands cultural pluralism rather than monotheism. Thus, going from capacity-building to competence development demands systemic, structural, and cultural transformation of PD design and delivery. Barriers that must be removed, structural (access, equity), pedagogical (depth, relevance), and ethical-cultural (justice, dignity), must be addressed locally through locally tailored infrastructure, custom learning models, teacher voice and well-being inclusion, and ethical frameworks on data, diversity, and sustainability.

Table 1 highlights the structural, pedagogical, and ethical-cultural barriers in Teacher Professional Development (TPD), illustrating how gaps in infrastructure, context, and inclusivity hinder meaningful participation. It underscores the need for equity-focused and contextually responsive strategies to ensure sustainable impact.

Table 1. Summary of the Challenges in Teacher Professional Development

Category	Key Challenges	Specific Issues	Implications
4.1 Structural Barriers	**Infrastructure Gaps & Digital Divide**	- Limited internet access (only 24% rural households online, NFHS-5, 2021) - Lack of devices - Power outages - Inadequate technical support - Absence of ICT policies/ budgets	Symbolic rather than meaningful access; limited completion of TPD modules; inability to apply digital pedagogy
	Urban–Rural & Socio-Economic Disparities	- Urban teachers have better access & networks - Rural teachers face poor working conditions, high student-teacher ratios, language/digital literacy gaps - Gendered barriers for female teachers	One-size-fits-all TPD reproduces privilege and inequity; weak localization of competence building
4.2 Pedagogical Challenges	**Technophobia & Resistance to Change**	- Fear/distrust of technology - Anxiety over automation/ job loss - Administrative overload - Coercive adoption methods	Leads to disengagement and superficial compliance; hinders transformative learning
	Overreliance on Standardized ICT Training	- Tool-focused rather than pedagogy-focused - Lack of design principles - No contextual adaptation	Limits transferability; fails in resource-constrained classrooms; stifles creativity
	Lack of Contextual Relevance	- Ignoring linguistic, cultural, curricular diversity - Minimal attention to local challenges (inclusive ed, multigrade classrooms)	Low motivation, poor retention; teachers as passive consumers instead of co-creators
4.3 Ethical & Cultural Issues	**Screen Time & Mental Health**	- Eye strain, sleep disturbance, burnout - Unrealistic expectations during pandemic	Risks de-professionalization; neglect of teacher well-being
	Data Privacy & Algorithmic Bias	- Lack of consent/transparency - Surveillance culture - Bias in algorithms - No redressal for misuse	Undermines trust; reinforces systemic discrimination
	Linguistic & Cultural Marginalization	- Hindi/English dominance in PD platforms - Urban, middle-class, dominant caste bias	Epistemic injustice; alienation of minority-language teachers; neglect of community-rooted pedagogy

5. SHIFTING PARADIGMS: COMPETENCY-BASED TEACHER DEVELOPMENT

The rise of new media has reshaped teaching and learning, challenging a re-thinking of teacher preparation and help. Standard capacity building centered on equipment use, though present-day contexts call for competency-based teacher development (CBTD)—a paradigmatic change that highlights adaptive expertise, ethical engagement, critical reflection, andcollaborative agency. CBTD moves beyond passive exposure to technology toward deliberate, inclusive, and lasting professional growth. This particular section explores 3 important dimensions of CBTD: (1) its core features, (2) participatory and also collaborative models, and (3) integration within continuous, contextual ecosystems.

5.1 Core Features of Competency-Based Models

5.1.1 Adaptive Learning and Personalization

A vital thing about competency-based teacher development (CBTD) is its emphasis on adaptive, personalized learning pathways customized to educators' goals, contexts, and needs (Darling-Hammond et al., 2017). Unlike one-size-fits-all models, CBTD allows teachers to select timelines, formats, or modules, backed by micro credentialing in places like inclusive technology, electronic assessment, or maybe honest AI. These routes frequently utilize formative assessments to offer quick responses, fostering reflection and refinement (Trust & Horrocks, 2016). Frameworks such as DigCompEdu (Redecker, 2017) and UNESCO's ICT CFT (UNESCO, 2022) further offer analysis tools to evaluate proficiency and also guide development. Adaptive learning therefore reframes PD like a responsive trip that honors teacher agency, diversity, and variability.

5.1.2 Reflective Practice and Feedback Loops

Competency development is grounded in manifestation, moving teachers beyond important tech use toward crucial inquiry into pedagogy, learner response, andpersonal context. Schön's (1992) "reflective practitioner" frames teaching as reflection on and in action. In CBTD, this is discovered through electronic portfolios, peer and self-assessment, coaching, and action research. Such practices build metacognition, helping teachers question assumptions, adapt techniques, and also assess ethical implications, for instance, analyzing exactly how AI tools shape creativity or maybe just how screen time policies impact attention. Feedback from colleagues plus mentors fosters dialogic learning (Lave & Wenger, 1991), deepening practice through dialogue instead of isolated content consumption.

5.1.3 Ethics, Values, and Digital Citizenship

Competence in electronic pedagogy must be morally grounded. In an era of surveillance, exclusion, algorithmic bias, and misinformation, teachers need much more than specialized ability, they have to understand the political and social implications of technology (Selwyn, 2021). Professional development must embed electronic ethics and citizenship, emphasizing privacy, critical media literacy, inclusive and safe online behavior, awareness of algorithmic bias, and advocacy for UDL. For example, a teacher utilizing a behavior tracking app must assess how it manages the information, the way it might stereotype learners, and also if it supports inclusive pedagogy (Livingstone & Helsper, 2007). Digital competence hence becomes inseparable from learner agency, social justice, and democratic values, positioning teachers as ethical decision-makers and public intellectuals.

5.2 Participatory and Collaborative Learning Models

5.2.1 Learning Communities and Peer Mentoring

Competency-based professional development (CBTD) rejects teaching as an isolated profession, emphasizing communities of practice (Wenger, 1998). Peer knowledge exchange, collaborative inquiry, and mentoring improve motivation, retention, and effectiveness when supported institutionally (Avalos, 2011; Lieberman & Miller, 2014). In India, grassroots learning circles in rural and tribal regions show just how peer-led PD could be much more sustainable as well as culturally relevant than top-down workshops.

5.2.2 Co-Design of Digital Content

Competence grows through innovative authorship, not passive adoption. Involving teachers in co-designing OERs, translating, localizing modules, establishing context-based assessments, and electronic storytelling increases ownership, motivation, and expert identity (Beetham & Sharpe, 2013). Co-design likewise democratizes knowledge creation, amplifying marginalized voices.

5.2.1 Teachers as Curators and Facilitators

Amid abundant electronic online resources, teachers need to serve as critical curators, evaluating materials for accessibility, accuracy, and bias; adapting them for learner diversity; and also facilitating inquiry through brand new media. Below, teachers shift from "sage on the stage" to "guide on the side," empowered as reflective, independent facilitators of collaborative learning.

5.3 Continuous and Contextual Learning Ecosystems

5.3.1 Lifelong Learning

Competency development is a lifelong process formed by changing learner needs, goals, and technologies (Darling-Hammond et al., 2017). Professional development should provide flexible, anytime, anywhere opportunities; recognize informal learning; support self-assessment and personalized trajectories; and also employ micro-credentials or digital badges to draw growth. Platforms such as SWAYAM, Edmodo, and Coursera are able to function as lifelong learning networks when stuck with pedagogical depth, reflection, and then customization.

5.3.2 Linking Pre-Service and In-Service Development

A significant gap in teacher training is the disconnection between pre-service education, which introduces pedagogy and ICT, and in-service programs, which frequently emphasize compliance and short-term goals. Competency-based systems should incorporate these stages right into a seamless continuum by embedding electronic pedagogy in B.Ed. and D.El.Ed. curricula, making sure mentors model skilled practices, building alumni networks for knowledge exchange, and adopting performance-based assessments to observe growth across career stages. Such coherence strengthens long-term impact, professional identity, and sustainability (Opfer & Pedder, 2011).

5.3.3 Integration with Institutional Mission and Vision

Competency-based teacher development (CBTD) has to be lodged in institutional culture, not treated as an add-on. Administrators and policymakers must align PD with institutional objectives of equity, addition, and innovation; set aside protected time for learning; involve teachers in policy and curriculum design; and also identify teacher leadership. Such environments promote lifelong learning, collaboration, and reflection, encouraging teachers and enhancing learner outcomes as well as school resilience. CBTD shifts professional development out of fixed, compliance-driven education to powerful, participatory, and, moreover, morally grounded systems. Its core principles, adaptive learning, co-design, ethical awareness, collaboration, reflective practice, and institutional integration, create an interdependent ecosystem of growth. Recognizing the possibility of new media in education requires reimagining teachers as designers, collaborators, facilitators, and critical thinkers in electronic spaces. Competence is therefore not really a checklist but a transformative capacity, reshaping pedagogy, policy, and society.

The last portions of the chapter will provide designs, case studies, andpolicy recommendations to further illustrate exactly how this particular paradigm could be enacted in practice.

6. INNOVATIVE PRACTICES AND MODELS

The transformation of teacher professional development (TPD) in the electronic era demands modern techniques that transcend standard workshop-based formats. With all the rise of new media technologies and evolving pedagogical paradigms, professional development must be more powerful and interactive, along with contextually embedded. This particular section explores two large categories of development in teacher development, hybrid and blended versions, along with experiential and also reflective models highlighting pedagogical philosophies, strategies, and the tools that underpin them.

6.1 Blended and Hybrid Professional Development Models

Hybrid and blended models incorporate the versatility and also scalability of internet learning together with the contextual depth and also relational richness of synchronous or face-to-face engagement. They provide teachers opportunities to get into quality content, take part in collaborative reflection, and put on new strategies inside their very own classrooms, all while keeping expert autonomy.

6.1.1 MOOCs, Webinars, and Online Coaching

Significant Open Online Courses (MOOCs) have emerged as a favorite format for large-scale teacher development. Platforms like SWAYAM (India), edX, and Coursera, along with FutureLearn, offer MOOCs on topics ranging from electronic pedagogy to inclusive training and subject-specific instruction. These classes frequently feature multimedia lectures, quizzes, and discussion boards, along with peer assessment activities, enabling asynchronous and self-paced learning. While

MOOCs are cost-effective and accessible, their efficacy improves significantly when incorporated with follow-up support, coaching, or mentorship. Internet coaching, through tools such as Zoom, Google Meet, or maybe WhatsApp groups that enables personalized feedback and sustained engagement. A study suggests that coaching models are definitely more powerful compared to one-time workshops, particularly whenever they concentrate on job-embedded practice and foster inquiry-based reflection (Kraft, Blazar, & Hogan, 2018). Webinars, both live and recorded, enable teachers to keep up with current trends and equipment. Nevertheless, their impact is amplified when paired with reflection journals, case discussions, or follow-up tasks, which foster active construction of expertise compared to passive consumption.

6.1.2 Mobile-Based Microlearning

In contexts where time, bandwidth, andresources are limited, especially in low-income or rural areas, mobile-based microlearning provides an important option. These models deliver short, focused learning units (3-7 minutes each) by smartphones, frequently utilizing apps, YouTube videos, podcasts, or perhaps messaging platforms such as Telegram or WhatsApp. For example, the DIKSHA platform in India offers mobile-accessible teacher training modules in regional languages, aligned with national curriculum standards. Teachers are able to access bite-sized learning objects, quizzes, and infographics, including videos, along with reflective prompts. Microlearning helps with just-in-time learning, permitting teachers to resolve classroom issues on the go. It supports constant learning, accommodates various schedules, and also encourages self-regulated professional development (Buchem & Hamelmann, 2010). Additionally, it complements formal education by enabling exploration, reinforcement, and revision of niche topics. Nevertheless, for microlearning to be impactful, it should be pedagogically designed, sequenced meaningfully, contextualized for neighborhood needs, and also stuck with opportunities for reflection and feedback.

6.2 Experiential and Reflective Models

While online and blended modes expand access and flexibility, true professional transformation usually comes from experiential learning in which teachers take part in reflection, experimentation, and practice-based inquiry. Experiential models draw from Kolb's (1984) learning cycle is application, conceptualization, reflection, and experience, and also highlight the improvement of praxis: the fusion of theory and practice through critical reflection (Freire, 1970).

6.2.1 Digital Sandboxes and Learning Labs

Electronic sandboxes are safe, low-stakes environments where teachers can test out new resources, instructional strategies, or maybe electronic content with no fear of failure. These may be internet simulations, collaborative playgrounds, or maybe in-house tech labs whereby educators explore tools like interactive whiteboards, AR/VR platforms, AI writing assistants, or maybe gamification apps. For instance, a school may create a "sandbox classroom" with varied ed tech tools and get teachers to co-plan and simulate lessons. Such hands-on, discovery-oriented settings help teachers develop creativity, curiosity, and confidence, key competencies for navigating electronic teaching (Beetham & Sharpe, 2013). Learning labs extend the idea into organized, action-oriented modules whereby teachers collaboratively design, check, and also perfect educational methods. They frequently involve cycles of design thinking and peer responses, along with iterative improvement, which makes them perfect for advertising educational innovation and design literacy.

6.2.2 Action Research in Classrooms

Action research is an excellent way for teachers to become systematic inquirers about their own practice. Here teachers choose a classroom problem to solve, design an intervention, collect data, and reflect on outcomes. The cycle of planning, acting, observing, and reflecting improves classroom practice as well as research orientation. For example, a teacher may examine "Does the flipped classroom video increase engagement for slow learners?" or "How do online polling tools change formative assessment?" Action research helps teachers to:

- Tailor solutions to their unique context
- Engage in data-informed decision-making
- Contribute to the professional knowledge base
- Develop agency and self-efficacy (Cochran-Smith & Lytle, 2009)

In the Indian context, action research has been institutionalized in several states through SCERTs and SSA programs. However, sustained impact requires scaffolding, mentorship, documentation support, and opportunities for dissemination.

6.2.3 Reflective Journaling and Professional Portfolios

Teachers need reflection. Practices like reflective journaling and digital portfolios enable educators to analyze classroom decisions, learner responses, and ethical dilemmas to increase metacognitive awareness and document professional development (Schon, 1992). Digital platforms like Google Docs, Padlet, Mahara, and Canvas allow multimodal journaling, peer feedback, and e-portfolios for appraisal, self-evaluation, and sharing of best practices. Looking forward, teacher professional development must involve diversification, personalization, and transformation. Innovative models such as MOOCs, microlearning, learning labs, action research, journaling, and portfolios allow flexible, teacher-centered alternatives to rigid training. Yet innovation must be grounded in pedagogy and ethics, responsive to teachers' contexts, and supportive of agency.

Table 2 provides a consolidated summary of the innovative practices and models in Teacher Professional Development (TPD) discussed above. It highlights how different approaches—ranging from blended and mobile-based models to experiential and reflective practices—can foster flexibility, creativity, and inclusivity. At the same time, the table underscores the need for contextual adaptation, infrastructural support, and sustained mentoring to ensure meaningful outcomes.

Table 2. Summary of Innovative Practices and Models in Teacher Professional Development

Category	Model / Approach	Key Features	Benefits	Considerations / Limitations
6.1 Blended & Hybrid Professional Development	**MOOCs, Webinars & Online Coaching**	- Self-paced multimedia content - Peer forums, quizzes - Coaching via Zoom/Meet/WhatsApp	Scalable, cost-effective, flexible; supports continuous learning; enhanced impact with mentorship	Risk of passive learning; needs follow-up tasks and feedback
	Mobile-Based Microlearning	- 3–7 min learning units - Delivered via apps, podcasts, videos, messaging apps - Local language content	Just-in-time learning; adaptable to rural/low-resource contexts; supports self-regulated PD	Needs careful sequencing, contextualization, and reflective prompts
6.2 Experiential & Reflective Models	**Digital Sandboxes & Learning Labs**	- Safe, hands-on experimentation spaces - Explore AR/VR, gamification, interactive whiteboards - Collaborative design & simulation	Builds confidence, creativity, design literacy; fosters innovation	Requires infrastructure, facilitation, and time allocation

continued on following page

Table 2. Continued

Category	Model / Approach	Key Features	Benefits	Considerations / Limitations
	Action Research in Classrooms	- Teachers identify problems, design interventions, collect/ analyze data - Iterative improvement cycles	Context-specific solutions; strengthens agency & research skills; contributes to knowledge base	Needs mentorship, documentation, and dissemination support
	Reflective Journaling	- Ongoing written, audio, or visual reflection - Focus on metacognition, classroom experiences, and ethical dilemmas	Enhances self-awareness, critical thinking, and professional judgment	Requires discipline, prompts, and safe sharing environments
	Professional Portfolios	- Curated evidence of growth: lesson plans, recordings, feedback, student work - Digital or physical formats	Supports appraisal, certification, goal-setting; shares best practices	Must be intentional and tied to learning goals

6.3 Case Studies

While theories and models supply conceptual clarity, it's the based encounters of implementation that usually spotlight the actual potential, and pitfalls of teacher professional development (TPD). This area draws from illustrative national and global case studies that showcase just how electronic innovation, contextual adaptation, and teacher agency intersect in substantial ways. These examples not only validate the strategies mentioned in earlier sections but also additionally underscore the range of pathways whereby professional competence may be grown.

6.3.1 National Case Studies (India)

6.3.1.1 DIKSHA: Digital Infrastructure for Knowledge Sharing

Launched in 2017 by the Ministry of Education, the DIKSHA platform is India's flagship electronic repository for teacher training and classroom resources. Created as a multilingual, modular, and mobile-friendly platform, DIKSHA offers self-paced master development content aimed at state curricula and also NEP 2020 recommendations (MoE, 2020). Main features include:

- QR-coded textbook integration
- Microlearning modules with certification

- Interactive videos, simulations, and assessments
- Contextual content in over 30 Indian languages

A study by Jandhyala (2020) found that DIKSHA significantly improved teachers' access to training resources, particularly in remote regions. However, it also noted limitations, such as low digital literacy, inconsistent internet access, and limited engagement with reflective or constructivist pedagogy. Despite these challenges, DIKSHA represents an innovative, scalable PD model that bridges geography, language, and resource barriers.

6.3.1.2 SWAYAM: A National MOOC Initiative

The SWAYAM (Study Webs of Active Learning for Young Aspiring Minds) is a national initiative providing more than 2000 classes, including teacher training modules. Created by institutions such as NCERT, NIOS, and IGNOU, these MOOCs offer content in several disciplines with integrated assessments and credit transfer (SWAYAM, 2022). A critical improvement is its integration of peer discussion boards, downloadable content for offline access, and teacher upskilling in electronic pedagogy. Courses such as "Pedagogy of Science" or "ICT in Education" encourage serious engagement with technology consumption. A crucial result of SWAYAM is its open access ethos—making certain expert learning isn't constrained by institutional affiliation. Nevertheless, the absence of personalized field-based reflection, action-oriented assignments, and support is still a limitation (Singh, 2019; Azhar & Ahmad Rashid, 2025).

6.3.2 International Case Studies

6.3.2.1 SELFIE Tool - European Commission

The SELFIE (Self-reflection on Effective Learning by Fostering the Usage of Innovative Educational Technologies) device, created by the European Commission, is an electronic framework that can help schools assess just how efficiently they're utilizing technology in teaching and learning (European Commission, 2021).

Key features include:

- Anonymous self-assessment surveys for teachers, students, and administrators
- Customized feedback reports
- Insights to develop digital action plans for whole-school development

SELFIE fosters collective ownership of electronic transformation, as it engages many stakeholders in the evaluation operation. Around two million people across seventy-six countries used SELFIE, usually as a precursor to school-wide PD initiatives. The tool exemplifies a data-driven, participatory type of professional development that moves beyond specific ability acquisition to institutional capacity building (Redecker, 2021).

6.3.2.2 OpenLearn – The Open University, UK

OpenLearn, a free learning platform by The Open University, offers more than 1000 short courses, including a robust collection of PD modules for teachers. These include "Supporting Children's Mental Health," "Becoming an Inclusive Educator," and "Digital Literacy for Educators."

Distinctive features of OpenLearn:

- Certificates of participation
- Integration of multimedia and scenario-based learning
- Open badges for micro-credentials

OpenLearn's emphasis on versatility, open access, and inclusive design makes it popular among educators in the Global South, like India and sub-Saharan Africa. Scientific studies indicate that OpenLearn fosters lifelong learning behavior, particularly when learners make use of the platform to address certain classroom challenges (Weller et al., 2018).

6.3.2.3 Teacher-Led Innovations in Low-Resource Settings

Several of probably the most impactful master development models emerge not from top-down platforms but from the grassroots new developments of teachers running in low-resource contexts. These examples highlight just how agency, creativity, and even collaboration are able to drive significant professional development, maybe even in the lack of semiformal structures.

6.3.2.4 Peer Learning Circles in Rural Maharashtra

For some government institutions in Maharashtra, teachers formed casual learning circles just where they met fortnightly to go over experiments, share strategies, and discuss classroom challenges with electronic resources. These group meetings, frequently carried out in school libraries or maybe community halls, were self-organized and driven by shared goals.

Teachers created lesson podcasts in Marathi, adapted open-source tools such as GeoGebra and Kahoot, and also exchanged peer feedback on WhatsApp. This particular model exemplifies situated expert learning, based in teachers' lived realities and sustained through mutual support as well as reflection (Nayak, 2020).

6.3.2.4 Radio-Based PD in Sub-Saharan Africa

In lands such as Kenya, Tanzania, and Nigeria, community radio stations are already utilized to broadcast weekly teacher education programs, primarily during COVID-19. These broadcasts are usually followed by mobile quizzes or maybe reflective discussions via SMS and WhatsApp. This particular version represents a low-tech feature that is inclusive and accessible, along with being contextually adaptive, overcoming electronic divides through innovative usage of legacy technologies (UNESCO, 2021).

6.3.2.5 The "Tech for Teaching" WhatsApp Group in Assam

In Assam, a team of upper-primary teachers began a WhatsApp set during the pandemic to go over the usage of Flipgrid, Google Forms, and YouTube in online classes. The group turned into a collaborative expert network, in which instructors shared lesson plans, mentored novices, and co-developed digital content. Additionally, they invited resource persons to do mini webinars, reflecting a bottom-up model of CPD that fosters teacher leadership and digital confidence. Their story, recognized by the Azim Premji Foundation (2022), underscores the possibility of teacher-led, mobile-enabled PD ecosystems. These diverse case studies indicate that originality in teacher professional development is able to emerge across scales, technologies, and cultural contexts. While national platforms like SWAYAM and DIKSHA leverage scale and infrastructure, overseas versions like OpenLearn and SELFIE provide reflective, inclusive frameworks. Above all, teacher-led innovations reaffirm the importance of contextual relevance, collaboration, and agency in professional learning. As electronic education will continue to develop, the best PD models are going to be the ones that are flexible but rigorous, scalable but private, and worldwide in vision yet community in practice.

7. INCLUSIVE AND EQUITABLE APPROACHES

equity and Inclusion should be main to teacher professional development (PD), not peripheral. In the electronic era, models that ignore diversity danger reinforcing exclusion. This specific section examines techniques, like Universal Design for Learning (UDL), assistive technologies, moreover culturally responsive pedagogy to make sure PD is inclusive for exclusive educators, rural teachers, and linguistically and culturally diverse communities.

7.1 Addressing Needs of Special Educators and Rural Teachers

Regardless of the promise of electronic transformation, the ability to access professional development (PD) stays uneven. Special educators frequently lack inclusive content and training for disability-specific pedagogy, while rural teachers face terrible connectivity, limited hardware, andlanguage barriers, excluding them from mainstream initiatives (UNESCO, 2021). Really inclusive PD should offer modules on assistive pedagogy, contextualized vernacular material, offline or low-tech solutions (e.g., SMS, radio, downloadable resources), as well as mentorship networks linking under-resourced and experienced educators. India's NISHTHA program, with modules on addition and foundational literacy in eleven languages, is a step ahead, but its top-down delivery and sensitive follow-up coaching undermine contextual relevance (KPMG, 2021).

7.2 UDL-Based Integration in Teacher Training

Universal Design for Learning (UDL) provides a robust pedagogical framework to ensure all learners, including those with disabilities, can access and engage with content meaningfully. Developed by CAST (Center for Applied Special Technology), UDL is based on three guiding principles (shown in figure 5):

- Multiple means of representation (how content is presented)
- Multiple means of action and expression (how learners demonstrate understanding)
- Multiple means of engagement (how learners are motivated and sustained)

Figure 4. Universal Design for Learning (UDL)

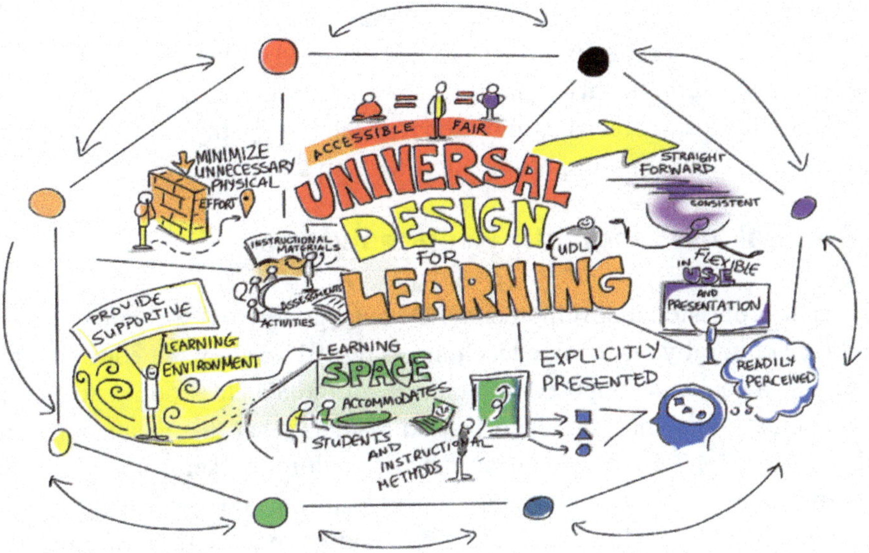

In the context of PD, UDL (see figure 4) can guide the design of inclusive training materials. For example:

- Use captioned videos and text-to-speech tools to make content accessible for teachers with hearing or visual impairments.
- Offer a choice of formats—videos, infographics, readings, podcasts—for diverse learner preferences.
- Encourage goal setting and self-assessment, particularly for teachers in non-traditional learning environments.

UDL-aligned PD helps educators not only build their own digital competence but also develop the capacity to implement inclusive pedagogy in their classrooms. Studies have indicated that teachers trained in UDL principles are more likely to differentiate instruction and adopt a strengths-based approach to disability (Rao, Smith, & Lowrey, 2017).

7.3 Accessibility Tools and Inclusive Digital Pedagogy

Accessibility in electronic learning isn't just technical but ethical. Teachers require training to meaningfully integrate assistive technologies like screen readers (NVDA, Braille displays, keyboard navigation, captions, and JAWS), along with multimodal assessments. Platforms such as DIKSHA are putting in accessibility features, but consciousness and usability training remain gaps. Inclusive pedagogy becomes further defined by designing activities with several modes of expression, fostering peer collaboration between learners with and without disabilities, and also embedding social-emotional learning. Professional development must provide teachers with challenges to ableist assumptions, develop empathy, and adjust strategies with techniques that support participation with no stigma.

7.4 Cultural and Linguistic Responsiveness

Teacher professional development (PD) must go beyond specialized education to embrace culturally responsive teaching (Gay, 2010), allowing educators to treat diversity as a source as opposed to a barrier. In India's classrooms, shaped by regional contexts, religions, castes, or varied dialects what this means is grounding curriculum in neighbourhood awareness, sharing culturally useful practices, critically examining biases in electronic resources, and fostering code-switching or bilingual techniques to allow for linguistic minorities and learners with disabilities (Singh, 2025). Instances like combining tribal ecological understanding in science teaching illustrate just how community voices enrich pedagogy. Ultimately, inclusive PD grounded in cultural responsiveness, assistive technologies, and UDL is crucial for democratizing training in the electronic age, representation, ensuring accessibility, and company for both learners and teachers. True development is not in sophisticated programs but rather in their power to add the excluded, amplify marginalized voices, and format education with equity, empathy, and sustainability.

8. FUTURE DIRECTIONS

In the electronic age, teachers should develop from transmitters of expertise to reflective practitioners, designers, and facilitators. This involves reimagining teacher professional development (TPD) as justice-oriented, inclusive, and continuous, with policies and practices that ensure sustainable agency and coherent impact.

- Policy Coherence and Contextual Relevance: Despite several initiatives, TPD is still fragmented, standardized, and detached from teachers' realities, particularly in multilingual and rural contexts (UNESCO, 2021; Mishra & Koehler, 2006). Coming reforms must incorporate policies across ministries, involve local actors in preparation, align pre-service and in-service curricula, and also follow participatory monitoring methods to evaluate inclusivity and adaptability.

- Agency, Voice, and Teacher Autonomy: Policy should shift from compliance to autonomy, recognizing teachers as change agents. Future directions normally include modular, personalized PD pathways; recognition of practice-based innovations; participatory governance in curriculum & resource design; and distributed leadership through teacher "tech champions." Research suggests that autonomy deepens and also sustains engagement (Webster-Wright, 2009; Fullan, 2007).
- Impactful and sustainable PD: one-off workshops and generic courses neglect to create long-lasting change. Rather, PD should construct combined ecosystems combining coaching, webinars, and MOOCs; stackable micro credentials; peer-led learning communities; and embedded reflective practices (journals, portfolios, and action research), along with feedback-driven improvement. The main objective needs to go from event-based to process-oriented, hierarchical to collaborative, and passive to co-creative, aligning with 21st-century visions of networked learning (Siemens, 2005; Hargreaves & Fullan, 2012).

9. RECOMMENDATIONS FOR STAKEHOLDERS

For Government and Policymakers

- Mandate Equity Standards in PD: Ensure inclusion of accessibility features, UDL frameworks, and content in regional languages.
- Budget for Continuous PD: Allocate dedicated funds for CPD, technology integration, and coaching support in schools.
- Policy Innovation Hubs: Create state-level or national innovation labs to pilot, evaluate, and scale innovative PD models.
- Data and Ethics Protocols: Develop regulatory frameworks around AI, learning analytics, and teacher monitoring tools to safeguard privacy and well-being.

For Educational Institutions

- Embed PD in Institutional Culture: Include structured time for PD in teachers' workload and performance appraisals.
- Create Digital Leadership Positions: Designate teacher mentors or ICT pedagogues who support others in their digital learning journey.

- Support Cross-Disciplinary Learning: Encourage collaboration between language, science, special education, and ICT faculties for integrated digital pedagogy.
- Facilitate Inclusive Infrastructure: Invest in assistive technologies, screen-reader-compatible platforms, and multimodal learning environments.

For Ed-Tech Companies and Developer

- Design with UDL and Accessibility Principles: Co-create tools with inputs from special educators, rural teachers, and diverse learners.
- Open Licensing and Localization: Promote OER platforms with Creative Commons licensing and multilingual content.
- Teacher Co-Creation Models: Involve teachers as design partners, beta testers, and evaluators in product development.
- Ethical AI Use in PD Platforms: Ensure algorithmic transparency, bias audits, and data consent protocols in personalized learning systems.

10. CONCLUSION

New media inclusion in education isn't just a technological shift but an epistemic, pedagogical, and cultural shift that recasts the teacher as a 21st-century agent of change. This chapter has advocated moving beyond capacity-building based on basic tool use and compliance to competence, defined as a dynamic, reflective, and adaptive practice. Competence involves more than technical proficiency: it involves pedagogical insight, critical awareness, collaboration, and ethical responsibility. Frameworks like TPACK, SAMR, DigCompEdu, and UDL offer significant scaffolding but are open to being used inclusively and in a context-sensitive manner. Policies (SDG 4, NEP 2020, UNESCO's ICT-CFT) have a progressive vision, but gaps in infrastructure, language equity, and responsiveness limit impact; platforms (DIKSHA, SWAYAM) can help but reach only a limited number of rural, marginalized teachers. Barriers like the digital divide, technophobia, and ethical risks call for a reimagining of professional development through blended learning, micro-credentialing, reflective journaling, and action research that see teachers as co-creators of knowledge and practice. In the long run, teacher professional development has to be viewed as a consistent, ethical, and collaborative process—central not just to adaptation to technological advancement but also to improving transformation, inclusion, and equity in educational systems around the world.

REFERENCES

Alim, H. S. (2016). Critical hip-hop language pedagogies: Combat, consciousness, and the cultural politics of communication. In *Language and social justice in practice*. Routledge.

Avalos, B. (2011). Teacher professional development in teaching and teacher education over ten years. *Teaching and Teacher Education*, *27*(1), 10–20. DOI: 10.1016/j.tate.2010.08.007

Azhar, A., & Ahmad Rashid, R.-A. (2025). A bird's eye-view of MOOCs for pedagogical knowledge and technical skills development of teachers in India. *International Journal of Research and Innovation in Social Science*, *9*(6), 4691–4705. DOI: 10.47772/IJRISS.2025.906000357

Azim Premji Foundation. (2022). Stories of practice: Teachers and school leaders in action during. *COVID, 19*. https://azimpremjifoundation.org

Beetham, H., & Sharpe, R. (Eds.). (2013). *Rethinking Pedagogy for a Digital Age: Designing for 21st Century Learning* (2nd ed.). Routledge., DOI: 10.4324/9780203078952

Buchem, I., & Hamelmann, H. (2010). Microlearning: A strategy for ongoing professional development. eLearning Papers, 21(1), 1–15.

CAST. (2018). Universal design for learning guidelines version 2.2. Retrieved from: http://udlguidelines.cast.org. Accessed on 12.09.2025.

Cochran-Smith, M., & Lytle, S. L. (2009). *Inquiry as stance: Practitioner research for the next generation*. Teachers College Press.

Cuban, L. (2001). *Oversold and underused: Computers in the classroom*. Harvard University Press. DOI: 10.4159/9780674030107

Darling-Hammond, L., Hyler, M. E., & Gardner, M. (2017). *Effective teacher professional development*. Learning Policy Institute. DOI: 10.54300/122.311

European Commission. (2021). SELFIE: Supporting schools in digital age. Retrieved from: https://ec.europa.eu/education/schools-go-digital/selfie_en. Accessed on 23.09.2025.

Freire, P. (1970). *Pedagogy of the oppressed*. Continuum.

Fullan, M. (2007). *The new meaning of educational change* (4th ed.). Teachers College Press.

Gay, G. (2010). *Culturally responsive teaching: Theory, research, and practice* (2nd ed.). Teachers College Press.

Giroux, H. A. (1988). *Teachers as intellectuals: Toward a critical pedagogy of learning*. Bergin & Garvey Publishers, Inc.

Giroux, H. A. (2011). *On critical pedagogy*. Bloomsbury Publishing.

Hargreaves, A., & Fullan, M. (2012). *Professional capital: Transforming teaching in every school*. Teachers College Press.

International Institute for Population Sciences (IIPS), & ICF. (2021). National Family Health Survey (NFHS-5), 2019–21: India: Volume I. Mumbai: IIPS. http://rchiips.org/nfhs

Jayalakshmi, P., & Uma Rani, K. (2024). National Education Policy 2020: Prospects & Challenges. KY Publications. http://www.kypublications.com/BOOKS/NEP%20 2020_28-8-2024.pdf

Koehler, M. J., & Mishra, P. (2009). What is technological pedagogical content knowledge? *Contemporary Issues in Technology & Teacher Education*, *9*(1), 60–70. https://citejournal.org/volume-9/issue-1-09/general/what-is-technological -pedagogicalcontent-knowledge

Kolb, D. A. (1984). *Experiential learning: Experience as the source of learning and development*. Prentice Hall., http://academic.regis.edu/ed205/Kolb.pdf

Kozma, R. B. (2008). Comparative analysis of policies for ICT in education. In Voogt, J., & Knezek, G. (Eds.), *International handbook of information technology in primary and secondary education* (Vol. 20, pp. 1083–1096). Springer., DOI: 10.1007/978-0-387-73315-9_68

KPMG. (2021). *NISHTHA programme evaluation report*. Ministry of Education, Government of India.

Kraft, M. A., Blazar, D., & Hogan, D. (2018). The effect of teacher coaching on instruction and achievement: A meta-analysis of the causal evidence. *Review of Educational Research*, *88*(4), 547–588. DOI: 10.3102/0034654318759268

Lave, J., & Wenger, E. (1991). *Situated learning: Legitimate peripheral participation*. Cambridge University Press. DOI: 10.1017/CBO9780511815355

Lieberman, A., & Miller, L. (2014). Teachers as professionals: Evolving definitions of professional development. In Martin, L. E., & Kragler, S. D. (Eds.), *Handbook of professional development in education* (pp. 3–20). Guilford Press.

Livingstone, S., & Helsper, E. J. (2007). Gradations in digital inclusion: Children, young people and the digital divide. *New Media & Society*, *9*(4), 671–696. DOI: 10.1177/1461444807080335

Ministry of Education. (2022). DIKSHA: One nation one digital platform. Retrieved from" https://diksha.gov.in/. Accessed on 12.08.2025.

Ministry of Education (MoE). (2020). National education policy 2020. Government of India. https://www.education.gov.in/sites/upload_files/mhrd/files/NEP_Final_English_0.pdf

Mishra, P. (2019). Considering contextual knowledge: The TPACK diagram gets an upgrade. *Journal of Digital Learning in Teacher Education*, *35*(2), 76–78. DOI: 10.1080/21532974.2019.1588611

Mishra, P., & Koehler, M. J. (2006). Technological pedagogical content knowledge: A framework for teacher knowledge. *Teachers College Record*, *108*(6), 1017–1054. DOI: 10.1111/j.1467-9620.2006.00684.x

Nayak, P. (2020). Peer learning communities in rural Maharashtra: A bottom-up model for teacher professional development. *Contemporary Education Dialogue*, *17*(1), 120–134. DOI: 10.1177/0973184919890315

OECD. (2009). *Creating effective teaching and learning environments: First results from TALIS*. OECD Publishing., DOI: 10.1787/9789264068780-

Opfer, V. D., & Pedder, D. (2011). Conceptualizing teacher professional learning. *Review of Educational Research*, *81*(3), 376–407. DOI: 10.3102/0034654311413609

Puentedura, R. (2013). SAMR: A contextualized introduction. Retrieved from https://www.hippasus.com/rrpweblog/archives/2013/10/25/SAMRAContextualizedIntroduction.pdf

Rao, K., Smith, S. J., & Lowrey, K. A. (2017). UDL and inclusive practices in schools: A case study of three districts. *Exceptionality Education International*, *27*(1), 1–22. DOI: 10.5206/eei.v27i1.7723

Redecker, C. (2017). *European framework for the digital competence of educators: DigCompEdu*. Publications Office of the European Union., DOI: 10.2760/159770

Redecker, C. (2021). The SELFIE tool and digital competence development in schools. *European Journal of Education*, *56*(4), 529–544. DOI: 10.1111/ejed.12483

Sandu, A., & Taylor, C. (2025). Digital learning technologies usage during Covid-19 lockdowns. *British Educational Research Journal*, *51*(2), 607–628. DOI: 10.1002/berj.4092

Schön, D. A. (1992). *The reflective practitioner: How professionals think in action* (1st ed.). Routledge., DOI: 10.4324/9781315237473

Selwyn, N. (2021). *Education and technology: Key issues and debates* (3rd ed.). Bloomsbury.

Sharma, G., Mittal, R., & Zayan. (2023). Teacher Education in India's National Education Policy 2020: Knowledge Traditions, Global Discourses and National Regulations. Contemporary Education Dialogue, 20(2), 256-282. (Original work published 2023)DOI: 10.1177/09731849231168728

Siemens, G. (2005). Connectivism: A learning theory for the digital age. *International Journal of Instructional Technology and Distance Learning*, *2*(1), 3–10. http://www.itdl.org/Journal/Jan_05/article01.htm

Sing Yun, W. (2023). Digitalization challenges in education during COVID-19: A systematic review. *Cogent Education*, *10*(1), 2198981. Advance online publication. DOI: 10.1080/2331186X.2023.2198981

Singh, A. K. (2025). From policy to practice: Challenges and pathway for advancing multilingual education through India's national education policy 2020. Policy Futures in Education, 23(4), 746-765. (Original work published 2025)DOI: 10.1177/14782103251320532

Singh, N. (2019). SWAYAM–Indian MOOCs: An insider's perspective. *Asian Journal of Distance Education*, *14*(1), 47–55. https://www.asianjde.com/ojs/index.php/AsianJDE/article/view/301

SWAYAM. (2022). About SWAYAM. https://swayam.gov.in

Trilling, B., & Fadel, C. (2009). *21st century skills: Learning for life in our times*. Jossey-Bass/Wiley.

Trucano, M. (2015). Teachers, teaching and ICTs. World Bank EdTech Blog. Retrieved from: https://blogs.worldbank.org/edutech/teachers-teaching-and-icts. Accessed on 23.08.2025.

Trust, T., & Horrocks, B. (2016). 'I never feel alone in my classroom': Teacher professional growth within a blended community of practice. *Professional Development in Education*, *43*(4), 645–665. DOI: 10.1080/19415257.2016.1233507

Trust, T., & Whalen, J. (2020). Should teachers be trained in emergency remote teaching? Lessons Learned from the COVID-19 Pandemic. *Journal of Technology and Teacher Education*, *28*(2), 189–199. https://www.learntechlib.org/primary/p/215995/. DOI: 10.70725/307718pkpjuu

UNESCO. (2015). Transforming our world: The 2030 agenda for sustainable development. United Nations. Retrieved from: https://sdgs.un.org/goals/goal4. Accessed on 10.09.2025.

UNESCO. (2021a). Reimagining our futures together: A new social contract for education. Retrieved from: https://unesdoc.unesco.org/ark:/48223/pf0000379707. Accessed on 14.09.2025.

UNESCO. (2021b). Teacher support and professional development during COVID-19: Review of practices. Retrieved from: https://unesdoc.unesco.org. Accessed on 17.09.2025.

UNESCO. (2022). ICT competency framework for teachers: Version 3. Retrieved from: https://unevoc.unesco.org/home/ICT+CFT+Version+3 Accessed on 15.09.2025.

Voogt, J., Erstad, O., Dede, C., & Mishra, P. (2015). Under which conditions does ICT have a positive effect on teaching and learning? *Journal of Computer Assisted Learning, 31*(5), 491–511. DOI: 10.1111/jcal.12136

Warschauer, M. (2003). *Technology and social inclusion: Rethinking the digital divide*. MIT Press. DOI: 10.7551/mitpress/6699.001.0001

Webster-Wright, A. (2009). Reframing professional development through understanding authentic professional learning. *Review of Educational Research, 79*(2), 702–739. DOI: 10.3102/0034654308330970

Weller, M., Jordan, K., DeVries, I., & Rolfe, V. (2018). Mapping the open education landscape: Citation network analysis of historical open education literature. *Open Praxis, 10*(2), 109–126. DOI: 10.5944/openpraxis.10.2.822

Wenger, E. (1998). *Communities of practice: Learning, meaning, and identity*. Cambridge University Press., DOI: 10.1017/CBO9780511803932

Chapter 10
Empowering Educators for the Digital Age:
A Faculty Development Framework for New Media Integration

Sharika T. R.
https://orcid.org/0000-0003-2836-4407
Adi Shankara Institute of Engineering and Technology, India

Akshaya Jayaraj
https://orcid.org/0009-0009-5512-8240
Adi Shankara Institute of Engineering and Technology, India

S. Anila
https://orcid.org/0009-0003-6558-2304
Adi Shankara Institute of Engineering and Technology, India

Parvathy T. Nair
https://orcid.org/0009-0006-1309-4538
Adi Shankara Institute of Engineering and Technology, India

Chinnu Maria Varghese
Adi Shankara Institute of Engineering and Technology, India

Sanjuna K. R.
https://orcid.org/0009-0009-8802-1175
Adi Shankara Institute of Engineering and Technology, India

ABSTRACT

The technologically driven revolution in engineering education, driven by generative AI, immersive platforms, and emerging media tools, calls for an envisioned shift in faculty development. This chapter presents a comprehensive, evidence-informed Faculty Development Framework designed to meet the challenges of engineering educators in the changing landscape of education. Grounded in the pedagogy-first integration principles the structure proposes five consecutive stages—Orientation, Exploration, Practice, Feedback, and Mentoring that are each intended to boost

DOI: 10.4018/979-8-3373-5157-5.ch010

digital fluency, instructional innovation, and ethics of AI adoption. Embedding tool mapping, evaluation rubrics, and implementation models, the structure ensures adaptability and scalability. It not only readies faculty to successfully implement technology in teaching but also creates a culture of ongoing learning, cooperation, and academic honesty. The chapter is wrapped up with practical strategies for institutionalization, policy coordination, and long-term sustainability of new media practices in engineering education.

1. INTRODUCTION

In the fast-paced digital age of today, students are more attracted to engaging, bite-sized material such as social media reels and interactive websites than they are to one-hour lectures. The COVID-19 pandemic spurred an abrupt shift from blackboards to PowerPoint slides, but the move was largely superficial digitizing static lectures rather than reconsidering pedagogical strategies. In spite of the explosion in digital tools and emerging media technologies, the typical engineering classroom continues to be faculty-centred where students continue to be passive receivers instead of active learners. Strategies such as collaborative learning, flipped classrooms, and active learning are infrequently implemented, and this gap between student expectations and the instruction method of practice continues to widen. Today's students look for inclusive, participatory, and technologically rich learning spaces, but the majority of the faculty members are not oriented and confident enough to fulfil these expectations. This calls for an immediate necessity for formal faculty development programs that not only familiarize teachers with next-generation digital tools but also provide training on how to incorporate these meaningfully into their pedagogy.

In addition to that, engineering education is closely connected with hands-on skills, problem-solving, and innovation, areas that can be greatly developed using immersive technologies such as virtual laboratories, coding simulations, augmented reality (AR), collaborative tools such as Google Jamboard, and AI-powered assistants. Yet all these tools tend to go underused in foundational subjects because they lack awareness, training, or institutional buy-in. Faculty, particularly those educated in conventional pedagogies, can feel swamped by the accelerating pace of technical change and unsure how to connect these tools with learning objectives and assessment plans.

This chapter calls for a faculty development model specifically designed for the engineering educator, with an emphasis on allowing effective new media integration. Not simply to instruct the 'how' of tool usage, but to create a mindset change toward reflective, student-focused, and outcomes-oriented teaching. The framework suggested in the following draws on experiential evidence, institutional case studies, and feedback from faculty development workshops to detail a step-by-step digital empowerment strategy. Through systematic interventions, ongoing mentoring, and exposure to cost-free or low-cost media platforms, teachers can be well positioned to design classrooms that are dynamic, participatory, and responsive to the exigencies of digitally native learners.

1.1. The Digital Shift in Engineering Education

In the age of Instagram reel, YouTube short, and AI contents, student attention spans have shortened substantially, and their learning environment expectations are quite different now. The learners are used to instant feedback, visual narratives, and being engaged actively sadly the factors which are frequently not found in conventional engineering classrooms. All too often, much of higher education is still based on lectures, static slides, and a passive learning paradigm in which students are listeners, not contributors. This disconnect not only disengages, but it also reduces the effectiveness of instruction, particularly in an era in which sparking curiosity and maintaining motivation are more crucial than ever.

In this age of digital revolution in education creates a need for leaners to be co-creators using digital simulations, collaborative spaces, AR/VR labs, coding sandboxes, and AI capabilities as not just add-ons but as essential blocks of learning. Leaners definitely will need technical proficiency with these tools but more importantly pedagogical proficiency to integrate them meaningfully. With the interdisciplinary nature of today's engineering education have forced teaching students not just to get by, but to excel in a global, networked world.

1.2. Why Faculty Readiness Matters

Faculty preparedness in new media integration is not just about producing a completely digitized form of course materials or designing a fancy set of interactive videos and notes. Rather, it involves sparking something instilling curiosity and motivation in students to start exploring and working on their own. In the rapidly changing digital age, when students are already inundated with advanced technologies in their daily lives, the educator's role has to change from being a purveyor of content to a catalyst for inspiring, relevant learning.

Engineering faculty in particular have to play the role of change agents, mentors who bring in students to face real-world challenges, industry-specific technologies, and cross-disciplinary innovations that are outside the curriculum. Teaching the mechanics of a subject is not sufficient; instructors need to facilitate students' realization of its uses, its applicability, and its potential impact. It takes more than technology tools; it takes a change in mindset (UNESCO, 2021). Too often, resistance to change, technology, and pedagogical innovation is still one of the greatest hindrances among faculty members.

1.1. Digital Readiness in Indian Engineering Institutions

The use of digital media and tools in teaching engineering is still unequal among Indian institutions. While premier institutions usually take the lead in using smart classrooms, FDPs, and MOOC-based learning, mid- and low-ranked institutions still lag behind in terms of readiness and adoption. As can be seen in Figure 1, some 85% of high NIRF-ranked engineering schools have smart classroom facilities reported compared to only 60% and 35% reported by mid- and low-ranked schools, respectively. Likewise, higher faculty exposure to digital pedagogy training (FDPs) continues to be at 75% in high-ranked institutions while merely 50% and 25% of faculty in mid- and low-ranked institutions have had the same exposure. Use of MOOCs like SWAYAM also displays this trend, decreasing sharply from 70% in the highest-ranked institutions to only 20% in the lower-ranked ones. The gap highlights the imperative for organized and inclusive faculty development systems that can bridge the digital divide in Indian technical education. What we need is a comprehensive Faculty development framework which is globally accepted.

Figure 1. Digital readiness metrics in Indian engineering institutions, based on trends derived from publicly available AICTE reports, NIRF institutional data, and World Bank discussions on higher education digitalization (2022–2024).

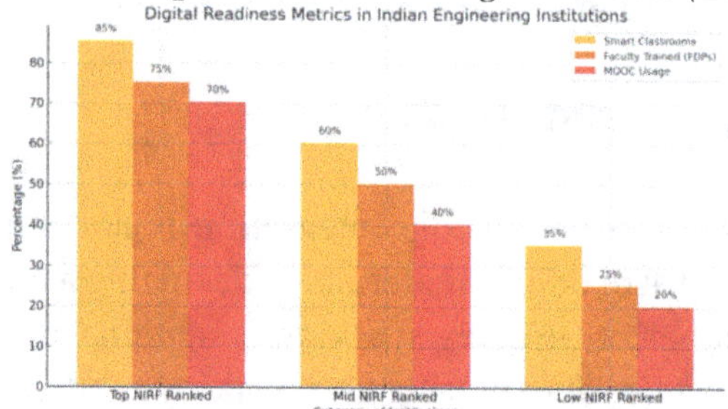

1.2. Objectives of the Chapter

This chapter seeks to respond to the immediate necessity of empowering engineering educators to transition into the fast-changing education ecosystem driven by digital transformation. The primary goals of the chapter are:

- To introduce a systematic framework for faculty development programs to enable engineering educators to phase in and implement digital tools, collaborative platforms, and active learning approaches into their curricula.
- To highlight the faculty's role as agents of change, tasked with inspiring students' curiosity, bringing in real-world problems, and incorporating new technologies like Artificial Intelligence, Augmented/Virtual Reality, simulation spaces, and interactive media.
- To provide actionable strategies, toolkits, and case-based examples that will allow engineering faculty to weave new media methodologies into their classrooms without a need for revamping the entire curriculum.
- To develop actionable policy and institutional suggestions for integrating digital pedagogy within AICTE and UGC-approved Faculty Induction and Refresher Courses, and to provide systemic scaffolding for media-enriched teaching.

Key Takeaways – Introduction

- Students expect interactive, tech-enabled learning, but classrooms remain faculty-centric.
- Digital tools lag due to low awareness, training gaps, and weak infrastructure.
- Faculty mindset change is key to adoption.
- Need for cost-effective, inclusive, policy aligned faculty development.

2. LITERATURE REVIEW

The transformation towards technology-enriched learning in engineering education has accelerated worldwide, spurred in part by digital change, changing student expectations, and systemic shocks such as the COVID-19 pandemic. This literature review integrates extant research on four main themes: faculty preparedness and impediments, the efficacy of flipped classrooms, shifting expectations of students, and the influence of national policies on digital pedagogy.

2.1. Faculty Preparedness and Technology Integration Barriers

Figure 2. Comparison between Traditional and Flipped Classroom Approach

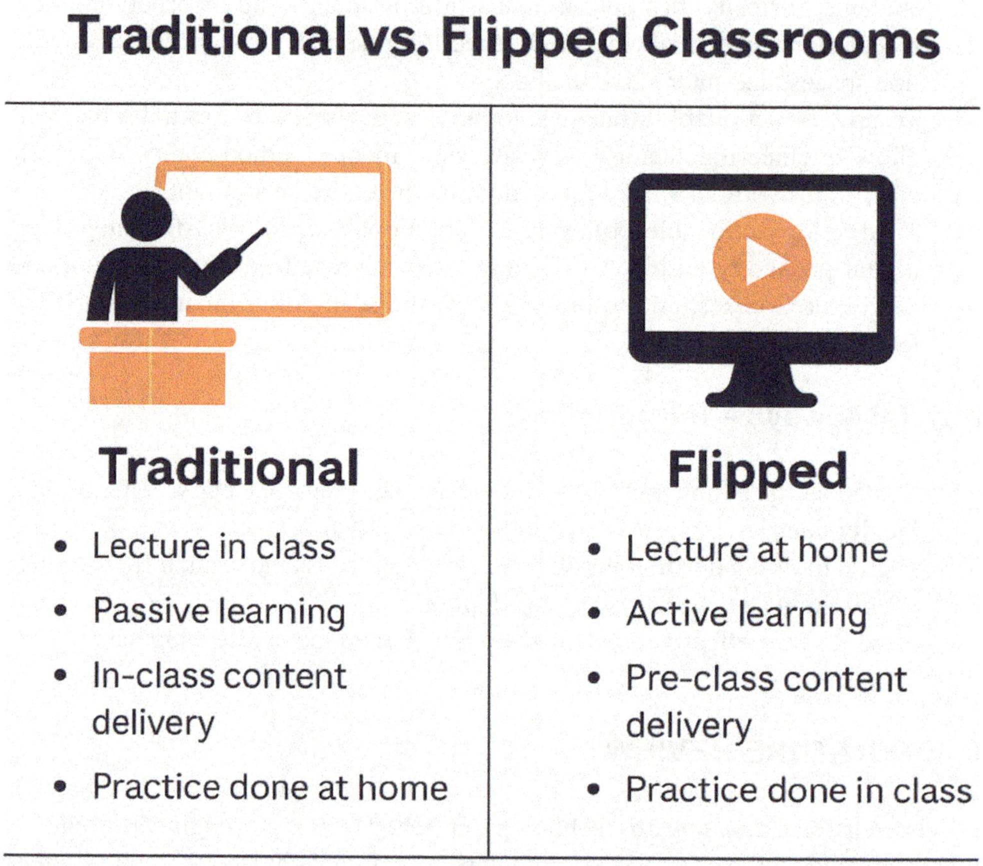

Faculty preparedness is the readiness of a teacher to use digital tools and innovative pedagogies. For engineering education, it means not only technical competence but also pedagogic flexibility. Mishra et al. (2020) explored Indian faculty preparedness in the sudden transition to online instruction due to the COVID-19 pandemic. Their research found that although the majority of faculty members were familiar with introductory tools such as PowerPoint and email, they were not trained to use advanced pedagogy tools in digital form, including Learning Management Systems (LMS), content authoring tools, and collaborative tools. These findings can be linked to the *Orientation* phase of the OEPFM (Section 5.2.1), which emphasizes structured induction and baseline skill-building before faculty engage in tool exploration.

In order to measure professional development experiences, Olmstead and Turpen (2016) created the Real-Time Professional Development Observation Tool (R-PDOT), which gauges the interactive nature of faculty training sessions. What they found was that a large number of STEM faculty development programs did not model active learning strategies that they were trying to implement.

2.2. Effectiveness of Flipped Classrooms in Engineering

One of the strongest digital pedagogies that have been studied in recent years is the flipped classroom model: lecture material is covered outside of class (through videos or readings), leaving face-to-face time for active, problem-solving work. Gilboy et al. (2021) demonstrated that flipped classroom methods in mechanical engineering enhanced student engagement, conceptual understanding, and attitudes towards learning compared to traditional lectures. Likewise, Srivastava et al. (2024) assessed flipped learning within an upper-level electrical engineering course and found major improvements in performance when interactive pre-class material was combined with in-class problem-solving exercises. The findings affirm the flipped classroom's possibility of revolutionizing sophisticated engineering instruction through active learning.

Student Expectations in an Age of Digitalism

Today's students, particularly those in engineering and technology, are digital natives and look for flexible, interactive, and media-rich learning experiences. Current research highlights that such learners are more inclined toward modular, self-paced online models combined with collaborative, problem-based classroom experiences. For instance, Rahman et al. (2024) concluded that engineering students interacted with blended learning more effectively when facilitated by bite-sized digital modules and peer interaction, echoing the fact that they are accustomed to platforms such as YouTube and Coursera.

Likewise, Al-Abri & Rahim (2023) pointed out how flipped classrooms in STEM fields enhance student responsibility and active engagement through the redefinition of lecture material as asynchronous study and the utilization of class time for design, troubleshooting, and applied learning. These results affirm the necessity of pedagogy-led digital integration that enables students to manage learning speed while allowing teachers to function as facilitators and mentors.

Table 1. Challenges Faced by Faculty and Opportunities with New Media Integration Comprehension

Aspect	Challenges Faced by Faculty	Opportunities with New Media Integration
Technological Familiarity	Limited exposure beyond PowerPoint, LMS, and email	Access to open-source tools (Jupyter Notebooks, Tinkercad, GeoGebra, Moodle, etc.)
Pedagogical Shifts	Hesitance to adopt active learning or interdisciplinary approaches	Encourages collaborative, flipped, or project-based learning strategies
Content Delivery	Traditional lectures dominate	Interactive tools (e.g., simulations, AR apps, coding platforms) enhance student focus
Assessment Methods	Reliance on summative exams	Enables formative assessment through quizzes, peer reviews, and real-time feedback tools
Student Engagement	Low due to passive learning models	Increases with tools like Padlet, Google Forms, Mentimeter, and virtual labs
Institutional Support	Lack of structured training or incentives	Government and institutional schemes (AICTE ATAL, SWAYAM, NPTEL FDPs) support upskilling
Time Constraints	Pressure to complete syllabus limits innovation	Modular use of tools allows partial, scalable integration
Interdisciplinary Demands	Difficulty in adapting to fast-changing, multi-domain industry needs	New media enables exposure to AI, IoT, simulation, and design thinking in early semesters

2.3. Existing Faculty Development Models

Worldwide, faculty development initiatives are being reframed to match the increasing demand for digital pedagogy and 21st-century learning frameworks. In the United States, programs such as the Center for the Integration of Research, Teaching and Learning (CIRTL) are centred on evidence-informed teaching strategies and digital technologies for STEM instructors. Advance HE (formerly Higher Education Academy) of Australia provides teaching fellowships that incorporate professional education in blended and online settings. The UK Professional Standards Framework (UKPSF) focuses on ongoing improvement in teaching through the use of technology-enhanced learning environments. National Institute of Education (NIE) in Singapore conducts digital literacy courses for university lecturers to integrate e-learning, gamification, and flipped classrooms. In India, AICTE schemes, UGC-HRDCs, and NITTTRs offer induction and refresher courses, albeit still mostly based on traditional approaches such as PPT or simple ICT tools.

As reported by UNESCO Institute for Information Technologies in Education (IITE) and OECD (OECD, 2023), nations are turning more towards blended professional development approaches. These typically involve MOOC-based material alongside local support. An example is Finland's "Innokas" initiative that mixes pedagogical innovation with digital preparedness for teachers of all disciplines.

Table 2. Related Works Comparison

Region/Source	Model or Study	Key Focus	Outcome
Germany – Wehling et al. (2021)	Fast-track Flipped Training with H5P	Digital content creation training	Faculty gained confidence with tech-enhanced instruction
Brazil – Chaves & Lage (2021)	Engineering flipped course using Moodle	Tech integration in classroom	Higher student performance and faculty openness
Global – UNESCO IITE (2021)	Digital TPD policies and frameworks	Blended PD via MOOCs & mentoring	Country-level innovation in teacher skill development

2.4. Indian Policy and Platform Support

India's learning environment has addressed these challenges through a variety of national efforts to encourage digital pedagogy. Initiatives such as SWAYAM, NPTEL, Virtual Labs, and AICTE's Faculty Development Programs are evidence of this dedication. These sites provide open-access courses, virtual simulations, and micro-credentialing opportunities for students and faculty.

In short, the studies examined here not only reflect common barriers and enablers of faculty digital adoption but also inform the design of the OEPFM phases directly, as charted in Table 3, such that every stage of the framework is evidence-based.

Table 3. Summarized Literature Review

Literature Source	Key Finding	OEPFM Phase Applied	How it Informs the Framework
Mishra et al. (2020)	Lack of advanced digital tool training in faculty	Orientation	Includes structured induction modules covering LMS, content creation, and collaboration tools
van Alten et al. (2019)	Flipped learning improves STEM outcomes	Practice	Encourages redesign of course modules into flipped formats
Turnbull et al. (2018)	Students prefer flexible, modular learning	Exploration & Practice	Encourages trial of modular e-learning before full integration
Connolly et al. (2016)	Peer-supported communities boost adoption	Mentoring	Embeds peer mentoring circles post-FDP
Freeman et al. (2014)	Active learning reduces failure rates	Practice	Makes active learning design a mandatory FDP deliverable

Key Takeaways – Introduction

- Students prefer interactive, tech-rich learning, but most classrooms stay faculty-centric.
- Digital tools remain underused due to low awareness, training gaps, and poor support.
- Need for structured, inclusive, policy-aligned faculty development.
- Goal: Provide a practical model for integrating new media in teaching.

3. NEW MEDIA TOOLS FOR ENGINEERING EDUCATION

In the changing environment of engineering education, new media technologies are acting as agents for active, learner-centered learning. These range from simulation environments and virtual laboratories to shared whiteboards, interactive video tools, AR/VR spaces, and AI-driven tutoring systems. They are remaking the learning and teaching of complex engineering concepts and the ways in which they are comprehended. To cope with drastic transformation of digital space involves creating classrooms where learners act as co-creators. They utilize digital simulations, collaborative spaces, AR/VR labs, coding sandboxes, and AI capabilities as not just add-ons but as essential blocks of learning and with technical proficiency with these tools but more importantly pedagogical proficiency to integrate them meaningfully. The biggest challenge in engineering education is moving forward with interdisciplinary learning and teaching students not just to get by, but to excel in a global, networked world.

3.1. Collaborative Tools (Jamboard, Miro, Padlet, GitHub Classroom)

Pandamic have taught us classroom is not about the four walls and blackboard and shown as a window to a new collaborative world stimulating peer interaction, instant feedback, and experiential involvement. There are a variety of tools available focusing on this collaborative learning keeping a means by allowing students and teachers to co-author knowledge, iterate designs, and coordinate thinking in physical and virtual spaces. The combination of tools like Google Jamboard, Miro,

Padlet, and GitHub Classroom gives engineering educators cross-platform options for problem-based learning, project organization, and interactive sessions.

The relative illustration (Figure 3) within this section facilitates a summary of the essential functions, pedagogical strengths, and implementation issues related to each site. The summary can be used by faculty members to match tool choice with course goals, learning styles of students, and readiness of the infrastructure.

Figure 3. Collaborative Digital Tools in Engineering

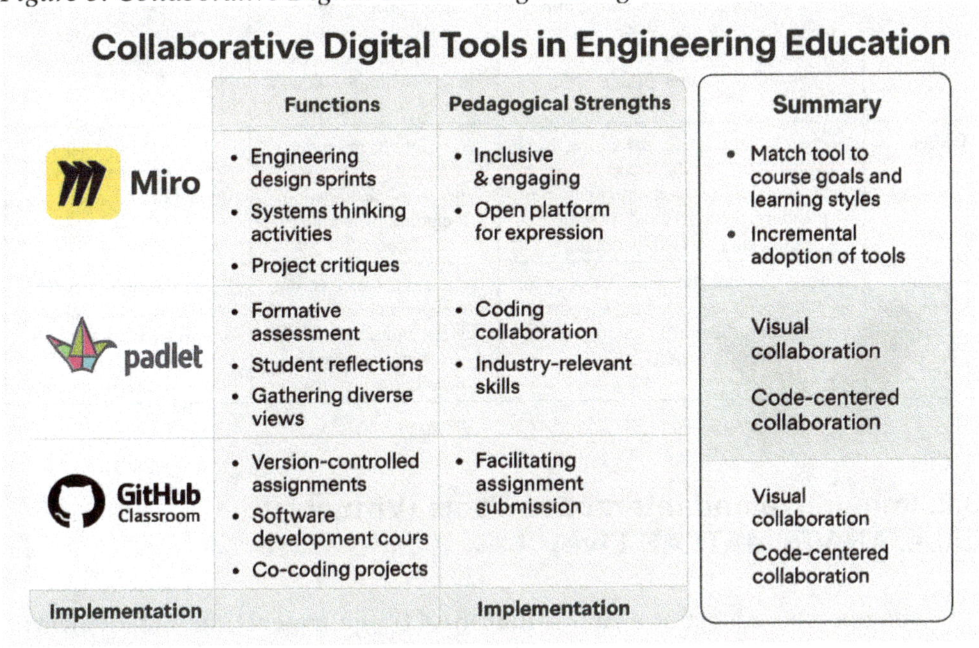

Through incorporating tools that facilitate visual collaboration and code-centered collaboration, this framework addresses the multi-modal requirements of engineering education, equipping students to not only learn, but to construct, test, and create in tandem within a digitally enhanced context. Table 4 below showcase the summary of these tools.

Table 4. Collaborative Tools Comparison Table

Tool	Description & Typical Use	Strengths for Engineering Learning	Limitations / Considerations
Google Jamboard	Cloud-based digital whiteboard—supports real-time collaborative drawing, sticky notes, images. Frequently used in live brainstorming or peer-annotation sessions. (Education Express)	Easy to set up; supports real-time visual collaboration; works across devices—ideal for group design thinking and virtual labs.	Google is phasing it out; limited advanced features compared to other tools; may lack long-term support. (Reddit, Reddit)
Miro	Robust visual collaboration platform with templates for flowcharts, mind maps, diagramming. Widely adopted in project-based and systems-design education. (Saima, Educate Me)	Excellent for brainstorming, group modeling, system mapping; integrates with GitHub, Slack, and teaching workflows.	Free version limited to three boards; can be complex for beginner users.
Padlet	Virtual bulletin board that allows users to post notes, media, links on shared walls in real time. Used for collaborative planning, feedback, and reflection. (Collegenp, en.wikipedia.org)	Very intuitive; supports multimedia posts; increases participation, including from quieter students.	Limited free usage; board management and moderation features are basic.
GitHub Classroom	A workflow tool connecting Git/GitHub with course assignments; supports version control and collaborative coding projects. (arXiv, arXiv)	Excellent for team coding, version control, peer review, and project-based learning in software development courses.	Requires familiarity with Git; may require initial training for both faculty and students.

3.2. Immersive and Interactive Tools (Virtual Labs, AR/VR, MATLAB Live)

As engineering education adapts to Industry 4.0 requirements, the employment of immersive and interactive technologies is increasingly revolutionizing conventional pedagogy. Technologies like Virtual Labs, Augmented/Virtual Reality (AR/VR) platforms, and MATLAB Live are allowing students to engage with complicated systems, visualize abstract principles, and experiment virtually despite geographical lab constraints.

Virtual Labs, including those funded by India's Ministry of Education (https://www.vlab.co.in/), enable students to remotely perform experiments in areas such as fluid mechanics, digital electronics, and control systems. AR/VR tools like Labster, Unity-based simulations, or EON Reality platforms provide immersive 3D environments where students can engage with engineering machinery, circuits, and mechanical systems in a lifelike manner. Such experiences foster spatial reasoning, systems thinking, and hands-on problem solving all critical skills in engineering. According to Sharma et al. (2020), the use of AR/VR in engineering education has significantly improved student motivation and conceptual understanding, especially in courses like thermodynamics and structural analysis.

MATLAB Live Editor helps to combines code with text, graphics, and equations to make interactive lessons and simulations. It permits live coding demonstrations, dynamic plotting, and inlined quizzes making it the perfect teaching tool for signal processing, control systems, and data analysis.

Table 5. Immersive and Interactive Tools Comparison

Feature / Tool	Virtual Labs (e.g., VLab)	AR/VR Platforms (e.g., Labster, Unity)	MATLAB Live Editor
Primary Purpose	Simulated lab experiments	Immersive 3D learning experiences	Interactive coding and computation
Best Used For	Core experiments, electronics, physics	Thermodynamics, mechanical systems	Data analysis, control systems
Hardware Required	PC/Internet	VR headset (optional), PC/ Tablet	PC with MATLAB
Student Engagement	Moderate	High (due to immersive interactivity)	High (interactive + real-time code)
Ease of Use (Faculty)	Easy	Moderate to High (needs setup)	Moderate
Accessibility	High (Web-based, Govt-supported)	Medium (some tools are paid/licensed)	Medium (requires MATLAB license)
Learning Outcomes	Procedural understanding	Conceptual + spatial learning	Analytical + computational thinking
Cost	Mostly Free	Varies (some freemium)	Paid (MATLAB required)
Scalability	High	Medium	High
Real-World Application	Moderate	High	Very High

3.3. Generative AI and LLMs

With the advent of Generative AI and Large Language Models (LLMs), engineering education is being revolutionized. Platforms such as ChatGPT, GitHub Copilot, and EduAI systems (e.g., Elicit, Explainpaper) are transforming the way faculty and students go about content creation, code generation, writing, and even concept ideation.

These AI technologies are not only providing automations but are also acting as smart collaborators to offer personalized support, scaffolding for intricate tasks, and feedback in real time. In engineering, where computational thinking and problem-solving are integral, the use of these models enables quick prototyping, debugging, conceptual clarity, and research writing. Notably, if introduced with appropriate academic support, they aid in ethical AI use, critical thinking, and digital literacy.

The limitation of the integration of such Generative AI and LLM based system is that they depend on understanding AI limitations, such as hallucinations, bias, and over reliance underscoring the importance of faculty preparedness, student orientation, and explicit usage guidelines. Table 5 presents a comprehensive evaluation of present Generative AI and LLMs solely for education point of you.

Table 6. Generative AI and LLMs Tools for Teaching Comparison

Tool/ Platform	Primary Use in Education	Best For	Input Type	Output Type	Limitations	Cost
ChatGPT	Concept explanation, content drafting	Writing help, programming, Q&A	Text prompts	Text, code, ideas	May hallucinate; lacks sources	Free+/Pro
GitHub Copilot	AI pair programming, code generation	Writing functions, suggesting syntax	Code context	Inline code suggestions	May suggest buggy code	Paid (edu free)
Elicit / EduAI	Research support, literature extraction	Summarizing papers, forming questions	Queries or papers	Citations, summaries	Limited domain knowledge	Mostly Free
Explainpaper	Paper simplification using LLMs	Understanding scientific content	PDF Upload	Simplified summary	May skip complex math/ logics	Free

In engineering fields where problem solving, computing, and analysis are integral, such AI-driven platforms can boost productivity, foster self-learning, and even facilitate creative ideation in design subjects. Research workflows are also being streamlined, as the likes of Elicit aid literature review creation and Explainpaper aid unscrambling dense academic text for first-time researchers.

Critical awareness is needed for their substantial integration, though. Challenges like AI hallucinations (generating plausible but false outputs), data bias, intellectual property issues, and student dependence have to be met with organized digital literacy training. It is the responsibility of faculty members to help them in this change by illustrating ethical use of AI, incorporating AI as a complementary tool and not a substitute, and drawing line on academic guidelines for AI-aided submissions. It is critical to educate students not only in employing these tools, but also on questioning their outputs, authenticating information, and comprehending how models are constructed and constrained.

Mechanical and civil engineering are also seeing huge benefits by integrating generative AI. Mechanical engineering students use LLMs to explain simulation outcomes, solve thermodynamic and fluid mechanics problems, and create documentation for CAD workflows. ChatGPT, for example, assists with explaining heat transfer principles or with optimizing design parameters, while Copilot aids in developing simulation environment scripts. In civil engineering, AI technologies assist with creating structural analysis reports, streamlining regulatory reports, and assessing environmental factors. Explainpaper assists students to break down long research papers, with other LLMs assisting in generating project estimates and managing construction documents.

While there are the advantages, however, the use of LLMs in engineering education comes with a responsibility. While these tools foster creativity, independent inquiry, and engaged learning, they also carry dangers if used uncritically. Over-dependency can lead to shallow knowledge, intellectual dishonesty, or misuse of flawed outputs. Therefore, teachers must include AI literacy in the curriculum so students can recognize boundaries such as hallucinations, bias, or lack of contextual knowledge. Lastly, incorporating generative AI and LLMs in engineering curricula is a turning point in education. They are not just redefining teaching methodologies but also promoting the development of new skills like moral thinking, inter-disciplinary thinking, and critical examination of knowledge offered by AI.

Key Takeaways – New Media Tools for Engineering Education

- New media technologies are transforming engineering education to more active, learner-centered styles.
- Collaborative tools (Jamboard, Miro, Padlet) and immersive technologies (Virtual Labs, AR/VR) facilitate peer learning and experimentation outside conventional labs.
- LLMs and generative AI provide assistance with coding, research, and customized learning—demanding ethical and assisted usage.
- Successful adoption requires both technical skills and good pedagogy to effect effective, policy-related integration.

4. CHALLENGES FACED BY ENGINEERING FACULTY

Engineering professors everywhere are confronted with complex challenges as they strive to keep up with changing educational needs and new technologies. The shift from more conventional, instructor-centered pedagogy toward student-centered models; focusing on active learning, flipped classrooms, and online platforms has opened doors and imposed stress. One major hindrance is insufficient pedagogical training in instructional design and integration of digital tools. As per a UNESCO global report (UNESCO, 2021), while digital infrastructure is enhancing globally, faculty preparedness to engage these facilities meaningfully and effectively is still uneven, with most instructors lacking confidence in choosing and implementing educational technologies meaningfully. This is most starkly seen in STEM fields, where delivering intricate content through interactive and remote facilities requires both pedagogical flexibility and technical mastery. Faculty tend to be concerned about the time commitment needed to create new media-based activities and still satisfy performance demands in research, administration, and student guidance (ASEE, 2020).

Additionally, the increasing use of AI-based learning tools—like ChatGPT, MATLAB Live, and virtual labs creates an additional complexity. Not only are faculty expected to learn and apply these tools, but they are also supposed to teach students their appropriate ethical and effective usage. For example, the IEEE-TEMS 2022 education report highlights that although AI tools provide robust assistance for personalization and automation, without proper training of faculties, their misuse could contribute to academic dishonesty or surface-level understanding (IEEE-TEMS, 2022).

4.1. Digital Skill Gap and Mindset Resistance

While there is increasing need for digitally empowered education, the main challenge at present takes the form of a digital skill gap among engineering faculty members. Most teachers, especially those who have been trained in pre-digital pedagogies, tend to find themselves without the requisite competencies to leverage new media tools, coding environments, and AI-based systems efficiently within their pedagogy. The World Bank's "Digital Skills in Tertiary Education" (2020) report highlights that even if infrastructure exists, human capital preparedness is a bottleneck in realizing successful digital transformation within education. This is not just a technical but also a pedagogic skills gap teachers might be unable to shift from didactic lecturing to student-centered, collaborative practices digital tools require.

Adding to that is the problem of mindset resistance a fear or reluctance on the part of faculty to learn new, unfamiliar tools or to change longstanding teaching practices. This resistance can be based on fear of failure, perceived lack of relevance, or added cognitive burden in learning and implementing new systems without sufficient training or institutional support. Study by Rienties et al. (2017) on learning technologies adoption by faculty concluded that intrinsic motivation and peer support were the principal drivers of adoption, while perceived complexity and time constraints were the main inhibitors. Digital initiatives in most engineering colleges, especially in resource-restricted environments, are implemented without concurrent professional development programs, furthering resistance instead of mitigating it.

4.2. Infrastructure and Accessibility Issues

Though digital engineering education is fraught with great potential, the success of these initiatives greatly depends on strong infrastructure and universal access. In developing and developed countries alike, inequalities exist in high-speed internet access, availability of digital devices, and reliable electricity—all central to effective digital learning opportunities. It was found in India through the All-India Survey on Higher Education (AISHE) 2021–22 that fewer than 60% of institutions of higher learning had totally digital classrooms or high-speed internet facilities on campuses. This digital divide is even greater among rural areas or tier-2 and tier-3 cities, where most engineering colleges have low-bandwidth facilities and old computing equipment.

At a global level, the 2023 Digital Learning Readiness Report by UNESCO (UNESCO, 2021) underscored that infrastructure constraints still pose a major stumbling block to large-scale implementation of digital learning, especially among lower- and middle-income nations. Even in institutions that are well-supported, discrepancies in hardware reliability, software licenses, and user support mechanisms cause discontinuity in digital participation. Additionally, the adoption of BYOD (Bring Your Own Device) models tends to shortchange students from underprivileged socio-economic populations who have no resources to purchase laptops or tablets compatible with the most up-to-date educational software.

Another frequently neglected area is accessibility for students and instructors with disabilities. Much educational software and content types are still non-compliant with global accessibility standards (e.g., WCAG 2.1), restricting inclusivity. Engineering education, being so dependent upon simulations, code environments, and design tools, offers even greater obstacles if digital systems are not universally accessible.

Solving these issues involves systemic investment—both in the modernization of campus infrastructure and the creation of inclusive digital ecosystems. Cloud platforms, open educational resources (OER), and state-supported digital public goods (like India's SWAYAM or DIKSHA portals) can fill gaps, but only when accompanied by persistent policy attention and localized response. In the absence of equal access, digital change will be an instrument of exclusion, not empowerment, in engineering education.

4.3. Ethics, Data Privacy, and Misuse of AI

As engineering education becomes more integrated with digital software and AI-based platforms, the ethical aspects related to data utilization, privacy, and adopting technology responsibly have become even more imperative. Generative AI applications like ChatGPT, GitHub Copilot, and others harvest, process, and even store users' data in order to improve functionality; leaving questions regarding the extent of control for faculty and students over their online presence. In an academic setting, where intellectual property and sensitive interactions are at hand, unauthorized use or sharing of material created or stored through these systems poses serious privacy issues.

At the global level, the OECD's 2023 (OECD, 2023) Policy Framework for Responsible AI in Education warns that if not with robust governance, AI can worsen current disparities or be utilized to police students instead of assisting them. For instance, AI proctoring systems or plagiarism check software have been denounced for unclear algorithms and biased flagging procedures, inappropriately impacting underrepresented students. Likewise, engineering schools employing AI for observing student performance should be transparent, obtain informed consent, and be fair in interpreting data.

Yet another ethical issue comes from excessive usage or blind adoption of AI aids, resulting in plagiarism or reduced criticality. Since LLMs can write essays, code answers, and even design documents, there is a danger that students can pass off AI-generated work as their own. The European Commission's (European Commission, 2022) Guidelines for Trustworthy AI (2022) emphasize ensuring human control, transparency, and accountability factors still not present in most higher education implementations.

Teachers have the double task of encouraging digital literacy, as well as ethical thinking. This involves assisting learners in grasping the limitations of AI (e.g., hallucinations or bias), instructing them on the ramifications of model training data, and highlighting the value of originality and academic integrity. In addition, institutions need to establish definitive policies on the use of AI within courses, protect student data under policies such as India's Digital Personal Data Protection Act (2023) or GDPR in the EU, and create AI ethics committees to review implementation.

Table 7. AI Use Guidelines for Classrooms – Checklist

Guideline	Purpose	Example Implementation
Plagiarism Prevention	Ensure AI-generated content does not replace student's original work	Use plagiarism + AI detection tools before accepting lab reports
Bias Awareness	Avoid reinforcing gender, cultural, or technical biases	Train faculty to prompt AI tools with inclusive datasets and review outputs critically
Transparency in AI-Assisted Grading	Maintain fairness and accountability in evaluation	Inform students when AI is used to assist in grading coding assignments
Data Privacy Compliance	Protect student data when using AI platforms	Avoid uploading identifiable student work to public AI tools

continued on following page

Table 7. Continued

Guideline	Purpose	Example Implementation
Human Oversight	Keep educators in the decision-making loop	Use AI for preliminary assessment but validate grades manually
Educational Value Alignment	Ensure AI use supports learning objectives	Encourage students to use AI for brainstorming, not for full project completion

Key Takeaways

- Instructors are pressured to undertake student-centric, digital pedagogy, without training and institutional support.
- Gaps in skills, change resistance, and unequal infrastructure exacerbate the digital divide.
- Ethical AI issues—plagiarism, prejudice, privacy—require explicit classroom regulations.
- Remedies require focussed upskilling, infrastructure enhancement, and an innovation culture.

5. PROPOSED FACULTY DEVELOPMENT FRAMEWORK

To overcome the digital divide and successfully incorporate new media tools in engineering education, there is a need for a well-designed and visionary Faculty Development Framework. This suggested framework prioritizes a multistage capacity-building methodology based on digital fluency, pedagogical innovation, and ethical integration of AI.

Figure 4. Proposed Faculty Development Framework

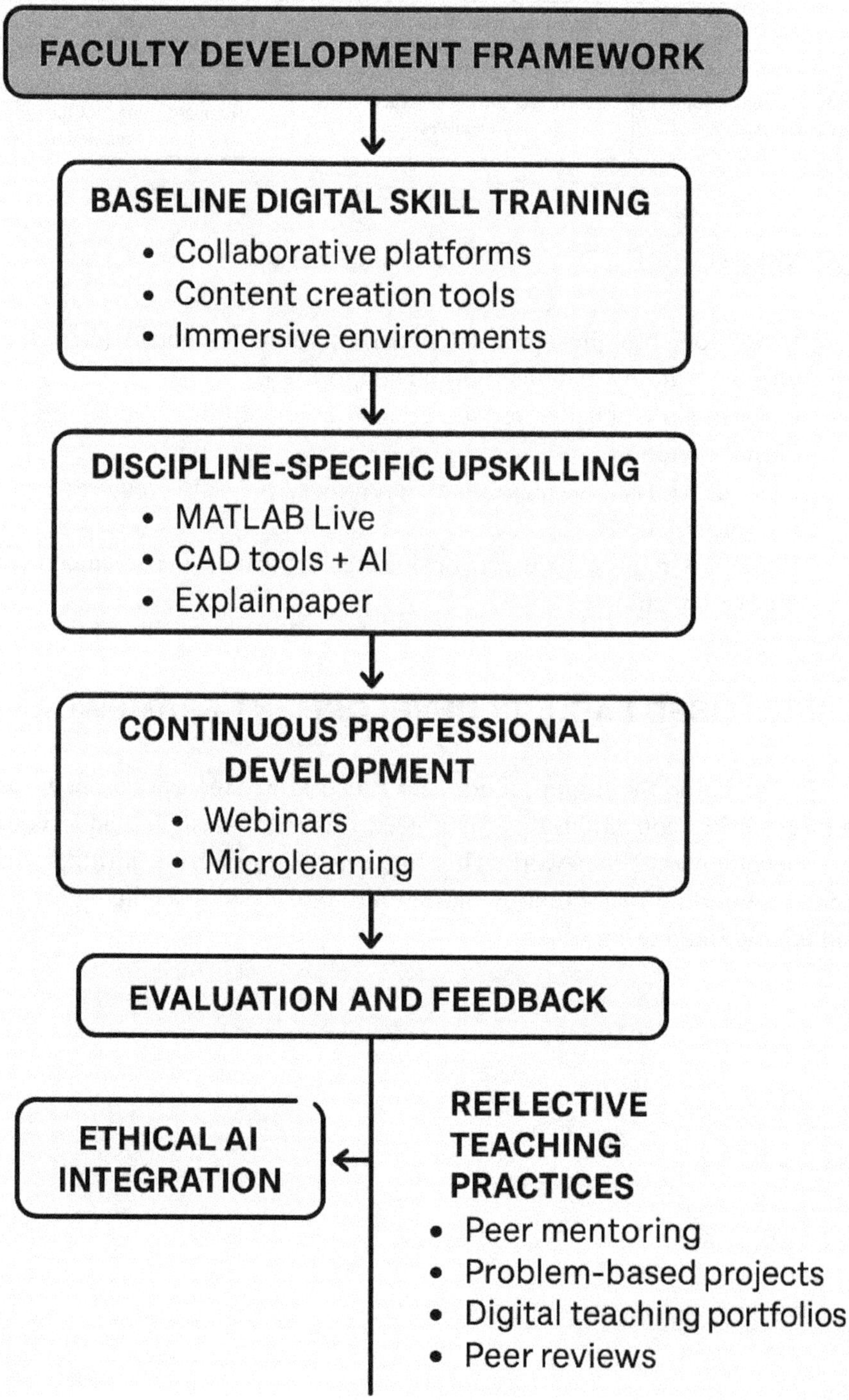

The model starts with baseline digital skill training that familiarizes all faculty members with necessary tools such as collaborative platforms (Padlet, GitHub Classroom), content creation tools (Canva, OBS Studio), and immersive environments (Virtual Labs, AR/VR modules).

Our proposed OEPFM model presents a new contribution through its pedagogy-first approach, in which technology use is always anchored in substantive teaching learning practices and not just tool adoption. It is also differentiated by our five phased developmental framework; Orientation, Exploration, Practice, Mentoring, and Change Management representing a systematic progression of faculty development, a pattern that is rarely observed with current models. Furthermore, the inclusion of generative AI and immersive media in faculty development is a progressive focus that goes beyond conventional professional education, and through this, the framework becomes innovative and contextually applicable for engineering education.

5.1. Core Principles: Pedagogy First, Tool Later

Embedded at the core of successful digital integration in engineering education is the principle: "Pedagogy First, Tool Later." This strategy demands that decisions about teaching are based on pedagogical purpose rather than the availability or newness of technology. The procedure begins with the determination of what to teach, and then selecting the best instructionally sound strategies for teaching, and only after that determining which digital tools can effectively accommodate those approaches.

This principle is consistent with established instructional design models like Backward Design (Wiggins & McTighe, 2005) and the TPACK model (Mishra & Koehler, 2006). Backward Design promotes starting with specific learning objectives, followed by establishing acceptable evidence of learning (assessment), and ending with planning for learning experiences and instruction. The TPACK model also states that authentic technology integration can be achieved only when technological knowledge (TK), pedagogical knowledge (PK), and content knowledge (CK) converge.

For instance, if the pedagogical objective is conceptual scaffolding in electrical engineering, tools such as MATLAB Live Editor or Jupyter Notebooks can be utilized for step-by-step problem visualization. When the objective is formative assessment and feedback, low-barrier instruments such as Google Forms or peer-reviewed quizzes in GitHub Classroom can support real-time analytics and adaptive support.

The "Pedagogy First" position sidesteps the pitfalls of techno-determinism—whereby pedagogy is influenced by tools instead of pedagogy informing tool use. It also protects against tool fatigue, whereby teaching staff have several platforms without discernible instructional benefit. This approach also enables sustainable adoption of technology, in which tools are brought together with intent, effectiveness, and scalability.

Figure 5. Pedagogy Used for the proposed FDP framework

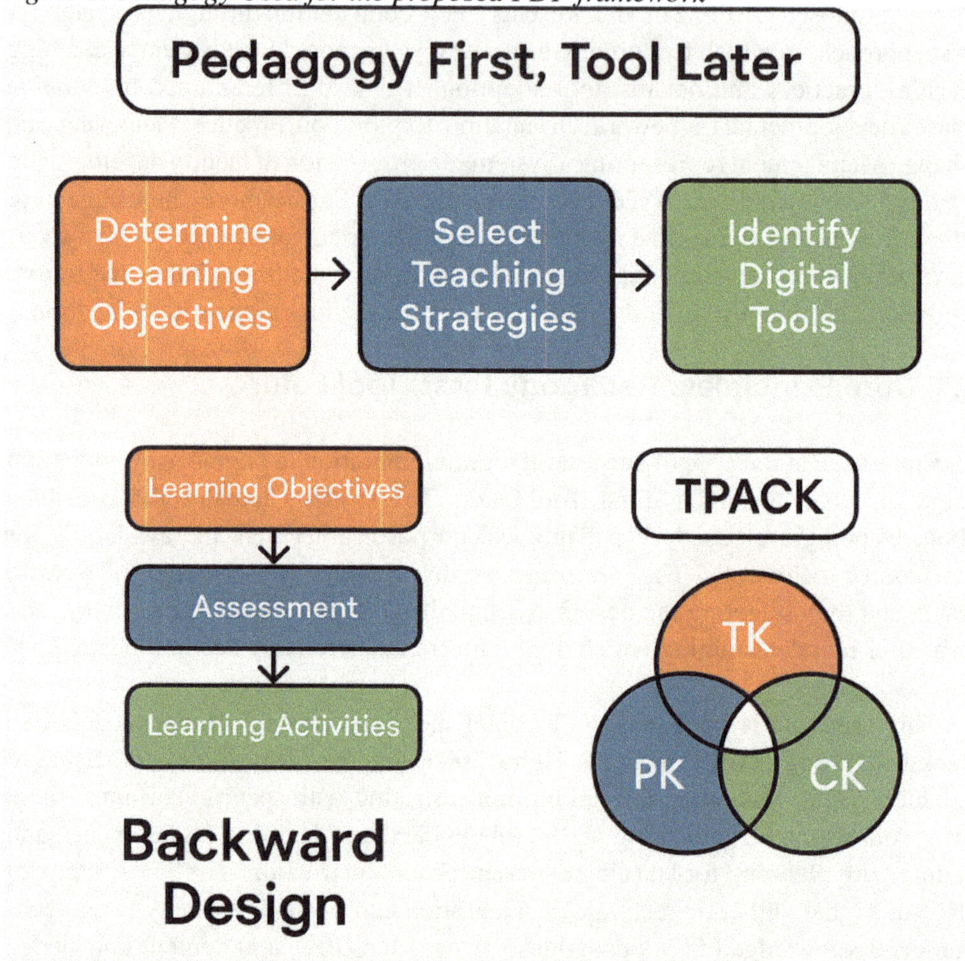

5.2. Proposed Framework: Orientation, Exploration, Practice, Feedback, Mentoring

To truly convert engineering faculty into adaptive digital teachers, a strong, cyclical, and evidence-based faculty development system needs to be put in place. This model—grounded in learning science, TPACK (Technological Pedagogical Content Knowledge), Adult Learning Theory, and Instructional Systems Design

(ISD)—suggests a systematic five-phase model: Orientation → Exploration → Practice → Feedback → Mentoring (OEPFM). Each phase is grounded in actionable strategies, tools, and outcomes to allow scalability and sustainability.

5.2.1. Orientation: Building Pedagogical and Digital Foundations

The Orientation phase introduces instructors into core concepts of instructional design, digital ethics, and basic digital literacy. Instructors do self-assessment of their own digital competencies through tools such as the DigCompEdu framework. Workshops acquaint them with legal and ethical aspects such as data privacy, algorithmic bias, accessibility, and academic integrity in the use of AI. Global case studies of initiatives like MIT Open Learning and NPTEL contextualize the feasibility and urgency of using educational technology in a variety of different teaching contexts. This stage introduces the tone of pedagogical ownership and critical consideration.

5.2.2. Exploration: Tool Evaluation and Contextual Adaptation

Faculty are invited to explore and contrast a number of different tools applicable to their subject matter during Exploration. They are introduced to discipline-specific platforms and AI tools pertinent to their instruction. For example, a chemical engineering professor can try MATLAB Live and LabArchives, while a computer science professor can try GitHub Copilot or ChatGPT to generate code.

5.2.3. Practice: Building and Pilot-Trying Tech-Enriched Pedagogy

The Practice stage entails implementing chosen tools into course elements like assignments, labs, and evaluations. Instructors create tech-enhanced lesson plans or flipped modules, mimic AI-augmented lab testing, and develop interactive learning objects with H5P, OBS Studio, or Google Workspace. They test with generative AI to jointly create rubrics, quizzes, or learning prompts and see their deployment in test environments. This stage depends significantly on iterative design and tweaking guided by real-time feedback, connecting theory to real-world classroom requirements.

5.2.4. Feedback: Continuous Refinement Through Data and Dialogue

Feedback is accessed through a triangulated process of peer observation, student comment, and learning analytics. Faculty are provided with evidence-based information through LMS dashboards (e.g., learner engagement data, quiz performance analytics), while qualitative feedback is collected via student focus groups and reflective journals. Faculty share their redesigned modules in roundtable sessions, where feedback is used to synthesize to inform future iterations. A culture of peer review and evidence-informed pedagogy is developed.

5.2.5. Mentoring: Sustaining Growth Through Recognition and Community

Mentoring turns this process into a sustainable model by instilling support systems like peer coaching, expert clinics, and micro-credentialing. Veteran faculty members mentor newer faculty members with best practices through systematic mentoring cycles. Communities of practice are established using collaborative tools like Microsoft Teams, LinkedIn Learning, or IEEE Collabratec to extend discourse and innovation beyond the formal program. Instructors are invited to expose their portfolios and accumulate stackable credentials to enhance career development. Table 8 showcase the mapping of proposed FDP framework phases to pedagogical tools and outcomes

Table 8. Mapping Framework Phases to Pedagogical Tools and Outcomes

Phase	Sample Tools/Platforms	Pedagogical Purpose	Outcome Indicator
Orientation	DigCompEdu, ADDIE Model	Establish digital readiness and design mindset	Baseline competency profile
Exploration	ChatGPT, MATLAB Live, Jamboard	Discover context-appropriate tools	Tool-Outcome mapping matrix
Practice	H5P, OBS Studio, Google Forms	Apply tools in teaching and assessments	Interactive content, AI-generated quizzes
Feedback	LMS Analytics, Peer Rubrics	Gather data-driven and peer input	Learner analytics, peer review reports
Mentoring	Accredible, IEEE CoPs	Support continuous upskilling	ePortfolios, badges, certification logs

Figure 6. Proposed FDP Framework

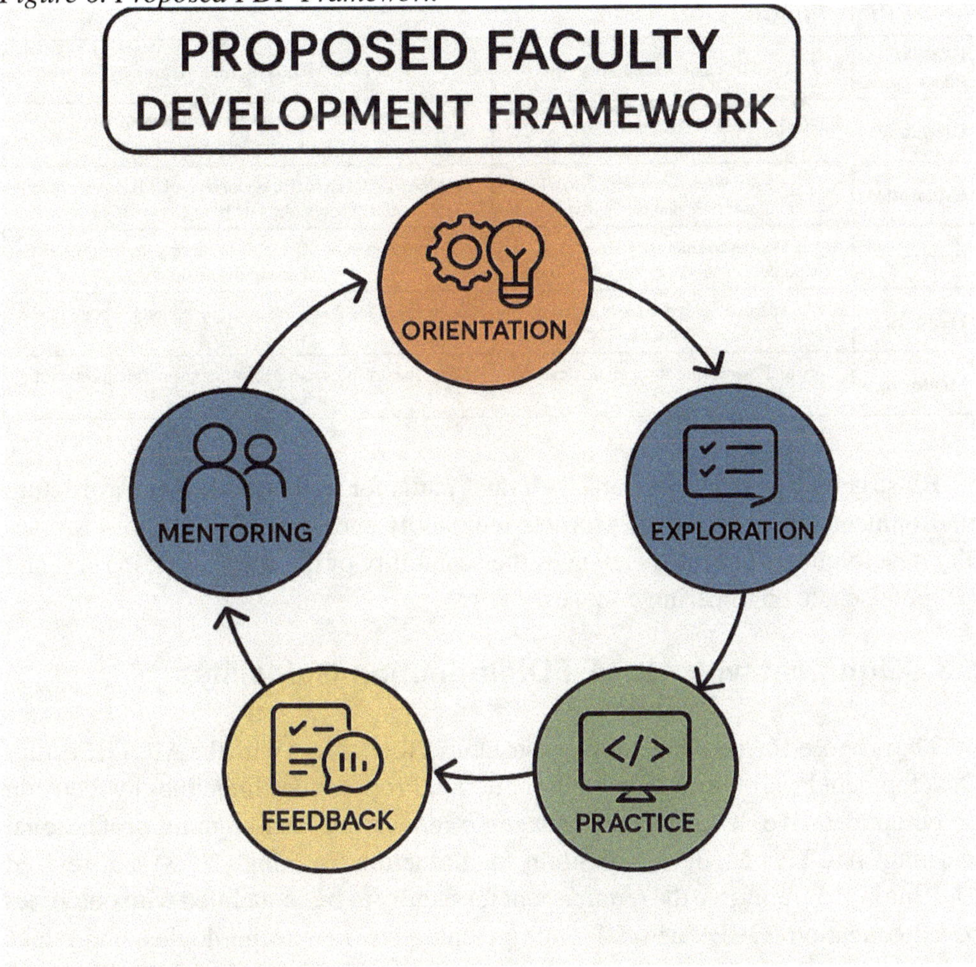

This adjustment substitutes costly platforms with low-cost, offline, or free alternatives, without sacrificing learning results. Table 9 shows the Comparation of High-Infrastructure vs Low-Infrastructure Strategies for OEPFM Phases

Table 9. Comparative Table: High-Infrastructure vs Low-Infrastructure Strategies for OEPFM Phases

OEPFM Phase	High-Infrastructure Strategy	Low-Infrastructure Strategy
Orientation	Interactive webinars on Zoom/MS Teams with real-time polls	Pre-recorded videos shared via WhatsApp/Telegram; printed guides for self-paced learning
Exploration	Hands-on workshops with AR/VR simulations & licensed software	SWAYAM/NPTEL offline videos on USB drives; open-source tools like GIMP or LibreOffice
Practice	LMS-based interactive modules (Moodle, Blackboard) with AI plugins	Google Forms or offline Excel templates for quizzes; local group discussions
Feedback	AI-enabled analytics dashboards & survey tools	Paper-based feedback forms digitized later; phone-based voice feedback
Mentoring	Virtual mentoring through dedicated LMS discussion forums	Peer mentoring groups on WhatsApp/Telegram with scheduled check-ins

By structuring the framework with dual paths for high- and low-infrastructure environments, institutions can promote inclusivity and equal opportunities for faculty development. This also enhances the scalability of the framework in rural and resource-scarce engineering colleges.

5.3. Alignment with AICTE FDP/Induction Guidelines

The proposed faculty development structure is consistent with the AICTE Faculty Development Programme (FDP) and Induction Programme Guidelines by focusing on comprehensive development, pedagogic innovation, and ongoing professional learning. AICTE's Model Curriculum for Induction Training (2018) and revised FDP initiatives reinforce the requirement for faculty to be acquainted with outcome-based education (OBE), active learning techniques, new technologies, and ethics in research and teaching—all of which are part of the five-stage OEPFM model (Orientation, Exploration, Practice, Feedback, Mentoring).

Digital preparedness, instructional design innovation, and ethical integration of technology—underscored in AICTE's FDP themes like "Learning Management Systems," "AI in Teaching," and "Universal Human Values"—are directly aligned with the Orientation and Exploration stages of the framework suggested here. The DigCompEdu Framework, TPACK model, and SAMR taxonomy are also in synergy with AICTE's support for competency-based faculty development. The provision of generative AI tools, virtual labs, and interactive content creation tools facilitates AICTE's mission to develop techno-pedagogical competencies among teachers in the implementation of NEP 2020.

In addition, the Mentoring stage supports AICTE's initiative towards Institutional Faculty Mentorship by creating peer coaching, community of practice, and micro-credentialing frameworks. These allow faculty to emerge as independent learners and drivers of institution-building capacity, aligning with the "train-the-trainer" culture promoted in AICTE Quality Improvement Programs (QIP).

Figure 7. Proposed Faculty Development Framework aligning TPACK model with digital tools and pedagogical strategies across Orientation, Exploration, Practice, Feedback, and Mentoring stages for engineering education.

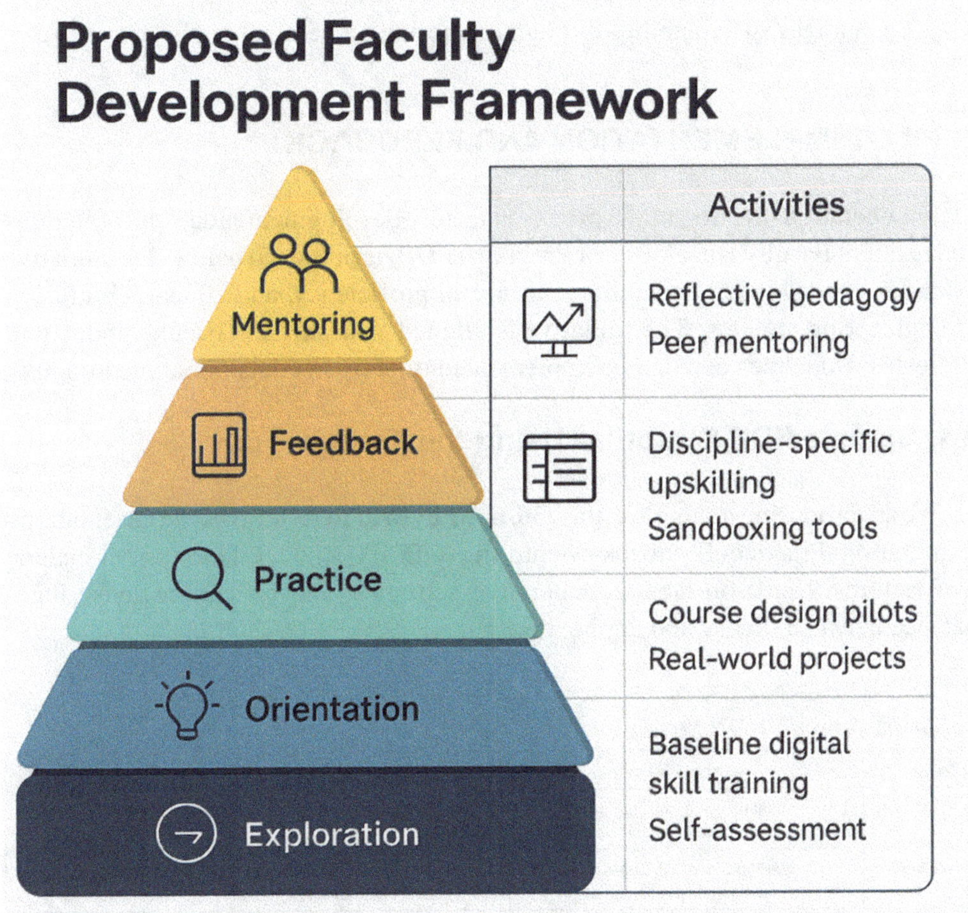

Essentially, this model does not only conform to Indian national standards it extends them by blending international digital competency standards, AI fluency, and evidence-based pedagogy to ensure that faculty are prepared for 21st-century engineering education.

Key Takeaways

- OEPFM provides a clean, scalable roadmap for new media integration in engineering education.
- Supports "Pedagogy First" to maintain learning at the centre.
- Makes adjustments for low-resource environments for broader outreach.
- Compliant with AICTE/NEP 2020 and international digital teaching best practices.
- Encourages sustainability through mentoring and ethical application of AI.

6. PILOT IMPLEMENTATION AND FEEDBACK

For operationalization of the proposed faculty development model, an ambitious and resilient Faculty Development Program (FDP) is proposed below. The initiative prioritizes pedagogical authenticity, technical proficiency, and ethical AI infusion in engineering streams. The initiative is aligned with AICTE Faculty Induction/ Refresher guidelines and can be implemented directly in educational institutions.

6.1. Sample FDP Structure Using the Framework

We are proposing a sample **5-day, 30-hour hybrid FDP** follows the Orientation–Exploration–Practice–Feedback–Mentoring (OEPFM) model. The sessions include live lectures, hands-on labs, collaborative activities, and reflections, ensuring a balance between theory and application.

Table 10. Sample FDP Structure

Phase	Activities	Tools/Techniques	Expected Outputs
Orientation	Instructional design basics, digital literacy, tech acceptance models	DigCompEdu, Jamboard, Mentimeter	Baseline digital fluency report
Exploration	Exploration of AI/LLMs an d media tools per discipline	ChatGPT, GitHub Copilot, Virtual Labs, EduAI	Tool-context matrix by department
Practice	Tech-enhanced course design, flipped modules, generative assessment techniques	H5P, OBS Studio, Google Forms	Working model of lesson/ activity
Feedback	Peer review, student simulation feedback, self-reflection	LMS analytics, Padlet, Peer rubrics	ePortfolio with lesson redesigns
Mentoring	Showcasing best practices, community-building	Microsoft Teams, LinkedIn, Accredible	Mentoring plan + community of practice setup

To test the proposed Faculty Development Framework for New Media Integration, a hypothetical pilot implementation plan is presented below. This plan is intended for one engineering department as a controlled entry point, with expansion to other departments contingent upon outcomes. Though at this point this is a conceptual pilot, it uses practical action with respect to AICTE FDP guidelines and realistic timelines so that it can be rolled out immediately by an institution. Faculty digital competence is the emphasis, the incorporation of new media tools into the curriculum, and measurable impact through qualitative and quantitative measures.

Table 11. Proposed Pilot Plan Table

Day/Session	FDP Topic	Mode of Delivery	Tools Demonstrated	Expected Learning Outcome	Evaluation Metric
Day 1 (AM)	Orientation to New Media in Engineering Education	In-person	PPT, Case Studies	Understand scope & importance of new media	Pre-FDP digital competency survey
Day 1 (PM)	Introduction to Generative AI & LLMs	Hands-on Workshop	ChatGPT, EduAI, GitHub Copilot	Apply AI tools for content & code generation	Task completion accuracy
Day 2 (AM)	Immersive Tools for Concept Delivery	Virtual Lab Session	MATLAB Live, AR/VR Demos	Simulate engineering experiments	Learner self-efficacy rating
Day 2 (PM)	Designing Interactive Assessments	Online	Kahoot, Mentimeter	Create engaging formative assessments	Peer review scores
Day 3 (AM)	Ethics & Responsible AI Use	Seminar + Case Discussion	AI Ethics Toolkit	Apply ethical frameworks to tool use	Scenario-based evaluation
Day 3 (PM)	Implementation Planning	Group Activity	Google Jamboard	Draft new media lesson plan	Rubric-based assessment of lesson plan
Post-FDP (2 weeks later)	Follow-up Mentoring & Feedback	Online	LMS Forum, Zoom	Reflect & refine teaching integration	Post-FDP survey & LMS analytics

6.2. Feedback and Refinement Plan

The Feedback and Refinement phase guarantees that the FDP stays responsive, evidence-informed, and in continuous improvement. Feedback is obtained using a mix of pre/post surveys, daily reflection, peer review, and LMS analytics to examine both pedagogical effectiveness and tool take-up. Participants provide redesigned lesson parts as part of an e-portfolio, which are reviewed by peers and mentors via structured rubrics. Daily reflection meetings and community exhibitions promote a culture of continuous improvement. These learnings not only inform personal development but also enable institutions to iterate on the FDP framework for wider scalability and reach.

Table 12. Feedback Method

Feedback Method	Purpose	Tools Used
Pre/Post Surveys	Measure digital/pedagogical growth	DigCompEdu, Google Forms
Daily Exit Tickets	Capture immediate insights	Padlet, Slido
LMS Analytics	Monitor engagement and effectiveness	Moodle/Canvas dashboards
Peer Review & Capstone	Facilitate constructive feedback on modules	Rubrics, PeerScore Sheets
ePortfolio Submission	Showcase redesigned tech-enhanced content	Google Sites, Accredible

6.2.1. Feedback Assessment

Feedback must be assessed using metric rubrics combined with qualitative observations to provide both formal measurement and rich understanding. Self-assessments by faculty participants must be conducted before and after the program, using metrics such as DigCompEdu or the TPACK model, to rate confidence and competence on scales related to digital pedagogy, tool skills, and AI ethics. Session-level feedback can be taken using a 4-point Likert scale rubric to assess relevance, clarity, interactivity, and applicability. The insights obtained are subsequently evaluated in order to determine recurring gaps or needs, which are utilized for enhancing module content, instructional strategy, and support measures in later versions of the FDP. Table show sample rubrics for FDP.

Table 13. Sample Rubrics for FDP

Criteria	Excellent (4)	Good (3)	Fair (2)	Needs Improvement (1)
Relevance of Content	Fully aligned with teaching needs; highly applicable	Mostly relevant with practical insights	Somewhat relevant; limited applicability	Unclear relevance to teaching practice
Clarity of Presentation	Concepts clearly explained; highly engaging	Clear but lacked some examples	Somewhat unclear; few concrete examples	Confusing or difficult to follow
Tool Usability & Access	Tool/platform was easy to use and access	Some learning curve but manageable	Difficult to use without support	Very hard to access or use

continued on following page

Table 13. Continued

Criteria	Excellent (4)	Good (3)	Fair (2)	Needs Improvement (1)
Pedagogical Integration	Clearly demonstrated classroom integration	Mentioned classroom use but lacked depth	Briefly addressed use in pedagogy	No clear pedagogical context provided
Interactivity & Engagement	Highly interactive with hands-on activities	Moderately interactive	Limited interaction	Mostly lecture-based or passive
Confidence Boost	Greatly improved my confidence to apply this	Improved confidence with some uncertainty	Slight improvement in confidence	Did not improve confidence

The table 8 is a planned 1-week Faculty Development Program organized based on the suggested framework. Each session is designed to blend theory and practice, with a focus on imparting pedagogical methods and tool proficiency in the context of new media and generative AI integration into engineering instruction.

Table 14. Sample FDP Schedule

Day	Session Title	Mode	Tools Used	Learning Outcome
Day 1	Reimagining Pedagogy & Digital Literacy	Hybrid (Live + LMS)	DigCompEdu, Mentimeter, Jamboard	Baseline self-assessment & digital goals
Day 2	Leveraging Generative AI in Engineering	Synchronous	ChatGPT, GitHub Copilot, Explainpaper	Use LLMs for ideation, code, content creation
Day 3	Interactive Module & Media Design	Hands-on	OBS Studio, H5P, Virtual Labs	Create a flipped or simulation-based module
Day 4	Ethics and Responsible AI in Classrooms	Live + Discussion	Data Ethics Canvas, Explainpaper	Develop classroom guidelines for AI use
Day 5	Capstone + Mentoring for Sustainable Practice	Showcase	Padlet, Microsoft Teams, Accredible	Present final redesign; join/lead faculty network

Key Takeaways

- Sample 5-day hybrid course with the OEPFM model.
- Combination of pedagogy, AI tools, and ethics.
- Hands-on, practical sessions for actual classroom application.
- Ongoing feedback for optimization.
- Aligns with AICTE norms and can be replicated in other departments.

7. RECOMMENDATIONS FOR ENGINEERING INSTITUTIONS

In order to effectively integrate new media and generative AI tools into mainstream engineering education, institutions need to have a strategic and multi-stakeholder approach. Top leadership should emphasize incorporating digital pedagogy into institutional policy and make specific funding allocations for technology-aided teaching. Engineering institutions are requested to set up in-house digital learning cells or teaching excellence centers that offer continuing faculty training against AICTE and NBA standard.

7.1. Integrating Framework into AICTE FDPs/Short-term Courses

The new faculty development model can be easily incorporated into current AICTE-approved FDPs and short-term training programs by matching its phases Orientation, Exploration, Practice, Feedback, and Mentoring against the mandated AICTE Faculty Training modules. Orientation and Exploration can be incorporated into the early days to address pedagogical theory, readiness for digital technology, and introduction to cutting-edge technologies such as generative AI, LLMs, and AR/VR. The Practice and Feedback phases can be aligned to hands-on sessions and microteaching exercises, where the faculty develop and implement tech-enabled lesson plans.

7.2. Policy Recommendations

For systematic uptake of digital tools and generative AI in engineering education, policy measures are essential at both institution and national levels. First, statutory institutions such as AICTE and UGC should revise curriculum guidelines for faculty development courses by incorporating obligatory modules on frontier technologies, digital pedagogy, and ethical use of AI. Accrediting agencies like NBA must include digital readiness and pedagogical innovation in the rubrics they use to evaluate faculty. Additionally, funding policies need to focus on building infrastructure for digital experiment labs and providing incentives for faculty members pursuing certified upskilling in educational technology. Finally, policies in institutions should foster a culture of innovation through the encouragement of interdisciplinary work, fellowships for faculty in EdTech, and reward of digitally enhanced teaching portfolios during performance evaluations and promotions.

For ensuring equitable and sustainable adoption of the OEPFM in engineering education, policy interventions need to be specific, quantifiable, and linked with existing regulatory frameworks. In the Table 15 we have a consolidation of the same.

Table 15. Policy Recommendations

Policy Area	Actionable Recommendation	Responsible Body	Measurement/Verification
Faculty Digital Competency	Mandate completion of **AICTE-approved micro-credentials in digital pedagogy** for career advancement and promotions.	AICTE	Verification of digital badges/ micro-certificates during promotion review.
Technology Mentorship	Require institutions to maintain **active tech-mentorship programs** for faculty, audited as part of **NBA accreditation cycles**.	NBA	Accreditation checklist includes evidence of mentorship meetings, logs, and outcomes.
Funding & Innovation	Introduce **government grants** tied to demonstrable faculty-led digital innovations in teaching, including open educational resources and AI integration.	Ministry of Education / State Govts.	Grant disbursement linked to annual reports of digital teaching projects and student engagement analytics.

7.3. Accessibility Integration in Engineering Education

In order to ensure that the Open Education and Pedagogy First Model (OEPFM) can serve all learners, engineering professors must incorporate accessibility features which can help tackle both physical and cognitive barriers.

Table 16. Key Engineering-Specific Accessibility Strategies

Accessibility Area	Engineering Challenge	Proposed Solution	Tool/Example
Equations & Formulas	Complex math notation often unreadable by screen readers	Use MathML for native accessibility or EquatIO for visual + auditory rendering	MathML, EquatIO
Laboratory Simulations	Hands-on labs inaccessible for motor-impaired students	Offer VR-enabled labs with adaptive controllers	Labster VR with accessibility features
Course Syllabi & Materials	Rigid formats limit flexibility for diverse learners	Use UDL-compliant syllabus templates with multiple representation formats	CAST UDL Templates
CAD & Engineering Drawings	CAD files not interpretable by screen readers	Provide alternative text descriptions or tactile 3D printed models	Fusion 360 + Tactile 3D Prints
Programming Assignments	Color-coded IDEs hinder color-blind learners	Use high-contrast and customizable theme IDE settings	VS Code Accessibility Themes

7.4. Sustainable Implementation Strategies

For effective and long-term incorporation of new media and generative AI into engineering education, sustainability needs to be integrated into the implementation plan. Institutions need to set up permanent digital learning cells or teaching innovation center's with the mandate for ongoing faculty support, tool assessment, and resource curating. These centers can partner with AICTE-certified training providers and EdTech startups to provide regular micro-credentialed courses and refresher FDPs. Incorporating the faculty development framework proposed into annual academic schedules guarantees continuity and consistency with institutional objectives. For ensuring budgetary and administrative sustainability, proposals can be incorporated into Quality Improvement Programs (QIP), TEQIP programs, or industry-funded innovation grants. Ultimately, a viable implementation strategy appreciates that faculty development is not an event but a dynamic, ongoing process that has to evolve with pedagogical and technological advancements.

7.5. Change Management for OEPFM Adoption

Effective application of the Open Education and Pedagogy First Model (OEP-FM) needs to be planned change management to address institutional resistance, workload issues, and budgetary limitations. The below methods can ensure smoother implementation:

Table 17. Department Buy-In Proposal Template

Section	Details to Include
Objective	Briefly explain the benefits of OEPFM integration for teaching quality and student outcomes
Alignment	Map framework benefits to institutional vision, NAAC/NBA criteria, and AICTE FDP guidelines
Expected ROI	Estimate potential time savings, student engagement increase, and quality improvement
Pilot Scope	Suggest starting with 1–2 courses in a semester
Resource Needs	List tools, training hours, and technical support required
Evaluation Plan	Include metrics such as pre/post faculty digital competency, grading turnaround time, and student satisfaction

Key Takeaways

- Include digital pedagogy in institutional policies and budgets.
- Create digital learning/teaching excellence centres for ongoing faculty training.
- Integrate OEPFM phases into AICTE FDPs with theory, practice, and mentoring.
- Make faculty micro-credentials mandatory and link funding to innovation.
- Ensure accessibility with tools and strategies for all learners
- Sustain change through peer mentoring, regular updates, and innovation grants.
- Start small with pilot courses, track results, and align with institutional goals.

8. BROADER IMPLICATIONS AND FUTURE DIRECTIONS

The implementation of our OEPFM model is likely to face institutional issues like resistance to change, budget constraints, and digital literacy deficiencies, but these can be overcome through leadership, specific policies, and ongoing mentorship. The methodology is also scalable and flexible, being translatable across discipline and into different contexts in both developed and developing nations. It should be researched further by conducting longitudinal studies to evaluate long-term effect and increase the model's precision, as well as incorporating emerging technologies like AI-based analytics and virtual reality technologies to enhance its applicability.

9. CONCLUSION

The speedy development of generative AI and new media technologies poses both a threat and an unprecedented challenge for engineering education. By embracing a rigorous, research-based faculty development process prioritizing pedagogy over technology, institutions can enable instructors to not only adapt but drive such a transformation. When carefully integrated into current academic frameworks such as AICTE-approved FDPs and short-term programs, this model builds teaching efficacy, encourages innovation, and develops long-term digital literacy. Successful execution of such a program relies on sustained institutional support, regular review, and policy-making that is inclusive in nature. With collective effort, engineering institutions can develop a future-capable teaching community capable of guiding the next generation of globally skilled engineers.

REFERENCES

AICTE. (2018). AICTE Training and Learning (ATAL) Academy Faculty Development Programme Guidelines. All India Council for Technical Education. Retrieved from: https://www.aicte-india.org/atal

AICTE. (2019). Model Curriculum for Induction Training Program for Faculty Members (FDP). New Delhi: All India Council for Technical Education. Available at: https://www.aicte-india.org/sites/default/files/FDP%20Handbook.pdf

AICTE. (2020). National Educational Alliance for Technology (NEAT) Scheme. AICTE. Retrieved from: https://neat.aicte-india.org/

Al-Abri, S., & Rahim, N. (2023). *Faculty development for strengthening online teaching capability: A mixed-method study*. PubMed Central.

ASEE. (2020). Profiles of Engineering and Engineering Technology by Institution. American Society for Engineering Education. https://ira.asee.org

Chaves, M., & Lage, A. (2021). Using Moodle and flipped classrooms in an engineering mechanics course. *International Journal of STEM Education*, *8*, 48. https://stemeducationjournal.springeropen.com/articles/10.1186/s40594-021-00302-2. DOI: 10.1186/s40594-021-00302-2

Connolly, M. R., Savoy, J. N., Lee, Y. G., & Hill, L. B. (2016). Building teaching careers: The CIRTL network's impact on early career STEM faculty. *CBE Life Sciences Education*, *15*(3), ar38. https://www.lifescied.org/doi/full/10.1187/cbe.15-12-0267. DOI: 10.1187/cbe.15-12-0267 PMID: 27543637

European Commission. (2022). Ethics Guidelines for Trustworthy AI. https://digital-strategy.ec.europa.eu/en/library/ethics-guidelines-trustworthy-ai

Freeman, S., Eddy, S. L., McDonough, M., Smith, M. K., Okoroafor, N., Jordt, H., & Wenderoth, M. P. (2014). Active learning increases student performance in science, engineering, and mathematics. *Proceedings of the National Academy of Sciences of the United States of America*, *111*(23), 8410–8415. https://www.pnas.org/content/111/23/8410. DOI: 10.1073/pnas.1319030111 PMID: 24821756

Freeman, S., Eddy, S. L., McDonough, M., Smith, M. K., Okoroafor, N., Jordt, H., & Wenderoth, M. P. (2014). Active learning increases student performance in science, engineering, and mathematics. *Proceedings of the National Academy of Sciences of the United States of America*, *111*(23), 8410–8415. DOI: 10.1073/pnas.1319030111 PMID: 24821756

. Gilboy, M. B., Heinerichs, S., & Pazzaglia, G. (2021). *Active learning through flipped classroom in mechanical engineering: improving students' perception of learning and performance.* International Journal of STEM Education, 8(12). SpringerOpen

IEEE-TEMS. (2022). *AI in Engineering Education: Opportunities and Ethical Challenges.* IEEE Technology and Engineering Management Society.

Ministry of Electronics and IT. India. (2023). Digital Personal Data Protection Act. https://www.meity.gov.in/digital-personal-data-protection-act-2023

Mishra, L., Gupta, T., & Shree, A. (2020). Online teaching-learning in higher education during lockdown period of COVID-19 pandemic. *International Journal of Educational Research Open, 1*, 100012. DOI: 10.1016/j.ijedro.2020.100012 PMID: 35059663

Mishra, L., Gupta, T., & Shree, A. (2020). Online teaching-learning in higher education during lockdown period of COVID-19 pandemic. *International Journal of Educational Research Open, 1*, 100012. Advance online publication. DOI: 10.1016/j.ijedro.2020.100012 PMID: 35059663

Mishra, P., & Koehler, M. J. (2006). Technological Pedagogical Content Knowledge: A framework for integrating technology in teacher knowledge. *Teachers College Record, 108*(6), 1017–1054. DOI: 10.1111/j.1467-9620.2006.00684.x

OECD. (2023). Policy Framework for Responsible AI in Education. https://www.oecd.org/education/edtech/policy-framework-ai-education.pdf

Olmstead, A., & Turpen, C. (2016). Evaluating Professional Development Work with the Real-Time Professional Development Observation Tool (R-PDOT). *Physical Review. Physics Education Research, 12*(2), 020136. DOI: 10.1103/PhysRevPhysEducRes.12.020136

. Rahman, M., Damanhouri, A., & Mahmud, R. (2024). *Enhancing engineering education through virtual reality: A systematic study on immersive engineering education practices.* ResearchGate (Open Access).

Rienties, B., Brouwer, N., & Lygo-Baker, S. (2017). The effects of online professional development on higher education teachers' beliefs and intentions towards learning facilitation and technology. *Teaching and Teacher Education, 63*, 113–123. DOI: 10.1016/j.tate.2016.12.001

Sharma, P., Srivastava, R., & Malik, R. (2020). *Impact of AR/VR on Conceptual Learning in Engineering Education.* Open Access Journal of Engineering Education Innovations.

Srivastava, A., ... (2024). Evaluating the effectiveness of flipped learning in an upper-division undergraduate electrical engineering course. Discover Education. Springer.

UNESCO. (2021). *Reimagining our futures together: A new social contract for education.* https://unesdoc.unesco.org/ark:/48223/pf0000379707

UNESCO. (2021). AI and Education: Guidance for Policy-makers. https://unesdoc.unesco.org/ark:/48223/pf0000376709

UNESCO IITE. (2021). Digital transformation of education: Teacher professional development. Moscow: UNESCO Institute for Information Technologies in Education. https://iite.unesco.org/publications/digital-transformation-of-education-teacher-professional-development/

van Alten, D. C. D., Phielix, C., Janssen, J., & Kester, L. (2019). Effects of flipping the classroom on learning outcomes and satisfaction: A meta-analysis. *Educational Research Review*, *28*, 100281. DOI: 10.1016/j.edurev.2019.05.003

Wehling, M., Thomeczek, C., & Seidl, M. (2021). Fast-track flipping – Preparing medical faculty for online teaching with digital tools. *BMC Medical Education*, *21*, 395. Advance online publication. https://bmcmededuc.biomedcentral.com/articles/10.1186/s12909-021-02784-8. DOI: 10.1186/s12909-021-02784-8 PMID: 34158039

Wiggins, G., & McTighe, J. (2005). *Understanding by Design* (2nd ed.). ASCD., https://www.ascd.org/books/understanding-by-design-2nd-edition

World Bank. (2020). Digital Skills in Tertiary Education and the Labour Market in Developing Countries. https://documents.worldbank.org/en/publication/documents-reports/documentdetail/306711611349330106

Chapter 11
Artificial Intelligence and Adaptive Learning Technologies

Ramkrishna Dikkatwar
University of Mumbai, India

Mittal Mohite
https://orcid.org/0000-0002-0238-2044
Sri Balaji University, Pune, India

Sonal Sharma
https://orcid.org/0000-0003-4853-5349
Thakur Institute of Management Studies and Research, Mumbai, India

P. Selvakumar
https://orcid.org/0000-0002-3650-4548
Department of Science and Humanities, Nehru Institute of Technology, Coimbatore, India

Sujay Mugaloremutt Jayadeva
https://orcid.org/0000-0003-2252-9071
JSS Academy of Higher Education and Research, Mysuru, India

Manjunath T. C.
https://orcid.org/0000-0003-2545-9160
Rajarajeswari College of Engineering, India

ABSTRACT

Artificial Intelligence (AI) is profoundly reshaping the landscape of education, transforming traditional teaching and learning paradigms through automation, personalization, and data-driven insights. As educational institutions strive to meet the diverse needs of 21st-century learners, AI technologies offer unprecedented opportunities to enhance learning experiences, streamline administrative processes, and support educators in delivering more effective and inclusive instruction. AI's role in education is multifaceted—ranging from intelligent tutoring systems and automated assessment tools to adaptive learning platforms and virtual teaching assistants—each contributing to a more responsive and personalized educational

DOI: 10.4018/979-8-3373-5157-5.ch011

environment. Routine processes such as grading multiple-choice assessments, tracking attendance, managing records, and scheduling meetings can be efficiently handled by AI-powered systems. This allows timely interventions, ensuring that support is provided before problems escalate.

THE ROLE OF ARTIFICIAL INTELLIGENCE IN EDUCATION

Artificial Intelligence (AI) is profoundly reshaping the landscape of education, transforming traditional teaching and learning paradigms through automation, personalization, and data-driven insights. As educational institutions strive to meet the diverse needs of 21st-century learners, AI technologies offer unprecedented opportunities to enhance learning experiences, streamline administrative processes, and support educators in delivering more effective and inclusive instruction. AI's role in education is multifaceted—ranging from intelligent tutoring systems and automated assessment tools to adaptive learning platforms and virtual teaching assistants—each contributing to a more responsive and personalized educational environment. Routine processes such as grading multiple-choice assessments, tracking attendance, managing records, and scheduling meetings can be efficiently handled by AI-powered systems. This allows timely interventions, ensuring that support is provided before problems escalate. Automation thus reduces the administrative burden on educators while enhancing institutional efficiency and student success. In the classroom, AI is driving innovation through intelligent tutoring systems (ITS) and virtual assistants. These technologies can deliver individualized instruction and provide support outside of traditional classroom hours. ITS tools simulate one-on-one tutoring by offering hints, explanations, and personalized feedback based on student interactions. Furthermore, AI contributes to curriculum design and instructional strategies by analyzing vast amounts of data to identify trends and learning gaps. Learning analytics enable educators to assess teaching methods in real time. AI tools can recommend pedagogical strategies, suggest improvements, and even generate custom learning materials aligned with students to enhance instructional quality and learner outcomes.

AI is also revolutionizing assessment and feedback mechanisms in education. Beyond simple grading automation, AI systems can evaluate written responses, essays, and project work. These tools provide timely, objective, and consistent feedback, reducing human bias and facilitating faster grading processes. Additionally, AI can help design formative progress, thereby offering a dynamic learning experience that continually responds to learners' evolving needs. In higher education and professional training, AI supports lifelong learning and skill development through intelligent recommendation systems. These systems suggest courses, resources, and career pathways goals, and previous trends use algorithms to personalize learning journeys, keeping learners engaged and aligned with their personal and professional aspirations. Rather than replacing teachers, AI augments their capabilities by handling routine tasks, offering instructional insights, and enabling more personalized engagement with students. Mentoring, guiding learners in critical thinking, creativity, collaboration, and ethical use of technology. Educator training and professional development are essential to help them harness AI effectively and integrate it meaningfully into their pedagogy. Conclusion: The role of Artificial Intelligence is both transformative and expansive, supporting inclusive education, enhancing assessments, and guiding curriculum design. AI stands as a catalyst for educational innovation. However, its implementation must be guided by ethical principles, inclusive policies, and continuous stakeholder engagement to ensure that its benefits are accessible to all. As technology continues to evolve, the partnership between AI and human educators will be crucial in creating a future-ready education system that nurtures the potential of every learner.

BENEFITS OF AI-DRIVEN LEARNING TECHNOLOGIES

Artificial Intelligence (AI)-driven learning in the landscape, which enhances the quality, accessibility, efficiency, and personalization of education across diverse settings. As schools, universities, and training institutions increasingly integrate AI into their instructional frameworks, it becomes evident. From predictive analytics, AI-driven tools are empowering both learners and educators in unprecedented ways. These benefits span pedagogical innovation, administrative efficiency, and long-term. Prominent benefits of AI-driven learning technologies include classroom models that apply individual students' varying styles, or systems, which are capable of analyzing preferences and behavior (Avalekar U A., et al, 2025). This allows them to deliver, supplement, and offer timely feedback. For example, AI-powered platforms like Squirrel AI and Knewton dynamically modify instructional paths to suit each learner, ensuring that students neither fall behind nor become disengaged due to a lack of challenge. This personalization fosters greater learner autonomy and improves academic outcomes by helping students master content at their own pace. In addition to personalization, efficiency, and time savings are key advantages offered by time-consuming and instructional multiple-choice quizzes, checking homework, managing student data, and scheduling. Furthermore, AI systems can generate real-time analytics and reports that help teachers track progress, identify learning gaps, and adjust instruction accordingly. By minimizing administrative overhead and enhancing decision-making with data-driven insights, AI helps streamline both teaching and learning processes.

AI-driven technologies also promote continuous and adaptive learning, enabling students to receive instruction and feedback anytime, anywhere. Learning is no longer confined to the classroom or restricted to set hours (Strielkowski W., et al, 2025). With AI-enabled chatbots, virtual tutors, and mobile learning applications, students can access academic assistance 24/7. These systems provide immediate answers to questions, explanations of complex topics, and encouragement, which are particularly valuable in remote learning environments. Inclusivity and accessibility represent another significant benefit of AI-driven learning technologies. AI tools help break down barriers for students with disabilities, those from diverse linguistic backgrounds, and individuals with limited access to traditional educational resources. For instance, speech recognition, text-to-speech, and language translation tools make learning materials accessible to visually impaired students, learners with dyslexia, and non-native speakers. Real-time captioning and transcription services powered by AI also assist students with hearing impairments. AI enhances student engagement and motivation through interactive and gamified learning experiences. Intelligent learning platforms can incorporate elements such as adaptive quizzes, real-time feedback, progress badges, and personalized learning paths, which sustain learner interest and drive intrinsic motivation. These gamified approaches appeal particularly to digital-native students who thrive in immersive and responsive environments. Additionally, AI can analyze engagement data to identify when a student is losing interest or struggling with content, prompting timely interventions or changes in instructional strategy to re-engage the learner (Bahri N A S., et al, 2023). In higher education and corporate training, AI supports career readiness and skill development by identifying knowledge gaps, suggesting relevant learning pathways, and aligning educational experiences with market needs. Personalized recommendation engines can suggest courses, certifications, and learning resources tailored to individual goals and job trends. This targeted approach learning learners navigate a rapidly evolving job market, leveraging learners' content, their career aspirations, prior learning, and industry trends, thereby supporting informed and strategic skill development. Traditional assessments often provide delayed results, limiting the opportunity for timely improvement. AI-enabled tools, on the other hand, can instantly evaluate assignments, provide detailed feedback, and guide learners through mistakes. These capabilities support the formative assessment process, performance-adapted learning continuously. Furthermore, AI detects patterns in student errors and misconceptions, allowing for targeted remediation and more effective learning interventions (Sumathy V., et al, 2024). AI also promotes collaboration and knowledge sharing through intelligent networking platforms. These tools can connect learners with peers, mentors, and experts based on shared interests, skill levels, and learning goals. Lastly, AI enables continuous improvement of educational content by analyzing how learners interact with it. AI systems can identify which content is most effective, which sections lead to confusion or drop-off, and how learners progress through modules. Content creators and educators can use this feedback to iteratively refine materials, optimize instructional design, and enhance learning outcomes.

HOW ADAPTIVE LEARNING TECHNOLOGIES WORK

Technologies advancement, data analytics, and cognitive science preferences, performance. At their core, dynamic presentation of educational sequence of instruction, and the pacing of lessons, involves continuous analysis of behavioral progress. These technologies mark a departure from traditional linear learning approaches by offering a more flexible, responsive, and individualized method of teaching and learning that supports mastery, engagement, and efficiency. The foundation of adaptive learning lies in data collection and analysis (Raimi L., et al, 2024). As learners interact with digital platforms—by answering questions, reading texts, watching videos, completing exercises, or participating in simulations—every action generates data. This includes correct and incorrect responses, time spent on each question or concept, frequency of attempts, engagement levels, click patterns, and even emotional cues (in advanced systems). These data points are captured in real time and fed into sophisticated algorithms that evaluate the learner's knowledge state, skills, strengths, and weaknesses. This ongoing evaluation, the system constructs a learner profile or model—a dynamic, evolving representation of the individual's learning journey. This model helps the adaptive system understand where the learner currently stands in terms of mastery and what concepts they are ready to tackle next. The learner profile is continuously refined as more data is gathered, ensuring that instructional decisions are increasingly accurate and personalized (Essa S G., et al, 2023). Once the learner model is established, the system uses decision-making algorithms—often powered byto determine most appropriate instructional content and sequence. These algorithms analyze which concepts need reinforcement, which can be skipped, and what type of content delivery (videos, simulations, text, quizzes, etc.) is most effective for the learner. Related to fractions, the system might recognize a gap in their understanding of division and redirect them to foundational lessons before progressing further. Conversely, if a learner demonstrates strong proficiency, the system may accelerate their progress or introduce more challenging material to maintain engagement.

Adaptive learning systems typically operate within a learning loop that includes four primary stages: diagnosis, instruction, assessment, and feedback. Diagnosis:

The system evaluates the learner's current level of understanding through initial assessments or by analyzing early interactions. This diagnostic phase is essential for establishing a baseline and identifying prior knowledge, misconceptions, and learning gaps. Instruction: Based on the diagnosis, the system selects and delivers personalized instructional content. This could include readings, multimedia resources, practice problems, and interactive activities designed to target specific learning objectives. The content is tailored not just in terms of difficulty, but also in format and instructional strategy. Assessment: Continuous or formative assessments are embedded within the learning experience. These include quizzes, drag-and-drop exercises, simulations, or scenario-based tasks that measure comprehension and application in real time. Feedback: Immediate feedback is provided to the learner, which may include explanations of correct and incorrect answers, hints, and suggestions for further practice (Kem D., 2022). Feedback also flows back to the system, updating the learner model and refining the personalization process. A key component of adaptive learning is content mapping—the structuring of educational content into a hierarchical or networked map of interconnected concepts and skills. This content map allows the system to identify prerequisite relationships between topics and understand which knowledge areas need to be mastered before advancing. Content is tagged with metadata that indicates difficulty level, skill type, pedagogical purpose, and instructional strategy. The system uses this metadata to align content delivery with the learner's needs and context. Several adaptive learning platforms illustrate these principles in practice. For instance, platforms like ALEKS (Assessment and Learning in Knowledge Spaces) use knowledge space theory to determine what students know and what they are ready to learn next. Knewton personalizes learning experiences by continuously analyzing learner data and adapting content delivery accordingly.

DreamBox Learning for mathematics combines adaptive technology with engaging game-like environments, adjusting not only the difficulty of problems but also the way they are presented to suit the learner's style and needs. Despite their many advantages, adaptive learning technologies also face challenges and limitations (Mehra J., et al, 2025). Developing high-quality, adaptive content requires significant investment in instructional design, metadata tagging, and algorithm training. Furthermore, the effectiveness of adaptive systems depends heavily on their personalization or reinforcement of existing inequalities. In conclusion, adaptive learning technologies work by continuously collecting and analyzing learner data, constructing dynamic learner profiles, and using intelligent algorithms to deliver personalized instruction that evolves with the learner. These systems enable a shift from standardized, linear education to individualized, responsive learning pathways that support mastery, engagement, and equity. Technologies hold tremendous transformative potential by being efficient.. However, realizing this potential requires thoughtful integration, robust content development, and ethical safeguards. For educators, adaptive learning becomes a powerful ally in delivering high-quality education for all.

PERSONALIZED LEARNING WITH AI-DRIVEN ADAPTIVE SYSTEMS

Personalized learning, empowered by AI-driven adaptive systems, represents a transformative shift in modern education—moving from a standardized, one-size-fits-all approach to a dynamic, learner-centered model that recognizes and responds to the individual needs, preferences, skills, and learning styles of each student. At the heart of this transformation is the integration of artificial intelligence technologies that enable real-time customization of educational content, pacing, and support. Relevant, adaptive are designed to continuously collect and analyze learner data, generate intelligent insights, and tailor instruction to ensure that every student is supported on a unique learning path toward mastery and success (Limbore N V., et al, 2025). The foundation of personalized learning through AI begins with data-driven learner profiling. As students engage with digital learning platforms, AI systems gather a wide array of data points—such as the types of questions attempted, time spent on tasks, patterns of correct and incorrect responses, preferred content formats, and engagement levels. This data is synthesized to build a comprehensive, dynamic learner profile that evolves with each interaction. The learner profile becomes the basis for understanding a student's current knowledge level, strengths, challenges, cognitive preferences, and emotional responses to content, allowing the system to make informed instructional decisions in real time. Once a learner profile is established, AI algorithms sequence, complexity, and modality of instructional materials specific to algebra might require additional scaffolding, visual aids, or targeted practice exercises may accelerate the pace or present more challenging problems to maintain engagement. This level of adaptivity ensures that students are neither left behind nor held back, allowing them to progress at a pace that aligns with their readiness and motivation (Taylor D L., et al, 2021). Personalized learning through AI not only increases academic efficiency but also reduces student frustration and promotes sustained interest. Content differentiation is another key aspect of personalized learning powered by AI. Different preferences may grasp concepts through visualizations, prefer text-based explanations, or hands-on practice. AI-driven platforms are capable of delivering content in multiple formats tailored to the learner's preferred learning style. Advanced systems may also factor in neurodiversity, language proficiency, or previous educational exposure to curate content that is accessible, inclusive, and aligned with the learner's context. This granular level of personalization ensures that learning is not only effective but also equitable and empowering.

Powerful personalized learning (ITS) behavior involves a tutor offering adaptive instructional strategies, adjusting content delivery in response to student inputs. ITS tools can diagnose misconceptions, offer step-by-step help, and recommend targeted exercises. For instance, Carnegie Learning's MATHia or Pearson's MyLab platforms use AI to simulate one-on-one instruction, allowing students to receive individualized attention that would be difficult to scale in traditional classroom environments. These systems can redirect students to foundational content when necessary, introduce enrichment tasks when appropriate, and optimize review cycles based on retention patterns. By leveraging spaced repetition, retrieval practice, and predictive analytics, AI systems ensure that learners receive instruction that is both effective and efficiently timed for long-term retention (Soelistianto F A., et al, 2024). Motivation and engagement are also enhanced through personalized learning with AI. Gamification elements such as badges, progress bars, achievement levels, and interactive challenges can be integrated into adaptive systems to keep students motivated. Furthermore, personalization agency relevance engages deeply with content that matches their interests, goals, and abilities. AI can also track motivational patterns and intervene when signs of disengagement are detected, adjusting content delivery or recommending new learning strategies to re-engage the learner. Personalized learning with AI extends beyond traditional academic subjects. In higher education and tools trajectories, career aspirations, and industry previous experiences. Coursera and edX recommend courses, certifications, and skill-building activities aligned with a learner's goals. This helps learners build tailored educational portfolios that enhance employability and lifelong learning. In corporate settings, AI supports workforce upskilling and reskilling by matching employees with relevant training modules and monitoring competency development over time. AI should augment, not replace, the human element of education. Teachers bring emotional intelligence, cultural awareness, creativity, and ethical judgment—qualities that AI cannot replicate (Yekollu R K., et al, 2024). The most effective personalized learning ecosystems are those in which technology and human educators collaborate synergistically. Professional development is necessary to equip teachers with the skills and confidence to use AI tools effectively and to interpret data insights in pedagogically sound ways. Furthermore, the success of personalized learning depends on infrastructure and access. In regions with limited digital resources, implementing AI-driven systems can be challenging. Bridging the digital divide by equitable devices, connectivity, and digital literacy is essential to prevent the deepening of educational inequalities. Governments, technology providers inclusive ecosystems support personalized learning.

INTELLIGENT TUTORING SYSTEMS FOR PERSONALIZED LEARNING

are revolutionizing the educational landscape by enabling highly AI-powered simulations of one-on-one human tutoring, guiding students through content while responding in real time. The core strength of an ITS diagnosis learner misunderstandings, adjust instructional strategies, and tailor content delivery to maximize learning efficiency and mastery. As a result, intelligent tutoring systems are playing a pivotal role in engaging diverse learners across disciplines and educational levels. One of the key components of intelligent tutoring systems is the learner model, a constantly evolving representation of the student's knowledge state, skills, preferences, and learning behaviors. This model is built and refined through continuous data collection as the student interacts with the system (Ivanenkov Y A., et al, 2023). Each response, action, hesitation, and request for help contributes to a deeper understanding of the learner's profile. Based on this model, the ITS makes real-time decisions about the most appropriate instructional content, level of difficulty, pacing, and feedback strategy to use. ITS platforms typically follow a four-component architecture: the domain model, the student model, the pedagogical model, and the user interface. Domain Model: component subject matter that ITS is designed to teach. It includes facts, concepts, problem-solving procedures, and rules that define correct and incorrect solutions. The domain model allows the ITS to assess the learner's responses accurately and identify what they know and where they need help. Student Model: As mentioned, this is the evolving representation progress updated as the learner interacts with the system and is used to guide personalized instructional decisions. Pedagogical Model: This component determines how to teach the content. It selects instructional strategies, provides feedback, decides when to review or reteach concepts, and manages the pacing and sequencing of lessons. It may also choose motivational interventions to encourage persistence.

User Interface: This is the medium through which learners interact with the system. It must be intuitive, accessible, and engaging, often incorporating multimedia elements like animations, voiceovers, interactive exercises, and simulations. This formative feedback loop helps reinforce learning, correct misconceptions, and build confidence. In advanced ITS systems, feedback is not merely corrective but also diagnostic and strategic, offering hints or prompts based on the learner's specific misunderstanding (Zhu C., et al, 2023). For example, if a student consistently misapplies a mathematical principle, the ITS might direct them to foundational concepts or offer alternative problem-solving techniques. Intelligent tutoring systems are particularly effective in STEM disciplines, where problem-solving processes can be broken down into logical steps. Similarly, platforms such as AutoTutor or Andes Physics Tutor provide support in science and physics by analyzing student input and guiding them with Socratic questioning. Beyond STEM, ITSs are increasingly being applied in language learning, writing, and reading comprehension. Tools like Duolingo and Grammarly use natural language processing (NLP) to evaluate student input, assess grammar and vocabulary use, and offer real-time corrections. Writing tutors such as My Writing Coach or Turnitin's Revision Assistant analyze essay structure, argument clarity, and coherence, offering students personalized feedback to strengthen their writing skills. These tools not only improve academic performance but also develop critical communication abilities.

Students can access instruction and practice at any time, allowing for flexible and autonomous learning outside of traditional classroom hours. This is particularly valuable for remote learning, adult education, or learners in underserved regions where qualified teachers may be scarce. It also serves as a valuable tool for differentiated instruction within classrooms, allowing educators to manage diverse learning needs more effectively by assigning tailored ITS modules to students based on their proficiency levels and goals. In addition to academic content, intelligent tutoring systems are evolving to support metacognitive and affective learning. Some ITS platforms can detect emotional states such as confusion, boredom, or frustration by analyzing user input, facial expressions (in systems equipped with cameras), or interaction patterns (Okonji N N., et al, 2025). These systems adapt their responses accordingly—slowing down the pace, offering encouragement, or presenting material in a different format. This emotional awareness helps maintain learner engagement and fosters a supportive digital learning environment that is sensitive to students' mental and emotional needs. It also offers educators powerful analytics and insights into student performance. Dashboards provide real-time data on learner progress, error patterns, time on task, and skill mastery. Teachers can use this data to identify struggling students, differentiate instruction, and inform pedagogical decisions. Additionally, ITS can suggest interventions, supplementary materials, or adjustments to instructional plans based on individual and group learning trends. This integration of AI and human instruction enhances educational effectiveness and supports evidence-based teaching practices. Despite their many benefits, intelligent tutoring systems face challenges and limitations. Developing high-quality ITS requires significant investments in subject matter expertise, instructional design, AI modeling, and user interface design. Moreover, ITSs are more effective in domains where learning can be structured logically; applying them to open-ended or abstract disciplines—such as philosophy, ethics, or creative arts—remains more complex (Chowdhary S., et al, 2025). Another challenge is ensuring cultural sensitivity and inclusivity, as ITS systems must be designed to accommodate diverse learners, languages, and educational contexts without bias. Furthermore, ITSs are not intended to replace human teachers. While they can replicate many cognitive aspects of instruction, they cannot substitute the emotional, social, and ethical dimensions of education that only human educators can provide. The ideal learning environment is one where ITS and educators collaborate—AI handles routine instruction, assessment, and feedback, while teachers focus on mentoring, fostering collaboration, and guiding students through complex thinking and interpersonal growth. By combining AI, cognitive science, and real-time data analysis, these systems deliver individualized instruction that supports student mastery, engagement, and autonomy. Whether in classrooms, homes, or workplaces, ITS can enhance learning outcomes, provide flexible access to quality instruction, and empower both learners and educators. As these systems continue to evolve, addressing their limitations and integrating them thoughtfully with human teaching will be essential to realizing their full potential in creating inclusive, effective, and future-ready learning environments.

ACCESSIBILITY AND INCLUSIVITY WITH AI-DRIVEN LEARNING

AI-driven learning systems environments where learners of all abilities, backgrounds, and languages can thrive. By breaking down traditional barriers to education—be they physical, cognitive, linguistic, or socio-economic—AI is enabling more inclusive participation and ensuring that learning opportunities are not limited by circumstance. Educational technology powerful means long-standing inequities and a just supportive academic landscape. Moreover, AI enhances language accessibility by enabling real-time translation and multilingual support. AI-powered translation tools can automatically convert text, audio, and video into multiple languages, making it possible for non-native speakers and multilingual learners to access content in their preferred language (Coates J M., et al, 2025). This is particularly beneficial in globalized classrooms or diverse educational settings where students speak various languages. AI language models can also assist with grammar correction and vocabulary enhancement, helping students who are learning a second language to improve their academic writing and comprehension. This fosters greater inclusivity by ensuring that language is not a barrier to understanding or participation. In terms of cognitive inclusivity, AI-driven learning platforms can adapt instruction to accommodate different learning styles, paces, and preferences. These features make learning more accessible to students who may not thrive under traditional, one-size-fits-all instruction. AI also supports inclusivity by bridging the digital divide through intelligent, low-bandwidth platforms and offline capabilities. In many regions, especially in rural or under-resourced communities, internet access and technological infrastructure remain limited. AI can optimize educational tools for use in low-connectivity environments, offering downloadable modules, offline assessments, and local data processing features. Additionally, AI systems can be embedded in affordable hardware solutions such as smartphones or tablets, expanding reach to marginalized populations (Yang S., 2024). By designing with equity in mind, AI-driven educational technologies help ensure that learners in all socio-economic contexts can access high-quality education. Another critical area where AI promotes accessibility is through emotion and behavior recognition technologies that support social and emotional learning (SEL). These systems use facial recognition, voice analysis, and behavioral tracking to identify signs of emotional distress, disengagement, or confusion in students. Teachers and support staff can be alerted in real time, enabling timely interventions for students who may be struggling silently due to emotional, psychological, or social challenges. In inclusive classrooms where students face a wide range of mental health issues or trauma-related experiences, these AI capabilities provide educators with valuable insights to offer empathetic, informed support.

AI also facilitates inclusive assessment practices by designing evaluations that are flexible and adaptive. Traditional exams often disadvantage students with different learning needs or those from varied cultural and linguistic backgrounds. AI systems can deliver assessments in diverse formats—visual, auditory, interactive—and can modify the level of difficulty, reduce anxiety, promote fairness, and ensure that assessments measure true understanding rather than test-taking skills or cultural familiarity. AI can also flag potentially biased or inaccessible test items, supporting educators in creating more equitable evaluation instruments (Lin C C., et al, 2023). AI tools enhance this approach by recommending alternative formats (e.g., audio versions of text, interactive simulations, translated materials), offering various ways for students to demonstrate understanding (e.g., spoken responses, digital portfolios, video projects), and customizing motivation strategies based on student interests and learning profiles. These innovations ensure that instructional materials and activities are accessible from the outset, rather than retrofitted as accommodations. In higher education and workforce training, AI is improving accessibility through career readiness and skill-building platforms tailored to learners with diverse abilities. These platforms assess individual strengths, suggest relevant courses or certifications, and simulate job-related tasks in an accessible format. For example, virtual labs, gamified training modules, and AI-powered mock interviews can be customized for learners with physical or cognitive disabilities. Educators, technologists, policymakers, disability advocates, linguists, and learners themselves must work together real world (Bradáč V., et al, 2022). Government institutions should support inclusive AI development through funding, research, regulation, and open-access initiatives. Teacher training is also essential so that educators can confidently leverage AI tools and ensure their implementation is aligned with inclusive pedagogical practices. In conclusion, AI-driven learning technologies represent a powerful force for accessibility and inclusivity in education. From assistive technologies and multilingual support to adaptive assessments and emotionally responsive systems,

AI enables learners of all abilities and backgrounds to participate meaningfully in the educational process. As we move toward digital, global, critical, and inclusive intentionally when implemented with care and equity at the forefront, AI can transform education into a truly accessible and inclusive experience for every learner, regardless of their starting point.

CHALLENGES IN IMPLEMENTING AI-DRIVEN LEARNING TECHNOLOGIES

The immense for transforming successful implementation in learning environments is fraught with numerous challenges. The integration of AI-driven learning technologies requires not only substantial technical infrastructure but also cultural, pedagogical, institutional, and ethical adaptations. As educational institutions, educators, and policymakers work to embrace these technologies, they must navigate a complex landscape of barriers that can hinder the full realization of AI's potential. These challenges include issues related to ethics, technological limitations, resistance to change, lack of digital literacy, infrastructure disparities, financial constraints, and algorithmic bias, among others. Inequitable Access and Infrastructure Disparities: The digital divide significantly affects the equitable implementation of AI-driven learning technologies (Terzieva V., et al, 2022). In many low-income regions or under-resourced communities, schools and students lack modern critical components for using AI-powered platforms effectively. These disparities can widen existing educational inequalities, as students in affluent areas benefit from cutting-edge tools while others fall further behind. Additionally, rural and marginalized schools may not have the IT staff or technical support required to maintain AI systems. Bridging these infrastructure gaps requires coordinated investment from governments, the private sector, and international organizations, which is often lacking or inconsistently applied. High Implementation Costs and Limited Budgets: Deploying AI technologies in education involves high purchases, training programs, and schools, particularly public institutions, operate under tight budgets that prioritize core needs like teacher salaries, infrastructure repair, and curriculum resources. As a result, investing in AI is not always feasible. Even when funding is available, the long-term costs associated with updates, technical support, and data storage can be prohibitive. For smaller institutions and developing countries, the financial burden of implementing and sustaining AI systems poses a significant obstacle (Peng C., et al, 2023). Lack of Digital Literacy Among Educators and Learners: For AI-driven technologies to be effective, educators and students alike must possess a certain level of digital literacy. Unfortunately, many teachers lack training in digital pedagogy or familiarity with AI concepts, leading to underutilization or misuse of available tools. Resistance to adopting new technologies can stem from fear, uncertainty, or past negative experiences with edtech. Similarly, students who are unfamiliar with digital platforms or who struggle with basic technological skills may find AI systems difficult to navigate. Without ongoing professional development, technical support, and curriculum integration strategies, the adoption of AI remains inconsistent and shallow.

Quality Assurance and Evaluation: Determining the effectiveness of AI-driven learning technologies is another significant challenge. While many products claim to improve engagement or outcomes, there is limited peer-reviewed research validating these claims. Educators and decision-makers need rigorous, evidence-based frameworks to evaluate the quality, reliability, and impact of AI tools. Without standardized metrics or independent reviews, schools may adopt technologies based on marketing hype rather than proven benefits. Building a culture of research and continuous feedback around AI implementations is necessary to refine practices and ensure meaningful learning gains (Saborío-Taylor S., et al, 2024). Legal and Regulatory Gaps: There are limited international standards or national regulations for schools and universities. As a result, institutions often operate in a regulatory gray area with little guidance on procurement, data handling, accountability, and intellectual property rights. This ambiguity creates uncertainty and increases the risk of misuse or legal liability. Clear, enforceable policies at the local, national, and international levels are needed to provide a legal framework that supports innovation while protecting students and educators. Human Element and Emotional Connection: While AI excels at processing information and providing data-driven insights, it lacks the emotional intelligence, empathy, and cultural awareness that human educators bring to the classroom. Maintaining a balance between automation and personal connection is vital for holistic development. Implementation of learning technologies for personalized learning (Nisha Angeline M., et al, 2025). However, realizing this vision requires confronting and addressing a range of challenges. From ethical concerns and infrastructure gaps to institutional resistance and algorithmic bias, these obstacles are complex and interdependent. Overcoming them will demand collaboration among educators, technologists, policymakers, researchers, and learners. By approaching implementation with foresight, transparency, and inclusivity, educational systems can navigate the challenges facing learners.

BIAS AND FAIRNESS IN AI-DRIVEN EDUCATION

AI systems personalize learning, educators. However, without careful design, implementation, and oversight, these technologies can unintentionally perpetuate, amplify, or even introduce new forms of inequality and discrimination, not mere flaws deeply rooted sociotechnical issues stemming from data quality, algorithm design, systemic inequities, and limited stakeholder inclusion. Ensuring driven education is just a foundational requirement, creating inclusive, equitable, and just learning environments. Impacts of Bias on Educational Equity: When AI systems are biased, they can negatively impact students in several ways: Discriminatory recommendations: AI-based recommendation engines might favor courses, materials, or learning paths for certain demographics while limiting options for others (Upadhyaya A N., et al, 2025). For example, a career counseling AI might steer female students away from STEM disciplines due to biased historical data. Unfair assessments: Automated grading tools or plagiarism detectors may misclassify content or assign lower scores based on writing styles, cultural references, or dialectical differences not aligned with mainstream academic norms. Differential support: AI tutors and adaptive learning platforms might prioritize certain student profiles while neglecting others, leading to unequal learning opportunities. Stereotype reinforcement: If educational content delivery systems present biased narratives, they may reinforce harmful stereotypes or exclude diverse perspectives. In effect, biased AI systems risk creating a stratified educational experience where fairness is undermined, particularly for historically marginalized students such as those from racial minorities, linguistic minorities, socioeconomically disadvantaged backgrounds, students with disabilities, or non-traditional learners. Cultural Sensitivity and Contextual Awareness: Fairness also involves cultural and contextual sensitivity. Many AI tools are designed in global tech hubs without adequate localization or understanding of regional educational contexts (Chemnad K., et al, 2024). For instance, a reading-level detection system trained on Western literature might not perform well when applied to texts from African or Asian cultures. Similarly, voice recognition technologies used in language learning may struggle with regional accents or dialects, leading to the penalization of students who speak differently. In multilingual and multicultural classrooms, fairness demands that AI systems be capable of recognizing and supporting linguistic diversity, varying cognitive styles, and culturally relevant content. Localization, language adaptability, and collaborative design with local educators are essential for avoiding cultural imperialism and technological exclusion.

Inclusion of Diverse Stakeholders: Fairness in AI is best achieved when a wide array of voices is included in the design, deployment, and governance processes. This includes: Educators, who understand pedagogical goals and classroom realities. Students, whose lived experiences can highlight unintended impacts (Roshanaei M., et al, 2023). Parents who have a stake in their children's learning. Policy-makers and administrators who ensure systemic alignment. Ethicists and sociologists, who examine broader social implications. Participatory design practices, co-creation workshops, and advisory councils that reflect diversity in race, gender, disability, and geography can help build socially just systems. Examples and Case Studies: Several real-world incidents highlight the need for fairness in AI-driven education: In the UK, the 2020 A-level grading controversy revealed how algorithmic grading unfairly penalized students from disadvantaged schools, sparking public outcry and policy reversal. In the U.S., predictive policing-style algorithms used by some districts to monitor student behavior were found to disproportionately target students of color. Automated proctoring tools have been criticized for flagging students with darker skin tones more frequently due to flawed facial recognition algorithms (Lin C C., et al, 2023). These examples demonstrate how poorly designed AI systems can have life-altering consequences in educational contexts and why fairness must be a design priority from the outset. Pathways Toward Equitable AI in Education: Achieving fairness in AI-driven education is a long-term endeavor. The following strategies can help: Investing in diverse datasets that reflect all learner types. Developing fairness-focused curricula for AI engineers and educators. Creating independent auditing bodies to assess fairness in educational technologies, empowering communities to participate in AI oversight and governance. Promoting global equity by ensuring AI tools are affordable and culturally adaptable.

DATA PRIVACY AND SECURITY IN AI-DRIVEN LEARNING

transform educational significance becomes paramount in technologies, personal educators, and institutions. Includes not only academic records but also behavioral data, biometric information, geolocation, and even emotional analytics. While this data fuels the intelligence analytics tools, it also presents unprecedented risks to individual privacy, institutional integrity, and the broader ethical use of digital moral, legal, and pedagogical. The Nature of Data in AI-Driven Learning: In the education process, diverse forms of personalized experiences optimize content delivery, assess performance, and provide feedback in real-time. The types of data typically used include: Personal Identifiable Information (PII): Name, date of birth, student ID, address, and contact details (Chinta S V., et al, 2024). Academic data: Grades, test scores, coursework, attendance, and learning progress. Behavioral data: Clickstream data, time spent on tasks, engagement patterns, and keystroke dynamics. Biometric and sensory data: Facial recognition for attendance, eye tracking for attention monitoring, or voice analysis in language learning tools. Psychological and emotional data: Responses to emotionally intelligent tutoring systems, sentiment analysis of discussion posts, or stress-level indicators. This complex and often sensitive data is what enables AI systems to adapt content, offer feedback, and make predictive insights. However, the scope and depth of data collection also make it susceptible to breaches, misuse, unauthorized access, or unethical profiling. Risks and Challenges to Data Privacy in AI-Driven Learning: Educational systems have several related risks: Data over-collection and surveillance. Many AI tools collect more data than necessary, sometimes without explicit consent, resulting in surveillance-like monitoring of students. Lack of informed consent: Students, parents, and even educators often do not fully understand. Third-party data sharing: Educational institutions frequently partner with edtech companies, raising concerns about data being shared or sold to third parties, including advertisers, without proper oversight. Profiling and discrimination: AI systems may develop profiles that could impact students' access to resources, track placement, or career advice based on biased or incomplete data (Keshta I., 2022). Data breaches and cyberattacks: Schools and educational platforms are increasingly targeted by cybercriminals due to their high value. These concerns highlight governance policy frameworks that safeguard privacy while enabling innovation. Balancing Innovation with Privacy: Undeniably can deliver personalized learning, streamline administration, and unlock powerful analytics for student support. However, privacy must not be sacrificed at the altar of innovation. Striking the right balance involves: Risk-benefit analysis: Evaluating the educational value of AI tools against potential privacy risks. Stakeholder involvement: Engaging educators, students, parents, and data protection officers around adoption. Impact assessments: Conducting Data Protection Impact Assessments (DPIAs) before deploying AI systems that handle personal data. Feedback loops: Establishing mechanisms for users to report concerns, challenge decisions made by AI, or request redress in case of misuse.

Figure 1. Process to implement Adaptive Learning Technology

The Role of Educational Leaders and Policymakers: Education leaders create a culture of use. Their responsibilities include: Establishing data privacy policies at the institutional level. Vetting AI tools for compliance and ethical standards before integration. Facilitating professional development on digital ethics and privacy. Advocating for national or regional frameworks that specifically govern AI in education. Supporting the creation of student data rights charters and promoting data literacy as a core component of digital citizenship education. Student and Parent Empowerment: Protecting privacy is not solely the duty of institutions and developers (Alhitmi H K., et al, 2024). Students and parents also need to be empowered: Education and awareness: Teaching students and families about their digital rights, how to manage privacy settings, and how to identify and respond to breaches. Participation in governance: Encouraging students and parents to contribute to data governance policies, review AI tools, and voice concerns. Tools for control: Providing dashboards or user interfaces that allow individuals to manage data permissions, download records, and view AI-generated insights. Case Studies and Real-World Examples: instances illustrate both pitfalls and potential data privacy AI education. In 2020, several schools using online proctoring tools faced backlash when students' webcams were used without adequate consent or clarity, raising concerns about invasive surveillance. In 2021, a university's AI grading system was accused of assigning lower scores to non-traditional learners, revealing the importance of explainability and appeal mechanisms. On the positive side, some AI learning platforms have adopted robust consent models and anonymized data analytics, allowing schools to benefit from insights without compromising individual privacy (Lokhande M., et al, 2025). AI-driven learning holds tremendous promise to revolutionize education through personalization, real-time feedback, and data-driven insights. However, these benefits cannot come at the cost of compromising student privacy and data security. As stewards of future generations, educators, developers, and policymakers must adopt a principled and proactive approach to managing data in the age of AI. This includes ensuring transparency, maintaining consent and control, minimizing data collection, and building robust security infrastructures. Ultimately, the goal is to create learning environments where AI empowers rather than exploits—where students thrive in an ecosystem that respects their rights, safeguards their privacy, and upholds the highest standards of ethical integrity. Only then can AI fulfill its potential as a force for good in education.

THE FUTURE OF AI IN EDUCATION: OPPORTUNITIES AND CHALLENGES

Artificial Intelligence presents a dynamic frontier marked by transformative possibilities and complex challenges accessible are poised to fundamentally reshape educational systems, pedagogies, and learning experiences across the globe. From hyper-personalized to predictive analytics, inclusive education strategies, and unprecedented integration, these raise critical questions around equity, accountability, and evolving. Understanding the opportunities and anticipating the challenges will be essential for shaping an AI-augmented future that is equitable, effective, and human-centered (Ivanashko O., et al, 2024). Opportunities for Transformation: Intelligent Tutoring and On-Demand Support: (ITS) chatbots promise to make support accessible 24/7. These tools can mimic one-on-one tutoring by diagnosing misconceptions, answering questions, and providing scaffolded feedback. Unlike human tutors, AI tutors are scalable and cost-effective, making high-quality instruction more widely available. These systems are especially beneficial in under-resourced settings, offering learning continuity where teacher shortages persist. Future iterations may integrate multimodal communication—text, voice, gesture, and facial recognition—for even more natural and effective interactions. Real-Time Feedback and Continuous Assessment: Traditional assessments often provide limited and delayed feedback. AI enables continuous, formative assessment through real-time monitoring of student interactions and performance. It can detect subtle indicators of learning, such as hesitation or error patterns, and offer immediate, personalized feedback. This fosters a growth-oriented mindset and encourages iterative learning (Adeshola I., et al, 2024). AI-driven assessments can also reduce bias by focusing on objective data rather than subjective grading, and they can support competency-based education by evaluating mastery rather than seat time. Lifelong and Just-in-Time Learning: The future of work demands continuous reskilling and upskilling. AI-powered platforms can support lifelong learning by offering just-in-time, modular content tailored to individual career goals and competency gaps. With the ability to recommend user profiles market demands, it can bridge the gap between education and employability. As education moves beyond traditional age-based stages, AI can facilitate learning that is flexible, on-demand, and learner-centered.

Challenges on the Horizon: Algorithmic Bias and Ethical Concerns: result in unfair treatment, especially for students from marginalized backgrounds. For example, predictive analytics tools that suggest academic tracking could disproportionately label certain demographics as at risk, reinforcing systemic disparities. Ensuring fairness, transparent algorithms, datasets, Ethical guidelines oversight bodies will be crucial to prevent discriminatory practices and uphold students' rights. Digital Divide and Inequitable Access: In low-income and rural areas, limited internet connectivity, outdated devices, and a lack of technical support hinder the implementation of AI tools. This digital divide threatens to widen the gap between privileged and underserved learners (Kuleto V., et al, 2021). Future efforts must focus on ensuring that AI technologies are affordable, scalable, and designed with inclusivity in mind. Public-private partnerships and government initiatives will be vital to bridging access gaps. Regulatory and Policy Gaps: in education, regulations guide its ethical and effective use, pressing on protection, AI procurement, intellectual property, and commercial exploitation, misuse, or fragmented implementation. Governments, international bodies, and educational stakeholders must work collaboratively to establish global standards and local guidelines that ensure responsible AI integration. Sustainability and Long-Term Viability: AI systems require regular updates, maintenance, and infrastructure to remain effective. Many educational institutions struggle with sustainability issues due to limited budgets or reliance on external vendors. The fast-paced evolution of AI also raises questions about technological obsolescence and long-term planning (Becker B A., et al, 2023). To ensure sustainability, schools and universities must develop strategic plans for AI adoption that include cost-benefit analysis, lifecycle management, and ongoing stakeholder engagement. To navigate this future successfully, stakeholders—including governments, educators, technologists, students, and communities—must engage in continuous dialogue, co-design equitable solutions, and establish robust policies to govern AI use responsibly. By harnessing AI with intentionality and foresight, education can evolve to meet the diverse needs of 21st-century learners, preparing them not only for the jobs of the future but also for lifelong growth, critical thinking, and social responsibility.

CONCLUSION

Redefining landscape by more immersive and engaging. As the technology matures, educators and institutions around the world are exploring innovative ways to enrich both the process and learning journeys. Enhanced learning experiences facilitated by AI extend beyond simple automation or digitization; they involve dynamic interactions, data-driven personalization, real-time support, and interactive environments that actively engage learners. By integrating AI into educational ecosystems, it is possible to meet diverse learner needs, optimize effective pedagogical strategies. Personalization at the Core of Enhanced Learning: Traditional often struggles to accommodate pace, style, and preferences. Powered platforms can overcome this limitation by adapting content delivery history. Through continuous data analysis, these systems curate personalized learning paths, recommend resources, and adjust instruction in real-time. This kind of tailored education fosters deeper engagement, increased motivation, and improved academic performance. Moreover, AI can help identify gaps in knowledge that may otherwise go unnoticed in traditional settings. Learning analytics tools track user interactions, test responses, and engagement patterns, giving instructors and learners valuable insights into areas needing reinforcement. This feedback loop not only boosts retention but also encourages a growth mindset by showing students how they are progressing and where they can improve. Real-Time Feedback and Immediate Reinforcement: AI offers the capability for instantaneous, context-sensitive feedback, transforming the way learners interact with educational material. Unlike traditional feedback, which is often delayed and generalized, AI can provide precise, real-time responses tailored to the learner's specific input. For instance, in writing platforms like Grammarly or Quill, AI evaluates grammar, structure, and clarity, offering suggestions that help students improve their communication skills on the spot. Similarly, coding platforms powered by AI can detect syntax errors or logical flaws and provide suggestions for improvement immediately. Kind of allows them to make corrections and understand their mistakes while the information is still fresh. It creates an iterative learning cycle where learners are not punished for errors but are instead guided toward mastery. Such an environment reduces anxiety and enhances confidence, particularly in complex or skill-based subjects like mathematics, science, and programming. Adaptive Learning and Continuous Monitoring: Adaptive learning platforms use a learner's dynamic modifications to the flow to suit their level of understanding. These systems continuously monitor user behavior—such as time spent on tasks, incorrect responses, and patterns in clicks or pauses—and use this data to adapt instruction accordingly. This ensures that learners are neither overwhelmed by complexity nor bored by redundancy. Platforms like Knewton or Smart Sparrow demonstrate how adaptive technology can deliver a truly individualized learning experience. Specifically in algebra, we may revisit foundational topics, offer additional examples, or change the mode of delivery (e.g., from text to video). Such responsiveness ensures optimal pacing and maximizes learning efficiency.

AI as a Collaborative Learning Partner: AI is not just a passive tool—it can act learning Intelligent agent. Chatbots and virtual tutors simulate dialogue-based learning environments that mimic human tutoring. These tools can answer questions, offer explanations, pose counterarguments, and even prompt reflection, helping students think critically and problem-solve independently. For example, AI chatbots like Khanmigo (from Khan Academy) and Squirrel AI provide conversational, Socratic-style learning experiences that encourage students to explore concepts deeply rather than memorize facts. These agents can also monitor emotional cues (through text sentiment or biometric data) to detect confusion, boredom, or frustration and adjust their tone or approach accordingly. This kind of emotional intelligence can foster a sense of companionship and support, particularly in self-paced or remote learning environments. Furthermore, AI-powered collaboration tools can group students based on learning styles, goals, or performance metrics, enabling peer-to-peer interaction and project-based learning. These smart systems promote social learning, which is known to improve retention, motivation, and communication skills. Enhanced Teacher Effectiveness and Resource Optimization: While AI is often seen as a learner-centric technology, it equally enhances the capabilities of educators, administrative attendance, content curation, and dedicates time to mentorship. Advanced assist teachers in designing personalized lesson plans, developing assessments aligned with learning objectives, and analyzing class-wide performance data for strategic planning. For instance, AI tools can evaluate student essays not just for grammar, but also for coherence, argument strength, and originality, providing scores and qualitative feedback. Teachers can use this information to identify trends in learning, differentiate instruction, and provide tailored support. Moreover, AI can be used for specific learner profiles, guiding professional development and pedagogical refinement. In essence, AI serves as a co-pilot for educators, enhancing their decision-making, reducing cognitive load, and amplifying their impact. Fostering Inclusivity and Equitable Access: AI-enhanced learning environments are particularly effective in addressing diverse learner needs, including those with physical, cognitive, or linguistic challenges. Assistive technologies powered by AI—such as screen readers, automated captioning, and real-time translation—break down barriers and students. Detect when learners are disengaged or struggling and trigger support interventions, such as alerts for tutors or customized content adjustments. Additionally, AI platforms can recommend culturally responsive materials and avoid bias through inclusive design practices. This ensures that learners from various backgrounds see themselves reflected in the curriculum, which fosters belonging and engagement.

REFERENCES

Adeshola, I., & Adepoju, A. P. (2024). The opportunities and challenges of ChatGPT in education. *Interactive Learning Environments*, *32*(1), 33–51. DOI: 10.1080/10494820.2023.2253858

Alhitmi, H. K., Mardiah, A., Al-Sulaiti, K. I., & Abbas, J. (2024). Data security and privacy concerns of AI-driven marketing in the context of economics and business field: An exploration into possible solutions. *Cogent Business & Management*, *11*(1), 2393743. DOI: 10.1080/23311975.2024.2393743

Avalekar, U. A., Mehta, V., Mishra, B. R., Prasanna, L., Rajlakshmi, P. V., Manjunath, T. C., & Selvakumar, P. (2025). The current advances in AI-driven education. In Babulak, E. (Ed.), *Educational AI humanoid computing devices for cyber nomads* (pp. 173–196). IGI Global Scientific Publishing., DOI: 10.4018/979-8-3693-8985-0.ch008

Bahri, N. A. S., Anuar, N. B., & Azmi, A. A. S. (2023). Benefits of AI-driven learning platform in engineering education context. *IACSIT International Journal of Engineering and Technology*, *15*, 329–340. DOI: 10.46492/ijet.v15i3.139

Becker, B. A., Denny, P., Finnie-Ansley, J., Luxton-Reilly, A., Prather, J., & Santos, E. A. (2023). Programming is hard—or at least it used to be: Educational opportunities and challenges of AI code generation. In *Proceedings of the 54th ACM Technical Symposium on Computer Science Education* (Vol. 1, pp. 500–506). DOI: 10.1145/3545945.3569759

Bradáč, V., Smolka, P., Kotyrba, M., & Průdek, T. (2022). Design of an intelligent tutoring system to create a personalized study plan using expert systems. *Applied Sciences (Basel, Switzerland)*, *12*(12), 6236. DOI: 10.3390/app12126236

Chemnad, K., & Othman, A. (2024). Digital accessibility in the era of artificial intelligence—Bibliometric analysis and systematic review. *Frontiers in Artificial Intelligence*, *7*, 1349668. DOI: 10.3389/frai.2024.1349668 PMID: 38435800

Chinta, S. V., Wang, Z., Yin, Z., & Hoang, N. (2024). FairAIED: Navigating fairness, bias, and ethics in educational AI applications. arXiv Preprint, arXiv:2403.14321. https://doi.org//arXiv.2403.14321DOI: 10.48550

Chowdhary, S., Selvakumar, P., Sangeetha, B., Sarvaani, V. V., Anute, N., & Sharma, M. (2025). The role of social capital in entrepreneurial development. In Martínez-Falcó, J., Sánchez-García, E., & Marco-Lajara, B. (Eds.), *Support networks for entrepreneurs: Social capital and strategic collaborations* (pp. 311–338). IGI Global Scientific Publishing., DOI: 10.4018/979-8-3693-9836-4.ch013

Coates, J. M., Santhanalakshmi, K., Dinesh, N., Gandhimathi, S., & Chandel, P. S. Mohit, & Selvakumar, P. (2025). Assessment and evaluation in transnational staff development. In G. Morris & J. Ye (Eds.), Training and development in transnational higher education (pp. 387–406). IGI Global Scientific Publishing. DOI: 10.4018/979-8-3373-1897-4.ch019

Essa, S. G., Celik, T., & Human-Hendricks, N. E. (2023). Personalized adaptive learning technologies based on machine learning techniques to identify learning styles: A systematic literature review. *IEEE Access : Practical Innovations, Open Solutions*, *11*, 23400–23420. DOI: 10.1109/ACCESS.2023.3276439

Ivanashko, O., Kozak, A., & Knysh, T. (2024). The role of artificial intelligence in shaping the future of education: Opportunities and challenges. *Futurity Education*, *4*(1), 126–146. DOI: 10.57125/FED.2024.03.25.08

Ivanenkov, Y. A., Polykovskiy, D., Bezrukov, D., Zagribelnyy, B., Aladinskiy, V., Kamya, P., Aliper, A., Ren, F., & Zhavoronkov, A. (2023). Chemistry42: An AI-driven platform for molecular design and optimization. *Journal of Chemical Information and Modeling*, *63*(3), 5867–5876. DOI: 10.1021/acs.jcim.2c01191 PMID: 36728505

Kem, D. (2022). Personalised and adaptive learning: Emerging learning platforms in the era of digital and smart learning. *International Journal of Social Science and Human Research*, *6*(2), 109–117. DOI: 10.47191/ijsshr/v5-i2-02

Keshta, I. (2022). AI-driven IoT for smart health care: Security and privacy issues. *Informatics in Medicine Unlocked*, *30*, 100990. DOI: 10.1016/j.imu.2022.100903

Kuleto, V., Ilić, M., Dumangiu, M., Ranković, M., Martins, O. M. D., Păun, D., & Mihoreanu, L. (2021). Exploring opportunities and challenges of artificial intelligence and machine learning in higher education institutions. *Sustainability (Basel)*, *13*(18), 10424. DOI: 10.3390/su131810424

Limbore, N. V., Anute, N., Ahluwalia, G. K., Chordiya, P. B., Kalshetti, P., & Selvakumar, P. (2025). Ethical leadership and corporate responsibility. In Harriott, S. (Ed.), *Innovative approaches to managing conflict and change in diverse work environments* (pp. 193–218). IGI Global Scientific Publishing., DOI: 10.4018/979-8-3693-9556-1.ch009

Lin, C. C., Huang, A. Y. Q., & Lu, O. H. T. (2023). Artificial intelligence in intelligent tutoring systems toward sustainable education: A systematic review. *Smart Learning Environments*, *10*(1), 35. DOI: 10.1186/s40561-023-00260-y

Lin, C. C., Huang, A. Y. Q., & Yang, S. J. H. (2023). A review of AI-driven conversational chatbots implementation methodologies and challenges (1999–2022). *Sustainability (Basel)*, *15*(5), 4012. DOI: 10.3390/su15054012

Lokhande, M., John Deva Prasanna, D. S., Selvakumar, P., Ragupathi, T., Vaissnave, V., & Manjunath, T. C. (2025). Novel ML algorithms for healthcare. In A. Ajibesin, N. G. N., & S. Thangavel (Eds.), Synergizing data envelopment analysis and machine learning for performance optimization in healthcare (pp. 113–134). IGI Global Scientific Publishing. DOI: 10.4018/979-8-3373-0081-8.ch005

Mehra, J., Madaan, S., & Balu, N. Mohit, Selvakumar, P., & Manjunath, T. C. (2025). The ubiquitous internet and smart computation available 24/7 for anyone and anywhere. In E. Babulak (Ed.), Educational AI humanoid computing devices for cyber nomads (pp. 247–270). IGI Global Scientific Publishing. DOI: 10.4018/979-8-3693-8985-0.ch010

Nisha Angeline, M., Selvakumar, P., Gupta, M. K., Nazar, N., Elumalai, D., & Bhattacharya, S. (2025). Emerging materials for energy storage and environmental applications. In K. Muduli, B. Moharana, S. Ales, & D. Biswal (Eds.), Using computational intelligence for sustainable manufacturing of advanced materials (pp. 53–72). IGI Global Scientific Publishing. DOI: 10.4018/979-8-3693-7974-5.ch003

Okonji, N. N., & Igwe, E. A. (2025). Prospects and challenges of personalized learning through artificial intelligence–driven adaptive learning systems in N. *International Journal of Education in Developing Areas*, *3*, 45–59. DOI: 10.30534/ijeda/2025/003112025

Peng, C., Xia, F., Naseriparsa, M., & Osborne, F. (2023). Knowledge graphs: Opportunities and challenges. *Artificial Intelligence Review*, *56*(11), 13071–13102. DOI: 10.1007/s10462-023-10465-9 PMID: 37362886

Raimi, L., Bamiro, N. B., & Lim, S. A. (2024). Two facets of AI-driven applications for sustainable learning and development: A systematic review of tech-entrepreneurial benefits and threats to creative learning. Social Responsibility. *Technology and Sustainable Development*, *12*, 88–110. DOI: 10.1108/S2043-052320240000023012

Roshanaei, M., Olivares, H., & Lopez, R. R. (2023). Harnessing AI to foster equity in education: Opportunities, challenges, and emerging strategies. *Journal of Intelligent Learning Systems and Applications*, *15*(4), 123–145. DOI: 10.4236/jilsa.2023.154009

Saborío-Taylor, S., & Rojas-Ramírez, F. (2024). Universal design for learning and artificial intelligence in the digital era: Fostering inclusion and autonomous learning. International Journal of Professional Development. *Learners and Learning*, *6*(2), ep2408. Advance online publication. DOI: 10.30935/ijpdll/14694

Soelistianto, F. A., Andrasmoro, D., Yusriati, Y., Mardiati, M., & Fawait, A. B. (2024). The impact of adaptive learning technology on improving students' concept understanding. *Journal of Computer Science Advancements*, *2*(3), 12–22. DOI: 10.70177/jsca.v2i3.1176

Strielkowski, W., Grebennikova, V., Lisovskiy, A., Rakhimova, G., & Vasileva, T. (2025). AI-driven adaptive learning for sustainable educational transformation. *Sustainable Development (Bradford)*, *33*(2), 1012–1030. DOI: 10.1002/sd.3221

Sumathy, V., & Navamani, G. (2024). AI-driven personalized learning: Enhancing student success through adaptive technologies. Science. *Information Technology & Applications*, *16*, 147–160. DOI: 10.1234/sita.2024.016

Taylor, D. L., Yeung, M., & Bashet, A. Z. (2021). Personalized and adaptive learning. *Innovations in STEM Higher Education*, *3*, 45–60. DOI: 10.21825/istem.v3i1.10186

Terzieva, V., Ivanova, T., & Todorova, K. (2022). Personalized learning in an intelligent educational system. In Lecture Notes in Networks and Systems (Vol. 556, pp. 13–23). DOI: 10.1007/978-3-031-17601-2_2

Upadhyaya, A. N., Debnath, P., Rani, P., Selvakumar, P., Manjunath, T. C., & Bhattacharya, S. (2025). AI-based disaster prediction and early warning systems. In Mobo, F. (Ed.), *AI and emerging technologies for emergency response and smart cities* (pp. 55–74). IGI Global Scientific Publishing., DOI: 10.4018/979-8-3693-9770-1.ch003

Yang, S. (2024). Intelligent tutoring system algorithm: Enhance personalized learning experience. In *International Conference on Frontier Computing* (pp. 112–118). https://doi.org/DOI: 10.1007/978-3-031-49402-7_14

Yekollu, R. K., Bhimraj Ghuge, T., & Sunil Biradar, S. (2024). AI-driven personalized learning paths: Enhancing education through adaptive systems. In *Lecture Notes in Computer Science* (Vol. 13890, pp. 98–112). Smart Education and Smart e-Learning Conference., DOI: 10.1007/978-3-031-45890-3_7

Zhu, C., Sun, M., Luo, J., Li, T., & Wang, M. (2023). How to harness the potential of ChatGPT in education? *Knowledge Management & E-Learning*, *15*, 1–18. DOI: 10.34105/kmel.23.15.1

Chapter 12
GenAI:
Opportunities, Disruptions, and the New Learning Paradigm

Sajad Ahmad Mir
https://orcid.org/0000-0001-6887-4925
Presidency University, Bangalore, India

Revati Ramrao Ramrao Rautrao
https://orcid.org/0000-0001-7803-8699
Dr. D.Y. Patil B-School, India

Navneet Saini
https://orcid.org/0009-0002-5234-3200
Rayat Bahara University, Mohali, India

Anita Choudhary
https://orcid.org/0000-0003-2957-131X
DBS Global University, India

A. V. Senthil Kumar
https://orcid.org/0000-0002-8587-7017
Nehru Institute of Information Technology and Management, India

Shallu Sehgal
https://orcid.org/0009-0007-1260-5399
Shoolini Institute of Life Sciences and Business Management, India

Nasir Ahmad Ganaie
https://orcid.org/0000-0001-6781-834X
University of Kashmir, India

Aditi R. R. Khandelwal
https://orcid.org/0000-0003-3503-1985
IIS University, India

ABSTRACT

Generative Artificial Intelligence (GenAI) is emerging as a transformative force in higher education, offering vast opportunities to personalize learning, enhance pedagogy, and streamline institutional processes. This chapter explores both the potential benefits, and the disruptive challenges associated with implementing and applying GenAI in academic settings. It highlights the integration of tools such as Khanmigo, Eduaide.ai, and ChatGPT to support instruction, automate administrative workflows, and improve student engagement. A three-phase implementation framework—pilot testing, faculty training with ethical orientation, and scalable deployment—is proposed. Additionally, platforms like Squirrel AI and ClassPoint

DOI: 10.4018/979-8-3373-5157-5.ch012

AI demonstrate the application of GenAI in adaptive learning and skill development. Emphasizing the need for AI literacy and ethical governance, it positions GenAI not merely as a technological tool but as a strategic driver of inclusive, responsible, and future-ready education.

INTRODUCTION

Artificial Intelligence (AI) has evolved rapidly over the past decade, influencing sectors ranging from healthcare to finance. In particular, the emergence of Generative AI (GenAI) represents a transformative leap forward, especially in the domain of education (Singh et al., 2024). Unlike traditional AI systems focused on automation or data analysis, GenAI is capable of generating original content—text, images, simulations, and assessments—by leveraging large language models trained on extensive datasets (Cordero et al., 2024). This evolution signals a new learning paradigm rooted in adaptability, personalization, and learner-centered innovation (Baig & Yadegaridehkordi, 2025).

THE RISE OF GENERATIVE AI IN EDUCATION

Generative AI refers to a group of artificial intelligence structures that can create new materials, whether it is text, images, audio, and video, by absorbing patterns that can be identified in the data sets that already exist (Rasul et al., 2024). In the effort to acquire this ability, these models are based on deep-learning paradigms, neural-network structures, and transformer-based networks, and they often produce results that are not distinguishable between results produced by humans (Akinwalere & Ivanov, 2022). The architectures acquire structural and distributional regularities of input data, which allows generating original content based on these regularities. GenAI does not merely interpret or copy forms that already exist, in this sense it human tends to simulate another kind of creativity and in this way, it blurs the line between machine and person, which creates human work. Some key constituent technologies are GPT, DALL·E, and Codex, which have proved to perform exceptionally well when applying the methods of natural-language processing, generating images, and generating code in respective applications (Zhang & Dong, 2024). GPT has mastered the ability of producing high-quality texts like a human, which makes it a suitable tool in chatbots, creating content and translating languages. DALL·E, in turn, uses textual prompts to create images, which allows generating visual artefacts when needed (Wang et al., 2023). Codex is a code synthesis tool, which achieves its main goal by automatically generating a code fragment or a complete program based on a natural-language instruction; thus, simplifying the process of writing software and teaching programming (Prather et al., 2024).The AI development in the educational sector is a new phenomenon, which can be called a transition to augmentation as opposed to automation, where the competencies of a machine would be complementary as opposed to substitutionary to those of a human (Baig & Yadegaridehkordi, 2025). Past educational technologies tended to be along the lines of automation of the administrative aspect of educational activities, assessment, scheduling, and content delivery. GenAI offers a radically new paradigm, enhancing cognitive, creative and decision-making abilities of both educators and learners (Elkhodr & Gide, 2025). With this ability, GenAI can improve the field of learning by automating administrative tasks, personalizing the contents, and providing high-quality analytic capabilities, thereby differing drastically with traditional educational technologies (Wu et al., 2024). Automation to augment has long represented the movement not only towards increased technological maturity, but also a symbiotic swerve in pedagogical focus, whereby AI is viewed less as a substitute agent and more of a co-learner in the instruction process. Examples of representative GenAI platforms in use today are ChatGPT, Eduaide and Khanmigo among others that have their own functionalities and uses. ChatGPT makes it possible to create, answer questions, and dialog while working with versatile text (Hasanein & Sobaih, 2023). Eduaide offers support to the packet preparation of lessons, tests, and creation of individual feedback to instructors. Khan Academy has developed Kahnmigo an intelligent tutoring system and personalized learning that scaffolds learning of students in consumption of educational content. These empirical implementations do not only support the practical value of GenAI, but also the ability to democratize educational access to high quality and flexibly adaptive support.

GenAI is a paradigmatic system to offer individualised and dynamic learning experiences and personalising learning content, providing immediate feedback, and continuously adjusting instructions based on the personal specifications of learners (Chan & Lee, 2023). GenAI algorithms aim to identify the gaps in knowledge and work out customised paths to learning based on the study and examination of performance data and learning patterns. Additionally, AI platforms also produce customized learning material that syncs with unique learning progression through a thorough study of the student data (Zhang et al., 2023). This instructive model further means precise guidance and teaching of learners thus maximising cognitive performance. GenAI-based systems also allow instant feedback on the actual task submission, detecting the errors and suggesting the recommended responses, which will reassure the understanding of the task and keep the learners interested in studying. In comparison to the fixed tools of education, GenAI will create an interactive learning climate, which will constantly change based on the efforts the learners will input, interact and master. This kind of responsiveness not only improves cognitive outcomes and increases mastery learning by differentiating pace, content and support to the learner profile. Characteristics of these systems to further personalise education also incorporate the different possibilities of their use in response to students with special individualised needs such as learning disabilities or even language barriers and thus this type of adaptation of the system allows the educator to create truly inclusive learning conditions.

GenAI promotes equity by predicting and supporting the needs of heterogeneous learners via the creation of personalised learning instructional content, the use of assistive technologies, and the implementation of personal assistance. With the help of AI-based algorithms, they are translating content into different languages, providing audio descriptions to visual materials, and providing text to speech services to those who cannot read or who have problems with reading and thus, facilitating a more accessible and inclusive world. Moreover, in adaptive learning platforms, the teaching tempo and level of challenge is dynamically altered based on performance with additional support provided to the poor performers and additional challenge provided to the top performers. This two-fold ability: to intervene simultaneously on tracks with delays and on accelerated tracks makes GenAI an expanding apparatus that differentiates education. Through the involvement of AI in the learning tools, the system will help the students with different learning needs be assisted in a personalized way and realise their full educational potential (Chetry, 2024).

ENHANCED CREATIVITY AND ENGAGEMENT

It has been thoroughly researched that storytelling, simulation, and content creating software with the help of AI enhance creativity and student involvement in studying situations (Kamalov & Gurrib, 2023). GenAI will be able to offer story concepts, character outlines and plot structures in the process providing the learners with inspirational ideas in their creative writing tasks. Some applications also allow co-creation, which is the interactive process in which learners create narratives together. Such co-constructive algorithm heralds the shift between passive consumption of content and active formulation of the narrative, further intensifying the involvement with the imaginative agency. One additional use of AI is interactive simulations and the world, which allow using experiences to explore conceptual material, such as virtual science labs or reconstructions of history. These immersion processes serve as cognitive scaffolds, which allows a connection between theory and practice. Similarly, GenAI places the learners in an interactive environment created by AI to perform spatial reasoning, scenario-based decision-making, and real-time feedback process that is not a common element of traditional learning pedagogies.

Co-creation power of AI allows learners to become active participants in the process of education development to make them feel like the owner and the investor of their learning. With the AI tools, students could create photos, videos, and multimedia presentations, thus convey ideas and provoke an understanding of new multimodal forms. Such an extended notion of academic literacy appreciates both textual and visual, spatial, and performative modes of teaching and learning. Such collaborative projects where students create the content with the help of AI support teamwork and communication as well as problem-solving skills. The AI in such environments is not a tool, but a creative agent itself, fostering human-AI collaboration in line with the emerging approach to the development of future-ready skills.

TEACHER SUPPORT AND EFFICIENCY

GenAI is a technology-based learning system whereby the planning, evaluation, and various other administrative tasks are automated, and teachers get more time to individually instruct learners and maintain unbroken contacts with them (Hazzan-Bishara et al. 2025). The lesson designs generated by AI-integrated platforms can meet the curricular requirements, specifically identified learning objectives, and performance indicators, eliminating the necessity to overwork by manually recalculating parameters. Some of them also give extensive libraries with the ready-made lesson plans, which can be modified by the teachers according to the peculiarities of their classrooms. In regard to evaluation, AI algorithms can be used to grade objective tests including multiple choice exams and standardized tests and provide real time feedback removing the administrative burden. Automating such tasks helps the teachers to focus on higher-order tasks, such as mentorship of students, project-based pedagogy and facilitation of his-order thinking processes.

In addition to being a very rigid automation GenAI is an instructional decision-support system, and it is able to provide data-informed suggestions of differentiated instruction. Analysing the performance patterns, AI systems will detect the unnoticed gaps in learning and suggest specific interventional actions and support measures. The insights give teachers the power to dynamically gain access to make formative, data-driven instructional decisions in order to improve the accuracy and effectiveness of personalized learning. Instructors will be able to alter the teaching practices, adjust homework, and choose additional learning resources to students that need assistance, thus making the teaching environment supportive and inclusive that the mainstream practices face significant challenges to duplicate on a larger scale.

LIFELONG LEARNING AND SKILL DEVELOPMENT

The recent trends around continuous learning, and microlearning, currently enabled by AI-powered systems, are changing the paradigm of lifelong learning and upskilling, making it prospective rather than retrospective in outlook. The education of the learners is offered in the form of bite-sized and just-in-time content modules, with the algorithm-based next step recommendations that helped to attain the knowledge and competencies (Dabingaya 2022). Through consideration of individual time-related restrictions, interests, and contextual factors, these systems lead to extremely versatile, self-determining and transferrable study designs, thus expanding the reach to a wide range of populations. In that regard, reskilling and upskilling with the help of GenAI play a specific role as modern labour markets are now highly volatile. Such platforms establish a skill gap through systematic learning analytics and develop a personalized training schedule and online allowance that is professional and competitive (Chan & Lee 2023). This in fact creates a two-way interactive process between education and employability by providing a direct correlation between skills learnt and labour-market needs in other words GenAI creates a dynamic feedback loop between education and employability. Besides, the systems provide customized career pathways, dynamically adjusted skill-juice-test tracking, artificial intelligence-driven job matching and make informed career choices that can, subsequently, introduce social and economic mobility. Therefore, GenAI reflects in the principles of Education 4.0 due to the nature of teaching that is individually tailored and performance driven. At the same time, these systems enable learning institutions to produce customized contents and monitor the performance of students in real time and hence improve the learning outcomes. In contrast to the traditional pedagogical methods, AI-assisted learning creates an ecosystem that revolves around the learners and dynamically changes with cognitive-analytics, behavioural evidence, and personal development. The system plans an instructional approach based on each learner by relying on knowledge-based research on learning style, power, and preference. However, the effectiveness of AI-enhanced learning is subject to active participation of teachers that act as designers, interpreters of data, and custodians of ethics in AI integration. Teachers are not just consumer of these technologies; they are as much co-producers of the unique learning process so that the pedagogical integrity is maintained and the wellbeing of the students is protected.

BACKGROUND AND IMPORTANCE

Higher education is undergoing a significant transformation driven by digitalization and the demand for flexible, personalized learning experiences. GenAI offers an opportunity to enhance pedagogical design, automate routine academic processes, and foster deeper student engagement. It holds particular promise in enabling adaptive content delivery, real-time feedback, multilingual support, and customized assessments. These features align with 21st-century educational goals centered on digital fluency, critical thinking, and inclusivity (Sharma et al., 2025).

Problem Statement

Despite its growing presence, the integration of GenAI into educational institutions remains inconsistent, unregulated, and in many cases, experimental. There is widespread excitement about GenAI's capacity to automate lesson planning, assessment, and administrative workflows. However, there is equal concern about unresolved issues such as data security, algorithmic discrimination, academic honesty, and equitable access—issues that, if left unaddressed, can widen digital divides and erode trust in academic processes.

Research gap and Evidence

Although current literature documents the potential of GenAI to increase educational efficiency, improve access, and foster personalized learning, there remains a critical gap in interdisciplinary and ethical frameworks guiding its adoption. Existing studies often focus on GenAI's technical capabilities, yet few address how educational institutions can implement these tools safely, inclusively, and in alignment with academic values. Moreover, empirical evidence on GenAI's classroom effectiveness is still emerging, and institutional case studies are limited in scope. Educator preparedness, AI literacy, and the absence of comprehensive policy frameworks further hinder large-scale, responsible adoption.

Aim of the Chapter

This chapter aims to explore the dual impact of GenAI as both a catalyst for educational innovation and a source of systemic disruption. It investigates how GenAI tools like Khanmigo, Eduaide.ai, ChatGPT, Squirrel AI, and ClassPoint AI are reshaping teaching and learning practices, while also raising fundamental concerns around ethics, regulation, and equity. A structured, three-phase implementation framework is proposed, emphasizing pilot testing, faculty training, and scalable deployment with ongoing monitoring. The chapter seeks to answer the guiding question: How might educational institutions ensure a safe, inclusive, and ethically responsible transition to GenAI-powered learning?

CHAPTER OBJECTIVES

- To understanding whether Generative AI can transform teaching, learning and administrative processes in higher education and ways in which this potential can be unlocked.
- To critically discuss the ethical, pedagogical and equity related concerns of using GenAI tools.
- To put forward a fair common ground by incorporating GenAI ethical overall behaviour without tampering academic integrity, inclusiveness, and educational ideals.
- To determine viable interdisciplinary action plans between educators, technologists, and policy makers.
- With a view to emphasizing the practices with innovative solutions to the challenge of digital divide, algorithmic bias, and privacy of personal data in educational systems based on AI.

RESEARCH METHODOLOGY

The chapter has been anchored in the qualitative, descriptive and analytical methodology where only a secondary source of data has been used. The study was then presented by carrying out a comprehensive literature review of the published text covering peer-reviewed journal articles, book chapters, policy, and institutional reports that focused on describing the role of Generative AI (GenAI) in higher education. It used all reliable academic databases as a source of all the data, such as Scopus, Elsevier, PubMed, SpringerLink, and Web of Science, which gave this study both credibility and academic rigour. Systematic searching through keywords was conducted to include relevant literature through the use of keywords that included Generative AI, Higher Education, AI in Teaching and Learning, Ethical Challenges in AI, and Technology-Driven Pedagogy. The expected search was kept down to a few years back since it was necessary to stay relevant to the recent trends and discussion. Sources that offer viable theoretical, empirical evidence and critical political analysis were considered. The chosen material was evaluated and arranged in the theme to retrieve major patterns, continuous trends, and opportunities and challenges related to adopting GenAI in academia. The focus was laid on learning the pedagogical, administrative, and ethical aspects of this technological change. Synthetising dissimilar standpoints presented in a broad spectrum of scholarly studies, the chapter attempts to introduce an extensive and unpartisan report on the transformational prospects of GenAI in higher education. Despite the fact that no primary data was collected, solid and differentiated secondary sources are used in the research and become a good basis to develop an idea of the discussion and strategic observations. The approach will make the findings of this study effectively supportable in terms of the previous academic literature and in accordance with the world discussion today about the use of artificial intelligence in the educational field.

Disruptions and Challenges in the New Paradigm

The implementation of Generative AI (GenAI) technologies in education has ushered in a new paradigm, offering transformative opportunities while simultaneously presenting critical challenges—particularly in the realm of academic integrity and assessment. As GenAI tools become more accessible and sophisticated, their application in academic tasks has raised serious concerns. Increasingly, students are using these tools to generate essays, complete assignments, and even answer examination questions, resulting in rising instances of AI-assisted plagiarism and cheating (Cordero et al., 2024). This misuse of GenAI challenges the foundations of ethical academic practice. The boundaries between original, student-authored work and machine-generated content are becoming difficult to distinguish. Educators and academic institutions often lack the technical expertise to reliably identify AI-generated submissions, which leads to a growing credibility crisis in evaluation practices (Sadeghpour et al., 2025). AI-generated content often mirrors human writing in tone, coherence, and structure, rendering conventional plagiarism detection methods inadequate. Given these disruptions, a shift in assessment strategies is imperative. Institutions must implement process-based assessment models that emphasize real-time cognitive engagement, creativity, and practical application of knowledge rather than final written outputs alone (Francis et al., 2025). Such a transformation prioritizes the learner's thinking process and reduces reliance on deliverables that can be easily replicated by GenAI systems.

To address these challenges proactively, educational institutions are applying hybrid assessment frameworks that combine traditional evaluation techniques with digital practices. These approaches not only measure academic performance but also promote critical thinking, ethical reasoning, and digital literacy. The implementation of AI-literacy modules into curricula is an essential step in this direction. By equipping students with an understanding of both the capabilities and limitations of GenAI, institutions can foster a culture of responsible and informed AI usage. This strategic application of AI-awareness strengthens the validity of academic assessments and promotes integrity-driven learning (Khlaif et al., 2024). Ultimately, the academic challenges posed by GenAI are not merely technical—they reflect deeper philosophical and pedagogical shifts. As the line between human and machine-generated work continues to blur, educational systems must redefine how they understand learning, originality, and academic trust. Aligning technological innovation with ethical and responsible pedagogical practices will ensure that genuine learning outcomes are achieved in this new paradigm.

Educationalist Willingness and Struggle

The success of GenAI implementation into the educational sphere directly depends on the readiness and willingness of educators to follow the trend of emergent technologies. There is an emphatic lack of AI literacy and the lack of dedicated training that is one of the major reasons why it is hard to integrate the GenAI tools on a robust level into the classroom. Despite the potential game-changing ability of pedagogy-enhanced AI, a significant percentage of teachers face limited knowledge, the lack of technical skills, and fears about the loss of employment (Delello et al., 2025). A class of issues which also reinforce resistance are issues of classroom control, pedagogical shifts of paradigm and management issues in a broader context. The empirical data indicate that poor foundational knowledge about AI may lead to the decreased self-efficacy of educators, thus decreasing their inclination to experiment with GenAI tools or adopt them (FİLIZ et al., 2025). The many teachers are worried that they will be replaced by AI or lose their professional freedom, which further enshrined resistance to the uptake (Hur, 2024). This is a fine-grained reading of the realization that the understanding of resistance needs to be broadened past the technological obstacle.

Ethical and Legal Dilemmas

The integration of genomic artificial intelligence (GAI) in education adds a complex galaxy of ethical and legal issues, which has to be patiently navigated, in order to achieve responsible and equitable adoption of GAI in education. The first in this list of concerns is the danger that any AI system, using the past as its training grounds, will fall into recreating what has been called and termed algorithmic bias to the extent of creating and bringing about even greater stereotypes in society. This kind of bias may be realized during tasks to create content and automated assessment, and it can produce biased or biased results (Al-Zahrani, 2024). This causes inequalities that can threaten the inclusive and equitable nature of learning spaces especially, for students of marginalized communities. Eradicating these prejudices is also critical when it comes to enhancing fair and equal educational results. Similar concerns are privacy, data protection and consent. A prosperous functioning of GAI systems frequently involves the use of massive amounts of personal data, but the gathering, storing and processing of these data prompts significant questions to their confidentiality and informed consent. The sensitive material of students can be even disclosed or exploited without strict security under these conditions, thus causing violation of their rights and damages to their well-being (Ng et al., 2025). Also, its use of obscure AI functions hinders tracking of decision-making procedures, which causes a lack in accountability in the case of wrong decision systems or face inequitable treatment. It is also problematic because of the misuse of the GAI tools, as students are sending assignments using the AI-generated content without proper verification and reference (Choi, 2025). At the same time, some issues were raised in relation to the unreliability of AI products as a source of facts, increased reliance on AI assistance, and the possible loss of critical thinking skills (Giannakos et al., 2024). Another innovative aspect is the socio-psychological hazards of AI supervision in teaching, or rather the hazards of AI supervision in teaching on student autonomy, inspiration, and confidence (Vieriu & Petrea, 2025). The implementation of AI to carry out monitoring and automatic evaluation of behaviour can also create the culture of control instead of cooperation, damage the faculty-student relationships by turning them into observational-based interactions. Therefore, it is necessary to re-conceptualize the AI ethics within the education settings by focusing on student empowerment, transparency, and human control in order to exploit the potential advantages of GAI and ensure a set of fundamental values of education are not overlooked.

RETHINKING PEDAGOGY IN THE GENAI ERA

GenAI makes us reconsider the pedagogical practice so that learners can operate in an environment where artificial and human intelligence can interact frictionlessly. Its adoption in education requires it to make a paradigm shift in teaching mode to shift away from the conventional, rote-based model to the inquiry-based and project-based models of learning. Memorization and factual knowledge learning tendencies have become outdated as technologies continue to evolve to a point where AI can provide anyone with the desired information in a fraction of a second and execute automatized processes replacing them. Therefore, pedagogical focus should be moved to the development of the higher-order skills and abilities: critical thinking, creativity, and ability to solve complex problems, which have been and always will be the highest priority of human beings and will never be substituted in the 21 st century. Engaging the learner through knowledge construction and the method of active learning facilitates more remarkable cognitive learning and increases long-term retention (Dickey et al., 2023). Project-based learning provides students with the ability to face real-life and real-world problems with interdisciplinary methods, whereas inquiry-based learning promotes intellectual involvement and self-reliance through the questioning, searching, and building knowledge. The integration of GenAI solutions has started to transform the educational environment offering virtually unlimited options in personalization of the learning process, content development, and streamlining of the educational processes. However, it, in turn, creates new pedagogical and ethical challenges that need to be planned and restructured (Krause et al., 2025). The responsible and best possible implementation of GenAI assumes that educators have the potential to acquire the required technical knowledge, the pedagogical strategies, and moral awareness that would allow embedding these tools into the teaching contexts (Machado et al., 2025). This need poses a complete change in professional growth that will not only have the technical education in mind but the reflective and ethical implementation of AI. The focus on pedagogical change should be emphasized in parallel with the use of AI, and it has become apparent that human instruction concerns need to be repositioned toward the learning methods of inquisition and ethics as well as human collaboration and interaction instead of simply tacking AI-oriented tools on preexisting infrastructures. This change can transform the role of educators into both supporters and essential agents of the transformation who determine the fate of AI-enhanced learning. The bigger picture is that the aim is to have learners ready to succeed in an AI-based world: the ability to think critically, solve problems dynamically, and learn throughout life. Through investing in teacher preparation and encouragement of timely and inclusive pedagogical frameworks, learning facilities can emerge with the certainty that GenAI results in progressive instruction, power, and instruction equality.

POLICY, REGULATION AND GOVERNANCE

The role of GenAI in education practice will be determined by the creation of powerful policies, regulations, and governance systems (Gentile et al., 2023). Unless specified courses of action, it remains unclear how to ethically and responsibly use AI in the field of education. Extensive governance borders are primarily needed to safeguard the reasonableness, equitable utilization of AI in educational facilities and the issue of data privacy, bias, and responsibility in algorithms. Government authorities, teachers, and technologists need to join forces in order to provide clear guidelines and policies on how GenAI is used in education (Kooli 2023). Otherwise, the problem of the injustice of AI tools implementation might reinforce the exaltation of disparities and undermine the faith of the people in educational establishments. Besides that, they should also foster the transparency and accountability of the development and deployment of AI systems. The multidisciplinary nature of the topic of ethical governance of AI in education will involve not only educators but policymakers, technologists, and ethicist as well (Nguyen et al., 2022). Incorporation of transparency and accountability will help educational organizations to create trust towards the AI systems as well as building a culture of responsible innovation.

The implementation of such systems should be under the prescriptions of ethical AI to avoid causing any harm or preserve fairness (Diantama, 2023). Defining AI in measurement and education and developing ethical standards It has been these aspects that the Special Interest Group on AI in Measurement and Education under the National Council of Measurement in Education has set upon itself to define and advance research on this subject (Bulut et al., 2024). To promote ethical use of AI in education, different stakeholders have come up with guidelines to promote this (Bulut & Beiting-Parrish, 2024).

Coming up with specific ethical AI standards specific to educational facilities presents a new sense of responsibility. Educational establishments have the role to control the implementation of AI, avoid misuse, and protect the psychological health of students by developing new guidelines and rules. An active policy-making system integrated into the institutional environment signifies the paradigm change and a responsible AI innovation in education. Through the creation of consistent policies and procedures, educational facilities will be able to develop secure, equal learning environments that take advantage of the opportunities presented by AI without exposing themselves to the risks involved. This kind of protection safeguards students and teachers and fosters a healthy level of ethical usage, inspired responsible innovations and maintains trust in AI technologies (Holmes et al., 2021).

The adoption of ethics in the use of AI by institutions will help in creating an ethical environment of using such powerful tools so that they contribute to learning experiences and futures and that there is no unlevel playing field with the use of such powerful tools by colleges and universities (Gouseti et al., 2024). Ethics in the context of AI in education is a requirement providing the solution to peculiarities and benefits of the field. One of such applications is the detection of AI-created plagiarism, the promotion of academic integrity, and education principles (Adams et al., 2023). Institutions can prevent this type of unethical conduct by defining the lines of expectations, and its outcomes regarding AI-based cheating to create an environment of academic integrity. The education programs and awareness campaigns play no less vital role in making students and educators aware of how they must use AI responsibly.

CURRICULUM TRANSFORMATION AND ADAPTATION

With the integration of Generative AI (GenAI) into the educational setting, it is important to provide not only the technological tools but to transform the curriculum and make it oriented towards the preparation of students to live in the world with AI. This transformation should be more focused on developing critical thinking, creativity, problem-solving, and collaboration because these competencies will help students to use AI and protect and advance unique human abilities (Delello et al., 2025). Instead of relying on their traditional pedagogical routines, educators need to create learning activities in which higher-order thinking is prioritized, as it empowers students to use AI in innovative ways and that are relevant to the context. Furthermore, it is essential to incorporate the understanding of AI in the basic curriculum, instead of a separate skill. This should be a deeper knowledge on how AI-based systems can be used, as well as its ethical, social and cultural implications (Chee et al.2024). Combining literacy in AI and rich curriculum in ethical thinking and innovation, schools can raise a generation of students who are technologically competent and socially responsible at the same time. This kind of integration promotes the investigation of the creative potential among students and the creation of an ethical foundation of the responsible application of AI, in which educational establishments will take the initiative of drafting context-sensitive policies considering local values and expectations (Yusuf et al., 2024). This culturally sensitive policy development as well as individualistic and dynamically based learning conditions enables students and solves the issue over misuse. Educators can be key to introducing these norms and thus create the norm of classroom level, which will make it easier to responsible and informed interaction with AI (Grieve et al., 2021).

Additionally, institutions need to focus on capacity building in terms of constant professional development so that teachers could have competencies they need to integrate GenAI into their pedagogical practice. To overcome issues pertaining to equity of access to AI resources and teacher readiness, both educators and researchers, and policymakers need to work collaboratively to not leave any learner behind (FILIZ et al., 2025). Lastly, the ethical framework in which GenAI will be integrated should be strong and should incorporate ethical rules and principles such as transparency, accountability, and fairness of systematic algorithms (Al-Zahrani, 2024). Such principles should no longer be mere talk but should be integrated to the design structure of education technologies and practices. Such a position locates ethical deliberation as a fundamental part of the curriculum, and not as a second thought. Overall, with the ongoing changes in the AI field, the important thing is constant communication, cross-sector cooperation, and scalable approaches that would make GenAI become a transformative and accommodating driver in the educational sector (Dwivedi et al., 2023).

EXAMPLES OF GLOBAL INITIATIVES OR GOVERNMENT RESPONSES

The growth of Generative AI (GenAI) has forced many governments and several educational institutions across the globe to design proactive solutions to the opportunities and challenges that arise with it. Several countries have developed their national AI strategies that outline plans to incorporate AI in various sectors where education was singled out as one of the major areas of focus (Bhuyan et al., 2025). The goal of these plans is to catalyse innovation, instil best principles of using AI, and implement a baseline competence in AI among the people. UNESCO, as an example, has issued international standards and principles of the responsible use of AI in education, with the main focus on human rights, inclusivity, and sustainability as the three cardinal requirements that guide the implementation of AI into learning settings. Concurrently, numerous nations are enhancing AI-centred training programs and professional growth concepts in a bid to enable students as well as teachers to acquire the necessary expertise to perform successfully in an AI-laden educational system.

At the same time, specific competency frameworks aimed at teachers with regard to AI have become popular ("AI Competency Framework for Teachers," 2024). These frameworks would help teachers gain the knowledge and skills to implement AI in a way that is embedded into pedagogical practice in a significant manner as compared to replacing human instruction. What is more, educational policies based on ethical values can help to develop an ethical attitude towards the use of AI in the classroom. Aware of the international scope of the AI impact, the drive towards transnational cooperation and the development of the cross-border norms of AI ethics and regulation is also gathering momentum. This direction indicates the beginning of a convergence to common ethical standards and teaching-based standards of AI competency, which as a whole can bring about greater coherence and equality in the integration of AI into learning institutions. Since GenAI continues to advance, the future course of action will require a continued interdisciplinary effort, external policy update, and creation of responsive learning environments. This planning does not only encourage ethical implementation of GenAI technologies but also progresses towards an inclusive and open access to quality, individualized learning experience (Pratschke, 2023).

THE NEED TO PROMOTE PRUDENT AI ON EDUCATIONAL PROGRAMS

They need to incorporate AI literacy in the course programs in both primary and higher education. The development of the curriculum ought to be geared towards the ability to think critically, problem-solve, and reasoning morally. With the help of educating students about the basics of AI, education institutions will be able to give them the power to act as responsible and informed users of AI-related technologies (Goertzel et al., 2007). GenAI is a two-sided sword and may become a problem, i.e., only dangerous to students, in case it is not properly applied (Wang et al., 2023). Properly applied and with clear guidelines, GenAI can become a powerful instrument along the learning path of students. The incorporation of AI in learning needs powerful and evidence-based studies to inculcate ethical accountability (Bozkurt et al., 2024). In the promotion of AI-incorporated education experiences, teachers are an integral part since they provide guided support and promote digital literacy and critical thinking (Chan & Lee, 2023). Teachers will also help in promoting the safe and responsible use of GenAI through provision of rules and expectations (Elkhodr & Gide, 2025).

Another way through which the digital literacy can be promoted by teachers is by integrating it in the curriculum- teaching skills to students on how to evaluate the online information, how algorithms work and how to preserve their privacy in the age of digitization. Through supplying students with such competencies, education allows them to develop a better ability to operate AI in an accountable way and overcome the digital world complexity. There is also the need to educate teachers and make them competent users of AI and capable of integrating it into the classroom (Zhang et al., 2023). Programs of AI literacy must be introduced in such a way that educators are proficient in the use of AI and know its fundamental mechanisms (Tzirides et al., 2024). Teachers will need to know how to make use of AI regarding their abilities as well as their limitations (Ma et al., 2024). How well the integration of AI in education turns out to be largely depends on the educator's humanity themselves, so their AI literacy is the major determinant. In the modern world of education, AI literacy is a skill that teachers and students need to have (Otero et al., 2023). This is a transition of the classic digital literacy to a more comprehensive, AI-specific one, including insights into the workings of algorithms, their ethical aspect, and the knowledge of data-based systems. The level of AI literacy among teachers has a direct link with the higher quality of education and the composition of student achievements (Yang et al., 2025). It has to have technical and human aspects of AI and consider the ethical, social, and emotional situations of integrating AI (Cassidy et al., 2023).

Because not all current users of AI will obtain formal training consisting of AI training, the current AI literacy will establish to what extent users will be able to keep up with emerging technologies and AI-based workflows (Carolus et al., 2023). The development of AI literacy is not only associated with the absence of failures in education but also with the overall social and political empowerment (Chee et al., 2024). The education on how AI works, and its limitations and social outcomes will be a form of background knowledge necessary among people to formulate approaches to dealing with emergent applications of AI. This awareness, or what is currently known as AI literacy, is becoming a fundamental requirement in achieving citizenship in the 21ist century. The concept of AI literacy can be explained as knowledge and skills regarding comprehension, working with and analysing AI systems and their output (Lintner, 2024). It also comprises a concept, algorithms, and apps within different disciplines. It is essential to introduce AI literacy in learning programs of any educational level (Otero et al., 2023). The incorporation of literacy in AI is a new educational requirement which is to enable learners to operate in the society that has the AI enhancement with competence and ethics (Zhang et al., 2023). Individuals will have to be AI literate to keep up to date and take an active part in the context of becoming more AI-cantered in the new reality (Gu & Ericson, 2025).

IMPLEMENTATION AND APPLICATION OF GENAI IN HIGHER EDUCATION

The active use of Generative AI (GenAI) instruments in the sphere of higher education is gradually becoming common around the globe. Multiple institutions are already starting to digitize their academic and administrative processes by using AI-based platforms. As an example, Khanmigo, an AI-based tutor created on the basis of the OpenAI technology GPT, which is widely used in the U.S. in classrooms to facilitate customized tutoring, delivering dynamic hints, adaptive courses to students (Wang et al., 2023). Eduaide.ai, likewise, is tracking teachers to rationalize the arrangement of lesson plans, creation of quizzes and provision of real-time feedback depending on curriculum goal (Hasanein & Sobaih, 2023). Practically, GenAI may be implemented on several levels. The tools used at the instructional level include ChatGPT and ClassPoint AI that can co-create essay prompts, simulate class debates, and assist multilingual students through content translation in real-time. As an example, in the University of South Australia, academic staff tested the possibility of using ChatGPT to create lesson summaries and discussion prompts, which were said to have improved interest and participation in the classes (Baig & Yadegaridehkordi, 2023). Some of the tasks being automated at the administrative level are admission queries, schedule-making, and plagiarism checking with the help of GenAI tools that will allow teachers to dedicate their time to instructional approaches that actually make a difference.

DISCUSSION

The infiltration of Generative AI (GenAI) into higher education is a turning point that will change pedagogical practices and curriculum planning and alter the governing role of institutions. The necessity to consider the dual effect of GenAI which is the radical potential, and, at the same time, convoluted issues is urgently demanded, and this chapter is responsive to it. It also places the discussion in the background of education in the 21ist century highlighting the high-level need to reconsider teaching and learning in digitally augmented learner-centric manner. An analysis of past academic literature shows that GenAI technologies are accelerating adaptive learning and customized content creation as well as streamlined administrative procedures (Baig & Yadegaridehkordi, 2025). Nevertheless, with all these advantages, there are also hazards in the literature, ABF, threat to academic integrity, and data privacy drawbacks, and increased digital divides (Francis et al., 2025). This paper, through the combination of knowledge found in cross-disciplinary sources, provides insight into the further comprehension of the mentioned problems and supports the idea of ethical, inclusive, and human-cantered integration of AI. This analysis has much scientific implications. It calls policymakers, teachers and technology developers to forge frameworks that sustain academic values and uses of AI tools as a positive rather than as a negative. The chapter also signals the necessity to conduct digital literacy training, well-developed data protection measures, and open AI governance systems in the learning institutions. Moving forward the research future could be enormous as the study can be conducted in a scientific way of linking long-term GenAI impacts on the performance of learners, faculty, and cultures of institutions. Also, a comparative analysis of the education systems worldwide may offer subtle understandings of the context-related issues and achievements. This publication is timely and needed in a systematic development of works on educational innovation. It self-strengthens the necessity of not approaching GenAI as a technology upgrade, but as a driver of meaningful, ethical and sustainable change to higher education.

FINDINGS

In this chapter, a comprehensive analysis of the up-to-date literature allowed devious a few essential facts about the introduction of Generative AI (GenAI) into the academic process. To start with, GenAI has an eye-opening potential of changing the traditional teaching and learning experiences by embedding more individualization, automated teaching and learning systems, and learner-focused pedagogies. Nevertheless, there is a significant disparity between the speed of technological development and the readiness of educators to efficiently implement and use AI-based tools that demonstrate the necessity of training faculties and institutional-level support. Additionally, the literature discloses continuous moral complications that pertain to GenAI, especially with regards to the matters of bias in algorithms, integrity of AI generated content as well as the privacy of student data. Such worries are aggravated by the currently low level of effective regulatory or ethical frameworks in present structures of education. Notwithstanding such constraints, new strategies have appeared in organizations. The significant facilitators of responsible and equitable use of GenAI are mentioned as interdisciplinary cooperation, a program on AI literacy within teacher education, and inclusive policy to create. Lastly, the results point to the significance of building thorough, equity-concentrated models in the effort to eliminate the digital gap and guarantee that the advantages of AI in learning are obtainable to all students, notwithstanding the disparities in finance and social-economic time.

CONCLUSION

The chapter critically evaluated the necessity of measuring the implementation of Generative AI (GenAI) in higher education, which is a field that undergoes a rapid technological change, but with great pedagogical, ethical, and infrastructural uncertainties. With the help of an extensive variety of scholarly textual studies, the chapter managed to distinguish that GenAI, although promising in personalization of learning, automatization of administrative affairs, and increased engagement of students, can be implemented successfully only to the extent that educators are ready and willing to integrate it, ethical issues related to the immersion into the digital realm exist, and digital divide concerns. The main findings indicate that there is a huge mismatch between the trend in the rapid development of GenAI technologies, and the preparation of educational establishments to use them safely and responsibly. The questions of algorithmic bias, the authenticity of AI-generated content and data privacy on the part of students became burning questions. Nevertheless, some effective measures were also found such as interdisciplinary cooperation, capacity building of educators as well as the creation of effective policy frameworks to guarantee the equitable and ethical implementation. The practice and theoretical implications of the given research are rather considerable. In practice, it needs institutions to invest in the AI literacy, inclusive infrastructure, and responsible patterns of governance. On a theoretical level, it helps to add to the rising debate about the social-technical trends in AI-based education, promoting a balanced approach to it that will not override the humanistic principles of the academic community. Although it is an overall study, the study is limited by the use of secondary sources of data, which could not embody fully the emerging developments on the ground or regional differences. Empirical studies, investigation along the lines of longitudinal study, and cross-cultural investigations are all areas that could be helpful in substantiation and expansion of the ideas discussed here in the future. This chapter reiterates that the future of GenAI in higher education will not only depend on the technology but rather there will be much to be suggested with the kind, ethical and inclusion driven implementation. Higher education has the potential to turn GenAI into a force of positive and inclusive innovation by empowering educators and safeguarding the interest of learners.

REFERENCES

AI competency framework for teachers. (2024). In UNESCO eBooks. UNESCO. https://doi.org/DOI: 10.54675/ZJTE2084

Al-Zahrani, A. M. (2024). Unveiling the shadows: Beyond the hype of AI in education. *Heliyon, 10*(9), e30696. Advance online publication. DOI: 10.1016/j.heliyon.2024.e30696 PMID: 38737255

Baig, M. I., & Yadegaridehkordi, E. (2023). Factors influencing academic staff satisfaction and continuous usage of generative artificial intelligence (GenAI) in higher education. *International Journal of Educational Technology in Higher Education, 22*(1), 5. Advance online publication. DOI: 10.1186/s41239-025-00506-4

Bhuyan, S. S., Sateesh, V., Mukul, N., Galvankar, A., Mahmood, A., Nauman, M., Rai, A., Bordoloi, K., Basu, U., & Samuel, J. (2025). Generative Artificial Intelligence Use in Healthcare: Opportunities for Clinical Excellence and Administrative Efficiency. *Journal of Medical Systems, 49*(1), 10. Advance online publication. DOI: 10.1007/s10916-024-02136-1 PMID: 39820845

Chan, C. K. Y., & Lee, K. K. W. (2023). The AI generation gap: Are Gen Z students more interested in adopting generative AI such as ChatGPT in teaching and learning than their Gen X and millennial generation teachers? *Smart Learning Environments, 10*(1), 60. Advance online publication. DOI: 10.1186/s40561-023-00269-3

Chetry, K. K. (2024). Transforming Education: How AI is Revolutionizing the Learning Experience. *International Journal of Research Publication and Reviews, 5*(5), 6352–6356. DOI: 10.55248/gengpi.5.0524.1277

Choi, Y. (2025). Integrating ChatGPT into the Design of 5E-Based Earth Science Lessons. *Education Sciences, 15*(7), 815. DOI: 10.3390/educsci15070815

Cordero, J., Torres-Zambrano, J., & Cordero-Castillo, A. (2024). Integration of Generative Artificial Intelligence in Higher Education: Best Practices. *Education Sciences, 15*(1), 32. DOI: 10.3390/educsci15010032

Dabingaya, M. (2022). Analyzing the Effectiveness of AI-Powered Adaptive Learning Platforms in Mathematics Education. *Interdisciplinary Journal Papier Human Review, 3*(1), 1–7. DOI: 10.47667/ijphr.v3i1.226

Delello, J. A., Sung, W., Mokhtari, K., Hebert, J., Bronson, A., & Giuseppe, T. D. (2025). AI in the Classroom: Insights from Educators on Usage, Challenges, and Mental Health. *Education Sciences, 15*(2), 113. DOI: 10.3390/educsci15020113

Diantama, S. (2023). Pemanfaatan Artificial Intelegent (AI) Dalam Dunia Pendidikan. *DEWANTECH Jurnal Teknologi Pendidikan, 1*(1), 8–14. DOI: 10.61434/dewantech.v1i1.8

Dwivedi, Y. K., Kshetri, N., Hughes, L., Slade, E., Jeyaraj, A., Kar, A. K., Baabdullah, A. M., Koohang, A., Raghavan, V., Ahuja, M., Albanna, H., Albashrawi, M. A., Al-Busaidi, A. S., Balakrishnan, J., Barlette, Y., Basu, S., Bose, I., Brooks, L., Buhalis, D., & Wright, R. (2023). Multidisciplinary perspectives on opportunities, challenges and implications of generative conversational AI for research, practice and policy. *International Journal of Information Management, 71*, 102642. DOI: 10.1016/j.ijinfomgt.2023.102642

Elkhodr, M., & Gide, E. (2025). Integrating Generative AI in Cybersecurity Education: Case Study Insights on Pedagogical Strategies, Critical Thinking, and Responsible AI Use. https://doi.org/DOI: 10.48550/ARXIV.2502.15357

Filiz, O., Kaya, M. H., & Adıgüzel, T. (2025). Teachers and AI: Understanding the factors influencing AI integration in K-12 education. *Education and Information Technologies, 30*(13), 17931–17967. Advance online publication. DOI: 10.1007/s10639-025-13463-2

Francis, N. J., Jones, S., & Smith, D. P. (2025). Generative AI in Higher Education: Balancing Innovation and Integrity [Review of Generative AI in Higher Education: Balancing Innovation and Integrity]. British Journal of Biomedical Science, 81. Taylor & Francis. https://doi.org/DOI: 10.3389/bjbs.2024.14048

Gentile, M., Città, G., Perna, S., & Allegra, M. (2023). Do we still need teachers? Navigating the paradigm shift of the teacher's role in the AI era. *Frontiers in Education, 8*, 1161777. Advance online publication. DOI: 10.3389/feduc.2023.1161777

Giannakos, M. N., Azevedo, R., Brusilovsky, P., Cukurova, M., Dimitriadis, Y., Hernández-Leo, D., Järvelä, S., Mavrikis, M., & Rienties, B. (2024). The promise and challenges of generative AI in education. *Behaviour & Information Technology*. Advance online publication. DOI: 10.1080/0144929X.2024.2394886

Hasanein, A. M., & Sobaih, A. E. E. (2023). Drivers and Consequences of ChatGPT Use in Higher Education: Key Stakeholder Perspectives. *European Journal of Investigation in Health, Psychology and Education, 13*(11), 2599–2614. DOI: 10.3390/ejihpe13110181 PMID: 37998071

Hazzan-Bishara, A., Kol, O., & Levy, S. (2025). The factors affecting teachers' adoption of AI technologies: A unified model of external and internal determinants. *Education and Information Technologies, 30*(11), 15043–15069. Advance online publication. DOI: 10.1007/s10639-025-13393-z

Hur, J. W. (2024). Fostering AI literacy: Overcoming concerns and nurturing confidence among preservice teachers. *Information and Learning Science*. Advance online publication. DOI: 10.1108/ILS-11-2023-0170

Kamalov, F., & Gurrib, I. (2023). New Era of Artificial Intelligence in Education: Towards a Sustainable Multifaceted Revolution. arXiv (Cornell University). https://doi.org//arxiv.2305.18303DOI: 10.48550

Khlaif, Z. N., Ayyoub, A. A., Hamamra, B., Bensalem, E., Mitwally, M. A. A., Ayyoub, A., Hattab, M. K., & Shadid, F. (2024). University Teachers' Views on the Adoption and Integration of Generative AI Tools for Student Assessment in Higher Education. *Education Sciences*, *14*(10), 1090. DOI: 10.3390/educsci14101090

Kooli, C. (2023). Chatbots in Education and Research: A Critical Examination of Ethical Implications and Solutions. *Sustainability (Basel)*, *15*(7), 5614. DOI: 10.3390/su15075614

Krause, S., Dalvi, A., & Zaidi, S. K. (2025). Generative AI in Education: Student Skills and Lecturer Roles. https://doi.org/DOI: 10.48550/ARXIV.2504.19673

Ng, B. Y., Li, J., Tong, X., Ye, K., Yenne, G., Chandrasekaran, V., & Li, J. (2025). Analyzing Security and Privacy Challenges in Generative AI Usage Guidelines for Higher Education. https://doi.org/DOI: 10.48550/ARXIV.2506.20463

Nguyen, A., Ngo, H. N., Hong, Y., Dang, B., & Nguyen, B.-P. T. (2022). Ethical principles for artificial intelligence in education. *Education and Information Technologies*, *28*(4), 4221–4241. DOI: 10.1007/s10639-022-11316-w PMID: 36254344

Pratschke, B. M. (2023). Generativism: the new hybrid. arXiv (Cornell University). https://doi.org//arxiv.2309.12468DOI: 10.48550

Rasul, T., Nair, S., Kalendra, D. R., Balaji, M. S., Santini, F. de O., Ladeira, W. J., Rather, R. A., Yasin, N., Rodriguez, R. V., Kokkalis, P., Murad, M. W., & Hossain, M. U. (2024). Enhancing academic integrity among students in GenAI Era: A holistic framework. *International Journal of Management Education*, *22*(3), 101041. DOI: 10.1016/j.ijme.2024.101041

Sadeghpour, M., Arakala, A., & Rao, A. (2025). Generative AI in Collaborative Academic Report Writing: Advantages, Disadvantages, and Ethical Considerations. https://doi.org/DOI: 10.48550/ARXIV.2504.08832

Sharma, A., Shailendra, S., & Kadel, R. W. (2025).. . *Experiences with Content Development and Assessment Design in the Era of GenAI.*, *1*, 1–5. Advance online publication. DOI: 10.1109/CSEE64583.2025.00008

Singh, N., Chaudhary, V., Singh, N., Soni, N., & Kapoor, A. (2024). Transforming Business with Generative AI: Research, Innovation, Market Deployment and Future Shifts in Business Models. arXiv (Cornell University). https://doi.org//arxiv.2411.14437DOI: 10.48550

Vieriu, A. M., & Petrea, G. (2025). The Impact of Artificial Intelligence (AI) on Students' Academic Development. *Education Sciences*, *15*(3), 343. DOI: 10.3390/educsci15030343

Wang, N., & Lester, J. C. (2023). K-12 Education in the Age of AI: A Call to Action for K-12 AI Literacy. *International Journal of Artificial Intelligence in Education*, *33*(2), 228–232. DOI: 10.1007/s40593-023-00358-x

Zhang, C., Schießl, J., Plößl, L., Hofmann, F., & Gläser-Zikuda, M. (2023). Acceptance of artificial intelligence among pre-service teachers: A multigroup analysis. *International Journal of Educational Technology in Higher Education*, *20*(1), 49. Advance online publication. DOI: 10.1186/s41239-023-00420-7 PMID: 36743849

Zhang, Y., & Dong, C. (2024). Unveiling the Dynamic Mechanisms of Generative AI in English Language Learning: A Hybrid Study Based on fsQCA and System Dynamics. *Behavioral Sciences (Basel, Switzerland)*, *14*(11), 1015. DOI: 10.3390/bs14111015 PMID: 39594315

Chapter 13
Exploring User Experience in Virtual and Desktop Animation Interfaces From a Usability Perspective

Ezwan Mohd Mokhtar
https://orcid.org/0000-0001-8006-8803
Taylor's University, Malaysia

Muhammad Aiman Mohd Zubir
PlayStation Studios, Malaysia

Marco Gillies
Goldsmiths, University of London, UK

ABSTRACT

User experience (UX) plays a vital role in animation learning, especially when comparing immersive virtual reality (VR) and traditional desktop interfaces. This study investigates UX differences between Autodesk Maya (desktop-based) and Tvori (VR-based) interfaces among 40 animation students using a within-subject usability design. Four UX dimensions, Attractiveness, Stimulation, Perspicuity, and Efficiency were assessed through the User Experience Questionnaire (UEQ), accompanied by semi-structured interviews. Results revealed that VR significantly outperformed desktop tools in Attractiveness and Stimulation, indicating higher engagement. However, no significant difference was found in Perspicuity and Efficiency, suggesting comparable usability. Qualitative feedback highlighted VR immersive

DOI: 10.4018/979-8-3373-5157-5.ch013

appeal and motivational potential, but also lead to discomfort. However, desktop interfaces were seen as structured and efficient. The study concludes that while VR enhances emotional engagement, a hybrid interface approach may better balance engagement with usability in animation learning.

INTRODUCTION

In the era of increasingly digital education, animation technology has become an important component in the field of visual communication design and creative education. Animation software not only serves as a technical tool for the production of visual content, but also as a pedagogical medium that supports exploration, creativity, and deeper learning experiences (Banerjee, Chowdhury, & Yein, 2023). In animation education in particular, the user experience of the interface plays a major role in determining the extent to which students can effectively understand and master the animation process.

Virtual Reality (VR) technology has emerged as a new approach to enhancing the effectiveness of the learning experience through a comprehensive immersive environment. In the context of art and design education, VR allows students to 'enter' a three-dimensional animation space and interact directly with visual objects using body gestures or special control devices. This concept of interaction provides new pedagogical potential that is not offered by traditional interfaces such as desktop or WIMP (Windows-Icons-Mouse-Pointer) (Pei, Fu, & Jiang, 2023). WIMP interfaces remain widely used in the industry due to their stability, accuracy, and flexibility in animation production, especially through software such as Autodesk Maya. However, their complexity and lack of intuitiveness for new users often cause cognitive stress and lack of emotional engagement among students (Gaarsdal, Wolff, & Madsen, 2022).

Although the use of VR in education is gaining ground, there are several key issues that remain unresolved. Studies have shown that students often experience fatigue, disorientation, and negative cognitive effects after using VR systems for extended periods of time (Pei et al., 2023). In addition, not all students have the same level of comfort when interacting with immersive three-dimensional environments, which can sometimes trigger physical discomfort and visual fatigue. In addition, VR interface design has yet to reach the standards of consistency and usability found in desktop interfaces (Pallavicini, Pepe, & Minissi, 2019).

In the context of Malaysia, the challenges in integrating VR-based animation interfaces are also closely related to the limited access to technology, user familiarity, and pedagogical support. Most animation students have been accustomed to WIMP-based systems since the beginning of their studies, making the transition to

VR systems a challenging experience. Furthermore, the lack of empirical comparative studies between these two systems from a user experience perspective makes technology selection more dependent on perceptions or current trends, rather than solid evidence (Banerjee et al., 2023).

This study aims to evaluate and compare the user experience among animation students when using two different types of animation interfaces: one immersive (using Tvori, a VR software) and the other traditional desktop (using Autodesk Maya). This evaluation will be conducted using the UEQ and supported by semi-structured interviews to gain a more contextual and in-depth understanding. This study not only evaluates the technical effectiveness of the interface but also examines how the interaction design and user engagement affect motivation and learning effectiveness in the context of learning animation.

This study attempts to address the following research objectives. First, to identify factors that influence user engagement in VR and desktop-based animation interfaces among animation students. Second, to analyse the level of usability of VR and desktop animation interfaces based on the dimensions of Learnability and Efficiency. Third, to explore students' perceptions and experiences of the advantages and constraints of using VR and desktop animation in the context of learning and animation production.

This study is expected to contribute to the field of animation learning and teaching by providing empirical evidence that systematically compares user experiences of VR and desktop-based animation interfaces. The findings of this study can help animation educators to plan more student-centred teaching strategies, taking into account the emotional, motivational, and cognitive dimensions influenced by interface design. This can directly improve pedagogical effectiveness and student engagement in the learning process. In terms of student learning development, this study provides exposure to how students interact with new technologies and the extent to which such technologies can support the development of their creative, technical, and affective skills. By identifying more stimulating and user-friendly interfaces, students can build greater confidence and focus on animation production, thereby strengthening their overall learning experience. In the context of the animation industry, the findings of this study have the potential to help industry players understand the needs of end-users in the educational context. It is important to design tools that are more intuitive, adaptive, and relevant to current trends in digital animation learning environment. This study also contributes to the strengthening of user experience design practices in the creative industry.

LITERATURE REVIEW

Technological developments in creative education, especially in the field of animation, have opened up a wide space to explore user experience (UX) through various interfaces including conventional desktop interfaces and virtual reality (VR) interfaces. In the context of animation learning, user experience plays an important role in determining the effectiveness of student interaction with digital systems and content. Therefore, various studies have been conducted to evaluate the effectiveness of interfaces based on dimensions such as emotional involvement, usability, and learning effectiveness in virtual and desktop environments. Previous studies have shown that although VR offers a high immersive experience, challenges such as cognitive load, physical discomfort, and accessibility are still major barriers. On the other hand, desktop interfaces still dominate due to their structural stability and efficiency even though the level of involvement may be lower. Therefore, this literature review explores the academic debate related to UX in animation learning, focusing on the comparison between VR and desktop interfaces, examining the challenges in creative learning environments, identifying existing research gaps, and establishing a conceptual framework based on the User Experience Questionnaire (UEQ) model. This review also aligns the results of past studies with current findings to formulate the research's contribution to the animation education landscape more comprehensively.

User Experience (UX) in Animation Learning

The role of User Experience (UX) is increasingly significant in digital learning environments, especially in the context of animation education that requires active interaction with software interfaces. A study by Banerjee et al. (2023) showed that virtual reality (VR) tools in industrial design education can enhance visual appeal and interactivity, two important elements in increasing student engagement. This is in line with the findings by Pei et al. (2023) who found that intuitive VR interface design has a positive impact on user experience in digital museums, which can be applied in the context of animation education.

User experience in the context of animation education depends not only on aesthetics and interactivity, but also on the navigation efficiency and functionality of the tool. Thamrongrat et al. (2023) found that although VR provides higher emotional engagement compared to desktop interfaces, cognitive load and physical fatigue are major challenges. This shows a conflict between emotional engagement and usability, in line with the issues raised in this study. Rodriguez-Garcia et al. (2024) emphasized that VR tools need to undergo comprehensive usability validation before being widely used in training and teaching. A study by Queiroz et al.

(2022) also reinforced this finding when they found that VR can increase student motivation and attention, but learning effectiveness is still influenced by how the interaction is designed. The level of immersion and interactivity has a direct impact on learning achievement but needs to be balanced with task design and student cognition (Petersen et al., 2022). Therefore, the implementation of new technologies in animation needs to be centered on design principles that emphasize a balance between aesthetics, navigational effectiveness, and student cognitive level. User experience in animation learning is not just about visual enjoyment, but needs to take into account functionality, navigational effectiveness, and a balance of mental load experienced by students. for the purpose of improving pedagogy in the field of animation.

Engagement in Immersive and Desktop Interfaces

Student engagement with the interface is a critical factor in influencing learning effectiveness. Immersive experiences through virtual reality (VR) technology are often associated with higher levels of emotional engagement compared to traditional desktop-based interfaces. A study by Pei et al. (2023) found that the use of VR interfaces in digital museums successfully increased visitors' sense of presence and interest in 3D content, a similar effect was also reported in animation learning that required high levels of visual interaction. This immersive effect is supported by Banerjee et al. (2023) in the context of industrial design education, which showed that students experienced higher engagement when they physically interacted with animated objects in a virtual space. However, this high engagement does not come without a cost. A prolonged use of VR can lead to physical fatigue and cognitive overload, especially in complex tasks such as sequential animation. The imbalance between high emotional engagement and work efficiency raises questions about the overall pedagogical effectiveness of VR.

In direct comparison with desktop interfaces, while VR is more engaging, students still value the stability and structured work layout of desktop software. Maya, for example, offers a more systematic environment and facilitates the management of technical elements of animation such as keyframes and rigging. Gaarsdal et al. (2022) showed that users in industrial training are more likely to choose desktop interfaces for tasks that require precise control. In another study, Pallavicini et al. (2019) compare immersive and non-immersive games shows that although VR provides high emotional engagement, users still have difficulty maintaining attention when there are visual distractions and navigational pressures. Therefore, while VR enriches the experience, it needs to be strategically combined with traditional interface elements to achieve a balance between engagement and work effectiveness.

Usability in Animation Interfaces

Usability ensures that interfaces can be accessed and used effectively by students in creative learning contexts. In animation, software such as Autodesk Maya represents a desktop-based interface (WIMP) that emphasizes stability, precision, and organised layout. A virtual reality-based (VR) interfaces such as Tvori focus on intuitive control and natural body interaction. However, although VR can increase emotional engagement, it does not necessarily lead to improvements in usability such as efficiency and ease of learning. VR interfaces require a high level of user-centred design to ensure that users do not feel confused or cognitively overloaded (Thamrongrat et al., 2023). The use of desktop interfaces that have long been used in the animation industry such as Maya is still preferred due to its ability to support a systematic workflow, especially in technical tasks such as keyframe editing. This is due to the interface structure that helps users navigate more easily and maintain consistency of work.

Challenges in UX for Creative Learning Environments

One of the main challenges is the physical discomfort and fatigue experienced in using virtual reality (VR) environments, which can affect students' motivation and concentration (Pei et al., 2023; Tang et al., 2022). In Thamrongrat et al. (2023), users reported eye strain and headaches when using VR headsets for prolonged periods. Students also face high cognitive load when having to adapt to new interfaces such as VR animation tools that require complex body coordination and various movements (An & Kaplan-Rakowski, 2024; Petersen et al., 2022). Similarly, Radianti et al. (2020) asserted that unfriendly system design can undermine the effectiveness of VR pedagogy in higher education. Barrett et al. (2022) study also showed that student performance did not necessarily improve in 3D or VR environments, and in some cases, was better in traditional desktop environments.

Another challenge is the lack of clear pedagogical guidance in designing VR interactions, causing students to lose focus or not effectively achieve learning objectives (Craig & Kay, 2023). The lack of meaningful interactivity and limited control over learning elements also reduce the effectiveness of the overall user experience. Li et al. (2021) emphasized that VR interfaces such as SpArc provide opportunities for greater creativity but admit the challenges in terms of 'learnability' and motion control compared to traditional desktop software such as Maya.

Rationale of the Study

Current studies have focused largely on the effectiveness of VR use in education, particularly in terms of student motivation and engagement (Guerra-Tamez, 2023; Queiroz et al., 2022). However, there is a lack of direct comparative studies between VR and desktop animation interfaces in the context of actual animation learning and how students evaluate usability aspects such as Learnability and Efficiency.

Most studies have focused more on VR applications in the fields of science and health (Birbara et al., 2020; Petersen et al., 2022), rather than animation art and design. This creates a need to empirically evaluate the impact of VR and desktop-based animation interfaces on the user experience (UX) in animation education itself. Banerjee et al. (2023) and Pei et al. (2023) have confirmed the importance of UX evaluation, however their scope is still limited to the context of industry and digital museums, games, not to the design of animated curricula.

UEQ Model

The User Experience Questionnaire (UEQ) framework consists of six main dimensions, namely Attractiveness, Perspicuity, Efficiency, Dependability, Stimulation, and Novelty (Laugwitz et al., 2008). However, in this study, we chose to focus on the dimensions of Attractiveness and Stimulation to assess engagement, and Perspicuity and Efficiency for usability. According to Schrepp et al. (2014), this dimension allows for the measurement not only of the technical efficiency of the interface, but also of the system's ability to build emotional connections with users, an important aspect in creative learning.

The UEQ can be adapted (Schrepp et al. (2017) for various contexts including VR and digital learning environments, where the aspects of novelty and stimulation affect users' motivation and interest in digital interactions. The selection of UEQ dimensions in this study shows a deep consideration of the suitability of the user context, who often interact with VR and desktop systems for a long period of time.

The past studies indicate that although VR technology has high potential in enhancing emotional engagement and conceptual understanding, issues such as cognitive load, visual fatigue, and accessibility remain major barriers in creative learning environments. More conventional desktop interfaces tend to provide efficiency and stability in animation production but fall short in terms of emotional engagement and interaction novelty. The UEQ assessment highlights the need to holistically understand usability dimensions such as attractiveness, stimulation, perspicuity, and efficiency across both platforms.

METHODOLOGY

This study was designed to evaluate and compare the user experience between two different animation interfaces, Autodesk Maya (desktop) and Tvori (virtual reality) among animation students. The choice of method was based on the need to understand not only the technical competence of users, but also their perceptions, motivations, and emotions when interacting with the software. The selection of methods are appropriate to the study objectives is fundamental to the reliability of the findings.

Research Design

This study used a within-subject experimental design to compare the user experience (UX) between two animation interfaces, Autodesk Maya (desktop-based) and Tvori (virtual reality-based). The within-subject design was chosen because each participant underwent both conditions, allowing for direct comparisons in the same situation, thus reducing individual variance between participants (Creswell, 2014). This approach is particularly useful in intervention studies when small changes in the independent variable are expected to affect the dependent variable (Field, 2018).

The Autodesk Maya was used as a alternative for traditional computer-based animation software (WIMP-Windows, Icons, Menus, Pointer), while Tvori was chosen as a representation for a virtual reality environment that allows for physical interaction and natural movement. Both software were used by participants to perform an animation task using 3D characters, involving "hand-waving" actions in two different emotional expressions of happy and sad.

Data Collection

This study was carried out systematically through two main methods: quantitative questionnaires and semi-structured qualitative interviews. Quantitative data were collected using the User Experience Questionnaire (UEQ), while qualitative data were obtained through interview sessions after user testing. The combination of these two approaches allowed researchers to evaluate the user experience comprehensively, in line with the mixed-method approach recommended by Creswell (2014).

The UEQ was used to measure six dimensions of user experience: Attractiveness, Perspicuity, Efficiency, Dependability, Stimulation and Novelty. It uses a seven-point semantic scale and has been proven to have high internal reliability (Schrepp, Hinderks, & Thomaschewski, 2017). This questionnaire was distributed in the form of a bilingual Google Form to ensure participants' understanding of technical terms.

Semi-structured interview sessions were conducted individually after each participant completed both animation tasks using Autodesk Maya and Tvori. Interview questions were designed based on the UEQ structure and were supplemented with follow-up questions (probes) to delve into participants' perceptions of the interface and user interactions. According to Braun and Clarke (2006), this interview approach allows researchers to identify themes and patterns underlying participant responses. The data collection process was conducted in a controlled environment, taking into account comfort, safety, and adherence to research ethics. All sessions were recorded and stored for further analysis.

Sampling

This study employed purposive sampling, which is a deliberate sampling technique based on certain criteria related to the objectives of the study. According to Creswell (2014), purposive sampling allows researchers to select the most suitable participants to provide in-depth information about the phenomenon being studied, especially in the context of mixed studies.

A total of 40 animation students were selected. This selection involved Diploma and Bachelor's level students who have an interest and basic knowledge in 2D or 3D animation. Priority was given to students who had never used virtual reality technology, to ensure that user reactions to the new interface could be observed more objectively.

The selected participant population was individuals who had the potential to understand and perform animation tasks practically, in line with the requirements of the within-subject design used. This method is also in line with Patton's (2002) recommendation that selecting participants based on specific criteria can increase the effectiveness of qualitative and mixed studies.

Instrument

The main instrument used in this study was the User Experience Questionnaire (UEQ) developed by Schrepp, Hinderks and Thomaschewski (2017). The UEQ is a questionnaire that assesses user experience based on six main dimensions, namely Attractiveness, Perspicuity, Efficiency, Dependability, Stimulation, and Novelty.

However, for the purpose of this study, we presented only four dimensions, namely Attractiveness, Stimulation, Perspicuity, and Efficiency. The selection of these dimensions was based on the study objectives which focused on the balance between user engagement and usability in the context of animation learning.

The use of partial scales from the UEQ is also in line with previous research practices that screen dimensions based on specific analytical needs (Schrepp et al.,

2017). Each item was assessed using a seven-point Likert scale with pairs of opposite words, and the score was calculated as an average for each dimension.

Procedures

All participants were tested individually and separately in this study. However, in unavoidable circumstances, there were sessions involving small groups of 2 to 3 participants. It was found that the presence of more than one participant increased their motivation, self-confidence, and their tendency to talk more.

Before the experiment was conducted, all participants were required to select a time slot by appointment in a schedule sheet provided online. On the day of the experiment, each participant was asked to sit at a table that had been prepared in the experimental room as soon as they arrived. The study was divided into three parts:

Part 1: Briefing, Initial Disclosure, Consent Form and Demographic Information

A brief briefing and demonstration were given by the researcher to explain the experimental process and how to use the Autodesk Maya software, the Tvori virtual reality application, and how to operate the Oculus Quest headset and controllers. During the VR demonstration, participants could see the internal display of the Tvori environment through the laptop screen.

Depending on the level of awkwardness or discomfort experienced by the participants, some of them were given the opportunity to briefly try out the VR experience to understand how to use the headset and controllers during the demonstration session.

After agreeing to participate in this study, participants were given written instructions on the study procedures, followed by signing the Consent Form. Next, they were asked to fill in demographic information via an online form using Google Form. The briefing and demonstration session took approximately 10 to 15 minutes.

Part 2: Treatments for Each Condition

After the briefing session was completed, participants were asked to perform Condition 1. They were instructed to animate a character using Autodesk Maya software, a Desktop-based animation software commonly used by most participants. To facilitate the task, an existing character named Andy Rig that had been equipped with a rig system was used. To navigate the Maya interface, a three-button mouse with a scroll wheel was used to allow the user to zoom in/out, pan left/right, and rotate the viewport.

Participants were given two tasks to animate the action of waving their hands with different expressions: happy (fast movement) and sad (slow movement). All participants' activities in Condition 1 were recorded and stored in a special folder for the participants on the researcher's laptop. After the participants completed the tasks, they were required to answer a post-experimental User Experience Questionnaire (UEQ) about their experience using Maya. Participants were asked to rate the experience based on their interactions with the interface in that condition. Upon completion, participants proceeded to the second condition in the experiment.

For Condition 2, participants were asked to animate characters using virtual reality-based animation software, Tvori. This software was relatively new to most participants. At the beginning, the researcher helped participants put on the Oculus Quest headset and hold the controllers in their left and right hands. Participants showed excitement when they could see the virtual environment through the Tvori interface.

Since most participants were first-time users of the VR environment, they felt awkward in operating the device and the environment. In most situations, the researcher had to give instructions to the participants to navigate the Tvori interface. The task given was the same as in Condition 1: an animation of waving hands with happy (fast movement) and sad (slow movement) expressions. Participants were free to choose an existing character that had been rigged in the Tvori application to use.

All activities of participants in Condition 2 were recorded and saved in their respective folders on the researcher's laptop. After completing the task, participants were asked to answer a UEQ questionnaire to evaluate their experience using Tvori on their interaction with the interface. The total time taken by participants to complete Condition 1 and Condition 2 was around 30 to 45 minutes, depending on the participant's skill level and level of familiarity with using Maya and Tvori.

Part 3: Post-Test Interview

After all experimental conditions were completed, a brief semi-structured interview session was conducted. Ten basic questions were prepared as a guide for this session, and follow-up questions (probing) were used if necessary to obtain more in-depth information. Participants were reminded that the interview session would be audio-recorded as part of the qualitative data collection for this study.

The estimated duration of the interview session was between 20 and 30 minutes, depending on the number of participants involved in each session. At the end of the session, participants were given RM10 as a token of appreciation after completing the session. The entire experimental session including briefing, task implementation, and interview took approximately 1 hour and 20 minutes for each participant. The step-by-step experimental procedure adopted in this within-subject usability study is as shown in Figure 1, encompassing briefing, task performance, UEQ assessments, and a concluding interview.

Figure 1. Flowchart of the experimental procedure for the usability study

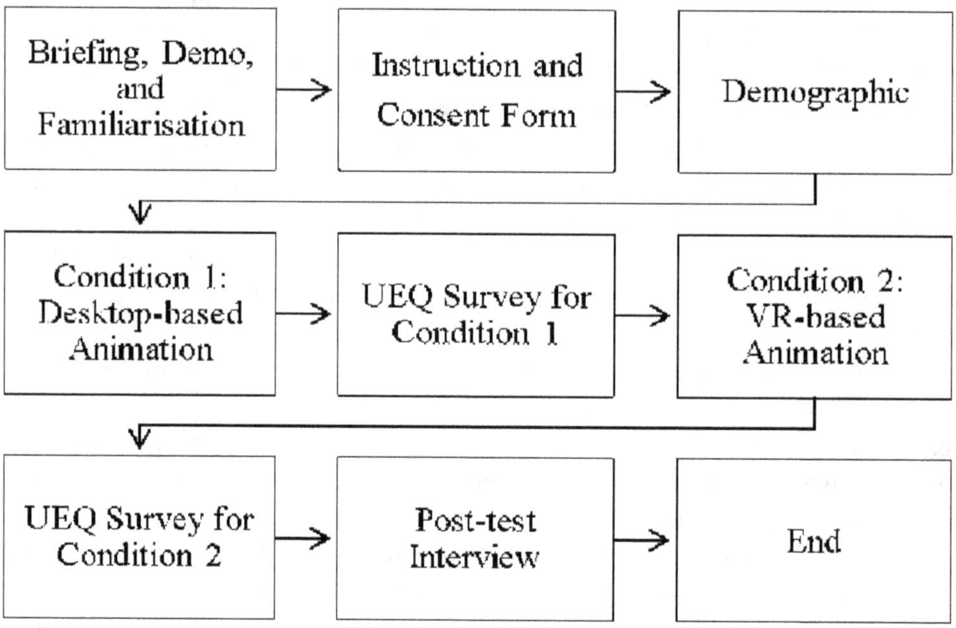

Data Analysis

The data analysis process in this study was carried out through two approaches in line with the mixed-methods strategy, namely quantitative analysis of questionnaire data and qualitative analysis of interview data. This approach allowed researchers to obtain a holistic picture of user experiences of desktop animation interfaces and virtual reality, as recommended by Creswell (2014).

For quantitative analysis, scores from the User Experience Questionnaire (UEQ) were analyzed using descriptive and inferential statistics, including a two-tailed t-test to determine significant differences between two conditions (Autodesk Maya and Tvori). The UEQ measures six scales of user experience and uses a seven-point Likert scale from -3 to +3. According to Schrepp et al. (2017), this test is suitable for assessing usability and user satisfaction in interactive technology environments.

For qualitative data, semi-structured interviews were analyzed using thematic analysis methods based on the Braun and Clarke (2006) approach. Interview transcriptions were done verbatim and analyzed to identify main themes based on the six UEQ scales. Coding was done manually and reviewed to ensure consistency of interpretation (inter-rater reliability), a process that is important to ensure the validity of qualitative data (Patton, 2002). These two approaches contribute to a more comprehensive understanding of how users evaluate and respond to different animation software usage experiences.

Ethical Considerations

This study adheres to the principles of research ethics as outlined by Creswell (2014), including the need for ethical approval, informed consent, and confidentiality and protection of participant data. The ethical approval form was submitted to the *Research Ethics and Integrity Sub-Committee (REISC)* via EAF1 form. All participants were informed of the study objectives, methods, and their right to withdraw without consequence. The informed consent form was provided in two languages (Malay and English) to ensure a clear understanding of the study content and process (Patton, 2002). All data collected, including video recordings and transcriptions, were stored securely and will not be disclosed without permission. This is in line with the principles of integrity, accountability, and confidentiality in social research (Babbie, 2013).

Data Validity and Reliability

The study emphasises the aspects of validity and reliability to ensure that the quality of the data obtained is high and reliable. In the context of quantitative data, the User Experience Questionnaire (UEQ) instrument used has gone through a process of construction and empirical evaluation by experts and shows high internal reliability (Cronbach's Alpha) values across the six scales tested (Schrepp, Hinderks, & Thomaschewski, 2017). The UEQ has also been widely used in user interface studies and has been proven valid for assessing user experience in technological environments (Laugwitz, Held, & Schrepp, 2008).

For qualitative data, validity is obtained through data triangulation, namely by comparing themes from interviews with the UEQ dimensions. In addition, cross-coding (inter-coder reliability) was performed by two independent researchers to ensure consistency in the interpretation of themes (Braun & Clarke, 2006). According to Patton (2002), the use of more than one researcher in analysing data can increase reliability and reduce individual bias. A systematic approach to the evaluation of instruments and analytical methods has helped ensure that the data obtained are valid and reliable to answer the research questions.

FINDINGS

This section presents the findings of the study based on quantitative and qualitative analyses obtained from an in-subject study involving 40 animation students. The study assessed the user experience of two animation interfaces, Autodesk Maya (desktop) and Tvori (virtual reality) by focusing on four key dimensions of UX: Attractiveness, Stimulation, Perspicuity, and Efficiency. Quantitative data were obtained through a User Experience Questionnaire (UEQ), while qualitative data were obtained from semi-structured interviews. These findings are analysed separately and integrated in the conclusion section to provide a comprehensive understanding of the user experience in the context of animation learning.

Quantitative Findings

This section discusses the quantitative findings based on the User Experience Questionnaire (UEQ) which was used to assess user experience in four main dimensions: Attractiveness, Stimulation, Perspicuity, and Efficiency. A total of 40 animation students were involved in this study and evaluated two software, namely Autodesk Maya (desktop) and Tvori (VR). A within-subject design method was used, where each participant tried both interfaces and provided a rating based on their experience. The UEQ scores were statistically analysed using a paired t-test to identify whether there was a significant difference in user perceptions of the two software as shown in Table 1 below.

Table 1. Average UEQ Score for Maya and Tvori by UX Dimension

UEQ Dimension	Autodesk Maya (Desktop)	Tvori (VR)	Score Difference	p-value	Interpretation
Attractiveness	1.48	2.09	0.61	0.0072	Significant, VR is more interesting
Stimulation	1.17	2.16	0.99	0.0002	Significant, VR is more fun
Perspicuity	1.53	1.87	0.34	0.1037	Not significant, equivalent
Efficiency	1.29	1.78	0.49	0.0716	Not significant, almost equivalent

Attractiveness

Attractiveness refers to the general assessment of the aesthetic pleasure and satisfaction experienced by the user. Based on the analysis, Tvori recorded an average score of 2.09, while Maya recorded 1.48. This difference was statistically significant ($p = 0.0072$), indicating that animation students were more attracted to the visual and interactive experiences offered by virtual reality interfaces.

Factors contributing to this finding included the perception of three-dimensional depth, intuitive motion control, and greater visual engagement. Many participants stated that they felt more "immersed" in the animation world when using Tvori, making the overall experience more enjoyable and emotionally engaging.

Stimulation

The second dimension, Stimulation, refers to the level of motivation and excitement that users feel while using the software. The average score for Tvori is 2.16, significantly higher than 1.17 for Maya, with a statistically significant difference ($p = 0.0002$). This indicates that the use of virtual reality in an animated environment has a significant positive effect on the emotional engagement of users.

Participants reported feeling more active and enthusiastic when they were able to move objects directly using their hands or controllers. The ability to stand, move and control objects in a virtual space gives the sensation of being part of the animated world being created. This is in contrast to Maya which, although efficient, is more static and based on keyboard and mouse interaction.

Perspicuity

Perspicuity refers to the degree to which users find it easy to learn the interface and functions of the system. The average score obtained for Maya is 1.53, while Tvori obtained 1.87. Although this difference favours Tvori, it is not statistically significant ($p = 0.1037$). This reflects that both systems are almost equivalent in terms of learnability, or in other words, easy for students to understand and learn.

Several participants stated that even though they were trying Tvori for the first time, navigating the virtual space and using the controls were easy to understand after a short training session. At the same time, Maya is easier for students with a digital design background, since its interface is more conventional and has been commonly used in teaching in higher education institutions. This balance shows the advantages of both platforms in supporting the learning process, depending on the context and skill level of the user.

Efficiency

The Efficiency dimension assesses the extent to which users can perform tasks quickly and efficiently. The average score for Tvori is 1.78, while Maya scores 1.29, with a nearly significant difference in scores ($p = 0.0716$). This indicates that while Tvori has the potential to offer a more flexible and faster work experience, the advantage is not statistically significant compared to Maya.

Some participants reported that the ease of physically moving objects in virtual space speeds up the basic animation process. However, for more technical tasks that require precise control such as rigging or keyframe editing, Maya is still seen as a more stable and structured platform. Thus, these findings reflect that efficiency is relative, depending on the type of task and the skill level of the user.

The quantitative findings show that VR offers significantly higher levels of emotional engagement (Attractiveness & Stimulation) compared to Maya (desktop). However, there is no significant difference in terms of learnability and efficiency between the two systems. These results indicate that virtual reality has great potential in increasing the motivation and interest of animation students, but from the aspect of work and learning efficiency, a combined or hybrid approach may be more suitable to ensure overall effectiveness in teaching animation. The next section will discuss the qualitative findings obtained from the participant interviews to deepen the understanding of user perceptions more comprehensively.

Qualitative Findings

The qualitative findings obtained from semi-structured interviews with participants after they tried two animation interfaces, Autodesk Maya (desktop) and Tvori (VR). The thematic analysis method used was based on the approach of Braun and Clarke (2006), which involves the process of identifying themes, coding data, and interpreting meaning based on the participants' narratives. This analysis focused on users' perceptions of the learning experience, emotional involvement, usability, and cognitive challenges encountered while using both interfaces. Four main themes were identified and presented as in Table 2 below.

Table 2. Themes, Codes, and Participant Quotes

Theme	Coding	Participant Quotes
Engagement and Emotions in VR	Virtual world is fun, immersive, visually appealing	"I feel like I'm in the real world... a very immersive experience." (Participant 05)
	Virtual reality is more interactive	"VR makes me more enthusiastic. It feels fun when I can move objects in space." (Participant 09)
Cognitive Load and Discomfort Fatigue	Quickly, visual fatigue, input overload	"I get tired quickly using VR, there are many things to control with my hands and head." (Participant 12)
	Feeling disoriented in virtual space	"I get dizzy when I'm in VR for too long, sometimes I feel disoriented." (Participant 07)
Structure and Routine in Virtual	Organized screen, complete tools, easier focus	"Virtual is more organized, all the tools are on one screen. It's easier to focus." (Participant 18)
	Work process is more efficient and consistent	"I like the way Maya organizes work, there is a timeline, there are shortcuts. More efficient." (Participant 15)
Learning and Adaptation	Both are easy to learn, but VR takes time	"Both are easy to learn, but Maya is easier to understand because you are used to using it." (Participant 03)
	Need to get used to the controls in the 3D space	"Tvori is also easy, but it takes time to get used to the space and controls." (Participant 10)

Theme 1: Engagement and Emotion in VR

A large number of participants stated that they were more emotionally engaged when using the virtual environment in Tvori. They described the experience as enjoyable and "alive", as they could control the animated objects directly with their hands, not just a mouse or keyboard. One participant (Participant 05) stated:

"I felt like I was in the real world... a very immersive experience."

The virtual environment provided a high sense of presence, where participants felt they were truly present in the animation workspace. This was consistent with the high scores on the Stimulation dimension in the quantitative findings, where VR demonstrated greater ability to foster engagement.

Theme 2: Cognitive Load and Discomfort

However, the virtual space experience also comes with challenges. Several participants reported cognitive and physical fatigue after using Tvori for extended periods of time. The head and hand-based control of movement, as well as the need to stand and move actively, led to fatigue and loss of concentration. Participant 12 said:

"I get tired quickly using VR, there are many things to control with my hands and head."

Some participants also reported dizziness and disorientation:

"I get dizzy when I'm in VR for too long, sometimes I feel disoriented." (Participant 07)

These findings suggest that while VR offers an engaging experience, it can also have cognitive effects that affect work efficiency in the long term. Thus, this proves that the level of engagement does not necessarily mean better efficiency.

Theme 3: Structure and Routine in Maya

In contrast to immersive virtual environments, Maya was identified as more structured and routine. Maya's interface provided a static layout and was more familiar to students, especially those with experience with digital design software. Participant 18 stated:

"Maya is more organised, all the tools are on one screen. It's easier to focus."

This advantage makes Maya more suitable for tasks that require deep focus and management of complex elements such as keyframes and timelines. Another participant (Participant 15) also supported this view:

"I like the way Maya organizes work, there's a timeline, there's shortcuts. It's more efficient."

This is in line with the quantitative findings in the Efficiency dimension, where the difference between the two systems was not significant, but the experience of working with Maya was more stable and structured.

Theme 4: Learning and Adaptation

Most participants agreed that both software were easy to learn, but Maya had the advantage of familiarity because it had been used in previous classes. Tvori, on the other hand, although interesting, required time to adapt to the 3D environment and body control. According to Participant 03:

"Both are easy to learn, but Maya is easier to understand because you are used to it."

However, participants also showed interest in exploring and adapting to Tvori, as stated by Participant 10:

"Tvori is also easy, but it takes time to get used to the space and controls."

This perception indicates that learning through VR is achievable, but it requires more time and practice to build natural navigation and body control skills.

The interview findings indicate that animation students responded positively to the use of VR in terms of emotional engagement and enjoyment, but at the same time were aware of the challenges that come with the technology, such as fatigue and loss of concentration. Autodesk Maya remains relevant as an efficient and stable tool for systematic animation production. Both tools show their own potential, and these findings support the suggestion that a hybrid approach between VR and desktop should be explored in the teaching and learning of animation.

The quantitative findings show that Tvori (VR) scores significantly higher in two dimensions, namely Attractiveness and Stimulation, indicating that animation students feel more attracted, emotionally involved and motivated when using the VR platform. Interactive and immersive elements such as the use of three-dimensional space, free movement and realistic visuals have a positive impact on students' perceptions of the animation learning experience.

However, for the other two dimensions, namely Perspicuity and Efficiency, no significant differences were recorded. This shows that in terms of ease of learning and efficiency in performing tasks, both interfaces are almost equivalent. Maya is seen to have the advantage in terms of a more systematic work structure and a work environment that students are used to, while Tvori requires some adaptation time but is still easy to master.

Qualitative findings further support these findings through four main themes identified. The first theme emphasizes high emotional engagement in VR, where participants expressed a sense of excitement and enjoyment of working in a virtual world that resembles reality. The second theme touches on the cognitive burden experienced when using VR for long periods of time, including visual fatigue and disorientation. The third theme discusses how Maya provides a more organized and focused work experience, suitable for tasks that require concentration and precision. Finally, the fourth theme shows that both software can be learned effectively, but the rate of adaptation depends on the background and level of exposure of the students.

The findings of this study indicate that VR has great potential to increase student engagement and motivation in animation learning. However, these advantages need to be balanced with an efficient work structure and reduce the risk of cognitive fatigue. Therefore, a hybrid approach between desktop and VR is proposed as the optimal strategy in the design of future animation teaching curricula. This approach is able to leverage the strengths of both platforms to produce interesting, meaningful and effective learning experiences.

DISCUSSION

The findings of this quantitative study show that VR-based animation interfaces score significantly higher on the Attractiveness and Stimulation dimensions than desktop interfaces. This is in line with previous studies that have found that VR environments can increase student motivation and engagement in animation learning through a more enjoyable and immersive experience (Guerra-Tamez, 2023; Petersen, Petkakis, & Makransky, 2022). User experience in this context is not only seen in terms of aesthetic perception, but also in terms of how the virtual environment affects students' emotions and cognitive engagement (Allcoat et al., 2021).

However, the findings show that there is no significant difference in terms of Perspicuity and Efficiency between the two interfaces. This implies that while VR increases emotional engagement, it does not necessarily guarantee an increase in technical usability or task effectiveness (Pei, Fu, & Jiang, 2023). A study by Lamberti, Cannavò and Montuschi (2020) also noted that VR often poses challenges in terms of physical fatigue, spatial disorientation and relearning requirements for new users, which can potentially affect efficiency.

This comparison also highlights the gap between emotion and work structure: VR is more prone to high emotional engagement but less in terms of systematic structure, while desktop offers a more robust and conventionally understandable workflow for students (Thamrongrat et al., 2023). Therefore, the need for a hybrid approach that combines the strengths of both platforms should be considered in future animation instructional designs.

Qualitative findings from participant interviews yielded four significant main themes in comparing virtual reality (VR) and desktop-based animated interfaces, namely emotional engagement, cognitive load, interaction effectiveness, and physical comfort.

First, emotional engagement was reported to be higher in VR environments due to the realistic 3D visuals and immersive virtual presence. One participant stated: "I felt like I was in the animated world itself." This phenomenon can be linked to the embodied learning theory that emphasizes the simultaneous physical and cognitive experience in the learning process (Khorasani et al., 2023). Queiroz et al. (2022) also reported that immersion in VR increased student engagement through emotional and presence elements.

However, participants also reported a high cognitive load in using VR. One quote state: "I get tired easily and have a hard time focusing when wearing a headset for long periods of time." This is consistent with Allcoat et al.'s (2021) finding that VR tends to increase cognitive load due to the complexity of navigation and multitasking required.

In terms of interaction effectiveness, desktop interfaces are seen as more efficient and organized, especially for technical tasks such as modeling and editing. One participant said: "Using the desktop is easy, I know the shortcuts, and the work goes faster." This reflects the value of efficiency and learnability as outlined in the UEQ model (Laugwitz et al., 2008).

Finally, the issue of physical comfort is also an important factor. Prolonged use of VR headsets causes discomfort such as dizziness and fatigue. Birbara et al. (2020) also confirms this issue as a major challenge in VR environments for education.

Although VR offers advantages in emotional engagement and presence, it faces limitations in terms of cognitive and physical load, while desktop interfaces still maintain advantages in terms of effectiveness and comfort. These findings reinforce the need for a balanced approach to instructional design that combines the advantages of both technologies.

RELATIONSHIPS BETWEEN QUANTITATIVE AND QUALITATIVE FINDINGS

The findings of this study show a convergent relationship between quantitative and qualitative data, particularly in terms of emotional engagement, usability, and comfort of using the animated interface. The Stimulation and Attractiveness dimensions in the UEQ questionnaire found that VR interfaces scored higher than desktop interfaces. This finding was also supported by qualitative data, where participants stated that VR provided a "more immersive" and "closer to the real world" experience, thus indicating a higher level of emotional engagement (P7, P12).

However, the qualitative data also detailed challenges that could not be captured through the questionnaire. Although the Efficiency score for the desktop interface was higher, interviews revealed that the organized work structure and conventional functionality allowed students to complete tasks more quickly and comfortably. One participant stated, "I know the shortcuts and functions of Maya because I am used to it, so I work faster, and I am not very tired" (P4). This shows that although VR is attractive in terms of engagement, it requires higher physical and cognitive energy – an aspect that is not fully captured through quantitative instruments alone.

The interview findings also revealed a high cognitive load in VR use. Although Perspicuity showed a moderate score in the quantitative data, participants reported that they needed longer to adapt to the controls in the VR environment. This phenomenon is consistent with the Cognitive Load theory that states that complex interactions can interfere with learning if not carefully designed (Sweller et al., 2019; Tang et al., 2022).

On the other hand, there was no significant conflict between the quantitative and qualitative findings. On the contrary, the qualitative findings helped to clarify nuances that were not captured by the UEQ instrument. For example, aspects of physical comfort in VR use—such as dizziness or eye discomfort—were not included in the UEQ dimensions but were mentioned by several participants. This suggests that while UEQ is appropriate for assessing user experience in terms of design perception, it may not be comprehensive enough to assess physiological or emotional factors in depth (Allcoat et al., 2021).

Implications for User Interface

The findings of this study provide significant guidance in shaping more effective and user-friendly user interface designs in learning contexts. From a user experience (UX) perspective, the high emotional engagement aspect of virtual reality (VR) interfaces shows great potential to increase student motivation and interest. However, challenges such as physical fatigue and high cognitive load need to be overcome with a design approach that considers the balance between emotional arousal and technical efficiency (Banerjee et al., 2023; Petersen et al., 2022).

An ideal design should integrate high interactivity elements such as direct object manipulation, immediate feedback, and engaging visualizations, yet not cognitively burdensome for the user (Guerra-Tamez, 2023). The development of animation-based learning systems is also recommended to include adaptive features that allow users to adjust the level of complexity of interactions according to their respective abilities and needs (Allcoat et al., 2021). A balance between emotionally stimulating aesthetic elements and efficient work structures can support pedagogical effectiveness and ensure a fun and sustainable learning experience.

Implications for Animation Teaching and Learning

The high emotional engagement aspect of VR-based interfaces shows the potential to increase students' motivation and interest in animation learning. This is in line with the findings of Queiroz et al. (2022) who stated that students showed deeper understanding and higher engagement when using a more immersive medium such as VR.

However, the advantages in terms of interactivity and immersive experience offered by VR need to be balanced with technical efficiency and a more structured work structure as found in desktop software. This is important to ensure that students do not experience excessive cognitive fatigue, as reported by An and Kaplan-Rakowski (2024) in the context of informal learning using VR.

From an educational practice perspective, instructors can design hybrid learning activities, combining the advantages of VR for exploration and emotional stimulation, and desktop for more systematic and technical animation production. This will allow students with different learning styles, whether visual, kinaesthetic, or reflective, to absorb knowledge more effectively (Allcoat et al., 2021).

The results of this study suggest that pedagogical approaches in animation education should not be one-dimensional but rather adapt instructional design to the varying needs of students, and consider a balance between interactivity, emotion, and work efficiency.

Strengths and Limitations of the Study

This study features several important methodological strengths. The use of a mixed methods approach, which combines quantitative data through the UEQ questionnaire and qualitative data through semi-structured interviews, allows for data triangulation that strengthens the validity of the findings (Schrepp et al., 2014; Hinderks et al., 2019). This strategy allows researchers to more comprehensively understand the user experience, including emotional dimensions, cognitive load, and technical proficiency of VR-based and desktop animation interfaces. Furthermore, the selection of participants consisting of animation students provides an authentic and relevant study context with real-world applications in animation teaching and learning.

However, this study also has several limitations. The small sample size and limited to only one institution affect the generalizability of the findings to a broader student population (Pei et al., 2023). In addition, the uneven context of exposure to VR technology among participants contributed to prior experience bias, particularly in perceptions of comfort and effectiveness of VR use (Tang et al., 2022). Technical issues associated with the use of VR devices such as disorientation and fatigue also pose challenges for participants in optimally evaluating the interface (Birbara et al., 2020). The implications of these limitations need to be considered in interpreting the study results and planning further studies.

Recommendations for Future Research

This study has opened up a range of possibilities in understanding the user experience of VR-based and desktop-based user interfaces in learning contexts. While the findings show the advantages and limitations of both platforms, future research could expand the scope by investigating the integration of gamification elements into animated interfaces. Elements such as visual rewards, points systems, or graded achievements have the potential to increase student engagement emotionally and motivationally (Queiroz et al., 2022; Guerra-Tamez, 2023).

It is appropriate to propose a comparison between various immersive platforms such as mixed reality (MR) and augmented reality (AR) to assess the effectiveness of more layered and responsive learning experiences (Craig & Kay, 2023; Radianti et al., 2020). This is important given that intensive VR use can sometimes cause fatigue and discomfort, and therefore a lighter approach such as AR may be a suitable alternative in the context of animated education. It is recommended that future studies use a more diverse sample in terms of skill levels, institutions, and cultural backgrounds to increase the generalizability of the findings.

CONCLUSION

This study has identified various dimensions of user experience (UX) in the use of virtual reality (VR) and desktop-based animation interfaces among animation students. The main findings show that VR interfaces tend to increase students' emotional engagement, motivation, and enjoyment, while desktop interfaces show advantages in terms of work structure efficiency and high usability. However, constraints such as physical fatigue, cognitive load, and interaction effectiveness issues in VR environments still limit the overall learning experience.

A thematic discussion of the findings shows three main themes that emerge: (1) Emotional Engagement, which is more pronounced in VR, but causes cognitive fatigue and distraction (Pei et al., 2023; Allcoat et al., 2021); (2) Efficiency and Usability, which are better in desktop animation tools such as Autodesk Maya because students are more familiar with linear structures and keyboard/mouse controls (Barrett et al., 2022; Rodriguez-Garcia et al., 2024); and (3) Holistic User Experience, where students stated that the combination of strengths of both types of interfaces can create a more balanced and effective learning experience.

All these findings directly support the three formulated objectives of the study, namely: (i) to identify factors that influence user engagement, (ii) to analyse the level of usability of the interface, and (iii) to explore students' perceptions of the strengths and limitations of VR and desktop animation interfaces. It also answers the problem statement that states the lack of motivational elements in desktop interfaces, fatigue in VR use, and the gap in instructional design that has not integrated the advantages of both types of interfaces.

The main contribution of this study is in offering a deeper understanding of UX in animation learning, thus contributing to more immersive instructional design and responsive to students' learning styles. This study is also able to enrich pedagogical practices and the development of animation education technology at the higher education level.

ACKNOWLEDGMENT

The authors would like to express their sincere gratitude to all who have supported and contributed to this research. Special thanks to collaborators and participants whose insights and cooperation greatly enriched the study. This research received no specific grant from any funding agency in any sectors. The authors also appreciate the constructive feedback provided by the anonymous reviewers, which significantly helped improve the quality of this article.

REFERENCES

Allcoat, D., Hatchard, T., Azmat, F., Stansfield, K., Watson, D., & von Mühlenen, A. (2021). Education in the digital age: Learning experience in virtual and mixed realities. *Journal of Educational Computing Research*, *59*(5), 795–816. DOI: 10.1177/0735633120985120

An, Y., & Kaplan-Rakowski, R. (2024). Examining Adults' Enjoyment, Challenges, and Cognitive Load in Informal Learning with High-Immersion Virtual Reality. *TechTrends*, *68*(6), 1118–1128. DOI: 10.1007/s11528-024-00999-2

Babbie, E. R. (2013). *The practice of social research* (13th ed.). Wadsworth Cengage Learning.

Banerjee, S., Chowdhury, A., & Yein, N. (2023). User experience evaluation of a virtual reality tool used for 3D modelling in industrial design education: A study in the Indian context. *Designs*, *7*(5), 105. DOI: 10.3390/designs7050105

Barrett, R. C. A., Poe, R., O'Camb, J. W., Woodruff, C., Harrison, S. M., Dolguikh, K., Chuong, C., Klassen, A. D., Zhang, R., Joseph, R. B., & Blair, M. R. (2022). Comparing virtual reality, desktop-based 3D, and 2D versions of a category learning experiment. *PLoS One*, *17*(10), e0275119. DOI: 10.1371/journal.pone.0275119 PMID: 36201546

Birbara, N. S., Sammut, C., & Pather, N. (2020). Virtual reality in anatomy: A pilot study evaluating different delivery modalities. *Anatomical Sciences Education*, *13*(4), 445–457. DOI: 10.1002/ase.1921 PMID: 31587471

Braun, V., & Clarke, V. (2006). Using thematic analysis in psychology. *Qualitative Research in Psychology*, *3*(2), 77–101. DOI: 10.1191/1478088706qp063oa

Craig, C., & Kay, R. (2023). A Systematic Overview of Reviews of the Use of Immersive Virtual Reality in Higher Education. *Higher Learning Research Communications, 13*(2). Advance online publication. DOI: 10.18870/hlrc.v13i2.1430

Creswell, J. W. (2014). *Research design: Qualitative, quantitative, and mixed methods approaches* (4th ed.). SAGE Publications.

Field, A. (2018). *Discovering statistics using IBM SPSS statistics* (5th ed.). SAGE Publications.

Gaarsdal, J., Wolff, S., & Madsen, C. B. (2022). Evaluating immersive animation authoring in an industrial VR training context. *Proceedings of the 14th International Conference on Signal Processing Systems (ICSPS 2022)*, 809–817. IEEE. DOI: DOI: 10.1109/ICSPS58776.2022.00147

Guerra-Tamez, C. R. (2023). The impact of immersion through virtual reality in the learning experiences of art and design students: The mediating effect of the flow experience. *Education Sciences, 13*(2), 185. Advance online publication. DOI: 10.3390/educsci13020185

Hinderks, A., Schrepp, M., Domínguez Mayo, F. J., Escalona, M. J., & Thomaschewski, J. (2019). Developing a UX KPI based on the User Experience Questionnaire. *Computer Standards & Interfaces, 65*, 38–44. DOI: 10.1016/j.csi.2019.01.007

Khorasani, S. et al. (2023). *Hands-on or hands-off: Deciphering the impact of interactivity on embodied learning in VR. Computers & Education: X Reality*, 3, 100037. DOI: 10.1016/j.cexr.2023.100037

Lamberti, F., Cannavò, A., & Montuschi, P. (2020). Is immersive virtual reality the ultimate interface for 3D animators? *Computer, 53*(4), 36–45. DOI: 10.1109/MC.2019.2908871

Laugwitz, B., Held, T., & Schrepp, M. (2008). Construction and evaluation of a user experience questionnaire. In Holzinger, A. (Ed.), *HCI and usability for education and work* (pp. 63–76). Springer., DOI: 10.1007/978-3-540-89350-9_6

Li, B., Said, I., Kirova, L., Blokhina, M., & Kang, H. J. (2021). SpArc: A VR animating tool at your fingertips. In Proceedings of the 27th ACM Symposium on Virtual Reality Software and Technology (VRST '21) (Article 95, 1–3). DOI: 10.1145/3489849.3489920

Pallavicini, F., Pepe, A., & Minissi, M. E. (2019). Gaming in Virtual Reality: What Changes in Terms of Usability, Emotional Response and Sense of Presence Compared to Non-Immersive Video Games? *Simulation & Gaming, 50*(2), 136–159. DOI: 10.1177/1046878119831420

Patton, M. Q. (2002). *Qualitative research and evaluation methods* (3rd ed.). SAGE Publications.

Pei, X., Fu, S., & Jiang, T. (2023). An empirical study on user experience evaluation of VR interface in digital museums. *Data and Information Management, 7*(4), 100057. DOI: 10.1016/j.dim.2023.100057

Petersen, G. B., Petkakis, G., & Makransky, G. (2022). A study of how immersion and interactivity drive VR learning. *Computers & Education, 179*, 104429. DOI: 10.1016/j.compedu.2021.104429

Queiroz, A. C. M., Fauville, G., Herrera, F., Leme, M. I. da S., & Bailenson, J. N. (2022). Do Students Learn Better With Immersive Virtual Reality Videos Than Conventional Videos? A Comparison of Media Effects With Middle School Girls. Technology, Mind, and Behavior, 3(3: Autumn). DOI: 10.1037/tmb0000082

Radianti, J., Majchrzak, T. A., Fromm, J., & Wohlgenannt, I. (2020). A systematic review of immersive virtual reality applications for higher education: Design elements, lessons learned, and research agenda. *Computers & Education, 147*, 103778. DOI: 10.1016/j.compedu.2019.103778

Rodriguez-Garcia, B., Ramírez-Sanz, J. M., Miguel-Alonso, I., & Bustillo, A. (2024). Enhancing Learning of 3D Model Unwrapping through Virtual Reality Serious Game: Design and Usability Validation. *Electronics (Basel), 13*(10), 1972. DOI: 10.3390/electronics13101972

Schrepp, M., Hinderks, A., & Thomaschewski, J. (2014). Applying the User Experience Questionnaire (UEQ) in Different Evaluation Scenarios. In Marcus, A. (Ed.), *Design, User Experience, and Usability: Theories, Methods, and Tools for Designing the User Experience* (Vol. 8517, pp. 383–392). Springer., DOI: 10.1007/978-3-319-07668-3_37

Schrepp, M., Hinderks, A., & Thomaschewski, J. (2017). Construction of a benchmark for the User Experience Questionnaire (UEQ). *International Journal of Interactive Multimedia and Artificial Intelligence, 4*(4), 40–44. DOI: 10.9781/ijimai.2017.445

Schrepp, M., Hinderks, A., & Thomaschewski, J. (2017b). Design and Evaluation of a Short Version of the User Experience Questionnaire (UEQ-S). *International Journal of Interactive Multimedia and Artificial Intelligence, 4*(6), 103–108. DOI: 10.9781/ijimai.2017.09.001

Tang, Q., Wang, Y., Liu, H., Liu, Q., & Jiang, S. (2022). Experiencing an art education program through immersive virtual reality or iPad: Mediating effects of presence and extraneous load on enjoyment, attention, and retention. *Frontiers in Psychology*, *13*. Advance online publication. DOI: 10.3389/fpsyg.2022.957037 PMID: 36186296

Thamrongrat, P., Khundam, C., Pakdeebun, P., & Mohd Nizam, D. N. (2023). Desktop vs. headset: A comparative study of user experience and engagement for flexibility exercise in virtual reality. *Emerging Science Journal*, *7*(4), 698–710. DOI: 10.28991/ESJ-2023-07-04-03

KEY TERMS AND DEFINITIONS

Animation Learners: The animation learners in this study were undergraduate animation students who underwent immersive and desktop interface testing. They represented real users in assessing their experience and proficiency in using animation tools for 3D character creation tasks.

Desktop (WIMP) Interface: Windows, Icons, Menus, and Pointers (WIMP)-based desktop interfaces are traditionally used via a keyboard and mouse. In this study, Autodesk Maya represents the desktop approach commonly used by students in the animation production process.

Usability Testing: The usability testing was used in this study to assess students' proficiency in using both animation interfaces. It measured aspects such as clarity, task effectiveness, and the level of user satisfaction in completing a simple animation task.

Usability: Usability refers to the extent to which the interface is easy to use, understand, and allows students to complete animated tasks efficiently. This study compared the usability between virtual and desktop interfaces in terms of understanding, accuracy, and reliability.

User Engagement: User engagement refers to the level of attention, interest, and active interaction of students while using both animated interfaces. This study observed how visual and interactive features in the interface could stimulate or distract students' attention.

User Experience (UX): User experience refers to the overall perception and emotional response of users when interacting with virtual and desktop animation interfaces. This study evaluated aspects such as effectiveness, ease of use, enjoyment, and user satisfaction in the context of digital animation learning.

User Experience Questionnaire (UEQ): The UEQ was used to assess six dimensions of user experience, namely Attraction, Comprehension, Efficiency, Reliability, Stimulation, and Uniqueness. This study used the UEQ to compare students' perceptions of virtual and desktop interfaces in the context of animation.

Virtual Reality (VR) Interface: A virtual reality interface is a computer-generated 3D environment that allows animation students to interact using immersive technologies such as controllers and head-mounted displays (HMDs). This study uses the Tvori platform as a proxy for such immersive interfaces.

Chapter 14
VR to Stimulate:
The Extended of Expertise of Psychology Lecturer to Use VR in Psychology Module – A Case Study

Siti Aminah Binti Harun
https://orcid.org/0000-0002-1107-5978
Universiti Malaya Wales, Malaysia

Walton Wider
INTI International University, Malaysia

Muhammad Ashraf Fauzi
Universiti Malaysia Pahang Al-Sultan Abdullah, Malaysia

Nur Salimah Alias
https://orcid.org/0000-0002-6256-9302
Universiti Malaysia Perlis, Malaysia

Vishalini R. Sivaperegasam
https://orcid.org/0009-0001-8446-2151
Universiti Malaya-Wales, Malaysia

ABSTRACT

The purpose of this study is to explore and support the model fit in explaining the possible determinants of VR implementation readiness among Psychology Lecturer. This finding involved lecturer participants and partial least square structural equation modeling (PLS-SEM) was used to analyze the data. TPB theory emphasized two main determinants in arguing the intention of readiness towards VR implementation.

DOI: 10.4018/979-8-3373-5157-5.ch014

These certain determinants exhibit their measurable and perceived characteristics. Data was collected via an online questionnaire survey as the research design used in this study was quantitative. The respondents were Malaysian ranging from 26 to 44 years old. The measurement model specifies the construct's internal consistency reliability (0.811-0.850) denoting strong internal consistency reliability. Convergent validity shows indicator loadings passed the threshold value of 0.60, discriminant validity analyzed via the (HTMT) which shows satisfactory lower threshold value of 0.80. All the determinants exert a significant on readiness, while subjective norm has no significant.

INTRODUCTION

Lecturing theoretical facts is part of clear understating measure which reflects students understanding to explore, yet there were some pedagogies should be considered. Alternatives and approaches came through centuries with applicable to reach the main learning outcome to be fulfil. Lecturer with clear mindset will available to learn and adopt, communication, cleared objectives and multiplayer indicate the teaching to be effective yet it must reach the student experience of learning to be satisfied and understanding. Technology also will main the important part in this application, which comply with readiness of lecturer to used Virtual Reality (VR) as one of alternate to teaching methodology and promote effective and affiant learning of individual.

Psychology is one of the programs that may seem theoretical and practice must enclose the elements, hence the learning must be an interactive in making sure the certain element can see practicable, which virtual reality will share this scenario and promote leaning effectiveness. Readiness is accepting this digital technology compared to more modern models' studies and factors behind it. Lecturer with knowledge and higher module understanding will trying the best to comply with syllabus and accreditation which intentionally follows the trends and practice with current technology. Is not only in subject matters of academic for psychology programme, but psychology practiced difference sectors may experiences of readiness, as they later will coordinate or supervised the students in industrial training for psychology.

Studies have indicated that the digital transformation has the capacity to impact any sector or organization (Naji et al., 2024; Maki et al., 2022; Matt et al., 2015). Although digital transformation was incorporated into construction practices early on, it is also simplifying the process to better meet the needs and preferences of modern users or generations.

Additionally, virtual reality makes it possible to simulate intricate interactions, such giving feedback or settling disputes inside a group therapy session, which is one of the courses in the level 6 psychology curriculum. Through these immersive experiences, participants can safely improve their communication and emotional control abilities. (Christofi et al., 2022; Kamińska et al., 2019). Engaging with virtual characters also facilitates the simulation of unresponsive relationships caused by economic status, self-expression, and ethnic pressure—all of which are growing increasingly significant in today's society (Dubiel et al., 2025).

As to the author, the framework of this conceptual model will be established by the research findings output, restricting it to solutions that concentrate on the use of virtual reality in soft skills in professional or educational contexts. In this research, it is explained how virtual reality may be used to teach soft skills in an efficient manner by creating interactions that are tailored to the end psychology students. Studies on virtual reality 's application in therapy or changing health-related behaviors, might, nevertheless, be directly tied to the setting of soft skills education. In order to get more specific goals and clearly defined of psychology lecturer readiness research's framework, author emphasis additional variables like expertise, awareness and virtual reality tools assisted into soft skills learning.

Despite the undergraduate requirements for psychology programs are in line with Malaysian Qualifications Agency (MQA) requirements, various psychology students may have varying learning styles. Students have amazing opportunity to visualize and showcase their designs through virtual reality. On the other hand, nothing is known about how the immersive virtual reality experience might enhance design education. The function of co-created (with students) virtual reality modules in educational psychology chapters is examined in this study. with an activity that focuses on the specifics of the theories' creation in the application of psychology, with a particular emphasis on pedagogy construction. In order to provide psychology lecturers with useful insights and frameworks for leveraging the new learning resources, this paper attempts to outline the pedagogical opportunities and difficulties of implementing virtual reality.

The author believes that by using this study framework findings of psychology lecturers readiness, it will be possible to obtain helpful findings that will raise the level of preparedness and intention to integrate virtual reality in psychology courses. In order to enable engagement with both real and virtual objects and situations, psychology lecturers will use their expertise in pedagogy, a fundamental area of psychology, to help their students see the actual world alongside realistic virtual objects. The students' real-world surroundings are replaced by a fully immersive digital environment created by virtual reality. It allows interaction with virtual objects and sights by immersing the user in a completely fabricated digital environment. In terms of hardware, virtual reality makes use of hand-navigating devices and immersive headsets. Virtual reality is a new paradigm in human-computer interaction that is primarily achieved using virtual reality technologies. It may also be installed using smartphones, tablets, and other devices with screens to show students augmented scenarios in real time.

In the quickly changing educational landscape of today, it is essential to comprehend the use and potential of virtual reality in higher education, particularly in such disciplines like psychology. It has been demonstrated that virtual reality enhances learning in a number of ways, including skill development, retention, and engagement. (Andalib & Monsur, 2024).

LITERATURE - READINESS OF PSYCHOLOGY LECTURE TOWARDS VR

Understanding the antecedents in each crisis, will promotes the extensive understanding in solving the crisis, yet the crisis must have the level assessment, in order to increase or decrease. The readiness, will define through many kinds of components. One of the components will testify through model testing with complete practices of data which will infer the certain group population. As in this research, the group of lecturers comply for difference generation perspectives, but through learning and training standard by Malaysian Qualification Accreditation, lecturer may face the same kind of syllabus of training in technologies practices.

The level of readiness should be understandable by the position of duties as lecturer and accepted with clear compromise especially in Psychology which promotes trend understating and captured. Psychologies programme which indicates the study in giving the best practice services must have better and reliable readiness. The future must foresee as the industrial services effectiveness for learning outcome and engage with students learning time as industrial need may succeed for both components in assessment based on creation modules for accreditation and completed syllabus in Psychology programme. The level of use of technologies and their most relevant applications in the industrial services towards educating and awareness making it possible to measure the level of adoption of these technologies (Ribeiro et al., 2024)

Literature – VR practice components

Virtual Reality may seem the best ideal to practice all the theoretical studies in Psychology. The main idea to show the ideal response from those whom practice the syllabus in psychology and creating the possible scenario may reflects. This is important for future graduates to understand the situation and make believe the super expecting to handle the scenario. This is the best way to speed up the understand, comprehended the knowledge and test the information received through visual practice using VR, especially lecturer in psychology. Competence and highly reliable of therapeutic may be introversion impose the given idea to students in understand more. In order to enhance the professional services qualities like lecturer and consultants, reality technology to be introduce for example virtual reality in study courses. The purpose of the study is to form a complex for improving the professional qualities of trainers based on virtual and additional reality technology (Kuspanov et al., 2024).

Lecturing represents one of the services that provides the medium to improve students via innovative formulation and encourage successful instruction. Digital technology creates trustworthy data that is exposed to successive generations. In order to make this digital technology believable, train in gaudily became the variable consonant. Outcome Based Education's (OBE) success will also be aided by a clear curriculum and regulated accreditation. Digital transformation has been made possible by the quick development of digital technology in many industries. By means of the phases of problem orientation, organizing students to learn, directing individual and group investigations, developing and presenting work results, and analyzing and evaluating the problem-solving process, the analysis's findings illustrate how the use of problem-based learning models can enhance students' capacity for creative thought. According to the recent study's findings, problem-based learning approaches have been successful in enhancing students' capacity for original thought, fluency, flexibility, and elaboration (Benu, et al., 2025). Effective problem-based learning activities in virtual reality will improve psychology education, particularly behavioral learning theory, which depends on a distinct stimulus-response relationship.

Integrating creativity and innovation into the university curriculum varies significantly across educational systems and countries (Fauzi et al., 2021). The best opinions as we can see from Indonesia. Scientific discoveries and technical developments have impacted Indonesia's e-learning system redesign. This exciting curriculum could have a big influence on Indonesian education going forward (Kyritsi and Davis, 2021). For instance, author visiting a laboratory in Pekan Baru, Indonesia, which encourages engaging virtual reality practice, demonstrates the participatory concept of virtual reality development. In another counties like Scotland, the Scottish Curriculum for Excellence (SCE), which emphasizes creativity as a fundamental element of teaching and learning, is a ray of hope in other nations like Scotland. It acknowledges how crucial creativity is to the growth of critical thinking and problem-solving abilities (Isabirye, et al, 2025).

Recent studies by Edwin also demonstrate that academic discussion, critical reflection, blended learning, inquiry-based learning, and clinical simulation can all promote critical thinking. Digital technology, community connections, interdisciplinary projects, and interprofessional education all foster collaboration. Project-based learning, augmented reality, artificial intelligence, maker education, and methodologies all foster creativity. Digital media, mentoring, narrative-based learning, and simulation training all improve communication (Edwin, et al., 2025).

Therefore, the framework model that this author proposed is evolving as important players in Malaysia's education sectors gradually recognize and embrace the many opportunities and related advantages of utilizing digital tools and technologies to enhance the performance and results of learning outcomes-based education (OBE) in psychology at the undergraduate level.

The alignments of the activities created by psychology instructors are crucial, regardless of whether they passed the test. The storyboard can include artwork, all of the learning objectives that have been set up, and any information that corresponds with a specific outcome. This makes the storyboard a vital place to apply virtual reality. The labelling can be relevant results for several tasks, the entire page, or how we set up the goal and results of virtual reality experiments or implementation. The storyboard's layout makes the notion presented obvious. In virtual reality -assisted tools, storyboard builders are crucial, and their knowledge is included in table 4's results according to MQA specifications. Depending on the organization, the specific outcome, and the verbing, other words may be used. Three or four determinants make up virtual reality -assisted tools' widgets, which can communicate each learning module's goal in a psychological program. Social tools, such as the understanding of external elements in TPB and the addition of a variable to determine the preparedness of psychology lecturers, irrespective of age or location, to adopt virtual reality practice. All of these factors, particularly the ambition to use virtual reality tools, affect the psychology lecturer's preparedness.

Under the direction of Sengupta, psychology was first studied as a scientific discipline in India in 1905 and as a university course at the University of Calcutta in 1916. Shortly after, India started to professionalize psychology as early as the 1920s, carving a professional niche for dynamic psychology. India, one of the nations with the fastest rate of digitalization through software engineering, places a strong emphasis on innovation and encourages the use of virtual reality. It attempted to provide the fundamentals by creating official training courses in applied psychology and a psychoanalysis course for psychology majors at the University of Calcutta (Manickam & Sruthi, 2025).

As to the author, the use of virtual reality technology and the knowledge of psychology lecturers will result in certain stimulated interactive boards that will improve psychology lesson delivery, particularly in modules that include illustrations, such as Biological Psychology and Sensation. To improve psychology education, some storyboard elements might be more appealing to the younger generation. Certain storyboards may have varied formatting depending on the century, such as SCOM, which was most commonly used in the 1990s. To comprehend the learning objectives in psychology, it is highly likely that some topics must begin with the experience of a psychology instructor.

New ideas for understanding educators' ready for supported virtual reality tools or assisted technologies, particularly those instructing based on theories and models, were added in recent studies in 2025 together with the out-of-date research on readiness.

The goal of navigating these experts' discussions is to better understand virtual reality practice in psychology by applying the new conceptual model theories for expanded TPB. It's critical to divide the materials according to specialized knowledge in order to foster creativity and increase user-teacher interaction.

In terms of widget comprehension for completion, the content may vary. Both open-ended and closed-ended activities are possible. These few factors could change depending on the psychology program's conception. When using virtual reality, everything must be in line with the psychology lecturer's expertise. Using multiple-step selection to either solve the problem or assess the cases will return to the essential concepts of psychology education, which fosters a deeper comprehension of psychology courses. In order to have a high level of engagement and an interactive virtual reality implementation session, the employment of Artificial Intelligence (AI) assistance will involve additional socialization duties. The commission for scoring the engagement erupted. The score could be utilized by the psychology lecturer to randomly assign tasks in virtual reality storyboards or aided software. Apparently to the author, this framework test will provide statistical support and thorough references for psychology researchers to expand on this concept in order to enhance psychology learning theories and make psychology programs dependable and user-friendly in digital technology.

In 2024, Andalibn and associates examined virtual reality applications across a range of educational domains, verifying that implementing virtual reality technologies improved student learning. Virtual reality enables exploratory learning, allowing students to test creative solutions in a risk-free setting and replicate real-world situations that might not be otherwise available (Andalibn & Monsur, 2024).

The outcomes of the author's research expecting that the use of virtual reality technology in education, especially in courses on construct applied psychology, improves the learning process by giving students information-building strategies or steps to follow, while reducing behavior risk factors, fostering enjoyment, and integrating with other psychological theories. This bolsters the case for using virtual reality in psychology courses like clinical psychology, perception, and sensation and motivation in order to create a cooperative and engaging learning environment.

METHODOLGY ANALYSIS; EXPLORING MODEL FIT R^2 & PATH COEFFICIENT TOWARDS READINESS TO VR

This study explores the model fit of readiness. Psychology lecture consist clear antecedents to understand the imply technologies especially virtual reality practice. Through PLS-SEM this study integrates all possible determinants to understand readiness behavior. The particular idea in extent to give evidence towards the idea of readiness with clear discussion towards variable. The main objective of this study, to prepare the services, accreditation body and syllabus practice suggested the virtual reality practice in Psychology Programs subjects or module in order to promote more interactive learning and understand among undergraduate level. Psychology lecture ranges from 26 to 44 years old had clear rules to be a part of the those experts and practice the model features, in making sure students understand, but with virtual reality readiness components, it will give more scientific evidence in order this virtual reality practice can be assimilate in clear rule listed by accreditation bodies especially for APA standards.

To assess the theoretical effectiveness of virtual reality's readiness implementation along six different variables under external (subjective norms and VR tools) and internal (PBC, Attitude, Experts and Awareness) factors. Respondent sampling stratified clear among 68 psychology lecture compline 0.005% from each fourteen state in Malaysia. Tested model fit will comply through R^2 value assumptions. Value of R^2 provide information about the dependent variables (endogenous) the extent of variation created by the independent variables (exogenous). Higher R^2 values suggest that the structural model can predict. In SmartPLS, the exogenous to endogenous variables were being tested for structural model by using the path coefficient indicator value, and t-values. Variance will communicate all determinants either to be justice for theory fitting. Most of the listed variable must exceed the 50%, which indicate complete determinants identifier. Authors believe this method of analysis complied more reliable statistic evidence.

In order to be justified and pondering by accredited body, syllabus committee and psychology practices the clear methodology analysis must be used, with clear gap and sample inferring. It is a matter of time, more testifying model fit will be computed through these studies and become one the main idea triggered. This is the future understanding compliance in making sure studying psychology and enrolling into psychology under graduate level programme will become more reliable and vibrant.

RESULT ANALYSIS

Results shown Intention was able to explain 60.8% of the variance in six main factors. It manages to explain the readiness implementation towards VR. For the six predictors on VRRD, the coefficient of determination, R^2 was 0.608. PBC, AWR ($\beta = 0.261$, $p< 0.001$), EXPERT ($\beta = 0.450$, $p< 0.01$), and ATT ($\beta = 0.004$, $p< 0.001$), were found to have positive relationship towards VRRD, thus supporting H1. Meanwhile for VRTools ($\beta = 0.339$), and Subjective Norm ($\beta = -0.091$), were found to be insignificant towards VRRD, thus only VRTools supporting H2.

Result Discussion Hypothesis 1: H1: Internal has positive influence on readiness of VR implementation

The readiness elements include attitude, the TPB variable PBC, and one external variable, awareness. Based on the analysis of those aspects, the author believes that three determinants influence the components that they impact. The theory of planned behavior and the norm activation model are the two primary psychological theories that are most commonly applied and acknowledged in the study of such problems. The theory of planned behavior (TPB) was put forth by Ajzen in 1985 and 1991.

To test the implementation of virtual reality's theoretical efficacy across internal (PBC, Attitude, Awareness and Experts), author considered expertise to consider theory-driven training design, which increases the potential to better understand what features of virtual reality promote psychology lecturer and how they do so. The results of this study provide a clear theoretical analysis of the advantages, disadvantages, and prospects of implementing virtual reality readiness among psychology lecturers. These also provide more insightful recommendations and encourage additional discussion.

The author's results are also in line with the Manickam research findings in 2025, which highlight the unmistakable proof of expert determinants. In this regard, virtual reality holds great promise, especially for the instruction of technical or procedural knowledge. However, existing literature also acknowledges the advantages of psychomotor skills, particularly visual scanning, affective skills, which are linked to controlling emotional reactions in stressful situations, and cognitive and observational abilities connected to spatial and visual information which explain through virtual reality implementation (Manickam et al.,2025).

H1 findings show any new practice in humans will be easier to comprehend if the inner modifier's emphases are emphasized. The legitimate retention of memories that show a strong desire to succeed will be dragged by internal struggle. Internal elements, like as attitude, PBC, and expertise, are typically driven by internal capabilities. One of the trustworthy theories with a strong intuition for attitude is TPB.

However, when combined with the expertise variable, it still demonstrates the irreversible HTMT and significance, which also mirrors the responders, a psychology lecturer who represents the accreditation and syllabus committee.

There were many researches communize the idea of TPB, but when induce with extended variable showing less than 50% variance which affect the Psychology Lecturer readiness towards virtual reality implementation. Respected with region factors, regardless of demographic factors, these will be declined as the training purpose already given in OBE and Accredited awareness. Clearly the experts which one of the indicators or a must component must be settled before people involved in Psychology services and pedagogies.

Industry partners will be future sample, which indicate the industrial need will give statistically variance in theoretical testing in future study. Likewise, researcher intend to explore more on the locus of perceived behavior control in proposed extended TPB by injecting the expert's variable.

The idea that psychology lecturer mentions virtual reality as one of the tools for introducing the greatest psychological modules during a lecture session may be expanded upon by expert variables. The underlying cause of the age difference in GAP between the new and older lecturers may be a difference in awareness of virtual reality. The majority of the preparedness demonstrates personal willingness for the purpose of psychological development. Although there is no clear difference in readiness between the older and younger lectures, someone with knowledge can be thought of as someone who is willing to teach the psychology module utilizing virtual reality.

Based on the findings, the author believes that PBC and preparedness attitudes among psychology lecturers meet the requirements for comprehending psychological themes, which can be significantly in line with the activities or chapter advancement of psychology modules. Module theories will be used as part of that, as the characteristics of the psychology lecturer will govern how the virtual preparation exercise is understood to manage behavior. It is anticipated that the psychology module will provide knowledge that interacts and will entice students to learn psychology, particularly the applied theories. If it is demonstrating the portion of applied theories in psychology, many psychology modules' model theories will be more specific to particular circumstances in psychological behavior research. As psychology lecturers, attitudes may appear to have the best psychological qualities since they will provide brilliant concepts for behavioral modification and psychological thought.

Biological psychology, health psychology, and cognitive psychology are examples of modules that might appear more credible if they are demonstrated via the process, providing clear and stimulating images of how psychology functions in the brain. The concepts of reading, writing, and typing with Cisco software may be included into psychology programs. employing software such as Kahoot and returning to conventional methods such as physical and restricted access. Active learning will keep students and instructors interested and enhance learning.

Engaging psychology lecturers helps students learn and stay motivated in their education. Students will be encouraged to learn more and participate more if this interactive learning is demonstrated in psychology modules through virtual reality practice. Maintaining student engagement is the biggest problem; effectively utilizing virtual reality will highlight the generational divide between the lecturer and the pupils. One technology that makes it clearer how to engage and connect with the Malaysian population's Alpha, Beta, and Gen Z is virtual reality. Recent studies by Kuspanov (2024) also appear to support H1 findings.

It may appear from recent studies that different regions affect the lecture. Due to the fact that virtual reality will be more engaging when students use their phones in lecture, it is possible that students could become easily detached. Hold courses could be stimulated by virtual reality to regain attention. Engaging with virtual reality stimulation and the resulting interactive storyboards lesson is enjoyable. Utilizing specific software in relation to virtual reality practices in order to maximize device idea of virtual reality preparedness among psychology instructors will result from the use of pairing in virtual reality practices and interaction (Isabirye, et al, 2025).

According to the author's attempt to elucidate the significance of expert factors in this investigation, this result is consistent with a 2025 Elaish' bibliometric analysis study. Since virtual reality technology offers immersive and captivating learning experiences, it has the potential to improve teaching and learning outcomes in the classroom. Although the use of virtual reality in educational settings is becoming more popular, more research is required to fully comprehend its pedagogical efficacy and address related issues and difficulties. To learn more about the current status of virtual reality integration in education, this bibliometric study thoroughly examines 1,157 pertinent papers from the Science Citation Index Expanded (SCI-EXPANDED) and the Social Science Citation Index (SSCI) (Elaish et al., 2025).

The analysis revealed variation in virtual reality adoption and research output across countries and institutions, underscoring the importance of collaboration and knowledge-sharing in the field. Key research areas and trends, such as the use of virtual reality for skill development and training, were identified. Additionally, the study highlighted the need for more research on the pedagogical effectiveness of virtual reality. The findings carry practical implications for guiding future research shaping policy decisions and advocating for a concerted effort to harness virtual reality's capabilities in education. This study serves as a practical roadmap, promoting the implementation and improvement of virtual reality technology and fostering equitable and inclusive educational practices.

Hypothesis 2: H2: External has positive influence on readiness of VR implementation

In simple terms, education is the goal of the syllabus, which upholds the spirit of psychology. In order to ensure that psychology education is both participatory and transparent, the technique taught through psychology theory are implied in future student responses. With regard to training, the same accreditation, and the objectives of OBE, the goals became certified, and virtual reality or any other digital or comprehend technologies must be applied to satisfy the future preferences of undergraduate level students. Graduates of psychology schools around the world might be endowed with a variety of psychology lectures readiness and intention. H2 may appear to be a valid reference to the extended TPB framework, according to the author's findings. According to the author's 2025 study, many of the studies that discussed VR techniques worldwide also included the generational divide between lecturers and students.

This is significant since the present Z generation and the upcoming Beta generation might end up being this Z generation's future students. There is a rebroadcast, and it needs to be in line with what is taught in schools for the generation that has demonstrated a definite readiness and passion for technology, particularly digital technology, in their day-to-day lives (Harun et al., 2024). In actuality, TPB already demonstrates the importance of the subjective norms' variable in relation to daily intention actions. As we examine the point of view of availability for sources like intent, thumbing tools, and others, it causes a lower threshold when awareness is introduced into the model framework in this study and exhibits a lower reaction. External factors continuously divert the Awareness and Subjective Norm in virtual reality implementation because of the limited access of internet, sources and community sharing.

When using a combination of pedagogies for virtual reality practice, role-playing techniques might not seem to work well with virtual reality -assisted technologies. Students act out a situation relevant to the subject area by assuming roles (such as professionals, stakeholders, or historical individuals). The reason it's interactive promotes the application of theory to practice, empathy, and problem-solving skills.

According to the author's H2 findings, students will benefit from additional practice with quick enactments in virtual reality visualizations that survive longer in working memory and are recalled to be expected in long-term memory. Specifically, the theories of clinical psychology, personality, and counseling will be represented. Literally altering the virtual reality tools with individual or group assistance. Understanding the positive purpose to be ready for virtual reality implementation in psychology modules was carried out by student involvement and virtual reality -assisted technologies.

Author finding shown as H2, Psychology lecturer subjective norm through Contemporary teaching and learning involves the development of virtual reality tools that are ready for implementation, as well as the benefit of having a deeper understanding of psychology modules such as industrial and organizational psychology, motivation and sensation, and an introduction to psychology. Although the knowledge principle is more significant, the goal of psychology classes is to satisfy the achievement of both CLOs and PLOs. Therefore, the use of virtual reality in the psychology module would put the practical 5 and affective 3 to the test. As the story comes to a close, the greatest incentive to learn will come from more engagement with virtual reality tools. Virtual reality practice will also feel meaningful in accordance with group activities. The group will attempt to engage students' skills and relate the aspects of psychology that are most effective in practical idea sessions to real-world activities.

These authors finding are accordance with current study by Manousou, (2025). Typical lecture versus interactive teaching methodology, which includes five methods: role-playing, flipped classroom, problem-based learning, and the jigsaw method. Since both psychology lecturer components focused on the problem that applied pedagogy to answer using virtual reality supported tools, the case study employing virtual reality is more engaging. Consider how virtual reality stimulation in psychology modules could help students better understand the instances. As a scientific discipline, psychology may be comparable to other disciplines in that it uses virtual reality to help solve problems and provide support.

The jigsaw method is the easiest technique for virtual reality specialists to create a storyline in virtual reality, according to the author's findings in H2. Its participatory nature promotes accountability, collective learning, and peer education. It is the psychology lecturer's responsibility to split the audience up into groups, show a short text or movie to each group, and then bring them back together to go over the key ideas.

Jigsaw methods is the most effective pedogagy approached in intuiting the virtual reality practice, especially when the output of this research study clearly mentioned of virtual reality expertise determinants. Special group will cover certain CLOs module in psychology and as virtual reality applied this approaches and presented to assess the knowledge through assisted software like Figma and fixed Jammed .

Psychology numerical topics are now better understood thanks to innovative teaching techniques like problem-based learning, modeling, interactive technologies, and gamification. Students' motivation and engagement rose as a result of the diaries' assistance in understanding their own learning progress. The visualization of statistical or numerical in Statistical Psychology, Research Method and Psychological Testing modules processes was enhanced by the use of virtual reality implementation. The integration of cutting-edge technologies into the educational process and to enhance methodological approaches to numerical instruction in higher education. (Коберник, 2025).

According to the author, the H2 result was consistent with the findings of the 2025 study, which suggests that the importance of cultivating lecturer' creative and original thinking skills, as well as the part these skills play in scientific research procedures in virtual reality. In order to address issues like the introduction of new pedagogical technologies, the efficient organization of scientific research, and the modernization of the management system, the research examines current scientific studies and real-world experiences pertaining to the development of leadership creative competence within the Uzbek educational system. The paper also offers practical suggestions for the development of creative competency as well as an inventive management paradigm (Ismoilov, 2025).

In order to encourage critical thinking through both synchronous and asynchronous interactions in e-learning environments, psychology lecturer need purposefully modify their educational approaches which trying to implement the virtual preality practices. According to research, well-designed remote learning digital environments can support cognitive growth and the acquisition of critical thinking-related abilities such student autonomy, metacognitive awareness, and self-directed learning. (Manousou, 2025).

In any educational context, incorporating cutting-edge tactics and ideas into different teaching modalities like problem-based learning and collaborative learning will cultivate essential traits in students. Examining how problem-based learning and collaborative learning affect character development in open and distance learning (Karunanayaka, 2025).

Student identification and determinants may be impacted by the virtual reality readiness objective. Students can practice problem-based learning using software-assisted activities like wool clap and virtual reality. Apple apps also advertise this virtual reality method. Given that virtual reality learning environments have a positive impact on students' learning satisfaction, it is crucial to identify the key components of these environments that foster this enjoyment, according to Wiafe and colleagues' 2025 findings, which align with the author's H2 findings on VR-Tools. This study examined the psychological effects of persuasive elements in a persuasive immersive virtual reality learning environment on students' learning satisfaction (Wiafe et al., 2025).

Figure 1. Structural Model Testing Results

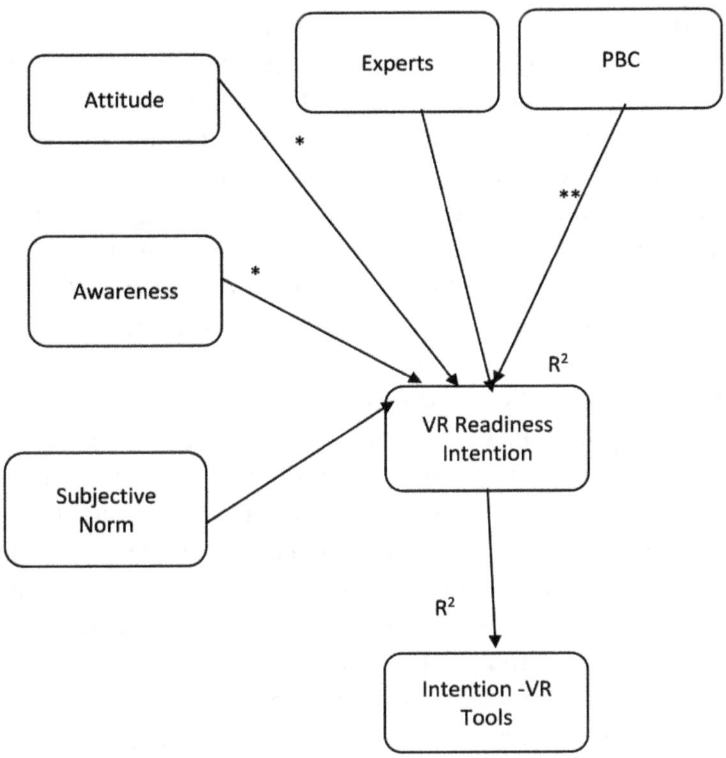

CONCLUSION

Collaboration and knowledge-sharing are crucial in the industry, as the investigation showed differences in virtual reality usage and research output between nations and universities. The use of virtual reality for training and skill development was selected as one of the main research areas and trends. The study on experts factors also emphasized the necessity for additional investigation into virtual reality's pedagogical efficacy. This study framework of extended TPB Model have intended in directing future studies, influencing legislative choices, and promoting a determined attempt to fully utilize virtual reality's potential in the lecturing. By encouraging the adoption and advancement of virtual reality technology and supporting inclusive and equitable teaching methods, this author study finding of H1 and H2 acts as a useful direction.

Model testing also became a tool for projecting the concept. Psychologists, particularly those who specialize in communicating with the public, must take into account unforeseen factors. We may develop the virtual reality practice into succession to reflect the psychology program adhering to the ideal trans and subjects to generation norms. Throughout the centuries, the people who practice the psychology lesson may have different attitudes and preferences. They may also stand still by adhering to the accreditation standards. The proposed framework would allow researchers and construction course experts to develop an evaluation tool similar to the analytical hierarchy process (AHP) or structural equation model (SEM) that would measure and rate a psychology undergraduate's readiness for digital transformation at the university level.

The pre-construction, construction, and facility management stages might all employ this paradigm. Current framework of Virtual reality research in psychology was developed as a result of this research to help facility management companies, clients, organizations, contractors, and designers understand how digital transformation is implemented in their respective domains and to support decision-makers in setting up action to adapt related technologies in their respective phases. Phases follow through the accreditation with two prospective regions, like western and eastern, which may also vary the virtual reality readiness. Universiti Malaya Wales, which practices the Dual Award Programme, may contribute to this model fit framework and projects a futuristic and interactive program of psychology, delivered at Universiti Malaya Wales. Universiti Malaya Wales Dual Award programmes are given the opportunity to study for a United Kingdom degree in Malaysia, and are offered in collaboration with partner university, the University of Wales Trinity Saint David (UWTSD). As a future graduate, student will receive certification from both Universiti Malaya Wales and UWTSD.

Virtual reality practicing may give future experiences when applied to these two universities, and may communicate more effectively with psychology practice in Malaysia and the United Kingdom. Through these our psychologist study findings, the framework may appear to highlight the relevance of virtual reality practice among psychology lecturers and engage with a futuristic syllabus that may comply with the different seasons in the United Kingdom and promotes interactive learning with the ideal of cross-cultural learning. Psychology students can also be assured of the strength and quality, as the courses are structured, monitored, and assessed by two different institutions, both Universiti Malaya Wales and the University of Wales Trinity Saint David.

Virtual reality practice will be more prominent as basic of this model testing framework from this study, which are both universities Universiti Malaya Wales and the University of Wales Trinity Saint David, are recognised for offering a curriculum that is vocationally relevant, addressing the needs of employers and creating a meaningful impact on communities by equipping graduates with the essential skills to thrive in an ever-evolving world. Through collaborations, these two universities strive to provide more individuals with the opportunity to benefit from higher education and to use their skills and knowledge to benefit society.

Universiti Malaya Wales is an institution that takes the initiative to understand this virtual reality, deliberately assisted with Apple Play, Apple Tutor, and more. One of the pillars implemented the idea of virtual reality practice through assisted software like Open Learning and focused on a few public and private universities in Malaysia, for example, UTHM, IMU, HELP, and UKM. These additional initiatives prompt psychology lecturers to be more proactive in understanding this digitally assisted behavior. Psychologists analyze these common assisted behaviors. Right, the virtual reality implementation will be more vital and reliable psychologically at Universiti Malaya Wales comprehended these ideas and believes this is important for implementing current trends and information coherence with the advancement technologies like virtual reality practicing, especially in the Malaysian setting.

Universiti Malaya Wales has created these moves to be clearer about how psychology stands and the vision of the psychology programme in communicating and creating, also producing reliable graduates who attempt to follow the current practice in generation and evaluation. These include the virtual reality practice. Entitle the courses, module, and subjects in psychology, experts are important, and the readiness towards that niche must be shaken with statistical evidence through repetitive research in psychology, including extensively tested, reliable theories and models in psychology.

Through granted research by psychology lecturers, the common encouraged activities through collaboration between public and private universities is through learning exposure by the Virtual reality storyboard practice research. Storyboard with a list of activity ideas for the completion task of psychology modules. For example, an analogy in an Artificial Intelligence assistant tool for implementing a virtual reality development activities program. An Apple teacher journey may encounter an assessment before the item in the storyboard for virtual reality intervention. Finally, analyze the user competitiveness, especially for psychology lecturer experts, as the first move to enhance the course psychology engagement. Course navigation can be one of the key areas of engagement between the user and designers. So, it's really possible for psychology studies to be more reflective and engaged. It's really happening for current research; this kind of gamification may be the key for program coordinators to implement virtual reality into certain topics that are reliable for the appearance engagement and reflection.

Recommended future studies also can be integrated between neuropsychologist and psychologist. Psychologists and neuropsychologists might collaborate on suggested future research. In order to assess the effectiveness of teaching psychology students about the relationships between brain structures and spatial visualization, virtual reality has been used into psychology modules, chapters, syllabuses, and instructional programs. Using three-dimensional (3D) depiction of anatomy contents, certain technologies have been put into place to make learning anatomy easier. One technology that shows promise in this area is augmented reality (AR). To visualize the morphological and functional details of the brain, a mobile augmented reality application was created.

Additionally, the author actively invests in a suicidal intent study mobile app application that helps divert attention from suicidal intent, raises awareness of mental health care, and encourages higher gurdian interaction to learn about psychology, all of which help to market psychology programs in Malaysia through initiatives from psychology lecturers with expertise. Recent bibliometric analyses of completed exams for visuospatial ability, anatomical knowledge, learning objectives, and technological experience were examined by the author as part of that.

ACKNOWLEDGMENT

Authors wishing to acknowledge assistance or encouragement financial & institutional support, under academic allocation funding Universiti Malaya Wales (RMC/2024/11- UM-Wales Internal Research Grant 2024).

REFERENCES

Andalib, S. Y., & Monsur, M. (2024). Co-created virtual reality (VR) modules in landscape architecture education: A mixed methods study investigating the pedagogical effectiveness of VR. *Education Sciences*, *14*(6), 553. DOI: 10.3390/educsci14060553

Benu, S., & Natonis, H. Y. (2025). Improving Students' Creative Thinking Abilitiesthrough Problem Based Learning Model. *International Journal of Christian Education and Philosophical Inquiry*, *2*(3), 42–51.

Christofi, M., Lamprinakos, G., Nguyen, D. K., & Tran, P. T. (2025). Digital strategy design and digital transformation: A review and future research directions. *International Marketing Review*, 1–22.

Dubiel, A., Kamińska, D., Zwoliński, G., Ramić-Brkić, B., Agostini, D., & Zancanaro, M. (2025). Virtual reality for the training of soft skills for professional education: Trends and opportunities. *Interactive Learning Environments*, *33*(5), 1–21. DOI: 10.1080/10494820.2025.2450634

Edwin, E., Widiana, I. W., Lasmawan, I. W., & Suharta, I. G. P. (2025). Curriculum transformation towards future education. *Prima Magistra: Jurnal Ilmiah Kependidikan*, *6*(2), 122–132.

Elaish, M. M., Yadegaridehkordi, E., & Ho, Y. S. (2025). Publication performance and trends in virtual reality research in education fields: A bibliometric analysis. *Multimedia Tools and Applications*, *84*(10), 6999–7026. DOI: 10.1007/s11042-024-19238-0

Fauzi, M. A., Harun, S. A., Martin, T., Paiman, N., & Firdaus Hussin, M. S. (2021). Smartphone Addiction among Young Adolescents: Integration of Flow Theory and Fear of Missing Out. *International Journal of Information & Management Sciences*, *32*(1).

Harun, S. A., & Alias, N. S. (2015). Culture Changes and Personality Types Relationship among UTM International Academic Staff. *International Education Studies*, *8*(13).

Harun, S. A., & Ibrahim, M. F. (2024). Virtual reality & current practices (an introduction to widad farokam). *Jurnal Pembangunan Sosial*, *27*, 69–87. DOI: 10.32890/jps2024.27.4

Harun, S. A. B., Kasim, N. M., Jinnah, A. B. M. A., Fahmi, F. B., Sundaralinggam, N. A., Khalili, D. A. B., & Saharudin, N. W. N. B. (2020, May). Widad Psychetra Door (WPD) as New Mobile Application (APPS). *Journal of Physics: Conference Series*, *1529*(5), 052097.

Harun, S. A., Noor, A. A. M., Khair, N. N. S., Saharudin, N. W. N., & Pei, T. P. (2018). Openness Personality among Autistic Children Teachers in Malaysia. A Case Study in One Private Centre. *Global Business and Management Research*, *10*(3), 465.

Harun, S. A., Yusof, J. N., Ibrahim, A., & Abdullah, N. (2015). Rationalizing the Limitation of Passive Students through Contextual Teaching. *Journal of Management Research*, *7*(2), 295.

Ibrahim, M. F. B., Rahman, N. B., Zulkafli, M. H. B., Kasim, N. B., & Harun, S. A. (2021, April). Widad FAROKAM – Virtual System. In Journal of Science and Management Research (7 (April), 23-29). Wardah Publishing.

Isabirye, A. K., Moloi, K. C., Lebelo, R. S., & Khan, S. (2025). Cultivating Creativity and Innovation in the School Curriculum for the 21st Century: Opportunities and Challenges. *Journal of Ecohumanism*, *4*(3), 334–348. DOI: 10.62754/joe.v4i3.6647

Ismoilov, S. (2025). Formation Of Creative Competence Of Leading Personnel In Higher Education Institutions. *International Journal of Artificial Intelligence*, *1*(1), 381–386.

Kamińska, D., Sapiński, T., Wiak, S., Tikk, T., Haamer, R. E., Avots, E., & Anbarjafari, G. (2019). Virtual reality and its applications in education: Survey. *Information (Basel)*, *10*(10), 318.

Karunanayaka, S. P. (2025). Promoting Professional Practice in Education through Innovative Thinking. *Journal of Innovative Practices in Education*, *1*(1), 1–8. DOI: 10.4038/jipe.v1i1.1

Kyritsi, K., & Davis, J. M. (2021). Creativity in primary schools: An analysis of a teacher's attempt to foster childhood creativity within the context of the Scottish Curriculum for Excellence. *Improving Schools*, *24*(1), 47–61.

Kuspanov, N., Botagariyev, T., Ryskaliyev, S., Doshybekov, A., Syzdykov, A., & Gabitov, A. (2024). The influence of information technology on the professional readiness of future trainers in Kazaksha kures. *Retos: nuevas tendencias en educación física, deporte y recreación*, (51), 365-372.

Maki, O.; Alshaikhli, M.; Gunduz, M.; Naji, K.K.; Abdulwahed, M. (2022). Development of digitalization road map for Healthcare Facility Management. IEEE Access 2022, 10, 14450–14462.

Manickam, L. S. S., & Sruthi, E. S. (2025). Competencies Based Professional Psychology Course In India. *Indian Journal of Psychology*.

Manousou, E. (2025). Critical Thinking in Distance Education: The Challenges in a Decade (2016–2025) and the Role of Artificial Intelligence. *Education Sciences*, *15*(6), 757. DOI: 10.3390/educsci15060757

Matt, C., Hess, T., & Benlian, A. (2015). Digital Transformation Strategies. *Business & Information Systems Engineering*, *57*(5), 339–343. DOI: 10.1007/s12599-015-0401-5

Naji, K. K., Gunduz, M., Alhenzab, F., Al-Hababi, H., & Al-Qahtani, A. (2024). Assessing the Digital Transformation Readiness of the Construction Industry Utilizing the Delphi Method. *Buildings (Basel, Switzerland)*, *14*(3), 601. DOI: 10.3390/buildings14030601

Ribeiro, D. B., Coutinho, A. D. R., Satyro, W. C., Campos, F. C. D., Lima, C. R. C., Contador, J. C., & Gonçalves, R. F. (2024). The DAWN readiness model to assess the level of use of Industry 4.0 technologies in the construction industry in Brazil. *Construction Innovation*, *24*(2), 515–536. DOI: 10.1108/CI-05-2022-0114

Wiafe, I., Ekpezu, A. O., Gyamera, G. O., Winful, F. B. P., Atsakpo, E. D., Nutrokpor, C., & Gulliver, S. R. (2025). Learning satisfaction in virtual reality: The role of persuasive design. *International Journal of Human-Computer Interaction*, *41*(17), 11021–11037. DOI: 10.1080/10447318.2024.2440205

Коберник, Г. І., & Kobernyk, H. (2025). Innovative approaches to the formation of mathematical competence of future primary school teachers. Scientific Bulletin of Mukachevo State University. Series. *Pedagogy and Psychology*, *11*(1), 71–81.

Chapter 15
Digital Creativity: The Influence of Thinking Styles on Motivation in Video Production Education

Wan Nor Ashiqin Wan Ali
https://orcid.org/0000-0003-2489-2843
Universiti Malaysia Perlis, Malaysia

Wan Ahmad Jaafar Wan Yahaya
https://orcid.org/0000-0002-8605-0062
Universiti Sains Malaysia, Malaysia

ABSTRACT

This study examines the link between thinking styles; legislative, executive, and judicial, and students perceived motivation in digital creativity education. Guided by Sternberg's Mental Self-Government Theory and Keller's ARCS model, it compares learner-paced (DVC-LS) and system-paced (DVC-SS) instructional approaches. Findings reveal that legislative thinkers show greater intrinsic motivation in learner-paced settings, while executive and judicial thinkers respond better to structured, system-paced environments. The results highlight the importance of aligning instructional design with learners' cognitive styles to enhance motivation and engagement in digital creativity education. This alignment can support more personalized, effective learning experiences and inspire sustained interest in creative digital tasks.

DOI: 10.4018/979-8-3373-5157-5.ch015

INTRODUCTION

Motivation is a foundational element of effective learning, particularly in skill-based disciplines such as digital video production. Keller's ARCS model, comprising attention, relevance, confidence, and satisfaction, underscores the importance of designing learning environments that sustain engagement and encourage persistence (Keller, 2016). Within such environments, individual differences in thinking styles can play a significant role in shaping how students interact with instructional content and respond to learning stimuli (S. Chen, 2022; Emamipour & Esfandabad, 2013; Grigorenko & Sternberg, 1997). This study explores the interplay between thinking styles; legislative, executive, and judicial, and perceived motivation, with a focus on learner-paced and system-paced instructional designs in digital video production education.

Digital creativity has emerged as a vital competency in contemporary education, aligned with global trends that emphasize innovation, communication, and media literacy. It involves the ability to use digital tools and platforms to conceive, design, and produce original content. In the context of higher education, digital creativity enables students to engage in meaningful knowledge construction and self-expression, fostering deeper learning and cognitive development.

In digital video production, digital creativity is not limited to technical execution; rather, it entails a multidimensional process that includes narrative development, visual composition, editing, and critical reflection. Students are required to apply creative problem-solving skills and aesthetic judgment while working with various multimedia elements. The complex and iterative nature of this process makes sustained motivation essential, particularly as students navigate technical challenges and conceptual decision-making.

Furthermore, the development of digital creativity often requires learners to work autonomously and engage in self-regulated learning. The ability to take initiative, revise ideas, and manage creative workflows reflects a high degree of learning agency. However, such autonomy must be carefully scaffolded to accommodate diverse learner profiles. Instructional design that fails to consider cognitive preferences may inadvertently hinder engagement and limit creative expression.

In this regard, understanding how students' thinking styles influence their motivation within different instructional contexts becomes increasingly relevant. Legislative thinkers typically prefer tasks that allow for self-direction and innovation, executive thinkers excel in structured environments with clear expectations, and judicial thinkers are inclined toward critical analysis and evaluation. Aligning instructional pacing with these preferences may enhance motivational outcomes and promote deeper engagement in digital creativity tasks.

Accordingly, this study aims to examine the relationship between thinking styles and motivation in digital video production, comparing the effects of learner-paced and system-paced instructional modes. By contextualizing these findings within the broader discourse on personalized learning and digital creativity, this research contributes valuable insights for the design of effective, inclusive, and engaging creative learning environments in higher education.

LITERATURE REVIEW

Thinking Styles and Motivation

Sternberg's Mental Self-Government (MSG) theory categorizes thinking styles as preferred ways individuals govern their mental activities, analogous to forms of government. Legislative thinkers derive motivation from creative autonomy and task ownership. Executive thinkers are driven by structured guidelines, while judicial thinkers find satisfaction in evaluating and refining their work (Al-Thani et al., 2014). Legislative thinkers prefer to create their own rules and tasks, making them well-suited for open-ended assignments that allow innovation and independent exploration (Sternberg, 1997). This style aligns closely with project-based learning and inquiry-driven environments, where motivation stems from self-expression and the freedom to approach tasks in novel ways.

Executive thinkers, on the other hand, thrive in environments with clear expectations, step-by-step procedures, and concrete objectives. They are motivated when tasks have predefined goals and are guided by established criteria. In digital learning contexts, such students may perform best when provided with templates, rubrics, and structured timelines that offer predictability and reduce ambiguity. Their engagement increases when they feel confident in their ability to meet instructor-defined goals effectively.

Judicial thinkers are analytical and critical in nature. They prefer tasks that involve comparing, contrasting, critiquing, and making evaluative judgments. These learners are motivated when given opportunities to reflect on multiple perspectives, assess the quality of digital artifacts, or engage in peer review. Within digital creativity education, judicial thinkers may be particularly drawn to activities that require evaluating multimedia work, refining production based on feedback, and articulating rationale for design choices.

Research suggests that aligning instructional strategies with students' thinking styles can significantly impact motivation and performance (Fan & Zhang, 2009). When students are placed in environments that complement their preferred cognitive approaches, they are more likely to experience increased interest, effort, and persistence. Conversely, a mismatch between instructional design and thinking style may lead to disengagement or underperformance. This alignment is particularly relevant in digital creativity, where tasks often require a blend of divergent thinking, technical skills, and reflective judgment.

Incorporating thinking styles into the instructional design of digital creativity education offers the potential to personalize learning experiences and improve motivational outcomes. Educators who recognize and adapt to these cognitive preferences can better scaffold student engagement by offering varied pathways to success. For instance, providing options for both independent and guided video projects, or offering analytical as well as generative roles in collaborative production, can cater to different styles. Such differentiated approaches not only support motivation but also contribute to a more inclusive and responsive learning environment.

Digital Video Production and Motivation

Digital video production requires technical and creative skills, making it an ideal context to explore motivation. Studies show that self-paced learning enhances intrinsic motivation by fostering control and engagement (Huang et al., 2020). As a multidisciplinary process, digital video production integrates elements of storytelling, cinematography, sound design, editing, and visual effects. This convergence of cognitive, technical, and artistic domains challenges students to manage complex workflows while maintaining a coherent creative vision. The need to synthesize multiple skill sets can be both stimulating and overwhelming, making motivation a key determinant of learning outcomes and sustained effort throughout the production process.

Motivational factors in video production are often linked to autonomy, relevance, and perceived competence, components emphasized in Keller's ARCS model. When learners perceive that a project is meaningful and aligned with their interests, they are more likely to invest time and energy into it. Additionally, the iterative nature of video editing, drafting, revising, and refining content, can reinforce a sense of competence and satisfaction as students witness the tangible results of their progress (Kellems et al., 2020). These motivational drivers are particularly potent in environments that support creativity and student choice.

Digital video projects also provide authentic contexts for learning, which can increase extrinsic and intrinsic motivation. Real-world relevance, such as producing videos for campus events, community awareness, or digital portfolios, enhances the significance of the learning task and encourages students to meet higher standards. The use of digital tools mirrors industry practices, further reinforcing the value of learning and potentially influencing students' career aspirations. These connections help establish a motivational bridge between academic goals and personal development.

Instructional pacing significantly influences motivation in digital video education. Learner-paced environments often empower students to take ownership of their learning process, promoting deeper engagement and flexibility in decision-making. However, not all students thrive in unstructured settings. System-paced instruction, with fixed timelines and guided checkpoints, can support learners who benefit from external structure and accountability. By examining how different pacing modes interact with individual thinking styles, educators can better support diverse learners in achieving both creative and academic goals.

In summary, digital video production is a rich educational medium for studying motivation due to its blend of autonomy, creativity, collaboration, and technical challenge. It not only serves as a tool for content delivery but also as a means of active knowledge construction. As students navigate the creative process, their motivational states are influenced by how instruction is designed and paced, making it essential to align pedagogical strategies with learner needs and cognitive preferences.

Segmenting Principle and Motivation

Learner-paced instruction aligns with Keller's confidence and satisfaction dimensions, enabling students to feel in control. System-paced instruction supports relevance and attention by providing consistent structure (Mayer & Pilegard, 2014). The segmenting principle, derived from multimedia learning theory, suggests that breaking information into smaller, manageable parts enhances cognitive processing and reduces overload (Mayer, 2009). This approach is particularly relevant in complex learning environments such as digital video production, where students must process multiple streams of information simultaneously, visual, auditory, and procedural. Segmenting allows learners to absorb content at their own pace, which fosters a sense of mastery and reinforces motivation through progressive success.

In learner-paced environments, students can pause, review, and repeat content based on their individual needs, which promotes self-regulation and autonomy, key components of intrinsic motivation (Clark & Mayer, 2016). When students feel that they can manage their own learning, their confidence increases, and they are more likely to persist through challenges. This autonomy also supports personalization, as learners can focus on areas where they feel less competent while advancing more quickly through familiar content.

System-paced instruction, while less flexible, plays a crucial role in maintaining attention and ensuring consistency. For some learners, particularly those with executive or judicial thinking styles, structured pacing helps reduce ambiguity and anxiety, allowing them to stay focused and aligned with course expectations.

Systematic sequencing of content and fixed deadlines can also encourage time management and discipline, both of which are essential in project-based learning contexts such as video production.

Research indicates that the effectiveness of pacing strategies is influenced by the complexity of the material and the learner's cognitive characteristics (Moreno & Mayer, 2007). For novice learners, system-paced instruction may prevent premature disengagement by scaffolding the learning process. In contrast, more advanced learners may benefit from learner-controlled environments that allow for deeper exploration and creativity. Therefore, applying the segmenting principle with consideration to learners' motivational profiles and thinking styles can lead to more effective instructional design.

In sum, the segmenting principle serves not only as a cognitive scaffold but also as a motivational tool. By aligning pacing strategies with learners' needs and cognitive styles, educators can enhance motivation through a balanced integration of structure and autonomy. In digital creativity education, where learners navigate complex tasks involving technical and creative decision-making, thoughtful application of the segmenting principle may significantly improve both engagement and learning outcomes.

The Role of Thinking Styles in Shaping Digital Creativity in Education

The concept of *digital creativity* has gained increasing attention in educational research due to the growing demand for innovation, digital literacy, and self-expression among 21st-century learners. Digital creativity refers to the capacity to generate original ideas or products using digital tools, integrating technical skills with imaginative thinking to produce multimedia content such as videos, animations, digital stories, and interactive media (Snelson, 2018; van Laar et al., 2020). As digital tools become more accessible and embedded in educational settings, fostering creativity through technology is recognized as a key strategy for preparing learners for dynamic, knowledge-based economies (Jenson & Droumeva, 2016).

Creativity in digital environments is inherently multifaceted. It involves ideation, experimentation, collaboration, problem-solving, and iterative refinement. These elements are especially pronounced in digital video production, where learners must conceptualize narratives, apply aesthetic principles, and manipulate complex technologies. Motivation and cognitive preferences play an essential role in supporting learners as they navigate these challenges (Chen et al., 2021; Georgiou & Kyza, 2018). However, not all students approach creative tasks in the same way, and differences in thinking styles may influence how they engage with digital creativity tasks.

Sternberg's theory of mental self-government offers a useful lens to examine the interaction between thinking styles and digital creativity. According to Clarke et al. (2010), individuals possess distinct thinking styles; legislative, executive, and judicial, that reflect their preferred ways of processing information and solving problems. Legislative thinkers are idea-oriented, enjoying tasks that allow for innovation and design. Executive thinkers prefer structured tasks with clear guidelines, while judicial thinkers gravitate towards analytical and evaluative tasks. These cognitive orientations influence how students respond to instructional strategies and creative opportunities in digital contexts.

Empirical studies support the link between thinking styles and creative output. Stanley and Zhang, (2018) found that legislative thinkers often demonstrate higher creativity scores, as they are more comfortable with ambiguity and less constrained by external instructions. In contrast, executive thinkers may require more scaffolding to engage in creative tasks, but they can excel when the task is framed with clear procedures. Judicial thinkers, while not always generative in their ideas, often contribute by enhancing the quality of creative work through critical analysis and structured refinement. These distinctions suggest that tailoring digital creativity instruction to thinking styles can enhance both engagement and creative performance.

Moreover, the integration of digital creativity into education has implications for personalized learning. Researchers have emphasized the importance of matching instructional design with cognitive preferences to optimize learner motivation and achievement (Israel-Fishelson & Hershkovitz, 2020; Vandewaetere & Clarebout, 2011). For example, providing legislative learners with autonomy in choosing creative tools or project directions can foster deeper engagement, whereas executive learners may benefit from guided templates or step-by-step tutorials. For judicial learners, opportunities to critique peer work or evaluate multiple solutions can activate their motivation and cognitive strengths. By aligning digital creativity tasks with thinking styles, educators can create more inclusive and effective learning environments that support diverse learners (Wan Ali et al., 2024; Wan Ali et al., 2024).

Integrating Cognitive Styles and Motivational Models

Sternberg's theory of Mental Self-Government (MSG) provides a framework for understanding learners' cognitive styles as "preferred ways of governing one's mental activity" across five dimensions: functions (legislative, executive, judicial), forms (monarchic, hierarchic, oligarchic, anarchic), levels (global vs. local), scope (internal vs. external), and leanings (liberal vs. conservative). Importantly, styles are not rigid categories but tendencies that influence how individuals approach problem-solving, creativity, and decision-making. Recent research emphasizes that thinking styles moderate the relationship between learning environments and creative performance, showing that classroom climate can be experienced quite differently depending on students' style profiles (Lin et al., 2024).

In parallel, Keller's ARCS model (Attention, Relevance, Confidence, Satisfaction) continues to serve as a practical, evidence-based framework for embedding motivational elements into instructional design. Systematic reviews between 2023 and 2025 confirm that ARCS interventions consistently improve engagement, persistence, and achievement across disciplines and modalities, with the strongest effects observed when combined with technology-enhanced or active-learning pedagogies (Fang et al., 2024; Mei et al., 2025; Zhou & Zhang, 2025). For example, ARCS-based strategies in flipped classrooms have been shown to increase students' confidence and deepen learning outcomes (Zhou & Zhang., 2025).

The integration of MSG and ARCS offers a more nuanced way to design instruction. MSG highlights the diversity of learners' cognitive preferences, while ARCS provides motivational levers to sustain engagement across these differences. Rather than endorsing the widely critiqued "matching hypothesis" of learning styles, which meta-analytic evidence continues to refute (Ryong, Lee, & Lee, 2024), the MSG–ARCS synthesis suggests a choice-based design approach. This means offering flexible learning pathways aligned with both motivational needs and style preferences, allowing students to self-select tasks or supports that resonate with their preferred modes of thinking.

For example, legislative thinkers, who prefer generating their own rules or projects, may thrive when given open-ended design challenges framed with ARCS principles: attention-grabbing problem contexts, authentic relevance, scaffolds for building confidence, and opportunities for public recognition of solutions. In contrast, executive thinkers may benefit from structured, step-by-step tasks that provide clarity, incremental confidence-building, and satisfaction through mastery feedback. Judicial thinkers, with their evaluative preference, may be best engaged through debate, peer review, and critique tasks embedded in ARCS motivational scaffolding.

Other MSG dimensions can be aligned similarly. Global thinkers may respond well to ARCS strategies that begin with conceptual maps and overarching narratives, while local thinkers may prefer detailed checklists and micro-feedback cycles. Internal-scope learners can be motivated through self-paced reflective practices, whereas external-scope learners may be engaged through peer collaboration and public showcases of their work. Finally, liberal-leaning students (preferring novelty) may find ARCS-driven satisfaction in innovative tasks, while conservative-leaning learners (preferring structure) may gain confidence and satisfaction from stable routines and exemplars.

In sum, integrating MSG and ARCS provides an inclusive framework that supports learner diversity without resorting to simplistic "matching" claims. Recent evidence supports the idea that environments designed with multiple motivational entry points can foster engagement, creativity, and persistence across varied learner profiles (Lin et al., 2024; Mei et al., 2025). This makes the MSG–ARCS integration a compelling basis for contemporary instructional design in higher education and beyond.

Table 1. Comparative Analysis of Sternberg's Thinking Styles and Keller's ARCS Model

Thinking Style (Sternberg)	Core Preference	Motivational Alignment (Keller ARCS)	Instructional Strategy	Recent Supporting Studies (2023–2025)
Legislative	Autonomy, creativity, innovation	Attention, Satisfaction	Project-based, flexible navigation, open-ended tasks	Chen et al. (2023); Wan Ali et al. (2024)
Executive	Structure, rules, clear directions	Relevance, Confidence	Templates, guided steps, sequential modules	Zhang (2023); Castro-Alonso et al. (2024)
Judicial	Analysis, evaluation, critique	Confidence, Satisfaction	Peer review, evaluative rubrics, critique-based activities	Georgiou & Kyza (2024); Li & Chen (2025)

Table 1 presents a comparative analysis of Sternberg's thinking styles alongside Keller's ARCS motivational model, demonstrating how cognitive preferences can be meaningfully aligned with motivational strategies in instructional design. Learners with a **legislative style**, who value autonomy, creativity, and innovation, align most strongly with the ARCS components of *Attention* and *Satisfaction*; they are best supported by project-based learning, flexible navigation, and open-ended tasks that stimulate curiosity and provide a sense of accomplishment, as highlighted in recent studies by Chen et al. (2023) and Wan Ali et al. (2024). Conversely, **executive-style learners**, who prefer structure, rules, and clear directions, are closely associated with *Relevance* and *Confidence* in the ARCS model; instructional strategies such as templates, guided steps, and sequential modules have been shown to enhance their performance and motivation (Zhang, 2023; Castro-Alonso et al., 2024). Finally, judicial thinkers, who thrive on analysis, evaluation, and critique, align well with *Confidence* and *Satisfaction*; they respond positively to activities such as peer review, the use of evaluative rubrics, and critique-based learning, which strengthen both mastery and validation of their evaluative abilities (Georgiou & Kyza, 2024; Li & Chen, 2025). Taken together, the table underscores that integrating MSG thinking styles with ARCS motivational strategies allows educators to design flexible, responsive learning environments that accommodate cognitive diversity while sustaining learner motivation.

METHODOLOGY

Research Design

This study adopted a quasi-experimental 2×3 factorial design to examine the interaction effects between instructional modes and students' thinking styles on perceived motivation in a digital video learning environment. The two instructional modes compared were:

i. DVC-LS: Learner-paced segmented digital video courseware.
ii. DVC-SS: System-paced segmented digital video courseware.

Participants were further grouped into three categories based on their thinking styles, as identified by Sternberg's Thinking Styles Inventory (TSI), forming the second independent variable. This design allowed for the analysis of both main effects and interaction effects between instructional method and cognitive disposition on students' motivation levels.

Figure 1. Factorial design layout showing DVC modes (DVC-LS, DVC-SS) crossed with Thinking Styles

		Independent Variable	
		DVC-LS	DVC-SS
Moderator Variable	Legislative		
	Executive		
	Judicial		

Participants

The sample consisted of 180 first-year undergraduate students from four Malaysian Technical University Network (MTUN) institutions. Participants ranged in age from 19 to 22 years, were proficient in English, and possessed good ICT skills. All participants owned smartphones and had basic computer knowledge, but limited exposure to digital video production and computational thinking (CT).

Participants' thinking styles were identified using the Thinking Styles Inventory (TSI) (Sternberg & Wagner, 1992), and they were then assigned to experimental groups based on their respective style classifications and instructional mode.

Instruments

Motivation Survey

Students' motivation was measured using an adapted version of Keller's Instructional Materials Motivation Survey (IMMS) (Keller, 2009), which includes 36 items across four key dimensions: Attention, Relevance, Confidence, and Satisfaction. This survey was administered after the intervention, and responses were recorded using a 5-point Likert scale (1 = Strongly Disagree, 5 = Strongly Agree).

Digital Video Courseware (DVC)

Two instructional interventions were developed to support the teaching of digital video production. This version allowed learners to:

Table 2. Comparison between DVC-LS and DVC-SS

DVC-LS	DVC-SS
Navigate freely across modules.	Modules were locked sequentially.
Control video playback (pause, play, scroll).	Learners progressed linearly.
Access content non-linearly.	Playback control was limited to mute and audio on/off.
Revisit materials for self-paced review.	Designed for structured, guided learning.

Table 2 compares the features of two digital video courseware modes: DVC-LS (learner-paced segmenting) and DVC-SS (system-paced segmenting). In DVC-LS, students could freely navigate across modules, access content non-linearly, and control video playback with functions like pause, play, and scrolling, offering high autonomy and flexibility. This mode allowed learners to revisit content at their own pace, fostering a self-directed and creative learning experience. In contrast, DVC-SS followed a structured, linear design where modules were locked sequentially, playback controls were minimal (limited to mute and audio on/off), and progression was tightly guided by the system. This setup emphasized order and consistency but limited opportunities for learner-driven exploration and digital creativity. Some examples of user interfaces of DVC-LS and DVC-SS can be referred to as Figure 2 and Figure 3.

Figure 2. User interface of DVC-LS vs DVC-SS (a).

<table>
<tr><th>Mode 1: DVC-LS (Learner-paced predefined segment)</th><th>Mode 2: DVC-SS (System predefined segment)</th></tr>
<tr><td>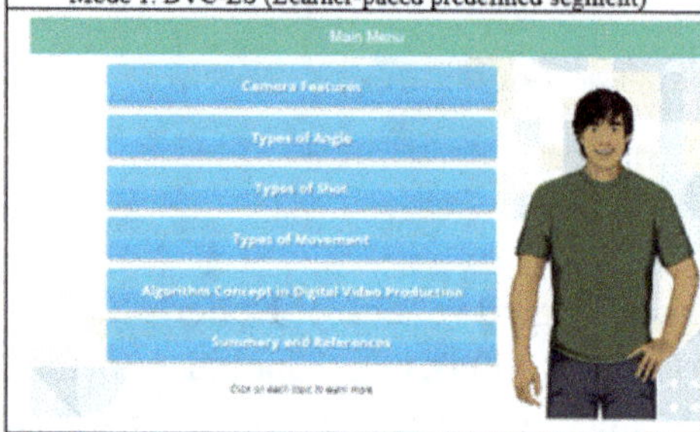
</td><td>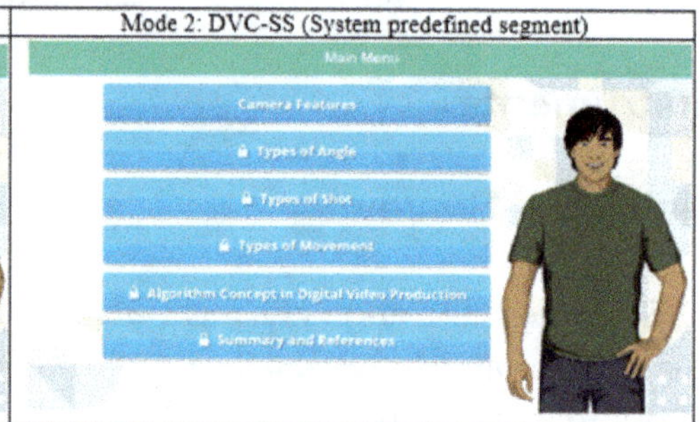
</td></tr>
<tr><td>Students are able to choose any module from the courseware to learn first.</td><td>Students are required to follow the flow of the main menu. Students are not able to select which module they want to learn first. The next incoming modules are locked until student completed to learn the first module.</td></tr>
</table>

Figure 3. User interface of DVC-LS vs DVC-SS (b)

<table>
<tr><td>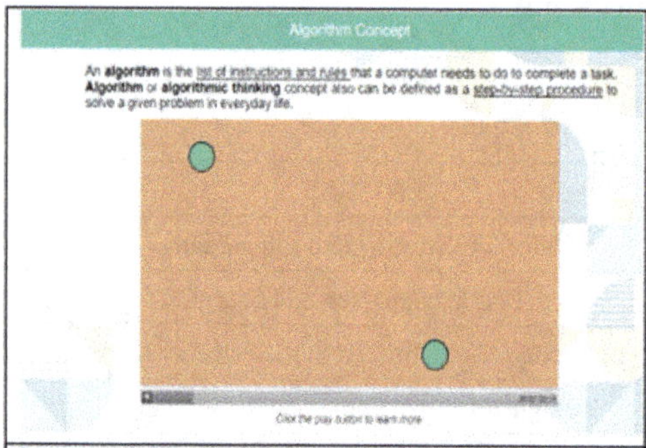
</td><td>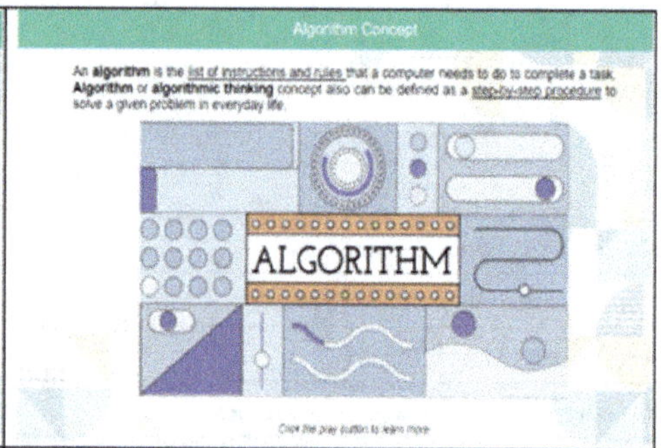
</td></tr>
<tr><td>Students are able to control the video presentation (pause, play, and scroll video) according to their preferreable learning pace.</td><td>Students are not able to control the video presentation. Students only have limited control provided by the courseware such as speaker to mute or play the audio.</td></tr>
</table>

Both modes integrated Computational Thinking (CT) algorithmic thinking via flowchart scaffolding, along with Gagné's Nine Events of Instruction (Gagne et al., 2005) and Mayer's Cognitive Theory of Multimedia Learning (CTML) principles (Mayer, 2009). Specifically, the Segmenting Principle was employed to distinguish between learner-controlled and system-controlled delivery (Castro-Alonso et al., 2021).

Table 3. DVC-LS and DVC-SS instructional features

Feature	DVC-LS (Learner-paced)	DVC-SS (System-paced)
Navigation	Free	Sequential
Control	Full (pause, scroll, replay)	Minimal (mute only)
Pacing	User-controlled	System-controlled
Module Access	Non-linear	Linear
Replay	Allowed	Restricted
CT Flowchart Activity	Learner-driven	Guided step-by-step

Table 3 shows the comparison between DVC-LS (learner-paced) and DVC-SS (system-paced) highlights key differences in learner autonomy and control, which directly influence digital creativity. DVC-LS offered flexible learning experience with free navigation, full control over playback (including pause, scroll, and replay), user-controlled pacing, non-linear module access, and the ability to replay content at will. It also featured learner-driven computational thinking (CT) flowchart activities, encouraging active exploration and decision-making. In contrast, DVC-SS presented a more rigid structure, with sequential navigation, minimal control (mute only), system-determined pacing, linear content access, restricted replay, and guided step-by-step CT activities. These constraints limit learners' creative freedom, suggesting that DVC-LS better supports motivation through enhanced digital creativity.

Courseware Development Framework

The development of the courseware for this project was guided by the Integrated Waterfall-ADDIE Model, a hybrid framework that merges the systematic rigor of software engineering methodologies with the pedagogical grounding of instructional design. This model, initially discussed by Eller (2015) and further elaborated by Wan Ali and Wan Yahaya (2023), allows developers to address both the technical aspects of multimedia software construction and the learning sciences underpinning instructional effectiveness. By aligning software development practices with established instructional strategies, the framework ensured that the resulting courseware was not only technically robust but also pedagogically sound, scalable, and learner centered.

The model adopted in this study contained **six** key phases; analysis, design, development, evaluation, testing, and implementation, presented in Figure 4. While these phases appear sequential, the integration of ADDIE principles allows for iterative refinement, meaning that feedback loops were embedded throughout the process. Each stage is discussed in detail below, with attention to its contribution to both instructional quality and learner experience.

Figure 4. Diagram of the Integrated Waterfall-ADDIE Model showing all six phases.

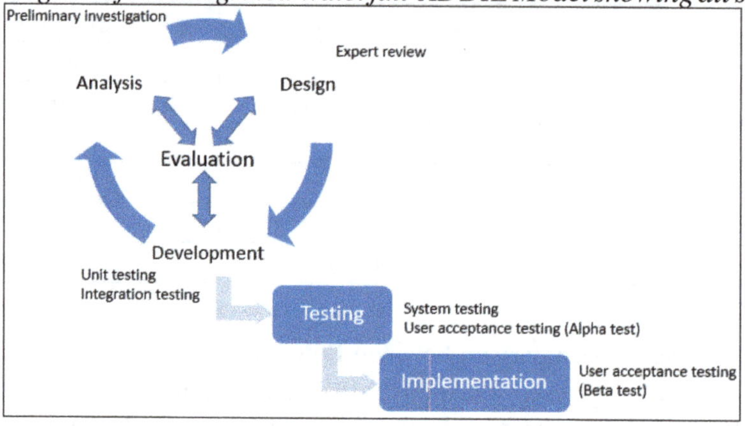

Phase 1: Analysis

The first phase, analysis, formed the foundation of the entire development process. This stage involved a systematic examination of the instructional problem, identification of learning gaps, and articulation of learner needs. Needs analysis tools such as surveys, interviews, and curriculum document reviews were employed to gather relevant data. For instance, attention was paid to the cognitive, affective, and psychomotor demands of the intended learners, who were primarily young adults. The process also clarified the scope of the content, ensuring that topics were both relevant to the curriculum and meaningful to learners' real-world applications.

Instructional objectives were formulated based on Bloom's taxonomy, with attention to ensuring progression from lower-order skills (e.g., comprehension) to higher-order skills (e.g., critical thinking and problem-solving). This alignment established clear benchmarks for the subsequent phases and allowed measurable learning outcomes to be articulated. In essence, the analysis stage served as the "diagnostic" process, ensuring that the courseware addressed authentic needs rather than offering generic or misaligned content.

Phase 2: Design

The design phase translated analytical findings into instructional blueprints. Central to this stage was the adoption of Gagné's Nine Events of Instruction, which provided a structured approach to sequencing content and learner interactions. For example, attention-grabbing introductions (Event 1) were paired with clear objectives (Event 2), scaffolded presentation of content (Events 4–5), and opportunities for practice and feedback (Events 6–7).

In addition, Cognitive Theory of Multimedia Learning (CTML) principles, as articulated by Mayer (2009), were systematically embedded. These included:

- Signaling to highlight key concepts,
- Spatial and temporal contiguity to ensure that related text, audio, and visuals were presented together,
- Coherence and redundancy reduction to avoid extraneous information,
- Modality to balance visual and auditory channels, and
- Personalization through conversational tone and relatable examples.

The design stage also included storyboard development which has been designed based on CTML principles (Loranger et al., 2010; Mayer, 2009), which mapped content flow, multimedia elements, and interactive components. Storyboards functioned as communication tools between subject matter experts, instructional designers, and multimedia developers, ensuring alignment before actual production began.

Phase 3: Development

During the development phase, the abstract designs were transformed into functional learning materials. The multimedia courseware was constructed using a combination of industry-standard tools: Articulate 360 for e-learning module creation, Adobe Photoshop for image editing and visual design, and Powtoon for animated video segments.

Multimedia assets were carefully selected and developed to maximize learner engagement without overloading working memory. For example, animations were used to illustrate complex processes that would be difficult to convey through static text alone, while audio narration complemented visuals to leverage dual-channel processing as suggested by CTML. The development team also prioritized young adult user interface (UI) guidelines, ensuring that layouts were intuitive, navigation was consistent, and extraneous elements were minimized.

This stage was not purely linear; rather, iterative prototypes were generated and subjected to formative reviews. Feedback cycles allowed incremental refinements, ensuring that errors were addressed before full-scale production.

Phase 4: Evaluation

The evaluation phase ensured that the courseware met both pedagogical and usability standards. Expert reviews and user testing were carried out using heuristic checklists for usability, the System Usability Scale (SUS) for overall user satisfaction, and NASA-TLX metrics to assess cognitive workload.

Expert evaluators included subject matter specialists and instructional designers, who assessed alignment with curricular goals, appropriateness of learning strategies, and adherence to multimedia learning principles. User testing involved representative learners, who provided feedback on clarity, usability, and engagement.

Evaluation was conducted iteratively, meaning that multiple rounds of feedback were integrated until both experts and users judged the courseware to be effective. This phase validated not only the instructional design but also the technical soundness of the multimedia environment.

Phase 5: Testing

While evaluation focused on pedagogical quality, the testing phase addressed system performance and learner experience refinement. Here, systematic quality assurance procedures were applied to identify and correct technical issues such as broken links, interface glitches, or animation synchronization problems.

Testing also examined the "flow" of the learner experience, ensuring that transitions were smooth, instructions were clear, and interactive elements worked as intended. Beta testing with small learner groups simulated authentic classroom use, allowing real-time observations of engagement and potential confusion points. These findings were crucial in refining the courseware before large-scale rollout.

Phase 6: Implementation

The final stage, implementation, involved actual deployment in classroom and pilot settings. Educators were briefed on facilitation strategies, while learners engaged with the courseware under semi-controlled conditions. This phase allowed the collection of real-world usage data, highlighting not only the effectiveness of the instructional strategies but also practical concerns such as technological accessibility, time management, and learner preferences.

The implementation phase served as a bridge between design and practice, confirming that the courseware could function as a sustainable instructional tool within authentic educational environments.

Integration of Multimedia Learning Principles

Throughout all six phases, multimedia learning principles (Loranger et al., 2010; Mayer, 2009) served as guiding heuristics. Signaling was used to draw attention to essential information; contiguity principles ensured coherence between words and visuals; and redundancy reduction prevented cognitive overload from duplicated narration and on-screen text. Likewise, modality principles balanced visual and auditory information, while personalization strategies introduced conversational tones and relatable examples to enhance learner connection.

By deliberately incorporating these principles, the courseware avoided common pitfalls such as cluttered screens, irrelevant visuals, or monotonous narration. Instead, learners experienced materials that were cognitively efficient, engaging, and pedagogically purposeful.

Learner-Centered Design Considerations

Finally, the design placed strong emphasis on the needs of young adult learners, who often value simplicity, relevance, and intuitive digital interactions. This demographic tends to have high exposure to digital media but also low tolerance for poorly designed interfaces. As such, the courseware emphasized minimal extraneous load, clear navigation cues, and authentic examples that connected learning content to real-life applications.

By doing so, the framework ensured not only compliance with instructional design theory but also resonance with the lived experiences and preferences of its intended users.

The Integrated Waterfall-ADDIE Model provided a comprehensive and structured approach for developing the courseware, blending systematic software engineering with evidence-based instructional design. Through its six phases, analysis, design, development, evaluation, testing, and implementation, the framework allowed for iterative refinement, strong alignment with multimedia learning principles, and sensitivity to learner needs. The result was a courseware product that was pedagogically robust, technologically reliable, and attuned to the expectations of young adult learners. This approach underscores the importance of hybrid frameworks in bridging theory and practice in modern instructional design.

RESULTS AND DISCUSSION

Digital Creativity and Motivation

The study investigated how digital creativity embedded in courseware design impacts student motivation, analyzed through ANOVA tests. The independent variable was the mode of digital video courseware: *learner-paced segmenting* (DVC-LS) versus *system-paced segmenting* (DVC-SS). The dependent variable was students' motivation scores, assessed using Keller's IMMS.

Significant Motivation Difference by Courseware Mode

The mean motivation score for students using DVC-LS (learner-paced courseware) was 4.484, while the mean score for those using DVC-SS (system-paced courseware) was 4.128. This notable difference indicates that students felt more motivated when they had control over their learning experience, as offered by DVC-LS. The higher mean score suggests that features such as flexible navigation, the ability to pause and replay content, and learner-driven interaction contributed positively to their engagement and intrinsic motivation. In contrast, the lower score for DVC-SS implies that the rigid, system-controlled structure may have limited students' sense of autonomy and creative involvement, leading to reduced motivation.

Furthermore, the one-way ANOVA revealed a significant difference in motivation between the two modes, [$F(1, 190) = 71.706$, $p < .001$, $\eta p^2 = .274$]. This large effect size shows that allowing learners to control pace, sequence, and engagement with content, key elements of digital creativity significantly enhance motivation.

While the two-way ANOVA showed no significant differences in motivation *within* thinking styles when exposed to the same mode. Legislative, executive, and judicial groups all responded similarly within each courseware type. The post-hoc test results showed significant differences in motivation across all three thinking styles: legislative, executive, and judicial, when comparing the two courseware types (DVC-LS vs. DVC-SS) (as referred to Table 4). For legislative thinkers, who prefer autonomy and creativity, motivation was significantly higher with DVC-LS (mean difference $\Delta M = 0.182$, $p = .000$), aligning with their preference for self-directed learning. Executive thinkers, who thrive in structured environments but still benefit from interaction, also showed a larger motivational gain with DVC-LS ($\Delta M = 0.400$, $p = .000$), suggesting that even structured learners are more engaged when given digital control. The largest difference was observed among judicial thinkers ($\Delta M = 0.474$, $p = .000$), indicating that critical, evaluative learners are highly motivated by environments that offer flexibility, control, and opportunities for digital creativity.

Table 4. Mean Motivation Scores by Thinking Style and Mode

Thinking Style	DVC-LS Mean	DVC-SS Mean	Difference	Sig.
Legislative	4.421	4.239	0.182	.000
Executive	4.496	4.096	0.400	.000
Judicial	4.531	4.057	0.474	.000

These results suggest that digital creativity, operationalized through learner-paced design, benefits all learners regardless of cognitive profile. Features like freedom to explore, manipulate, and construct knowledge, core to digital creativity, boost motivation and engagement in multimedia learning environments.

Discussion based on Thinking Styles

Legislative Thinkers

The findings indicate that legislative thinkers demonstrated significantly higher motivation when engaging with the learner-paced predefined segment courseware (DVC-LS). This group, characterized by a preference for autonomy and independent decision-making, benefited greatly from the DVC-LS design, which afforded substantial control over the learning process. Features such as module selection, video playback control, and non-linear navigation aligned with their intrinsic motivation to explore and structure learning independently.

The results support the Mental Self-Government (MSG) Theory, which posits that individuals with legislative thinking styles prefer environments that offer opportunities for creativity and self-direction. The DVC-LS environment enabled these learners to take ownership of their learning pace and structure, resulting in increased engagement and motivational scores. This is consistent with prior research that suggests learner control enhances cognitive engagement and motivation (Brown, 2001; Mayer & Pilegard, 2014).

Executive Thinkers

In contrast, executive thinkers, who favor structured, directive learning environments, exhibited stronger motivation when interacting with the system-paced predefined segment courseware (DVC-SS). Although the overall motivational gain was higher in DVC-LS, executive learners responded more positively to the clear, step-by-step sequencing in DVC-SS. This mode reduced the cognitive load associated with decision-making and better suited their preference for clearly outlined tasks and expectations.

This observation aligns with studies suggesting that executive learners are more comfortable with instructional settings that are externally guided and rule-bound (Zhang, 2002; Lin et al., 2001). The linear progression of DVC-SS supported their learning preferences, thereby enhancing motivational outcomes within this subset of learners.

Judicial Thinkers

Judicial thinkers, known for their evaluative and analytical tendencies, displayed balanced motivation across both DVC-LS and DVC-SS conditions. Although their motivation levels were not significantly higher in either mode, judicial learners scored the highest in self-efficacy. This suggests that their confidence in managing and evaluating learning tasks was sustained regardless of control or pacing format.

Judicial thinkers' ability to critique and assess learning materials may explain their adaptability to both learning modes. Their motivation was reinforced by opportunities for critical reflection, supported by structured content in DVC-SS and flexible navigation in DVC-LS. These findings resonate with literature indicating that judicial learners are generally more self-assured and cognitively resilient when engaging with analytical tasks (Fan, 2016; Cheng & Sin, 2021).

Implications for Instructional Design

The differential responses among legislative, executive, and judicial thinkers have important implications for instructional design. The results underscore the value of personalized digital courseware, wherein learning environments are adapted to suit individual cognitive preferences:

i. Legislative learners benefit most from learner-controlled formats that offer autonomy and flexible navigation.
ii. Executive learners require highly structured content with sequential access and clear directions to maintain motivation.
iii. Judicial learners thrive in analytically rich environments, regardless of pacing, as long as critical thinking opportunities are present.

The integration of computational thinking (CT), particularly algorithmic thinking through flowcharts and scaffolding, further supports learner engagement across all styles. This approach not only enhances motivation and self-efficacy but also cultivates 21st-century skills critical for academic and professional success.

Consequently, instructional designers and educators should consider combining learner-paced segmentation with cognitive style awareness to create adaptive, engaging, and effective multimedia learning environments. Such alignment fosters sustained motivation, improves knowledge retention, and supports diverse learners in technology-enhanced settings.

Table 5. Implications for Instructional Design across Diverse Learner Contexts

Learner Context	Instructional Design Implications	Digital Creativity Application	Example
TVET Students	Hands-on, structured modules	Video tutorials with stepwise scaffolding	Technical training videos in electronics
Online Learners	Self-paced, adaptive systems	Gamified interactive platforms	MOOCs with embedded ARCS elements
Creative Industry Trainees	Autonomy, collaborative projects	Portfolio-based video production	Team-based storytelling projects

Table 5 highlights how instructional design can be adapted to different learner contexts by integrating motivational strategies and digital creativity tools. For TVET students, learning is best supported through hands-on and structured modules that emphasize step-by-step skill acquisition; in this context, scaffolded video tutorials are effective for demonstrating technical processes such as electronics training. Online learners, by contrast, benefit from self-paced and adaptive systems that provide flexibility and autonomy, with gamified platforms and MOOCs enhanced by ARCS elements sustaining attention, ensuring relevance, and building confidence through adaptive feedback. Meanwhile, creative industry trainees require instructional designs that promote autonomy, collaboration, and innovation; portfolio-based video production and team storytelling projects allow them to experiment, showcase skills, and produce industry-relevant outputs while remaining motivated by authentic, project-based learning experiences. Collectively, the table underscores that instructional design must be context-sensitive, ensuring that digital creativity applications align with learners' needs, professional goals, and motivational drivers.

CONCLUSION

This study demonstrates the influence of thinking styles on motivation in digital video production education, highlighting the significance of designing instructional materials that accommodate diverse cognitive profiles. When digital video courseware is aligned with students' thinking styles, whether through learner-paced or system-paced segmenting, learners are more likely to experience heightened engagement, confidence, and satisfaction. These findings affirm that personalization in digital learning environments not only improves knowledge retention but also promotes motivation, which is vital in creative fields like digital video production.

Digital creativity plays a central role in fostering motivation and learning effectiveness in multimedia environments. In the context of this study, the integration of computational thinking (CT) algorithmic flowcharts, dynamic visuals, and interactive modules enabled students to experiment with creative decision-making processes.

The courseware's design encouraged students to explore camera angles, movements, and editing techniques, which served as both technical and artistic challenges. Such digital creativity tasks cultivate critical 21st-century skills, including problem-solving, self-expression, and innovation, that are essential in media-related disciplines.

Moreover, the findings suggest that instructional designs that promote digital creativity—such as allowing students to control the pacing and sequencing of their learning, empower learners to take ownership of their creative process. The ability to pause, replay, and navigate flexibly through digital content supports a constructivist learning experience where students build knowledge through active exploration. This creative freedom not only sustains intrinsic motivation but also enhances students' capacity to apply theoretical concepts in practical, meaningful ways, which is crucial in fields like digital storytelling and video production.

Future research should explore how further enhancements in digital creativity, through gamification, augmented reality, virtual production environments, or collaborative digital platforms, might amplify student engagement and learning outcomes. Investigating how these emerging technologies interact with thinking styles could provide richer insights into designing inclusive and inspiring educational experiences. Such studies would contribute to the development of innovative pedagogies that prepare learners for the evolving demands of creative industries in the digital age.

REFERENCES

Al-Thani, A., Al-Thani, T., & Semmar, Y. (2014). Investigating the relationship between students' Tthinking styles, self-efficacy for learning, and academic performance at Qatar University. *American International Journal of Social Science, 3*(2), 172–179. www.aijssnet.com

Ali, W., Ashiqin, W. N., & Yahaya, W. W. A. J. (2023). Computational Thinking Self-Efficacy Perception for Progressive Learning in Malaysia: A Study of Validity and Reliability. In *Comparative Research on Diversity in Virtual Learning: Eastern vs. Western Perspectives* (p. 19). DOI: 10.4018/978-1-6684-3595-3.ch001

Ali, W. N. A. W., & Yahaya, W. A. J. W. (2024). Optimizing Acceptance Testing: Evaluating Digital Video Courseware With System Usability Scale (SUS) and NASA-TLX Workload Metrics. In *Power of Persuasive Educational Technologies in Enhancing Learning* (pp. 419-436). IGI Global Scientific Publishing.

Brown, K. G. (2001). Using computers to deliver training: Which employees learn and why? *Personnel Psychology, 54*(2), 271–296. DOI: 10.1111/j.1744-6570.2001.tb00093.x

Castro-Alonso, J. C., Koning, B. B. De, Fiorella, L., & Paas, F. (2021). *Five strategies for optimizing instructional materials: Instructor- and learner-managed cognitive load*. 1379–1407.

Chen, L., Zeng, S., & Wang, W. (2021). The influence of emotion and learner control on multimedia learning. *Learning and Motivation, 76*(September), 101762. DOI: 10.1016/j.lmot.2021.101762

Chen, S. (2022). Predictive roles of thinking styles in coping strategies among Mainland postgraduate students in Hong Kong. *Frontiers in Psychology, 12*(January), 1–12. DOI: 10.3389/fpsyg.2021.693637 PMID: 35153883

Clark, R. C., & Mayer, R. E. (2016). E-learning and the science of instruction: Proven guidelines for consumers and designers of multimedia learning. In *Essential resources for training and HR professionals* (Fourth). Pfeiffer A Wiley Imprint.

Clarke, T. A., Lesh, J. J., Trocchio, J. S., & Wolman, C. (2010). Thinking styles: Teaching and learning styles in graduate education students. *Educational Psychology, 30*(7), 837–848. DOI: 10.1080/01443410.2010.510794

Eller, R. (2015). Implementing design into instruction: Intersections between the Waterfall model and ADDIE model. *Assumption University-EJournal of Interdisciplinary Research (AU-EJIR), 1*(1), 63–69.

Emamipour, S., & Esfandabad, H. S. (2013). Developmental study of thinking styles in Iranian students university. *Procedia - Social and Behavioral Sciences, 84*(1997), 1736–1739. DOI: 10.1016/j.sbspro.2013.07.023

Fan, W., & Zhang, L. F. (2009). Are achievement motivation and thinking styles related? A visit among Chinese university students. *Learning and Individual Differences, 19*(2), 299–303. DOI: 10.1016/j.lindif.2008.10.005

Fang, X., Ng, D. T. K., Leung, J. K. L., & Xu, H. (2024). The applications of the ARCS model in instructional design, theoretical framework, and measurement tool: A systematic review of empirical studies. *Interactive Learning Environments, 32*(10), 5919–5946. DOI: 10.1080/10494820.2023.2240867

Gagne, R. M., Wager, W. W., Golas, K. C., & Kelle, J. M. (2005). *Principle of instructional design* (5th ed.). Thomson Learning Inc.

Georgiou, Y., & Kyza, E. A. (2018). Relations between student motivation, immersion and learning outcomes in location-based augmented reality settings. *Computers in Human Behavior, 89*(March), 173–181. DOI: 10.1016/j.chb.2018.08.011

Grigorenko, E. L., & Sternberg, R. J. (1997). Styles of thinking, abilities, and academic performance. *Exceptional Children, 63*(3), 295–312. DOI: 10.1177/001440299706300301

Huang, R., Tlili, A., Yang, J., & Chang, T.-W. (2020). The Chinese experience in maintaining undisrupted learning in COVID-19 outbreak. In *Handbook on Facilitating Flexible Learning During Educational Disruption* (Issue March). Beijing: Smart Learning Institute of Beijing Normal University. https://www.researchgate.net/publication/339939064

Israel-Fishelson, R., & Hershkovitz, A. (2020). Persistence in a game-based learning environment: The case of elementary school students learning computational thinking. *Journal of Educational Computing Research, 58*(5), 891–918. DOI: 10.1177/0735633119887187

Jenson, J., & Droumeva, M. (2016). Exploring media literacy and computational thinking: A game maker curriculum study. *Electronic Journal of e-Learning, 14*(2), 111–121.

Kellems, R. O., Eichelberger, C., Cacciatore, G., Jensen, M., Frazier, B., Simons, K., & Zaru, M. (2020). Using video-based instruction via augmented reality to teach mathematics to middle school students with learning disabilities. *Journal of Learning Disabilities, 53*(4), 277–291. DOI: 10.1177/0022219420906452 PMID: 32065040

Keller, J. M. (2016). Motivation, learning, and technology: Applying the ARCS-V motivation model. *Participatory Educational Research*, *3*(2), 1–15. DOI: 10.17275/per.16.06.3.2

Lin, S., Duan, W., Wang, Y., & Duan, H. (2024). Thinking style moderates the impact of the classroom environment on language creativity. *Journal of Intelligence*, *12*(1), 5. DOI: 10.3390/jintelligence12010005 PMID: 38248903

Loranger, H., McCloskey, M., Nielsen, J., McKloskey, M., & Nielsen, J. (2010). *College students (ages 18-24) on the web* (2nd ed.). Nielsen Norman Group.

Mayer, R. E. (2009). Multimedia learning. In *Psychology of Learning and Motivation - Advances in Research and Theory* (2nd ed.). Cambridge University Press., DOI: 10.1017/CBO9780511811678

Mayer, R. E., & Pilegard, C. (2014). Basic principles of multimedia learning. In Mayer, R. E. (Ed.), *The Cambridge Handbook of Multimedia Learning* (pp. 316–344). Cambridge University Press. DOI: 10.1017/CBO9781139547369.016

Mei, Q., Chan, N. N., Gill, R. S., Subramaniam, N., Motevalli, S., & Ang, C. S. (2025). Impact of attention, relevance, confidence, satisfaction (ARCS) model on teaching effectiveness in higher education: A systematic review. *Discover Education*, *4*(1), 252. DOI: 10.1007/s44217-025-00674-5

Moreno, R., & Mayer, R. (2007). Interactive multimodal learning environments: Special issue on interactive learning environments: Contemporary issues and trends. *Educational Psychology Review*, *19*(3), 309–326. DOI: 10.1007/s10648-007-9047-2

Ryong, K., Lee, D., & Lee, J. G. (2024). Chatbot's complementary motivation support in developing study plan of e-learning English lecture. *International Journal of Human-Computer Interaction*, *40*(10), 2641–2655. DOI: 10.1080/10447318.2022.2163786

Snelson, C. (2018). Video production in content-area pedagogy: A scoping study of the research literature. *Learning, Media and Technology*, *43*(3), 294–306. DOI: 10.1080/17439884.2018.1504788

Stanley, D., & Zhang, Y. (2018). Student-produced videos can enhance engagement and learning in the online environment. *Online Learning : the Official Journal of the Online Learning Consortium*, *22*(2), 5–26. DOI: 10.24059/olj.v22i2.1367

Sternberg, R. J. (1997). The concept of intelligence and its role in lifelong learning and success. *The American Psychologist*, *52*(10), 1030–1037. DOI: 10.1037/0003-066X.52.10.1030 PMID: 9329294 van Laar, E., van Deursen, A. J. A. M., van Dijk, J. A. G. M., & de Haan, J. (2020). Determinants of 21st-century skills and 21st-century digital skills for workers: A systematic literature review. *SAGE Open*, *10*(1), 2158244019900176. Advance online publication. DOI: 10.1177/2158244019900176

Vandewaetere, M., & Clarebout, G. (2011). Can instruction as such affect learning? the case of learner control. *Computers & Education*, *57*(4), 2322–2332. DOI: 10.1016/j.compedu.2011.05.020

Wan Ali, W. N. A., Wan Yahaya, W. A. J., Syed Idrus, S. Z., & Yaacob, M. N. F. (2024). Fostering Motivation In Tvet Students : The Role Of Learner-Paced Segments And Computational Thinking In Digital Video. [AJTLHE]. *ASEAN Journal of Teaching & Learning in Higher Education*, *16*(2), 215–232. DOI: 10.17576/ajtlhe.1602.2024.01

Zhou, Q., & Zhang, H. (2025). Flipped classroom teaching and ARCS motivation model: Impact on college students' deep learning. *Education Sciences*, *15*(4), 517. DOI: 10.3390/educsci15040517

Compilation of References

Abdelsalam, M., & Mostafa, M. (2025). *Bridging the Digital Divide: AI, VR, and AR for Equitable K-12 Education*. https://papers.ssrn.com/sol3/papers.cfm?abstract_id=5124551

Abeywardena, I. S. (2023). OXREF: Open XR for Education Framework. *International Review of Research in Open and Distance Learning*, *24*(3), 185–206. DOI: 10.19173/irrodl.v24i3.7109

Adeshola, I., & Adepoju, A. P. (2024). The opportunities and challenges of ChatGPT in education. *Interactive Learning Environments*, *32*(1), 33–51. DOI: 10.1080/10494820.2023.2253858

Adil, M., Song, H., Khan, M. K., Farouk, A., & Jin, Z. (2024). 5G/6G-enabled metaverse technologies: Taxonomy, applications, and open security challenges with future research directions. *Journal of Network and Computer Applications*, *223*, 103828. DOI: 10.1016/j.jnca.2024.103828

Adnan, N. I., Ramli, S., & Ismail, I. N. (2021). Investigating the usefulness of TikTok as an educational tool. [IJPTL]. *International Journal of Practices in Teaching and Learning*, *1*(2), 1–5. https://ir.uitm.edu.my/id/eprint/52140/

Agbo, F. J., Sanusi, I. T., Oyelere, S. S., & Suhonen, J. (2021). Application of Virtual Reality in Computer Science Education: A Systemic Review Based on Bibliometric and Content Analysis Methods. *Education Sciences*, *11*(3), 142. DOI: 10.3390/educsci11030142

Agrawal, A. V., Pitchai, R., Senthamaraikannan, C., Balaji, N. A., Sajithra, S., & Boopathi, S. (2023). Digital Education System During the COVID-19 Pandemic. In *Using Assistive Technology for Inclusive Learning in K-12 Classrooms* (pp. 104–126). IGI Global. DOI: 10.4018/978-1-6684-6424-3.ch005

AI competency framework for teachers. (2024). In UNESCO eBooks. UNESCO. https://doi.org/DOI: 10.54675/ZJTE2084

AICTE. (2018). AICTE Training and Learning (ATAL) Academy Faculty Development Programme Guidelines. All India Council for Technical Education. Retrieved from: https://www.aicte-india.org/atal

AICTE. (2019). Model Curriculum for Induction Training Program for Faculty Members (FDP). New Delhi: All India Council for Technical Education. Available at: https://www.aicte-india.org/sites/default/files/FDP%20Handbook.pdf

AICTE. (2020). National Educational Alliance for Technology (NEAT) Scheme. AICTE. Retrieved from: https://neat.aicte-india.org/

Ajidarma, S. G. (2011). *Panji Tengkorak: Kebudayaan dalam Perbincangan*, KPG (Kepustakaan Populer Gramedia)

Ajidarma, S. G. (2021). *Ngobrolin Komik.* Pabrik Tulisan.

Akcanca, N. (2020). An alternative teaching tool in science education: Educational comics. *International Online Journal of Education & Teaching*, *7*, 1550–1570.

Akour, M., & Alenezi, M. (2022). Higher education future in the era of digital transformation. *Education Sciences*, *12*(11), 784. DOI: 10.3390/educsci12110784

Al-Abri, S., & Rahim, N. (2023). *Faculty development for strengthening online teaching capability: A mixed-method study*. PubMed Central.

AlAfnan, M. A. (2024). Social media personalities in Asia: Demographics, platform preferences, and behavior based analysis. *Studies in Media and Communication*, *12*(3), 349–363. DOI: 10.11114/smc.v12i3.6925

Alam, D. A. (2023). *Connectivism Learning Theory and Connectivist Approach in Teaching and Learning: A Review of Literature, 12*(2).

Albikawi, Z. F. (2023). Anxiety, depression, self-esteem, internet addiction, and predictors of cyberbullying and cybervictimization among female nursing university students: A cross-sectional study. *International Journal of Environmental Research and Public Health*, *20*(5), 4293. DOI: 10.3390/ijerph20054293 PMID: 36901301

Aleixo, P. A., & Sumner, K. (2017). Memory for biopsychology material presented in comic book format. *Journal of Graphic Novels & Comics*, *8*(1), 79–80. DOI: 10.1080/21504857.2016.1219957

Alhitmi, H. K., Mardiah, A., Al-Sulaiti, K. I., & Abbas, J. (2024). Data security and privacy concerns of AI-driven marketing in the context of economics and business field: An exploration into possible solutions. *Cogent Business & Management*, *11*(1), 2393743. DOI: 10.1080/23311975.2024.2393743

Ali, W. N. A. W., & Yahaya, W. A. J. W. (2024). Optimizing Acceptance Testing: Evaluating Digital Video Courseware With System Usability Scale (SUS) and NASA-TLX Workload Metrics. In *Power of Persuasive Educational Technologies in Enhancing Learning* (pp. 419-436). IGI Global Scientific Publishing.

Ali, W., Ashiqin, W. N., & Yahaya, W. W. A. J. (2023). Computational Thinking Self-Efficacy Perception for Progressive Learning in Malaysia: A Study of Validity and Reliability. In *Comparative Research on Diversity in Virtual Learning: Eastern vs. Western Perspectives* (p. 19). DOI: 10.4018/978-1-6684-3595-3.ch001

Alim, H. S. (2016). Critical hip-hop language pedagogies: Combat, consciousness, and the cultural politics of communication. In *Language and social justice in practice*. Routledge.

Allcoat, D., Hatchard, T., Azmat, F., Stansfield, K., Watson, D., & von Mühlenen, A. (2021). Education in the digital age: Learning experience in virtual and mixed realities. *Journal of Educational Computing Research, 59*(5), 795–816. DOI: 10.1177/0735633120985120

Allison, J., Hwang, G.-J., Mayer, R. E., Pellas, N., Karnalim, O., de Freitas, S., Ng, O.-L., Huang, Y.-M., Hooshyar, D., Seidman, R. H., Al-Emran, M., Mikropoulos, T. A., Schroeder, N. L., Roscoe, R. D., & Sanusi, I. (2025). From Generative AI to Extended Reality: Multidisciplinary Perspectives on the Challenges, Opportunities, and Future of Educational Computing. *Journal of Educational Computing Research, 63*(6), 1327–1363. DOI: 10.1177/07356331251359964

Al-Rahmi, W., Othman, M. S., & Yusuf, L. M. (2015). The role of social media for collaborative learning to improve the academic performance of students and researchers in Malaysian higher education. *International Review of Research in Open and Distance Learning, 16*(4). Advance online publication. DOI: 10.19173/irrodl.v16i4.2326

Al-Thani, A., Al-Thani, T., & Semmar, Y. (2014). Investigating the relationship between students' Tthinking styles, self-efficacy for learning, and academic performance at Qatar University. *American International Journal of Social Science, 3*(2), 172–179. www.aijssnet.com

Al-Zahrani, A. M. (2024). Unveiling the shadows: Beyond the hype of AI in education. *Heliyon, 10*(9), e30696. Advance online publication. DOI: 10.1016/j.heliyon.2024.e30696 PMID: 38737255

Andalib, S. Y., & Monsur, M. (2024). Co-created virtual reality (VR) modules in landscape architecture education: A mixed methods study investigating the pedagogical effectiveness of VR. *Education Sciences, 14*(6), 553. DOI: 10.3390/educsci14060553

Anderson, B., R O'G. (2016). *Mitologi dan Toleransi Orang Jawa*, MataBangsa, Yogyakarta, 4th print, Translated from *Mythology and the tolerance of the Javanese*, 1965

Andrey, J., Evans, B., & Rathi, A. (2021). Digital inequities in education: Infrastructure, access, and opportunity. *Journal of Digital Equity*, *3*(2), 45–62.

Anute, N., & Geetali Tilak, . (2024). Revolutionizing e-Learning with AR, VR, and AI. *The Scientific Temper*, *15*(04), 3122–3126. DOI: 10.58414/SCIENTIFICTEMPER.2024.15.4.20

An, Y., & Kaplan-Rakowski, R. (2024). Examining Adults' Enjoyment, Challenges, and Cognitive Load in Informal Learning with High-Immersion Virtual Reality. *TechTrends*, *68*(6), 1118–1128. DOI: 10.1007/s11528-024-00999-2

Aqib, M. A., Ekawati, R., & Khabibah, S. (2024). A modified Technological Pedagogical and Content Knowledge (TPACK) framework: A systematic literature review. Multidisciplinary Reviews, 8(6), Article 2025167.

Arco, L. J. P. (2023, March). Possibilities and limitations of social media in education processes during the pandemic: The teachers perspective. In *CTE Workshop Proceedings* (Vol. 10, pp. 315-325). https://doi.org/DOI: 10.55056/cte.552

ASEE. (2020). Profiles of Engineering and Engineering Technology by Institution. American Society for Engineering Education. https://ira.asee.org

Ashraf, M. A., Mollah, S., Perveen, S., Shabnam, N., & Nahar, L. (2022). Pedagogical Applications, Prospects, and Challenges of Blended learning in Chinese higher Education: A Systematic review. *Frontiers in Psychology*, *12*, 772322. Advance online publication. DOI: 10.3389/fpsyg.2021.772322

Asmae, M. (2025). Artificial Intelligence and Augmented Reality: Revolutionizing E-Learning for the Education of Tomorrow. International Journal of Innovative Science and Research Technology, 2053–2059. DOI: 10.38124/ijisrt/25feb1307

Astaño, J. L. (2025). Bibliometric analysis of studies on nanolearning and microlearning. *International Journal of Studies in Education and Science*, *6*(2), 240–256. DOI: 10.46328/ijses.144

Astleitner, H., & Schlick, S. (2025). The social media use of college students: Exploring identity development, learning support, and parallel use. *Active Learning in Higher Education*, *26*(1), 231–254. DOI: 10.1177/14697874241233605

Avalekar, U. A., Mehta, V., Mishra, B. R., Prasanna, L., Rajlakshmi, P. V., Manjunath, T. C., & Selvakumar, P. (2025). The current advances in AI-driven education. In Babulak, E. (Ed.), *Educational AI humanoid computing devices for cyber nomads* (pp. 173–196). IGI Global Scientific Publishing., DOI: 10.4018/979-8-3693-8985-0.ch008

Avalos, B. (2011). Teacher professional development in teaching and teacher education over ten years. *Teaching and Teacher Education*, *27*(1), 10–20. DOI: 10.1016/j.tate.2010.08.007

Azhar, A., & Ahmad Rashid, R.-A. (2025). A bird's eye-view of MOOCs for pedagogical knowledge and technical skills development of teachers in India. *International Journal of Research and Innovation in Social Science*, *9*(6), 4691–4705. DOI: 10.47772/IJRISS.2025.906000357

Azhari, A., Toms, Z., Pavlopoulou, G., Esposito, G., & Dimitriou, D. (2022). Social media use in female adolescents: Associations with anxiety, loneliness, and sleep disturbances. *Acta Psychologica*, *229*, 103706. DOI: 10.1016/j.actpsy.2022.103706 PMID: 35973307

Azim Premji Foundation. (2022). Stories of practice: Teachers and school leaders in action during. *COVID*, *19*. https://azimpremjifoundation.org

Babbie, E. R. (2013). *The practice of social research* (13th ed.). Wadsworth Cengage Learning.

Baddeley, A. D. (2000). The episodic buffer: A new component of working memory? *Trends in Cognitive Sciences*, *4*(11), 417–423. DOI: 10.1016/S1364-6613(00)01538-2

Bahri, N. A. S., Anuar, N. B., & Azmi, A. A. S. (2023). Benefits of AI-driven learning platform in engineering education context. *IACSIT International Journal of Engineering and Technology*, *15*, 329–340. DOI: 10.46492/ijet.v15i3.139

Baig, M. I., & Yadegaridehkordi, E. (2023). Factors influencing academic staff satisfaction and continuous usage of generative artificial intelligence (GenAI) in higher education. *International Journal of Educational Technology in Higher Education*, *22*(1), 5. Advance online publication. DOI: 10.1186/s41239-025-00506-4

Banerjee, S., Chowdhury, A., & Yein, N. (2023). User experience evaluation of a virtual reality tool used for 3D modelling in industrial design education: A study in the Indian context. *Designs*, *7*(5), 105. DOI: 10.3390/designs7050105

Barocas, S., & Selbst, A. D. (2016). Big data's disparate impact. *California Law Review*, *104*, 671.

Barrett, D. J. (2008). *MediaWiki*. O'Reilly Media, Inc.

Barrett, H. (2023). Rethinking digital portfolios: Fostering reflection and engagement. *Educational Technology Journal*, *12*(1), 45–60.

Barrett, R. C. A., Poe, R., O'Camb, J. W., Woodruff, C., Harrison, S. M., Dolguikh, K., Chuong, C., Klassen, A. D., Zhang, R., Joseph, R. B., & Blair, M. R. (2022). Comparing virtual reality, desktop-based 3D, and 2D versions of a category learning experiment. *PLoS One*, *17*(10), e0275119. DOI: 10.1371/journal.pone.0275119 PMID: 36201546

Bartle, R. (1996). Hearts, clubs, diamonds, spades: Players who suit MUDs. *Journal of MUD Research*, *1*(1), 19–34.

Basilotta-Gomez-Pablos, V., Matarranz, M., & Casado, R. (2022). Teacher digital competence and its impact on assessment practices. *Education and Information Technologies*, *27*(1), 975–993.

Battipede, E., Giangualano, A., Boffi, P., Clerici, M., Calvi, A., Cassenti, L., Cialini, R., Weghe, T. L., Addimando, L., Lanzi, P. L., & Gallace, A. (2024). *Physics Playground: Insights from a Qualitative-Quantitative Study about VR-Based Learning*. ArXiv., DOI: 10.1007/978-3-031-88881-6_8

Becker, B. A., Denny, P., Finnie-Ansley, J., Luxton-Reilly, A., Prather, J., & Santos, E. A. (2023). Programming is hard—or at least it used to be: Educational opportunities and challenges of AI code generation. In *Proceedings of the 54th ACM Technical Symposium on Computer Science Education* (Vol. 1, pp. 500–506). DOI: 10.1145/3545945.3569759

Beetham, H., & Sharpe, R. (Eds.). (2013). *Rethinking Pedagogy for a Digital Age: Designing for 21st Century Learning* (2nd ed.). Routledge., DOI: 10.4324/9780203078952

Benu, S., & Natonis, H. Y. (2025). Improving Students' Creative Thinking Abilitiesthrough Problem Based Learning Model. *International Journal of Christian Education and Philosophical Inquiry*, *2*(3), 42–51.

Bernard, R. M., Borokhovski, E., Schmid, R. F., Tamim, R. M., & Abrami, P. C. (2014). A meta-analysis of blended learning and technology use in higher education: From the general to the applied. *Journal of Computing in Higher Education*, *26*(1), 87–122. DOI: 10.1007/s12528-013-9077-3

Bhowmick, D., & Sarma, I. B. D. (2021). Micro-learning: An Effective E-learning Resource with Poor Net Connectivity. In *Virtual and Classroom Learning in Higher Education: A Guide to Effective Online Teaching* (pp. 76–96). Bentham Science Publishers.

Bhuyan, S. S., Sateesh, V., Mukul, N., Galvankar, A., Mahmood, A., Nauman, M., Rai, A., Bordoloi, K., Basu, U., & Samuel, J. (2025). Generative Artificial Intelligence Use in Healthcare: Opportunities for Clinical Excellence and Administrative Efficiency. *Journal of Medical Systems*, *49*(1), 10. Advance online publication. DOI: 10.1007/s10916-024-02136-1 PMID: 39820845

Bijl, A., Veldkamp, B. P., Wools, S., & de Klerk, S. (2024). Serious games in high-stakes assessment contexts: A systematic literature review into the game design principles for valid game-based performance assessment. *Educational Technology Research and Development*, *72*(4), 2041–2064. DOI: 10.1007/s11423-024-10362-0

Birbara, N. S., Sammut, C., & Pather, N. (2020). Virtual reality in anatomy: A pilot study evaluating different delivery modalities. *Anatomical Sciences Education*, *13*(4), 445–457. DOI: 10.1002/ase.1921 PMID: 31587471

Boelens, R., De Wever, B., & Voet, M. (2017). Four key challenges to the design of blended learning : A systematic literature review. *Educational Research Review*, *22*, 1–18. DOI: 10.1016/j.edurev.2017.06.001

Bond, M., Marin, V. I., Dolch, C., Bedenlier, S., & Zawacki-Richter, O. (2021). Digital transformation in higher education: Tools, practices, and pedagogies. *Australasian Journal of Educational Technology*, *37*(4), 1–15.

Bonneff, M. (2008). *Komik Indonesia*. Kepustakaan Populer Gramedia.

Brackenbury, T., & Kopf, L. (2022). Serious Games and Gamification: Game-Based Learning in Communication Sciences and Disorders. *Perspectives of the ASHA Special Interest Groups*, *7*(2), 482–498. DOI: 10.1044/2021_PERSP-21-00284

Bradáč, V., Smolka, P., Kotyrba, M., & Průdek, T. (2022). Design of an intelligent tutoring system to create a personalized study plan using expert systems. *Applied Sciences (Basel, Switzerland)*, *12*(12), 6236. DOI: 10.3390/app12126236

Brailovskaia, J., Teismann, T., & Margraf, J. (2018). Cyberbullying, positive mental health and suicide ideation/behavior. *Psychiatry Research*, *267*, 240–242. DOI: 10.1016/j.psychres.2018.05.074 PMID: 29940454

Braun, V., & Clarke, V. (2006). Using thematic analysis in psychology. *Qualitative Research in Psychology*, *3*(2), 77–101. DOI: 10.1191/1478088706qp063oa

Brigham, T. J. (2015). An Introduction to Gamification: Adding Game Elements for Engagement. *Medical Reference Services Quarterly*, *34*(4), 471–480. DOI: 10.1080/02763869.2015.1082385

Brooke, J. (1996). SUS: A "Quick and Dirty" Usability Scale. In *Usability Evaluation In Industry*. CRC Press.

Brown, J. S., Collins, A., & Duguid, P. (1989). Situated Cognition and the Culture of Learning. *Educational Researcher*, *18*(1), 32–42. DOI: 10.3102/0013189X018001032

Brown, K. G. (2001). Using computers to deliver training: Which employees learn and why? *Personnel Psychology*, *54*(2), 271–296. DOI: 10.1111/j.1744-6570.2001.tb00093.x

Buchem, I., & Hamelmann, H. (2010). Microlearning: A strategy for ongoing professional development. eLearning Papers, 21(1), 1–15.

Burdea, G. C., & Coiffet, P. (2024). *Virtual Reality Technology* (Third). John Wiley & Sons.

Burke, D., Crompton, H., & Nickel, C. (2025). The Use of Extended Reality (XR) in Higher Education: A Systematic Review. *TechTrends*, *69*(5), 998–1011. Advance online publication. DOI: 10.1007/s11528-025-01092-y

Burnell, K., Meter, D. J., Andrade, F. C., Slocum, A. N., & George, M. J. (2025). The effects of social media restriction: Meta-analytic evidence from randomized controlled trials. *SSM. Mental Health*, *7*, 100459. DOI: 10.1016/j.ssmmh.2025.100459

Caballero-Hernandez, J. A., Palomo-Duarte, M., & Dodero, J. M. (2017). Skill assessment in learning experiences based on serious games: A Systematic Mapping Study. *Computers & Education*, *113*, 42–60. DOI: 10.1016/j.compedu.2017.05.008

Caladine, R. (2008). *The future of rich media, learning management systems, and content management systems.*, DOI: 10.4018/978-1-59904-732-4.ch016

Campbell, J. (1949). *The hero with a thousand faces*. Pantheon Books.

Cao, X., Masood, A., Luqman, A., & Ali, A. (2018). Excessive use of mobile social networking sites and poor academic performance: Antecedents and consequences from stressor-strain-outcome perspective. *Computers in Human Behavior*, *85*, 163–174. DOI: 10.1016/j.chb.2018.03.023

CAST. (2018). Universal design for learning guidelines version 2.2. Retrieved from: http://udlguidelines.cast.org. Accessed on 12.09.2025.

Castro-Alonso, J. C., Koning, B. B. De, Fiorella, L., & Paas, F. (2021). *Five strategies for optimizing instructional materials: Instructor- and learner-managed cognitive load*. 1379–1407.

Chabris, C. F. (1999). Brief exposure to Mozart music does not enhance spatial ability: A meta-analysis. *Current Directions in Psychological Science*, *8*(4), 131–134.

Chamorro-Atalaya, O., Flores-Velásquez, C. H., Olivares-Zegarra, S., Dávila-Ignacio, C., Flores-Cáceres, R., Arévalo-Tuesta, J. A., Cruz-Telada, Y., & Suarez-Bazalar, R. (2024). Microlearning and nanolearning in higher education: A bibliometric review to identify thematic prevalence in the COVID-19 pandemic and post-pandemic context. *International Journal of Learning. Teaching and Educational Research*, *23*(4), 279–297. DOI: 10.26803/ijlter.23.4.15

Chan, C. K. Y., & Lee, K. K. W. (2023). The AI generation gap: Are Gen Z students more interested in adopting generative AI such as ChatGPT in teaching and learning than their Gen X and millennial generation teachers? *Smart Learning Environments*, *10*(1), 60. Advance online publication. DOI: 10.1186/s40561-023-00269-3

Chatzakou, D., Leontiadis, I., Blackburn, J., Cristofaro, E. D., Stringhini, G., Vakali, A., & Kourtellis, N. (2019). Detecting cyberbullying and cyberaggression in social media. [TWEB]. *ACM Transactions on the Web*, *13*(3), 1–51. DOI: 10.1145/3343484

Chaves, M., & Lage, A. (2021). Using Moodle and flipped classrooms in an engineering mechanics course. *International Journal of STEM Education*, *8*, 48. https://stemeducationjournal.springeropen.com/articles/10.1186/s40594-021-00302-2. DOI: 10.1186/s40594-021-00302-2

Chemnad, K., & Othman, A. (2024). Digital accessibility in the era of artificial intelligence—Bibliometric analysis and systematic review. *Frontiers in Artificial Intelligence*, *7*, 1349668. DOI: 10.3389/frai.2024.1349668 PMID: 38435800

Chen, L., Zeng, S., & Wang, W. (2021). The influence of emotion and learner control on multimedia learning. *Learning and Motivation*, *76*(September), 101762. DOI: 10.1016/j.lmot.2021.101762

Chen, S. (2022). Predictive roles of thinking styles in coping strategies among Mainland postgraduate students in Hong Kong. *Frontiers in Psychology*, *12*(January), 1–12. DOI: 10.3389/fpsyg.2021.693637 PMID: 35153883

Chen, S., Diao, Y., & Zhang, J. (2011, September). Social media: Communication characteristics and application value in distance education. In *2011 International Conference on Electrical and Control Engineering* (pp. 6774-6777). IEEE. https://doi.org/DOI: 10.1109/ICECENG.2011.6056919

Cherner, T., & Fegely, A. (Eds.). (2023). *Bridging the XR technology-to-practice gap: Methods and strategies for blending extended realities into classroom instruction.* AACE, Association for the Advancement of Computing in Education.

Chetry, K. K. (2024). Transforming Education: How AI is Revolutionizing the Learning Experience. *International Journal of Research Publication and Reviews, 5*(5), 6352–6356. DOI: 10.55248/gengpi.5.0524.1277

Choi, Y. (2025). Integrating ChatGPT into the Design of 5E-Based Earth Science Lessons. *Education Sciences, 15*(7), 815. DOI: 10.3390/educsci15070815

Chouhan, N., Khan, A., Shah, J. Z., Hussnain, M., & Khan, M. W. (2021). Deep convolutional neural network and emotional learning based breast cancer detection using digital mammography. *Computers in Biology and Medicine, 132*, 104318. DOI: 10.1016/j.compbiomed.2021.104318 PMID: 33744608

Chounta, I.-A. (2024). *The State of Artificial Intelligence and Education Across Europe—Education—Www.coe.int.* Education. https://www.coe.int/en/web/education/-/the-state-of-artificial-intelligence-and-education-across-europe-2

Chowdhary, S., Selvakumar, P., Sangeetha, B., Sarvaani, V. V., Anute, N., & Sharma, M. (2025). The role of social capital in entrepreneurial development. In Martínez-Falcó, J., Sánchez-García, E., & Marco-Lajara, B. (Eds.), *Support networks for entrepreneurs: Social capital and strategic collaborations* (pp. 311–338). IGI Global Scientific Publishing., DOI: 10.4018/979-8-3693-9836-4.ch013

Chowdhury, E. K. (2024). Examining the benefits and drawbacks of social media usage on academic performance: a study among university students in Bangladesh. *Journal of Research in Innovative Teaching & Learning*. https://doi.org/DOI: 10.1108/JRIT-07-2023-0097

Christofi, M., Lamprinakos, G., Nguyen, D. K., & Tran, P. T. (2025). Digital strategy design and digital transformation: A review and future research directions. *International Marketing Review*, 1–22.

Christy, K. R., & Fox, J. (2014). Leaderboards in a virtual classroom: A test of stereotype threat and social comparison explanations for women's math performance. *Computers & Education, 78*, 66–77. DOI: 10.1016/j.compedu.2014.05.005

Chugh, R., & Ruhi, U. (2018). Social media in higher education: A literature review of Facebook. *Education and Information Technologies, 23*(2), 605–616. DOI: 10.1007/s10639-017-9621-2

Chu, X., Yang, S., Sun, Z., Jiang, M., & Xie, R. (2022). The association between cyberbullying victimization and suicidal ideation among Chinese college students: The parallel mediating roles of core self-evaluation and depression. *Frontiers in Psychiatry*, *13*, 929679. DOI: 10.3389/fpsyt.2022.929679 PMID: 35845449

Cinar, O., Rafferty, K., Cutting, D., & Wang, H. (2024). AI-Powered VR for Enhanced Learning Compared to Traditional Methods. *Electronics (Basel)*, *13*(23), 4787. DOI: 10.3390/electronics13234787

Cipriano, C., Strambler, M. J., Naples, L. H., Ha, C., Kirk, M., Wood, M., Sehgal, K., Zieher, A. K., Eveleigh, A., McCarthy, M., Funaro, M., Ponnock, A., Chow, J. C., & Durlak, J. (2023). The state of evidence for social and emotional learning: A contemporary meta-analysis of universal school-based SEL interventions. *Child Development*, *94*(5), 1181–1204. DOI: 10.1111/cdev.13968 PMID: 37448158

Clark, R. C., & Mayer, R. E. (2016). E-learning and the science of instruction: Proven guidelines for consumers and designers of multimedia learning. In *Essential resources for training and HR professionals* (Fourth). Pfeiffer A Wiley Imprint.

Clarke, T. A., Lesh, J. J., Trocchio, J. S., & Wolman, C. (2010). Thinking styles: Teaching and learning styles in graduate education students. *Educational Psychology*, *30*(7), 837–848. DOI: 10.1080/01443410.2010.510794

Coates, J. M., Santhanalakshmi, K., Dinesh, N., Gandhimathi, S., & Chandel, P. S. Mohit, & Selvakumar, P. (2025). Assessment and evaluation in transnational staff development. In G. Morris & J. Ye (Eds.), Training and development in transnational higher education (pp. 387–406). IGI Global Scientific Publishing. DOI: 10.4018/979-8-3373-1897-4.ch019

Cochran-Smith, M., & Lytle, S. L. (2009). *Inquiry as stance: Practitioner research for the next generation*. Teachers College Press.

Connolly, M. R., Savoy, J. N., Lee, Y. G., & Hill, L. B. (2016). Building teaching careers: The CIRTL network's impact on early career STEM faculty. *CBE Life Sciences Education*, *15*(3), ar38. https://www.lifescied.org/doi/full/10.1187/cbe.15-12-0267. DOI: 10.1187/cbe.15-12-0267 PMID: 27543637

Corbeil, J. R., Khan, B. H., & Corbeil, M. E. (2021). Microlearning in the digital age. *Taylor and Francis. Doi*, *10*, 9780367821623.

Cordero, J., Torres-Zambrano, J., & Cordero-Castillo, A. (2024). Integration of Generative Artificial Intelligence in Higher Education: Best Practices. *Education Sciences*, *15*(1), 32. DOI: 10.3390/educsci15010032

Craig, A. B. (2013). *Understanding Augmented Reality: Concepts and Applications* (1st ed.). Morgan-Kaufmann.

Craig, C., & Kay, R. (2023). A Systematic Overview of Reviews of the Use of Immersive Virtual Reality in Higher Education. *Higher Learning Research Communications, 13*(2). Advance online publication. DOI: 10.18870/hlrc.v13i2.1430

Creswell, J. W. (2014). *Research design: Qualitative, quantitative, and mixed methods approaches* (4th ed.). SAGE Publications.

Crogman, H. T., Cano, V. D., Pacheco, E., Sonawane, R. B., & Boroon, R. (2025). Virtual Reality, Augmented Reality, and Mixed Reality in Experiential Learning: Transforming Educational Paradigms. *Education Sciences, 15*(3), 303. DOI: 10.3390/educsci15030303

Csikszentmihalyi, M. (1990). *Flow: The psychology of optimal experience*. Harper & Row.

Cuban, L. (2001). *Oversold and underused: Computers in the classroom*. Harvard University Press. DOI: 10.4159/9780674030107

Dabingaya, M. (2022). Analyzing the Effectiveness of AI-Powered Adaptive Learning Platforms in Mathematics Education. *Interdisciplinary Journal Papier Human Review, 3*(1), 1–7. DOI: 10.47667/ijphr.v3i1.226

Dafiotis, P., Sylaiou, S., Stylianidis, E., Koukopoulos, D., & Fidas, C. (2025). Evaluating Uses of XR in Fostering Art Students' Learning. *Multimodal Technologies and Interaction, 9*(4), 36. DOI: 10.3390/mti9040036

Darling-Hammond, L., Hyler, M. E., & Gardner, M. (2017). *Effective teacher professional development*. Learning Policy Institute. DOI: 10.54300/122.311

Das, S., Lekhya, G., Shreya, K., Shekinah, K. L., Babu, K. K., & Boopathi, S. (2024). Fostering Sustainability Education Through Cross-Disciplinary Collaborations and Research Partnerships: Interdisciplinary Synergy. In *Facilitating global collaboration and knowledge sharing in higher education with generative AI* (pp. 60–88). IGI Global Scientific Publishing.

Das, A. K., & Singh, A. K. (2022). Comics: An Alternative Medium for Education and Social Progress. *ECS Transactions, 107*(1), 8847–8854. DOI: 10.1149/10701.8847ecst

DataReport. (2025, January). Digital 2025: Global overview report. https://datareportal.com/reports/digital-2025-global-overview-report

Deci, E. L. (1971). Effects of externally mediated rewards on intrinsic motivation. *Journal of Personality and Social Psychology, 18*(1), 105–115. DOI: 10.1037/h0030644

Deci, E. L., Koestner, R., & Ryan, R. M. (1999). A meta-analytic review of experiments examining the effects of extrinsic rewards on intrinsic motivation. *Psychological Bulletin, 125*(6), 627–668. DOI: 10.1037/0033-2909.125.6.627 PMID: 10589297

Deci, E. L., & Ryan, R. M. (1985). *Intrinsic motivation and self-determination in human behavior*. Plenum Press. DOI: 10.1007/978-1-4899-2271-7

Deci, E. L., & Ryan, R. M. (2000). The "what" and "why" of goal pursuits: Human needs and the self-determination of behavior. *Psychological Inquiry, 11*(4), 227–268. DOI: 10.1207/S15327965PLI1104_01

Dede, C. (2009). Immersive Interfaces for Engagement and Learning. *Science, 323*(5910), 66–69. DOI: 10.1126/science.1167311 PMID: 19119219

Dede, C., Salzman, M. C., Loftin, R. B., & Sprague, D. (1999). Multisensory Immersion as a Modeling Environment for Learning Complex Scientific Concepts. In Feurzeig, W., & Roberts, N. (Eds.), *Modeling and Simulation in Science and Mathematics Education* (pp. 282–319). Springer New York., DOI: 10.1007/978-1-4612-1414-4_12

Delello, J. A., Sung, W., Mokhtari, K., Hebert, J., Bronson, A., & Giuseppe, T. D. (2025). AI in the Classroom: Insights from Educators on Usage, Challenges, and Mental Health. *Education Sciences, 15*(2), 113. DOI: 10.3390/educsci15020113

Demuyakor, J. (2020). Analysis of social media utilization by students in higher education: A critical literature review of Ghana. *Journal of New Media and Mass Communication, 6*(1), 1–7. DOI: 10.18488/journal.91.2020.61.1.7

Denojean-Mairet, M., López-Pernas, S., Agbo, F. J., & Tedre, M. (2024). A literature review on the integration of microlearning and social media. *Smart Learning Environments, 11*(1), 46. DOI: 10.1186/s40561-024-00334-5

Desiderio, L., Poutrain, S., Karda, M., & Kazantzidou, D. (2024). Using Artificial Intelligence And Leveraging Nano And Microlearning For Enhanced Language Acquisition: A Comprehensive Approach. *EdMedia+ Innovate Learning*, 175–185.

Deterding, S., Dixon, D., Khaled, R., & Nacke, L. (2011). From game design elements to gamefulness: Defining gamification. *Proceedings of the 15th International Academic MindTrek Conference*, 9-15. DOI: 10.1145/2181037.2181040

Diantama, S. (2023). Pemanfaatan Artificial Intelegent (AI) Dalam Dunia Pendidikan. *DEWANTECH Jurnal Teknologi Pendidikan, 1*(1), 8–14. DOI: 10.61434/dewantech.v1i1.8

Dicheva, D., Dichev, C., Agre, G., & Angelova, G. (2015). Gamification in education: A systematic mapping study. *Journal of Educational Technology & Society, 18*(3), 75–88.

Dos Santos, V. de F., Balbino, J., Bueno, A. J. A., Ghisi, K. M., Bessa, W. A., Souza, O. G., & Austríaco-Teixeira, P. (2025). FROM BLACKBOARD TO CLOUD. *HOW EDUCATION IS MOVING TO ALL-DIGITAL ENVIRONMENTS, 7*(6), 32475–32487. DOI: 10.56238/arev7n6-193

Dubiel, A., Kamińska, D., Zwoliński, G., Ramić-Brkić, B., Agostini, D., & Zancanaro, M. (2025). Virtual reality for the training of soft skills for professional education: Trends and opportunities. *Interactive Learning Environments, 33*(5), 1–21. DOI: 10.1080/10494820.2025.2450634

Dumitru, C., Radovici, M. C. M., Rasiti, G., & Veselinović, L. (2023). Science and learning in the digital era. *Der Donauraum, 63*(1–2), 83–98. DOI: 10.7767/dedo.2023.63.1-2.83

Dweck, C. S. (2006). *Mindset: The new psychology of success.* Random House.

Dwinggo Samala, A., Bojić, L., Bekiroğlu, D., Watrianthos, R., & Hendriyani, Y. (2023). Microlearning: Transforming education with bite-sized learning on the go—Insights and applications. [iJIM]. *International Journal of Interactive Mobile Technologies, 17*(21).

Dwivedi, Y. K., Kshetri, N., Hughes, L., Slade, E., Jeyaraj, A., Kar, A. K., Baabdullah, A. M., Koohang, A., Raghavan, V., Ahuja, M., Albanna, H., Albashrawi, M. A., Al-Busaidi, A. S., Balakrishnan, J., Barlette, Y., Basu, S., Bose, I., Brooks, L., Buhalis, D., & Wright, R. (2023). Multidisciplinary perspectives on opportunities, challenges and implications of generative conversational AI for research, practice and policy. *International Journal of Information Management, 71*, 102642. DOI: 10.1016/j.ijinfomgt.2023.102642

Dyulicheva, Y. Y., & Glazieva, A. O. (2021, December 18). *Game based learning with artificial intelligence and immersive technologies: An overview.* S&SE@*SW 2021: 4th Workshop for Young Scientists in Computer Science & Software Engineering*, Kryvyi Rih, Ukraine.

Edwin, E., Widiana, I. W., Lasmawan, I. W., & Suharta, I. G. P. (2025). Curriculum transformation towards future education. *Prima Magistra: Jurnal Ilmiah Kependidikan*, *6*(2), 122–132.

Eickelmann, B., Gerick, J., & Koop, C. (2017). ICT use in teaching and learning: A cross-national analysis. *Computers & Education*, *104*, 1–14.

Einstein, D. A., Dabb, C., & Fraser, M. (2023). FoMO, but not self-compassion, moderates the link between social media use and anxiety in adolescence. *Australian Journal of Psychology*, *75*(1), 2217961. DOI: 10.1080/00049530.2023.2217961 PMID: 40666004

Elaish, M. M., Yadegaridehkordi, E., & Ho, Y. S. (2025). Publication performance and trends in virtual reality research in education fields: A bibliometric analysis. *Multimedia Tools and Applications*, *84*(10), 6999–7026. DOI: 10.1007/s11042-024-19238-0

Elkhodr, M., & Gide, E. (2025). Integrating Generative AI in Cybersecurity Education: Case Study Insights on Pedagogical Strategies, Critical Thinking, and Responsible AI Use. https://doi.org/DOI: 10.48550/ARXIV.2502.15357

Eller, R. (2015). Implementing design into instruction: Intersections between the Waterfall model and ADDIE model. *Assumption University-EJournal of Interdisciplinary Research (AU-EJIR), 1*(1), 63–69.

Emamipour, S., & Esfandabad, H. S. (2013). Developmental study of thinking styles in Iranian students university. *Procedia - Social and Behavioral Sciences, 84*(1997), 1736–1739. DOI: 10.1016/j.sbspro.2013.07.023

Erstad, O., Černochová, M., Knezek, G., Furuta, T., Takami, K., & Liang, C. (2024). Social and Emotional Modes of Learning Within Digital Ecosystems: Emerging Research Agendas. *Technology. Knowledge and Learning*, *29*(4), 1751–1766. DOI: 10.1007/s10758-024-09775-w

Ertmer, P. A., & Ottenbreit-Leftwich, A. T. (2019). Teacher beliefs and technology integration practices. *Journal of Research on Technology in Education*, *51*(1), 1–15.

Essa, S. G., Celik, T., & Human-Hendricks, N. E. (2023). Personalized adaptive learning technologies based on machine learning techniques to identify learning styles: A systematic literature review. *IEEE Access : Practical Innovations, Open Solutions*, *11*, 23400–23420. DOI: 10.1109/ACCESS.2023.3276439

European Commission. (2021). SELFIE: Supporting schools in digital age. Retrieved from: https://ec.europa.eu/education/schools-go-digital/selfie_en. Accessed on 23.09.2025.

European Commission. (2022). Ethics Guidelines for Trustworthy AI. https://digital-strategy.ec.europa.eu/en/library/ethics-guidelines-trustworthy-ai

Extremera, N., Quintana-Orts, C., Mérida-López, S., & Rey, L. (2018). Cyberbullying victimization, self-esteem and suicidal ideation in adolescence: Does emotional intelligence play a buffering role? *Frontiers in Psychology*, *9*, 367. DOI: 10.3389/fpsyg.2018.00367 PMID: 29623058

Fang, X., Ng, D. T. K., Leung, J. K. L., & Xu, H. (2024). The applications of the ARCS model in instructional design, theoretical framework, and measurement tool: A systematic review of empirical studies. *Interactive Learning Environments*, *32*(10), 5919–5946. DOI: 10.1080/10494820.2023.2240867

Fan, W., & Zhang, L. F. (2009). Are achievement motivation and thinking styles related? A visit among Chinese university students. *Learning and Individual Differences*, *19*(2), 299–303. DOI: 10.1016/j.lindif.2008.10.005

Farinella, M. (2018). The potential of comics in science communication. *JCOM, Journal of Science Communication*, *17*(01), Y01. DOI: 10.22323/2.17010401

Fauzi, M. A., Harun, S. A., Martin, T., Paiman, N., & Firdaus Hussin, M. S. (2021). Smartphone Addiction among Young Adolescents: Integration of Flow Theory and Fear of Missing Out. *International Journal of Information & Management Sciences*, *32*(1).

Febriyanti, P., Santoso, R. B. (2023). *Nilai Keislaman dalam Cerita Wayang Kulit dengan Lakon Babad Alas Wanamarta di Kabupaten Karanganyar*, Jurnal Keislaman, Volume 06, Nomor 01, Maret 2023

Ferrera, R. (2023). Nano Learning: An Analysis of The Bite-Sized Discussions on Tiktok. *Available at SSRN* 4524968. DOI: 10.2139/ssrn.4524968

Field, A. (2018). *Discovering statistics using IBM SPSS statistics* (5th ed.). SAGE Publications.

Filiz, O., Kaya, M. H., & Adıgüzel, T. (2025). Teachers and AI: Understanding the factors influencing AI integration in K-12 education. *Education and Information Technologies*, *30*(13), 17931–17967. Advance online publication. DOI: 10.1007/s10639-025-13463-2

Forman, T., Kenney, B., & Wheeler, D. (2020). Barriers to digital participation: Socioeconomic and geographic perspectives. *International Journal of Digital Literacy*, *12*(3), 89–105.

Francis, N. J., Jones, S., & Smith, D. P. (2025). Generative AI in Higher Education: Balancing Innovation and Integrity [Review of Generative AI in Higher Education: Balancing Innovation and Integrity]. British Journal of Biomedical Science, 81. Taylor & Francis. https://doi.org/DOI: 10.3389/bjbs.2024.14048

Freeman, S., Eddy, S. L., McDonough, M., Smith, M. K., Okoroafor, N., Jordt, H., & Wenderoth, M. P. (2014). Active learning increases student performance in science, engineering, and mathematics. *Proceedings of the National Academy of Sciences of the United States of America, 111*(23), 8410–8415. https://www.pnas.org/content/111/23/8410. DOI: 10.1073/pnas.1319030111 PMID: 24821756

Freire, P. (1970). *Pedagogy of the oppressed.* Continuum.

Fullan, M. (2007). *The new meaning of educational change* (4th ed.). Teachers College Press.

Furnham, A., & Bradley, A. (1997). Music while you work: The differential distraction of background music on the cognitive test performance of introverts and extraverts. *Applied Cognitive Psychology, 11*(5), 445–455. DOI: 10.1002/(SICI)1099-0720(199710)11:5<445::AID-ACP472>3.0.CO;2-R

Gaarsdal, J., Wolff, S., & Madsen, C. B. (2022). Evaluating immersive animation authoring in an industrial VR training context. *Proceedings of the 14th International Conference on Signal Processing Systems (ICSPS 2022)*, 809–817. IEEE. DOI: DOI: 10.1109/ICSPS58776.2022.00147

Gagné, R. M. (1985). *The conditions of learning and theory of instruction* (4th ed.). Holt, Rinehart & Winston.

Gagne, R. M., Wager, W. W., Golas, K. C., & Kelle, J. M. (2005). *Principle of instructional design* (5th ed.). Thomson Learning Inc.

Galindo-Domínguez, H., Bezanilla, M. J., & Campo, L. (2025). Relationship between social media use and critical thinking in university students. *Education and Information Technologies, 30*(5), 6641–6665. DOI: 10.1007/s10639-024-12953-z

Gallego-Duran, F. J., Villagra-Arnedo, C. J., Satorre-Cuerda, R., Compan-Rosique, P., Molina-Carmona, R., & Llorens-Largo, F. (2019). A guide for Game-Design-Based Gamification. *Informatics (MDPI), 6*(4), 49. DOI: 10.3390/informatics6040049

Garcia-Bonete, M.-J., Jensen, M., & Katona, G. (2019). A practical guide to developing virtual and augmented reality exercises for teaching structural biology. *Biochemistry and Molecular Biology Education, 47*(1), 16–24. DOI: 10.1002/bmb.21188 PMID: 30475432

Garcia-Ruiz, M. A., Santana-Mancilla, P. C., & Gaytan-Lugo, L. S. (2019). A usability study of an interactive auditory display for supporting learning of molecular structure. *Proceedings of EdMedia '19,* The Association for the Advancement of Computing in Education.

Garcia-Ruiz, M., Nasir, M., & Rahman, Z. (2023, May 15). *Using AI Software Tools to Support Teaching Coding: A Double-edged Sword. Upper Peninsula Teaching and Learning Conference (UPTLC)*, Lake Superior State University, Sault Ste. Marie, Michigan, USA.

Garcia-Ruiz, M., Santana-Mancilla, P., Gaytán-Lugo, L., & Iñiguez Carrillo, A. (2022). Participatory Design of Sonification Development for Learning about Molecular Structures in Virtual Reality. *Multimodal Technologies and Interaction, 6*(10), 1–20. DOI: 10.3390/mti6100089

Gardner, H. (1983). *Frames of mind: The theory of multiple intelligences*. Basic Books.

Garg, A., Sharma, R. B., Tripathi, S., Kumar, K. S., Varshney, A. K., & Sharma, A. (2025). AI-Powered Virtual Reality: Transforming Education Beyond Conventional Approaches. *2025 International Conference on Intelligent Control, Computing and Communications (IC3)*, 398–403. DOI: 10.1109/IC363308.2025.10956771

Gay, G. (2010). *Culturally responsive teaching: Theory, research, and practice* (2nd ed.). Teachers College Press.

Gentile, M., Città, G., Perna, S., & Allegra, M. (2023). Do we still need teachers? Navigating the paradigm shift of the teacher's role in the AI era. *Frontiers in Education, 8*, 1161777. Advance online publication. DOI: 10.3389/feduc.2023.1161777

Georgiou, Y., & Kyza, E. A. (2018). Relations between student motivation, immersion and learning outcomes in location-based augmented reality settings. *Computers in Human Behavior, 89*(March), 173–181. DOI: 10.1016/j.chb.2018.08.011

Ghahari, D., Chaharlangi, D., Bonato, S., Sliekers, S., Sockalingam, S., Ali, A., & Benassi, P. (2023). Educational Approaches Using Simulation for Psychiatric Risk Assessment: A Scoping Review. *Academic Psychiatry, 48*(1), 61–70. DOI: 10.1007/s40596-023-01836-z

Ghanbaripour, A. N., Talebian, N., Miller, D., Tumpa, R. J., Zhang, W., Golmoradi, M., & Skitmore, M. (2024). A Systematic Review of the Impact of Emerging Technologies on Student Learning, Engagement, and Employability in Built Environment Education. *Buildings (Basel, Switzerland), 14*(9), 2769. DOI: 10.3390/buildings14092769

Giannakos, M. N., Azevedo, R., Brusilovsky, P., Cukurova, M., Dimitriadis, Y., Hernández-Leo, D., Järvelä, S., Mavrikis, M., & Rienties, B. (2024). The promise and challenges of generative AI in education. *Behaviour & Information Technology*. Advance online publication. DOI: 10.1080/0144929X.2024.2394886

Giroux, H. A. (1988). *Teachers as intellectuals: Toward a critical pedagogy of learning*. Bergin & Garvey Publishers, Inc.

Giroux, H. A. (2011). *On critical pedagogy*. Bloomsbury Publishing.

Goffman, E. (1967). *Interaction ritual: Essays on face-to-face behavior*. Pantheon Books.

Gopi, B., Kokila, M. S., Bibin, C. V., Sasikala, D., Howard, E., & Boopathi, S. (2024). Distributed technologies using AI/ML techniques for healthcare applications. In *Social Innovations in Education, Environment, and Healthcare* (pp. 375–396). IGI Global.

Gottfried, J. (2024). Americans' social media use. *Pew Research Center, 31*. https://janeaddams-il.aauw.net/files/2025/04/Soc-media-use-Americans.pdf

Goulart, V. G., Liboni, L. B., & Cezarino, L. O. (2022). Balancing skills in the digital transformation era: The future of jobs and the role of higher education. *Industry and Higher Education, 36*(2), 118–127. DOI: 10.1177/09504222211029796

Grassini, S. (2025). Beyond Textbooks: AI, XR, and the New Era of Learning. In *Futuristic Insights on Education Components—How education can meet the demands of an ever-changing world.* UNESCO Regional Center for Educational Planning.

Graul, B., Rollins, M. L., Powers, N., & Della Corte, D. (2020). *Student created video content for assessment, experiential learning, and service.* ArXiv., DOI: 10.1119/5.0029343

Greenberg, M. T. (2023). *Evidence for social and emotional learning in schools.* Learning Policy Institute. DOI: 10.54300/928.269

Grigorenko, E. L., & Sternberg, R. J. (1997). Styles of thinking, abilities, and academic performance. *Exceptional Children, 63*(3), 295–312. DOI: 10.1177/001440299706300301

Guerra-Tamez, C. R. (2023). The impact of immersion through virtual reality in the learning experiences of art and design students: The mediating effect of the flow experience. *Education Sciences, 13*(2), 185. Advance online publication. DOI: 10.3390/educsci13020185

Güney, K. (2023). Considering the Advantages and Disadvantages of Utilizing Social Media to Enhance Learning and Engagement in K-12 Education. *Research in Social Sciences and Technology, 8*(2), 83–100. DOI: 10.46303/ressat.2023.13

Gu, Y., Feijoo-Garcia, M. A., Zhang, Y., Magana, A. J., Benes, B., & Popescu, V. (2024). An XR Environment for AI Education: Design and First Implementation. *2024 IEEE Conference on Virtual Reality and 3D User Interfaces Abstracts and Workshops (VRW)*, 157–162. DOI: 10.1109/VRW62533.2024.00032

Hajirasouli, A., & Banihashemi, S. (2022). Augmented reality in architecture and construction education: State of the field and opportunities. *International Journal of Educational Technology in Higher Education, 19*(1), 39. DOI: 10.1186/s41239-022-00343-9

Hall, A. (2011). *Illustration.* Laurence King Publishing.

Hallam, S., Price, J., & Katsarou, G. (2002). The effects of background music on primary school pupils' task performance. *Educational Studies, 28*(2), 111–122. DOI: 10.1080/03055690220124551

Hamari, J., Koivisto, J., & Sarsa, H. (2014). Does gamification work? A literature review of empirical studies on gamification. *Proceedings of the 47th Hawaii International Conference on System Sciences*, 3025-3034. DOI: 10.1109/HICSS.2014.377

Hamza-Lup, F. G., & White, S. (2018). Design and assessment for hybrid courses: Insights and overviews. arXiv. https://arxiv.org/abs/1811.07273

Han, S. (2022). Flipped classroom: Challenges and benefits of using social media in English language teaching and learning. *Frontiers in Psychology, 13*, 996294. DOI: 10.3389/fpsyg.2022.996294

Hanus, M. D., & Fox, J. (2015). Assessing the effects of gamification in the classroom: A longitudinal study on intrinsic motivation, social comparison, satisfaction, effort, and academic performance. *Computers & Education, 80*, 152–161. DOI: 10.1016/j.compedu.2014.08.019

Hargreaves, A., & Fullan, M. (2012). *Professional capital: Transforming teaching in every school.* Teachers College Press.

Harun, S. A. B., Kasim, N. M., Jinnah, A. B. M. A., Fahmi, F. B., Sundaralinggam, N. A., Khalili, D. A. B., & Saharudin, N. W. N. B. (2020, May). Widad Psychetra Door (WPD) as New Mobile Application (APPS). *Journal of Physics: Conference Series, 1529*(5), 052097.

Harun, S. A., & Alias, N. S. (2015). Culture Changes and Personality Types Relationship among UTM International Academic Staff. *International Education Studies, 8*(13).

Harun, S. A., & Ibrahim, M. F. (2024). Virtual reality & current practices (an introduction to widad farokam). *Jurnal Pembangunan Sosial, 27*, 69–87. DOI: 10.32890/jps2024.27.4

Harun, S. A., Noor, A. A. M., Khair, N. N. S., Saharudin, N. W. N., & Pei, T. P. (2018). Openness Personality among Autistic Children Teachers in Malaysia. A Case Study in One Private Centre. *Global Business and Management Research, 10*(3), 465.

Harun, S. A., Yusof, J. N., Ibrahim, A., & Abdullah, N. (2015). Rationalizing the Limitation of Passive Students through Contextual Teaching. *Journal of Management Research, 7*(2), 295.

Hasanein, A. M., & Sobaih, A. E. E. (2023). Drivers and Consequences of ChatGPT Use in Higher Education: Key Stakeholder Perspectives. *European Journal of Investigation in Health, Psychology and Education, 13*(11), 2599–2614. DOI: 10.3390/ejihpe13110181 PMID: 37998071

Hattie, J., & Timperley, H. (2007). The power of feedback. *Review of Educational Research, 77*(1), 81–112. DOI: 10.3102/003465430298487

Haw, S.-C., & Muthu, K. S. (2023). *Proceedings of the International Conference on Computer, Information Technology and Intelligent Computing (CITIC 2022)*. Springer Nature.

Ha, Y. K. (2025). Assessing Learning Outcomes in Simulation-based Education to Recognize and Respond to Deteriorating Patients in Nursing Education: A Scoping Review. *Journal of Korean Critical Care Nursing, 18*(1), 39–54. DOI: 10.34250/jkccn.2025.18.1.39

Hayikaleng, N. (2019) *The Effects of Using Dual-Coding Theory in Teaching English Reading Comprehension among Vocational Students at Narathiwat Technical College*, International Journal of Arts Humanities and Social Sciences Studies Volume 4 Issue 6 July 2019.

Hazzan-Bishara, A., Kol, O., & Levy, S. (2025). The factors affecting teachers' adoption of AI technologies: A unified model of external and internal determinants. *Education and Information Technologies, 30*(11), 15043–15069. Advance online publication. DOI: 10.1007/s10639-025-13393-z

Hilsmann, N., & Dodson, C. (2025). Mobile Microlearning in Continuing Professional Development for Nursing: A Scoping Review. *Journal of Continuing Education in Nursing*, *56*(2), 53–62. DOI: 10.3928/00220124-20250121-05 PMID: 39880017

Hinderks, A., Schrepp, M., Domínguez Mayo, F. J., Escalona, M. J., & Thomaschewski, J. (2019). Developing a UX KPI based on the User Experience Questionnaire. *Computer Standards & Interfaces*, *65*, 38–44. DOI: 10.1016/j.csi.2019.01.007

Hjellvik, S., Mallam, S., Giskeodegard, M. F., & Nazir, S. (2024). Review on competency Assessment instrumentation in computer-based simulation. Technology Knowledge and Learning, 2994), 2171-2200. https://doi.org/.DOI: 10.007/s10758-024-09735-4

Hmoud, M., Daher, W., & Ayyoub, A. (2025). From experience to engagement: A mixed methods exploration of learning environments using artificial intelligence and extended reality. *Frontiers in Education*, *10*, 1617132. Advance online publication. DOI: 10.3389/feduc.2025.1617132

Hofmann, R., Curran, S., & Dickens, S. (2021). Models and measures of learning outcomes for non-technical skills in simulation-based medical education: Findings from an integrated scoping review of research and content analysis of curricular learning objectives. *Studies in Educational Evaluation*, *71*, 101093. DOI: 10.1016/j.stueduc.2021.101093

Hofstede, G. (1980). *Culture's consequences: International differences in work-related values.* Sage Publications.

Holmes, W., Bialik, M., & Fadel, C. (2019a). Artificial Intelligence in Education Promises and Implications for Teaching and Learning. In *(1st ed.). Center for Curriculum Redesign: Boston, MA, USA. (2019).* Center for Curriculum Redesign. https://circls.org/primers/artificial-intelligence-in-education-promises-and-implications-for-teaching-and-learning

Holmes, W., Bialik, M., & Fadel, C. (2019b). Artificial Intelligence in Education Promises and Implications for Teaching and Learning. In *(1st ed.). Center for Curriculum Redesign: Boston, MA, USA. (2019).* Center for Curriculum Redesign. https://circls.org/primers/artificial-intelligence-in-education-promises-and-implications-for-teaching-and-learning

Holmes, W., & Tuomi, I. (2022). State of the art and practice in AI in education. *European Journal of Education*, *57*(4), 542–570. DOI: 10.1111/ejed.12533

Horvath, A., & Goldschmid, R. (2025). Extended Abstract—Immersive Education: Utilizing the Potential of Immersive Technologies in Computer Science Higher Education. *Immersive Learning Research - Academic*, 162–167. DOI: 10.56198/508qgt70

Howard, S. K., Tondeur, J., Ma, J., & Yang, J. (2021). Teacher technology integration and overload: Understanding the balance. *Technology, Pedagogy and Education, 30*(4), 469–484.

Huang, R., Tlili, A., Yang, J., & Chang, T.-W. (2020). The Chinese experience in maintaining undisrupted learning in COVID-19 outbreak. In *Handbook on Facilitating Flexible Learning During Educational Disruption* (Issue March). Beijing: Smart Learning Institute of Beijing Normal University. https://www.researchgate.net/publication/339939064

Hunicke, R., LeBlanc, M., & Zubek, R. (2004). MDA: A formal approach to game design and game research. *Proceedings of the AAAI Workshop on Challenges in Game AI*, 1-5.

Hur, J. W. (2024). Fostering AI literacy: Overcoming concerns and nurturing confidence among preservice teachers. *Information and Learning Science*. Advance online publication. DOI: 10.1108/ILS-11-2023-0170

Husain, G., Thompson, W. F., & Schellenberg, E. G. (2002). Effects of musical tempo and mode on arousal, mood, and spatial abilities. *Music Perception, 20*(2), 151–171. DOI: 10.1525/mp.2002.20.2.151

Hu, Y., Tutschku, K., Boeva, V., Goswami, P., Abghari, S., & Sundstedt, V. (2024). Towards an Ethical and Data Privacy Metrology for AI-Enriched Human-Centered XR Systems. *2024 IEEE International Conference on Metrology for eXtended Reality, Artificial Intelligence and Neural Engineering (MetroXRAINE)*, 119–124. DOI: 10.1109/MetroXRAINE62247.2024.10796457

Ibrahim, M. F. B., Rahman, N. B., Zulkafli, M. H. B., Kasim, N. B., & Harun, S. A. (2021, April). Widad FAROKAM – Virtual System. In Journal of Science and Management Research (7 (April), 23-29). Wardah Publishing.

IEEE-TEMS. (2022). *AI in Engineering Education: Opportunities and Ethical Challenges*. IEEE Technology and Engineering Management Society.

Immordino-Yang, M. H., & Damasio, A. (2007). We feel, therefore we learn: The relevance of affective and social neuroscience to education. *Mind, Brain and Education : the Official Journal of the International Mind, Brain, and Education Society, 1*(1), 3–10. DOI: 10.1111/j.1751-228X.2007.00004.x

International Institute for Population Sciences (IIPS), & ICF. (2021). National Family Health Survey (NFHS-5), 2019–21: India: Volume I. Mumbai: IIPS. http://rchiips.org/nfhs

Isabirye, A. K., Moloi, K. C., Lebelo, R. S., & Khan, S. (2025). Cultivating Creativity and Innovation in the School Curriculum for the 21st Century: Opportunities and Challenges. *Journal of Ecohumanism*, *4*(3), 334–348. DOI: 10.62754/joe.v4i3.6647

Isen, A. M. (2000). Positive affect and decision making. In M. Lewis & J. M. Haviland-Jones (Eds.), *Handbook of emotions* (2nd ed., pp. 417–435). Guilford Press.

Ismoilov, S. (2025). Formation Of Creative Competence Of Leading Personnel In Higher Education Institutions. *International Journal of Artificial Intelligence*, *1*(1), 381–386.

Israel-Fishelson, R., & Hershkovitz, A. (2020). Persistence in a game-based learning environment: The case of elementary school students learning computational thinking. *Journal of Educational Computing Research*, *58*(5), 891–918. DOI: 10.1177/0735633119887187

Ivanashko, O., Kozak, A., & Knysh, T. (2024). The role of artificial intelligence in shaping the future of education: Opportunities and challenges. *Futurity Education*, *4*(1), 126–146. DOI: 10.57125/FED.2024.03.25.08

Ivanenkov, Y. A., Polykovskiy, D., Bezrukov, D., Zagribelnyy, B., Aladinskiy, V., Kamya, P., Aliper, A., Ren, F., & Zhavoronkov, A. (2023). Chemistry42: An AI-driven platform for molecular design and optimization. *Journal of Chemical Information and Modeling*, *63*(3), 5867–5876. DOI: 10.1021/acs.jcim.2c01191 PMID: 36728505

Jabbour, D., Masri, J. E., Nawfal, R., Malaeb, D., & Salameh, P. (2023). Social media medical misinformation: impact on mental health and vaccination decision among university students. *Irish Journal of Medical Science (1971-)*, *192*(1), 291-301. https://doi.org/DOI: 10.1007/s1185-022-02936-9

Jäncke, L., & Sandmann, P. (2010). Music listening while you learn: No influence of background music on verbal learning. *Behavioral and Brain Functions : BBF*, *6*(1), 3. DOI: 10.1186/1744-9081-6-3

Jayalakshmi, P., & Uma Rani, K. (2024). National Education Policy 2020: Prospects & Challenges. KY Publications. http://www.kypublications.com/BOOKS/NEP%20 2020_28-8-2024.pdf

Jayalath, J., & Esichaikul, V. (2020). Gamification to enhance motivation and engagement in blended eLearning for technical and vocational education and training. *Technology Knowledge and Learning*, *27*(1), 91–118. DOI: 10.1007/s10758-020-09466-2

Jenson, J., & Droumeva, M. (2016). Exploring media literacy and computational thinking: A game maker curriculum study. *Electronic Journal of e-Learning*, *14*(2), 111–121.

John, A., & Bates, S. (2024). Barriers and facilitators: The contrasting roles of media and technology in social–emotional learning. *Social and Emotional Learning: Research, Practice, and Policy*, *3*, 100022. DOI: 10.1016/j.sel.2023.100022

Johnson, D. W., & Johnson, R. T. (1989). *Cooperation and competition: Theory and research*. Interaction Book Company.

Jones, S. M., McGarrah, M. W., & Kahn, J. (2025). Social and emotional learning: A principled science of human development in context. In *Social and Emotional Learning* (pp. 4–19). Routledge. DOI: 10.4324/9781003054573-2

Kalaiselvi, D., Ramaratnam, M., Kokila, S., Sarkar, R., Anandakumar, S., & Boopathi, S. (2024). Future developments of higher education on social psychology: Innovation and changes. In *Social Innovations in Education, Environment, and Healthcare* (pp. 146–169). IGI Global.

Kalogeras, S. (2019). The Practice of Transmedia Storytelling Edutainment in Media-Rich Learning Environments. In Advances in Educational Technologies and Instructional Design (pp. 149–164). DOI: 10.4018/978-1-5225-5915-3.ch008

Kamariddinovna, M. E. (2025). THE ROLE OF NANO-LEARNING IN DEVELOPING DIGITAL COMPETENCE AMONG FUTURE ENGLISH LANGUAGE TEACHERS. *AMERICAN JOURNAL OF EDUCATION AND LEARNING*, *3*(5), 335–341.

Kamińska, D., Sapiński, T., Wiak, S., Tikk, T., Haamer, R. E., Avots, E., & Anbarjafari, G. (2019). Virtual reality and its applications in education: Survey. *Information (Basel)*, *10*(10), 318.

Kamińska, D., Zwoliński, G., Laska-Leśniewicz, A., Raposo, R., Vairinhos, M., Pereira, E., Urem, F., Ljubić Hinić, M., Haamer, R. E., & Anbarjafari, G. (2023). Augmented Reality: Current and New Trends in Education. *Electronics (Basel)*, *12*(16), 3531. DOI: 10.3390/electronics12163531

Kapp, K. M. (2012). *The gamification of learning and instruction: Game-based methods and strategies for training and education*. Pfeiffer.

Karagiorgas, D. N., & Niemann, S. (2017). Gamification and Game-Based Learning. *Journal of Educational Technology Systems*, *45*(4), 499–519. DOI: 10.1177/0047239516665105

Karthikeyan, M., Vigilia, J. N., Sequeira, S. L., Priya, P. V., Ghamande, M. V., & Boopathi, S. (2024). NBA Implementation Across Engineering Disciplines for Driving Social Changes in India. In *Social Innovations in Education, Environment, and Healthcare* (pp. 240–265). IGI Global. DOI: 10.4018/979-8-3693-2569-8.ch012

Karunanayaka, S. P. (2025). Promoting Professional Practice in Education through Innovative Thinking. *Journal of Innovative Practices in Education*, *1*(1), 1–8. DOI: 10.4038/jipe.v1i1.1

Katsitadze, N., Kharadze, N., & Pirtskhalaishvili, D. (2025). The impact of social media on students' effective time management. *Baltic Journal of Economic Studies*, *11*(1), 200–210. DOI: 10.30525/2256-0742/2025-11-1-200-210

KAYALAR., F. (2022). Efficiency and Application of Nano-learning in Adult Education. *Proceedings of VIAC 2022 in Budapest*, 71.

Kearns, C., & Kearns, N. (2020). The role of comics in public health communication during the COVID-19 pandemic. *Journal of Visual Communication in Medicine*, *43*(3), 139–140. DOI: 10.1080/17453054.2020.1761248 PMID: 32643470

Kellems, R. O., Eichelberger, C., Cacciatore, G., Jensen, M., Frazier, B., Simons, K., & Zaru, M. (2020). Using video-based instruction via augmented reality to teach mathematics to middle school students with learning disabilities. *Journal of Learning Disabilities*, *53*(4), 277–291. DOI: 10.1177/0022219420906452 PMID: 32065040

Keller, J. M. (2016). Motivation, learning, and technology: Applying the ARCS-V motivation model. *Participatory Educational Research*, *3*(2), 1–15. DOI: 10.17275/per.16.06.3.2

Kem, D. (2022). Personalised and adaptive learning: Emerging learning platforms in the era of digital and smart learning. *International Journal of Social Science and Human Research*, *5*(2), 385–391. DOI: 10.47191/ijsshr/v5-i2-02

Kent, L., Snider, C., Gopsill, J., & Hicks, B. (2021). Mixed reality in design prototyping: A systematic review. *Design Studies*, *77*, 101046. DOI: 10.1016/j.destud.2021.101046

Keshta, I. (2022). AI-driven IoT for smart health care: Security and privacy issues. *Informatics in Medicine Unlocked*, *30*, 100990. DOI: 10.1016/j.imu.2022.100903

Kessing, D., Katzwinkel, T., & Löwer, M. (2024). Gamification as an innovative method in user experience design. *Proceedings of the Design Society*, *4*, 285–294. DOI: 10.1017/pds.2024.31

Khlaif, Z. N., Ayyoub, A. A., Hamamra, B., Bensalem, E., Mitwally, M. A. A., Ayyoub, A., Hattab, M. K., & Shadid, F. (2024). University Teachers' Views on the Adoption and Integration of Generative AI Tools for Student Assessment in Higher Education. *Education Sciences*, *14*(10), 1090. DOI: 10.3390/educsci14101090

Khlaif, Z. N., Mousa, A., & Sanmugam, M. (2024). Immersive Extended Reality (XR) Technology in Engineering Education: Opportunities and Challenges. *Technology. Knowledge and Learning*, *29*(2), 803–826. DOI: 10.1007/s10758-023-09719-w

Khlaif, Z. N., & Salha, S. (2021). Using TikTok in education: A form of micro-learning or nano-learning? *Interdisciplinary Journal of Virtual Learning in Medical Sciences*, *12*(3), 213–218.

Khorasani, S. et al. (2023). *Hands-on or hands-off: Deciphering the impact of interactivity on embodied learning in VR. Computers & Education: X Reality*, 3, 100037. DOI: 10.1016/j.cexr.2023.100037

Kiili, K. (2005). Digital game-based learning: Towards an experiential gaming model. *The Internet and Higher Education*, *8*(1), 13–24. DOI: 10.1016/j.iheduc.2004.12.001

Kirkpatrick, D. L., & Kirkpatrick, J. D. (2006). *Evaluating training programs: The four levels* (3rd ed.). Berrett-Koehler Publishers.

Koehler, M. J., & Mishra, P. (2009). What is technological pedagogical content knowledge? *Contemporary Issues in Technology & Teacher Education*, *9*(1), 60–70. https://citejournal.org/volume-9/issue-1-09/general/what-is-technological -pedagogicalcontent-knowledge

Koivisto, J., & Hamari, J. (2019). The rise of motivational information systems: A review of gamification research. *International Journal of Information Management*, *45*, 191–210. DOI: 10.1016/j.ijinfomgt.2018.10.013

Kolb, D. A. (1984). *Experiential learning: Experience as the source of learning and development*. Prentice Hall., http://academic.regis.edu/ed205/Kolb.pdf

Kolb, D. A., Boyatzis, R. E., & Mainemelis, C. (2001). Experiential Learning Theory: Previous Research and New Directions. In *Perspectives on Thinking, Learning, and Cognitive Styles*. Routledge.

Konecki, M., Konecki, M., & Vlahov, D. (2023). Using Virtual Reality in Education of Programming. *2023 11th International Conference on Information and Education Technology (ICIET)*, 39–43. DOI: 10.1109/ICIET56899.2023.10111156

Kooli, C. (2023). Chatbots in Education and Research: A Critical Examination of Ethical Implications and Solutions. *Sustainability (Basel), 15*(7), 5614. DOI: 10.3390/su15075614

Kourtesis, P. (2024). A Comprehensive Review of Multimodal XR Applications, Risks, and Ethical Challenges in the Metaverse. *Multimodal Technologies and Interaction, 8*(11), 98. DOI: 10.3390/mti8110098

Kozma, R. B. (2008). Comparative analysis of policies for ICT in education. In Voogt, J., & Knezek, G. (Eds.), *International handbook of information technology in primary and secondary education* (Vol. 20, pp. 1083–1096). Springer., DOI: 10.1007/978-0-387-73315-9_68

Коберник, Г. І., & Kobernyk, H. (2025). Innovative approaches to the formation of mathematical competence of future primary school teachers. Scientific Bulletin of Mukachevo State University. Series. *Pedagogy and Psychology, 11*(1), 71–81.

KPMG. (2021). *NISHTHA programme evaluation report.* Ministry of Education, Government of India.

Kraft, M. A., Blazar, D., & Hogan, D. (2018). The effect of teacher coaching on instruction and achievement: A meta-analysis of the causal evidence. *Review of Educational Research, 88*(4), 547–588. DOI: 10.3102/0034654318759268

Krashen, S. D. (1982). *Principles and practice in second language acquisition.* Pergamon Press.

Krause, S., Dalvi, A., & Zaidi, S. K. (2025). Generative AI in Education: Student Skills and Lecturer Roles. https://doi.org/DOI: 10.48550/ARXIV.2504.19673

Krippendorff, K. (1999). *Content Analysis: An Introduction of its Methodology.* SAGE Publications.

Krishnamoorthy, N., Chandrasekar, J., Saqib, M., Therasa, P., Ganesh, C. S., & Boopathi, S. (2025). The Role of CO-PO Mapping in NBA Accreditation Assessments: Enhancing Educational Quality and Outcomes. In *Hispanic Leadership in Higher Education* (pp. 89–118). IGI Global.

Kuleto, V., Ilić, M., Dumangiu, M., Ranković, M., Martins, O. M. D., Păun, D., & Mihoreanu, L. (2021). Exploring opportunities and challenges of artificial intelligence and machine learning in higher education institutions. *Sustainability (Basel), 13*(18), 10424. DOI: 10.3390/su131810424

Kundu, A. (2024). Teachers' readiness for integrating digital assessment in K–12 education. *Education and Information Technologies, 29*(2), 1457–1478.

Kuspanov, N., Botagariyev, T., Ryskaliyev, S., Doshybekov, A., Syzdykov, A., & Gabitov, A. (2024). The influence of information technology on the professional readiness of future trainers in Kazaksha kures. *Retos: nuevas tendencias en educación física, deporte y recreación*, (51), 365-372.

Kyritsi, K., & Davis, J. M. (2021). Creativity in primary schools: An analysis of a teacher's attempt to foster childhood creativity within the context of the Scottish Curriculum for Excellence. *Improving Schools, 24*(1), 47–61.

Lahiry, S., Choudhury, S., Chatterjee, S., & Hazra, A. (2019). Impact of social media on academic performance and interpersonal relation: A cross-sectional study among students at a tertiary medical center in East India. *Journal of Education and Health Promotion, 8*(1), 73. DOI: 10.4103/jehp.jehp_365_18 PMID: 31143790

Lamberti, F., Cannavò, A., & Montuschi, P. (2020). Is immersive virtual reality the ultimate interface for 3D animators? *Computer, 53*(4), 36–45. DOI: 10.1109/MC.2019.2908871

Lampropoulos, G., Keramopoulos, E., Diamantaras, K., & Evangelidis, G. (2023). Integrating Augmented Reality, Gamification, and Serious Games in Computer Science Education. *Education Sciences, 13*(6), 618. DOI: 10.3390/educsci13060618

Landers, R. N., & Landers, A. K. (2014). An empirical test of the theory of gamified learning: The effect of leaderboards on time-on-task and academic performance. *Simulation & Gaming, 45*(6), 769–785. DOI: 10.1177/1046878114563662

Larson, K., & Chambers, R. (2020a). AR in the Computer Programming Classroom: A Review of the Literature. *2020 IEEE International Conference on Teaching, Assessment, and Learning for Engineering (TALE)*, 436–443. DOI: 10.1109/TALE48869.2020.9368329

Laskar, J. H. (2024). Content-based learning to competency-based education: A paradigm shift. *Educational Reforms Journal, 18*(1), 99–110.

Laskar, J. H., Khatun, R., & Sarkar, M. C. (2023). Education. In *Resurgent India*. Ashok Yakkaldevi.

Laugwitz, B., Held, T., & Schrepp, M. (2008). Construction and evaluation of a user experience questionnaire. In Holzinger, A. (Ed.), *HCI and usability for education and work* (pp. 63–76). Springer., DOI: 10.1007/978-3-540-89350-9_6

LaValle, S. M. (2023). *Virtual Reality*. Cambridge University Press., https://lavalle.pl/vr/ DOI: 10.1017/9781108182874

Lave, J., & Wenger, E. (1991). *Situated learning: Legitimate peripheral participation*. Cambridge University Press. DOI: 10.1017/CBO9780511815355

Lee, J., & Lee, J. H. (2022). Effects of simulation-based education for neonatal resuscitation on medical students' technical and non-technical skills. *PLoS One*, *17*(12), e0278575. DOI: 10.1371/journal.pone.0278575

Li, B., Said, I., Kirova, L., Blokhina, M., & Kang, H. J. (2021). SpArc: A VR animating tool at your fingertips. In Proceedings of the 27th ACM Symposium on Virtual Reality Software and Technology (VRST '21) (Article 95, 1–3). DOI: 10.1145/3489849.3489920

Lickona, T. (1992). *Educating for Character; how Our School Can Teach Respect and Responsibility*. Bantam Books.

Lieberman, A., & Miller, L. (2014). Teachers as professionals: Evolving definitions of professional development. In Martin, L. E., & Kragler, S. D. (Eds.), *Handbook of professional development in education* (pp. 3–20). Guilford Press.

Limbore, N. V., Anute, N., Ahluwalia, G. K., Chordiya, P. B., Kalshetti, P., & Selvakumar, P. (2025). Ethical leadership and corporate responsibility. In Harriott, S. (Ed.), *Innovative approaches to managing conflict and change in diverse work environments* (pp. 193–218). IGI Global Scientific Publishing., DOI: 10.4018/979-8-3693-9556-1.ch009

Lin, C. C., Huang, A. Y. Q., & Lu, O. H. T. (2023). Artificial intelligence in intelligent tutoring systems toward sustainable education: A systematic review. *Smart Learning Environments*, *10*(1), 35. DOI: 10.1186/s40561-023-00260-y

Lin, C. C., Huang, A. Y. Q., & Yang, S. J. H. (2023). A review of AI-driven conversational chatbots implementation methodologies and challenges (1999–2022). *Sustainability (Basel)*, *15*(5), 4012. DOI: 10.3390/su15054012

Lin, C.-J., Lee, H.-Y., Wang, W.-S., Huang, Y.-M., & Wu, T.-T. (2025). Enhancing reflective thinking in STEM education through experiential learning: The role of generative AI as a learning aid. *Education and Information Technologies*, *30*(5), 6315–6337. DOI: 10.1007/s10639-024-13072-5

Lin, S., Duan, W., Wang, Y., & Duan, H. (2024). Thinking style moderates the impact of the classroom environment on language creativity. *Journal of Intelligence*, *12*(1), 5. DOI: 10.3390/jintelligence12010005 PMID: 38248903

Lipschitz, J. M., Pike, C. K., Hogan, T. P., Murphy, S. A., & Burdick, K. E. (2023). The engagement problem: A review of engagement with digital mental health interventions and recommendations for a path forward. *Current Treatment Options in Psychiatry*, *10*(3), 119–135. DOI: 10.1007/s40501-023-00297-3 PMID: 38390026

Livingstone, S., & Helsper, E. J. (2007). Gradations in digital inclusion: Children, young people and the digital divide. *New Media & Society*, *9*(4), 671–696. DOI: 10.1177/1461444807080335

Li, X., & Yang, Z. (2024). Rural-urban disparities in teachers' technological pedagogical content knowledge: Evidence from China. *Education and Information Technologies*, *29*(3), 2101–2120.

Lokhande, M., John Deva Prasanna, D. S., Selvakumar, P., Ragupathi, T., Vaissnave, V., & Manjunath, T. C. (2025). Novel ML algorithms for healthcare. In A. Ajibesin, N. G. N., & S. Thangavel (Eds.), Synergizing data envelopment analysis and machine learning for performance optimization in healthcare (pp. 113–134). IGI Global Scientific Publishing. DOI: 10.4018/979-8-3373-0081-8.ch005

Lombard, D. (1996). *Nusa Jawa Silang Budaya 1: Batas Batas Pembaratan*. Gramedia Pustaka Utama.

Loranger, H., McCloskey, M., Nielsen, J., McKloskey, M., & Nielsen, J. (2010). *College students (ages 18-24) on the web* (2nd ed.). Nielsen Norman Group.

Lorenzo, G., & Ittelson, J. (2022). Building reflective learners with e-portfolios. *Journal of Learning Technologies*, *8*(2), 112–128.

Luck, M., & Aylett, R. (2000). Applying artificial intelligence to virtual reality: Intelligent virtual environments. *Applied Artificial Intelligence*, *14*(1), 3–32. DOI: 10.1080/088395100117142

Lukose, J. M., & Agbeyangi, A. O. (2025). Is social media hindering or helping Academic Performance? A case study of Walter Sisulu University Buffalo City Campus. *arXiv preprint arXiv:2501.03611*. https://doi.org//arXiv.2501.03611DOI: 10.48550

Lysloff, R., Kant-Achilles, M., Seltmann, F., & Schumacher, R. (1992). *Review of Wayang Beber*, by M. Kant-Achilles, F. Seltmann, & R. *Asian Music*, *24*(1), 146–151. DOI: 10.2307/834457

Maciel-Saldierna, M., Méndez-Garavito, I. R., Elizondo-Hernandez, E., Fuentes-Orozco, C., González-Ojeda, A., Ramírez-Ochoa, S., Cervantes-Pérez, E., Vicente-Hernández, B., Vázquez-Sánchez, S. J., Chejfec-Ciociano, J. M., & Cervantes-Guevara, G. (2024). Social Media Use and Fear of Missing out: An Exploratory Cross-Sectional Study in Junior High Students from Western Mexico. *Pediatric Reports, 16*(4), 1022–1033. DOI: 10.3390/pediatric16040087 PMID: 39585041

Mahzunah, A. K., Sari, I. Y., Paradela, B. V., Murti, B., & Tursina, E. (2024). The Impact of Cyberbullying on Self-Harming Behavior and Suicidal Thoughts among Adolescents: A Meta-Analysis. *Journal of Health Promotion and Behavior, 9*(4), 357–369. DOI: 10.26911/thejhpb.2024.09.04.07

Maki, O.; Alshaikhli, M.; Gunduz, M.; Naji, K.K.; Abdulwahed, M. (2022). Development of digitalization road map for Healthcare Facility Management. IEEE Access 2022, 10, 14450–14462.

Malamed, C. (2009) Visual Language for Designer: Principles for Creating Graphics that People Understand. Rockport.

Mallek, F., Mazhar, T., Shah, S. F. A., Ghadi, Y. Y., & Hamam, H. (2024). A review on cultivating effective learning: Synthesizing educational theories and virtual reality for enhanced educational experiences. *PeerJ. Computer Science, 10*, e2000. DOI: 10.7717/peerj-cs.2000 PMID: 38855256

Manca, S., & Ranieri, M. (2016). Facebook and the others. Potentials and obstacles of social media for teaching in higher education. *Computers & Education, 95*, 216–230. DOI: 10.1016/j.compedu.2016.01.012

Manfredi, G., Erra, U., & Gilio, G. (2023). A Mixed Reality Approach for Innovative Pair Programming Education with a Conversational AI Virtual Avatar. *Proceedings of the 27th International Conference on Evaluation and Assessment in Software Engineering*, 450–454. DOI: 10.1145/3593434.3593952

Manickam, L. S. S., & Sruthi, E. S. (2025). Competencies Based Professional Psychology Course In India. *Indian Journal of Psychology.*

ManiMekalai. M., Veni, C., Agarwal, A., Joshi, A. A., Gururaja, H., & Boopathi, S. (2024). Harnessing VR and AR for sustainable smart manufacturing: Eco-friendly innovations. In *Reshaping environmental science through machine learning and IoT* (pp. 355–380). IGI Global Scientific Publishing.

Manousou, E. (2025). Critical Thinking in Distance Education: The Challenges in a Decade (2016–2025) and the Role of Artificial Intelligence. *Education Sciences, 15*(6), 757. DOI: 10.3390/educsci15060757

Manwaring, K. C., Larsen, R., Graham, C. R., Henrie, C. R., & Halverson, L. R. (2017). Investigating student engagement in blended learning settings using experience sampling and structural equation modeling. *The Internet and Higher Education*, *35*, 21–33. DOI: 10.1016/j.iheduc.2017.06.002

Marougkas, A., Troussas, C., Krouska, A., & Sgouropoulou, C. (2023). Virtual Reality in Education: A Review of Learning Theories, Approaches and Methodologies for the Last Decade. *Electronics (Basel)*, *12*(13), 2832. DOI: 10.3390/electronics12132832

Marpelina, L. & others. (2024). Revolutionizing history learning in the digital era: Transforming the way we learn. *KnE Social Sciences*, 912–927.

Marr, B. (2021). *Business trends in practice: The 25+ trends that are redefining organizations*.

Matt, C., Hess, T., & Benlian, A. (2015). Digital Transformation Strategies. *Business & Information Systems Engineering*, *57*(5), 339–343. DOI: 10.1007/s12599-015-0401-5

Ma, X., Liu, Q., & Zhang, W. (2025). The impact of multidimensional excessive social media use on academic performance: The moderating role of mindfulness. *Frontiers in Psychology*, *16*, 1579509. DOI: 10.3389/fpsyg.2025.1579509 PMID: 40625430

Mayer, R. E. (2009). Multimedia learning. In *Psychology of Learning and Motivation - Advances in Research and Theory* (2nd ed.). Cambridge University Press., DOI: 10.1017/CBO9780511811678

Mayer, R. E., & Pilegard, C. (2014). Basic principles of multimedia learning. In Mayer, R. E. (Ed.), *The Cambridge Handbook of Multimedia Learning* (pp. 316–344). Cambridge University Press. DOI: 10.1017/CBO9781139547369.016

McCloud, S. (1993). *Understanding Comic: The Invisible Art*. Kitchen Sink Press.

McCulloch, A., & Sinha, S. (2024). Portfolio practices for metacognitive skill development. *Reflective Education Quarterly*, *5*(1), 1–18.

McGonigal, J. (2011). *Reality is broken: Why games make us better and how they can change the world*. Penguin Press.

MCLeod. S. (2025, March 19). *Kolb's Learning Styles & Experiential Learning Cycle*. https://www.simplypsychology.org/learning-kolb.html

McLoughlin, C. (2011). Leading pedagogical change with innovative web tools and social media. In Encyclopedia of E-Leadership, Counseling and Training (pp. 1-11). IGI Global. DOI: 10.4018/javet.2011010102

Mehra, J., Madaan, S., & Balu, N. Mohit, Selvakumar, P., & Manjunath, T. C. (2025). The ubiquitous internet and smart computation available 24/7 for anyone and anywhere. In E. Babulak (Ed.), Educational AI humanoid computing devices for cyber nomads (pp. 247–270). IGI Global Scientific Publishing. DOI: 10.4018/979-8-3693-8985-0.ch010

Mei, Q., Chan, N. N., Gill, R. S., Subramaniam, N., Motevalli, S., & Ang, C. S. (2025). Impact of attention, relevance, confidence, satisfaction (ARCS) model on teaching effectiveness in higher education: A systematic review. *Discover Education*, *4*(1), 252. DOI: 10.1007/s44217-025-00674-5

Meng, Q., Yan, Z., Abbas, J., Shankar, A., & Subramanian, M. (2025). Human–computer interaction and digital literacy promote educational learning in pre-school children: Mediating role of psychological resilience for kids' mental well-being and school readiness. *International Journal of Human-Computer Interaction*, *41*(1), 16–30. DOI: 10.1080/10447318.2023.2248432

Merelo, J. J., Castillo, P. A., Mora, A. M., Barranco, F., Abbas, N., Guillén, A., & Tsivitanidou, O. (2023). Chatbots and messaging platforms in the classroom: An analysis from the teacher's perspective. *Education and Information Technologies*, *29*(2), 1903–1938. DOI: 10.1007/s10639-023-11703-x PMID: 37361787

Mhlongo, S., Mbatha, K., Ramatsetse, B., & Dlamini, R. (2023). Challenges, opportunities, and prospects of adopting and using smart digital technologies in learning environments: An iterative review. *Heliyon*, *9*(6), e16348. DOI: 10.1016/j.heliyon.2023.e16348

Ministry of Education (MoE). (2020). National education policy 2020. Government of India. https://www.education.gov.in/sites/upload_files/mhrd/files/NEP_Final_English_0.pdf

Ministry of Education. (2022). DIKSHA: One nation one digital platform. Retrieved from" https://diksha.gov.in/. Accessed on 12.08.2025.

Ministry of Electronics and IT. India. (2023). Digital Personal Data Protection Act. https://www.meity.gov.in/digital-personal-data-protection-act-2023

Mishra, L., Gupta, T., & Shree, A. (2020). Online teaching-learning in higher education during lockdown period of COVID-19 pandemic. *International Journal of Educational Research Open*, *1*, 100012. DOI: 10.1016/j.ijedro.2020.100012 PMID: 35059663

Mishra, P. (2019). Considering contextual knowledge: The TPACK diagram gets an upgrade. *Journal of Digital Learning in Teacher Education*, *35*(2), 76–78. DOI: 10.1080/21532974.2019.1588611

Mishra, P., & Koehler, M. J. (2006). Technological Pedagogical Content Knowledge: A framework for teacher knowledge. *Teachers College Record*, *108*(6), 1017–1054. DOI: 10.1111/j.1467-9620.2006.00684.x

Mohamed Hashim, M. A., Tlemsani, I., & Matthews, R. (2022). Higher education strategy in digital transformation. *Education and Information Technologies*, *27*(3), 3171–3195. DOI: 10.1007/s10639-021-10739-1 PMID: 34539217

Molina, E., & Medina, E. (2025). *AI Revolution in Higher Education*. The World Bank.

Moore, N., Ahmadpour, N., Brown, M., Poronnik, P., & Davids, J. (2022). Designing Virtual Reality–Based Conversational Agents to Train Clinicians in Verbal De-escalation Skills: Exploratory Usability Study. *JMIR Serious Games*, *10*(3), e38669. DOI: 10.2196/38669 PMID: 35793129

Moreno, R., & Mayer, R. (2007). Interactive multimodal learning environments: Special issue on interactive learning environments: Contemporary issues and trends. *Educational Psychology Review*, *19*(3), 309–326. DOI: 10.1007/s10648-007-9047-2

Moreno, R., & Mayer, R. E. (2000). A coherence effect in multimedia learning: The case for minimizing irrelevant sounds in the design of multimedia instructional messages. *Journal of Educational Psychology*, *92*(1), 117–125. DOI: 10.1037/0022-0663.92.1.117

Mubarak, A., Cao, H., & Zhang, Y. (2020). Digital divide and social inclusion: A review. *Sustainability*, *12*(20), 8588.

Mukasheva, M., Kalkabayeva, Z., & Pussyrmanov, N. (2023). Visualization of sorting algorithms in the virtual reality environment. *Frontiers in Education*, *8*, 1195200. Advance online publication. DOI: 10.3389/feduc.2023.1195200

Mulyono, S. (1983). *Simbolisme and Mistisisme dalam Wayang*. CV Haji Masagung.

Musbikin, I. (2010). *Serat Dewa Ruci: The Mystery of the Water of Life*. Diva Press.

Myara, J. (2024). The Applications and Uses of Immersive Virtual Reality: A Multisensory Approach to Effective and Efficient Academic Pedagogy. *PCOM Capstone Projects*. https://digitalcommons.pcom.edu/capstone_projects/52

Nacak, A., Bağlama, B., & Demir, B. (2020). Teacher candidate views on the use of YouTube for educational purposes. *Online Journal of Communication and Media Technologies, 10*(2), e202003. DOI: 10.29333/ojcmt/7827

Nagata, J. M., Memon, Z., Talebloo, J., Li, K., Low, P., Shao, I. Y., Ganson, K. T., Testa, A., He, J., Brindis, C. D., & Baker, F. C. (2025). Prevalence and patterns of social media use in early adolescents. *Academic Pediatrics, 25*(4), 102784. DOI: 10.1016/j.acap.2025.102784 PMID: 39800219

Naji, K. K., Gunduz, M., Alhenzab, F., Al-Hababi, H., & Al-Qahtani, A. (2024). Assessing the Digital Transformation Readiness of the Construction Industry Utilizing the Delphi Method. *Buildings (Basel, Switzerland), 14*(3), 601. DOI: 10.3390/buildings14030601

Nanjappa, S., Ghosh, V., Acharya, S., Mukerjee, H. S., & Stl, V. (2023). Microlearning in corporate settings: Practitioner perspectives. *Human Resource Development International, 26*(5), 655–662. DOI: 10.1080/13678868.2022.2160688

Nayak, P. (2020). Peer learning communities in rural Maharashtra: A bottom-up model for teacher professional development. *Contemporary Education Dialogue, 17*(1), 120–134. DOI: 10.1177/0973184919890315

Ng, B. Y., Li, J., Tong, X., Ye, K., Yenne, G., Chandrasekaran, V., & Li, J. (2025). Analyzing Security and Privacy Challenges in Generative AI Usage Guidelines for Higher Education. https://doi.org/DOI: 10.48550/ARXIV.2506.20463

Nguyen, A., Ngo, H. N., Hong, Y., Dang, B., & Nguyen, B.-P. T. (2022). Ethical principles for artificial intelligence in education. *Education and Information Technologies, 28*(4), 4221–4241. DOI: 10.1007/s10639-022-11316-w PMID: 36254344

Nguyen, H. T. L., Nakamura, K., Seino, K., & Vo, V. T. (2020). Relationships among cyberbullying, parental attitudes, self-harm and suicidal behavior among adolescents: Results from a school-based survey in Vietnam. *BMC Public Health, 20*(1), 476. DOI: 10.1186/s12889-020-08500-3 PMID: 32276608

Nicol, D. J., & Macfarlane-Dick, D. (2018). Formative assessment and self-regulated learning: A model and seven principles of good feedback practice. *Studies in Higher Education, 43*(5), 798–814.

Niemi, H., Harju, V., Vivitsou, M., Viitanen, K., Multisilta, J., & Kuokkanen, A. (2014). Digital Storytelling for 21 Century Skills in Virtual Learning Environments. *Creative Education, 05*(09), 657–671. DOI: 10.4236/ce.2014.59078

Ningtyas, P. K., Widarti, H. R., & Parlan, P. (2024). Exploring the Use of Social Media in Science Learning Environments: A Systematic Literature Review. *Journal of Science Learning*, *7*(2), 178–186. https://eric.ed.gov/?id=EJ1440831. DOI: 10.17509/jsl.v7i2.67071

Nisha Angeline, M., Selvakumar, P., Gupta, M. K., Nazar, N., Elumalai, D., & Bhattacharya, S. (2025). Emerging materials for energy storage and environmental applications. In K. Muduli, B. Moharana, S. Ales, & D. Biswal (Eds.), Using computational intelligence for sustainable manufacturing of advanced materials (pp. 53–72). IGI Global Scientific Publishing. DOI: 10.4018/979-8-3693-7974-5.ch003

Noble, E. R., Ask, T. F., & Knox, B. J. (2025). Tailored Extended Reality Environments for Education and Training in Cybersecurity: Engagement Beyond Awareness. *2025 IEEE Global Engineering Education Conference (EDUCON)*, 1–9. DOI: 10.1109/EDUCON62633.2025.11016494

Nukarinen, T., Rantala, J., Korpela, K., Browning, M. H., Istance, H. O., Surakka, V., & Raisamo, R. (2022). Measures and modalities in restorative virtual natural environments: An integrative narrative review. *Computers in Human Behavior*, *126*, 107008. DOI: 10.1016/j.chb.2021.107008

Nunez-Canal, M., de Obesso, M., & Perez-Sanchez, A. (2022). Assessing digital competence: Review of tools and methods. *Education Sciences*, *12*(6), 402.

Obourdin, G., de Maeyer, S., & Van den Bossche, P. (2024). Unlocking the power of immersive learning: The FAIRI instructional design proposition for adaptive immersive virtual reality. *Computers & Education: X Reality*, *5*, 100084. DOI: 10.1016/j.cexr.2024.100084

Odoom, D., Agyepong, L., Dick-Sagoe, C., & Mensah, E. O. (2025). Unveiling the social media landscape: Exploring factors influencing usage patterns among tertiary education students in Ghana. *Education and Information Technologies*, *30*(3), 3861–3883. DOI: 10.1007/s10639-024-12944-0

OECD. (2009). *Creating effective teaching and learning environments: First results from TALIS*. OECD Publishing., DOI: 10.1787/9789264068780-

OECD. (2023). Policy Framework for Responsible AI in Education. https://www.oecd.org/education/edtech/policy-framework-ai-education.pdf

Oestreich, J. H., & Guy, J. W. (2022). Game-Based Learning in Pharmacy Education. *Pharmacy (Basel, Switzerland)*, *10*(1), 11. DOI: 10.3390/pharmacy10010011

Okonji, N. N., & Igwe, E. A. (2025). Prospects and challenges of personalized learning through artificial intelligence–driven adaptive learning systems in N. *International Journal of Education in Developing Areas*, *3*, 45–59. DOI: 10.30534/ijeda/2025/003112025

Okorie, P. N., MacDowell, P., & Olson, B. (2024). Applying a Constructivist Approach to Designing Virtual Reality Experiences that Facilitate Authentic Learning for Adolescents. *The Journal of Applied Instructional Design*, *13*(4). Advance online publication. DOI: 10.59668/2033.18640

Oliveira, K. K. de S., & De Souza, R. A. (2022). Digital transformation towards education 4.0. *Informatics in Education*, *21*(2), 283–309.

Olmstead, A., & Turpen, C. (2016). Evaluating Professional Development Work with the Real-Time Professional Development Observation Tool (R-PDOT). *Physical Review. Physics Education Research*, *12*(2), 020136. DOI: 10.1103/PhysRevPhysEducRes.12.020136

Opfer, V. D., & Pedder, D. (2011). Conceptualizing teacher professional learning. *Review of Educational Research*, *81*(3), 376–407. DOI: 10.3102/0034654311413609

Oranje, A., Mislevy, B., Bauer, M. I., & Jackson, G. T. (2019). Summative Game-Based Assessment. In Advances in game-based learning (pp. 37-65). DOI: 10.1007/978-3-030-15569-8_3

Osborn-King, R. (2005). Can 'Blended Learning' Be Redeemed? *E-learning*, *2*(1).

Paananen, V., Kiarostami, M. S., Lik-Hang, L., Braud, T., & Hosio, S. (2023). From Digital Media to Empathic Spaces: A Systematic Review of empathy Research in Extended reality Environments. *ACM Computing Surveys*, *56*(5), 1–40. DOI: 10.1145/3626518

Packer, H., & Huang, F. (2025). Can China's universities power it to victory in the global AI race? *Times Higher Education (THE)*. https://www.timeshighereducation.com/depth/can-chinas-universities-power-it-victory-global-ai-race

Padmavathi, P., Thrimurthulu, V., Bharani, J., Sailaja, V., Kumar, N. M., & Boopathi, S. (2025). A Study on Integration of Deep Learning With IoT for Smart Engineering Solutions. In *Navigating Challenges of Object Detection Through Cognitive Computing* (pp. 125–158). IGI Global Scientific Publishing. DOI: 10.4018/979-8-3693-9057-3.ch005

Padmavathy, S., Gudipudi, N. R., & Boopathi, S. (2025). *Em povvering Small and Medium Enterprises Through Smart Technology and Talent Management.*

Palaus, M., Marron, E. M., Viejo-Sobera, R., & Redolar-Ripoll, D. (2024). Neural basis of video gaming: A systematic review of neuroimaging studies. *Frontiers in Human Neuroscience*, *18*, 123–145.

Pallavicini, F., Pepe, A., & Minissi, M. E. (2019). Gaming in Virtual Reality: What Changes in Terms of Usability, Emotional Response and Sense of Presence Compared to Non-Immersive Video Games? *Simulation & Gaming*, *50*(2), 136–159. DOI: 10.1177/1046878119831420

Panadero, E., & Alonso-Tapia, J. (2023). The role of peer assessment and self-assessment in promoting metacognitive skills. *Educational Psychology Review*, *35*(1), 299–315.

Patel, P., Torppa, M., Aro, M., Richardson, U., & Lyytinen, H. (2021). Assessing the effectiveness of a game-based phonics intervention for first and second grade English language learners in India: A randomized controlled trial. *Journal of Computer Assisted Learning*, *38*(1), 76–89. DOI: 10.1111/jcal.12592

Patton, M. Q. (2002). *Qualitative research and evaluation methods* (3rd ed.). SAGE Publications.

Pedroso, J. E., Tubola, L. F. A., & Aquidado, E. J. (2023). Facebook Messenger: As Means of Communication for Academic Inquiries. *Journal of Digital Learning and Distance Education*, *2*(2), 491–505. DOI: 10.56778/jdlde.v2i2.116

Pei, X., Fu, S., & Jiang, T. (2023). An empirical study on user experience evaluation of VR interface in digital museums. *Data and Information Management*, *7*(4), 100057. DOI: 10.1016/j.dim.2023.100057

Pekrun, R. (2014). Emotions and learning. [UNESCO International Bureau of Education.]. *Educational Practices Series*, *24*, 1–31.

Peng, C., Xia, F., Naseriparsa, M., & Osborne, F. (2023). Knowledge graphs: Opportunities and challenges. *Artificial Intelligence Review*, *56*(11), 13071–13102. DOI: 10.1007/s10462-023-10465-9 PMID: 37362886

Petersen, G. B., Petkakis, G., & Makransky, G. (2022). A study of how immersion and interactivity drive VR learning. *Computers & Education*, *179*, 104429. DOI: 10.1016/j.compedu.2021.104429

Petko, D., Prasse, D., & Cantieni, A. (2016). Perceived quality of educational technology use: Scale development and validation. *Computers & Education*, *92-93*, 27–36.

Pham, X. L., Nguyen, P. N., & Nguyen, T. H. (2023). Innovative approaches to learning: An examination of nano-learning research. *2023 14th IIAI International Congress on Advanced Applied Informatics (IIAI-AAI)*, 212–217.

Pirker, J., Dengel, A., Holly, M., & Safikhani, S. (2020). Virtual Reality in Computer Science Education: A Systematic Review. *26th ACM Symposium on Virtual Reality Software and Technology*, 1–8. DOI: 10.1145/3385956.3418947

Pomerantz, J., & Rode, R. (2020). Exploring the Future of Extended Reality in Higher Education. *EDUCAUSE Review*. https://er.educause.edu/articles/2020/6/exploring-the-future-of-extended-reality-in-higher-education

Pozzo, D. N., Roa, I. G., Gonzalez Beleño, C. A., Arévalo Fajardo, B. Y., Herrera Cantillo, C. P., & Guerrero, V. C. (2024). Perspectives and applications of virtual reality in higher education: An analysis of Latin America's publications. *Procedia Computer Science*, *238*, 962–967. DOI: 10.1016/j.procs.2024.06.120

Priya, P. K., & Boopathi, S. (2025). *Agile Approaches to Commercializing Agricultural Business: Strategies for.*

Puentedura, R. (2013). SAMR model: A model for integrating technology into teaching. [Original framework description].

Puentedura, R. (2013). SAMR: A contextualized introduction. Retrieved from https://www.hippasus.com/rrpweblog/archives/2013/10/25/SAMRAContextualizedIntroduction.pdf

Purnama, Y., & Asdlori, A. (2023). The role of social media in students' social perception and interaction: Implications for learning and education. [TACIT]. *Technology and Society Perspectives*, *1*(2), 45–55. DOI: 10.61100/tacit.v1i2.50

Purwanto, S. (2018). Pendidikan Nilai Dalam Pagelaran Wayang. *Jurnal Pendidikan Islam*, *06*(01), 1–30.

Queiroz, A. C. M., Fauville, G., Herrera, F., Leme, M. I. da S., & Bailenson, J. N. (2022). Do Students Learn Better With Immersive Virtual Reality Videos Than Conventional Videos? A Comparison of Media Effects With Middle School Girls. Technology, Mind, and Behavior, 3(3: Autumn). DOI: 10.1037/tmb0000082

Radianti, J., Majchrzak, T. A., Fromm, J., & Wohlgenannt, I. (2020). A systematic review of immersive virtual reality applications for higher education: Design elements, lessons learned, and research agenda. *Computers & Education*, *147*, 103778. DOI: 10.1016/j.compedu.2019.103778

Raimi, L., Bamiro, N. B., & Lim, S. A. (2024). Two facets of AI-driven applications for sustainable learning and development: A systematic review of tech-entrepreneurial benefits and threats to creative learning. Social Responsibility. *Technology and Sustainable Development, 12*, 88–110. DOI: 10.1108/S2043-052320240000023012

Rajkumar, V., Boopathi, S., & Jatav, S. S. (2024). Empowerment of Fisherwomen through Self-Help Groups: A Multidimensional Impact Assessment in Thoothukudi, Tamil Nadu, India. *Indian Journal of Extension Education, 60*(4), 47–52. DOI: 10.48165/IJEE.2024.60409

Ramadhani Fajri, B., Mohd Kamaruzaman, F., Omar, M., Lofandri, W., & Samala, A. D. (2025). Smart Teaching Factory: Integrating Extended Reality, Artificial Intelligence, and Animated Simulations for Transformative Vocational Education. *Salud, Ciencia y Tecnología, 5*, 1769. DOI: 10.56294/saludcyt20251769

Rana, S., & Chicone, R. (2025a). AI-Enhanced Virtual and Augmented Reality for Cybersecurity Training. In *Fortifying the Future* (pp. 101–131). Springer., https://ouci.dntb.gov.ua/en/works/7A561EB2/ DOI: 10.1007/978-3-031-81780-9_5

Ranaweera, M., & Mahmoud, Q. H. (2024). Deep Reinforcement Learning with Godot Game Engine. *Electronics (Basel), 13*(5), 985. DOI: 10.3390/electronics13050985

Rao, K., Smith, S. J., & Lowrey, K. A. (2017). UDL and inclusive practices in schools: A case study of three districts. *Exceptionality Education International, 27*(1), 1–22. DOI: 10.5206/eei.v27i1.7723

Rasul, T., Nair, S., Kalendra, D. R., Balaji, M. S., Santini, F. de O., Ladeira, W. J., Rather, R. A., Yasin, N., Rodriguez, R. V., Kokkalis, P., Murad, M. W., & Hossain, M. U. (2024). Enhancing academic integrity among students in GenAI Era: A holistic framework. *International Journal of Management Education, 22*(3), 101041. DOI: 10.1016/j.ijme.2024.101041

Rauscher, F. H., Shaw, G. L., & Ky, K. N. (1993). Music and spatial task performance. *Nature, 365*(6447), 611. DOI: 10.1038/365611a0

Rauschnabel, P. A., Felix, R., Hinsch, C., Shahab, H., & Alt, F. (2022). What is XR? Towards a Framework for Augmented and Virtual Reality. *Computers in Human Behavior, 133*, 107289. DOI: 10.1016/j.chb.2022.107289

Ravichandra, T., Mariappan, M., Padmaja, C., Barnikana, N. R., Saravanan, T., & Boopathi, S. (2025). Mapping the Growth of Pedagogical Content Knowledge Across Teaching Careers. In *Current Trends and Best Practices of Pedagogical Content Knowledge (PCK)* (pp. 151–182). IGI Global Scientific Publishing. DOI: 10.4018/979-8-3693-0655-0.ch006

Redecker, C. (2017). *European framework for the digital competence of educators: DigCompEdu*. Publications Office of the European Union., DOI: 10.2760/159770

Redecker, C. (2021). The SELFIE tool and digital competence development in schools. *European Journal of Education, 56*(4), 529–544. DOI: 10.1111/ejed.12483

Ribeiro, D. B., Coutinho, A. D. R., Satyro, W. C., Campos, F. C. D., Lima, C. R. C., Contador, J. C., & Gonçalves, R. F. (2024). The DAWN readiness model to assess the level of use of Industry 4.0 technologies in the construction industry in Brazil. *Construction Innovation, 24*(2), 515–536. DOI: 10.1108/CI-05-2022-0114

Rienties, B., Brouwer, N., & Lygo-Baker, S. (2017). The effects of online professional development on higher education teachers' beliefs and intentions towards learning facilitation and technology. *Teaching and Teacher Education, 63*, 113–123. DOI: 10.1016/j.tate.2016.12.001

Roberts, E., & Townsend, L. (2016). The contribution of the digital economy to rural development. *Local Economy, 31*(1-2), 129–147.

Rodriguez-Garcia, B., Ramírez-Sanz, J. M., Miguel-Alonso, I., & Bustillo, A. (2024). Enhancing Learning of 3D Model Unwrapping through Virtual Reality Serious Game: Design and Usability Validation. *Electronics (Basel), 13*(10), 1972. DOI: 10.3390/electronics13101972

Rojas, M. P., & Chiappe, A. (2024). Artificial Intelligence and Digital Ecosystems in Education: A review.Technology Knowledge and learning, 29(4), 2153-2170. DOI: 10.1007/s10758-024-09732-7

Romoser, C., Nelson, R., & Ferrill, T. (2024, April 1). *Recreational Therapists' Usability Perceptions of the Meta Quest 2 VR System. | EBSCOhost*. DOI: 10.18666/TRJ-2024-V58-I2-12077

Rosa, S. (2019) *Teaching Character Through Oral Stories in Indonesia And Malaysia*, Journal of Southeast Asian Studies, Volume 24(2), December 2019, 176-190, ISSN 1823-4127/e-ISSN 2600-8653

Roshanaei, M., Olivares, H., & Lopez, R. R. (2023). Harnessing AI to foster equity in education: Opportunities, challenges, and emerging strategies. *Journal of Intelligent Learning Systems and Applications, 15*(4), 123–145. DOI: 10.4236/jilsa.2023.154009

Rout, B., & Bhoi, M. T. (2024a). SEL and Technology: The Role of Digital Tools in Promoting Emotional and Social Skills. *International Journal for Research in Applied Science and Engineering Technology, 12*(12), 1584–1512. DOI: 10.22214/ijraset.2024.66086

Ryan, R. M., & Deci, E. L. (2000). Self-determination theory and the facilitation of intrinsic motivation, social development, and well-being. *The American Psychologist, 55*(1), 68–78. DOI: 10.1037/0003-066X.55.1.68

Ryan, R. M., & Deci, E. L. (2017). *Self-determination theory: Basic psychological needs in motivation, development, and wellness*. Guilford Publications. DOI: 10.1521/978.14625/28806

Ryong, K., Lee, D., & Lee, J. G. (2024). Chatbot's complementary motivation support in developing study plan of e-learning English lecture. *International Journal of Human-Computer Interaction, 40*(10), 2641–2655. DOI: 10.1080/10447318.2022.2163786

Saborío-Taylor, S., & Rojas-Ramírez, F. (2024). Universal design for learning and artificial intelligence in the digital era: Fostering inclusion and autonomous learning. International Journal of Professional Development. *Learners and Learning, 6*(2), ep2408. Advance online publication. DOI: 10.30935/ijpdll/14694

Sadallah, M. (2024). User-Centered Course Reengineering: An Analytical Approach to Enhancing Reading Comprehension in Educational Content. ArXiv. https://arxiv.org/abs/2412.11944

Sadeghpour, M., Arakala, A., & Rao, A. (2025). Generative AI in Collaborative Academic Report Writing: Advantages, Disadvantages, and Ethical Considerations. https://doi.org/DOI: 10.48550/ARXIV.2504.08832

Sadler, D. R. (1989). Formative assessment and the design of instructional systems. *Instructional Science, 18*(2), 119–144. DOI: 10.1007/BF00117714

Sadoski, M., Paivio, A., & Goetz, E. T. (1991). Commentary: A Critique of Schema Theory in Reading and a Dual Coding Alternative [Published By: International Literacy Association]. *Reading Research Quarterly, 26*(4), 463–484. DOI: 10.2307/747898

Sahoo, P., & Pradhan, J. S. (2025). Exploring the Role of Social Media in Promoting Collaborative Learning: A Systematic Review. *JOURNAL OF DIGITAL LEARNING AND DISTANCE EDUCATION, 3*(12), 1423–1435. DOI: 10.56778/jdlde.v3i12.502

Sailer, M., & Homner, L. (2020). The gamification of learning: A meta-analysis. *Educational Psychology Review, 32*(1), 77–112. DOI: 10.1007/s10648-019-09498-w

Salisi, J. C. V., Aravejo, M. C. V., Eguia, G. C., Maranan, R. S. B., & Du, M. R. (2019). Social media use, perceived depression and academic performance of college students in a Philippine Higher Education Institution. *Cabrini Journal of Allied Medicine, 3*(2), 0. https://www.academia.edu/download/75923790/10.-Social-Media-Use-Perceived-Depression-and-Academic-Performance-among-College-Students.pdf

Sandu, A., & Taylor, C. (2025). Digital learning technologies usage during Covid-19 lockdowns. *British Educational Research Journal, 51*(2), 607–628. DOI: 10.1002/berj.4092

Santosa, I. B. (2023). *Alam Batin Jagat Wayang*. DIVA Press.

Saravanan, S., Chandrasekar, J., Kumar, S. S., Patel, P., Shanthi, J. M., & Boopathi, S. (2024). The Impact of NBA Implementation Across Engineering Disciplines: Innovative Approaches. In *Enhancing Higher Education and Research With OpenAI Models* (pp. 229–252). IGI Global Scientific Publishing. DOI: 10.4018/979-8-3693-1666-5.ch010

Sarkar, R., Mahamuni, V. S., Chitra, M., Vijayakumar, M., Jefferson, K., & Boopathi, S. (2025). Integrating Innovation Tools and Technology in Educational Management. In *Planning Tools for Policy, Leadership, and Management of Education Systems* (pp. 121–154). IGI Global.

Sarkar, R., Shandilya, S., Anand, T., Sri, R. R., Dhanaraj, K., & Boopathi, S. (2025). Best Practices and Frameworks for Higher Education: Optimizing Learning Progressions Using Recent Tools. In *Driving Quality Education Through AI and Data Science* (pp. 51–72). IGI Global Scientific Publishing.

Sarkar, R., Parmar, D. V., Trivedi, N. B., Prabakaran, S., Chandra, S., & Boopathi, S. (2025). Pedagogical Contents Developments and Specialized Training for Teaching Careers. In *Global Practices in Inclusive Education Curriculum and Policy* (pp. 187–216). IGI Global.

Schellenberg, E. G. (2004). Music lessons enhance IQ. *Psychological Science, 15*(8), 511–514. DOI: 10.1111/j.0956-7976.2004.00711.x

Schellenberg, E. G. (2011). Examining the association between music lessons and intelligence. *British Journal of Psychology, 102*(3), 283–302. DOI: 10.1111/j.2044-8295.2010.02000.x

Schön, D. A. (1992). *The reflective practitioner: How professionals think in action* (1st ed.). Routledge., DOI: 10.4324/9781315237473

Schrepp, M., Hinderks, A., & Thomaschewski, J. (2014). Applying the User Experience Questionnaire (UEQ) in Different Evaluation Scenarios. In Marcus, A. (Ed.), *Design, User Experience, and Usability: Theories, Methods, and Tools for Designing the User Experience* (Vol. 8517, pp. 383–392). Springer., DOI: 10.1007/978-3-319-07668-3_37

Schrepp, M., Hinderks, A., & Thomaschewski, J. (2017). Construction of a benchmark for the User Experience Questionnaire (UEQ). *International Journal of Interactive Multimedia and Artificial Intelligence, 4*(4), 40–44. DOI: 10.9781/ijimai.2017.445

Schrepp, M., Hinderks, A., & Thomaschewski, J. (2017b). Design and Evaluation of a Short Version of the User Experience Questionnaire (UEQ-S). *International Journal of Interactive Multimedia and Artificial Intelligence, 4*(6), 103–108. DOI: 10.9781/ijimai.2017.09.001

Schwaiger, M. (2021). Europe Needs to Integrate Immersive Learning Quickly at All Education Levels – But How? What to Learn From 25 EU Projects in This Field. *Journal of Elementary Education, 14*(Spec.Iss), 63–85. DOI: 10.18690/rei.14.Spec.Iss.63-85.2021

Schwartz, R. W., Ayres, K. M., & Douglas, K. H. (2017). Effects of music on task performance, engagement, and behavior: A literature review. *Psychology of Music, 45*(5), 611–627. DOI: 10.1177/0305735617691118

Sebullen, M. T. (2023). Assessing Pre-Service Teachers' Perceptions of the Practicality of Social Media in the Educational Arena. *Cognizance journal, 3*(7), 58-70. https://www.researchgate.net/publication/372216086

Sekhar, K. C., Ingle, R. B., Banu, E. A., Rinawa, M. L., Prasad, M. M., & Boopathi, S. (2024). Integrating VR and AR for Enhanced Production Systems: Immersive Technologies in Smart Manufacturing. In *Human-Machine Collaboration and Emotional Intelligence in Industry 5.0* (pp. 90–112). IGI Global.

Selwyn, N. (2021). *Education and technology: Key issues and debates* (3rd ed.). Bloomsbury.

Setia, S., Tichy, M., Gilbert, F., & Tichy, M. L. (2024). Innovating social-emotional learning to enhance positive engagement of youth with social media: A comprehensive review of why and how. *Cureus, 16*(9). Advance online publication. DOI: 10.7759/cureus.70130 PMID: 39463555

Setiawan, E. (2017) *Makna Filisofi Wayang Purwa dalam Lakon Dewa Ruci*, Kontemplasi.

Sharma, D. M., Ramana, K. V., Jothilakshmi, R., Verma, R., Maheswari, B. U., & Boopathi, S. (2024). Integrating Generative AI Into K-12 Curriculums and Pedagogies in India: Opportunities and Challenges. *Facilitating Global Collaboration and Knowledge Sharing in Higher Education With Generative AI*, 133–161.

Sharma, G., Mittal, R., & Zayan. (2023). Teacher Education in India's National Education Policy 2020: Knowledge Traditions, Global Discourses and National Regulations. Contemporary Education Dialogue, 20(2), 256-282. (Original work published 2023)DOI: 10.1177/09731849231168728

Sharma, A., Shailendra, S., & Kadel, R. W. (2025).. . *Experiences with Content Development and Assessment Design in the Era of GenAI.*, *1*, 1–5. Advance online publication. DOI: 10.1109/CSEE64583.2025.00008

Sharma, P., Srivastava, R., & Malik, R. (2020). *Impact of AR/VR on Conceptual Learning in Engineering Education*. Open Access Journal of Engineering Education Innovations.

Shater, A., & Abualrish, M. A., & Al_manei, M. M. A. (. (2024). The Impact of Social Media Usage on Academic Performance: A Study of the Professional Educational Diploma Program in UAE. *American Journal of Education and Technology*, *3*(3), 71–79. DOI: 10.54536/ajet.v3i3.2996

Siemens, G. (2005). Connectivism: A Learning Theory for the Digital Age. *International Journal of Instructional Technology & Distance Learning*, *2*(1). http://www.itdl.org/Journal/Jan_05/article01.htm

Siemens, G. (2005). Connectivism: A learning theory for the digital age. *International Journal of Instructional Technology and Distance Learning*, *2*(1), 3–10. http://www.itdl.org/Journal/Jan_05/article01.htm

Silva, E. S., da Costa, W. P., de Lima, J. C., & Ferreira, J. C. (2025). Contribution of microlearning in basic education: A systematic review. *Education Sciences*, *15*(3), 302. DOI: 10.3390/educsci15030302

Sing Yun, W. (2023). Digitalization challenges in education during COVID-19: A systematic review. *Cogent Education*, *10*(1), 2198981. Advance online publication. DOI: 10.1080/2331186X.2023.2198981

Singh, A. K. (2025). From policy to practice: Challenges and pathway for advancing multilingual education through India's national education policy 2020. Policy Futures in Education, 23(4), 746-765. (Original work published 2025)DOI: 10.1177/14782103251320532

Singh, N. (2019). SWAYAM–Indian MOOCs: An insider's perspective. *Asian Journal of Distance Education*, *14*(1), 47–55. https://www.asianjde.com/ojs/index.php/AsianJDE/article/view/301

Slater, M. (2018). Immersion and the illusion of presence in virtual reality. *British Journal of Psychology*, *109*(3), 431–433. DOI: 10.1111/bjop.12305 PMID: 29781508

Smeda, N., Dakich, E., & Sharda, N. (2014). The effectiveness of digital storytelling in the classrooms: A comprehensive study. *Smart Learn. Environ.*, *1*(1), 6. DOI: 10.1186/s40561-014-0006-3

Snelson, C. (2018). Video production in content-area pedagogy: A scoping study of the research literature. *Learning, Media and Technology*, *43*(3), 294–306. DOI: 10.1080/17439884.2018.1504788

Soelistianto, F. A., Andrasmoro, D., Yusriati, Y., Mardiati, M., & Fawait, A. B. (2024). The impact of adaptive learning technology on improving students' concept understanding. *Journal of Computer Science Advancements*, *2*(3), 12–22. DOI: 10.70177/jsca.v2i3.1176

Song, Y., Chen, X., Hao, T., Liu, Z., & Lan, Z. (2019). Exploring two decades of research on classroom dialogue by using bibliometric analysis. *Computers & Education*, *137*, 12–31. DOI: 10.1016/j.compedu.2019.04.002

Sousa, M. J., Marôco, A. L., Gonçalves, S. P., & Machado, A. de B. (2022). Digital learning is an educational format towards sustainable education. *Sustainability (Basel)*, *14*(3), 1140. DOI: 10.3390/su14031140

Southgate, D. E., & Roscigno, V. J. (2009). The impact of music on childhood and adolescent achievement. *Social Science Quarterly*, *90*(1), 4–21. DOI: 10.1111/j.1540-6237.2009.00598.x

Soykan, E., Bastas, M., & Çakici, A. (2023). Digital transformation of education in the COVID-19 process and its psychological effects on children. *Frontiers in Education*, *8*, 1117458. DOI: 10.3389/feduc.2023.1117458

Speicher, M., Hall, B. D., & Nebeling, M. (2019). What is Mixed Reality? *Proceedings of the 2019 CHI Conference on Human Factors in Computing Systems*, 1–15. DOI: 10.1145/3290605.3300767

Spencer, A. D. (2025). *The Future of Immersive, AI-Driven, and Decentralized Technologies in Cybersecurity Education and Cyber Science*. RAIS Conference proceedings, Princeton, NJ.

Srivastava, A., ... (2024). Evaluating the effectiveness of flipped learning in an upper-division undergraduate electrical engineering course. Discover Education. Springer.

Stanley, D., & Zhang, Y. (2018). Student-produced videos can enhance engagement and learning in the online environment. *Online Learning : the Official Journal of the Online Learning Consortium*, *22*(2), 5–26. DOI: 10.24059/olj.v22i2.1367

Sternberg, R. J. (1997). The concept of intelligence and its role in lifelong learning and success. *The American Psychologist, 52*(10), 1030–1037. DOI: 10.1037/0003-066X.52.10.1030 PMID: 9329294

Strielkowski, W., Grebennikova, V., Lisovskiy, A., Rakhimova, G., & Vasileva, T. (2025). AI-driven adaptive learning for sustainable educational transformation. *Sustainable Development (Bradford), 33*(2), 1012–1030. DOI: 10.1002/sd.3221

Sumathy, V., & Navamani, G. (2024). AI-driven personalized learning: Enhancing student success through adaptive technologies. Science. *Information Technology & Applications, 16*, 147–160. DOI: 10.1234/sita.2024.016

SWAYAM. (2022). About SWAYAM. https://swayam.gov.in

Sweller, J. (1994). Cognitive load theory, learning difficulty, and instructional design. *Learning and Instruction, 4*(4), 295–312. DOI: 10.1016/0959-4752(94)90003-5

Tang, Q., Wang, Y., Liu, H., Liu, Q., & Jiang, S. (2022). Experiencing an art education program through immersive virtual reality or iPad: Mediating effects of presence and extraneous load on enjoyment, attention, and retention. *Frontiers in Psychology, 13*. Advance online publication. DOI: 10.3389/fpsyg.2022.957037 PMID: 36186296

Tapalova, O., & Zhiyenbayeva, N. (2022). Artificial intelligence in education: AIEd for personalised learning pathways. *Electronic Journal of e-Learning, 20*(5), 639–653. DOI: 10.34190/ejel.20.5.2597

Taylor, D. L., Yeung, M., & Bashet, A. Z. (2021). Personalized and adaptive learning. *Innovations in STEM Higher Education, 3*, 45–60. DOI: 10.21825/istem.v3i1.10186

Tene, T., Marcatoma Tixi, J. A., Palacios Robalino, M., Mendoza Salazar, M. J., Vacacela Gomez, C., & Bellucci, S. (2024). Integrating immersive technologies with STEM education: A systematic review. *Frontiers in Education, 9*, 1410163. Advance online publication. DOI: 10.3389/feduc.2024.1410163

Tenney, K., Stringer, B. P., LaTona-Tequida, T., & White, I. (2023). Conceptualizations and Limitations of STEM Literacy across Learning Theories. *Journal of Microbiology & Biology Education, 24*(1), e00168–e22. DOI: 10.1128/jmbe.00168-22 PMID: 37089236

Terzieva, V., Ivanova, T., & Todorova, K. (2022). Personalized learning in an intelligent educational system. In Lecture Notes in Networks and Systems (Vol. 556, pp. 13–23). DOI: 10.1007/978-3-031-17601-2_2

Thamrongrat, P., Khundam, C., Pakdeebun, P., & Mohd Nizam, D. N. (2023). Desktop vs. headset: A comparative study of user experience and engagement for flexibility exercise in virtual reality. *Emerging Science Journal, 7*(4), 698–710. DOI: 10.28991/ESJ-2023-07-04-03

Thompson, W. F., Schellenberg, E. G., & Letnic, A. K. (2011). Fast and loud background music disrupts reading comprehension. *Psychology of Music, 40*(6), 700–708. DOI: 10.1177/0305735611400173

Trilling, B., & Fadel, C. (2009). *21st century skills: Learning for life in our times.* Jossey-Bass/Wiley.

Triyono, M. B., Mutohhar, F., Kholifah, N., Nurtanto, M., Subakti, H., & Prasetya, K. H. (2023). Examining the mediating-moderating role of entrepreneurial orientation and digital competence on entrepreneurial intention In vocational education. *Journal of Technical Education and Training, 15*(1), 116–127. DOI: 10.30880/jtet.2023.15.01.011

Trucano, M. (2015). Teachers, teaching and ICTs. World Bank EdTech Blog. Retrieved from: https://blogs.worldbank.org/edutech/teachers-teaching-and-icts. Accessed on 23.08.2025.

Trust, T., & Horrocks, B. (2016). 'I never feel alone in my classroom': Teacher professional growth within a blended community of practice. *Professional Development in Education, 43*(4), 645–665. DOI: 10.1080/19415257.2016.1233507

Trust, T., & Whalen, J. (2020). Should teachers be trained in emergency remote teaching? Lessons Learned from the COVID-19 Pandemic. *Journal of Technology and Teacher Education, 28*(2), 189–199. https://www.learntechlib.org/primary/p/215995/. DOI: 10.70725/307718pkpjuu

Tsai, C.-Y., & Lai, Y.-C. (2022). Design and Validation of an Augmented Reality Teaching System for Primary Logic Programming Education. *Sensors (Basel), 22*(1), 389. DOI: 10.3390/s22010389 PMID: 35009929

Tversky, B., Morrison, J. B., & Betrancourt, M. (2002). Animation: Can it facilitate? *International Journal of Human-Computer Studies, 57*(4), 247–262. DOI: 10.1006/ijhc.2002.1017

Twenge, J. M., & Campbell, W. K. (2018). Associations between screen time and lower psychological well-being among children and adolescents. *Psychological Science, 29*(12), 1947–1954. PMID: 30406005

UDISE. (2025). School education statistics in India. Ministry of Education, Government of India.

UNESCO IITE. (2021). Digital transformation of education: Teacher professional development. Moscow: UNESCO Institute for Information Technologies in Education. https://iite.unesco.org/publications/digital-transformation-of-education-teacher-professional-development/

UNESCO. (2015). Transforming our world: The 2030 agenda for sustainable development. United Nations. Retrieved from: https://sdgs.un.org/goals/goal4. Accessed on 10.09.2025.

UNESCO. (2018). ICT competency framework for teachers (Version 3).

UNESCO. (2021). AI and Education: Guidance for Policy-makers. https://unesdoc.unesco.org/ark:/48223/pf0000376709

UNESCO. (2021). *Reimagining our futures together: A new social contract for education.* https://unesdoc.unesco.org/ark:/48223/pf0000379707

UNESCO. (2021a). Reimagining our futures together: A new social contract for education. Retrieved from: https://unesdoc.unesco.org/ark:/48223/pf0000379707. Accessed on 14.09.2025.

UNESCO. (2021b). Teacher support and professional development during COVID-19: Review of practices. Retrieved from: https://unesdoc.unesco.org. Accessed on 17.09.2025.

UNESCO. (2022). ICT competency framework for teachers: Version 3. Retrieved from: https://unevoc.unesco.org/home/ICT+CFT+Version+3 Accessed on 15.09.2025.

UNESCO. (2023, June 9). ICT Competency Framework for Teachers as a game changer for digital capacity building for teachers.

Upadhyaya, A. N., Debnath, P., Rani, P., Selvakumar, P., Manjunath, T. C., & Bhattacharya, S. (2025). AI-based disaster prediction and early warning systems. In Mobo, F. (Ed.), *AI and emerging technologies for emergency response and smart cities* (pp. 55–74). IGI Global Scientific Publishing., DOI: 10.4018/979-8-3693-9770-1.ch003

Vaithianathan, V., Subbulakshmi, N., Boopathi, S., & Mohanraj, M. (2024). Integrating Project-Based and Skills-Based Learning for Enhanced Student Engagement and Success: Transforming Higher Education. In *Adaptive Learning Technologies for Higher Education* (pp. 345–372). IGI Global.

Vaithianathan, V., Shastri, D. S., Nandakumar, V., Misba, M., Kumar, P. S., & Boopathi, S. (2025). NEP Policy Implementation Strategies in Education in India. In *Educational Philosophy and Sociological Foundation of Education* (pp. 325–356). IGI Global.

van Alten, D. C. D., Phielix, C., Janssen, J., & Kester, L. (2019). Effects of flipping the classroom on learning outcomes and satisfaction: A meta-analysis. *Educational Research Review, 28*, 100281. DOI: 10.1016/j.edurev.2019.05.003

van Laar, E., van Deursen, A. J. A. M., van Dijk, J. A. G. M., & de Haan, J. (2020). Determinants of 21st-century skills and 21st-century digital skills for workers: A systematic literature review. *SAGE Open, 10*(1), 2158244019900176. Advance online publication. DOI: 10.1177/2158244019900176

Van Mechelen, M., Smith, R. C., Schaper, M., Tamashiro, M., Bilstrup, K., Lunding, M., Petersen, M. G., & Iversen, O. S. (2022). Emerging Technologies in K-12 Education: A future HCI research agenda. *ACM Transactions on Computer-Human Interaction, 30*(3), 1–40. DOI: 10.1145/3569897

Vandewaetere, M., & Clarebout, G. (2011). Can instruction as such affect learning? the case of learner control. *Computers & Education, 57*(4), 2322–2332. DOI: 10.1016/j.compedu.2011.05.020

Vashisht, S. (2024). Enhancing Learning Experiences through Augmented Reality and Virtual Reality in Classrooms. 2024 2nd International Conference on Recent Advances in Information Technology for Sustainable Development (ICRAIS), 12–17. DOI: 10.1109/ICRAIS62903.2024.10811732

Vasilchenko, A., Li, J., Ryskeldiev, B., Sarcar, S., Ochiai, Y., Kunze, K., & Radu, I. (2020). Collaborative Learning & Co-Creation in XR. *Extended Abstracts of the 2020 CHI Conference on Human Factors in Computing Systems*, 1–4. DOI: 10.1145/3334480.3381056

Veckalne, R., & Tambovceva, T. (2022). The role of digital transformation in education in promoting sustainable development. *Virtual Economics, 5*(4), 65–86. DOI: 10.34021/ve.2022.05.04(4)

Venkatasubramanian, V., Chitra, M., Sudha, R., Singh, V. P., Jefferson, K., & Boopathi, S. (2024). Examining the Impacts of Course Outcome Analysis in Indian Higher Education: Enhancing Educational Quality. In *Challenges of Globalization and Inclusivity in Academic Research* (pp. 124–145). IGI Global Scientific Publishing.

Vieriu, A. M., & Petrea, G. (2025). The Impact of Artificial Intelligence (AI) on Students' Academic Development. *Education Sciences, 15*(3), 343. DOI: 10.3390/educsci15030343

Voogt, J., Erstad, O., Dede, C., & Mishra, P. (2015). Under which conditions does ICT have a positive effect on teaching and learning? *Journal of Computer Assisted Learning, 31*(5), 491–511. DOI: 10.1111/jcal.12136

Vygotsky, L. S. (1978). *Mind in society: The development of higher psychological processes*. Harvard University Press.

Wahyudi, A. (2012) Lakon Dewa Ruci: Cara Menjadi Jawa. Yogyakarta

Wallace, W. T. (1994). Memory for music: Effect of melody on recall of text. *Journal of Experimental Psychology. Learning, Memory, and Cognition*, *20*(6), 1471–1485. DOI: 10.1037/0278-7393.20.6.1471

Wan Ali, W. N. A., Wan Yahaya, W. A. J., Syed Idrus, S. Z., & Yaacob, M. N. F. (2024). Fostering Motivation In Tvet Students : The Role Of Learner-Paced Segments And Computational Thinking In Digital Video. [AJTLHE]. *ASEAN Journal of Teaching & Learning in Higher Education*, *16*(2), 215–232. DOI: 10.17576/ajtlhe.1602.2024.01

Wang, X., Zhao, X., & Yu, C. (2025). The influence of information and social overload on academic performance: the role of social media fatigue, cognitive depletion, and self-control. *Revista de Psicodidáctica (English ed.)*, 500164. https://doi.org/DOI: 10.1016/j.psicoe.2025.500164

Wang, N., & Lester, J. C. (2023). K-12 Education in the Age of AI: A Call to Action for K-12 AI Literacy. *International Journal of Artificial Intelligence in Education*, *33*(2), 228–232. DOI: 10.1007/s40593-023-00358-x

Wang, S., Wang, F., Zhu, Z., Wang, J., Tran, T., & Du, Z. (2024). Artificial intelligence in education: A systematic literature review. *Expert Systems with Applications*, *252*, 124167. DOI: 10.1016/j.eswa.2024.124167

Warschauer, M. (2003). *Technology and social inclusion: Rethinking the digital divide*. MIT Press. DOI: 10.7551/mitpress/6699.001.0001

Webster-Wright, A. (2009). Reframing professional development through understanding authentic professional learning. *Review of Educational Research*, *79*(2), 702–739. DOI: 10.3102/0034654308330970

Wehling, M., Thomeczek, C., & Seidl, M. (2021). Fast-track flipping – Preparing medical faculty for online teaching with digital tools. *BMC Medical Education*, *21*, 395. Advance online publication. https://bmcmededuc.biomedcentral.com/articles/10.1186/s12909-021-02784-8. DOI: 10.1186/s12909-021-02784-8 PMID: 34158039

Wei, Z., Liao, J., Lee, L., Qu, H., & Xu, X. (2025). Towards Enhanced Learning through Presence: A Systematic Review of Presence in Virtual Reality Across Tasks and Disciplines. ArXiv. https://arxiv.org/abs/2504.13845

Weller, M., Jordan, K., DeVries, I., & Rolfe, V. (2018). Mapping the open education landscape: Citation network analysis of historical open education literature. *Open Praxis, 10*(2), 109–126. DOI: 10.5944/openpraxis.10.2.822

Wenger, E. (1998). *Communities of practice: Learning, meaning, and identity*. Cambridge University Press., DOI: 10.1017/CBO9780511803932

Werbach, K., & Hunter, D. (2012). *For the win: How game thinking can revolutionize your business*. Wharton Digital Press.

What is human-centered AI? (2021, February 9). IBM Research. https://research.ibm.com/blog/what-is-human-centered-ai

Wiafe, I., Ekpezu, A. O., Gyamera, G. O., Winful, F. B. P., Atsakpo, E. D., Nutrokpor, C., & Gulliver, S. R. (2025). Learning satisfaction in virtual reality: The role of persuasive design. *International Journal of Human-Computer Interaction, 41*(17), 11021–11037. DOI: 10.1080/10447318.2024.2440205

Wiggins, G., & McTighe, J. (2005). *Understanding by Design* (2nd ed.). ASCD., https://www.ascd.org/books/understanding-by-design-2nd-edition

Wijayanti, F. (2023) *Analysis of Character Values in the History of Wayang Beber Wonosari, Gunung Kidul Regency, Special Region Province of Yogyakarta.* Nagri Pustaka: Journal of Education, Historical Studies, and Culture.

Winstone, N. E., Nash, R. A., Parker, M., & Rowntree, J. (2023). Engaging through feedback: Exploring student metacognition and the peer review process. *Assessment & Learning in Higher Education, 48*(2), 234–249.

World Bank. (2020). Digital Skills in Tertiary Education and the Labour Market in Developing Countries. https://documents.worldbank.org/en/publication/documents-reports/documentdetail/306711611349330106

World Benchmarking Alliance. (2021). Digital companies share experiences and best practices.

Yadav, U., Pitchai, R., Gopal, V., Kumar, K. S., Talukdar, M., & Boopathi, S. (2025). Powers of Higher Education Leadership: Navigating Policy and Management in Academic Institutions. In *Navigating Leadership and Policy Management in Education* (pp. 103–136). IGI Global.

Yang, G. (2008). Graphic Novels in the Classroom. *Language Arts, 85*(3), 185–192. DOI: 10.58680/la20086181

Yang, M., & Carless, D. (2022). Peer feedback as a tool for enhancing evaluative judgement in higher education. *Teaching in Higher Education, 27*(3), 343–360.

Yang, S. (2024). Intelligent tutoring system algorithm: Enhance personalized learning experience. In *International Conference on Frontier Computing* (pp. 112–118). https://doi.org/DOI: 10.1007/978-3-031-49402-7_14

Yan, H., Zhang, R., Oniffrey, T. M., Chen, G., Wang, Y., Wu, Y., Zhang, X., Wang, Q., Ma, L., Li, R., & Moore, J. B. (2017). Associations among screen time and unhealthy behaviors, academic performance, and well-being in Chinese adolescents. *International Journal of Environmental Research and Public Health, 14*(6), 596. DOI: 10.3390/ijerph14060596 PMID: 28587225

Yan, W., Lowell, V. L., & Yang, L. (2024). Developing English language learners' speaking skills through applying a situated learning approach in VR-enhanced learning experiences. *Virtual Reality (Waltham Cross), 28*(4), 167. DOI: 10.1007/s10055-024-01061-5

Yao, X., Zhao, J., Chao, W., Gao, D., Wang, M., & Zhao, G. (2025). Relationship Between Fear of Missing Out and Social Media Fatigue: Cross-Lagged Panel Design. *Journal of Medical Internet Research, 27*, e75701. DOI: 10.2196/75701 PMID: 40680183

Yaseen, H., Mohammad, A. S., Ashal, N., Abusaimeh, H., Ali, A., & Sharabati, A. (2025). The Impact of Adaptive Learning Technologies, Personalized Feedback, and Interactive AI Tools on Student Engagement: The Moderating Role of Digital Literacy. *Sustainability (Basel), 17*(3), 1133. DOI: 10.3390/su17031133

Yee, N. (2006). Motivations for play in online games. *Cyberpsychology & Behavior, 9*(6), 772–775. DOI: 10.1089/cpb.2006.9.772 PMID: 17201605

Yekollu, R. K., Bhimraj Ghuge, T., & Sunil Biradar, S. (2024). AI-driven personalized learning paths: Enhancing education through adaptive systems. In *Lecture Notes in Computer Science* (Vol. 13890, pp. 98–112). Smart Education and Smart e-Learning Conference., DOI: 10.1007/978-3-031-45890-3_7

Yerkes, R. M., & Dodson, J. D. (1908). The relation of strength of stimulus to rapidity of habit-formation. *The Journal of Comparative Neurology and Psychology, 18*(5), 459–482. DOI: 10.1002/cne.920180503

Yousef, A. M. F., Huang, R., Tlili, A., Garcia, M. B., Mahmoud, A. G., & Metwally, A. H. S. (2023). Small bites, big impact: The power of nanolearning. *International Conference on Smart Learning Environments*, 108–116. DOI: 10.1007/978-981-99-5961-7_12

Zainuddin, Z., Chu, S. K. W., & Othman, J. (2024). The evaluation of gamification implementation for adult learners: A scale development study based on andragogical principles. *Education and Information Technologies*, *29*(14), 18591–18620. DOI: 10.1007/s10639-024-12561-x

Zhang, C., Schießl, J., Plößl, L., Hofmann, F., & Gläser-Zikuda, M. (2023). Acceptance of artificial intelligence among pre-service teachers: A multigroup analysis. *International Journal of Educational Technology in Higher Education*, *20*(1), 49. Advance online publication. DOI: 10.1186/s41239-023-00420-7 PMID: 36743849

Zhang, Y., & Dong, C. (2024). Unveiling the Dynamic Mechanisms of Generative AI in English Language Learning: A Hybrid Study Based on fsQCA and System Dynamics. *Behavioral Sciences (Basel, Switzerland)*, *14*(11), 1015. DOI: 10.3390/bs14111015 PMID: 39594315

Zhou, Q., Wang, B., & Mayer, I. (2024). Understanding the social construction of the metaverse with Q methodology. *Technological Forecasting and Social Change*, *208*, 123716. DOI: 10.1016/j.techfore.2024.123716

Zhou, Q., & Zhang, H. (2025). Flipped classroom teaching and ARCS motivation model: Impact on college students' deep learning. *Education Sciences*, *15*(4), 517. DOI: 10.3390/educsci15040517

Zhuang, T., Xu, X., & Zhang, Y. (2024). Contextualizing and visualizing abstract theoretical knowledge for situated learning: Large-scale VR-supported higher education in China. *Virtual Reality (Waltham Cross)*, *29*(1), 4. DOI: 10.1007/s10055-024-01075-z

Zhu, C., Sun, M., Luo, J., Li, T., & Wang, M. (2023). How to harness the potential of ChatGPT in education? *Knowledge Management & E-Learning*, *15*, 1–18. DOI: 10.34105/kmel.23.15.1

Zhu, Y., & Jiang, H. (2025). Revolutionising education: The evolution, current landscape and future of digital learning. *International Journal of Smart Technology and Learning*, *4*(3), 278–295. DOI: 10.1504/IJSMARTTL.2025.146291

About the Contributors

Wan Nor Ashiqin Binti Wan Ali earned her PhD in Instructional Multimedia from Universiti Sains Malaysia (USM) in 2023 and is a Senior Lecturer at the Faculty of Intelligent Computing, Universiti Malaysia Perlis (UniMAP). Her expertise includes Instructional Multimedia, Information Technology, Computational Thinking, and Educational Technology. She has published widely in Scopus, Web of Science, and MyCite on multimedia learning, computational thinking, and digital courseware. Her research integrates cognitive multimedia principles with technology-enhanced education, focusing on reducing cognitive load for digital natives. She has also authored book chapters and co-authored books on web application development and human development. She contributes as a reviewer, editorial member, and internal examiner, and has received awards for innovations in instructional multimedia and cybersecurity. She continues advancing educational technology through impactful teaching and research.

Yasemin Gulbahar is a professor in the Department of Computer Education and Instructional Technologies (CEIT) of Ankara University. She received her PhD in CEIT from Middle East Technical University. Her research interests include e-Learning, instructional design, and pedagogy of teaching programming.

Syed Zulkarnain Syed Idrus is an Associate Professor at Universiti Malaysia Perlis (UniMAP), Malaysia. He began his tertiary education in 1995 at North Trafford College (NTC), Manchester, United Kingdom and received a Business & Technology Education Council (BTEC) National Diploma (ND) in Information Technology Applications in 1997. He then pursued for the bachelor degree course at the University of Manchester Institute of Science and Technology (UMIST), Manchester, United Kingdom and obtained a B.Sc. degree in Information Systems Engineering in 2001. After working for a short stint in private colleges, he pursued for his M.Sc. degree in the field of Computer Engineering and graduated in 2008 from the Universiti Malaysia Perlis (UniMAP), Malaysia. Finally, he completed his Ph.D. degree in Computer Science and Applications at the Université de Caen Basse-Normandie, Caen, France in 2015 specialising in computer security. To-date, he has written and co-authored over 250 articles including journal and conference papers with an h-index of 22, published 8 books and 2 patents. His expertise in computer security is notably well accepted, where he has been invited to sit as one of the editorial board members in numerous International Journals. For his continuous contributions and recognitions in research as well as career, he had been awarded with several prestigious awards both at national and international levels.

Mohd Noorulfakhri Yaacob, a Senior Lecturer at Universiti Malaysia Perlis (UniMAP), is a renowned expert in information technology, system development, and biometric research. Born on September 1, 1981, in Malaysia, he holds a Ph.D. in Communication and Information Technology from UniMAP (2021), a Master's in Information Technology from Universiti Utara Malaysia (2009), and a Bachelor's in Computer Science from Universiti Kebangsaan Malaysia (2003). With over 20 years of experience, Noorulfakhri has contributed significantly to system development, data center management, and national-level ICT projects. He has led the development of systems for the Ministry of Higher Education, including SUKIPT and ASEAN University Games. His research focuses on biometric authentication, particularly keystroke dynamics, with numerous publications in prestigious journals. A recipient of the I-RIA 2019 Silver Medal, Noorulfakhri is also a certified Professional Technologist (Ts.) and holds multiple IT certifications. Residing in Arau, Perlis, he is a dedicated academic, innovator, and family man committed to advancing technology and education.

***

A.V.Senthil Kumar is working as a Professor and Principal, Nehru Institute of Information Technology and Management, Coimbatore, India. He has worked as Professor and Director, PG and Research Department of Computer Applications, Hindusthan College of Arts & Science, Coimbatore, Tamilnadu for 15 years and as Senior Grade Lecturer in CMS College of Science and Commerce for 14 years. To his credit he has industrial experience for five years and teaching experience of 29 years. He has also received his Doctor of Science (D.Sc in Computer Science). He has to his credit 86 Book Chapters, 234 papers in International and National Journals, 85 papers in International Conferences in International and National Conferences, and edited 17 books and 3 Text books. He is as Associate Editor of IEEE Access. He is an Editor-in-Chief for many journals and Key Member for India, Machine Intelligence Research Lab (MIR Labs). He is an Editorial Board Member and Reviewer for various International Journals. He is also a Committee member for various International Conferences. He has guided 16 Ph.D scholars and guiding 3 Ph. D scholars now.

Nur Salimah binti Alias is a senior lecturer in the Department of Business at the Faculty of Business and Communication, Universiti Malaysia Perlis (UniMAP), Kangar, Perlis, Malaysia. She earned her PhD from Universiti Sains Malaysia (USM), Penang, Malaysia. Her research interests encompass social psychology, positive psychology, psychological well-being, and human interpersonal relationships. Additionally, she is co-authoring a series of books titled "Diges Kemanusian," intended for publication by Universiti Malaysia Perlis (UniMAP).

Ezwan Mohd Mokhtar is a lecturer at the School of Media and Communication, Taylor's University, Malaysia. His expertise lies in animation, user experience (UX), and immersive media. His research focuses on the intersection of animation learning and interface design to enhance engagement, creativity, and educational effectiveness.

Muhammad Aiman Mohd Zubir is a character artist at PlayStation Studios, Malaysia. Formerly a lecturer at Universiti Teknologi MARA (UiTM), he specializes in 3D character design, digital sculpting, and animation production. His professional and academic work explores the creative integration of art, technology, and storytelling in digital media.

Ramkrishna Dikkatwar is a distinguished Professor at Thakur Institute of Management Studies & Research (TIMSR), affiliated with the University of Mumbai, India. With a deep commitment to academic excellence and industry-relevant research, Dr. Dikkatwar brings extensive experience in teaching, research, and mentoring in the field of management education. His scholarly interests span across marketing, strategy, and innovation, and he has contributed to various national and international journals and conferences. As a respected academician, he plays a key role in shaping the intellectual and professional growth of students and fostering a culture of continuous learning and innovation at TIMSR.

Miguel A. Garcia-Ruiz graduated in Computer Systems engineering and obtained his MSc in Computer Science from the University of Colima, Mexico. Miguel received his PhD in Computer Science and Artificial Intelligence from the Centre for Research in Cognitive Science (COGS), University of Sussex, UK. Dr. Miguel Garcia-Ruiz took a virtual reality workshop at Salford University, England, and a computer graphics techniques internship at the Madrid Polytechnic University, Spain. Dr. Miguel Garcia-Ruiz has published various books and many scientific papers in academic journals, and has directed a video documentary about an introduction to virtual reality. Dr. Miguel was a Visiting Professor at the Faculty of Business and IT of the University of Ontario, Canada, where he participated in a research project on combating social deviations with technology, He was an

Assistant Professor with the School of Telematics, University of Colima, Mexico. Currently, Miguel is a Full Professor with the Faculty of Computer Science and Technology from Algoma University, Canada. Dr. Garcia-Ruiz was a member of Mexico's National System of Researchers (SNI) of the National Council of Science and Technology (CONACYT), and was awarded the Innovation Educator of the Year, given by the Sault Ste. Marie Innovation Centre (SSMIC) in 2015.

Marco Gillies is a Professor of Computing at Goldsmiths, University of London. His interdisciplinary research focuses on virtual reality, artificial intelligence, embodied interaction, and virtual humans. He is also known for his contributions to the use of full-body movement and the development of immersive media and social interaction in VR, AR and MR.

Abdullah Yasin Gunduz is an Associate Professor in the Department of Computer Technologies at Usak University, Turkiye. His research focuses on educational technology, artificial intelligence in education, flipped learning, gamification and e-learning. He has participated in several national and international research projects. His academic contributions aim to bridge the gap between innovative technologies and effective pedagogical practices.

Potchong M. Jackaria currently holds a rank of Assistant Professor under the Science and Mathematics Department of the College of Education, Mindanao State University Tawi-Tawi, College of Technology and Oceanography in Tawi-Tawi, Philippines. Prior to working at MSU, he had an extensive experience teaching in different public schools handling elementary level mathematics and later as school head. Asst. Prof. Jackaria obtained his master degree in Education in Administration and Supervision from MSU Tawi-Tawi College of Technology and Oceanography and a Master of Science Education Major in Mathematics from MSU-Iligan Institute of Technology. His research interests include mathematics teaching, contextualization, professional development and education policy.

Sujay Mugaloremutt Jayadeva is an Associate Professor in the Department of Health System Management Studies at JSS Academy of Higher Education & Research, Mysuru. With a strong academic foundation and a passion for advancing healthcare management education, Dr. Sujay has been actively involved in teaching, research, and academic leadership. His areas of expertise include health systems management, public health policy, and healthcare quality improvement. Committed to bridging the gap between academic theory and real-world healthcare challenges, he has contributed to numerous research projects and scholarly publications. At JSS Academy, he plays a pivotal role in nurturing future healthcare leaders and promoting excellence in health management education.

Sanjuna K. R is an Associate Professor in the Department of Computer Science and Engineering, Adi Shankara Institute Of Engineering And Technology where she has been serving since 5th August 2024. She holds a Ph.D. in Computer Science and Engineering from PRIST University, Thanjavur (awarded in March 2021), a Master of Engineering in Computer Science and Engineering from Mahendra Engineering College, Anna University (2008), and a B.Tech. in Information Technology from the School of Engineering, CUSAT (2006). With over 16 years of teaching experience, Dr. Sanjuna K. R has established herself as a dedicated academician and an accomplished researcher. Her areas of expertise include Image Processing, Data Warehousing and Data Mining, and Artificial Intelligence. Dr. Sanjuna has also demonstrated exceptional leadership abilities. She previously served as Head of the Department of Computer Science and Engineering at SNMIMT, and from March 2022 to October 2023, she held the position of Principal In-Charge at SNM Institute of Management and Technology, Maliankara. Her research contributions, published in reputed international journals and conferences, reflect her commitment to advancing knowledge and innovation in the field of Computer Science and Engineering.

Aditi R Khandelwal, is currently working as Associate Professor in the Department of Commerce at The IIS (deemed to be University), Jaipur. She completed her Ph.D in the year 2013 from University of Rajasthan. She is an alumna of ICFAI University, Hyderabad, from where she obtained her post graduate degree in Management (MBA). She has also completed M.Com in Business studies and Economic Analysis and Financial Management. She also holds Post Graduate diploma in Cyber Law and IPR. In her 16 years long academic career she has written 4 books, edited 3 Internationally published books, Published over 40 research papers which are not only published in national and international journals but are also scopus published and presented over 40 research papers in National and International Conferences. She has also been invited speaker in national and international colleges, universities and conferences. She has also received many awards for best papers in international conferences.

Gurashish Kour, a research scholar in the Department of Educational Studies, Central University of Jammu. Her interest areas are Experiential Learning, Environment Education, Artificial Intelligence, Sustainability, Media rich technologies.

Raj Madhu is a Research Scholar in the Department of Educational Studies at the Central University of Jammu. He holds an M.A. in Education from the University of Kalyani and has successfully qualified for the Junior Research Fellowship

(NET-JRF). His research interests encompass Educational Philosophy, Educational Technology, Inclusive Education, and the Indian Knowledge System (IKS), reflecting his commitment to advancing innovative and inclusive educational practices.

T.C. Manjunath was born on 6th February 1967. He did his B.E. from RV College of Engg. in 1989 (B'lore Univ), M.E. in Robotics & Automation from Govt.'s LD College of Engg., (Gujarat Univ., Ahmedabad) in 1992 with FCD-First Rank & PhD in Systems & Control Engg. from IIT Bombay in the year 2007, got best research scholar award for the entire IITB. He is currently working as the Dean Research (R & D) and as Professor in Dept. of Computer Science & Engg. with specialization in IoT, Cyber Security, Blockchain Technology in Rajarajeswari College of Engineering, Bengaluru, Karnataka. He has got a teaching (academic), research & administrative experience of more than 35+ years (10 years as Principal & 8 years as HoD, 1 year as Dean Research & rest as faculty) and has published more than 1500+ research papers in various national & international journals & conferences, with 175+ patents, 100+ book-chapters, 25 awards, 100s of Keynote talks and also published 25 text books in various field of science, engineering & technology, completed projects worth Rs. 9 Crores till date & guided 10 PhD scholars in VTU. He is a member of 30 Professional Society Chapters and is a fellow of IE, IETE, AMIEE, Sr. Member of IEEE and a chartered engineer.

Asit K. Mantry is a Professor and Head of the Department of Educational Studies at the Central University of Jammu, India. With over 15 years of academic and administrative experience, he has held previous positions at SRM University and Budha College of Education, where he also served as HoD and Officiating Principal. He holds a Ph.D. and M.Phil. in Education from Kurukshetra University and has qualified the UGC-NET. His research interests include educational leadership, integral education, action research, and teacher education. Prof. Mantry has authored and edited multiple books, published over 40 research articles in reputed national and international journals, and guided numerous M.Ed. and Ph.D. scholars. He is also a life member of the Indian Association of Teacher Education (IATE) and serves on several academic and administrative committees at CUJ.

Sajad Ahmad Assistant Professor I Public Administration I Political Science I Police Administration I Research Methodology Introduction I am a dedicated academician and researcher with a Ph.D. in Public Administration, committed to advancing knowledge through rigorous research and scholarly publications in esteemed Scopus-indexed journals. My academic journey is enriched by active participation in international conferences, contributing valuable insights to the field. My passion for education and research has driven me to create meaningful contributions in Public Administration, Political Science, Police Administration, and Research Methodology. Academic and Professional Journey My professional journey in academia began with a strong inclination toward teaching and research. Over the years, I have refined my pedagogical approaches, integrating innovative teaching methodologies with research-driven insights to enhance student learning outcomes. My academic career has been shaped by various teaching and research experiences, which have provided me with a comprehensive understanding of higher education's dynamic landscape.

Mittal Mohite is an Associate Professor and the Controller of Examinations at Sri Balaji University, Pune. With a strong academic background and extensive experience in higher education, Dr. Mohite plays a dual role in both academic leadership and institutional administration. As an Associate Professor, she is known for her engaging teaching style, research orientation, and commitment to academic excellence in Management. In her capacity as Controller of Examinations, she ensures the integrity, transparency, and smooth functioning of the university's examination and evaluation processes. Her strategic approach, attention to detail, and student-centric vision make her a pivotal contributor to both academic and administrative frameworks at Sri Balaji University.

Parvathy Nair is currently working as an Assistant Professor in the Department of Computer Science and Engineering at Adi Shankara Institute of Engineering and Technology. She completed her Bachelor's degree in Information Technology from Velalar College of Engineering and Technology, Erode, in 2011. She went on to pursue her Master's degree in Computer Science and Engineering from SMK Fomra Institute of Technology, Chennai, graduating in 2013. With a strong academic foundation and a passion for teaching, she has been actively contributing to the academic growth and technical skill development of her students.

Somang Nam is an Assistant Professor in the School of Computer Science at Algoma University, Canada. He was born in Bielefeld, Germany, in 1989. He received his HBSc. degree in Computer Science, with minors in Mathematics and Ethnomusicology, from the University of Toronto, Canada, in 2013. He obtained his MSc. degree in Computer Science from Toronto Metropolitan University, Canada, in 2016, and his PhD. degree in Human Factors, Industrial Engineering from the University of Toronto in 2021. His primary research interests include human factors, human–computer interaction, and accessibility.

Lydia A. Omar was born in July 12, 2004 in Pangutaran, sulu. Growing up in Lahnagan, Pangutaran, sulu, she developed an early interest in reading and writing. Lydia A. Omar pursued education at Mindanao State University-Tawi-Tawi College of Technology and Oceanography, where she focused on Bachelor of Secondary Education Major in Mathematics.

P. Selvakumar is currently an Associate Professor in the Department of Science and Humanities at Nehru Institute of Technology, Coimbatore, Tamil Nadu, India. Prior to joining Nehru Institute of Technology, he held positions as an Assistant Professor in the Department of Science and Humanities various engineering colleges in Coimbatore, Tamil Nadu, India, spanning from 2011 to 2023. Dr.P. Selvakumar's academic and research interests lie primarily in the field of phytochemistry. He has made significant contributions to his field, with an impressive record that includes 30 journal publications, 12 patents, and 20 conference papers. Additionally, he has organized 5 seminars and conferences, further demonstrating his commitment to academic and scientific exchange. Throughout his career, Dr. P.Selvakumar has been recognized for his dedication and excellence in teaching, having been honored with several awards, including the Best Teacher Awards. He holds a prominent position in the academic community, contributing actively to research.

Biswabhusan Pradhan is an Assistant Professor in the Department of Tourism and Travel Management at the Central University of Jammu. He holds a Master's degree in Tourism and Travel Management and is currently pursuing a Ph.D. in the same field. His research interests include educational leadership, smart tourism, and rural tourism. Mr. Pradhan has contributed to various reputed journals, showcasing his academic commitment and expertise in the evolving landscape of tourism studies.

Vishalini Sivaperegasam is a Psychology Lecturer at University Malaya-Wales. Her academic and professional focus lies in the fields of Counselling Psychology and Expressive Arts Therapy, where she actively integrates creative approaches into therapeutic practices and pedagogy. With a commitment to student-centered education and psychological wellbeing, her work emphasizes the healing power of narrative and arts within multicultural contexts. Vishalini continues to explore the intersections of cultural identity, mental health, and expressive modalities in both academic and applied settings.

Revati Ramrao Rautrao Associate Professor, is a scholar, HR expert, and educator with 20+ years of experience, known for her research in sustainability, AI in education, and women's empowerment.

Anila S is an Assistant Professor at Adi Shankara Institute of Engineering and Technology, where she has been dedicated to teaching since the beginning of her academic career in 2015. She holds a B.Tech degree in Information Technology from the College of Engineering, Kallooppara under CUSAT (2013), and an M.Tech in Cyber Forensics and Information Security from the same institution. Currently, she is pursuing her Ph.D. at Karunya Institute of Technology and Sciences, further deepening her expertise and commitment to research in the field of computer science.

Pedro C. Santana Mancilla is a full professor at the School of Telematics at the Universidad de Colima in Mexico. He earned his Ph.D. in Information and Communications Technology from the University of Vigo (Spain), a Master's degree in Engineering from the Autonomous University of Baja California (Mexico), and a degree in Telematics Engineering from the Universidad de Colima (Mexico). His research focuses on Human-Computer Interaction, intelligent systems and environments, the Internet of Things, smart transportation, and the development of support technologies for older adults and learning. He is a level 2 member of the National System of Researchers (SNII) of the Ministry of Science, Humanities, Technology, and Innovation (SECIHTI). He is a member of the Mexican Academy of Computing, where he coordinates the Academic Section on Human-Computer Interaction. Additionally, he serves as the president of the Mexican Association of Human-Computer Interaction and leads the research group "UCOL-CA-118: Intelligent, Interactive, and Accessible Environments" at the School of Telematics. His scientific work includes publications in books, journals, and conferences nationally and internationally.

Ratan Sarkar is an Assistant Professor in the Department of Education, Tezpur University (A Central University), Assam, India. Previously, he served nearly seven years as Assistant Professor in the Department of Teachers' Training (B.Ed.), Prabhat Kumar College, Contai (Vidyasagar University), and as Guest Faculty at National Institute for Empowerment of Persons with Intellectual Disabilities, Regional Centre, Kolkata. He holds a Ph.D. in Education from Pondicherry University, an M.Ed. and M.Phil. in Special Education from Ramakrishna Mission Vivekananda Educational and Research Institute, Belur Math, and an M.A. in Education and Technology from Tata Institute of Social Sciences, Mumbai. He began his academic journey with a B.Ed. in Special Education (Jadavpur University) and a B.A. in English (Hons) from Siliguri College (University of North Bengal), Darjeeling. Dr. Sarkar has published extensively in leading journals (SAGE, Springer, Routledge, Wiley), authored books, chapters, and reviews, and led projects under the Ministry of Education, Govt. of India. He works on inclusive education, educational technology, and policy advocacy to advance equitable learning ecosystems.

Sonal Sharma is an Associate Professor at Thakur Institute of Management Studies & Research, Mumbai, where she brings a wealth of academic expertise and research experience to the field of management education. With a strong background in organizational Behavior, she is committed to delivering high-quality, industry-relevant education. Dr. Sharma is actively engaged in scholarly research, conferences, and academic publications, contributing to thought leadership in her domain. Her dynamic teaching style, emphasis on practical application, and dedication to student development have earned her recognition as a respected educator and mentor. She plays a key role in shaping future business leaders and strengthening the academic foundation of the institute.

Sharika T. R. is an Assistant Professor in the Department of Computer Science and Engineering at Adi Shankara Institute of Engineering and Technology, Kerala, India. She is currently pursuing her Ph.D. in Computer Science and Engineering at Karunya Institute of Technology and Sciences, Coimbatore, with a research focus on Artificial Intelligence in education. With academic expertise spanning AI, Data Science, and Educational Technology, she is actively involved in teaching, mentoring, and digital curriculum enhancement. Her research interests include AI-driven learning environments, natural language processing, and e-learning technologies. She advocates for interdisciplinary, learner-centric teaching models and is committed to empowering educators through strategic faculty development and digital literacy.

Wan Ahmad Jaafar Wan Yahaya has been the Director of the Centre for Instructional Technology and Multimedia (PTPM) at Universiti Sains Malaysia (USM), Penang, since 2016. On 21 October 2025, he was appointed as the Deputy Vice-Chancellor (Student Affairs) of Universiti Sains Malaysia. He also serves as the President of the Malaysian Educational Technology Association (META). Additionally, he is the Chairman of the Technical Committee on Audio, Video, Information Technology, and Communication Equipment at the Department of Standard Malaysia, Ministry of International Trade and Industry Malaysia. He holds a PhD in Multimedia Education from the University of Leeds and a Master of Education (Computer in Education) from the University of Manchester, United Kingdom. Before that, he pursued a bachelor's degree at the University of Malaya, Malaysia. As the main supervisor, he has graduated 33 PhD students and has published more than 180 articles/papers in indexed journals such as Scopus, Web of Science (ISI), SCSI, SSCI, conference proceedings, and book chapters, primarily in the field of multimedia education. He has also presented over 18 speeches as a keynote and invited speaker, both nationally and internationally. Some of his innovative creations and projects have won gold awards and received special recognition in international innovation, invention, design, and technology competitions in Malaysia, Indonesia, Korea, and Geneva (Switzerland). In recognition of his outstanding contributions to the field of Educational Communications and Technology, he received the Thailand Association International Honor Award for the year 2023.

Index

A

C

D

E

F

G

H

I

L

M

N

P

R

S

T

www.ingramcontent.com/pod-product-compliance
Lightning Source LLC
LaVergne TN
LVHW062337300926
849161LV00007B/1730
* 9 7 9 8 3 3 7 3 5 1 5 7 5 *